VARIETIES OF MEMORY AND CONSCIOUSNESS

Essays in Honour of Endel Tulving

edited by

HENRY L. ROEDIGER, III
Rice University

FERGUS I.M. CRAIK
University of Toronto

LEA Lawrence Erlbaum Associates, Publishers
1989   Hillsdale, New Jersey   Hove and London

Lawrence Erlbaum Associates, Inc., Publishers
365 Broadway
Hillsdale, New Jersey 07642

Library of Congress Cataloging-in-Publication Data
Varieties of memory and consciousness : essays in honour of Endel
  Tulving / edited by Henry L. Roediger III, Fergus I.M. Craik.
      p. cm.
  Grew out of a conference, held at the University of Toronto in May
1987, to celebrate Endel Tulving's 60th birthday.
  Includes bibliographies and index.
  ISBN 0-89859-935-0
  Paperback ISBN: 0-8058-0546-x
  1. Memory—Congresses. 2. Memory—Physiological aspects—
Congresses. 3. Neuropsychology—Congresses. 4. Tulving, Endel—
Congresses. I. Tulving, Endel. II. Roediger, Henry L.
III. Craik, Fergus I. M.
  [DNLM: 1. Consciousness—congresses. 2. Memory—congresses.
BF371 V299 1987]
BF371.V34   1989
153.1'2—dc19
DNLM/DLC
for Library of Congress   88-36804
                                                           CIP

Printed in the United States of America
10 9 8 7 6 5 4 3 2 1

Contents

Preface

The present volume grew out of a conference held at the University of Toronto in May, 1987. The occasion was a celebration of Endel Tulving's 60th birthday. As organizers, we had envisioned a first-rate scientific conference that would also include social events worthy of the occasion. The three-day episode exceeded our expectations and we are pleased to present this volume in Endel's honour.

Endel Tulving in a unique figure in cognitive psychology. His research, writing, theories, and personality have strongly influenced everyone who attended the conference, and probably anyone who would be reading these words. A brief biographical sketch, taken from the *American Psychologist*, follows this Foreword. Endel's magnetism can be seen from the strong attraction of our conference, as it pulled in people from all over the world; Nobuo Ohta came from Japan, Don Thomson from Australia, Lars-Göran Nilsson from Sweden, and Donald Broadbent, John Gardiner, and Lawrence Weiskrantz from England. In addition, others came from all over the United States and Canada. Each session of the conference was attended by 75 to 100 people.

The conference was organized around four Endelian themes, with a session devoted to each. These were: Encoding and Retrieval Processes; Neuropsychology of Memory; Classificatory Systems for Memory; and Consciousness, Emotion, and Memory. In each session there were four speakers and a commentator, for a total of 20 participants over the three day event. We have chosen to organize the book along exactly the same lines. The primary departure from the conference proceedings is that Mortimer Mishkin presented an excellent paper at the conference, but could not contribute a chapter. We are happy that Morris Moscovitch, who could not attend the conference because of a prior commitment, has provided a chapter in the Neuropsychology section.

The conference was supported financially by the University of Toronto, by the Natural Sciences and Engineering Research Council of Canada, and by Lawrence Erlbaum Associates. We are deeply grateful for this help—the meeting, and the book that has grown out of it, would simply not have been possible without their assistance. We thank Suparna Rajaram and Kavitha Srinivas for their excellent work in producing both the author index and the subject index.

We believe that this volume is a fitting tribute to Endel Tulving, because it represents the cutting edge of research and thinking on some of the most important problems on which he has himself worked. The four main themes of the volume are interrelated and the contributions often fit together well, even in chapters from different sections. Because the writers heard the other presenters and read each others' drafts, they were able to integrate information from across the conference in the final forms of their chapters, to the benefit of the volume as a whole. We are pleased to present this volume to Endel as a token of our admiration, affection, and esteem.

Henry L. Roediger, III
Rice University

Fergus I. M. Craik
University of Toronto

List of Speakers at the Conference

Henry L. Roediger, III, Rice University
Fergus I. M. Craik, University of Toronto
Michael J. Watkins, Rice University
Roger Ratcliff, Northwestern University
Bennet B. Murdock, Jr., University of Toronto
Lawrence Weiskrantz, University of Oxford
Laird S. Cermak, Boston Veterans Administration Medical Center
Morris Moscovitch, University of Toronto
Mortimer Mishkin, National Institute of Mental Health
David S. Olton, The Johns Hopkins University
Marcel Kinsbourne, The Shriver Center
John R. Anderson, Carnegie-Mellon University
Donald Broadbent, University of Oxford
James H. Neely, State University of New York–Albany
Robert G. Crowder, Yale University
Lars-Göran Nilsson, University of Umeå
Robert A. Bjork, University of California—Los Angeles
Eric Eich, University of British Columbia
Daniel L. Schacter, University of Arizona
Larry L. Jacoby, McMaster University
Robert S. Lockhart, University of Toronto

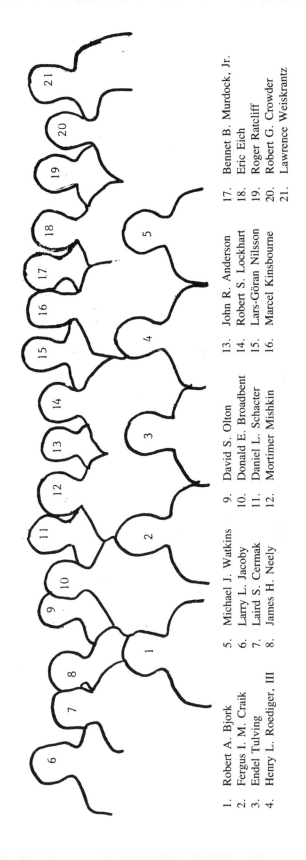

1. Robert A. Bjork
2. Fergus I. M. Craik
3. Endel Tulving
4. Henry L. Roediger, III
5. Michael J. Watkins
6. Larry L. Jacoby
7. Laird S. Cermak
8. James H. Neely
9. David S. Olton
10. Donald E. Broadbent
11. Daniel L. Schacter
12. Mortimer Mishkin
13. John R. Anderson
14. Robert S. Lockhart
15. Lars-Göran Nilsson
16. Marcel Kinsbourne
17. Bennet B. Murdock, Jr.
18. Eric Eich
19. Roger Ratcliff
20. Robert G. Crowder
21. Lawrence Weiskrantz

Endel Tulving: A Biographical Sketch

In 1983 Endel Tulving received the American Psychological Association's Award for Distinguished Scientific Contributions. The following citation and biography are reprinted, with permission, from the American Psychologist, *1984, 39, 265–267. Material in the last two paragraphs has been updated to reflect the situation in 1989.*

Citation

"For his penetrating insights into the nature of human memory. More than others, he has directed attention to one of the most important issues in the analysis of memory: the relationship between the encoding and the retrieval of mental events. He has developed elegant methods for studying the structure of memory traces. And he has brought into bold relief the concepts of subjective organization, availability versus accessibility, encoding specificity, and episodic versus semantic memory, all of which animate modern discussion of memory. An engaging colleague and a charismatic teacher who delights in puzzles and paradoxes, he has influenced scores of scientists both in and beyond North America."

Biography

Endel Tulving was born on May 26, 1927, in Estonia. His father was a judge in a small town, and the Tulving family lived in relative comfort until Estonia's forcible incorporation into the Soviet Union in 1940. In 1944, in the course of the war, Tulving, then 17, and his younger brother Hannes were separated from their home, parents, and country and taken to Germany. When the war ended, Tulving finished his high school education, worked for a while as a teacher and interpreter for the U.S. Army, and studied medicine at the University of Heidelberg. In 1949 he emigrated to Canada. After a summer's work as a farmhand and construction laborer, Tulving enrolled in the honour psychology program at the University of Toronto. In June 1950 he married Ruth Mikkelsaar, his high school sweetheart, and with her help worked his way through the university. He graduated with first class honors at the top of his class in 1953, spent a further year obtaining the master's degree, and then, with the help of a Harvard Foundation fellowship, went to do his doctorate at Harvard where he learned unforgettable lessons from such teachers as E. G. Boring, E. G. Heinemann, G. A. Miller, S. S. Stevens, and B. F. Skinner.

Tulving had completed all his course work and his dissertation, dealing with oculomotor adjustments and visual acuity, at the end of the summer of 1956 and returned to Toronto. At the urging of A. H. Shephard, one of Tulving's former professors, the Department of Psychology at Toronto had created a lecturer's position for him. Tulving found his new role challenging and rewarding. But there was no laboratory space, no equipment, and no money for research. This meant that if he was going to do any research it was going to be done without these usual paraphernalia. Natural candidates for such research included verbal learning. Tulving had had no training or experience in it, but the field did not seem to be highly technical, and that meant that anyone could try.

Like all others who have ever played the research game, Tulving soon found himself on two concurrent schedules of partial reinforcement, one administered by nature, the other by his peers. One of his early satisfactions was derived from pursuing an idea that had occurred to him at Harvard in a seminar on information theory taught by George Miller and Edwin Newman. The idea had to do with a method of measuring the amount of sequential constraint among items recalled on successive trials in a multitrial free-recall situation. The method of measurement suggested an experiment, the experiment yielded data, and the data needed some theoretical justification. Since, at Toronto, there was no great pressure to publish, Tulving took his time in searching for such justification, finally getting out the paper on subjective organization in 1962. One of his early disappointments was caused by the fact that the world largely ignored what he himself thought was the best paper in his first ten years as a practicing verbal learner, a paper that appeared in *Psychological Review* in 1964.

Meanwhile, the department at Toronto had been undergoing rapid changes under the leadership of Roger Myers, who had become chair in 1956, the same year that Tulving returned from Harvard. Myers was determined to put the department on the psychological map, and he went about his tasks imaginatively and forcefully. In addition to hiring a number of promising younger people, in 1960 he brought into senior positions Abram Amsel, Daniel Berlyne, and George Mandler. Tulving found himself well attuned to all three new stars and their ideas about the future of psychology and Toronto's part in it. He got along particularly well with Mandler, with whom he shared research interests and basic orienting attitudes toward the study of the mind, and from whom he learned new things about the "making, packaging, and selling" of science. It was Mandler who encouraged him to use the term *subjective organization* to refer to what his method measured; Tulving himself felt that the verbal learning establishment of the day would frown on such a soft-sounding, mushy term.

In other ways, too, Mandler's advice and help was invaluable, and his presence in Toronto during five years turned out to play a crucial role in Tulving's life. The establishment of the Ebbinghaus Empire (EE), the well-known research group at Toronto, consisting of faculty members interested in verbal learning, memory, and information processing, and their students, can be traced back to brown-bag lunches that Tulving had with Mandler in his office. Although it has had its ups and downs, the Ebbinghaus Empire has always served as a critical touchstone for the testing and honing of ideas of its members and a challenging forum for many visitors from North America and overseas who have addressed it. The regular members of the EE group include or have included people such as Fergus Craik, Eric Eich, Janet Metcalfe Eich, Arthur Flexser, Bert Forrin, Paul Kolers, Robert Lockhart, Colin MacLeod, Stephen Madigan, Gail McKoon, Bennet Murdock, Karalyn Patterson, Roger Ratcliff, Henry (Roddy) Roediger, Daniel Schacter, Norman Slamecka, Marilyn Smith, Donald Thomson, and Michael Watkins, among others. Tulving has collaborated with and been influenced by many of them.

Tulving had been imprinted on Boring's vaunted 80-hour week by the time he left Harvard. He says that he is now only dimly aware of the countless hours spent in work, but he remembers well the fun and excitement of it all. Finding out things about the human mind that no one else knew about, even if insignificant on the cosmic scale, was fun. Finding beauty and order in the data was exciting. Finding things that made no sense at all in terms of existing knowledge was outright thrilling.

In 1970, Tulving accepted a professorship at Yale, but a number of personal, environmental, and institutional problems conspired to lead him to the decision to return to Toronto. At that point, William McGuire, then chair at Yale, came up with a plan entailing joint professorship at Yale and at Toronto.

Tulving spent the 1972–1973 year at the Center for Advanced Study in the Behavioral Sciences at Stanford—''the best year in my life,'' he says—and then assumed his new role as a dual academic citizen. He would spend one term at Toronto and the other in New Haven visiting the other place once every few weeks during its ''off'' term.

Although he enjoyed this way of life, in the spring of 1974 he was obliged to become the chair of the department at Toronto, and the arrangement with Yale had to be terminated. Although there were some challenges and hence satisfaction to the chair's job, and although the period was interrupted by a most satisfying year spent in Oxford, most of the work that Tulving found himself doing as chair was mindless and useless. He was glad when his term ended in 1980 and he could return to teaching and research.

Tulving says that his research has been strongly influenced by two factors—accidental discoveries, and bright, stimulating collaborators and students. Almost without exception, all his interesting findings have been serendipitous. And many seemed to be critically dependent on his interaction with others. These observations have greatly influenced his personal philosophy of science.

Tulving says that he has lived a very happy, fulfilling, and fascinating life. In addition to the satisfaction that he has derived from his work, friends, students, and colleagues, he has been especially happy in his relationship with his family. His wife Ruth, after "putting hubby through," enrolled in the Department of Drawing and Painting at the Ontario College of Art, and graduated at the top of her class in 1960. She has remained professionally active to this day. She is a member of the Royal Canadian Academy and past president of the Ontario Society of Artists, the oldest organization of professional artists in Canada. Daughter Elo Ann, 38, has four academic degrees, including two in law from McGill University. She is a lawyer, having been admitted to the bar in 1982. She lives with her husband in London, Ontario. Daughter Linda, 32, graduated from the University of Toronto with a master's degree in psychology and received her M.D. at the University of Calgary. She is now in the private practice of medicine in Mississauga, Ontario. Ruth, Elo Ann, and Linda are Tulving's best friends and most loyal supporters, and he their greatest admirer.

Tulving is a Fellow of the Royal Society of Canada. He has received the Warren Medal of the Society of Experimental Psychologists, the Izaak Walton Killam Memorial Scholarship of the Canada Council, a Fellowship from the John Simon Guggenheim Memorial Foundation, the Award for Distinguished Contributions to Psychology as a Science of the Canadian Psychological Association. Tulving has been elected a Foreign Honorary Member of the American Academy of Arts and Sciences and a Foreign Associate of the U.S. National Academy of Science. He received the degree of Doctor of Philosophy, Honoris Causa, from the University of Umeå in Sweden, and has also received honorary degrees from the University of Waterloo and Laurentian University. In 1977–1978, he served as a Commonwealth Visiting Professor at the University of Oxford.

ENCODING AND RETRIEVAL PROCESSES

1

Explaining Dissociations Between Implicit and Explicit Measures of Retention: A Processing Account

Henry L. Roediger, III
Rice University

Mary Susan Weldon
University of California, Santa Cruz

Bradford H. Challis
Purdue University

Explicit measures of memory refer to tasks in which people are directly tested on episodes from their recent experience; in performing the tasks people are instructed to remember events and presumably are aware that they are recollecting recent experiences. Implicit measures of retention are those on which subjects are not told to remember events, but simply to perform some task; retention is measured by transfer from prior experience (relative to an appropriate baseline), and presumably conscious recollection is not necessarily involved (Graf & Schacter, 1985). Explicit memory tasks are the standard warhorses of the experimental psychologist's armamentarium for investigating memory: free recall, cued recall, recognition, and various judgments (frequency, modality, feeling-of-knowing, etc.). Implicit measures of retention are transfer tasks in which performance on the critical task is influenced by prior experience, without the prior experience necessarily being reflected on explicit measures. Examples of implicit tasks are reading inverted text, naming fragmented words or pictures, or naming words or pictures from brief displays. Great interest has recently been displayed in the relation between explicit and implicit measures of retention, because they are shown to behave differently as a function of many independent variables (Schacter, 1987). The purpose of the present chapter is to consider functional dissociations between these two classes of tasks and to sketch a theory rationalizing their interrelation.

The first section of the chapter reviews an approach to explaining dissociations developed within the domain of laboratory memory tasks. This approach is based on Tulving's (1983) ideas of the encoding/retrieval paradigm and the encoding specificity principle. These ideas are compared to similar notions from other domains, and the general heading of transfer-appropriate processing is used to refer to this class of ideas. We argue that the notion of transfer-appropriate processing permits an understanding of dissociations between explicit and implicit measures of retention. The second section briefly reviews dissociations between explicit and implicit measures of retention, as a function of both subject variables (e.g., amnesia produced by brain injury) and independent variables under experimental control (e.g., the levels of processing manipulation). The third section considers the standard explanations of functional dissociations between measures of retention in terms of differing memory systems, particularly the episodic/semantic distinction and the declarative/procedural distinction. Criticisms of these approaches are also briefly described. The fourth section is devoted to spelling out an alternative theory that, in many ways, embodies the notion of encoding specificity to explain the dissociations between explicit and implicit retention. The fifth section of the chapter is aimed at specifying these ideas better and providing further evidence about their validity. The sixth and final section addresses problems of the transfer-appropriate processing approach and suggests future research. The chapter is capped by a few concluding comments on the issues raised.

RETRIEVAL PROCESSES AND ENCODING SPECIFICITY

At the risk of considerable oversimplification, Endel Tulving's career can be marked by three primary lines of contribution. Although these overlap, one can point to the decade of the 1960s as concerned with the organization of memory, particularly subjective organization in multitrial free recall; to the 1970s as concerned with the effectiveness of retrieval cues and with recall/recognition comparisons; and to the 1980s with the issue of whether or not human memory is subserved by distinct systems. Of course, this division of Tulving's career into phases is imperfect, because the seed for the major issue of each decade was planted in the prior one. Thus concern with retrieval cues began in the 1960s (Tulving & Pearlstone, 1966) and with memory systems in the 1970s (Tulving, 1972). Nonetheless, the division proves useful in identifying the main thrust of research for the decade. The basic argument in the first three sections of this chapter maintains that Tulving uncovered important truths about memory in the 1970s—the encoding specificity decade—and that these ideas also work to explain the data taken as evidence for separate memory systems—functional dissociations among measures of retention (Roediger, 1984). These cryptic remarks are fleshed out later.

   Tulving and Pearlstone (1966) showed that category names could serve as excellent retrieval cues in aiding recall of words belonging to semantic categories, relative to performance under free recall conditions. The advantage of cued to free recall surpassed 200% in some of their conditions, which dramatizes the necessity for distinguishing between the information available in memory (what is stored) and the information accessible on a test (what can be retrieved under a particular set of test conditions). The quest to know what information a person has stored in memory and how it is organized will always founder on the fact that any procedure to assess these issues will only reveal what a person knows under a particular set of retrieval conditions. Thus theories of cognitive structure must always specify a set of retrieval conditions operating during testing (Anderson, 1978).

After Tulving and Pearlstone's (1966) impressive demonstration, interest grew in the factors that caused retrieval cues to be effective (e.g., Thomson & Tulving, 1970; Tulving & Osler, 1968). Numerous experiments were conducted to determine the necessary relation between retrieval cues and stored experiences for successful recollection. The general principle that emerged from numerous experiments came to be known as the encoding specificity principle (or hypothesis): ". . . recollection of an event, or a certain aspect of it, occurs if and only if properties of the trace of the event are sufficiently similar to the retrieval information" provided in the retrieval cues (Tulving, 1983). Many lines of evidence can be provided to support this assertion, but the most convincing conforms to the encoding/retrieval paradigm shown in Fig. 1.1 here. An experiment using the encoding/retrieval paradigm incorporates conditions in which both encoding and retrieval conditions are manipulated orthogonally. Usually experimenters wish to vary the similarity between encoding and retrieval conditions, a property illustrated by letters in Fig. 1.1. Encoding conditions A and B are crossed with retrieval conditions A' and B', which are similar to encoding conditions A and B, respectively. If the encoding specificity principle holds, performance in conditions A–A' and B–B' (where encoding and test conditions match) should be better than in conditions A–B' and B–A' in which the encod-

The Encoding/Retrieval Paradigm

		Retrieval Condition	
		A'	B'
Encoding Condition	A	A A'	A B'
	B	B A'	B B'

FIG. 1.1.   The encoding/retrieval paradigm. Minimally, two encoding conditions (A and B) are crossed with two retrieval conditions (A' and B'). Retention should be enhanced in conditions represented by cells in which the best match exists between study and test conditions (AA', BB') relative to the other conditions (AB', BA'). Adapted from Tulving (1983, p. 220).

ing and retrieval conditions match less well. Numerous experiments have re-vealed such effects (see Tulving, 1983, pp. 226–238, for 14 examples), so discussion here is limited to a single case that illustrates the point.

Morris, Bransford, and Franks (1977) reported an experiment dealing with the issue of how manipulations designed to influence the level of processing of studied stimuli affected performance on different types of memory tests. The usual expectation is that deeper, more meaningful processing should aid reten-tion compared to processing that encourages only shallow or superficial coding (Craik & Lockhart, 1972; Craik & Tulving, 1975). Morris et al. (1977, Experi-ment 1) crossed phonemic (or rhyme) and semantic (meaningful) conditions at both study and test. Subjects studied words such as EAGLE in sentence frames designed to effect either phonemic or semantic encoding ("____ rhymes with legal" or "____ is a large bird"). The subjects responded *yes* or *no* to each statement, and we consider results based on tests of items to which the subjects responded *yes* during study.

The subjects' memories were tested in two different ways. Half the subjects were tested on a standard recognition test in which studied words were inter-mixed with nonstudied words and the task was to identify the studied words. Morris et al. (1977) assumed that the subjects accomplished this task by referring to the meaning of the test words, and thus that one should expect better perfor-mance for words encoded semantically rather than phonemically. Indeed, just this pattern was found, as can been seen in the left column of Fig. 1.2. The other test used by Morris et al. was a rhyme recognition test. Subjects were told that the test items would include words that rhymed with the studied words and that they should discriminate these rhyming words from the distractors that did not rhyme with the targets. On this rhyme recognition test the standard levels of processing effect reversed, with phonemic encoding producing better perfor-mance than semantic encoding, in general conformity with the encoding specific-ity principle. The data are shown in the right column of Fig. 1.2. Similar experiments and results were reported by Fisher and Craik (1977) and McDaniel, Friedman, and Bourne (1978), although typically there was no advantage of rhyme encoding on the phonemic test. That is, the standard levels of processing effect disappeared but did not reverse on their versions of phonemic tests.

Several general lessons can be drawn from the research described in this section. First, the encoding/retrieval paradigm is useful for studying the interac-tive effect of encoding and retrieval conditions in order to investigate the encod-ing specificity hypothesis. Second, many demonstrations of cross-over interac-tions or functional dissociations have been found by researchers employing the encoding/retrieval paradigm. Even such robust effects as levels of processing can disappear (Fisher & Craik, 1977; McDaniel et al., 1978) or even reverse (Morris et al., 1977) under the appropriate test conditions. Tulving (1979) used such demonstrations to argue that the notion of levels of processing may be superfluous in describing data from such experiments; rather, such experiments

Retrieval Condition

		Semantic (A')	Rhyme (B')
Encoding Condition	Semantic (A)	.84	.33
	Rhyme (B)	.63	.49

FIG. 1.2. Transfer-appropriate processing. Study conditions biased encoding towards rhyme (phonemic) encoding or semantic encoding; test conditions were arranged to tap either one or the other dimension. Data are taken from Morris, Bransford, & Franks (1977, Experiment 1).

demonstrate the interactive nature of remembering as embodied in the encoding specificity principle, without need for separate "levels" of information to be postulated. Morris et al. (1977) made a similar argument, but cast their view under the rubric of transfer-appropriate processing. The general argument is similar to the encoding specificity principle, but (they argued) more general: study conditions foster good performance on later tests to the extent that the test permits appropriate transfer of the knowledge gained during study (see also Bransford, Franks, Morris, & Stein, 1979; Stein, 1978).[1] We return to this argument below as a possible avenue to understanding dissociations between explicit and implicit measures of retention.

DISSOCIATIONS BETWEEN EXPLICIT AND IMPLICIT MEASURES OF RETENTION

The main challenge of this chapter is to provide an account of dissociations between explicit and implicit measures of retention as a function of various independent and subject variables. First it is necessary to provide a brief review of such dissociations, but we do so by providing examples of important findings rather than by reviewing the literature exhaustively. Readers can consult recent excellent reviews by Shimamura (1986), Schacter (1987), and Richardson-Klavehn and Bjork (1988) for fuller treatments.

---

[1]Craik (1979) and Lockhart (1979) argued that the concept of different levels is still needed, in addition to the transfer-appropriate processing ideas, to account for the data in Fig. 1.2 and elsewhere. The reason is that performance is usually substantially better in the Semantic study–Semantic test condition than in Phonemic study–Phonemic test condition (see Fig. 1.2). Thus, even under transfer appropriate test conditions, deeper levels permit better performance. (But see Tulving, 1979, for an alternative view.)

Some form of distinction between explicit and implicit retention is quite old, being honored in the writings of many philosophers (see Schacter, 1987). Even within experimental psychology the distinction dates to Ebbinghaus's (1885/ 1964) great book (Roediger, 1985). However, modern interest in the distinction is relatively recent and has its origins in work with amnesic patients. Patients are classified as amnesic when some brain injury renders them seemingly incapable of retaining new experiences; more technically, they suffer a profound anterograde amnesia. Studies of famous cases such as H. M., whose amnesia was due to a temporal lobectomy, and other more typical forms of amnesia (e.g., numerous cases of Korsakoff's syndrome) led to the conclusion by about 1970 that amnesics were incapable of transferring verbal information from a relatively intact short-term store to a long-term memory (e.g., Baddeley & Warrington, 1970). Researchers were aware that even profound amnesics such as H. M. were capable of learning and retaining motor skills at about the same levels as were normal subjects (e.g., Corkin, 1968), but retention of verbal information in amnesics survived only at very low levels, if at all, after a period of brief distraction following its study.

This picture of retention in amnesics began to change around 1970 because of reports by Warrington and Weiskrantz (1968, 1970) indicating that amnesics occasionally showed normal levels of performance on certain verbal tests. These early claims were, of course, disputed and discussed because they seemed inconsistent with so much prior literature and thinking. But many more recent studies have confirmed Warrington and Weiskrantz's findings and have indicated the variables responsible for their occurrence. Their prototypic experimental study is considered here.

Warrington and Weiskrantz (1970, Experiment 2) presented four amnesic patients (three Korsakoffs and one with a temporal lobectomy) words to remember and then assessed their retention on four tests. Sixteen control patients without brain damage were similarly tested. Today we would probably classify two of the four tests as involving explicit retention (free recall and recognition) and two of the tests as involving implicit retention (completing fragmented words in which each letter was degraded, and completing words when given three-letter stems). In the latter two tests the measure of interest is repetition priming, or the advantage in completing the words due to prior study. (The words were selected so that they could not be completed in the fragmented form without prior study.)

The results for the two explicit memory tests, recall and recognition, are shown in the top panel of Fig. 1.3. As usual, the amnesic patients showed poorer retention than did the control subjects; if anything, the surprise is that amnesic patients performed as well as they did on these tests. The results in the bottom panel show performance of the two groups on the two implicit tests, and the interesting observation is that priming was intact for amnesic patients. They completed the words as well as the control patients in both cases. (The slight difference favoring controls given the three letter word stems was not signifi-

Explicit Tests

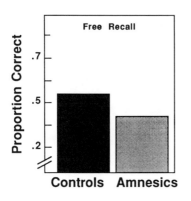

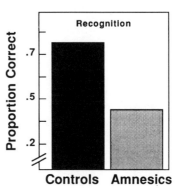

Implicit Tests

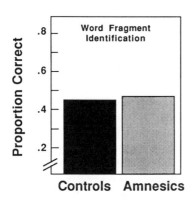

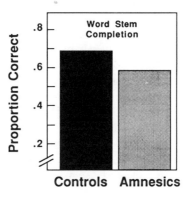

FIG. 1.3.   Intact retention of verbal information in amnesics. Amnesics performed more poorly than controls on explicit tests (recall and recognition), but showed equal priming on implicit tests (word fragment identification and word stem completion). Data from Warrington and Weiskrantz (1970, Experiment 2).

cant.) Thus, on what would now be called implicit tests of retention, amnesics performed as well as control subjects in retaining verbal information.

Similar results have now been obtained by many researchers using a number of different tasks. Shimamura (1986) has reviewed this research and found that amnesics show intact priming on at least eight different tasks, listed here in Table 1.1 along with an illustrative reference. Seven of the eight tasks use verbal materials, so intact retention of verbal materials (as measured implicitly) is well established.

TABLE 1.1
Tasks Showing Preserved Learning in Amnesia
(adapted from Shimamura's, 1986, review)

Task	Illustrative Study
1. Fragmented picture identification	Warrington & Weiskrantz (1968)
2. Word completion	Warrington & Weiskrantz (1970)
3. Lexical decision	Moscovitch (1982)
4. Perceptual identification	Nissen, Cohen, & Corkin (1981)
5. Spelling of homophones	Jacoby & Witherspoon (1982)
6. Preference judgments	Johnson, Kim, & Risse (1985)
7. Free association of related information	Gardner, Boller, Moreines, & Butters (1973)
8. Word completion with new associates	Graf & Schacter (1985)

Graf, Squire, and Mandler (1984) have reported an important condition necessary for establishing priming in at least some of these paradigms: the nature of the instructions given to the subjects. In their Experiment 3, amnesic and control subjects were tested with the same type of three-letter word stems as were used by Warrington and Weiskrantz (1970). However, subjects were given instructions either to use the stems as cues to recall words from the recently presented list (explicit memory instructions), or to produce any word that began with those three letters (implicit memory instructions). Graf et al. showed that when given explicit retention instructions, amnesics performed much worse than did normals; however, when given implicit instructions they showed the same level of priming. This demonstration is impressive, because the same overt cues (word stems) were used in both test conditions. Thus, the necessary condition for preserved priming in amnesics is not simply the presentation of powerful cues— if that were the case, amnesics should perform well on recognition tests—but also the instructions, set, or attitude subjects take toward the task. When amnesics are given indirect or implicit tests in which the memorial nature of the task is disguised, they perform at levels comparable to normal subjects. Thus, amnesics' ability to encode verbal information may be intact; their difficulty may be in gaining awareness of the stored information.

Many experiments with amnesics can thus be viewed as revealing a functional dissociation between a subject variable (brain damage or not) and different retention tests (explicit and implicit). However, similar dissociations can be seen within normal memory as a function of many independent variables. For example, Jacoby and Dallas (1981) manipulated levels of processing in the standard way and showed the usual powerful effects on an explicit recognition test, but no effect on the amount of priming in a perceptual identification test in which subjects had to name words presented quite briefly. That is, the amount of priming on the perceptual identification test was the same regardless of the level of processing the words received during prior presentation. Graf, Mandler, and Haden (1982) and Graf et al. (1984) reported little effect of levels of processing on priming in the word stem completion task, and Roediger, Weldon, Stadler, & Riegler (in preparation) replicated this finding and extended it to a different word completion test (completing words with letters omitted, e.g., c__a__p__g__e, for *champagne*).

Another experiment of this ilk reported by Jacoby (1983) is presented in some detail, because it is critical for the argument to be developed later. Jacoby had subjects study antonyms in one of three conditions. In the Context condition subjects saw *hot–COLD* and read the second word aloud; in the Generate condition subjects saw *hot–???* and were to generate the target; in the No Context condition they saw *XXX–COLD* and were to read the target aloud. Thus, in all three conditions subjects spoke the target word aloud, but the response was effected by different means; namely, processing the data in the No Context condition, processing the concept's meaning in the Generate condition, and presumably a mixture of these processes in the Context condition.

Following presentation of words under these three conditions, different groups of subjects received one of two different types of test. One was a standard recognition test in which studied targets were intermixed with new words and the task was to indicate the previously studied words. The results of this task are shown at the top of Fig. 1.4 and replicate the generation effect (Slamecka & Graf, 1978; Winnick & Daniel, 1970); that is, words generated during prior study were better recognized than those read with no relevant semantic context, with the context condition falling in between. Shown at the bottom of the figure is the amount of priming produced by these study conditions on the perceptual identification test (the percentage correct as a function of the prior study condition, compared to performance on nonstudied words). Now the pattern of results that was seen on the recognition test reverses, with best performance resulting from the No Context study condition and the least priming coming from the Generate study condition. Opposing patterns of performance on an explicit and implicit test provide the strongest form of functional dissociation and indicate that such dissociations are not limited to subject variables such as brain damage.

PREVALENT THEORETICAL ACCOUNTS
OF FUNCTIONAL DISSOCIATIONS

The most popular accounts of functional dissociations between memory measures are in terms of distinct memory systems. The general form of the argument is that performance of one memory system is reflected in one measure (say, recall or recognition) and operation of the other system is reflected in some other measure (say, priming in word stem completion). The leading candidates for the different systems are the episodic and semantic systems proposed by Tulving

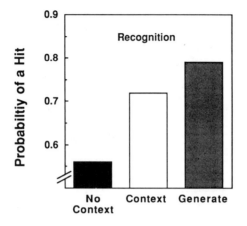

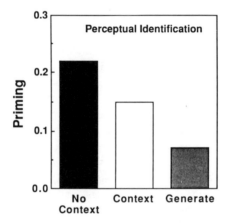

FIG. 1.4. Dissociation between retention measures in normals. Items generated during study were recognized better on a later test than items read during study, but read items produced greater priming than generated items in perceptual identification. Data from Jacoby (1983, Experiment 2).

(1972, 1983) and the procedural and declarative systems championed by Squire (1986, 1987), among others. After some preliminary remarks about memory systems, we briefly consider these two dichotomies.

Good a priori reasons exist for supposing that the human brain has several different means for representing information and permitting access to it. One argument comes from comparative psychology: It is difficult to believe that the human brain has not developed more systems to retain information than exist in simple organisms such as *aplysia,* which nevertheless do reveal the ability to learn (see Sherry & Schacter, 1987, for this comparative approach). Also, other cognitive systems such as vision have separate subsystems specialized to transmit different types of information about the world, such as localization of an object and its identity (Weiskrantz, 1986), so it is plausible that more than one memory system exists, too. Empirical evidence also exists from laboratory studies with monkeys (e.g., Mishkin & Appenzeller, 1987) and other mammals (e.g., Olton, this volume) that convincingly argues for distinct brain mechanisms underlying different forms of learning. However, the exact mapping of this elegant neuroscientific work onto the various memory systems proposed by those studying human memory is hazardous; certainly it is not enough for a theorist to say that others have found evidence for systems, and therefore they must be the systems proposed by the theorist. Rather, one would like the systems to have at least some surface resemblance and, as much as possible, to show that the same factors are at work in humans with certain patterns of brain damage and with animals similarly damaged through experimental means. Although tantalizing leads for such comparisons currently exist, in our opinion they are far from being well established at this point.

In this chapter we primarily consider evidence for distinct systems from functional dissociations in normal remembering, although at the end we return to the issue of dissociations in pathological cases (amnesics). Functional dissociations in both normal and pathological states have been viewed as critical evidence for the distinction between memory systems (see Squire, 1987; Tulving, 1983), so it seems fair to evaluate the distinction using this evidence.

The dissociations from the experiments by Warrington and Weiskrantz (1970) and Jacoby (1983) described earlier can be taken as strong support for the distinction between separate episodic and semantic memory systems. Tulving states that

> Experiments following the logic of experimental dissociation involve the manipulation of a single variable and comparison of the effects of the manipulation in two different tasks, one episodic, the other semantic. Dissociation is said to have occurred if it is found that the manipulated variable affects subjects' performance in different directions in the two tasks. . . The finding of dissociation would be regarded as support for the distinction between episodic and semantic memory systems. (Tulving, 1983, p. 73)

In the studies described earlier (and many others) recall and recognition (episodic tasks) are dissociated from priming in word stem completion and perceptual identification (semantic memory tasks).

Whether or not dissociation results should be taken as evidence for the episodic/semantic memory distinction has been questioned on various grounds by several commentators (e.g., Hintzman, 1984; McKoon, Ratcliff, & Dell, 1986;

Neely, this volume; Roediger, 1984). For example, the form of the interaction between independent variables and retention tests in normals is not predicted by the theory; that is, why should a variable such as generating versus reading (Jacoby, 1983) or levels of processing (Jacoby & Dallas, 1981) have large effects on episodic memory and no effect (levels) or an opposite effect (generating) on priming with a semantic memory task? And surely all dissociations between tasks should not necessarily reflect operation of different systems, or we would soon have evidence for many different systems (a recall system and a recognition system, for example). These and other vexing problems are yet to be worked out (see McKoon et al., 1986; and Tulving's, 1986, reply), but in the absence of a better theory, dissociations between memory measures might be taken as tentative evidence for the existence of separate systems.

The same dissociations used as evidence for the episodic/semantic distinction by Tulving are used as evidence for the declarative/procedural systems by Squire (1986, 1987). Recently Tulving (1984, 1985) has also argued that a distinction between these systems is needed. The classic distinction between declarative and procedural knowledge (Ryle, 1949) is between knowing that (stating knowledge propositionally) and knowing how (operating on the environment in ways difficult to verbalize, as in riding a bicycle). Both episodic and semantic memory would then be conceived as representing declarative or propositional subsystems distinct from procedural memory. One possible arrangement suggested by Squire (1987) is represented in Fig. 1.5, where it can be seen that several disparate abilities are represented in procedural memory. For example, both classical conditioning and priming in word stem completion are considered to reflect procedural memory. Note that this usage strains the usual meaning of the term, because completing word stems would seem to have a relatively light motor component, probably no greater than in a standard cued recall task (considered to be episodic and declarative).[2] Thus although tasks can be reasonably well assigned to reflect episodic or semantic memory by Tulving's criteria (Tulving, 1983, pp. 77–78), the situation becomes much more complicated once more memory systems are introduced and allowance is made for overlapping processes in the various systems and subsystems (Tulving, 1984). Indeed, others have argued that the concatenation of systems within systems has become too byzantine and complex (McKoon et al., 1986). Even though a priori considerations and ablation studies with animals may indicate separate neural systems for handling information, these neural paths may not represent anything like the distinct systems proposed in current theories. Weiskrantz (this volume) has noted that

---

[2]Of course, there is no necessary reason to adhere to the criterion of classifying tasks as procedural only if they involve heavy motor components. Kolers and Roediger (1984) argued for an approach involving "procedures of mind," whereby mental skills (perceiving, remembering, reading, thinking) could be conceived as having properties similar to physical skills. This approach is broadly congruent with the one proposed in the next section of this chapter.

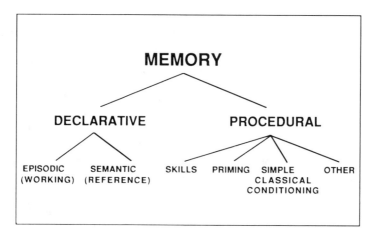

FIG. 1.5. A tentative taxonomy of memory proposed by Squire (1987). Declarative memory includes propositional and imaginal information that can be brought into consciousness. Procedural memory includes cognitive and motor skills, classical conditioning, habituation, sensitization, various perceptual effects, and other instances in which experience facilitates the engagement of specific cognitive operations.

nature provides neither pure lesions for disrupting systems nor pure tasks for measuring them, and he has endorsed a task analytic approach for an understanding of dissociations (see Moscovitch, 1984, for similar ideas). In the next section we propose an alternative to the systems approach that is both simpler and more complete in that it also provides a task analysis.

TRANSFER-APPROPRIATE PROCEDURES

The approach developed here borrows ideas from several predecessors. The general thrust of the argument resembles that of the encoding specificity hypothesis towards explaining encoding/retrieval interactions in episodic memory experiments, but the processing assumptions are slightly different. In particular, the present approach is based on Kolers' procedural viewpoint (Kolers, 1973, 1979; Kolers & Roediger, 1984), the transfer-appropriate processing ideas from the Vanderbilt group (Bransford et al., 1979; Morris et al., 1977; Stein, 1978), and a particular distinction introduced by Jacoby (1983). The component ideas are therefore not particularly novel, but their amalgamation is new, and they are being employed here for other means. The general ideas were stated in previous chapters by Roediger and Blaxton (1987b) and Roediger and Weldon (1987), but we develop them further here.

Four basic assumptions underlie our approach to explaining dissociations between explicit and implicit measures of retention. First, we assume that memory tests benefit to the extent that the operations required at test recapitulate or overlap the encoding operations performed during prior learning. This idea restates the proposal of many theorists (e.g., Kolers & Roediger, 1984; Morris et al., 1977; Tulving & Thomson, 1973, among others) and seems relatively uncontroversial. Second, we assume that explicit and implicit memory tests typically require different retrieval operations (or access different forms of information), and consequently will benefit from different types of processing during learning. This second assumption is spelled out more fully in the next two. The third assumption is that most explicit memory tests rely on the encoded meaning of concepts, or on semantic processing, elaborative coding, mental imagery, and the like. A wealth of evidence shows that variables such as levels of processing, elaborative coding in sentences or images, or meaningful organization in schemas enhances retention on explicit tests such as recall and recognition. We refer to explicit tests as requiring conceptually driven processing, following Jacoby (1983). The fourth assumption is that most standard implicit memory tests rely heavily on the match between perceptual processing during the learning and test episodes. As commonly used, many implicit tests (repetition priming in perceptual identification, lexical decision, fragment or stem completion, etc.) seem to tap the perceptual record of past experience, to borrow the phrase of Kirsner and Dunn (1985). We refer to these tests as data-driven (Jacoby, 1983). Thus, variations in conceptual processing will have little effect on such implicit memory tests, but variations in surface features between study and test will greatly affect priming. (On the other hand, variations only in surface features should have little effect on conceptually driven tests.)

We believe that a theory based on the four postulates stated previously can well explain the bulk of the experimental evidence usually interpreted as support for distinct memory systems. However, before taking on this challenge, let us clarify the approach by denying two erroneous inferences people have drawn from our previous writings. (a) We are not saying that all explicit memory tests are conceptually driven and all implicit memory tests are data-driven. In explicit tests, subjects are instructed to remember experiences; in implicit tests they are not. We describe later attempts to design explicit, data-driven tests and implicit, conceptually driven tests. Our assumption states that most implicit tests that have typically been used are data-driven, and most explicit tests are conceptually driven, but nothing inherent in the nature of explicit or implicit tests forces this correlation. (b) We do not consider the proposed distinction between data-driven and conceptually driven processing as a dichotomy into which all memory tasks can be placed, but rather as representing endpoints on a continuum. In the next section of the chapter we present ideas about how tasks can be classified and ordered along this continuum and what variables might influence placement of a task. We should add, too, that we do not mean to imply that the continuum of processing types is the only feature that permits a task analysis, but we do believe that it represents an important feature for reasons that will become clear.[3]

A first step is to account for dissociations between explicit and implicit tests produced by experimental variables. We use two examples and more appear in the next section. Consider first Jacoby and Dallas' (1981) finding that manipulation of levels of processing, by orienting tasks that directed subjects' attention to different features of words, produced large effects on recognition, but had no effect on the amount of priming in perceptual identification. This outcome was replicated by Graf and Mandler (1984) with the implicit test of word stem completion and by Roediger et al. (in preparation) with both word stem and word fragment completion. The explicit tests of recognition and recall are assumed to be primarily conceptually driven, and so should be affected by variations in processing induced by the standard levels of processing manipulation. On the other hand, the "data" (words) presented during the study phase are the same in each condition and presumably must be processed through the visual system to achieve lexical access no matter what further processing requirements are demanded. This processing of data, which is assumed to be relatively constant across the processing manipulations, therefore transfers equally to the data-driven implicit memory tests.

A welcome complement to this asymmetric dissociation (an effect on explicit retention, no effect on implicit retention) would be a dissociation in which an experimental variable had opposing effects on the two types of test. Jacoby (1983) provided just such an interaction in an experiment described earlier (see Fig. 1.4). Generating words during study produced better retention on an explicit memory test (recognition) than did reading them out of context, but the latter condition produced greater priming in perceptual identification than did generating. Blaxton (1985, Experiment 1) provided a conceptual replication of this finding using the explicit test of free recall and the implicit test of primed word fragment completion. Reading a word obviously involves more data-driven processing than generating it (a case in which the word is not seen), and thus transfers better to a data-driven test. Generating words from associative cues (hot–???) involves more elaborative processing than does reading the target (XXX–COLD), and therefore transfers better to a conceptually driven test. Thus, the procedural framework in which a distinction is drawn between the broad classes of data-driven and conceptually driven processes accounts well for the dissociations between explicit and implicit tests reviewed here.

The transfer-appropriate procedural approach does not provide the only account of these dissociations, however. They can be equally well described, albeit

---

[3]Data- and conceptually driven processing are considered as components of tasks, and one must be careful to distinguish the preponderance (or balance) of the two processing modes in a given situation, without denying that other features of the task are important, too. For example, dissociations between tests can be achieved by manipulating variables, such as word frequency, that may not affect the mode of processing (data-driven or conceptually driven).

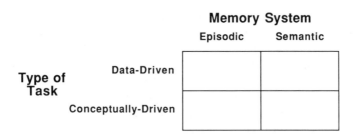

FIG. 1.6. Experimental design needed to distinguish between the effects of memory system (episodic/semantic) and type of processing (data-driven vs. conceptually driven) when interpreting dissociations among memory tests.

at a general level, in terms of distinct memory systems. Depending on one's preference, recognition and recall could be manifestations of operations in the declarative or episodic memory system(s), whereas priming on implicit tests could result from changes registered in the semantic or procedural systems. This approach could account for the general presence of dissociations between measures, although the transfer-appropriate processing approach has the advantage of accounting for the form of the interaction as well as its existence. Still, the dissociations reviewed above cannot be taken as decisive evidence favoring the transfer-appropriate procedures approach.

The reason for the indeterminacy of the issue based on the above data can be seen in Fig. 1.6, in which alleged memory systems form the columns and alleged modes of processing form the rows. These are two difficulties with the logic used by most researchers studying dissociations between measures. First, virtually all researchers have chosen to study dissociations between tasks tapping episodic and semantic memory (or declarative/procedural memory) by manipulating an independent variable and examining its effect on one measure of episodic memory and one measure of semantic memory. (The Warrington & Weiskrantz, 1970, experiment portrayed in Fig. 1.3 is a welcome exception.) With only one task representing each system or type of processing, any form of interaction can be interpreted as reflecting operation of the systems. A second problem, besides comparison of only two tasks, is that in virtually all previous experiments a confounding has existed between the system being tapped and the form of processing required by the tasks. Tests tapping episodic or declarative retention are almost always conceptually driven—free recall, cued recall with associative cues, or recognition memory. On the other hand, tests believed to tap semantic or procedural memory are usually data-driven—perceptual identification, word fragment and word stem completion, and lexical decision. The resulting interactions usually taken as evidence for different systems (or procedures) can thus always be given an account in terms of the alternate view.

Because dissociations are a prime source of evidence for the distinction between memory systems, we should ask how strong this evidence is. With regard to the picture in Fig. 1.6, do dissociations between measures of retention fall mainly between systems (the left and right columns), or can dissociations be found within systems, too? If dissociations between measures of retention are routinely found within systems, and if they are explicable by other principles, then dissociations between measures thought to reflect the operation of different systems must be given less weight as support for the systems viewpoint. Specifically, if dissociations between episodic (or semantic) memory tasks can be obtained, then one must either pursue post hoc arguments that postulate increasing numbers of memory systems, or seek a more parsimonious general principle that predicts such dissociations both within and between the alleged systems.

Let us first consider the case of possible dissociations within episodic memory, in the left hand column of Fig. 1.6. We need not review this evidence extensively, because experimental dissociations within episodic memory are so plentiful and well known. The numerous interactions in the standard encoding/retrieval paradigm (Fig. 1.1) that are taken as support for the encoding specificity principle all exemplify dissociations within episodic memory. One such dissociation is shown in Fig. 1.2, representing results from Morris et al. (1977). Dissociations within episodic retention are well established (see Tulving, 1983, chapter 11).

Fewer results are available to address the issue of dissociations within measures reflecting semantic (or procedural) memory, for the reason that few researchers have employed more than one test of semantic (procedural) memory in the same experiment under the same study conditions. One example revealing a strong dissociation within two semantic (procedural) tasks has been provided by Weldon and Roediger (1987, Experiment 4). They had subjects study a long series of pictures and words prior to an unspecified memory test. (Pictures represented easily named objects, and across subjects specific items were counterbalanced between the two modes of presentation.) After studying the words and pictures, different groups of subjects took one of two types of implicit memory test. One group was given the word fragment completion test, as employed by Tulving, Schacter, and Stark (1982), in which letters are omitted from words and subjects are told to complete the word. The second group was given a picture fragment naming test in which subjects were given severely degraded pictures and were told simply to name each with the first word to come to mind. In both implicit tests, one-third of the test items represented studied pictures, another third represented studied words, and a final third were nonstudied items that served as a baseline for measuring priming in the other conditions.

The results of the experiment are shown in Fig. 1.7, which portrays the amount of priming on each test as a function of study condition (words or pictures). As is apparent, pictures produced much greater priming than did words on the picture fragment identification test, whereas words produced greater prim-

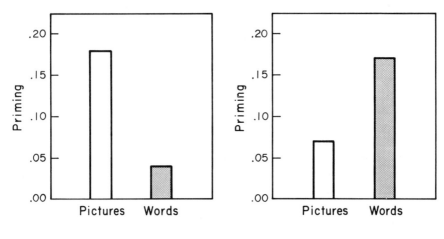

Picture Fragment Identification   Word Fragment Completion

FIG. 1.7.   Dissociation between two semantic memory tests. Pictures produced more priming than words on a picture fragment identification task, but words produced more priming on the word fragment completion test. Data from Weldon and Roediger (1987, Experiment 4).

ing than pictures on the word fragment completion test. The results show a strong dissociation between two semantic or procedural memory tests, and we suspect that many other interactions of this form could be produced.[4] Such dissociations within the semantic or procedural memory system are quite natural from the procedural view, because both word fragment completion and picture fragment identification are data-driven tests and thus the match between surface features in the study events and test stimuli should determine performance. The results in Fig. 1.7 conform exactly to this expectation. On the other hand, these data showing dissociations between two semantic or procedural tests are difficult to interpret within the systems framework, unless one is willing to postulate more systems. Indeed, perhaps the data in Fig. 1.7 support the operation of separate verbal and imaginal systems (Paivio, 1986) within semantic or procedural memory. But, if so, one would then be postulating three memory systems to explain four data points. Certainly the transfer-appropriate processing idea is more parsimonious.

The foregoing review indicates that it is probably as easy to discover experimental dissociations within memory systems, either episodic/semantic or pro-

---

[4]In a related endeavor, Witherspoon and Moscovitch (in press) show stochastic independence between two tests both thought to tap the semantic or procedural system. This demonstration undercuts the use of stochastic independence between tests tapping different systems as support for separate systems, just as the present analysis criticizes the use of functional independence as such a criterion.

cedural/declarative, as it is to find dissociations between systems. This lessens one's enthusiasm for considering dissociations between measures as crucial evidence in the debate about memory systems and their nature. Three experiments reported in a dissertation by Blaxton (1985) reinforce this view. Experiment 2 is described briefly, but the general logic of all three was the same. Blaxton developed four tests of memory that were intended to fill the four quadrants of Fig. 1.6, with there being two versions of episodic (or declarative, or explicit) tests and two types of semantic (or procedural or implicit) tests. One test of each type was considered to be data-driven and one was conceptually driven. The episodic, conceptually driven test was free recall and the data-driven, semantic memory test was word fragment completion. These tests comprised the usual confounded comparison used to produce dissociations between episodic and semantic memory. The other two tests were novel. The data-driven, episodic test was graphemic cued recall in which subjects were given cues that looked (and sounded) like the target word in the list. For example, subjects might be given a cue word such as HAMHOCK to serve as a retrieval cue for HEMLOCK, with the instruction that the cue shared surface features with the target, but no semantic features. (The test is episodic, because subjects were told to use the cues to retrieve members of the recently studied list.) The conceptually driven semantic memory measure was priming in answering general knowledge questions. Subjects were required to answer questions such as "What did Socrates drink at his execution?", with the relevant target (HEMLOCK) having been studied under various conditions or not at all. Instructions to subjects were simply to answer questions, and no reference was made to the prior list; the relation between the query and target was conceptual and did not depend on surface similarity. Hence the test was of semantic memory, and was conceptually driven.

The four test conditions described here were administered to different groups of subjects following two different study conditions in Blaxton's (1985) Experiment 2. The study manipulation was simply whether or not words were presented visually or auditorily within the study list, there being a block of words in each mode for subjects taking each test. Modality often has large effects on implicit memory tests (e.g., Jacoby & Dallas, 1981) and little or no effect on explicit tests of long-term memory (e.g., Murdock & Walker, 1969). The question addressed by Blaxton was whether this dissociation was inherent in tests tapping different memory systems, or was produced by different modes of processing at retrieval. She expected that modality would have large effects on data-driven tests in which test stimuli were presented visually and thereby matched better the study items presented visually, but that little or no modality effect would be apparent on conceptually driven tests, regardless of the putative memory system tested. The results fully confirmed this reasoning, as is apparent in Fig. 1.8. First, examine the lower left and upper right quadrants of the figure, which illustrate a typical dissociation between episodic and semantic memory. Modality had no statistically significant effect on free recall (with a slight auditory advantage), but visual presentation produced much greater priming than did auditory presentation in word fragment completion. However, examination of the two cells constituting the other diagonal leads to the conclusion that mode of processing, and not the memory system tapped, constitutes the basis for the dissociation. A modality effect was found on the other data-driven test, even though it tested episodic memory; but no modality effect was found on the other conceptually driven test, even though it tapped semantic memory. Fig. 1.8

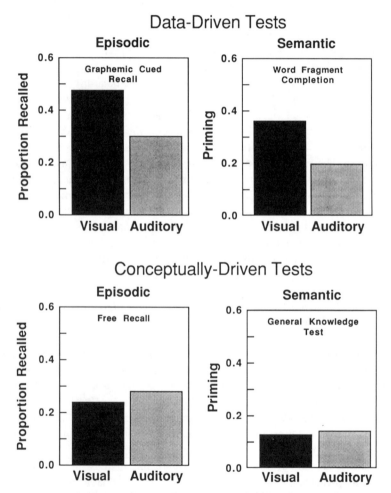

FIG. 1.8. Comparison of the effects of type of processing vs. memory system. The effects of study modality differ as a function of the type of processing involved in the retrieval tests, so that visual data-driven tests show large modality effects but conceptually-driven tests do not. Note that the distinction between episodic and semantic memory systems does not accommodate these results. Data from Blaxton (1985, Experiment 2).

shows that modality of presentation can produce dissociations within both episodic and semantic memory. The distinction between modes of processing provides a better account of the obtained dissociations in Blaxton's (1985) experiments than does postulation of memory systems, a statement that also aptly summarizes the gist of this section.

SPECIFYING THE TRANSFER
OF PROCEDURES APPROACH

Critics of the idea of memory systems have complained about the obscurity of the theorizing (e.g., McKoon et al., 1986), raising such central problems as how memory systems are defined, or how operational definitions may be provided that will permit unambiguous knowledge of what system a test taps. In other papers one of us has been similarly critical of the fuzziness of memory systems as they are usually postulated (Kolers & Roediger, 1984; Roediger, 1984; Roediger & Blaxton, 1987b). However, our own critics have remarked to us (in letters, reviews, and bemused public observations) that they do not perceive any great advantage in specificity of theorizing in our description of dissociations in terms of transfer-appropriate processing. In this section we attempt to address this issue, elaborating on the remarks made in prior sections. We illustrate our arguments with data mostly from the word fragment completion test, because it is the one we have used most extensively, but we believe that the argument holds for other data-driven tests, too.

To reiterate points made earlier, we argue (a) for a procedural approach in which emphasis is placed on the mental operations performed during learning experiences and during test episodes, and on the interrelation of the two; (b) that performance will benefit to the extent that procedures invoked by the test recapture those used during prior learning; and (c) that an important dimension for this account lies in whether procedures are directed more at surface features of stimuli during study and test (data-driven processing) or at the deeper meaning of the stimuli (conceptually driven processing). The first two assumptions are stated rather generally, but are so familiar in one form or another in many different theories of learning and memory that we feel no further need to defend them here. The challenge comes in arguing that the data-driven/conceptually driven distinction first applied in this area of inquiry by Jacoby (1983) deserves its privileged status.

At the risk of seeming hopelessly old-fashioned in these days of wild and woolly cognitive science, we propose to ground our theorizing in operational definitions of our concepts, with these buttressed by converging operations (Garner, Hake, & Ericksen, 1956). These steps have the advantage of making our theoretical concepts amenable to observation, communication, and disconfirmation.

Operational Definitions

The distinction between data-driven and conceptually driven processing is undeniably fuzzy in our prior writings (Roediger & Blaxton, 1987b; Roediger & Weldon, 1987), and so here we propose a straightforward operational definition that would classify any task that uses verbal materials as either data-driven or conceptually driven. The crucial comparison (following Jacoby, 1983) is between the No Context and the Generate conditions within a generation experiment, in which a word (or other material) is either presented to the subject to be read out of context (XXX–COLD), or is produced by the subject in response to a related semantic clue (hot–???).[5] We assume that reading a word without an appropriate semantic context involves data-driven processing, whereas generating a word from an associate or synonym involves conceptually driven processing. Thus, when the subject says "cold" following the display of XXX–COLD, we assume that the processes involved are largely bottom-up, or data-driven; on the other hand, when "cold" is spoken following "hot–???", we assume the processes involved are top-down, or conceptually driven (because no "data" for *cold* were displayed). Reading a word in context (hot–COLD), as in several of Jacoby's (1983) experiments, presumably involves both data-driven and conceptually driven processing.

From these assumptions, the following operational definitions of data-driven and conceptually driven tests follow: (a) Data-driven tests are those in which items studied in No Context conditions produce better performance than those studied under Generate conditions; and (b) conceptually driven memory tests are those in which items produced in Generate conditions produce performance superior to those studied in No Context conditions. Again, reading a word out of context involves data-driven processing, whereas generating it from associative clues involves conceptually driven processing.

Armed with these operational definitions, we can classify priming in perceptual identification as strongly data-driven (Jacoby, 1983), whereas typical recognition, free recall, and semantic cued recall tests are categorized as conceptually driven. (Recognition may have a small data-driven component—perceptual fluency as proposed by Jacoby & Dallas, 1981, or activation as proposed by Mandler, 1980—but others disagree; Watkins & Gibson, 1988.) Other explicit and implicit tasks can now be classified as data-driven or conceptually driven based on this operational definition. For example, Blaxton (1985, Experiment 1) sought to justify her classification of five tasks as data-driven or conceptually

---

[5]Note that the comparison recommended here is not the one used in standard generation effect experiments (e.g., Slamecka & Graf, 1978), which is between items read in context (hot–*cold*) and those generated (hot–???). This last comparison is useful for studying the generation effect, because study conditions are held constant except for overt presentation of the target. However, for purposes of distinguishing data-driven and conceptually driven processes, the No Context/Generate comparison is more appropriate.

TABLE 1.2
Proportion Correct from Blaxton (1985)

	Study Condition		
Type of Test	Generate	No Context	Nonstudied
Free recall	.30	.19	—
Semantic cued recall	.67	.51	.04
General knowledge questions	.50	.33	.25
Graphemic cued recall	.34	.45	.06
Word fragment completion	.46	.75	.27

driven based on a comparison of items studied in No Context and Generate conditions. Four of the five tasks (free recall, graphemic cued recall, word fragment completion, and answering general knowledge questions) were described previously, and the fifth test was semantic cued recall (e.g., POISON as a cue for HEMLOCK). Her basic results from the No Context/Generate comparison are shown in Table 1.2, where it can be seen that free recall, semantic cued recall, and priming on general knowledge questions can all be classed as conceptually driven (Generate greater than No Context), whereas graphemic cued recall and priming in word fragment completion are data-driven (No Context greater than Generate) by our operational definition.

Not all implicit memory tasks have been investigated sufficiently to know whether or not they should be classified as data-driven or conceptually driven, but priming in lowering visual duration thresholds (Winnick & Daniel, 1970; Clarke & Morton, 1983) and in the lexical decision task (Monsell, 1985; Neely & Tekman, in preparation) meet our criterion of No Context surpassing Generate conditions. We speculate that priming in word stem completion also will turn out to be data-driven by our definition. The important point is that any verbal task can be classified. For example, workers in social cognition have recently become interested in the role of priming on person perception (e.g., Srull & Wyer, 1980). In a typical paradigm, subjects are exposed to some material during a first phase in which (for example) many of the words have a hostile connotation. During an ostensibly unrelated second phase, they are asked to rate hypothetical people in terms of their personality traits when given various ambiguous behaviors. The measure of interest is how much the prior phase affects accessibility of the category (hostile) in describing the behaviors, compared to ratings of subjects who were not exposed to the material in the first phase. The general finding is large priming effects on measures of category accessibility that persist even over a delay of one week (Srull & Wyer, 1980). E. S. Smith and Branscombe (in press) asked whether category accessibility might qualify as a conceptually driven measure of implicit retention. They had subjects either read priming words in the first phase of an experiment, or generate them from conceptual clues. Later,

TABLE 1.3
Proportion Correct in Smith and Branscombe's (in press) Experiment

Type of Test	Study Condition		
	Generate	No Context	Nonstudied
Category accessibility	.52	.43	.34
Free recall	.61	.45	—
Word fragment completion	.43	.62	.41

on the category accessibility test, subjects were given a description of behaviors that were ambiguous and were asked to provide a one-word trait adjective to describe the behavior. Two other groups of subjects were given the same materials during the study phase but then were asked either to free recall the material or to complete words from fragments. (One set of traits was not presented during the study phase to assess priming on the category accessibility and word fragment completion tests.)

The results showed that priming in category accessibility can be classified as a conceptually driven implicit memory test, because the test revealed an advantage of items studied under Generate compared to No Context conditions. The basic results are shown in Table 1.3, where it can also be seen that a generation effect was obtained in free recall, but that No Context items produced superior priming to Generate items in primed fragment completion (replicating Blaxton, 1985). The Smith and Branscombe experiment illustrates well how a new implicit memory test can be classified as data-driven or conceptually driven via the No Context/Generate contrast (see also Srinivas & Roediger, in preparation).

Providing operational definitions for data-driven and conceptually driven processing in terms of the No Context/Generate contrast may pose problems, because the standard generation effect (involving a Context/Generate contrast) has recently been shown to be subject to numerous variables that may affect our definition. For example, it may disappear under between-subject conditions (Begg & Snider, 1987; Slamecka & Katsaiti, 1987; but see Hirshman & Bjork, 1988; McDaniel, Waddill, & Einstein, 1989) and with low-frequency words (Nairne, Pusen, & Widner, 1985). Also, if the generation procedure is data-driven and the test is data-driven, then one might expect positive generation effects, or an advantage of Generate to Read (Gardiner, 1988; Nairne, 1988). Thus in applying our definition, one should bear in mind the clearest comparison, as specified in Jacoby (1983): (a) the No Context condition should involve reading words in a neutral context to enhance data-driven processing during study, and the Generate condition should involve producing words with minimal overt data (letters) specifying the target word; (b) the generation process must be driven by a conceptually related context, such as a synonym, antonym, or associate; and (c) a within-subjects contrast at study is preferred, to show opposite effects on the two classes of test with study conditions held constant.

We turn attention now to converging operations to specify tests as data-driven or conceptually driven. In brief, data-driven tests should be greatly affected by manipulations of surface information between study and test and relatively immune to manipulations involving conceptual elaboration. Conversely, conceptually driven tests should be little affected by manipulations of surface information, but strongly affected by conceptual elaboration.

Manipulation of Surface Variables

Earlier work by Roediger and Blaxton (1987b) presented considerable evidence that primed word fragment completion was greatly affected by surface variables, so here we provide just a brief review. The general notion is that if a task is defined as data-driven by No Context study conditions producing greater priming than Generate study conditions, then this test should also be greatly affected by other variations in surface information. Assuming a visual, linguistic test, these surface manipulations would include such things as modality (greater priming from visual rather than auditory study), symbolic form (greater priming from words rather than pictures), and language (greater priming from words in the same language as the test fragments, rather than from a different language). These same variables should reveal no effect or opposite effects on conceptually driven tests such as free recall. These predictions have been borne out for the word fragment completion test (see Durgunoğlu & Roediger, 1987; Roediger & Blaxton, 1987a; Weldon & Roediger, 1987).

A summary of evidence concerning surface variables appears in Fig. 1.9. Plotted on the ordinate is the amount of priming (proportion of completed fragments following study of the concept minus proportion completed without prior study) and on the abscissa is the type of stimulus change between study and test. A word of caution is in order, because the data presented in Fig. 1.9 were collected from several experiments using different subjects, materials, and item sets; nonetheless, the data appear orderly. On the far left appears the amount of priming obtained when little or no change exists between study and test in the format in which the items appear. When typography is changed between study and test (handprinted in uppercase letters, typed in lower case letters) priming drops somewhat, but when items were presented auditorily and tested visually much less priming occurred (Roediger & Blaxton, 1987a, Experiments 1 and 2). Interestingly, when words were presented auditorily but subjects were asked to imagine their appearance when typed, priming increased compared to the uninstructed auditory case (third column from the left compared to the fourth). When subjects studied pictures they showed slight but statistically significant priming on the word fragment completion test (Roediger & Weldon, 1987; Weldon & Roediger, 1987). The four columns on the far right reveal that little or no priming from other conceptual relations occurred in primed fragment completion. In completing a fragment such as _M_RE_L_ for UMBRELLA, subjects showed no statistically significant effect from prior study of a synonym of the

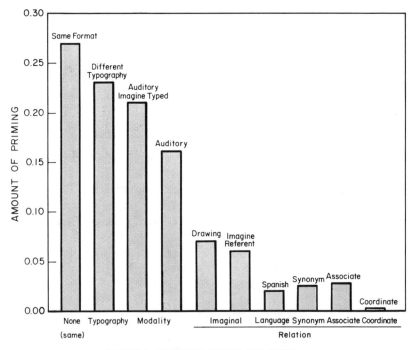

CHANGE BETWEEN STUDY AND TEST

FIG. 1.9.   Effects of surface variables on priming. Priming on the word fragment completion test declines as the match between the surface features of the study items and test fragments decreases. From Roediger and Blaxton (1987b).

concept (PARASOL), or an associate (RAIN), or a category coordinate (RAIN-COAT), or (for fluent bilinguals) a translation equivalent (PARAGUAS)–see Durgunoğlu and Roediger (1987) and Roediger and Challis (in preparation). (We return to the last manipulations in the next section.)

The general conclusion to emerge from Fig. 1.9 is that the amount of priming falls off as a function of the dissimilarity between the study and test events. The interpretation is that the procedures induced by processing of study and test events become increasingly dissimilar as a function of the perceptual dissimilarity. Although we cannot take space to review the literature here, a similar case can be made that repetition priming in perceptual identification, lexical decision, and word stem completion are also quite sensitive to manipulations of surface features, which agrees with our speculation above that these represent data-driven tests.

One problem for the notion that primed fragment completion constitutes a data-driven test is that the amount of cross-modal priming is so great, and yet the surface forms between auditory study and the visual fragment completion test are so different. If primed fragment completion is data-driven, why should cross-modal priming be so great? A tentative answer may be that priming in word fragment completion (and probably other data-driven tests) does not depend only on a match of low-level surface features, but may depend as well on higher-level processes involved in word recognition ("lexical memory," as some would have it). Auditory and visual word recognition may involve overlapping processes at these higher levels, even though some other procedures may be mode specific. Kolers (1975) studied transfer in reading of transformed text in which reading a misoriented sentence of text was preceded by subjects either (a) reading the sentence in the same transformed orientation, (b) reading it in normal orientation, (c) hearing it read to them, or (d) hearing it in an alternate language that the subjects knew well. Transfer in speed of reading the target sentence occurred for all four study conditions, but these were ordered as given above from (a) to (d), with the last two conditions about equal. He interpreted the data as indicating that comprehension in all four study conditions necessitated procedures that were used in reading the target sentences later, but more procedures were shared when the prior sentence was read in inverted orientation. Tananhaus, Flanigan, and Seidenberg (1980) have reported evidence consistent with the idea that orthographic features of words are automatically generated even when people only hear the words. Such features would help support priming on data-driven tests. Thus the extensive cross-modal priming in word fragment completion (as well as in word stem completion; Graf, Shimamura, & Squire, 1985) may provide an important key in determining what processes are involved in repetition priming (see Weldon, 1988).

Manipulation of Conceptual Information

The second converging operation for definition of tasks as primarily data-driven or conceptually driven is that manipulation of conceptual operations should affect performance on conceptually driven tests but have little effect (or an opposite effect, depending on the match in procedures between study and test events) on data-driven tests. A wealth of evidence supports the idea that levels of processing (Craik & Lockhart, 1972), imagery (Paivio, 1986), organization (Tulving, 1968), and other forms of elaborative processing have large positive effects in performance on conceptually driven tasks such as free recall and recognition. The issue is then whether parallel effects are found in data-driven tests; on the present account they should not occur, or should occur only weakly if the task has a small conceptually driven component. In general, evidence from perceptual identification falls in line, because Jacoby and Dallas (1981) reported no effect of levels of processing on priming while finding a large effect on recognition. Graf and Mandler (1984) and Graf, Squire, and Mandler (1984) generally replicated this finding with primed word stem completion, although they often found a weak trend toward a "levels" effect across experiments. Roediger et al. (in preparation) found no levels of processing effect in primed word fragment completion, nor in word stem completion. Similarly, Carroll, Byrne, and Kirsner (1985) found no effect of processing level on repetition priming in picture naming or in perceptual identification of pictures, and Kirsner, Milech, and Standen (1983) found no effect of levels in the lexical decision task (but see Duchek & Neely, in press).

Turning to other research with primed fragment completion, so far every experiment has produced results exactly as expected. For example, Weldon and Roediger (1987, Experiment 1) had subjects study pictures and words and then take either a free recall test or the word fragment completion test. Pictures are thought to provide richer encoding than words, either through multiple codes (Paivio, 1986) or through stronger representation of semantic information (Nelson, 1979), so better performance would be expected for pictorial than verbal stimuli on conceptually driven tests. On the other hand, processes involved in the study of words (rather than pictures) should be more similar to those involved in word fragment completion. The results are shown in the top panel of Fig. 1.10 and conformed exactly to these expectations.

Durgunoğlu and Roediger (1987) included conditions in a larger experiment that exemplified the same logic. They showed fluent Spanish-English bilinguals a mixed list of Spanish and English words and then gave them either a free recall or a word fragment completion test, with the fragments always presented in English. Because Spanish was the dominant language for most of these subjects, one can probably assume a richer code for Spanish than for English words and, as shown in the lower panel of Fig. 1.10, they recalled Spanish words slightly better than English words. However, with the greater match from study of English words to completing English fragments, the reverse pattern was obtained on primed fragment completion. Thus, in both experiments the conditions that could be assumed to provide richer conceptual processing produced better performance on the conceptually driven test of free recall, but this trend was reversed on the data-driven fragment completion test.

Roediger and Challis (in preparation) tested the same prediction in a different way. In two experiments they presented subjects with a long list of words followed by either a free recall test or a word fragment completion test. Three study conditions were of primary interest: (a) words were presented once in the list (*elephant*), (b) words were presented twice (*elephant-elephant*), or (c) words were presented and followed by a conceptually related word (*elephant-pachyderm*). When two items were presented, the lag between them was also manipulated, from zero (massed presentation) up to 31 intervening items. We assumed that re-presentation of the word as in condition (b) would force subjects to reprocess both the surface features and the word's meaning, at least with spaced presentations when one could assume that the word would be fully reprocessed

Weldon and Roediger (1987)

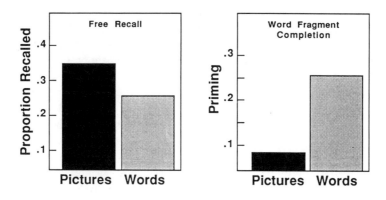

Durgunoğlu and Roediger (1987)

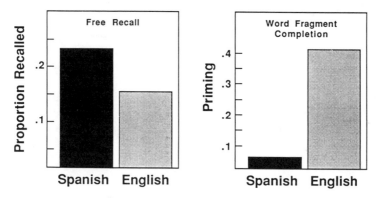

FIG. 1.10. Dissociation as a function of study format. In the top panel, pictures produced better performance than words on a conceptually driven free recall test, but words produced more priming than pictures on the data-driven word fragment completion test. Analogous results are shown in the bottom panel as a function of the language in which the words were studied. Data in the top panel are from Weldon and Roediger (1987, Experiment 1), and those in the bottom panel from Durgunoğlu and Roediger (1987).

(Jacoby, 1978). Thus positive effects would be expected on either data-driven or conceptually driven tests. On the other hand, for the conditions that involved conceptual repetition, subjects would be expected to elaborate the conceptual processes but (because of the dissimilarity in surface features) no further data-driven processing would be expected of the target item due to the repetition of the concept. Thus conceptual repetition should aid recall of *elephant* in free recall, but should leave unaffected the amount of priming in word fragment completion.

The results are shown in Fig. 1.11 for conditions in which presentations were spaced, combining data across two experiments so that each point is based on between 1,296 and 1,944 subject × item observations, depending on the condition. Free recall results, in the top panel, show that repetition of a word under spaced conditions produced a sizeable increment in recall compared to its single presentation. Of primary interest is the finding that conceptual repetition also enhanced recall of the target item, as predicted, but only about half as much. The primed fragment completion results appear in the bottom panel, where a different pattern is evident. Presenting the same word twice under spaced conditions enhanced the amount of priming, but conceptual repetition produced no benefit at all compared to priming from a single presentation. In Fig. 1.9 we showed results indicating that semantic priming does not occur in fragment completion, at least with a delay of some 15 minutes between study of a word (*pachyderm*) and test on its fragmented alternate form (__LEP__AN__); the results in the bottom of Fig. 1.11 extend this finding by showing that even when the target has been studied, conceptual repetition fails to enhance priming.

Taken together, the results from this section support the conclusion that the data-driven task of primed word fragment completion is insensitive to manipulations of conceptual factors. Little research exists as to whether or not the same conclusion holds for other implicit tests that we believe to be data-driven, but priming in perceptual identification and word stem completion show little or no effect of levels of processing. Also, presentation of pictures, or of words in an alternate language for bilinguals, produces little or no effect on priming in perceptual identification or lexical decision (e.g., Kirsner, Milech, & Stumpfel, 1986; Kirsner, Smith, Lockhart, King, & Jain, 1984).

Test Orientation

One other dimension critical to determining the nature of retention tests is test orientation or retrieval orientation (Graf & Mandler, 1984; Nelson, Canas, Bajo, & Keelean, 1987). This dimension refers to the instructions that subjects are given when tested. On explicit tests, subjects are given instructions to retrieve recent experiences; on implicit tests, subjects are usually given some sort of cue and simply told to produce the first thing to come to mind that somehow fits or completes the cue. We believe that implicit instructions, when given in conjunction with perceptually degraded test stimuli, constrain the subject to be primarily guided by the surface features of the cue. That is, data-limited test stimuli must be resolved on the basis of perceptual operations.

This conclusion is derived in part from experiments by Weldon and Roediger (1987; see too, Weldon, Roediger, & Challis, 1989). They found the usual pictorial advantage in free recall when people studied pictures rather than words,

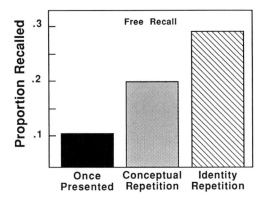

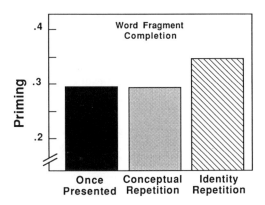

FIG. 1.11. Repetition effects in free recall and word fragment completion. Both identity repetitions (umbrella-umbrella) and conceptual repetitions (umbrella-parasol) improved free recall over single presentations. On the word fragment completion test, however, only identity
repetitions, which repeated identical surface forms, boosted priming
beyond levels obtained with single presentations. Data from Roediger
and Challis (in preparation).

but this reversed on priming in word fragment completion (see the top panel of
Fig. 1.10). Prior study of words produced greater priming than prior study of
pictures, which the authors attributed to the data-driven nature of the test. But
many other studies in the literature have shown that the picture superiority effect
is obtained in tests of word recognition (see Madigan, 1983). That is, prior study
of a picture of an elephant (instead of study of the word) supports better recognition of the word *elephant* on a later test. Yet surely the word *elephant* on the test

matches the studied word better than its pictorial counterpart. The test word in recognition should also provide a better match than the fragment, __LEP-__AN__, and yet primed fragment completion is a data-driven test and word recognition (where more data are presented) is not. Why? Test orientation must play a critical role. In fragment completion and other implicit tests subjects are told to produce the first thing that comes to mind in response to the fragment, which constrains them to be guided by surface features of the fragment. In standard slow-paced recognition tests, on the other hand, perceiving the word is easy; the challenge is to match the concept derived from the test word to the memories of recent experiences. Therefore, recognition is less affected by the match of perceptual processing between study and test events.

In summary, test instructions also play a role in determining processing mode. Although it is certainly possible to implement a data-driven episodic memory test, it is difficult to keep subjects focused on the perceptual nature of word cues and away from their meaning (Blaxton, 1985). Explicit test instructions seem to encourage conceptually driven processing, probably because we normally retrieve the meaning of events. Implicit test instructions, in conjunction with data-limited displays, probably encourage more superficial processing and attention to surface features. However, we suspect from our own work that when subjects are given cues perceptually similar to target items but with explicit instructions, it will be difficult to override data-driven retrieval (Roediger & Weldon, 1987; Weldon et al., 1989).

ADVANTAGES AND DISADVANTAGES
OF THE TRANSFER OF PROCEDURES APPROACH

We believe that the procedural approach described in this chapter accounts well for dissociations in remembering, at least for the bulk of the evidence collected from normal subjects. The ideas are similar to those proposed by Tulving and Thomson (1973), Morris et al. (1977), and Kolers and Roediger (1984) to account for numerous phenomena in other domains, so the breadth of explanatory power should be great. A major premise of this approach is that the existence of dissociations among measures of retention does not require postulation of special systems. As Kolers and Roediger (1984) noted, it is not the fact of "dissociations that needs to be explained, for that is the natural state of affairs; it is the characteristics of tasks—and relations among their underlying procedures—that needs explaining" (p. 439).

In this chapter we have tried to specify our ideas, particularly with regard to the distinction between data-driven and conceptually driven processing. We have provided an operational definition that should permit investigators to determine whether a particular task employing verbal materials is data-driven or conceptually driven. We have also specified converging operations. These statements permit falsification of the theory. For example, tasks classified as purely data-driven should not be affected by encoding variables that cause elaboration of processing, but should be affected by manipulations of surface features. Similarly, tasks determined to be conceptually driven by our litmus test of a positive generation effect should be unaffected by manipulations of surface variables, but should be influenced by elaborative factors. The procedural approach also predicts the form of an interaction or dissociation among study and test conditions, rather than simply predicting some dissociation.

The primary drawback we see in the procedural approach is its inability to account easily for certain phenomena found in amnesic patients. The primary impetus for our investigations of dissociations among memory measures came from observations in amnesic patients, so ideally we would like the ideas to apply forcefully to phenomena in that domain. And they do, but only up to a point. Perhaps the most natural extrapolation would be to argue that amnesics should show preserved priming on data-driven tests of retention, but not on conceptually-driven tests. The perceptual record may be intact for amnesics, so this story would go, but their brain injury may have rendered them incapable of deriving benefits from elaborative processing. A check of the data bearing on this hypothesis may be made by referring back to Table 1.1, which lists the tasks on which amnesics show preserved priming, according to Shimamura's (1986) review. The data-driven hypothesis of preserved priming works well for most of the tasks—repetition priming in completion of fragmented pictures and words, lexical decision, perceptual identification, and (arguably) for preference judgments and for spelling of homophones, although little is known about these last two tasks. However, preserved priming in free association tasks with semantic cues (e.g., Gardner, Boller, Moreines, & Butters, 1973) and in word completion with new associates (Graf & Schacter, 1985) cannot be covered by the simple view that preserved priming always reflects data-driven processing. Because preserved priming has been shown on what seem to be conceptually driven tasks, we must abandon the simplest extension of our ideas to the full range of amnesic tasks.

The failure of our theory to deal with the full range of preserved priming in amnesics is unfortunate, but we hardly see any reason to abandon it on that account. Part of the problem is simply the greater specificity of our views on what should be preserved. All the tasks in Table 1.1 might be said to reflect procedural knowledge, or alternatively the operation of semantic memory. But these terms and their contrasts (declarative and episodic, respectively) are not as well specified as are the postulated forms of processing discussed previously. We do not have operational definitions of either set of terms, much less a set of converging operations.

Moscovitch (1984) reviewed the literature on preserved priming in amnesia and concluded that three features appeared in all tasks on which preserved priming occurs. First, the tasks were highly structured so that the goals and means to achieve them were clear. Second, the strategies and responses needed to accomplish the tasks already existed in the subjects' repertoires. Third, task performance did not require reference to particular postmorbid episodes. One could posit a memory system that had just these properties, of course, and say that it was spared in amnesia, but we prefer Moscovitch's (1984; Moscovitch, Winocur, & McLachlan, 1986) functional approach that focuses on specification of the necessary and sufficient procedural requirements for determining preserved priming (see Weiskrantz, this volume, too).

CONCLUSIONS

We have argued for a theory emphasizing transfer-appropriate processing, and against the notion of separate memory systems, to explain dissociations among measures of retention. We now retreat from this hard line by making a few additional points in conclusion. First, as we noted earlier, it seems likely that more than one memory system exists in the human brain for comparative and phylogenetic reasons. The human brain is larger and more complex than any other brain and it seems likely that more complicated mechanisms exist than in many creatures with less complex neural structures and relatively simple abilities to learn. Second, elegant animal work by Mishkin and Appenzeller (e.g., 1987), Olton (this volume), and others clearly shows operation of different neural structures in various forms of learning. However, the direct relevance of this evidence for the particular theories advanced to account for preserved priming in amnesics, and other dissociations among memory measures, is not clear at this time. The reason is related to the first point: the animal work has been conducted with systems less complex than the human brain. The interesting observations from amnesics and from normals is that intact priming occurs even for verbal material, and thus work with rats or even monkeys may not uncover how this verbal information is represented. Third, we must admit that there is no inherent reason that an approach specifying both memory systems and something like processing modes or procedures cannot be partially correct. Neural structures require processing for their operation, and procedures must be carried out by the brain. A theory specifying both structural bases and processing assumptions is needed (Anderson, 1978), but those presently on the scene emphasize either structure to the relative neglect of processing assumptions (the systems approaches) or processing assumptions to the relative neglect of structure (our own approach). We defend our own bias at the present stage of knowledge as more fruitful, because it focuses attention on the procedural (behavioral) aspects of performance and deflects attention away from the metaphysics of identifying hidden systems and wondering in what complex arrangements they may be ordered. In contrast, our own approach lays out a program of research needed for its proper test, which will also provide a wealth of basic information about the tasks thought to reflect implicit retention.

ACKNOWLEDGMENTS

This research was supported by Grant RO1 HD15054 from the National Institute of Child Health and Human Development. The authors appreciate the comments of F. I. M. Craik, R. G. Crowder, J. M. Gardiner, J. H. Neely, M. A. McDaniel, and E. Tulving on an earlier version.

REFERENCES

Anderson, J. R. (1978). Arguments concerning representations for mental imagery. *Psychological Review, 85,* 249–277.

Baddeley, A., & Warrington, E. K. (1970). Amnesia and the distinction between long- and short-term memory. *Journal of Verbal Learning and Verbal Behavior, 9,* 176–189.

Begg, I., & Snider, A. (1987). The generation effect: Evidence for generalized inhibition. *Journal of Experimental Psychology: Learning, Memory, and Cognition, 13,* 553–563.

Blaxton, T. A. (1985). *Investigating dissociations among memory measures: Support for a transfer appropriate processing framework.* Doctoral dissertation, Purdue University.

Bransford, J. D., Franks, J. J., Morris, C. D., & Stein, B. S. (1979). Some general constraints on learning and memory research. In L. S. Cermak & F. I. M. Craik (Eds.), *Levels of processing in human memory* (pp. 331–354). Hillsdale, NJ: Lawrence Erlbaum Associates.

Carroll, M., Byrne, B., & Kirsner, K. (1985). Autobiographical memory and perceptual learning: A developmental study using picture recognition. *Memory & Cognition, 13,* 273–279.

Clarke, R., & Morton, J. (1983). Cross-modality facilitation in tachistoscopic word recognition. *Quarterly Journal of Experimental Psychology, 35A,* 79–96.

Corkin, S. (1968). Acquisition of motor skill after bilateral medial temporal-lobe excision. *Neuropsychologica, 6,* 255–266.

Craik, F. I. M. (1979). Levels of processing: Overview and closing comments. In L. S. Cermak & F. I. M. Craik (Eds.), *Levels of processing in human memory* (pp. 447–461). Hillsdale, NJ: Lawrence Erlbaum Associates.

Craik, F. I. M., & Lockhart, R. S. (1972). Levels of processing: A framework for memory research. *Journal of Verbal Learning and Verbal Behavior, 11,* 671–684.

Craik, F. I. M., & Tulving, E. (1975). Depth of processing and the retention of words in episodic memory. *Journal of Experimental Psychology: General, 104,* 268–294.

Duchek, J. M., & Neely, J. H. (in press). A dissociative word-frequency × levels-of-processing interaction in episodic recognition and lexical decision tasks. *Memory & Cognition.*

Durgunoğlu, A. Y., & Roediger, H. L. (1987). Test differences in accessing bilingual memory. *Journal of Memory and Language, 26,* 377–391.

Ebbinghaus, H. (1964). *Memory: A contribution to experimental psychology.* New York: Dover. (Originally published 1885; translated 1913)

Fisher, R. P., & Craik, F. I. M. (1977). The interaction between encoding and retrieval operations in cued recall. *Journal of Experimental Psychology: Human Learning and Perception, 3,* 153–171.

Gardiner, J. M. (1988). Generation and priming effects in word-fragment completion. *Journal of Experimental Psychology: Learning, Memory, and Cognition, 14,* 495–501.

Gardner, H., Boller, F., Moreines, J., & Butters, N. (1973). Retrieving information from Korsakoff patients: Effects of categorical cues and reference to the task. *Cortex, 9,* 165–175.

Garner, W. R., Hake, H., & Eriksen, C. W. (1956). Operationism and the concept of perception. *Psychological Review, 63,* 149–159.

Graf, P. & Mandler, G. (1984). Activation makes words more accessible, but not necessarily more retrievable. *Journal of Verbal Learning and Verbal Behavior, 23,* 553–568.

Graf, P., Mandler, G., & Haden, P. (1982). Simulating amnesic symptoms in normal subjects. *Science, 218,* 1243–1244.

Graf, P. & Schacter, D. L. (1985). Implicit and explicit memory for new associations in normal and amnesic subjects. *Journal of Experimental Psychology: Learning, Memory, and Cognition, 11,* 501–518.

Graf, P., Shimamura, A. P., & Squire, L. R. (1985). Priming across modalities and priming across category levels: Extending the domain of preserved function in amnesia. *Journal of Experimental Psychology: Learning, Memory, and Cognition, 11,* 386–396.

Graf, P., Squire, L. R., & Mandler, G. (1984). The information that amnesic patients do not forget. *Journal of Experimental Psychology: Learning, Memory, and Cognition, 10,* 164–178.

Hintzman, D. L. (1984). Episodic versus semantic memory: A distinction whose time has come— and gone? *The Behavioral and Brain Sciences, 7,* 240—241.

Hirshman, E., & Bjork, R. A. (1988). The generation effect: Support for a two-factor theory. *Journal of Experimental Psychology: Learning, Memory, and Cognition, 14,* 484–494.

Jacoby, L. L. (1978). On interpreting the effects of repetition: Solving a problem versus remembering a solution. *Journal of Verbal Learning and Verbal Behavior, 17,* 649–667.

Jacoby, L. L. (1983). Remembering the data: Analyzing interactive processes in reading. *Journal of Verbal Learning and Verbal Behavior, 22,* 485–508.

Jacoby, L. L. & Dallas, M. (1981). On the relationship between autobiographical memory and perceptual learning. *Journal of Experimental Psychology: General, 110,* 306–340.

Jacoby, L. L., & Witherspoon, D. (1982). Remembering without awareness. *Canadian Journal of Psychology, 32,* 300–324.

Johnson, M. K., Kim, J. K., & Risse, G. (1985). Do alcoholic Korsakoff's syndrome patients acquire affective reactions? *Journal of Experimental Psychology: Learning, Memory, and Cognition, 11,* 22–36.

Kirsner, K., & Dunn, J. (1985). The perceptual record: A common factor in repetition priming and attribute retention. In M. I. Posner & O. S. M. Marin (Eds.), *Mechanisms of attention: Attention and performance XI* (pp. 547–566). Hillsdale, NJ: Lawrence Erlbaum Associates.

Kirsner, K., Milech, D., & Standen, P. (1983). Common and modality-specific processes in the mental lexicon. *Memory & Cognition, 11,* 621–630.

Kirsner, K., Milech, D., & Stumpfel, V. (1986). Word and picture identification: Is representational parsimony possible? *Memory & Cognition, 14,* 398–408.

Kirsner, K., Smith, M. C., Lockhart, R. S., King, M.-L., & Jain, M. (1984). The bilingual lexicon: Language-specific units in an integrated network. *Journal of Verbal Learning and Verbal Behavior, 23,* 519–539.

Kolers, P. A. (1973). Remembering operations. *Memory & Cognition, 1,* 347–355.

Kolers, P. A. (1975). Specificity of operations in sentence recognition. *Cognitive Psychology, 7,* 289–306.

Kolers, P. A. (1979). A pattern-analyzing basis of recognition. In L. S. Cermak & F. I. M. Craik (Eds.), *Levels of processing in human memory* (pp. 363–384). Hillsdale, NJ: Lawrence Erlbaum Associates.

Kolers, P. A., & Roediger, H. L. (1984). Procedures of mind. *Journal of Verbal Learning and Verbal Behavior, 23,* 425–449.

Lockhart, R. S. (1979). Remembering events: Discussion of papers by Jacoby and Craik, Battig, and Nelson. In L. S. Cermak & F. I. M. Craik (Eds.), *Levels of processing in human memory* (pp. 77–85). Hillsdale, NJ: Lawrence Erlbaum Associates.

McDaniel, M. A., Friedman, A., & Bourne, L. E. (1978). Remembering the levels of information in words. *Memory & Cognition, 6,* 156–164.

McDaniel, M. A., Waddill, P. J., Einstein, G. O. (1988). A contextual account of the generation effect: A three factor theory. *Journal of Memory and Language, 27,* 521–536.

McKoon, G., Ratcliff, R., & Dell, G. S. (1986). A critical evaluation of the semantic/episodic distinction. *Journal of Experimental Psychology: Learning, Memory, & Cognition 12,* 295–306.

Madigan, S. (1983). Picture memory. In J. C. Yuille (Ed.), *Imagery, memory and cognition: Essays in honour of Allan Paivio* (pp. 65–89). Hillsdale, NJ: Lawrence Erlbaum Associates.

Mandler, G. (1980). Recognizing: The judgment of previous occurrence. *Psychological Review, 87,* **252–271.**

Mishkin, M., & Appenzeller, T. (1987). The anatomy of memory. *Scientific American, 256,* 80–90.

Monsell, S. (1985). Repetition and the lexicon. In A. W. Ellis (Ed.), *Progress in the psychology of language* (pp. 147–195). Hillsdale, NJ & London: Lawrence Erlbaum Associates.

Morris, C. D., Bransford, J. D., & Franks, J. J. (1977). Levels of processing versus transfer appropriate processing. *Journal of Verbal Learning and Verbal Behavior, 16,* 519–533.

Moscovitch, M. (1982). Multiple dissociations of function in amnesia. In L. Cermak (Ed.), *Human memory and amnesia* (pp. 337–370). Hillsdale, NJ: Lawrence Erlbaum Associates.

Moscovitch, M. (1984). The sufficient conditions for demonstrating preserved memory in amnesia: A task analysis. In L.R. Squire & N. Butters (Eds.), *The neuropsychology of memory* (pp. 104–114). New York: Guilford Press.

Moscovitch, M., Winocur, G., & McLachlan, D. (1986). Memory as assessed by recognition and reading time in normal and memory-impaired people with Alzheimer's disease and other neurological disorders. *Journal of Experimental Psychology: General, 115,* 331–347.

Murdock, B. B., & Walker, K. D. (1969). Modality effects in free recall. *Journal of Verbal Learning and Verbal Behavior, 8,* 665–676.

Nairne, J. S. (1988). The mnemonic value of perceptual identification. *Journal of Experimental Psychology, 14,* 248–255.

Nairne, J. S., Pusen, C., & Widner, R. L. (1985). Representation in the mental lexicon: Implications for theories of the generation effect. *Memory & Cognition, 13,* 183–191.

Neely, J. H., & Tekman, H. (in preparation). *Is the lexical decision task predominately data-driven or conceptually-driven?*

Nelson, D. L. (1979). Remembering pictures and words: Appearance, significance, and name. In L. S. Cermak & F. I. M. Craik (Eds.), *Levels of processing in human memory* (pp. 45–76). Hillsdale, NJ: Lawrence Erlbaum Associates.

Nelson, D. L., Canas, J. J., Bajo, M., & Keelean, P. D. (1987). Comparing word fragment completion and cued-recall with letter cues. *Journal of Experimental Psychology: Learning, Memory, and Cognition 13,* 542–552.

Nissen, M. J., Cohen, N. J., & Corkin, S. (1981). The amnesic patient H. M.: Learning and retention of perceptual skills. *Society for Neurosciences Abstracts, 7,* 235.

Paivio, A. (1986). *Mental representations: A dual coding approach.* New York: Oxford University Press.

Richardson-Klavehn, A., & Bjork, R. A. (1988). Measures of memory. *Annual Review of Psychology, 39,* 475–543.

Roediger, H. L. (1984). Does current evidence from dissociation experiments favor the episodic/semantic distinction? *The Behavioral and Brain Sciences, 7,* 252–254.

Roediger, H. L. (1985). Remembering Ebbinghaus. *Contemporary Psychology, 30,* 519–523.

Roediger, H. L., & Blaxton, T. A. (1987a). Effects of varying modality, surface features, and retention interval on priming in word fragment completion. *Memory & Cognition, 15*, 379–388.

Roediger, H. L., & Blaxton, T. A. (1987b). Retrieval modes produce dissociations in memory for surface information. In D. Gorfein & R. R. Hoffman (Eds.), *Memory and cognitive processes: The Ebbinghaus Centennial Conference* (pp. 349–379). Hillsdale, N.J.: Lawrence Erlbaum Associates.

Roediger, H. L., & Challis, B. H. (in preparation). *Effects of identity repetition and conceptual repetition on free recall and word fragment completion.*

Roediger, H. L., & Weldon, M. S. (1987). Reversing the picture superiority effect. In M. A. McDaniel & M. Pressley (Eds.), *Imagery and related mnemonic processes: Theories, individual differences, and applications* (pp. 151–174). New York: Springer-Verlag.

Roediger, H. L., Weldon, M. S., Stadler, M. A., & Riegler, G. H. (in preparation). *Direct comparison of word stems and word fragments in implicit and explicit retention tests.*

Ryle, G. (1949). *The concept of mind.* New York: Barnes & Noble.

Schacter, D. L. (1987). Implicit memory: History and current status. *Journal of Experimental Psychology: Learning, Memory, and Cognition, 13*, 501–518.

Sherry, D. F., & Schacter, D. L. (1987). The evolution of multiple memory systems. *Psychological Review, 94*, 439–454.

Shimamura, A. P. (1986). Priming effects in amnesia: Evidence for a dissociable memory function. *Quarterly Journal of Experimental Psychology, 38A*, 619–644.

Slamecka, N. J., & Graf, P. (1978). The generation effect: Delineation of a phenomenon. *Journal of Experimental Psychology: Human Learning and Memory, 4*, 592–604.

Slamecka, N. J., & Katsaiti, L. T. (1987). The generation effect as an artifact of selective displaced rehearsal. *Journal of Memory and Language, 26*, 589–607.

Smith, E. S. & Branscombe, N. (in press). Category accessibility as implicit memory. *Journal of Experimental Social Psychology.*

Squire, L. R. (1986). Mechanisms of memory. *Science, 232*, 1612–1619.

Squire, L. R. (1987). *Memory and brain.* New York: Oxford University Press.

Srinivas, K., & Roediger, H. L. (in preparation). *Testing the nature of two implicit tests: Dissociations between conceptually-driven and data-driven processes.*

Srull, T. K., & Wyer, R. S. (1980). Category accessibility and social perception: Some implications for the study of person memory and interpersonal judgments. *Journal of Personality and Social Psychology, 38*, 841–856.

Stein, B. S. (1978). Depth of processing reexamined: The effects of precision of encoding and test appropriateness. *Journal of Verbal Learning and Verbal Behavior, 17*, 165–174.

Tanenhaus, M. K., Flanigan, H., & Seidenberg, M. S. (1980). Orthographic and phonological code activation in auditory and visual word recognition. *Memory & Cognition, 8*, 513–520.

Thomson, D. M., & Tulving, E. (1970). Associative encoding and retrieval: Weak and strong cues. *Journal of Experimental Psychology, 86*, 255–262.

Tulving, E. (1968). Theoretical issues in free recall. In T. R. Dixon & D. L. Horton (Eds.), *Verbal behavior and general behavior theory* (pp. 2–36). Englewood Cliffs, NJ: Prentice-Hall.

Tulving, E. (1972). Episodic and semantic memory. In E. Tulving & W. Donaldson (Eds.), *Organization and memory* (pp. 381–403). New York: Academic Press.

Tulving, E. (1979). Relation between encoding specificity and levels of processing. In L. S. Cermak & F. I. M. Craik (Eds.), *Levels of processing in human memory* (pp. 405–428). Hillsdale, NJ: Lawrence Erlbaum Associates.

Tulving, E. (1983). *Elements of episodic memory.* New York: Oxford University Press.

Tulving, E. (1984). Relations among components and processes of memory. The *Behavioral and Brain Sciences, 7*, 257–263.

Tulving, E. (1985). How many memory systems are there? *American Psychologist, 40*, 385–398.

Tulving, E. (1986). What kind of hypothesis is the distinction between episodic and semantic memory? *Journal of Experimental Psychology: Learning, Memory, and Cognition, 12*, 307–311.

Tulving, E., & Osler, S. (1968). Effectiveness of retrieval cues in memory for words. *Journal of Experimental Psychology, 77,* 593–601.

Tulving, E., & Pearlstone, Z. (1966). Availability versus accessibility of information in memory for words. *Journal of Verbal Learning and Verbal Behavior, 5,* 381–391.

Tulving, E., & Thomson, D. M. (1973). Encoding specificity and retrieval processes in episodic memory. *Psychological Review, 80,* 352–373.

Tulving, E., Schacter, D. L., & Stark, H. A. (1982). Priming effects in word-fragment completion are independent of recognition memory. *Journal of Experimental Psychology: Learning, Memory, and Cognition, 8,* 336–342.

Warrington, E. K., & Weiskrantz, L. (1968). New method of testing long-term retention with special reference to amnesic patients. *Nature, 217,* 972–974.

Warrington, E. K., & Weiskrantz, L. (1970). Amnesic syndrome: Consolidation or retrieval? *Nature, 228,* 629–630.

Watkins, M. J., & Gibson, J. M. (1988). On the relation between perceptual priming and recognition memory. *Journal of Experimental Psychology: Learning, Memory, and Cognition, 14,* 477–483.

Weiskrantz, L. (1986). *Blindsight.* New York: Oxford University Press.

Weldon, M. S. (1988). *Mechanisms underlying data-driven retrieval.* Unpublished doctoral dissertation, Purdue University, West Lafayette, IN.

Weldon, M. S., & Roediger, H. L. (1987). Altering retrieval demands reverses the picture superiority effect. *Memory & Cognition, 15,* 269–280.

Weldon, M. S., Roediger, H. L., & Challis, B. H. (1989). The properties of retrieval cues constrain the picture superiority effect. *Memory & Cognition.*

Winnick, W. A., & Daniel, S. A. (1970). Two kinds of response priming in tachistoscopic recognition. *Journal of Experimental Psychology, 84,* 74–81.

Witherspoon, D., & Moscovitch, M. (in press). Stochastic independence between two implicit memory tests. *Journal of Experimental Psychology: Learning, Memory, and Cognition.*

2 On the Making of Episodes

Fergus I. M. Craik
University of Toronto

On a number of occasions Endel Tulving has stressed the central role of events and episodes in an analysis of memory. In Tulving's (1984) words, "The basic units of perceived time are events. An event is something that occurs in a particular place at a particular time. The closely related term 'episode' refers to an event that is part of an ongoing series of events" (p. 229). Also, "The basic unit of the conceptual analysis of episodic memory is an act of remembering that begins with an event perceived by the rememberer, and ends with recollective experience" (p. 229). Typically, a remembered event or episode consists of some focal elements (e.g., objects or actions) framed within a spatiotemporal context. The act of encoding serves to integrate the representations of the event with its context so that later presentation of part of the context (recall) or part of the focal event (recognition) can lead to *redintegration* of the entire encoded episode.

The integration of event and context is thus of crucial importance in the understanding of memory processes, yet very little is known about the factors that provide the mental 'glue' to hold elements together. The perceptual principles described by the Gestalt psychologists represent one attempt to grapple with the issue, as does other work in perception seeking to explain how a series of discrete visual fixations is transformed into a continuous whole (e.g., Kolers, 1973). In memory theory, the work on organization (e.g., Mandler, 1967; Miller, 1956; Tulving, 1962) is also relevant to some extent.

In this chapter I discuss two lines of work that bear on the problem; both are somewhat preliminary, but the ideas and findings are presented nonetheless in the hope that they draw attention to the issues and perhaps trigger debate.

INTEGRATION OF EVENT AND CONTEXT

The first line of work stems from an unpublished study carried out some years ago by Alan Allport. In turn, Allport's experiment was based on a study by Huppert and Piercy (1976) involving Korsakoff patients "who were severely amnesic by all the usual clinical criteria. Despite this, after being shown 80 target pictures, they could make 80% correct judgments on a yes/no recognition test one week later" (Huppert & Piercy, 1982). In the Huppert and Piercy experiment, Korsakoff and control subjects were first shown 80 pictures; these pictures were thus "familiar" to all subjects. The actual recognition memory experiment was carried out on the following day. The presentation list consisted of 40 completely new pictures plus 40 "familiar" pictures from Day 1 (the previous set). The recognition test was carried out 10 minutes later; it consisted of the 80 target items, plus 80 distractors, 40 of which were completely new, and 40 of which were also drawn from the "familiar" set presented on the preceding day. Although the recognition performance of the patients was poorer than that of the controls for both "new" and "familiar" items, the Korsakoffs' performance was disproportionately worse on the familiar pictures. It seemed that these amnesic patients knew that they had seen some items before, but were poor at discriminating those seen only on Day 1 from those presented again on Day 2. Further work described by Huppert and Piercy (1982) confirmed the notion that Korsakoff patients base their recognition on a nonspecific feeling of familiarity, and are impaired in their ability to form associations between items and their context of occurrence. This impairment of contextual integration would largely spare the patient's ability to recognize events, but would result in an inability to remember where and when the event occurred (see also Mandler, 1980).

Allport conjectured that division of attention during learning might have an analogous effect of impairing the integration of events and context in normal subjects. He therefore attempted to mimic this aspect of the amnesic syndrome in college subjects by having them learn a list of words while they also performed a mental arithmetic task. In greater detail, one group of subjects learned two lists of words under full-attention conditions; one list was presented in the kitchen of their student apartment and the second list was presented in the bedroom. A second group of subjects repeated the experiment under conditions of divided attention. Both groups were tested the following day—first for recognition of the words themselves and second for their ability to discriminate kitchen from bedroom words. The results showed that the divided-attention subjects *recognized* almost as many words as their full-attention counterparts (89% and 99% respectively) but the divided-attention subjects were relatively poor at context discrimination (46% correct compared with 95% correct for the full-attention controls). It seems that withdrawal of attention may impair contextual integration more than it impairs the ability to register and later recognize the event itself.

Some caution may be in order, however. The recognition performance of the control group is right on ceiling, so the possible interaction between divided attention and recognition/context recall certainly needs to be checked. This was the purpose of an experiment carried out by Ruth Ann Sanders (1985) as part of her Master's thesis. Sanders presented six lists of 10 words to be learned; the words were presented serially, visually, and in conjunction with a visual scene shown as a color slide projected next to each word. The scenes were colorful and distinctive (e.g., a market scene, an English garden, a beach scene, and the like). Subjects were told to learn the word list by associating each word with the adjacent scene; so if the word was "giraffe," they should envision a giraffe in the English garden, for example. Each word was exposed for 5 seconds, and the scenes were blocked—so that one scene stayed on for 10 successive words, was then replaced by another scene for the next 10 words, and so on until the 60 words (six scenes) had been presented. In addition to the control group of 18 young adult subjects learning the lists under full attention conditions, a further group of 18 young subjects learned the lists while simultaneously performing an auditory monitoring task (monitoring a continuous string of auditorily presented digits for "targets", defined as three successive odd digits, e.g., 391 or 715). This second group thus learned under divided-attention (DA) conditions. A third group was also run; this group consisted of 18 people aged 60–80 who learned the words under full-attention conditions. The older participants were mostly retired professional people; they lived at home and were in good health. They had volunteered to take part in experiments on memory and learning, and they were tested in the lab, as were the younger groups. A few minutes after the acquisition phase, subjects in all groups were first given a recognition memory test for the words themselves (60 targets + 60 distractors), and then a test in which the original 60 words were presented (in scrambled order) and subjects made a forced-choice decision regarding the scene with which each word had been presented in the first phase.

On the argument that older people may have reduced processing resources and so perform like young people under conditions of divided attention (Craik & Byrd, 1982), it was expected that both the young DA group and the old group would show a considerable reduction in the ability to assign context, but little if any reduction in recognition memory for the words, compared to the young full-attention group. (It should perhaps be stressed that the Young DA group performed the secondary task during acquisition only; during recognition and context testing all subjects performed under conditions of full attention.)

The results (Table 2.1) are expressed in terms of Hits minus False Alarms for both word recognition and context identification; they show that the expectations were borne out in the case of the old group, but that performance for the young DA group dropped as much in word recognition as it did in context identification.

TABLE 2.1
Proportions of Words Recognized and Contexts
Correctly Assigned by Three Groups (Hits Minus False Alarms
in Both Cases); Data from Sanders (1985)

Group:	Word Recognition	Context Identification
Young (full attention)	.86	.61
Young (divided attention)	.54	.27
Old (full attention)	.70	.22

In an attempt to gain some further insight into the relation between item recognition and context identification, the data from individual subjects in Sanders' experiment were examined in a scatter plot. What is the expected function linking the two variables? There are many possibilities, some of which are shown in Fig. 2.1. These hypothetical functions trace the changing relations between

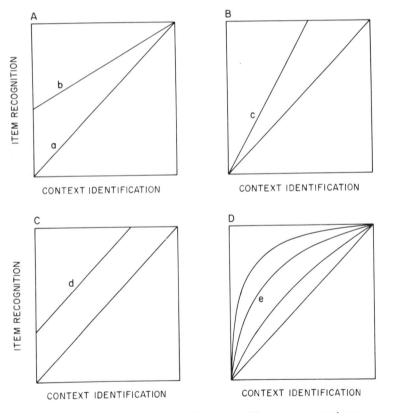

FIG. 2.1.   Hypothetical curves relating recognition memory and context identification.

item recognition and context identification as performance declines from perfect performance (the probabilities of both item recognition and context identification = 1.0) at the top right of each figure, towards the y axis, at which point context identification is at chance. Differences in performance might be associated with individual differences in encoding and retrieval, or with the withdrawal of sufficient time or "processing resources" to perform adequate encoding and retrieval operations. On the assumption that item recognition is as good or better than context identification, possible functions will lie in the top left half of the figure. Function a assumes that item recognition and context identification drop off at the same rate, whereas function b (also shown in Fig. 2.1A) is a linear version of Allport's suggestion, that context identification declines more rapidly than does item recognition. Function b also suggests that there is still substantial item recognition even when ability to identify context has reached chance levels. Function c (Fig. 2.1B) assumes that item recognition and context identification reach chance levels together, but that recognition reaches ceiling at a point where context identification is less than perfect. Figure 2.1C shows another variant, in which there is still substantial item recognition when context identification is at chance, and context identification is less than perfect when item recognition reaches the ceiling. Figure 2.1D shows a set of curvilinear relations between the two variables. In this case, item recognition and context identification converge at both 0.0 and 1.0; as resources or abilities decline from perfect performance, context identification drops off relatively rapidly at first, but then drops off slowly as performance approaches chance levels; conversely, item recognition drops off slowly at first, but then relatively rapidly.

The scatterplot data from Sanders' experiment are too variable to yield many clues as to which (if any) of the functions in Fig. 2.1 they resemble. To reduce the variability, the data from all three conditions (old subjects plus the two groups of young subjects) were treated as one pool of 54 observations (3 conditions × 18 subjects per group) and divided into six groups of 9 subjects each (regardless of their experimental condition) on the basis of item recognition scores. That is, the mean item-recognition and context-identification scores were calculated for successive sixths of the pooled observations. The resulting six data points are shown in Fig. 2.2. No formal curve-fitting has been attempted, but by inspection, functions of the type a and b do not seem at all likely. Functions of the type c, d, or e are better candidates, with d or e perhaps providing closer approximations. A function of type e is shown to illustrate the argument made later in the chapter. It is also possible, of course, that separate functions underlie each of the three experimental groups.

Two further studies have since been conducted in collaboration with Robin and Lorna Morris to gain further information about the relations between item recognition and context identification. The first study was simply an extension of Sanders' (1985) experiment; it was run in an attempt to generate more data points of the sort shown in Fig. 2.2. Two groups of 24 young subjects were tested, one

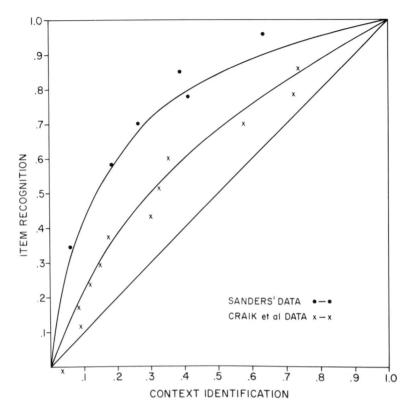

FIG. 2.2. Relations between item recognition and context identification. Data points ●———● are from Sanders (1985); points x———x are from an unpublished study by Craik, Morris, and Morris.

under full-attention conditions and the other under divided-attention conditions. Each subject was first familiarized with six distinctive scenes, then a series of 30 common concrete nouns was shown, with each word being presented along with one of the six pictures. In this case (unlike in Sanders' experiment) the pictures were not blocked, but changed from one trial to the next; however, in the series of 30 words, each picture was shown five times. For one series of 30 words, the successive word-picture pairs were presented at a 3-second rate. Each subject was also presented with two further series at a 5-second rate and a 7-second rate respectively. These further series used the same six pictures, but 30 new words in each case. The order of the three rate conditions was counterbalanced over subjects. The divided-attention group was treated identically, except that subjects carried out an auditory monitoring task while watching the word-picture pairs. As in Sanders' experiment, subjects were instructed to envision each word's referent in the context of its accompanying picture. After each series of

30 items, subjects were first given a word-recognition test (30 targets plus 60 distractors) and then a context-identification test in which the 30 words were re-presented and a forced-choice decision was made with respect to which of the six pictures had been shown with each word in the initial presentation.

The basic results are shown in Table 2.2. Clearly, performance on both item recognition and context identification drop as encoding time is reduced from 7 to 3 seconds; also, performance levels are substantially lower for the divided-attention group. But there is little evidence that performance declines more rapidly in context identification than it does in recognition. The differences between full- and divided-attention groups for item recognition scores are .29, .35, and .36 for the 3, 5, and 7-second conditions respectively, whereas the corresponding difference values for context identification are .26, .44, and .40 respectively. As in Sanders' data, then, there is little apparent support for All-port's suggestion that division of attention reduces the ability to remember context while having relatively little effect on recognition memory.

However, another analysis (suggested to me by Endel Tulving) is rather more supportive. If divided attention reduces the ability to integrate events and their context, the conditional probabilities of context identification, given successful item recognition, should be lower for the divided attention group. This is in fact the case; the conditional probabilities for the full attention group are .55, .71, and .68, for 3, 5, and 7-second presentation rates respectively, whereas the corresponding values for the divided attention group are .33, .35, and .37 respectively. These values are in good agreement with the data from Sanders' (1985) study when these latter data were similarly analyzed. The rate of presentation in Sanders' study was 5 seconds per word; the conditional probabilities of context identification given correct word recognition for the young–full attention, young–divided attention, and old groups were .69, .40, and .37 respectively.

The data in Table 2.2 were broken down into the 12 highest-scoring subjects (on the basis of recognition scores) and 12 lowest-scoring subjects, for each of the two groups. The two resulting sets of 6 data points are shown in Fig. 2.3. The full-attention data are reasonably well fitted by a straight line of type *b* (from Fig. 2.1), although a curvilinear function of type *e,* close to the positive diagonal, would also provide a good fit. The Divided-Attention points are clustered rather

TABLE 2.2
Proportions of Words Recognized and Contexts Identified
(Hits Minus False Alarms in Both Cases) for Two Groups
of Subjects and Three Rates of Presentation

Group:	Full Attention			Divided Attention		
Presentation rate (sec)	3	5	7	3	5	7
Word recognition	.48	.62	.66	.19	.27	.30
Context identification	.35	.56	.55	.09	.12	.15

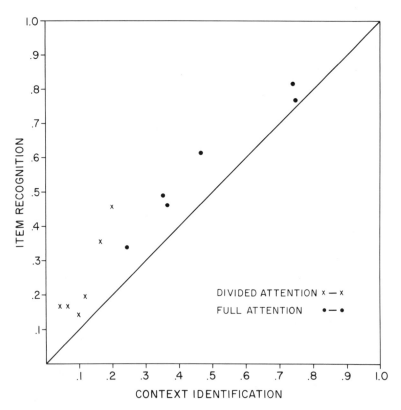

FIG. 2.3.   Relations between item recognition and context identification for Full Attention and Divided Attention groups.

close to the origin, and therefore do not yield an obvious function. A straight line of type c is a possibility, although a curvilinear function of type e, further from the positive diagonal than the Full-Attention curve, is not ruled out. To explore all possibilities, the 144 data points for the entire experiment (2 groups × 3 presentation rates × 24 subjects) were placed in one common pool, and then split down into 12 groups of 12 observations on the basis of recognition scores. The resulting data points are also shown in Fig. 2.2; they give a reasonable fit to a curvilinear function.

The possibility of a set of curvilinear functions relating item recognition and context identification suggested in Fig. 2.2 is highly speculative at this stage. It might well turn out that linear functions provide better fits, and that different conditions yield data points that lie on different functions. Nevertheless, a family of curvilinear functions is an attractive possibility, because such a model could embrace both Allport's original suggestion and the present data. That is, for a curvilinear function like the top leftmost function shown in Fig. 2.1D, recognition would decline much more slowly than context identification as performance dropped from 1.0 on both variables, and this is what Allport's experiment showed. For the model to be correct, however, recognition should decline relatively rapidly as chance levels are approached, and this appears to happen in the data shown in Fig. 2.2.

What might the parameter be of such a set of curves? That is, why might some lie close to the positive diagonal and others closer to the top left of the graph? One possibility is that events and contexts vary greatly in how easy or difficult subjects find it to form an integrated encoding of the two; some events fit naturally and easily into their contexts of occurrence, whereas others may be integrated quite poorly. In the latter case, as resources are withdrawn, recognition of the central event will remain relatively high at first whereas context identification or recall will be substantially impaired. On the other hand, when events and their contexts are well integrated, these two aspects of the overall situation will be less separable, and performance on the two variables will both decline as resources are withdrawn. Korsakoff patients (Huppert & Piercy, 1976, 1982) would fall on one of the upper left curves, as would older people (Sanders, 1985), but younger people (depending on the materials used) would tend to fall on a curve closer to the positive diagonal.

To explore this notion, Robin Morris, Lorna Morris, and I carried out a further experiment in which we attempted to manipulate the ease of integration of items and their contexts. We constructed sentences whose final words were either quite compatible with the context described in the first part of the sentence, or were arbitrary with respect to that context. We refer to the compatible series of sentences as the Integrated set, and the arbitrary sentences as the Non-integrated set. Examples of the sentences are:

Roger got to the parking lot and realized that he had lost his *keys*.

Graham was in the dining-room holding the *envelope*.

The first sentence is from the Integrated series and the second is from the Non-integrated set. In all there were 15 sentences in each set.

The rationale for the study was that if recognition of the final words from the sentences is plotted simultaneously with recall of the initial contextual part of the sentence, then data points from the Integrated set will fall on a curve (Fig. 2.1D) that is closer to the positive diagonal than will data points from the Non-integrated set. Specifically, as performance on the Non-integrated materials declines (due to time constraints or to resource limitations), ability to recall the context given the final word will fall off more rapidly than will recognition of the final word itself. In a sense, performance on the Non-integrated set should yield data that mimic the performance of the older subjects in Sanders' experiment. In contrast, recognition and recall performance from the Integrated sentences should tend to fall off at more similar rates, thereby mimicking results from the younger subjects in Sanders' experiment, and from the subjects whose data points form the lower curve in Fig. 2.2.

In overview, the sentences were presented serially to subjects who were told that memory for the last word (underlined) would be tested, but to learn the word in the context of the rest of the sentence. Later, recognition of the last words was tested (30 targets + 60 distractors) followed by a context recall test of the form:

Where was Roger when he realized that he had lost his keys?

Where was Graham when he was holding the envelope?

An attempt was made to generate different points on the hypothesized functions (shown in Fig. 2.1) by varying the time subjects has to study each sentence—either 5, 10, or 15 seconds. The design was thus three rates of presentation (5, 10, 15 seconds) × two types of sentence (Integrated/Non-integrated) with five exemplars in each combination. Forty-eight young subjects (mean age = 24.4) were tested—mostly in groups.

The results of the recognition (Hits minus False Alarms) and context recall tests are given in Table 2.3. Several points can be made from the data. First, performance on the Integrated sentences is superior to performance on the Non-integrated sentences. This is true of both recognition and recall, although the superiority of Integrated materials is greater for context recall; the result is the expected one and confirms that the Integrated/Non-integrated manipulation was successful. Second, for the Integrated sentences, the corresponding values of recognition and context recall are quite close (the average superiority of recognition is .02) showing that the points fall just above the positive diagonal in Fig. 2.1D. In contrast, the recognition values for the Non-integrated sentences are on average .19 higher than the corresponding recall values, showing that these points lie considerably above the positive diagonal. The data are plotted in Fig. 2.4. With only 3 data points per condition it is not possible to say anything very meaningful about the shapes of their underlying functions. At least they do not violate the proposed curvilinear model.

Although clearly this is work in its very early stages, the simultaneous manipulation of materials, subjects, and resources may shed some light on the factors

TABLE 2.3
Proportions of Words Recognized (Hits Minus False Alarms)
and Proportions of Contexts Recalled for Two
Sentence Types and Three Rates of Presentation

	Non-integrated Sentences			Integrated Sentences		
Rate of presentation:	5	10	15	5	10	15
Recognition	.42	.54	.61	.49	.63	.73
Context recall	.24	.36	.40	.46	.62	.70

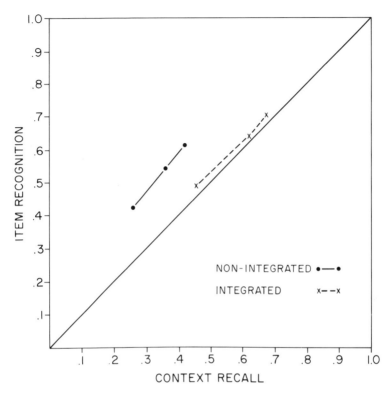

FIG. 2.4.   Recognition memory and context recall values from Integrated and Non-integrated sentences.

involved in contextual integration. The present results certainly leave the framework suggested in Fig. 2.1D as a possibility. Speculatively, time and amount of attention may trade off to determine where performance lies on a given function. In turn, the functions themselves may reflect the combination of subject and material differences that give rise to a particular degree of ease or difficulty with which that focal event and its context can be integrated—and therefore *redintegrated* at the time of retrieval.

What other factors besides subjects and materials affect the making of episodes? One candidate is the emotional impact of events, and I now report a preliminary experiment carried out to explore this issue.

THE ROLE OF AFFECT IN CONTEXTUAL INTEGRATION

There is strong anecdotal evidence that emotional events serve to create a particularly strong integration of events and their contexts. Brown and Kulik (1977) proposed the term "flashbulb memory" to denote the vivid remembering of contextual detail reported when people recall a dramatically emotional moment such as when they learned of President Kennedy's assassination. Michael Rubin and I have recently explored the possibility that much milder emotional events might act similarly to give rise to greater contextual integration. In one il-lustrative experiment we presented lists of twelve words for later free recall, and embedded in each list was a salient "target" word which was either a mildly emotional word (examples include breast, corpse, screw, lesbian, nipple, rapist) or the name of a major city (e.g., Lisbon, Dallas, Berlin, Calgary). The remain-ing words were nouns, five to seven letters in length, chosen at random from the Toronto word pool (Friendly, Franklin, Hoffman, & Rubin, 1982). Context was manipulated by presenting each word list auditorily, and spoken by one of four different tape-recorded speakers; "context identification" was thus memory for which speaker had presented a particular word. The four speakers had distinctive accents (Canadian female, South African female, Trinidadian male, Scottish male) and each presented four 12-word lists—so that a complete list was present-ed in one voice. The list presentations were preceded by each tape-recorded speaker presenting a short spoken biography of his or her background and present occupation, to familiarize subjects with the voices and to enable subjects to form an image of each speaker.

Each list contained one Target word (an emotional word for eight lists and a City word for the remaining eight), and the Target word was placed between serial positions three and nine. Each list also contained a designated Neutral control word, also in serial positions three and nine, but positioned at least one word away from the Target item. Other words of interest were the first (Primacy) and last (Recency) words in each list—we thought that Primacy words might show enhanced context identification and Recency words might show depressed identification of context (for example, negative recency may be associated with poorer contextual integration). Subjects were told that they would be asked to free-recall a random 8 of the 16 lists immediately after presentation, and that the remaining 8 lists would be tested later. They were told to attend to each voice and to relate each word to that speaker as it would help them to remember the words; however, subjects were not informed that they would later be asked to identify which speaker had presented a particular word.

Thirty-two subjects participated; words were presented at a 3-second rate, and the immediate free recall period was 1 minute; in the case of the 8 non-recalled lists a 30-second rest period was given. After all 16 lists had been presented and recalled (when requested), subjects were given a typed list consisting of the Primacy, Neutral, Target, and Recency words from all 16 lists. The 64 words were scrambled with respect to their list of origin. Subjects were reminded of the four speakers and were asked to recall which speaker had presented each of the 64 words.

The results are shown in Table 2.4. With respect to free recall, Primacy, Target, and Recency words were all recalled more frequently than were the

TABLE 2.4
Proportions of Words and Contexts
Recalled as a Function of Word Type

	Word Type				Target Type	
	Primacy	Neutral	Target	Recency	City	Emotional
Free recall	.62	.48	.70	.96	.70	.69
Voice identification	.49	.36	.48	.35	.44	.52

Neutral control words; City and Emotional words did not differ in their recall levels. The chance level for identification of original speaker's voice was .25, and Table 2.4 shows that all values are higher than this level. The context recall values for Primacy and Target words were reliably higher than those of Neutral words, but context recall for Recency words did not differ from the control level. When Target words were broken down into Emotional and City words, the effect is carried largely by the Emotional words.

It seems that item salience increases the ability to recall *context* as well as increasing item recall itself. This was true of Primacy words, of Emotional words, and of City words to a slight extent. The wider interest here is in the factors affecting the integration of events and contexts—it seems possible that emotional and unexpected events give rise to "flashbulb memories" although presumably of a much weaker sort than those occasioned by emotionally traumatic events. What are the crucial factors involved in this enhanced integration of events and their contexts of occurrence? One obvious mechanism is that salient events attract more attention, and that increased attention is associated with more elaborate processing of the event itself, and also with more integrative processing of events and their contexts. A question for further research is whether such enhancement of contextual integration is especially marked for events and contexts that are particularly compatible; that is, does item salience simply amplify pre-existing differences among items in event/context compatibility, or does salience "illuminate" *any* context in the way that the flashbulb effect imprints apparently arbitrary contexts onto the memory of emotionally traumatic incidents?

A further set of questions relates to the role of emotionality in such experimental situations. Do individual differences play a part? For example, do emotionally labile people show better context recall? Is the poor memory shown by older people associated with their 'flattened affect'? With respect to the underlying neurophysiology, Gold (1987) has recently discussed the evidence linking adrenaline release, and the associated rise in plasma glucose levels, with memory enhancement. Since it is known that emotional events are associated with the release of adrenaline (e.g., Frankenhaeuser, 1975), it is an interesting possibility that the emotional items in experimental lists also act via adrenaline release and increased blood glucose levels. It certainly makes sense biologically that emotionally significant events should be associated with enhanced memory for their time and place of occurrence (Brown & Kulik, 1977).

CONCLUSIONS

An understanding of how the stream of conscious experience is organized into events and episodes is central to our understanding of encoding and retrieval processes in episodic memory (Tulving, 1972, 1983). Features of objects and actions are presumably integrated through co-occurrence and mental contiguity; in turn, events are integrated with other events as a function of their similarity and relatedness in terms of an appropriate semantics. The integration of events with the ongoing spatio-temporal context is crucial for episodic *remembering*— as opposed to more primitive feelings of familiarity. It has been suggested that the processes of attention (or ''processing resources'') play an important role in this integration of events with their contexts; in addition, the experiment with Michael Rubin suggests that emotionality may further enhance such integration. Finally, the separation of resource and subject/material factors suggested by the results of the experiments with Ruth Ann Sanders and with Robin and Lorna Morris may lead to the development of more complete theories of episodic integration.

ACKNOWLEDGMENT

The research reported in this chapter was supported by Grant A8261 from the Natural Sciences and Engineering Research Council of Canada.

REFERENCES

Brown, R., & Kulik, J. (1977). Flashbulb memories. *Cognition, 5,* 73–99.

Craik, F. I. M., & Byrd, M. (1982). Aging and cognitive deficits: The role of attentional resources. In F. I. M. Craik & S. E. Trehub (Eds.), *Aging and cognitive processes* (pp. 191–211). New York: Plenum Press.

Frankenhaeuser, M. (1975). Sympathetic-adrenamedullary activity, behaviour, and the psychosocial environment. In P. H. Venables & M. J. Christie (Eds.), *Research in psychophysiology* (pp. 71–94). London: Wiley.

Friendly, M., Franklin, P. E., Hoffman, D., & Rubin, D. C. (1982). The Toronto word pool: Norms for imagery, concreteness, orthographic variables, and grammatical usage for 1,080 words. *Behavior Research Methods & Instumentation, 14,* 375–399.

Gold, P. E. (1987). Sweet memories. *American Scientist, 75,* 151–155.

Huppert, F. A., & Piercy, M. (1976). Recognition memory in amnesic patients: Effect of temporal context and familiarity of material. *Cortex, 12,* 3–20.

Huppert, F. A., & Piercy, M. (1982). In search of the functional locus of amnesic syndromes. In L. S. Cermak (Ed.), *Human memory and amnesia* (pp. 123–137). Hillsdale, NJ: Lawrence Erlbaum Associates.

Kolers, P. A. (1973). Some modes of representation. In P. Pliner, L. Krames, & T. Alloway (Eds.), *Communication and affect: Language and speech,* (pp. 21–44). New York: Academic Press.

Mandler, G. (1967). Organization and memory. In K. W. Spence & J. T. Spence (Eds.), *The psychology of learning and motivation* (Vol. 1, pp. 327–372). New York: Academic Press.

Mandler, G. (1980). Recognizing: The judgment of previous occurrence. *Psychological Review, 87,* 252–271.

Miller, G. A. (1956). The magical number seven, plus or minus two: Some limits on our capacity for processing information. *Psychological Review, 63,* 81–97.

Sanders, R. A. (1985). *Age differences in memory: Integration of event and context.* Unpublished master's thesis, University of Toronto.

Tulving, E. (1962). Subjective organization in free recall of unrelated words. *Psychological Review, 69,* 344–354.

Tulving, E. (1972). Episodic and semantic memory. In E. Tulving & W. Donaldson (Eds.), *Organization of memory* (pp. 381–403). New York: Academic Press.

Tulving, E. (1983). *Elements of episodic memory.* New York: Oxford University Press.

Tulving, E. (1984). Precis of elements of episodic memory. *The Behavioral and Brain Sciences, 7,* 223–238.

3 Willful and Nonwillful Determinants of Memory

Michael J. Watkins
Rice University

Memory of a stimulus object is of the object as it is experienced in conscious mind rather than of the object as it impinges upon the sensory receptors. In other words, what is remembered is the object as encoded[1]. The concern of this chapter is with the control of the encoding, and specifically with the extent to which the encoding is under the willful control of the rememberer.

This issue is, in my opinion, as important as any in cognitive psychology, and can be fairly said to have dominated the way memory has been conceptualized. And yet, paradoxically, it is an issue that has received remarkably little balanced discussion. Theorists have tended to adopt an extreme position and appear to have seen little of merit in the opposing position. An encapsulated history of the experimental study of memory illustrates the point.

Ebbinghaus (1885/1964) was balanced in his viewpoint but not in his research. This is hardly surprising. Memory and the other "higher mental processes" were, at the time, considered too complex to submit to the experimental method, and Ebbinghaus was aware that much of the complexity was attributable to willful control over the encoding process. It was natural, then, that in seeking to demonstrate that memory could in fact be explored by the experimental method, Ebbinghaus went to great lengths to keep willful control to a minimum. This he did by using nonsense syllables (which he assumed would be less prone to yield unwanted associations than would words or other stimuli he might have

---

[1]It is important to be clear that encoding is not being used here to refer to a hypothetical process whereby information is registered in a hypothetical memory trace. In one guise or another, the concept of memory trace is given central place in just about all memory theories, and in the author's view, this is a universal mistake (see Watkins, 1981).

used) and by reading them quickly and without adopting a "mnemotechnic" frame of mind.

Once the feasibility of exploring memory by experiment had been demonstrated, efforts to minimize the role of willful control lessened, and for a time both willful and stimulus control were permitted. With the advent of behaviorism, however, the idea of willful control was banished as antithetical to the official creed. To keep conflict between data and theory to a minimum, researchers abandoned the free recall procedure (or method of retained members, as it had been known) and turned almost exclusively to serial recall and paired associates procedures, in which encoding could be more reasonably considered as largely stimulus controlled. The questions posed in this research were also strongly stimulus oriented. The result was a kind of research that had much of the character of Ebbinghaus's original studies, although for reasons that were doctrinal rather than practical.

A philosophical viewpoint that disregarded willful control over encoding of a stimulus object missed so much of the very essence of psychology that a reaction was inevitable. Led by a few bold thinkers—Endel Tulving prominent amongst them— the reaction came in the late 1950s and early 1960s in the form of the information-processing revolution. So thoroughly did it change the way memory was conceptualized and researched that only rarely do today's research reports make reference to those dating from the behaviorist era. Willful control lies at the very heart of the new perspective. At first, its role was constrained by the widely held assumption that information flows in an orderly fashion through a fixed sequence of stores or other hypothetical structures. By the 1970s, however, so many difficulties had been raised with such a rigorously structural framework (see, e.g., Craik & Lockhart, 1972) that it had to be largely dismantled, with the result that willful control became free to operate virtually without constraint.

The case that Tulving and others made for incorporating the concept of willful encoding into our theorizing is a compelling one, and nowadays just about all memory researchers accept it. To be sure, its very success demonstrates that theoretical style in psychology is subject to enormous shifts, but now that willful encoding has been shown to submit well enough to the experimental method, it is unlikely ever to be ignored again—at least not as religiously as it was in the behaviorist era. Happily, willful encoding is here to stay.

But does this mean that the way memory theorists conceptualize encoding is now as it should be? I believe that it is not. The principal argument I make in this chapter is that the reaction against the mindlessness of behaviorism has gone too far, and that too little emphasis is being given to the role of nonwillful factors in the control of encoding. In making this argument, I begin with a brief review of some of the principal findings that have been offered in support of the current perspective. Then, I show that such findings tell only one side of the encoding story.

WILLFUL ENCODING

The ways in which encoding is willfully controlled can be categorized under the headings of *attention, organization,* and *rehearsal.* To be sure, this threefold classification has no deep theoretical significance, and it is unlikely to prove comprehensive. Moreover, the boundaries between the three processes are not only fuzzy, but also complicated by interactions. For example, whether the occurrence of an item can be brought to mind for subsequent rehearsal depends on how it was initially attended to and organized. Conversely, bringing an item back to mind provides an opportunity for additional attention or organization. And, to complete the triangle, attention may be necessary for organization. Despite these difficulties, the classification is useful for descriptive purposes. Let us, then, quickly sample the most influential forms of evidence for each of these processes in turn.

Attention

When two or more verbal messages are heard at the same time, it is generally not possible to follow more than one of them. The other message or messages are heard, but little is understood of their content. Dubbed the *cocktail party phenomenon,* this effect was subjected to intensive laboratory study in the early years of the information-processing era. The results of this research showed that, when directed to "shadow" a message arriving at one ear, a subject will subsequently show little if any memory for the contents of a second message arriving at the other ear (e.g., Cherry, 1953; Moray, 1959)—apart, that is, from a transient "echo" (e.g., Treisman, 1964; Glucksberg & Cowen, 1970). A related finding is the relatively poor recall of material presented while a subsidiary task is being performed. Much of this research has involved verbal to-be-remembered messages and nonverbal subsidiary tasks, and the general finding is that, although the subsidiary task does not block understanding of the verbal message, it does adversely affect how well it will subsequently be remembered (e.g., Anderson & Craik, 1974; Baddeley, Lewis, Eldridge, & Thomson, 1984).

Organization

The significance of organization as a means by which subjects control their encoding was demonstrated in the 1960s, most notably through influential research programs by Gordon Bower and Endel Tulving. Among the best-known demonstrations of Bower and his associates is a study in which subjects studied a set of 112 words arranged in four hierarchical patterns (Bower, Clark, Lesgold, & Winzenz, 1969). The words had been chosen such that they could be assigned to the hierarchy in a meaningful way. For example, the word *platinum* converged, along with *silver* and *gold,* on *rare;* which in turn converged, along with *common* and *alloys,* on *metals;* which in turn converged, along with *stones,* on *minerals.* For half of the subjects, whom we may call the meaningful group, the words were shown in just this arrangement. For the other half of the subjects, whom we may call the random control group, the same spatial pattern was used but the words were assigned to positions within the pattern at random. After three study-test trials, all of the subjects in the meaningful group recalled all 112 words, whereas subjects in the random control group averaged only 53 words.

Tulving (1962, 1964) investigated how people learned to recall a set of randomly selected words presented in the form of a single list. Although a different ordering of the words was used for each successive presentation of the list, the subjects showed a steadily increasing idiosyncratic consistency in the order in which they recalled the words. This trend led Tulving to conclude that list learning was a matter not of mere exposure to the words (or of stimulus control), but rather of the subjects' actively seeking out an organizing scheme.

Rehearsal

Rehearsal is widely regarded among cognitive psychologists as serving two distinct functions in the remembering process: First, as a device for retaining information in a hypothetical short-term store, and second, as a means for building up memory proper. Both of these functions are central to what for two decades has been the received view, or modal model, of memory—the two-store model (Atkinson & Shiffrin, 1968; Waugh & Norman, 1965). The most influential empirical support for the notion that memory is built up by rehearsal has been obtained with the overt rehearsal procedure, in which a list of items is presented slowly and the subjects rehearse by calling out items from earlier in the list. These responses are recorded for later analysis. The best-known study of this kind was conducted by Rundus (1971), who showed an impressive correlation between the total number of times an item is rehearsed and its probability of being recalled. The correlation weakened for items presented towards the end of the list, but this is just as would be expected from the modal model, for the last few items of the list are assumed to be reported on the basis of information held in the short-term store.

Some Finer Distinctions

The processes of attention, organization, and rehearsal may vary qualitatively as well as quantitatively. Qualitatively different forms of attention have been obtained with the use of different study or "orienting" tasks, with powerful effects on level of recall (e.g., Craik & Tulving, 1975; Hyde & Jenkins, 1969). Moreover, the relative effects of two orienting tasks depend on the recall situation (e.g., Barclay, Bransford, Franks, McCarrell, & Nitsch, 1974; Fisher & Craik,

1977), proving that the forms of encoding induced by the different orienting tasks really do vary in a qualitative way. Qualitatively different forms of organization can be reasonably presumed to characterize different mnemonic techniques. And qualitatively different forms of rehearsal have been demonstrated in a study from our own laboratory (Watkins, Peynircioglu, & Brems, 1984), in which an instruction to rehearse an item pictorially was found to enhance the effectiveness of pictorial cues but not of verbal cues in a subsequent memory test, whereas an instruction to rehearse verbally enhanced the effectiveness of verbal cues but not of pictorial cues.

The meaningful differentiation of attention and organization and rehearsal as encoding processes, to say nothing of differentiation within these processes, represents a level of complexity beyond the scope of behaviorism. But the inadequacies of behaviorism do not justify the tendency of contempory theorists to stress the role of willful control over the remembering process to the point of ignoring other sources of control. Let us take a look at these other sources.

NONWILLFUL ENCODING

For a stimulus object to be remembered, certain conditions that are beyond direct willful control must be met. For example, the would-be rememberer must be: reached by information emanating from the object; capable of picking up, or sensing, this information; and awake rather than asleep. Also, much of what is of value in a stimulus requires a special knowledge on the part of the subject. This point is illustrated by a contrast between Mozart and his lesser-known British contemporary, William Woodfall. Mozart was good not only at composing music, but also at remembering it. As a child, he heard Allegri's Miserere at the Sistine Chapel in Rome, and wrote down the score—a closely guarded secret—from memory. No less celebrated at the time was Woodfall's ability to report from memory, and with what everyone agreed was astonishing accuracy, parliamentary debates. These feats were probably domain-specific. It is unlikely that Mozart could have matched Woodfall in remembering debates or that Woodfall's memory could have occasioned consternation in the Sistine Chapel.

These prerequisites of memory are noncontroversial and are entirely ignored, but they do serve to establish beyond doubt that there is more to the determination of what gets remembered than willful control. Moreover, when the prerequisites are satisfied, nonwillful factors have a strong influence over the strength or durability of memory. As an obvious example, the likelihood of recalling a stimulus object increases monotonically with the duration of our exposure to it (e.g., Roberts, 1972). Other stimulus variables, although less well explored, are no less potent.

Some years ago, John Gardiner and I conducted an experiment to demonstrate the importance of eventfulness in the remembering process (Gardiner & Watkins, 1979). We presented a list of 100 words, each of which named a concrete object. The words were shown on index cards at a rate of one every 10 seconds. Following presentation, the subjects were given a test sequence of 200 words, including the 100 that comprised the study list, and their task was to identify as many words from the study list as they could. What was varied was the eventfulness of the item presentations in the study sequence. The control subjects studied the items in a normal, uneventful way. For subjects in the eventful condition, presentation of each item was made into an enriched event in which the experimenter produced the object named by the word and proceeded to perform appropriate actions: For *bucket,* he would perform a short slapstick routine; for *apple,* he would take a bite and comment on its taste; and so on. At test, subjects in the eventful group missed many fewer studied words and erroneously identified many fewer lure words than did subjects in the control group. In theory, the control subjects might have been able to compensate for the uneventfulness of their presentations by embellishing them in their minds, but the important point is that in practice they did not.

The case for nonwillful control over the remembering process does not rest solely on such clearly stimulus-bound factors. It can also be made from a consideration of attention, organization, and rehearsal—the very processes on which the case for willful encoding is grounded. Our earlier look at these processes revealed only half of the story, and we now need to look at the other half.

Attention

That attention is not totally willful is shown by a variety of phenomena, some striking, others more subtle. Among the more striking is the Stroop effect. Here, the subject is shown a list of color names, each printed in a color that conflicts with the color being named. The subject's task is to name as quickly as possible the colors in which the words are printed. It is frustratingly difficult, the problem being to repress the colors named by the words. A more subtle, although presumably related, phenomenon is the part-set cuing effect, which is the impairment in the recall of a subset of previously studied words that occurs when the remaining items are re-presented at the time of recall (e.g., Nickerson, 1984; Slamecka, 1968). The relation between the part-set cuing effect and the Stroop effect is brought out in a study conducted in our own laboratory (Watkins & Allender, 1987), in which subjects were found to be impaired in their ability to generate words of a specified category if they were hearing other words of that same category. In each of these cases, it is as though unhelpful stimuli cannot be suppressed, but capture at least some attention to the detriment of the task at hand.

Limits on how far the encoding process can be willfully controlled are also illustrated by the stimulus suffix effect. This refers to the impairment in the recall of a short list of spoken items that is brought about by the addition of a nominally irrelevant spoken item to the end of the list. As often as not, the to-be-recalled items are permutations of the digits 1 through 9, and the suffix item is *zero*. The subject is instructed to ignore the suffix item or to treat it merely as a recall signal. Compared to the recall of lists not followed by a suffix item, recall is reduced, especially for the last one or two items. Indeed, recall is impaired nearly as much by the suffix item as by the addition of a to-be-recalled item (e.g., Crowder, 1967; Dallett, 1965). Apparently, the subject has virtually no success at all in ignoring the suffix item.

Organization

The significance of willful organization should not be denied, but neither should it be exaggerated. The advantage of a meaningfully organized layout shown by the Bower, Clark, Lesgold, & Winzenz (1969) study is really evidence of stimulus organization rather than of a willful mental organization. Indeed, if willful organization came easily, subjects in the random control group would have had no difficulty in mentally rearranging the items into a layout as meaningful as the layout presented to the meaningful group, and the two groups would not have differed in their recall. That they did differ is therefore testimony to the difficulty of willful organization. Similarly, Tulving's (1962) experiment did reveal mastery of the list, but at the same time the mastery was slow and tortuous, a fact that also attests to the difficulty of willful organization.

In some sense, the organizationalists of the 1960s were the heirs of the Gestalt psychologists, but in another sense they were quite different. The Gestalt psychologists focused on organization, but not on willful control. For example, they demonstrated that for an array of objects of two physical kinds, each object is seen as belonging with the others of its own kind, regardless of the subject's intentions. And objects that are physically close are similarly seen as belonging together. In both cases, the organization is more appropriately attributed to the physical world outside of the perceiver rather than to the perceiver's willful control. The Law of Prägnanz (see Koffka, 1935; Wertheimer, 1938) remains as compelling as ever, and to at least this extent, a theoretical perspective that attributes organization to willful control is less than comprehensive.

Rehearsal

That rehearsal is regarded as willful is one aspect of the thoroughgoing distortion that the term has undergone to fit the prevailing theoretical perspective. The distortion has been discussed in some detail elsewhere (Watkins & Peynircioglu, 1982), and only the briefest of summaries can be given here.

In one respect, the term *rehearsal* is overextended. Thus, whereas the layman preserves the etymology of the term by retaining the core notion of repetition, the psychologist rejects this restriction and includes such notions as nonrepetitive "elaborative rehearsal." In what is probably the most comprehensive review of the rehearsal literature available to date, Johnson (1980) makes the point clearly: "Repetition is a frequently used strategy in rehearsal, but the two concepts are not synonymous. . . . A definition equating rehearsal with repetition is overly restrictive" (p. 265).

In most regards, however, memory researchers have used the term too narrowly. For example, whereas in general usage, rehearsal connotes an overt activity every bit as readily as it connotes a covert activity, memory researchers use the term almost exclusively in reference to covert activity. Also, rehearsal can be stimulus-based or memory-based. Actually, these may be considered as endpoints of a continuum, with, in some cases, the purpose of rehearsal being to wean the rehearser off the stimulus to an entirely memory-based performance. In memory research, rehearsal is restricted to the memory-based variant. Again, I cite Johnson (1980): "Rehearsal needs to be differentiated from external reexposures to the task. Such reexposures are simply additional learning trials, and there is no merit in dubbing such presentation trials as rehearsal. . . . All learning experiences may be viewed as preparation for future performances, but if rehearsal is to be a useful concept, the term should designate some particular subset of preparatory learning activities" (p. 265). Of most direct relevance to the present concern, researchers virtually always think of rehearsal as being under the control of the rehearser, but here again they are being transparently restrictive. We may be in control of rehearsing our own particular part in a play, but rehearsal of the play as such is under the control of the director.

And so it is that for cognitive psychologists rehearsal refers to an activity that is covert, memory-based, and subject-controlled. Thus defined, it has become a key concept in interpreting the results of learning and memory research. In my view, the role of rehearsal in this usage of the term is grossly exaggerated.

Although this is not the place for an evaluation of all of the relevant evidence (see Watkins & Peynircioglu, 1982, for a more comprehensive account), a few comments on the role of rehearsal in the free recall procedure are in order. Rehearsal has been invoked to account for findings from just about all of the standard memory paradigms (see Johnson, 1980), but nowhere within the experimenter's arsenal has it figured so importantly as in the free recall procedure. Presumably, the reason for this is that any mixing up of the order of the items during mental repetitions is not penalized in a free recall test.

As was noted earlier, the most influential empirical support for the hypothesis that rehearsal plays a key role in the free recall procedure comes from studies using the overt rehearsal technique. The validity of this support, however, is open to question. For one thing, the support is based on correlational evidence, which means that we cannot be sure that the greater likelihood of recall observed for the more rehearsed items is actually caused by the rehearsal. For a given subject trying to recall a given word list, some words will, for whatever reason, be easier to recall than others, and these words are not only more likely to be recalled in the official recall test that follows list presentation, but they are also more likely to be produced in the rehearsal intervals that follow each word presentation, for these intervals are, in reality, nothing more than a series of miniature recall tests. Thus, the support that the overt rehearsal procedure provides for the hypothesis that rehearsal promotes recall is nothing more than a correlation between two measures of recall. Another problem with the overt rehearsal procedure is that the instruction to report rehearsals aloud carries the danger of inducing rehearsal when none would otherwise occur.

A less problematic approach to evaluating the significance of rehearsal is to vary experimentally the amount of rehearsal that can be assumed to occur under the hypothesis that rehearsal does play a key role in the remembering process. Some of the research that has adopted this approach has focused on the serial position function obtained in a final free recall procedure. In this procedure, subjects are presented with a series of lists, each comprising a different set of words, for immediate free recall. They are subsequently given a grand recall test, in which they recall as many of the words as they can without regard to list of presentation. Early research with this procedure (e.g., Craik, 1970) had shown that the final recall serial position function—obtained by classifying each recalled word according to the position it had occupied within its presentation list—was characterized by a progressive reduction in level of recall across the last few within-list positions. This "negative recency" effect is exactly as predicted by the hypothesis that rehearsal controls recall, for if we assume that rehearsal stops when list presentation is complete, then there would be progressively fewer and fewer rehearsal opportunities as an item's presentation position nears the end of the list. And indeed, the overt rehearsal procedure has revealed just such a trend in number of rehearsals (Rundus, 1971). Subsequent research, however, has revealed the negative recency effect to have nothing to do with rehearsal, but instead to be the consequence of subjects switching the way in which they process the items when they think the end of the list is imminent. Thus, when list length was varied unpredictably from one list to the next so as to prevent the subjects from anticipating when a list would end, no negative recency effect was found (Watkins & Watkins, 1974). This finding has been confirmed when care is taken to eliminate the potentially confounding effects of initial recall (Watkins & Peynircioglu, 1982, Experiment 1). The implication is that, even in the free recall procedure, effective study of an item ceases with the presentation of the next item in the study list, and hence that there is no effective rehearsal.

THE PROBLEM OF DISTINGUISHING BETWEEN WILLFUL AND NONWILLFUL CONTROL

We have seen that, in the behaviorist era, the experimental study of memory was undertaken in the context of a theoretical perspective that stressed the role of stimulus control to the exclusion of willful control. Since then, a different per-

spective has prevailed, and theorizing has emphasized the will and all but neglected other sources of control. In my opinion, neither of these perspectives has,
or ever could, yield a satisfactory understanding of the memory process.

There can no longer be any doubt that the experimental method can explore
mental concepts in a meaningful way, but we should not overlook the context in
which the mind functions. The mind plays a biological role, reacting to, as well
as initiating actions upon, the physical world. For the most part, today's theories
fare little better in capturing this interaction than did those of the behaviorists.
The behaviorists adopted a theoretical perspective appropriate for a virtually
mindless organism more or less at the total mercy of its environment. Contemporary theories seem to be aimed at hypothetical organisms wrapped up in their
own mental processes and existing independently of the world they inhabit. It is
hard to imagine such organisms, for they do not and could not exist, but in
satirizing some of the more abstruse thinkers of his day, Jonathan Swift did as
good a job as we can hope for. He brought the intrepid Lemuel Gulliver into
contact with the Laputians, whom Gulliver described thus:

> Their heads were all reclined, either to the right or the left; one of their eyes turned
> inward, and the other directly up to the zenith. . . . I observed, here and there,
> many in the habit of servants, with blown bladders, fastened like a flail to the end
> of a stick, which they carried in their hands. In each bladder was a small quantity of
> dried peas, or little pebbles, as I was afterward informed. With these bladders they
> now and then flapped the mouth and ears of those who stood near them. . . . It
> seems the minds of these people are so taken up with intense speculations that they
> can neither speak nor attend to the discourses of others without being roused by
> some external action upon the organs of speech and hearing; for which reason,
> those persons who are able to afford it always keep a flapper . . . in their family, as
> one of their domestics; nor ever walk abroad or make visits without him. And the
> business of this officer is, when two, three, or more persons are in company, gently
> to strike with his bladder the mouth of him who is to speak, and the right ear of him
> or them to whom the speaker addresses himself. This flapper is likewise employed
> diligently to attend his master in his walks, and upon occasion to give him a soft
> flap on his eyes; because he is always so wrapped up in cogitation that he is in
> manifest danger of falling down every precipice, and bouncing his head against
> every post; and in the streets, of jostling others, or being jostled himself . . .

It seems to me that today's theories would at best be appropriate for people
even less in harmony with their environment than were the Laputians, who after
all could be brought up to a passable level of functioning with only a modest
amount of prompting. Applied to ordinary mortals, our theories do an extraordinarily poor job of capturing the effects of external factors. Consider again the
eventfulness study summarized earlier (Gardiner & Watkins, 1979). The finding
that eventful presentations are more memorable than are uneventful presentations
seems eminently plausible, but it is generally not well predicted by extant the-

orizing. This is not to say, of course, that contemporary theories cannot cope with the finding; indeed, they typically have sufficient degrees of freedom to cope with just about any finding. But Gardiner and I asked more of a theory: We asked not only that it accommodate our finding but that it could not just as easily accommodate the opposite finding. And by this criterion, such theories as we could think of did not fare well.

I should note that it would not be entirely appropriate to argue that there is nothing in today's theorizing that provides an even-handed framework for distinguishing between the stimulus object and potential rememberer as sources of encoding control; the notion of data-limited and resource-limited processing (Norman & Bobrow, 1975) would do just such a job. But this notion has not, as far as I know, been used in directing any general empirical investigations of the encoding stage of the memory process.

The distinction between willful and nonwillful control of encoding is not a clean one. For one thing, it is a facet of the distinction between free will and determinism, a distinction that has confounded philosophers for centuries and that shows no sign of being resolved any time soon. In the present context, two difficulties warrant mention. First, certain effects could be attributed to either willful or nonwillful control. As an example, I implied earlier that the effects of orienting task obtained in research on the depth-of-processing construct illustrated willful control, but because they were brought about by instructions, I could have argued just as forcefully that they were the result of stimulus control. In the world outside the laboratory, we may adopt a certain way of thinking about an item of information in an effort to remember it; alternatively, the way we think about the item, and hence our likelihood of remembering it, may be determined by external requirements. Second, the problem of distinguishing between willful and nonwillful sources of control is compounded by their manifold interactions. For instance, we can willfully optimize stimulus conditions. Indeed, we can change the environment in a way that meets the prerequisites of encoding. Thus, we put ourselves in a position to receive information, as by seeking out someone we wish to talk to or by going to a library, concert, or party. Or, conversely, we may seek to avoid receiving information in order to better attend to other information. We can even compensate, to some extent, for the limitation in the range over which our sensory systems function, as when we turn on a radio receiving set to transform radio waves into sound waves. And we surely have some measure of control over our sleeping schedule and our areas of expertise.

No doubt, such difficulties have discouraged psychologists from discussing the distinction between willful and nonwillful encoding and, no less importantly, from using the distinction as a framework for planning research. But the difference between the psychology of the behaviorists and that of today's information-processing researchers is as different as night and day, and, in at least an intuitive and informal way, much of the difference can be captured in terms of the locus of control over the encoding process. Keep in mind, too, that when we get right down to it, the distinction between night and day is blurred and arbitrary. But we still make it.

ACKNOWLEDGMENTS

The writing of this chapter was supported by the National Institute of Mental Health Grant MH35873. The author is grateful to John O. Brooks III, Elizabeth S. Sechler, and Olga C. Watkins for detailed comments on a draft version of the chapter.

REFERENCES

Anderson, C. M. B., & Craik, F. I. M. (1974). The effect of a concurrent task on recall from primary memory. *Journal of Verbal Learning and Verbal Behavior, 13*,107–113.

Atkinson, R.C., & Shiffrin, R. M. (1968). Human memory: A proposed system and its control processes. In K. W. Spence & J. T. Spence (Eds.), *The psychology of learning and motivation* (Vol. 2, pp. 89–195). New York: Academic Press.

Baddeley, A., Lewis, V., & Eldridge, M., & Thomson, N. (1984). Attention and retrieval from long-term memory. *Journal of Experimental Psychology: General, 113*, 518–540.

Barclay, J. R., Bransford, J.D., Franks, J. J., McCarrell, N. S., & Nitsch, K. (1974). Comprehension and semantic flexibility. *Journal of Verbal Learning and Verbal Behavior, 13*, 471–481.

Bower, G. H., Clark, M. C., Lesgold, A. M., & Winzenz, D. (1969). Hierarchical retrieval schemes in recall of categorized word lists. *Journal of Verbal Learning and Verbal Behavior, 8*, 323–343.

Cherry, E. C. (1953). Some experiments on the recognition of speech, with one and two ears. *Journal of the Acoustical Society of America, 25*, 975–979.

Craik, F. I. M. (1970). The fate of primary memory items in free recall. *Journal of Verbal Learning and Verbal Behavior, 9*, 143–148.

Craik, F. I. M., & Lockhart, R. S. (1972). Levels of processing: A framework for memory research. *Journal of Verbal Learning and Verbal Behavior, 11*, 671–684.

Craik, F. I. M., & Tulving, E. (1975). Depth of processing and the retention of words in episodic memory. *Journal of Experimental Psychology: General, 104*, 268–294.

Crowder, R. G. (1967). Prefix effects in immediate memory. *Canadian Journal of Psychology, 21*, 450–461.

Dallett, K. M. (1965). "Primary memory": The effects of redundancy upon digit repetition. *Psychonomic Science, 3*, 237–238.

Ebbinghaus, H. (1964). *Memory: A Contribution to Experimental Psychology*. New York: Dover. (Originally published 1885).

Fisher, R. P., & Craik, F. I. M. (1977). Interaction between encoding and retrieval operations in cued recall. *Journal of Experimental Psychology: Human Learning and Memory, 3*, 701–711.

Gardiner, J. M., & Watkins, M. J. (1979). Remembering eventful and uneventful word presentations. *Bulletin of the Psychonomic Society, 13*, 108–110.

Glucksberg, S., & Cowen, G. N. (1970). Memory for unattended auditory material. *Cognitive Psychology, 1*, 149–156.

Hyde, T. S., & Jenkins, J. J. (1969). Differential effects of incidental tasks on the organization of recall of a list of highly associated words. *Journal of Experimental Psychology, 82*, 472–481.

Johnson, R. E. (1980). Memory-based rehearsal. In G. H. Bower (Ed.), *The psychology of learning and motivation* (Vol. 14, pp. 263–307). New York: Academic Press.

Koffka, K. (1935). *Principles of Gestalt psychology.* New York: Harcourt.

Moray, N. (1959). Attention in dichotic listening: Affective cues and the influence of instructions. *Quarterly Journal of Experimental Psychology, 9,* 56–60.

Nickerson, R. S. (1984). Retrieval inhibition from part-set cuing: A persisting enigma in memory research. *Memory & Cognition, 12,* 531–552.

Norman, D. A., & Bobrow, D. G. (1975). On data-limited and resource-limited processes. *Cognitive Psychology, 7,* 44–64.

Roberts, W. A. (1972). Free recall of word lists varying in length and rate of presentation: A test of the total-time hypothesis. *Journal of Experimental Psychology, 92,* 365–372.

Rundus, D. (1971). Analysis of rehearsal processes in free recall. *Journal of Experimental Psychology, 89,* 63–77.

Slamecka, N. J. (1968). An examination of trace storage in free recall. *Journal of Experimental Psychology, 76,* 504–513.

Treisman, A. (1964). Monitoring and storage of irrelevant messages in selective attention. *Journal of Verbal Learning and Verbal Behavior, 3,* 449–459.

Tulving, E. (1962). Subjective organization in free recall of "unrelated" words. *Psychological Review, 69,* 344–354.

Tulving, E. (1964). Intratrial and intertrial retention: Notes towards a theory of free recall verbal learning. *Psychological Review, 71,* 219–237.

Watkins, M. J. (1981). Human memory and the information-processing metaphor. *Cognition, 10,* 331–336.

Watkins, M. J., & Allender, L. E. (1987). Inhibiting word generation with word presentations. *Journal of Experimental Psychology: Learning, Memory, and Cognition, 13,* 564–568.

Watkins, M. J., & Peynircioglu, Z. F. (1982). A perspective on rehearsal. In G. H. Bower (Ed.), *The psychology of learning and motivation* (Vol. 16, pp. 153–190). New York: Academic Press.

Watkins, M. J., Peynircioglu, Z. F., & Brems, D. (1984). Pictorial rehearsal. *Memory and Cognition, 12,* 553–557.

Watkins, M. J., & Watkins, O. C. (1974). Processing of recency items for free recall. *Journal of Experimental Psychology, 102,* 488–493.

Waugh, N. C., & Norman, D. A. (1965). Primary memory. *Psychological Review, 72,* 89–104.

Wertheimer, M. (1938). The general theoretical situation. In W. D. Ellis (Ed.), *A source book of Gestalt psychology* (pp. 1–11). New York: Harcourt.

4 Memory Models, Text Processing, and Cue-Dependent Retrieval

Roger Ratcliff
Gail McKoon
Northwestern University

An important concept championed by Tulving (1974, 1983) is the notion that retrieval conditions are critical in assessing memory: Memory cannot be assessed independently of retrieval, and a theoretical description of memory cannot be formulated without specification of the retrieval environment. In this chapter, we illustrate the profound influence that this view has had on the development and testing of memory models, and we show how the cue dependent view has begun to have an influence on research concerned with text processing.

MEMORY MODELS

There is a new generation of memory models that are more ambitious than models that were developed in the 1970s (with the notable exceptions of HAM [Anderson & Bower, 1973] and ACT [Anderson, 1976]). The new models attempt to deal with a range of phenomena across experimental paradigms at a level of detail that in the past has been found only in extremely limited models designed for a single task. In this chapter, five models that vary in their commitment to cue-dependent retrieval are considered and evaluated on the dimension of encoding/retrieval interaction. In models dealing with recall and recognition, the treatment of results from the recognition failure procedure is described because these results provide serious problems for superficial accounts of recognition and recall. In the models that do not deal with recall and recognition, the treatment of cue-target interactions is discussed.

In the recognition failure procedure, pairs of words are studied and then the second member of a pair is tested; in one test, the second member is presented by itself for recognition, and in another test, the first member of the pair is presented as a cue for recall of the second. The result of most importance is that under a variety of conditions, there is significant recall of words that were not recognized (Tulving & Thomson, 1973; Watkins & Tulving, 1975). It is this result that poses a serious problem for simple models of recall and recognition, and so it is used to evaluate models in this chapter.

ACT*, Anderson (1983)

This model assumes two different sources of knowledge, a declarative associative memory and a procedural production system. The declarative memory system is a traditional associative memory in which concepts are represented by nodes, and associations between concepts are represented by links between nodes. To account for results that show cue-dependent retrieval, Anderson used the idea that different senses of a word have different representations and thus are represented by different nodes in memory (see Reder, Anderson, & Bjork, 1974). This view has not changed since the ACT (Anderson, 1976) incarnation of his model.[1] Thus, *black* in the context of *train* would evoke the sense of *black* that includes dark soot on a steam train, whereas *black* in the context of *white* evokes the sense of black concerned with racial differences or the color of text on a page. Because there are different senses, retrieval of an item in a retrieval context will be a function of similarity (number of connections or paths in the network) between the encoded sense and the sense activated at retrieval, (Note that it is not necessary that senses are equated with dictionary meanings, as in Tulving and Watkins, 1977. For example, although "coconut" has only one dictionary meaning, it can have different features in different situations and these can be considered different senses.) The ACT* account of retrieval is similar to Tulving's (Tulving & Thomson, 1973) in many ways. It provides a way of grading the similarity between trace information and cue information and so could be viewed as providing an implementation of Tulving's views within the framework of ACT*.

Wiseman and Tulving (1975; see also Flexser & Tulving, 1978) showed that across a range of experiments, the probability of recognizing the target member of a pair conditionalized on correct cued recall of the target was almost independent of the probability of recognition not conditionalized on cued recall. In Anderson's (1983, p. 196) framework, the probability of retrieving a trace in memory from the target is independent of retrieving it from the cue, so that independence is expected. Anderson argued that the slight lack of independence is due to cases where the trace was never formed, and neither recall nor recognition succeeds (see also Begg, 1979). He also argued that the ACT* explanation is largely the same as Flexser and Tulving's (1978) explanation.

---

[1]Note that ACT is the 1976 memory model and ACT* is the 1983 memory model.

Diffusion Model, Ratcliff (1978)

Ratcliff developed a decision model designed to account for recognition performance across a range of experimental paradigms and several different measures. The model assumes that a cue (test probe) is compared with each item in memory in parallel. The goodness-of-match between the cue and each memory item drives a random walk (or in the continuous version, the diffusion process) so that the better the match, the faster the process moves to the positive boundary, and the poorer the match, the faster the process moves to the non-match boundary. Using the diffusion model, it is possible to account for reaction time, accuracy, the shape of the reaction time distribution, and growth of accuracy as a function of time, across a range of experimental paradigms (see Ratcliff, 1978; 1981; 1985; 1987; 1988; Ratcliff & McKoon, 1982).

The model is closely related to Tulving's view of cue-dependent processing because the model is phrased in terms of the goodness-of-match between the cue and each item in memory. In fact, the account is given in terms of a resonance metaphor in which the match between cue and target is used to drive the diffusion process. This is precisely the notion of cue-dependent retrieval. This model or closely related models (e.g., the discrete random walk) are candidates for integration with models of memory representation (like those considered next) because they allow a continuous source of goodness-of-match information to be integrated over time (the diffusion model) or allow a feature matching process to be used to determine goodness-of-match (simple random walk).

MINERVA 2, Hintzman (1986a)

Hintzman's MINERVA 2 (1986a) model is cue-dependent in that recall and recognition are both mediated by the relationship of a cue to all items stored in memory. The model represents an item as a vector of features. Each item is kept separate in memory, and at retrieval, the retrieval cue interacts with all items to produce an overall value of match. To understand how recognition failure of recallable words is explained, it is necessary to work through the details of recognition and cued recall. For associations, Hintzman assumed that the two items of a pair, the cue and target (A–B), are stored as separate parts of one memory vector. In pair recognition, the test vector (A–B) is compared to each vector in memory, and a value of similarity (essentially a correlation or dot product) is obtained. This similarity is cubed, and the resulting value is called activation. The activation values are summed over all items to give intensity, which is used in a standard signal detection procedure to predict recognition performance. For recognition of the B member of a pair alone, the B part of the vector is used as the probe with the rest of the vector being set to zero. The intensity is calculated in the same way as for pair recognition.

In cued recall, the A member of a studied pair is used as a probe into memory, and activation values of all vectors in memory are determined. The activation value for each vector then multiplies each element in it's own memory vector, and these vectors are summed over all memory items to produce an output vector. This produces an output vector in which the memory vectors with the strongest associations to a member (largest activation values) produce the largest contributions to the output vector. The B part of the output vector is then correlated with the B part of each vector in memory, and the largest correlation determines the strongest B member and thus determines cued recall. So recognition conditionalized on correct recall depends on both intensity and recall, and recognition depends on the intensity value. When these values are calculated, it is found that, under most conditions, the two measures are independent.

Hintzman (1986b) described several simulation experiments that explored recognition failure further. He argued that in MINERVA 2 there are two factors that produce opposite correlations between recognition and cued recall. First, for recognition, the greater the echo intensity (the more target features encoded), the greater the recognition rate. For cued recall, the more target features stored, the better the cued recall. Thus, recognition and recall are positively correlated as a function of the number of target features stored. However, the more cue features stored, the more strongly the cue probe can activate memory. Because the number of cue features encoded is independent of the number of target features, the overall effect of the number of cue features serves to dilute, but not neutralize, the size of the correlation. To produce the behavior of near independence of the model (and thus counteract the source of positive correlation), another factor must be involved. Hintzman identified this as *intralist similarity*. If another item has a B member similar to the target B, it will increase activation for recognition of the B member (because activations are summed over all items), and so increase recognition performance. However, for cued recall, the existence of a similar item will reduce the probability that that item will be recalled (i.e., have a larger match to the test target), thus producing a negative correlation. In combination, these factors are shown to give the required low degree of association between the two measures.

TODAM, Murdock (1982, 1983)

Murdock's (1982; 1983; see also Eich, 1982) model assumes a vector/feature representation for an item. Unlike Hintzman's model, all items are combined into a single memory trace; at encoding, the features of each item are added to a single memory vector. Associations are stored in this same vector by convolving the A and B members of a pair together and adding this convolution (also a vector) to the memory vector. This model, therefore, does not explicitly represent individual items. It is only at retrieval that the interaction between cue information and memory produces either a value of match that can be used as the basis for a recognition decision or a noisy vector that can be used to produce a name for recall.

For recognition, the interaction between the recognition cue and memory is given by the dot product between the test vector and the memory vector. In relating this scheme to cue-dependent retrieval, it can be seen immediately that it is impossible to determine what items are stored in memory independent of a retrieval cue. Thus, retrieval in this model is strongly dependent on an interaction between the retrieval cue and memory.

The situation is similar in cued and associative recall. For cued recall, the A member of the pair (given as a cue) is correlated with the memory vector to give another vector. This noisy retrieved vector must be compared with various candidates (in, for example, a lexicon that relates vectors to names of items) to obtain the name of the item—that is, it needs to be cleaned up. Again, independent of retrieval, there is no way to assess memory for this paired associate.

Murdock accounted for the phenomenon of retrieval failure of recallable words by noting that in his model, item information and associative information are independently computed and stored. So the relationship between the probability of recognition and probability of recognition given recall will be independent. Murdock argued that averaging over subjects with slightly different parameter values will lead to the slight correlation.

Murdock (1983) pointed out that the vector model is a concrete implementation of the cue-dependent view of memory, and that the only way to talk about encoded information sensibly is in terms of interactions with the retrieval cues. Because memory is a sum (combination) of items, each individually stored item is not itself present in memory but is only present in the memory vector. It is through the interaction of the retrieval cue with this memory vector that information about the presence or absence of the item in memory is obtained.

SAM, Gillund and Shiffrin
(1984; Raaijmakers & Shiffrin, 1981)

Gillund and Shiffrin's (1984) model can be interpreted as being radical, compared to the other models. It assumes that there are no associations between items ("images" in Gillund & Shiffrin, 1984; Raaijmakers & Shiffrin, 1981) in memory. Instead, associations are represented as strengths between retrieval cues and items in memory. It is worth stressing that this can be interpreted as meaning that there are no associations between images in long-term memory. Although no empirical or computational issues ride on this characterization, it is important to stress this point because it shows how the notion of cue dependence has become accepted theoretically.

Another way to describe this framework is in terms of a two-layer connectionist model. Cues at one layer are associated to items at another layer, but there are no connections between elements or nodes within a layer, no item-to-item

Retrieval Structure (Gillund & Shiffrin, 1984)

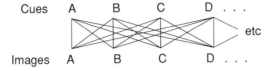

One Cue

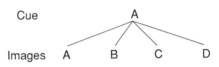

$$\text{Familiarity} = \sum_k S_{ak} = S_{aa} + S_{ab} + S_{ac} + \cdots$$

Two Cues

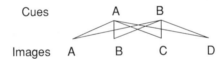

$$\text{Familiarity} = \sum_k S_{ak}S_{bk} = S_{aa}S_{ba} + S_{ab}S_{bb} + S_{ac}S_{bc} + \cdots$$

FIG. 4.1. Familiarity computations in the SAM model of Gillund and Shiffrin (1984). S_{ij} represents the strength of cue i to target j (so S_{ab}, for example, represents the strength for the cue A to target B link).

connections or cue-to-cue connections (see Fig. 4.1). Encoding strengthens connections between layers as in standard connectionist models, but the model differs from connectionist models in its retrieval assumptions.

The retrieval structure is built up during encoding: When items are stored in the short-term memory buffer together, strengths are built up from each item as a cue to each item as an image for all items in the buffer. At recognition, for a single retrieval cue, the strength of that cue to each item is summed across items. For more than one retrieval cue, the strengths of each cue to an item are multiplied, and these are summed over items. Thus, the way to view this model is consistent with Tulving's view of cue-dependent retrieval. What is important is the joint effectiveness of the retrieval cues in their interaction with memory.

The recall process is a search process that involves both sampling processes and recovery processes. A cue is used along with context to sample memory. One item is selected by this process, and then a recovery process proceeds that will, with some probability, recover the stored name of the item. Both of these processes are stochastic and given some cue, there is some probability that the correct item will not be selected for sampling. Even if the correct item is sampled, there is still some probability that it will not be recovered.

To account for recognition failure of recallable words, two main factors have to be considered. First, as noted previously, the recall process is a stochastic process; that is, there is variability in which items are sampled and then variability in the recovery process. This means that the recall process will be somewhat independent of recognition across items. A second factor is the effect of different contexts in recall and recognition. In the recognition test, the context may induce a different meaning than that induced at recall, and this would increase the independence of performance on these tests. Gillund and Shiffrin (1984, p. 27) argued that these two factors are sufficient to account for the phenomenon of recognition failure.

SUMMARY FOR MEMORY MODELS

It is worth classifying these memory models with respect to how they deal with recognition failure, how they stand on the dimension of cue dependence, and other discriminating factors. Table 4.1 presents this classification. It is interesting to note how much the explanations vary within the frameworks of these models. This suggests that it may be possible to test among these different accounts by experimentally varying factors that are assumed to be important in some models and not others. One common factor that does run through these models is the assumption that item and associative information are (somewhat) independent or that there are differences in information used in recall and recognition that are attributed to differences in context. This factor is quite consistent with Tulving's notion of encoding specificity.

CUE-DEPENDENT PRIMING

A question that arises about these memory models is what they contribute to our understanding of memory phenomena beyond fitting the data and accounting for experimental results in their domain of application. One response to this question is that they provide criteria for development of further theory (and after all, development of theory is the major aim of the scientific enterprise). A second response to this question is that they can provide alternative frameworks for examining existing phenomena and so provide competing models. For example,

TABLE 4.1
Classification of Memory Models

	Vector/ Node	Separate Items in Memory	Cue Dependent	Recognition Failure
ACT*	node	yes	no but mimics by using multiple senses of words	different senses of words so that recognition and recall are nearly independent
Diffusion model	either	yes	yes	no recall component but an extension would assume independent item and associative info.
MINERVA2	vector	yes	close but not phrased in these terms	interaction of factors—no. of encoded features produces positive correl. interitem similarity produces negative correl.
TODAM	vector	no	specific implementation of cue dep.	independent item and associative information
SAM	node	yes	yes	combination of stochastic recall process and context differences in recall and recognition

when we began to think about some data from a priming experiment on discourse processing in the context of Gillund and Shiffrin's cue-dependent model, we were able to develop an account of priming phenomena (Ratcliff & McKoon, 1988) that is an alternative to the currently popular and almost unchallenged spreading activation theory.

Our model for priming assumes that the prime and target are combined in a compound cue as in pair recognition in Gillund and Shiffrin (1984). Essentially, the strengths of the two cues (the prime and target) to an item in memory are multiplied and then summed over all items (see Fig. 4.1). So, if the prime and target are both connected to the same items in memory, then the result will be relatively large numbers multiplied together, leading to large values of familiarity. Thus, when the prime and target share associates, a large value of familiarity is obtained, and this in turn generates a fast reaction time (using a model such as the diffusion model, Ratcliff, 1978), that is, a standard priming effect in response latency. To have the subject respond mainly on the basis of the target and not the prime, the target is weighted more than the prime (see Gillund and Shiffrin's account of cued recognition, 1984). With these simple assumptions, it is possible to explain most effects within the priming literature by examining the contents of the compound cue (assumed to be the last two or possibly three items in short-term memory for single words, or the last few propositions for text).

Two variables that most directly illustrate the difference between the cue-dependent retrieval theory and spreading activation are the range of priming and decay of priming. Spreading activation is a mechanism that has been assumed to underlie retrieval of paths in memory that are then made available for evaluation (Anderson, 1976, 1983; Collins & Loftus, 1975). Thus, within the framework of a semantic network memory representation, the theory predicts that activation should spread for relatively long distances. On the other hand, the compound cue theory, as implemented in the Gillund and Shiffrin model, predicts that priming should only occur between items that have associates directly in common (items directly connected or connected by one mediating item). The data currently available (Balota & Lorch, 1986; de Groot, 1983) support the latter, that the range of priming only extends to near high associates. With respect to decay of priming, in most spreading activation models, rate of decay is a parameter that can vary over a range of values, but within the compound cue model, introducing an item between the prime and target will bump the prime out of the compound cue, and eliminate priming. In fact, many studies of priming show such rapid decay (e.g., Ratcliff, Hockley, & McKoon, 1985).

Although the priming model is formulated here within Gillund and Shiffrin's (1984) cue-dependent framework, it is possible to implement the model within other frameworks, such as Hintzman's and Murdock's (see Ratcliff & McKoon, 1988). To speak to the point concerning the use of these memory models, we reiterate that our compound cue model was only conceived in attempting to explain priming within the Gillund and Shiffrin framework. Although the Gillund and Shiffrin model was not developed to account for priming, it could be applied to priming in an insightful way. And, given this application, it became clear that the compound cue idea could also be implemented in the other frameworks.

Besides providing an illustration of the power of some current memory models, the compound cue theory also provides an alternative explanation of priming that is cue-dependent and thus consistent with Tulving's views on retrieval.

TEXT PROCESSING

Consideration of the interactions between encoding and retrieval processes leads to a broader range of issues in text processing research than in the more traditional areas of verbal learning. This is because the information relevant to a recognition or recall response is much less constrained when a studied text is the object of memory than when a list of words is the object. The information is less constrained because subjects, through early training and education, perceive their task as retrieving knowledge about a studied text, rather than retrieving an exact replica of the studied material. Thus, any particular retrieval decision will reflect some combination of information that was explicitly stated in a studied text and information that was contributed (inferred) by the subject.

The kinds of information that might be added by the subject to explicitly stated text information vary from inferences about the referent of a pronoun to inferences about "who did it" in a murder mystery. Intuitively, it seems that pronouns are understood quickly and easily during reading, and so we might like to argue that the connection between pronoun and referent (an inference) is explicitly encoded during reading. Then it would follow that this inferred information was no more subject to variable retrieval conditions than other information that was *explicitly* stated in the text. On the other hand, inferring the identity of a murderer is not easy; to do it, we have to stop reading, try to remember relevant information, and engage in active problem solving. We do not have the subjective feeling that the identity of the murderer is encoded into the text representation *during reading,* and we would expect that the probability of guessing the identity would vary widely as a function of different contextual cues.

To begin to study the large range of inference processes that lies between the extremes illustrated by these examples, it is useful to identify dimensions on which encoding–retrieval interactions can vary. In our work, we have made use of four such dimensions. The first is the *time course* of processing; the idea is that some kinds of inferred information are available relatively quickly at retrieval, whereas other kinds are available only after considerable processing time. Information that takes a relatively long time to generate at retrieval is usually information that involves additions at retrieval to what was understood during reading. Thus, to get a picture of the representation of a text without such additions, we often limit the retrieval time available to the subject.

When retrieval time is limited, then we can fill out the picture of a text representation by examining different *retrieval contexts* for specific test items. An example of this second dimension of encoding–retrieval interaction is that retrieval cues can vary in their specificity. With a retrieval cue that is not very specific, it is possible that no evidence at all will be obtained for some inference; it looks like the subject did not make the inference. But with a very specific retrieval cue, the same inference (whether it was made or not) might be uniquely determined, and the system would act as though the inference had been made at encoding. In other words, evidence for the presence of inferences in a text representation can be manipulated by alterations in the retrieval environment.

The effect of variations in retrieval environment will depend, to some extent, on third and fourth dimensions, the *strength* of the inference in question and the *specificity* of the inference. Some inferences might be encoded so strongly during reading that they are indistinguishable from explicitly stated information, and so relatively less subject to variations in retrieval environment. Other inferences might be made only minimally (weakly), and so be much more subject to retrieval factors. In addition, some inferences may be made very specifically ("the butler did it") or some not specifically ("some person or thing in the manor did it").

In the sections that follow, each of these four dimensions is discussed and illustrated by examples from empirical findings. However, before this, a brief review of earlier work on retrieval aspects of inference in text processing is presented (to provide a retrieval context for the next sections).

Retrieval and Inference Processing

The issue of cue-dependent retrieval has often been ignored in the domain of memory for textual information. The general (implicit) assumption has often been that any measure—recall, cued recall, recognition, or story summarization—gives a direct reflection of the memory representation of a text. However, some researchers have strongly criticized this assumption (Baillet & Keenan, 1986; Corbett & Dosher, 1978; McKoon & Ratcliff, 1980, 1981; Ratcliff & McKoon, 1978; Singer, 1978, 1979), and several empirical demonstrations have reinforced the criticisms.

One such demonstration was provided by Corbett and Dosher (1978). It had previously been claimed that instrumental inferences were formed during sentence encoding; that the concept "hammer" was encoded as part of the memory representation of "John pounded the nail." The logic behind this claim was that "hammer" was a good retrieval cue for the sentence about "John," even though "hammer" had not been explicitly stated (Paris & Lindauer, 1976). Corbett and Dosher showed that "hammer" was also a good retrieval cue for the sentence "John pounded the nail with a rock," where "hammer" would not be inferred as the instrument. Thus, the finding that a concept is a good retrieval cue cannot be taken as evidence that the concept was inferred during encoding. Instead the suggestion is that, at the time of retrieval, subjects are able to make use of the interaction between the retrieval cue (hammer) and the explicitly stated information (pounding the nail) to construct information that leads to a response.

Further evidence for such an interaction is shown in results from an experiment by Singer (1978). He used materials that varied in forward versus backward associations: "soup" is given as a high associate to "ladle" but the corresponding high associate to "soup" is not "ladle" but "spoon." If an instrument is inferred *during* reading of a sentence about stirring soup, then that instrument will be "spoon" (because "spoon" is a high associate of "soup") and "spoon" will be a good recall cue for the sentence. But if an instrument is not inferred during reading, but functions as a good recall cue because of retrieval processes, then the best cue will be one from which "soup" can be generated, that is, "ladle." In fact, in Singer's experiment, "ladle" was a better recall cue than "spoon."

These experiments provided evidence of the importance of retrieval processes to research on inference. However, they do not give any indication of how the retrieval processes are operating, that is, they do not give any clear picture of the text representation. For example, it might be that an instrument for stirring soup is encoded relatively strongly but unspecifically, so that retrieval processes simply add a bit of specificity. In this case, evidence for the inference would be expected to appear across a range of retrieval conditions. Alternatively, it could be that the instrument is encoded very weakly (or not at all), so that evidence for the inference would appear only with a relatively great amount of processing time or an extremely specific retrieval cue. Examples of empirical efforts to investigate these issues are the topics of the next sections.

Time Domain of Processing

One variable that is rarely used in research that examines encoding–retrieval interactions is the time course of processing (see Tulving, 1983, chap. 11). However, processes must evolve over time, and the more time available, the more processing will get accomplished. So, measures of response time and measures from procedures in which time for processing is controlled will provide important sources of information for theory development.

Procedures that limit the time available for retrieval processes are especially useful in text research because the range of such retrieval processes is so large. Without time pressure of any sort, that is with recall or story summarization, subjects are free at the time of the memory test to generate many *additions* to the information retrieved about a text, and to form many new inferences about the text. They are also free to delete or discount retrieved information from their responses (cf. Baillet & Keenan, 1986). If retrieval time is tightly restricted, then the possibility of such additions and deletions is reduced, and responses reflect more directly the information that was encoded at the time of reading.

One way to divide up the dimension of the time course of processing is to contrast automatic processes with strategic processes (Posner & Snyder, 1975). An automatic response to some test event does not require conscious processing, occurs relatively quickly, and occurs even when the probability of that type of event is so low that subjects would not be expected to develop a strategy for responses to the event. A strategic response does require conscious attention, takes a relatively long time, and is more likely to occur when probability is high enough for subjects to develop strategies.

In much of our work, we have limited retrieval time in an effort to ensure that responses were the result of automatic, rather than strategic, processes. Specifically, we have used procedures that measure priming, defined as the amount of facilitation given by one item to the response to a subsequent item. For example, if subjects studied two sentences, "The baby hit the concrete" and "The freak met the debutante," then we might contrast recognition speed and accuracy for the target word "concrete" when it was primed by a word from the same sentence, "baby," and when it was primed by a word from another sentence, "freak." Typically, we find facilitation in the first case relative to the second. Three aspects of the procedure ensure that the facilitation is due to automatic processes: the time between presentation of prime word and target test word (SOA) is short (e.g., 150 msec); subjects are under speed instructions; and the probability that a prime and target come from the same sentence is relatively low so that subjects would not be expected to develop strategies based on expecting a target to be from the same sentence as a prime.

Given that the facilitation is automatic, then it can be used to measure the degree of association in memory between the two concepts represented by the prime and target words. For a studied text, the association might be between two explicitly stated concepts from a text, as in the "baby–concrete" example, between an explicitly stated concept and some other concept that was not stated explicitly but could potentially be inferred, or between an explicitly stated concept and some unstated concept related to the text by general knowledge (through *semantic memory,* in Tulving's terms).

If we accept the automatic–strategic distinction, then it provides a clear theoretical rationale for arguing that priming procedures can reveal the associations that make up the memory representation of the organization of concepts. If, instead, automatic and strategic processes are viewed as two ends of a continuum, on which automatic processing is simply the lack of time for much strategic processing to take place, then priming procedures still have validity. When there is little time for processing, then relative amounts of facilitation will reflect relative degrees of association between concepts.

In the following sections, empirical examples show that the evidence for some kinds of inferences changes as retrieval conditions are moved from fast and automatic to slower and more strategic, and that with automatic processing, inferences can be cue-dependent.

Elaborative Inferences

In our work on text processing, we were faced with the issue of cue-dependent retrieval most directly in attempts to study elaborative inferences. A frequent question in text research has been whether readers make inferences of prediction: Given a sentence about an actress falling off a fourteenth-story roof, does the reader infer, or elaborate the text to include, the result that the actress died? The inference seems quite compelling, so it is plausible (and consistent with past theoretical claims) that the representation of the text encoded into memory would include the information that the actress died.

With respect to elaborative inferences of the kind given in the actress example, we examined three dimensions of retrieval conditions (McKoon & Ratcliff, 1986, 1987, 1988b); we varied the time available at retrieval for processing, we varied the retrieval context, and we varied the strength (and/or specificity) of the inference.

To vary the time available for retrieval processing, we compared the effects of a cue expressing the to-be-inferred event (e.g., the word "dead") on cued recall performance and speeded recognition performance (McKoon & Ratcliff, 1986). The idea was that subjects use much more time to make their responses in cued recall than in recognition. With cued recall, subjects read a list of sentences that included predicting sentences like the actress sentence, and control sentences that included many of the same words as the predicting sentences but did not predict the target events. After a delay of several minutes after list presentation, subjects were given a list of single word cues (the target events like "dead") and were asked to write down the sentence that corresponded to each cue. Subjects recalled 23 percent of the sentences that predicted the cue word, but only 4 percent of the control sentences. In the past, this kind of result has been taken to demonstrate that predicted events are inferred during reading of predicting sentences and encoded into memory with the sentences.

With speeded recognition, the same predicting and control texts were used with a study–test procedure. On each trial, subjects read two sentences, and then were presented with a list of test items. Each test item was made up of a prime word and a target word. The subjects were required to decide whether the target had appeared in one of the two studied texts, and to respond at a deadline of 650 msec after the target was presented. With this deadline, subjects can respond consistently at the required time, and differences across conditions show up in accuracy rates. For the target items that expressed predictable events (e.g., the word "dead"), the correct response was "no." With a neutral word as prime (the word "ready," used consistently throughout the experiment), the results were that there was little difference in accuracy between the predicting and the control sentences. Thus, the results suggest that subjects did *not* make an inference during reading about predictable events.

Obviously, the results of the cued recall and speeded recognition experiments are at variance. With cued recall, subjects have the time to employ strategies that lead to recall of the predicting sentences from the target cues. But with speeded recognition, subjects must rely on fast automatic processes, and they have insufficient time to add information to the cue to build the connection between the cue and a studied sentence that would lead to successful retrieval. Of course, there were other differences in procedure between the cued recall and recognition experiments, but it is certainly plausible that the critical difference was the time available for retrieval processing.

One possible conclusion from these results is that elaborative inferences of the predictable events kind are not encoded during reading; the basis for this conclusion is that there is no indication of such inferences in speeded recognition; successful cued recall would be attributed entirely to strategic retrieval processes. However, this conclusion would ignore the importance of studying inferences under a range of retrieval contexts. Conclusions about the content of the memory representation of a text cannot be based on only one retrieval context. In fact, when the retrieval context was changed in the recognition experiment by using a word from the studied sentence ("actress") as a prime instead of the neutral prime, the error rate on the predicted event targets ("dead") was much higher for predicting study sentences than control study sentences.

The overall pattern of results for inferences about predictable events can be understood in terms of associations between retrieval cues and information in memory. The association between a predicted event by itself (or with a neutral prime) and a studied predicting sentence in memory is not strong enough to give errors in speeded recognition. But for a combined cue of the predicted event plus a prime from the sentence, the association is strong enough to give errors. The picture of the memory representation given by these associations is one in which the inference about the predicted event is encoded in some minimal way; for example, for "death", the encoded inference might be "something bad."

It was this idea, that inferences might be encoded minimally, that suggested to us that inferences might vary in strength, a third dimension in addition to the dimensions of the time course of processing and retrieval context. To test the strength notion, we used a new set of predicting and control sentences, in which there were many words that were semantically associated to the predicted event (McKoon & Ratcliff, 1988b). For example, the predicting sentence for the target word "sew" was "The housewife was learning to be a seamstress and needed practice so she got out the skirt she was making and threaded her needle," and the control sentence was "The housewife was a careless seamstress, and when she dropped an unthreaded needle on the floor, she didn't find it until she stepped on it days later." For these materials, there are the same words semantically associated to the target "sew" in both the predicting and control sentences, yet only in the case of the predicting sentence would the housewife actually be expected to sew. With the strong semantic associations to support the inference for the predicting sentence, the target word by itself (with the neutral prime) was strongly enough associated to the memory representation to give significantly more errors with the predicting sentences than the control sentences.

This work on elaborative inferences begins to address the issues of cue-dependent retrieval in text processing. We have obviously just begun to take the first steps in examining the interactions of retrieval and inference processes, but so far, the results indicate that we can tease apart some of the factors that operate at the time of retrieval.

Aspects of Meaning

Another kind of inference that has received a great deal of attention in the text-processing literature concerns the different features of meaning of words. The features necessary for comprehension in one context may be different than in another context. For example, comprehension of a text about painting a picture of a tomato may be more likely to include the information that tomatoes are red than a text about rolling a tomato across the floor, when neither text states explicitly that "tomatoes are red." In studying this kind of inference, we were surprised to learn just how wide-ranging the effects of retrieval context could be.

In our experiments (McKoon & Ratcliff, 1988a; see Table 4.2), we were concerned with retrieval when processing was speeded, and varying retrieval context under this condition. On each trial of a study–test experiment, subjects read three short texts, and then were presented with a series of true/false test sentences. Some of the sentences could only be verified with respect to the studied texts, whereas others could be verified by general knowledge (i.e., without having read the texts at all). The interesting test sentences were those

TABLE 4.2

Matching Version:

This still life would require great accuracy. The painter searched many days to find the color most suited to use in the painting of the ripe tomato.
Target test sentence: Tomatoes are red. (True)
Priming test sentences:
      The still life would require great accuracy. (True)
      Newspapers are reading material. (True)
Filler test sentences:
      The painter searched for many days. (True)
      Balloons are heavy. (False)
Mismatching Version:

The child psychologist watched the infant play with her toys. The little girl found a tomato to roll across the floor with her nose.
Target test sentence: Tomatoes are red. (True)
Priming test sentences: The child psychologist watched the infant. (True)
                    Newspapers are reading material. (True)
Filler test sentences:
      The little girl played with her toys. (True)
      Balloons are heavy. (False)

that expressed features of meaning of nouns when the nouns had appeared in a studied text but the features of meaning had not been stated explicitly. The features of meaning either matched the meaning of the text (as "tomatoes are red" matches the text about painting a picture of tomatoes in Table 4.2) or did not match the meaning of the text (as "tomatoes are red" does not match the text about rolling a tomato). One retrieval context was an immediately preceding test sentence that had nothing to do with any studied text (e.g., "Newspapers are reading material," true by general knowledge). In this context, responses for the target sentences were equally fast in the matching and mismatching conditions. This might be taken to suggest that readers do not infer different aspects of meaning for different uses of nouns. But, as with predictable events, changing the retrieval context changes the picture of the memory representation. When the immediately preceding test sentence was from a studied story, then responses to matching target test sentences were faster and more accurate than responses to mismatching target test sentences. The difference between the matching and mismatching sentences was present both when the preceding test sentence was from the same text as the target and when it was from a different text.

Overall, as with the predictable events inferences, the picture given by varying retrieval conditions can be understood in terms of associations between retrieval cues and memory. A cue made up of a sentence like "tomatoes are red" plus another general-knowledge sentence (that has nothing to do with any studied text) is not strongly associated to information in memory about recently studied texts. On the other hand, a cue made up of "tomatoes are red" plus a sentence from any studied text is associated to recently studied information. The strength of that association depends on whether the two sentences refer to the same text and on whether "tomatoes are red" matches the meaning of a studied text.

Summary for Text Processing

For text-processing research, the most important consequence of considering the notion of cue-dependent retrieval is that the questions to be asked are completely changed. Previously, questions have always been concerned with whether readers make some specific kind of inference. Instead, as suggested by Tulving's theoretical work and the empirical work discussed previously, the questions must become what retrieval conditions give evidence for some kind of inference, and more generally, what retrieval factors are important for memory for textual information. This shift in research toward encoding–retrieval interactions leads to a greater emphasis on retrieval processes than has been the case in the past. For one example, further research is needed to investigate the dimension that ranges from fast automatic retrieval processes to slow strategic processes. For another, we need to try to understand how information that is not available easily and quickly, such as the connection between two thematically related stories, can be calculated and become available with time (cf. Seifert, McKoon, Abelson, & Ratcliff, 1986).

CONCLUSION

The future of research in the two domains of memory models and text processing looks quite rosy. For memory, there are several competing models that do an impressive job of accounting for a wide range of data. These models are now being compared and contrasted, and attempts are being made to understand what features of the models provide predictive power in specific domains. Part of this development is the introduction of nonlinear processes into the models (e.g., Gillund & Shiffrin, 1984, products of strengths; Hintzman, 1986a,b, cubing strengths), and these new architectures provide challenges in understanding the bases of the predictions of the models. Along with this development of memory models, the parallel and more visible development of connectionist models and their nonlinear characteristics has also led to a rich theoretical domain of investigation. As noted earlier, within this domain of study, the issue of encoding–retrieval interactions is proving to be important in developing and evaluating the models.

The domain of text processing has been relatively inactive over the last few years (compared with the late 1970s). We feel that there will soon be a renaissance fueled partly by developments in theory in linguistics and, to a lesser extent, in computer science. In addition, the development of rapid priming techniques offers experimental procedures to test advances in theory. As illustrated previously, we expect that encoding–retrieval interactions will play an important role in advances in this area.

Although this chapter has reviewed these two areas of research somewhat independently, we find considerable cross-fertilization between the areas. One example was the new theory of priming phenomena, which was driven by data from text processing and theory from a current memory model (Gillund & Shiffrin; 1984). Often, we find heuristic value in qualitatively applying memory models to empirical data from text research to guide subsequent theoretical and empirical questions. Generally, an important target is the development of memory models that will apply not only to traditional memory paradigms, but also to empirical phenomena in the domains of text processing and text memory.

ACKNOWLEDGMENT

This research was supported by NSF grant BNS 85 10361 to Roger Ratcliff, NIH grant HD18812 to Gail McKoon, and NSF grant BNS 85 16350 to Gail McKoon.

We thank John Anderson, James Neely, and Henry Roediger for their useful comments on this chapter.

REFERENCES

Anderson, J. R. (1976). *Language, memory, and thought.* Hillsdale, NJ: Lawrence Erlbaum Associates.

Anderson, J. R. (1983). *The architecture of cognition.* Cambridge, MA: Harvard University Press.

Anderson, J. R., & Bower, G. H. (1973). *Human associative memory.* Washington, DC: Winston.

Baillet, S. D., & Keenan, J. M. (1986). The role of encoding and retrieval processes in the recall of text. *Discourse Processes, 9,* 247–268.

Balota, D. A., & Lorch, R. F. (1986). Depth of automatic spreading activation: Mediated priming effects in pronunciation but not in lexical decision. *Journal of Experimental Psychology: Learning, Memory, and Cognition, 12,* 336–345.

Begg, I. (1979). Trace loss and the recognition failure of unrecalled words. *Memory and Cognition, 7,* 113–123.

Collins, A. M., & Loftus, E. F. (1975). A spreading-activation theory of semantic processing. *Psychological Review, 82,* 407–428.

Corbett, A. T., & Dosher, B. A. (1978). Instrument inferences in sentence encoding. *Journal of Verbal Learning and Verbal Behavior, 17,* 479–491.

de Groot, A. M. B. (1983). The range of automatic spreading activation in word priming. *Journal of Verbal Learning and Verbal Behavior, 22,* 417–436.

Eich, J. M. (1982). A composite holographic associative recall model. *Psychological Review, 89,* 627–661.

Flexser, A. J., & Tulving, E. (1978). Retrieval independence in recognition and recall. *Psychological Review, 85,* 153–171.

Gillund, G., & Shiffrin, R. M. (1984). A retrieval model for both recognition and recall. *Psychological Review, 19,* 1–65.

Hintzman, D. (1986a). "Schema abstraction" in a multiple-trace memory model. *Psychological Review, 93,* 411–428.

Hintzman, D. (1986b). *Judgments of frequency and recognition memory in a multiple-trace memory model.* (Tech. Rep. No. 86-11). Eugene: University of Oregon.

McKoon, G., & Ratcliff, R. (1980). Priming in item recognition: The organization of propositions in memory for text. *Journal of Verbal Learning and Verbal Behavior, 19,* 369–386.

McKoon, G., & Ratcliff, R. (1981). The comprehension processes and memory structures involved in instrumental inference. *Journal of Verbal Learning and Verbal Behavior, 20,* 671–682.

McKoon, G., & Ratcliff, R. (1986). Inferences about predictable events. *Journal of Experimental Psychology: Learning, Memory, and Cognition, 12,* 82–91.

McKoon, G. (1988). *The use of on-line lexical decision probes to investigate inference processes.* Manuscript submitted for publication.

McKoon, G., & Ratcliff, R. (1988a). Contextually relevant aspects of meaning. *Journal of Experimental Psychology: Learning, Memory, and Cognition, 14,* 331–343.

McKoon, G., & Ratcliff, R. (1988b). Semantic association and elaborative inference. In press, *Journal of Experimental Psychology: Learning, Memory, and Cognition.*

Murdock, B. B. (1982). A theory for the storage and retrieval of item and associative information. *Psychological Review, 89,* 609–626.

Murdock, B. B. (1983). A distributed memory model for serial-order information. *Psychological Review, 90,* 316–338.

Paris, S., & Lindauer, B. K. (1976). The role of inference in children's comprehension and memory for sentences. *Cognitive Psychology, 8,* 217–227.

Posner, M. I., & Snyder, C. R. (1975). Attention and cognitive control. In R. L. Solso (Ed.), *Information processing and cognition: The Loyola symposium* (pp. 55–85). Hillsdale, NJ: Lawrence Erlbaum Associates.

Raaijmakers, J. G. W., & Shiffrin, R. M. (1981). Search of associative memory. *Psychological Review, 88,* 93–134.

Ratcliff, R. (1978). A theory of memory retrieval, *Psychological Review, 85,* 59–108.

Ratcliff, R. (1981). A theory of order relations in perceptual matching. *Psychological Review, 88,* 552–572.

Ratcliff, R. (1985). Theoretical interpretations of speed and accuracy of positive and negative responses. *Psychological Review, 92,* 212–225.

Ratcliff, R. (1987). More on the speed and accuracy of positive and negative responses. *Psychological Review, 94,* 277–280.

Ratcliff, R. (1988). Continuous versus discrete information processing: Modeling the accumulation of partial information. *Psychological Review, 95,* 238–255.

Ratcliff, R., Hockley, W. E., & McKoon, G. (1985). Components of activation: Repetition and priming effects in lexical decision and recognition. *Journal of Experimental Psychology: General, 114,* 435–450.

Ratcliff, R., & McKoon, G. (1978). Priming in item recognition: Evidence for the propositional structure of sentences. *Journal of Verbal Learning and Verbal Behavior, 20,* 204–215.

Ratcliff, R., & McKoon, G. (1982). Speed and accuracy in the processing of false statements about semantic information. *Journal of Experimental Psychology: Human Learning and Memory, 8,* 16–36.

Ratcliff, R., & McKoon, G. (1988). A retrieval theory of priming in memory. *Psychological Review, 95,* 385–408.

Reder, L. M., Anderson, J. R., & Bjork, R.A. (1974). A semantic interpretation of encoding specificity. *Journal of Experimental Psychology, 102,* 648–656.

Seifert, C. M., McKoon, G., Abelson, R.P., & Ratcliff, R. (1986). Memory connections between thematically similar episodes. *Journal of Experimental Psychology: Learning, Memory, and Cognition, 12,* 220–231.

Singer, M. (1978, August). *The role of explicit and implicit recall cues.* Paper presented at the meeting of the American Psychological Association, Toronto.

Singer, M. (1979). Processes of inference during sentence encoding. *Memory and Cognition, 7,* 192–200.

Tulving, E. (1974). Cue-dependent forgetting. *American Scientist, 62,* 74–82.

Tulving, E. (1983). *Elements of episodic memory.* New York: Oxford University Press.

Tulving, E., & Thomson, D. M. (1973). Encoding specificity and retrieval processes in episodic memory. *Psychological Review, 80* 352–373.

Tulving, E., & Watkins, O. C. (1977). Recognition failure of words with a single meaning. *Memory and Cognition, 5,* 513–522.

Watkins, M. J., & Tulving, E. (1975). Episodic memory: When recognition fails. *Journal of Experimental Psychology: General, 104,* 5–29.

Wiseman, S., & Tulving, E. (1975). A test of confusion theory of encoding specificity. *Journal of Verbal Learning and Verbal Behavior, 14,* 370–381.

5 The Past, the Present, and the Future: Comments on Section 1

Bennet B. Murdock, Jr.
University of Toronto

In their opening remarks to the conference from which this volume came, the organizers suggested that we both commemorate the past and anticipate the future. In my remarks, I make three main points. The first deals with the past, the second with the present, and the third with the future. For the past, I review very briefly previous work on context as an encoding variable. For the present, I play the role of a gadfly and cast a critical eye on the use of experimental separation as a means of providing evidence for multiple memory systems. For the future, I suggest one direction in which the field might be (and in my view should be) moving.

As is quite clear from the chapters in this section, the work of Tulving and his colleagues has been quite influential in calling attention to the role of context as an important variable in human memory. Is this a new insight, one that earlier investigators of memory failed to appreciate? In a word, the answer is "no." Consider this quotation from McGeoch's (1932) classic article on forgetting and the law of disuse:

> It follows that forgetting, in the sense of functional inability or loss, may result from a lack of the proper eliciting stimulus, even when interpolated events have not been such as to bring the material below the threshold of recall at the time.
>
> The absence of the necessary stimulus will occur as a result of change in the stimulating context of the individual. At least until learning has been carried far beyond the threshold, the learner is forming associations, not only intrinsic to the material which is being learned, but also between the parts of this material and the manifold features of the context or environment in which the learning is taking place. (p. 365)

TABLE 5.1
Transfer as a Function of Changed Conditions at Recall

Conditions	Percent Recalled
Same syllables (Control)	67.76
1st letter of 1st syllable changed	40.15
2nd letter of 1st syllable changed	59.85
1st and 2nd letter of 1st syllable changed	39.38
1st letter of 2nd syllable changed	40.93
2nd letter of 2nd syllable changed	53.86
1st and 2nd letters of 2nd syllable changed	37.65

Note: From Yum (1931, p. 73).

By 1932, there was also experimental data demonstrating the effect of context on memory. As noted later by McGeoch (1946):

> Pan's data show an intimate relation between the recall of paired associates and the presence of incidental contextual words. Removal during recall of a context logically related to the response word and present throughout learning decreased recall. On the other hand, if the context had been varied during learning, this effect was diminished. Change from an old context to a new one at recall yielded a decrement, but introduction, during recall, of a context logically related to the response word increased recall. (pp. 502–503)

The study by Pan (1926) was entitled, "The influence of context upon learning and recall," and the comment by McGeoch suggests that the results were not completely unnoticed by others in the field.

The results from another early study by Yum (1931) are shown in Table 5.1. Subjects learned a list of nonsense-syllable paired associates and then were tested for recall under various conditions. The results showed that recall decreased as a function of changed stimulus conditions (changes in the A members of the A–B paired associates), and this would be "context" in the intrinsic sense of McGeoch. Further experiments in the same paper showed similar results for meaningful words and for pictures.

Such results seemed to be common knowledge in the field. As stated by Hovland (1951) in his chapter in the S. S. Stevens Handbook:

> A fourth important factor in forgetting is the alteration of the stimulating conditions from the time of learning to that of the measurment of retention. Forgetting occurs when some of the stimuli present during the original learning are no longer present during recall, or when new stimuli are present that evoke competing responses sufficiently strong to block those originally learned. Relevant stimuli are both external (like the furniture in the room in which we learn, the apparatus, the experimenter, etc.) and internal (resulting from posture, responses made during

learning, etc.). Reduced recall has been shown when learning has been in one location, and testing in another . . . The gradient of generalization discussed above operates in the determining the amount of such transfer. Similarly, when words are learned with one color background, recall is reduced when the background is changed . . . Case studies have also shown that a language learned in one context is poorly retained in a different context but is quickly relearned when the original context is restored. (p. 676)

Given this early work, why has Tulving's contribution been so influential? It is not just old wine in new bottles; the old wine was consumed and not replenished. With the ascendancy of interference theory in the late 1950s and early 1960s, this traditional wisdom was replaced by a different emphasis. Concern shifted to storage effects rather than retrieval effects: retroactive and proactive effects, their mechanisms, and their consequences. One cannot claim that context effects were disputed, but they were certainly not the center of attention.

It may be hard to appreciate how dominant a role interference theory played at this time, and it provided the framework for much of the research on verbal learning and memory. Tulving felt that, by de-emphasizing context, the research on interference theory was neglecting an important variable, and this led to the encoding specificity principle. This principle reestablished the importance of context beyond all doubt, and it is an important part of our current understanding of learning and memory.

To turn to the present, my second point deals with the logic of experimental separation as a means of establishing the existence of separate memory systems (see also the Roediger, Weldon, and Challis chapter in this volume). If there are separate memory systems, then some sort of experimental separatation should be possible. The converse does not follow; experimental separation does not imply (in the strict sense) separate memory systems. Because the enterprise (of demonstrating an experimental separation, then claiming evidence for separate systems) seems so popular today, a word of caution may not be out of order.

Let me illustrate my point with a particular example. A study by Watkins and Watkins (1977) reported a lovely experimental separation of primacy and recency in the serial-position curve of serial recall. They found that word frequency had an appreciable affect on primacy but little or no effect on recency, whereas mode of presentation (auditory or visual) had an appreciable effect on recency but little or no effect on primacy. These data are shown in the top half of Fig. 5.1.

In an application of a distributed-memory model to serial-order effects, Lewandowsky and Murdock (in press) fitted these data with their model, and the fitted data are shown in the bottom half of Fig. 5.1. I think it will be acknowledged that the agreement between observed and fitted is quite close; in particular, the fitted data shows the same clear pattern of experimental separation as the observed data. Are there two separate memory systems, one responsive to the effect of word frequency but not modality, the other responsive to the effect of modality but not word frequency?

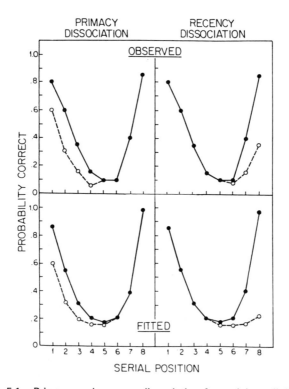

FIG. 5.1.   Primacy and recency dissociation for serial recall. The observed primacy dissociation is due to high versus low frequency
words, whereas the observed recency dissociation is produced by different presentation modalities (auditory and visual). The data are from
Watkins and Watkins (1977). The bottom panels show the fits of a
distributed memory model with one parameter affecting primacy but
not recency, and another parameter affecting recency but not primacy.
(Figure 20 from Lewandowsky and Murdock, in press.)

Not according to our single-system model. Without going into detail, suffice
it to say that there are several free parameters in the model, and it so happens that
one of them can produce primacy differences without recency differences,
whereas another can produce recency differences without primacy differences. It
is not even necessary to detail what these parameters are, or how they work. The
point should be clear; a model with a single memory system can explain the
experimental separation as due to the differential effects of the experimental
variables on the model parameters.

What do we mean by a single-memory system? Although there are various
interpretations of this phrase, here we mean a memory system in which different
types of information (e.g., item information, associative information, or propositional information) is stored in a common memory (e.g., vector, matrix, or set of

connections). The alternative (multiple memory systems) is one in which different types of information are stored in separate memories. When we find an experimental separation, it could be due to separate memory systems or it could be due to the action of different parameters within a single memory system. So, theoretically, the result is inconclusive.

I should state that I am not opposed to experimental separations of this sort; quite the contrary, they can be quite illuminating. Nor am I saying that there *aren't* separate memory systems. Indeed, there probably are. Human memory is probably organized first by mode of presentation (Murdock, 1974), so different memory stores corresponding to different sensory modalities would constitute a multiple-memory system. My only point is that experimental separation in and of itself is not sufficient to validate the claim.

The point about experimental separation is a theoretical issue, and my third and final point concerns theory. What does the future hold in store? Or, better, in what directions can we most profitably move if we are to continue to advance the study of human memory beyond its current state? I would suggest that our theoretical understanding lags far behind our experimental and methodological sophistication, and the best hope for the future lies in the development and testing of theories and models.

This is not a particularly popular view with some of my colleagues, although feelings are mixed. However, in Chapter 4, Ratcliff and McKoon present a convincing argument for the importance of theory, and I can do no better than echo their views. Basically, our goal is understanding, and understanding is not description. We need theories and models to deepen and broaden our understanding.

The search for new phenomena is exciting and exhilerating, but we also have a responsibility to explain our old phenomenon. In the early stages of a science, we need stable and reliable data, and the more facts we have the better. We have passed that stage in the memory area. We have our facts firmly in place. Our data base is a reliable and impressive set of findings about many aspects of human memory, perhaps not quite as precise as that of physics and chemistry, but probably as good as, say, some branches of the neurosciences.

Given this extensive and impressive set of data, we need to increase our understanding of the mechanisms and processes involved in the storage and retrieval of information from memory. Such an explanation requires a theory or a model. Our successes to date have not been too impressive, but this is probably our best hope for continuing progress in the field.

ACKNOWLEDGMENTS

This research was supported by Grant APA 146 from the Natural Sciences and Engineering Research Council of Canada. The author thanks Marcia Johnson for helpful comments on the manuscript.

REFERENCES

Hovland, C. I. (1951). Human learning. In S. S. Stevens (Ed.), *Handbook of experimental psychology* (pp 613–689). NY: Wiley.

Lewandowsky, S., & Murdock, B. B., Jr. (in press). Memory for serial order. *Psychological Review*.

McGeoch, J. A. (1932). Forgetting and the law of disuse. *Psychological Review, 39,* 352–370.

McGeoch, J. A. (1946). *The psychology of human learning.* New York: Longmans-Green.

Murdock, B. B., Jr. (1974). *Human memory: Theory and data.* Potomac, MD: Laurence Erlbaum Associates.

Pan, S. (1926). The influence of context upon learning and recall. *Journal of Experimental psychology, 9,* 468–491.

Yum, K. S. (1931). Transfer as a function of changed conditions at recall. *Journal of Experimental Psychology, 14,* 68–82.

Watkins, O. C., & Watkins, M. J. (1977). Serial recall and the modality effect: Effects of word frequency. *Journal of Experimental Psychology: Human Learning and Memory, 3,* 712–718.

II NEUROPSYCHOLOGY

6 Remembering Dissociations

L. Weiskrantz
University of Oxford

One of the truly gratifying developments over the past decade, and one to which Endel Tulving and his clinical colleagues have made particular contributions, has been the marriage between theory construction in human experimental psychology and research findings in neuropsychology. For the latter to be of any use for the former, conclusions and inferences must be capable of being cast in terms of independent or interacting parallel pathways, or in ordered sequences of hierarchies of processes along given pathways, including feedback loops upon that pathway. Needless to say, this is so only if the theoretical flow diagrams are themselves cast in such terms. But, in neuropsychology, the raw data are always cast in the form: Lesion X produces Deficit on Task A. If one substitutes "Treatment" (e.g., a drug, sensory deprivation, stress, etc.) for "Lesions" and substitutes "Behavioral Outcome" for "Deficit", then precisely the same logic applies, and so the issues have much wider application (cf. Weiskrantz, 1968a). What I explore here is how we go from those simple conjunctions in the raw data to inferences that are in a useful form. Having considered some of these general principles in the first part of the chapter, I then follow up with some evidence about dissociations that lead one to inferences about multiple memory systems.

In neuropsychology, as it is practiced today, there are two approaches, sometimes it seems, two cultures, that derive naturally from neuropsychologists collectively, but not necessarily individually, having quite practical responsibilities as well as a deep curiosity about the mind-brain question. There are those who have an abiding and important practical concern, often driven by the everyday needs of the clinical scene, who wish to describe and treat patients with similar clusters of deficits, typically drawn from common aetiological sources. There are those, on the other hand, who focus on particular pieces of neuropsychological evidence, sometimes derived from just a single case, as being decisive for drawing distinctions of particular interest, irrespective of nosological, epidemiological, or aetiological considerations. I argue that the second of these cultures is more productive for theory application, which is the main concern here, although it has its obvious limitations in the practical sphere (at least in the short-term) and in certain other respects, and that the first culture can be positively misleading for drawing theoretical inferences. The difficulty is that the members of these two cultures sometimes both address the same theoretical issues, generating conclusions that reflect quite different considerations.

THREE ASSERTIONS
AND THEIR IMPLICATIONS

I start with three dogmatic propositions with which I think most practicing neuropsychologists would agree. The first is that there is no such entity as a "pure" behavioral task, that is, a task that reflects only a single process or capacity. Even the "simplest" task, whether it be finger tapping or an unconditioned reflex, entails attention, wakefulness, motivation, sensory adaptation levels, and so on. When we turn to the types of tasks that are typically used in cognitive neuropsychology—for example, recognition memory—the point is both more obvious and more complex.

The second assertion concerns an assumption that remains implicit in neuropsychological research (indeed, in the study of all treatment effects); namely that there *can* be a "pure" deficit. That is, it is possible in principle, albeit not always in practice, to give a coherent and unitary characterization of a breakdown; for example, an increase, let us say, in a sensory threshold, or a slower rate of dark adaptation, or a more rapid rate of short-term forgetting. By unitary I mean that only a single process be involved, and by coherent I mean that the deficit must be describable and interpretable in terms that relate to the characterization of normal behavior and not to bizarre or ad hoc categories generated de novo. (If it can be related to a physiological substrate with properties that allow causal inferences, so much the better, but that is another matter.) Perhaps not all neuropsychological practitioners will accept this assumption—and the traditional critics of neuropsychology, who argue that it is no more than the study of uninterpretable perturbations, would certainly reject it. I have examined the issue much more fully elsewhere (Weiskrantz, 1968a). Here I merely assert that the foregoing assumption must be fulfilled for the findings of neuropsychology to be transcribable to human experimental psychology (and vice versa), as historically and pragmatically they patently have been.

The third assertion, I am sure, will not be in dispute. It is that lesions of the brain, whether structural or chemical, typically affect a multiplicity of pathways. Therefore, as a practical matter, even if the second assumption is accepted, the typical neuropsychological outcome is very likely to be complex and to involve more than a single deficit. Even if the most extreme "localizationist" position is adopted, that is, that discrete regions of the brain are uniquely critical for discrete processes, as a matter of practical geometry and anatomy, lesions—and especially those imposed by disease rather than by experimenters—will involve a composite of intermingled regions.

As an aside, however, there are two features of the real nervous system, at least, that make the task somewhat more manageable for experimental manipulations and also, if one is fortunate, for the interpretation of clinical cases. The anatomical circuits flowing out from the regions of sensory input—for example, the striate cortex—do so not in a strictly serial manner, going to each way station as links in a chain. If that were the case, interruption of the circuit at any point would block transmission to any point beyond. Instead, the organization is of a leap-frogging character so that connections are made to a region but also bypass that region (cf. Cowey, 1979). This means that very specific effects might be assigned to subregions so that if any is selectively damaged, there could well be a selective loss of a particular capacity without interference with the rest of the circuit. This feature of the nervous system, which naturally leads to a modular view, is one of the ways in which it is different from the electronic devices with which comparisons were sometimes made in the past. (Also, the brain carries its own evolutionary history in its anatomical organization, unlike artificial analogs.) The second point is that it seems possible, even likely, that comparable principles of anatomical and functional organization will apply to several sensory systems (cf. Jones & Powell, 1970). Such common anatomical flow diagrams enable one to exploit this feature of redundancy in one's interpretations.

Let us return to our three propositions: that single tasks are complex functionally, that lesions are typically multiple, but that nevertheless unitary deficits are possible in principle. What we wish to extract from the empirical findings is a conclusion that can be assigned to a particular locus in a theoretical structure, or lead to an inference that suggests a theoretical structure. What we want to avoid are conclusions that may impede such an assignment, or, of course, conclusions that are themselves unwarranted.

The first point that must follow from the three propositions is that no firm conclusions can be reached by studying treatment effects on only a single task, no matter how seductive it may be for other reasons; for example, if one considers that one has a "prototypical" task in animals that really is homologous to a task to which the human amnesic patient may be differentially sensitive. This is because it will not be possible to say which one or more of the various features of that task represents the weakness that leads to the measured deficit. In order to isolate a critical feature, if there be one, it is essential to study a spectrum of tasks in which various possible features are selectively arranged either to be present or absent.

It follows equally from the same argument that holding a task constant—

delayed non-matching from sample, let us say—and working one's way experimentally through a set of lesions in a putative anatomical circuit or some other set of loci, is subject to the same limitation. If each of several different lesions yields a deficit on a single task, we still do not know whether each is doing so for the same reason.

A second point concerns the interactions of lesion effects on a single task. Given that any single task involves a multiplicity of factors, any two lesions may appear to combine (or antagonize) their effects by acting on different factors; for example, one lesion might change motivation and the other might change skilled motor coordination, or one might change visual acuity and the other might change fineness of focused attention, and so on. The result may or may not be simple summation, as predicted by a principle of mass action. Thus, that a particular memory task is affected more severely by combined lesions (in the hippocampus and amygdala, shall we say?) does not permit the conclusion that both structures are contributing to the task in the same manner and that the lesion effects are merely summating quantitatively. This may be so, but again, without a minimum of at least two tasks one cannot draw such a conclusion. And when, as it happens, it is known from other evidence that these two lesions have quite different effects from each other on some other tasks, there is a reasonable presumption that they have different effects on this single task as well.

If it is always necessary to have more than one task in order to draw useful conclusions from the study of a single treatment effect, this brings us to the third point. It derives directly from the third assumption, that any particular treatment is highly likely to have multiple effects. The point is that such effects may be related in no interesting or causal way, but derive simply from anatomical proximity and intermingling that is incidental to one's analysis. Temporal lobe lesions in human beings can produce memory impairments. They can also produce visual field defects, not because there is a retino-geniculate projection to neurons in the temporal lobe, but because the radiation fibres from lateral geniculate to the striate cortex course through the white matter of the temporal lobe. Although it may be statistically of interest, nothing is added to the theoretical characterization of temporal lobe memory deficits to say that they can be accompanied by field defects, even if this association were a probable one. Again, there is no doubt that striate cortex lesions, which invariably *do* cause visual field defects, may often be associated with headaches and muscular tension. But a broken leg may also be associated with the same symptoms. A small tumor in the region of the inner ear can lead both to hearing loss and to a loss of balance. Let us extend the list to more contemporary examples: Parkinsons's Disease can lead to loss of motor control as well as to cognitive deficits. Korsakoff's Disease can lead to changes in sensory thresholds as well as to long-term memory loss. Korsakoff's Disease can lead to short-term memory as well as long-term memory deficits. Alzheimer's Disease can . . . : The list can be expanded indefinitely.

The question at issue is whether these associations of deficits are obligatory. If they are not, then it is parsimonious and prudent to consider that they reflect different and potentially independent processes. If a temporal lobe memory loss can occur in the absence of a visual field defect, then the two need have nothing to do with each other except that they are cerebral room-mates, or worse, components in a neuropsychological broth. Of course, if we with to arrange the most complete custodial care for temporal lobe patients, it may be prudent to assess their vision as well as their memory, just as it would be prudent to consider assigning a social worker to an alcoholic Korsakoff patient. These are issues of epidemiological and correlative profiles, and do not convey any causal significance whatever. A single case may be sufficient to demonstrate that one can occur without the other, even if 99 out of 100 other cases demonstrate a concordance.

But even the example of a single dissociation (e.g., memory loss without visual field defect) may not be good enough. It may be that patients differ in their sensitivities to one or another of the tests, so that a change in visual thresholds may be undetectable in some, or that the tests themselves are not of equal sensitivity; that is, one may be easier for the patient to pass than another. Not all clinical tests, indeed few of them, allow for a titration of the limits of the patient's capacity, and even when they do, there is often insufficient time to administer them to that end.

Double Dissociations: Relative versus Absolute

It is obvious, I hope, that we have come to the point of asserting the value of *double* dissociations. If a task is affected by one treatment, is unaffected by a second treatment, and if that second treatment does affect some further task that is unaffected by the first treatment, then we have satisfied the requirement of having more than one task per treatment, and we have at the same time shown that the failure of the first treatment to have an effect on the further task is not due to the insensitivity of that task. We now have reasonable grounds for suggesting that the two tasks in question can be assigned to different and potentially independent pathways in a theoretical structure. The conclusion does not follow with logical certainty (cf. Weiskrantz, 1968b); it is a pragmatic argument, but no less valuable for that.

Given the third assertion, that pathways may be intermingled and/or the lesion may be over-intrusive, it is not surprising that genuine double dissociations may often occur that are not absolute. That is, Lesion A may affect Task 1 severely, and also Task 2, but less severely. Conversely, Lesion B affects Task 2 severely and Task 1 less severely. This sometimes provides the basis for dismissive comments that some deficits are not "pure" and hence there is no specificity of processing. For example, it is often said that prosopagnosia (failure of recognition of familiar faces) is rarely if ever seen in isolation without other agnosic disorders. But the fact that different categories of meaningful items (including faces) can be affected *differentially* in different patients (Warrington, 1982a) can give rise to a rich set of inferences about specific dissociable processes, even though a "pure" disorder may be seen only rarely in any single patient. Empirically, the dissociations are just as real when they are relative as when they are absolute, although with relative double dissociations it remains unresolved, without further work, what the source of the residual deficit is on the minor of the two tasks for each lesion, that is, whether it is overlap of pathways, overinclusiveness of lesion, interaction between parallel pathways, or a general non-specific factor.

There is a subtle way in which a background of a hidden relative double dissociation can lead to a misleading conclusion when one is focused on a particular task that one is tempted to use as a kind of behavioral "assay" in going through a putative circuit. For example, a recognition or delayed non-matching-from-sample task can be tested with lesions at a number of different loci to define a "memory circuit". Some of those loci may not lie in the main focus, but nevertheless yield a deficit. For example, there may well be a deficit on delayed nonmatching *performance* caused by lesions of the inferotemporal cortex. But it has been claimed that this deficit is relatively mild compared to the deficit caused by lesions within the hippocampal system (e.g., the fornix) and very mild compared to the classical deficit in visual discrimination learning well known to be caused by inferotemporal lesions. Indeed, there is a pattern of double dissociation between inferotemporal and fornix lesions and their effects on visual discrimination learning and delayed recognition deficits, respectively (Gaffan & Weiskrantz, 1980). Therefore, a misleading conclusion may be reached about a continuous sequential circuit, even though the background evidence from dissociations makes the interpretation of a route along *parallel* pathways more parsimonious. The relative double dissociation between the two types of tasks may derive from the proximity of the pathways, or their intermingling *or* —recalling our opening assertion that all *tasks* are invariably impure— because visual recognition and visual discrimination learning tasks share some features in common.

But the very "impurity" of tasks to which our first pontifical assertion draws attention can sometimes work to a dissociative advantage, because a finer analysis of different phases or components of the "single" task may sometimes be possible, and these may dissociate. For example, continuing with the instance of delayed nonmatching in the monkey, it appears that inferotemporal lesions affect mainly the acquisition (or reacquisition) of the nonmatching rule itself, and have a less serious effect on delay *after* acquisition has been mastered. Conversely, fornix lesions do not impair the acquisition of the rule, but they differentially affect performance with increasing delays and lists (Gaffan & Weiskrantz, 1980). (It is possible that Mishkin, 1982, obtained a somewhat different result because his inferotemporal group never reached the same reacquisition criterion as the controls, and hence started the delay testing at a lower initial performance level.)

Associations and Hierarchies

We are still left, however, with those putatively obligatory associations of deficits associated with a single treatment; that is, when exceptions are not found to their joint occurrence for that particular lesion. Such associations can, in turn, be of three different types. Fortunately, the strategy that allows for their ultimate classification is similar in all three cases. The first type is of a hierarchical relationship. For example, the typical field defect caused by striate cortex lesions in humans is characterized by a loss of *awareness* for visual stimuli, whether they are black and white or colored, or moving or stationary (I am not talking about what might be possible in "blindsight"). If it can be shown that any of these can be singly dissociated, for example, that every striate cortical field defect is accompanied by losses in color as well as in black and white but that lesions elsewhere can yield a loss in color but not in black and white (and, of course, that this is not due to differences in sensitivity per se), then we have reason to place the striate locus higher in the hierarchy with regard to these two capacities.

Movement is even more interesting, because a patient with circumscribed brain lesions has recently been described, in whom a selective and severe impairment of the perception of movement (above a relatively low velocity) has been convincingly demonstrated. The perception of stationarity, and apparently all other visual functions are completely unaffected (Zihl, von Cramon, & Mai, 1983). And so this, too, can be thought of as a single dissociation that places movement further down the hierarchy in the output from striate cortex. The lesion appears to lie in a region homologous to that in the monkey (MT) in which neurons respond especially sensitively and selectively to moving visual stimuli. The single dissociation of color and movement perception respectively (and hence their double dissociation from each other) strongly suggests a modular organization beyond the striate cortex, supported also by both anatomy and electrophysiology.[1]

---

[1]There is a paradox regarding movement perception, because it has also been claimed that occipital brain lesions sometimes lead to the loss of perception of stationary stimuli but allow the perception of moving targets (Riddoch, 1917). Together with the previous case, this might be said to yield a double dissociation between disorders of perception of movement and of stationarity. It has been suggested, in fact, that the processing of movement can proceed via an independent pathway that bypasses the striate cortex altogether, most readily assigned to the midbrain pathway in a "two visual system" framework. It is known that total loss of striate cortex can still allow various types of visual discriminations to occur, including movement—but *also* of stationary stimuli (cf. Wieskrantz, 1986, for review). I suspect that the explanation of the Riddoch type of case might be rather simpler and have to do with moving stimuli being easier to detect than stationary ones under the typical conditions of visual field testing. When a patient has a relative but not an absolute field defect, that is, a raised visual threshold for detection, stationary stimuli might well be below threshold and moving ones above threshold, especially when visual adaptation is an important factor.

The second type of obligatory conjunction of deficits following a single treatment is when one is a secondary consequence of the other, although it is not an essential feature of the deficit conceptually, that is, not incorporated in an organized hierarchical scheme. For example, it may well be that patients with bilateral cortical blindness not only cannot see but invariably have damaged shins because they bump into obstacles. Deaf people may never go to musical concerts. Persons with Alzheimer's Disease may shun social interactions because they fail to recognize peers. To obtain single dissociations by showing that there are persons who always damage their shins even though they can see normally, or that there are non-concert-goers who are not deaf, is merely a trivial demonstration that there is more than one possible cause of a deficit, if deficit it be. That demonstration at least shows that the treatment is not the exclusive conjunct of the deficit, which is of some help theoretically. But the logic of the disentanglement in the case of the secondary consequential effect is the same as in the demonstration of hierarchies through single dissociations, even though conceptually they are distinguishable.

Also, in both of these examples, really important information can come from the rare single case. The rare patient who has normal long-term memory but severely impaired short-term memory is sufficient to demonstrate the lack of a necessary conjunction, even though they are characteristically conjoined in conditions such as Alzheimer's Disease. In other words, once again, the important information is derived from a dissociation, not from the announcement of a common association. It is not difficult to understand why the intensive study of particular single cases has become such a feature of recent neuropsychological research. Not only does the rare single case, if well chosen, show what is possible—after all, the conclusions drawn from the first explosion of the first atomic bomb also were based on a single case—but its importance in neuropsychology always lies in the disentanglement, that is, the dissociation, of a striking disorder from a background of otherwise intact performance.

Finally, of course, there are those obligatory conjunctions that are Gibraltar-like and hence may be entirely legitimate. If it were always the case, say, that a reduced digit span invariably co-occurred with a weakened "recency" component (in the free recall serial position effect), then there would be some value in considering them as a single package conceptually and in concluding that they reflect a single dysfunction. But one approaches the universal negative as an asymptote, not as an achievable goal in reality, and so once again the strategy must be to continue to seek other treatments or single cases, no matter how rare, to see if a dissociation emerges. But if one continues to find a conjunction even after exhaustive search, this bolsters one's confidence in suggesting a common conceptual basis that links the two deficits.

Throughout the whole of this discussion, I have been deliberately one-sided regarding the relationship between neuropsychology and theoretical structures.

Of course, the relationship is two-directional. The encouraging development of the past decade is the way theory has directed neuropsychological research *and* vice versa. It has the additional advantage of linking conceptualization to the real brain and not to a conceptual nervous system, which traditionally has been just another way of rewriting one's theory in the language of metaneurology.

I doubt if many neuropsychologists would disagree with the value of finding double dissociations, and so it might be thought that I am merely preaching to the converted—and with a doctrine that is far from novel. But one reason for venturing into the pontifical is to stress that the classification of many patient-groups is formed essentially for practical and custodial or aetiological reasons, and consequently there is an unfortunate temptation to accept referral of cases from this pool of "typical" cases, with their mixed deficits, for research purposes without careful screening for the pure and prototypical and without eliminating cases with mixed deficits that are known to be dissociable from the deficit of conceptual interest—and thus to argue from conjunctions to causation. A single "pure" case in the hand is worth an infinitude of mixed deficits. In fact, a cocktail of unanalyzed deficits can be almost uninterpretable, if one is lucky, or positively misleading, if one is unlucky. The information that is of conceptual value comes from careful dissection rather than from associative conglomeration.

MULTIPLE MEMORY SYSTEMS

Given our general conclusion that follows from the initial three assertions—that the minimal neuropsychological analysis designed for conceptual consumption requires comparisons across *both* a set of tasks *and* a set of lesions or treatments—let us turn to the domain in which Endel Tulving has contributed so richly, namely in drawing distinctions between types of memory processes. Using the evidence from dissociations, one can ask: How many potentially independent (but normally interacting) memory systems are suggested by neuropsychological findings? I have tried to deal with this question more fully elsewhere (Weiskrantz, 1987), and will restrict myself here to a rather sketchy summary of the evidence at both the human and (where relevant and possible) the animal level.

The general answer to the question of "how many?" is probably "many more than we know of," but it is convenient to group them into five main categories: (a) short-term memory; (b) knowledge and skills; (c) stable associative memory; (d) priming; and (e) event memory. All but the first would normally be classified as long-term memory systems, based on survivals over relatively long intervals. Within each of these categories can be found a variety of subcategories.

Short-Term Memory

The clearest evidence for a double dissociation between short-term memory and all the other long-term memory systems comes from the evidence of Saffran and Marin (1975), Shallice and Warrington (1970), Warrington, Logue, and Pratt (1971), and Warrington and Shallice (1969), of patients who perform poorly on Brown-Peterson type tasks, have severely abbreviated digit- or letter-spans, and a differentially reduced recency versus primacy effect in serial position curves in free recall. These patients can be normal on the entire range of long-term memory tasks. Conversely, patients with any of the long-term memory deficits—for example, those with the amnesic syndrome—can be quite normal on the very same short-term memory tasks on which the former patients are impaired (Baddeley & Warrington, 1970; Warrington, 1982b).

It seems reasonable to speculate that there are a number of dissociable short-term memory systems organized by modality or by the nature of the material being retained. The cases of Shallice and Warrington were more severely impaired with auditory than visual material. A suggestion has been advanced that simultanagnosia may reflect an analogous deficit in the visual mode (Kinsbourne & Warrington, 1962; cf. Warrington & Weiskrantz, 1973). The critical anatomical loci, in both instances, appear to be located posteriorly, in close approximation to the respective primary sensory regions. Depending on the functional character of the material for which accessibility decays rapidly (for whatever reason), one might expect different anatomical systems to be involved; thus, for example, in monkeys and human infants the prefrontal cortex might be implicated in short-term retention of spatial information of the *A not-B* type (Diamond, 1988; Diamond & Goldman-Rakic, 1983).

To the extent that in humans the short-term system can exploit verbal information in an acoustical code (Conrad, 1962) and hence can serve powerfully as a self-renewing rehearsal device, obviously no homologue will readily be found in animals (although animals can use non-symbolic motor patterns to bridge a temporal gap; Hunter, 1913). But there is no reason to deprive animals of a short-term memory system for items in visual and other sensory modes. Wright, Santiago, Sands, Kendrick, and Cook (1985) have convincingly demonstrated qualitatively similar U-shaped serial position functions in pigeons, monkeys, and humans using the same serial-probe picture recognition paradigm for each. Gaffan and Weiskrantz (1980) have reported evidence that the orderly decline in performance with increasing retention interval for monkeys in the delayed nonmatching paradigm is a genuine recency effect. Physiological evidence for animals also supports a conclusion that slowly and rapidly declining functions can be affected independently (Boast, Zornetzer, & Hamrick, 1975; Kesner & Conner, 1972).

Knowledge and Skill

Knowledge and skill systems include a number of different subsystems, no doubt with quite different anatomical substrates. All species of deficits within this category can be doubly dissociated from short-term memory deficits, from deficits of event memory, and probably also from all the other long-term memory deficits except priming (see below). One major subcategory consists of the "agnosic" disorders. There are striking examples of patients whose acquired knowledge of objects and persons, or other entities, becomes severely degraded (cf. Bauer & Rubens, 1985; Warrington, 1985), without this being explicable in terms of difficulties with more basic perceptual or other prerequisites. The agnosias cover more or less the whole range of categories of knowledge that adult humans possess, for example, topographagnosia, color agnosia, prosopagnosia, autotopagnosia, visual object agnosia. Although pure cases may be rare, dissociations among these various categories are found. And within each category there may well be highly specific and discrete losses, for example, for animate but not for inanimate objects (Warrington & Shallice, 1984). Especially instructive is the double dissociation between abstract and concrete words. The relationship between them has usually been thought to be hierarchical leading only to single dissociations (concrete + abstract impaired vs. only abstract impaired). But cases have now been reported of patients who show good retention of abstract words but impaired knowledge of concrete words (Warrington, 1975, 1981; Warrington & Shallice, 1984).

Learned motor skills, sometimes designated as one type of "procedural memory" (Cohen & Squire, 1980), can be selectively impaired in various forms of apraxia as well as in basal ganglia disorders such as Parkinson's Disease (cf. Paillard, 1982). It has been suggested that some types of "cognitive" rule-governed procedures may also be affected in Parkinson's Disease, overlapping with deficits associated with frontal lobe damage (e.g., card-sorting tasks).

Many aphasic and acquired dyslexic disorders are clearly examples of impairments of acquired knowledge or skill, and the analysis of evidence for dissociable subtypes lies at the heart of much contemporary research in human cognitive psychology. This type of disorder obviously may not easily be seen in animals, but knowledge systems as such, with large capacities and relatively permanent and static stores, are obviously not unique to human beings. Many animals acquire a large body of knowledge about the limits and layout of their territories and have a repertoire of the useful or undesirable objects within them, or the routes along which they navigate. The ability of pigeons to classify pictures of objects or scenes into categories of acquired knowledge is quite remarkable (Herrnstein, 1985). In the monkey, the anterior inferotemporal cortex is a reasonable candidate for the critical anatomical site for a visually mediated "prototypical object store" (Weiskrantz & Saunders, 1984).

A very well-studied example of the acquisition of specific knowledge is imprinting in birds. In several species, exposure to a particular object at a critical stage of development can give rise to a long-lasting and specific attachment. Horn and his colleagues have investigated the neural basis of the phenomenon in some detail and with much success (Horn, Rose, & Bateson, 1973; Horn, 1981, 1985). The specific learned attachment can be selectively impaired in chicks by lesions in the hyperstriatum, without impairing the acquisition or retention of learned visual discriminations. Horn has also suggested a double dissociation between imprinting to initially "neutral" objects and a "primed" preference for species-specific objects.

Stable Associative Memory

The category of stable associative memory is not easy to define rigidly, but the intention is to refer to any close, direct, and durable relationship of S-S or S-R conditioning, in the absence, or with a minimum, of mediating links or competing associations. The obvious examples are simple classical and instrumental conditioning. Excluded are associations that depend critically on recency or degree of familiarity, or shifting associates as in reversal tasks or random paired-associates. In the gray area lie learned discriminations based on instrumental reinforcement, which provide one (but not the only) route into an animal's knowledge system. Double dissociations between deficits in simple conditioning and other memory systems have not been directly demonstrated, but it is possible to speculate that they will. Certainly, this type of learning is well within the capacity of human amnesic patients (see the following) and very probably of patients with every other known clinical form of memory disorder; it is also of interest that neodecorticate rats still can demonstrate both instrumental and classical conditioning (Oakley, 1981; Oakley & Russell, 1977). On the other hand, Thompson and his colleagues (Donegan, Lowery, & Thompson, 1983; Lavond, Lincoln, & McCormick, 1983; Lincoln, McCormick, & Thompson, 1982; Mc-Cormick, Clark, Lavond, & Thompson, 1982) have implicated particular nuclei of the cerebellum (the medial dentate nucleus and the lateral interpositus nuclei) as having a critical role in classical conditioning in the rabbit for the nictitating membrane response and leg flexion responses. Yeo, Hardiman, and Glickstein (1984) have also implicated a small region of the cerebellar cortex in the same type of conditioning paradigm. It is the conditioned and not the unconditioned response that is abolished in acquisition or retention by lesions in these sites.

These double dissociations have been constructed here, thus, by comparisons between man and rabbit, but there is no reason to suppose that they would not occur within a single species. But even within this supposedly simple domain, further single dissociations are found. Thus, the cerebellar lesions that block conditioning of leg flexion to an aversive stimulus are reported *not* to have an effect on the heart-rate conditioned response established by such a stimulus

(Lavond et al., 1983). Therefore, the cerebellar role appears to be restricted to the striate musculature. It seems possible that this single dissociation could be extended into a double dissociation by considering lesions of the limbic lobe, which can have an effect on conditioned emotional responses.

Priming

Priming, the facilitation effected by performing a task on the further performance of itself or a similar task at a later time, is a capacity that appears to be highly resistant to destruction. No new information need be acquired; rather, the probability of performance is altered merely through its prior occurrence. The facilitation can be very long-lasting, without the subject necessarily being aware of it. No one has reported a selective loss of priming per se (although there are suggestions that it may sometimes be weakened in the amnesic syndrome). This may be because it has only recently been the focus of attention in human experimental psychology and has scarcely penetrated into the neurological domain. But there may well be reasons for doubting that it could be selectively lost as a general capacity, because it seems possible that priming would be ubiquitous within all of the major ganglia in the nervous system, including the spinal cord.

Priming has hardly been studied behaviorally in animals, but there may be physiological phenomena that are related. The phenomenon of *long-term potentiation* can be seen not only after repeated activation of structures such as the hippocampus, but also in many other regions of the nervous system, including the spinal cord, the autonomic nervous system, and pyramidal tract, among others; (cf. Anderson, 1977). Horn and Wiesenfield (in personal communication) have also seen it in the cat's lateral geniculate nucleus after repeated electrical stimulation of the optic tract. Also, the phenomenon of "kindling"— the gradual change in the tendency for certain structures such as the amygdala to develop autonomous electrical seizure discharges—may be related, and indeed has been suggested as a possible substrate for a general memory mechanism (Majkowski, 1981). If it is the case that priming is a widespread intrinsic property of neuronal ganglia, then obviously, a general loss of priming as a whole could never occur, although examination of specific losses could turn out to be of diagnostic value. It is much too early to know if even that will prove likely.

Amnesia and Event Memory

So much has been written about the amnesic syndrome, which for present purposes we are classifying as a defect in event memory, that it is not necessary to review either the clinical features or what is, by now, a very large experimental literature. What is clear is that amnesic patients, who do not acknowledge a phenomenal memory for an event or experience even a minute or two afterwards, need not be impaired in any of the other categories we have reviewed heretofore:

they can have normal short-term memory performance, they acquire motor and cognitive skills (but new usable knowledge may be more problematic), they show good conditioning and robust priming effects. Nor do any of those latter deficits, or combinations of them, yield the same pattern or possess the same quality as seen in the amnesic syndrome. An agnosic patient, for example, may very well be able to recall the experience of not being able to identify the meaning of a particular object or class of objects.

It is still a matter of some debate as to what is the best conceptual characterization of the amnesic syndrome (Tulving, 1983), and I do not intend to enter into that debate here: The clinical manifestations are clear enough. Whatever is wrong with the amnesic patient is dissociable from other memory deficits previously considered. But within this syndrome, it does seem reasonable to dissociate verbal from nonverbal components of the syndrome: Right hemisphere lesions can affect nonverbal event memory in isolation (e.g., yes/no recognition of faces) and left hemisphere lesions yield comparable deficits for verbal material.

It is also the case that some of the strictures that emerged in the first section of this chapter concerning the difference between the associative and dissociative approaches to the subject, can sometimes be very aptly illustrated in the field of amnesia. For example, many amnesic patients suffer from multiple deficits that are known to be dissociable from the amnesic state as such, such as short-term memory deficits. If one studies patients who have *both* short-term and long-term impairments, it is easy to see how conceptual analysis might be difficult or that one might be tempted to locate the site of difficulty near the input or encoding stage. It is also possible to see how artificial dichotomies might arise due to fortuitous differential, but non-obligatory associations that arise from differences in sites of interruption of circuits, leading to a supposed taxonomy of amnesia that reflects these associations rather than the core. I have dwelled on these points at some length elsewhere with specific reference to the amnesic syndrome (Weiskrantz, 1985). It is, all the same, encouraging to see the dissociative attitude making a more common intrusion into clinical studies.

One of the major developments, as many are aware, is that possible homologies between the human amnesic state and similar states in animals are at last becoming realized (Gaffan, 1974; Mishkin, 1982; Squire & Zola-Morgan, 1983; Warrington & Weiskrantz, 1982; Weiskrantz, 1982). For many years, there seemed to be a puzzling but intractable impasse. It is now clear that deficits in something akin to event memory, as exemplified in tasks such as delayed recognition or delayed matching/nonmatching, can be dissociated in animals from discrimination learning, conditioning, and the retention of the skill of performing in the task per se; that is, remembering rules. Equally, discrimination learning deficits can occur independently of deficits in recognition (although these double dissociations are sometimes hard to appreciate from examination of putative circuit diagrams often shown, which suggest a serial circuit between the focus for deficits of visual discrimination learning and recognition, whereas the demonstrated dissociations suggest that parallel pathways obtain). It is also extremely interesting, and important, to find that qualitatively similar dissociations appear to emerge within the forward anatomical projections of the structures that were implicated in their earlier stages (Bachevalier & Mishkin, 1986; Mishkin, Malamut, & Bachevalier, 1984).

CONCLUDING COMMENTS

Finally, coming full circle and returning to the theme in the first half of the chapter, I do not wish to underplay the difficulties inherent in the interpretation of neuropsychological evidence. Of course, lesions can yield uninterpretable and even bizarre symptoms, even when they can be dissociated. And it is often difficult, if one is attempting to isolate possible circuits for particular capacities based on real anatomy, to separate effects on fibers of passage or more distant effects from more direct effects on the target cell bodies: The example of the effects of temporal lobe lesions that incidentally damage visual radiation fibers and thus cause visual field defects is one that we understand; how many do we not understand? Nevertheless, in this connection it is encouraging to see the development of specific agents that selectively affect fibers or cells, and labelling techniques are developing apace. One hardly need repeat well-worn homilies about how enormously complex the nervous system is. Developmental factors introduce their own fascinating complexities—the examples I have chosen were almost all drawn from findings with adults. But neuropsychology, no more than any other discipline, is not required to account for all perturbations or to embrace variance for the benefit of the skeptics. Imagine the difficulty a physicist would have in accounting for the exact paths of falling leaves—he might attempt to reduce or account for variance by studying different species of leaves, in different seasons, over a range of wind speeds, humidity, and so forth. It seems unlikely that he will ever become a Gallileo by so doing.

Aside from the difficulties that stem from complexity per se, there are two issues that arise in the study of dissociations that require at least some comment. First, given the profusion of dissociations that neuropsychologists are turning up, are we to end up with Humpty Dumpty fragmented into an infinitude of independent bits and pieces? One answer to this has already been touched on, namely that single dissociations permit inferences about hierarchical arrangements, as in the examples discussed in the visual system and the joint dependence of certain capacities on an input from striate cortex. All of the sensory systems have this general organization. In this sense, it is appropriate to call "modular" capacities of the visual system, such as color and motion, visual subcomponents. Again, object agnosias can be fractionated by double dissociation, but the breakdowns appear to be at levels within a hierarchical tree structure. Agnosias for abstract names, in contrast, do not fit a tree structure, and their dissociation from object agnosias (Warrington, 1975, 1981; Warrington & Shallice, 1984) implies a non-hierarchical independence from them. And so, if one wishes to, one can call meaning for animate versus inanimate objects subcomponents of a larger meaning system. They are separate branches of a larger tree. Depending on whether one is gazing upwards or downwards, it is equally important to know that there are separate branches as it is to know that there is a trunk. It is also important to know that there are other concepts that require structures more like bamboo than trees. But the point to bring out here is that combinations of single and double dissociations allow inferences to be generated about ordering and structure.

There is also another less fundamental sense in which it may be legitimate and helpful to talk of independent capacities being subcomponents of a "system," namely when these invariably come into play simultaneously in normal behavior. Thus, in classical avoidance conditioning (e.g., leg flexion) there will always be an autonomic and a striate muscular activity, even though it appears that the mechanisms of their involvement in conditioning are dissociable. The example also makes it clear that the terms that one uses depend on pragmatics, the level of analysis, and the focus of attention. Autonomic responses are also part of another framework involved in the adaptation to emergency, and striated musculature is involved in motor skills. There is no implication from the study of dissociations that one must consider the dissociates to be rigid atomic fragments.

But a more basic contributor to the ordering of the findings is sometimes available, namely, physiological and anatomical information about the structures themselves that are involved in the brain disorders. To the extent that these domains themselves can be ordered into systems, it is appropriate to consider that disorders within them be so grouped. Again, with the visual system this is perhaps self-evident, although the recent evidence that supports a "modular" view of certain visual capacities concentrated in structures beyond the striate cortex was far from self-evident before it was discovered (Zeki, 1981; cf. Cowey, 1979). But going well outside a sensory system as such, strong inferences are being drawn, for example, about a possible system for event memory based on some of the anatomical connections of the medial temporal lobe (e.g., Mishkin, 1982). Of course, the identification of the relevant anatomy is further bolstered by the neuropsychological findings that are themselves guided by the anatomical background and tracer studies.

The second issue that requires comment concerns the status of the potentially dissociable components or systems and how they *interact* in the intact organism. Neuropsychology by itself cannot reveal the nature of their normal interaction. Of course, at a superficial level, one can derive some inferences by comparing a deficit with the control state. Something is revealed about how short-term memory (STM) interacts with aspects of long-term memory (LTM) by seeing how LTM is altered in a patient with a pure STM deficit. But at a deeper level, one is guided by theoretical concerns in experimental psychology itself. Appeal to a theoretical concept like "rehearsal loop" is one way of linking STM and LTM.

But, conversely, its status in the theoretical structure is severely constrained by the neuropsychological evidence. Serial processing is difficult to entertain when there is evidence of parallel pathways.

Quite aside from this intrinsic theoretical interest in the contents of dissociations themselves, there are two other reasons why a dissociative strategy as applied to the domain of memory might have value. The first concerns physiological mechanisms and embodiments. If the dissociations suggested are real, then it is clear that the neural mechanisms for each are likely not only to be qualitatively very different, but also their anatomical distribution within the vertebrate nervous system must also be very different. Priming, for example, it was suggested, appears to be a widespread property of ganglionic substrates. Knowledge systems, on the other hand, must depend on very specific and probably nondispersed domains (although possibly distributed among cells within these limited domains) and probably are critically dependent wholly or mainly on cerebral cortex in mammals. Specific knowledge acquired in imprinting is dependent critically on one specific region of the chick brain. We have seen that there is quite a different locus for one aspect of classical conditioning than for other forms of learning. The circuitry implicated in event memory, which appears to involve two parallel but interacting systems, each limbic as well as diencephalic, again has a different disposition and distribution from other systems.

At present, the relations between these dissociable systems and synaptic mechanisms are not known, but it seems very rash to assume that all systems work the same way at the synaptic level, for example, that facilitation in priming involves the same synaptic process as in knowledge acquisition. It may also be premature to consider that information gleaned from studying an associative mechanism in a simple organism, such as *Aplysia,* will extend as an explanatory mechanism to other forms of memory not found in simple creatures. For example, I consider it rather doubtful that *Aplysia* has event memory, but even if it does, we have seen that it is dissociable from associative conditioning.

The second point is practical. We started by pointing out the multiplicity of deficits that are seen following even a circumscribed lesion. But the severe degenerative diseases that are such an endemic and intractable problem today typically involve multiple lesions, often anatomically widely dispersed, and thus implicate several of the systems discussed here. It seems highly likely that these different systems also use different transmitters and have a different underlying neurochemistry, and hence are potentially amenable to different patterns of neurochemical treatments. The study of dissociations can help not only to specify the components of the disorders that apply in individual cases, but also help to concoct the appropriate treatment. With a cocktail of deficits, it may be necessary to apply a cocktail of treatments. Even if this is not a practical recipe (drug firms do not like to produce cocktails and physicians dislike them because the proportions cannot easily be varied) and treatment must be carried out sequentially, the individual responses of components of the syndrome to treatment will add practical elucidation of the dissociations themselves.

The dissociative approach seizes upon these particular phenomena with which it can either "spot weld" a conceptual relationship or drive a wedge between two psychological domains. We have concentrated mainly on memory domains here, but there are no major areas of psychology, including that of awareness and consciousness, where comparable examples could not be discussed. Neuropsychology also takes the results of these conceptual operations and inferences to guide the further study of brain dysfunction, which it does in relation to anatomy, physiology, and neurochemistry, all of which bolster conceptualization at the neuronal level when these sources converge, which at the same time feeds back upon theory in the psychological domain, which guides further neuropsychological enquiry, and so forth. Neuropsychology is therefore at the crossroads between neurobiology, the neurological clinic, and experimental psychology. *These*, at last, are associative partners that one can embrace and from whom dissociations are not sought.

REFERENCES

Anderson, P. (1977). Long-lasting facilitation of synaptic transmission. In *Functions of the septo-hippocampal system* (p. 102). Ciba Foundation Symposium 58. Amsterdam: Elsevier.

Bachevalier, J., & Mishkin, M. (1986). Visual recognition impairment follows ventromedial but not dorsolateral prefrontal lesions in the monkey. *Behavioural Brain Research, 20,* 249–261.

Baddeley, A. D., & Warrington, E. K. (1970). Amnesia and the distinction between long- and short-term memory. *Journal of Verbal Learning and Verbal Behavior, 9,* 176–189.

Bauer, R. M., & Rubens, A. B. (1985). Agnosia. In K. M. Heilman & E. Valenstein (Eds.), *Clinical neuropsychology* (2nd ed., pp. 187–241). New York: Oxford University Press.

Boast, C. A., Zornetzer, S. F., & Hamrick, M. R. (1975). Electrolytic lesions of various hippocampal subfields in the mouse: Differential effects on short- and long-term memory. *Behavioral Biology, 14,* 85–94.

Cohen, N. J., & Squire, R. L. (1980). Preserved learning and retention of pattern-analyzing skill in amnesia: Dissociation of "knowing how" and "knowing that". *Science, 210,* 207–210.

Conrad, R. (1962). An association between memory errors and errors due to acoustic masking of speech. *Nature, 193,* 1314–1315.

Cowey, A. (1979). Cortical maps and visual perception. The Grindley Memorial Lecture. *Quarterly Journal of Experimental Psychology, 31,* 1–17.

Diamond, A. (1988). Differences between adult and infant cognition: Is the crucial variable presence or absence of language? In L. Weiskrantz (Ed.), *Thought without language* (pp. 337–370). Oxford: Oxford University Press.

Diamond, A., & Goldman-Rakic, P. S. (1983). Comparison of performance on a Piagetian object permanence task in human infants and rhesus monkeys: Evidence for involvement of prefrontal cortex. *Neuroscience Abstracts (Part I), 9,* 641.

Donegan, N. H., Lowery, R. W., & Thompson, R. F. (1983). Effects of lesioning cerebellar nuclei on conditioned leg-flexion responses. *Neuroscience Abstracts, 100,* 7.

Gaffan, D. (1974). Recognition impaired and association intact in the memory of monkeys after transection of the fornix. *Journal of Comparative and Physiological Psychology, 86,* 1100–1109.

Gaffan, D. & Weiskrantz, L. (1980). Recency effects and lesion effects in delayed non-matching to randomly baited samples by monkeys. *Brain Research, 196*, 373–386.

Herrnstein, R. J. (1985). Riddles of natural categorization: In L. Weiskrantz (Ed.), *Animal intelligence* (pp. 129–144). London: The Royal Society.

Horn, G. (1981). Neural mechanisms of learning: An analysis of imprinting in the domestic chick. *Proceedings of the Royal Society (London), 213B*, 101–137.

Horn, G. (1985). *Memory, imprinting, and the brain. An enquiry into mechanism.* Oxford: Oxford University Press.

Horn, G., Rose, S. P. R., & Bateson, P. P. G. (1973). Experience and plasticity in the central nervous system. *Science, 181*, 506–514.

Hunter, W. S. (1913). The delayed reaction in animals and children. *Behavior Monographs, 2*, (1, Serial No. 6).

Jones, E. G., & Powell, T. P. S. (1970). An anatomical study of converging pathways in the cerebral cortex of the monkey. *Brain, 93*, 793–820.

Kesner, R. P., & Conner, H. S. (1972). Independence of short- and long-term memory: A neural system analysis. *Science, 176*, 432–434.

Kinsbourne, M., & Warrington, E. K. (1962). A disorder of simultaneous form perception. *Brain, 85*, 461–486.

Lavond, D. G., Lincoln, J. S., & McCormick, D. A. (1983). Effect of bilateral cerebellar lesions on heart-rate and nictitating membrane/eyelid conditioning in the rabbit. *Neuroscience Abstracts,* 189.1

Lincoln, J. S., McCormick, D. A., & Thompson, R. F. (1982). Ipsilateral cerebellar lesions prevent learning of the classically conditioned nictitating membrane eyelid response. *Brain Research, 242*, 190–193.

McCormick, D. A., Clark, G. A., Lavond, D. G., & Thompson, R. F. (1982). Initial localization of the memory trace for a basic form of learning. *Proceedings of the National Academy of Sciences, USA. 79*, 2731–2735.

Majkowski, J. (1981). Brain electrical stimulation: Kindling and memory aspects. *Acta Neurologica Scandinavia, 64* (Suppl. 89), 101–108.

Mishkin, M. (1982). A memory system in the monkey. In D. E. Broadbent & L. Weiskrantz (Eds.), *The neuropsychology of cognitive function* (pp. 85–95). London: The Royal Society.

Mishkin, M., Malamut, B., & Bachevalier, J. (1984). Memories and habits: Two neural systems. In G. Lynch, J. L. McGaugh, & N. M. Weinberger (Eds.), *Neurobiology of learning and memory* (pp. 65–77). New York: Guilford Press.

Oakley, D. A. (1981). Performance of decorticated rats in a two-choice visual discrimination apparatus. *Behavioural Brain Research, 3*, 55–69.

Oakley, D. A., & Russell, I. S. (1977). Subcortical storage of Pavlovian conditioning in the rabbit. *Physiology and Behavior, 18*, 931–937.

Paillard, J. (1982). Apraxia and the neurophysiology of motor control: In D. E. Broadbent & L. Weiskrantz (Eds.), *The neuropsychology of cognitive function* (pp. 111–134). London: The Royal Society.

Riddoch, G. (1917). Dissociation of visual perceptions due to occipital injuries, with especial reference to the appreciation of movement. *Brain, 40*, 15–57.

Saffran, E., & Marin, O. (1975). Immediate memory for word lists and sentences in a patient with deficient auditory short-term memory. *Brain and Language, 2*, 420–433.

Shallice, T., & Warrington, E. K. (1970). Independent function of verbal memory stores: A neuropsychological study. *Quarterly Journal of Experimental Psychology, 22*, 261–273.

Squire, L. R., & Zola-Morgan, S. (1983). The neurology of memory: The case for correspondence between the findings for human and nonhuman primate. In J. A. Deutsch (Ed.), *The physiological basis of memory* (2nd ed., pp. 199–267). New York: Academic Press.

Tulving, E. (1983). *Elements of episodic memory.* Oxford: Oxford University Press.

Warrington, E. K. (1975). The selective impairment of semantic memory. *Quarterly Journal of Experimental Psychology, 27,* 635–657.

Warrington, E. K. (1981). Concrete word dyslexia. *British Journal of Psychology, 72,* 175–196.

Warrington, E. K. (1982a). Neuropsychological studies of object recognition. In D. E. Broadbent & L. Weiskrantz (Eds.), *The neuropsychology of cognitive function* (pp. 15–33). London: The Royal Society.

Warrington, E. K. (1982b). The double dissociation of short- and long-term memory deficits. In L. S. Cermak (Ed.), *Human memory and amnesia.* Hillsdale, NJ: Lawrence Erlbaum Associates.

Warrington, E. K. (1985). Agnosia: The impairment of object recognition. In J. A. M. Frederiks (Ed.), *Handbook of clinical neurology* (vol. 1, pp. 333–349). London: Elsevier Science.

Warrington, E. K., Logue, V., & Pratt, R. T. C. (1971). Anatomical localization of selective impairment of auditory-verbal short-term memory. *Neuropsychologia, 9,* 377–387.

Warrington, E. K., & Shallice, T. (1969). The selective impairment of auditory verbal short-term memory. *Brain, 92,* 885–896.

Warrington, E. K., & Shallice, T. (1984). Category specific semantic impairments. *Brain, 107,* 829–854.

Warrington, E. K., & Weiskrantz, L. (1973). An analysis of short-term and long-term memory deficits in man. In J. A. Deutsch (Ed.), *The physiological basis of memory* (pp. 365–395). New York: Academic Press.

Warrington, E. K., & Weiskrantz, L. (1982). Amnesia: A disconnection syndrome? *Neuropsychologia, 20,* 233–247.

Weiskrantz, L. (1968a). Treatments, inferences, and brain function. In L. Weiskrantz (Ed.), *Analysis of behavioral change* (pp. 400–414). New York: Harper & Row.

Weiskrantz, L. (1968b). Some traps and pontifications. In L. Weiskrantz (Ed.), *Analysis of behavioral change* (pp. 415–429). New York: Harper & Row.

Weiskrantz, L. (1982). Comparative studies of amnesia. In D. E. Broadbent & L. Weiskrantz (Ed.), *Neuropsychology of cognitive function* (pp. 97–109). London: The Royal Society.

Weiskrantz, L. (1985). On issues and theories of the human amnesic syndrome. In N. M. Weinberger, J. L. McGaugh, & G. Lynch (Eds.), *Memory systems of the brain: Animal and human cognitive processes* (pp. 380–415). New York: Guilford.

Weiskrantz, L. (1986). *Blindsight. A case study and implications.* Oxford: Oxford University Press.

Weiskrantz, L. (1987). Neuroanatomy of memory and amnesia: A case for multiple memory systems. *Human Neurobiology, 6,* 93–105.

Weiskrantz, L., & Saunders, R. C. (1984). Impairments of visual object transforms in monkeys. *Brain, 107,* 1033–1072.

Wright, A. A., Santiago, H. C., Sands, S. F., Kendrick, D. F., & Cook, R. G. (1985). Memory processing of serial lists by pigeons, monkeys and people. *Science, 229,* 287–289.

Yeo, C. H., Hardiman, M. J., & Glickstein, M. (1984). Discrete lesions of the cerebellar cortex abolish the classically conditioned nictitating membrane response of the rabbit. *Behavioural Brain Research, 13,* 261–266.

Zeki, S. (1981). The mapping of visual functions in the cerebral cortex. In Y. Katsuki, R. Norgren, & M. Sato (Eds.), *Brain mechanisms of sensation* (pp. 105–128). New York: Wiley.

Zihl, J., von Cramon, D., & Mai, N. (1983). Selective disturbance of movement vision after bilateral brain damage. *Brain, 106,* 313–340.

7 Synergistic Ecphory and the Amnesic Patient

Laird S. Cermak
Memory Disorders Research Center
Boston Veterans Administration Medical Center
Boston University School of Medicine

The overriding message that I have received from Endel Tulving's work is that memory is a process, not a depository. His study of the relationship between encoding at acquisition and the process of reconstruction at retrieval has become central to my own research. His influence has greatly structured my search for those places in the processing of information that are impaired in the amnesic patient. In addition, his thesis has provided the rationale for my belief that there is no such thing as a single or "core" amnesia. If Tulving is correct that memory is a process, then amnesia must be a consequence of deficient processing. Deficient processing might occur at various places along a processing continuum for different patients. The net result would be an inability to acquire and retain new information, but the processing factors contributing to this outcome might not be identical for all patient populations. The purpose of the present chapter is to depict some of these processing deficits and to show how research with amnesic populations can be used to differentiate amongst types of processing abilities.

THE DISTINCTION BETWEEN ANALYTIC AND ENCODING DEFICITS

A distinction between analysis and encoding is one that has had to be made because investigators of the amnesic syndrome have discovered that the general definition of an encoding deficit as an input disorder covers too many sins (Cermak, in press). It is clear that all amnesics are inept in storing or encoding new information, but they seem to differ in the extent to which they can adequately analyze incoming information. Some amnesics (alcoholic Korsakoff patients) appear incapable of automatically detecting semantic features of verbal information, whereas other amnesic patients (e.g., a post-encephalitic patient in particular) can perform such analysis. This distinction between analysis and encoding obviously needs further definition. However, prior to such a specific discussion, it is necessary to briefly review the history of the study of encoding deficits in amnesia.

Initially, theorists who proposed that amnesia could be explained as due to encoding deficits (Cermak 1972, 1975, 1979; Kinsbourne & Wood, 1975) argued that amnesic patients' memory disorder was *directly* related to an impairment in the way they took in information. Several experiments (Cermak & Butters, 1972; Cermak, Butters, & Gerrein, 1973; Cermak, Butters, & Moreines, 1974; Cermak, Naus, & Reale, 1976) demonstrated that amnesic Korsakoff patients spontaneously encoded only shallow (visual) features of verbal information, as opposed to deep (semantic) ones. These impairments were documented using Wickens' (1970) release from proactive inhibition technique (Cermak, Butters, & Moreines, 1974), which demonstrated that amnesic Korsakoff patients' increased sensitivity to interference during retrieval was related to a lack of semantic encoding. This was exemplified by the fact that the amount of proactive interference (PI) release demonstrated by these patients varied with the encoding requirements of the verbal materials. Korsakoff patients demonstrated normal PI release when the verbal materials involved only rudimentary categorizations (e.g., letters vs. numbers), but showed absolutely no release when the stimulus materials involved semantic differences, such as the taxonomic difference between animals and vegetables. Thus, these amnesics' retrieval deficit was seen as a direct result of their inability to spontaneously encode material on the basis of its semantic features.

In order to further investigate the influence of these semantic encoding deficits on retrieval attempts by amnesics, an encoding-specificity procedure, developed by Thomson and Tulving (1970), was used. In this procedure, Korsakoff patients were given a list of 12 word pairs consisting of a capitalized to-be-remembered (TBR) word and an associated word printed in lower case letters above it. The patient was instructed to memorize each TBR word and to pay attention to the small related word as it could be used to help him or her remember the critical word. Then the patient was given 12 cue words and told to write down the TBR word that the cue brought to mind in the blank space next to each cue. Five different input–output relationships were investigated: (a) S-S, in which a strongly associated cue word occurred at input and again at output; (b) W-W, in which the same weakly associated cue word occurred at input and output; (c) S-W, in which a strong associate was presented at input, but a weak associate at output; (d) W-S, in which a weak associate was presented at input, but a strong one at output; and (e) O-O, in which no cues were given with the targets at either study or test. The outcome (Cermak, Uhly, & Reale, 1980) revealed that Korsakoff patients profited by strong associate encoding and retrieval cues (as evidenced by S-S recall above both O-O and W-S), but failed to show the same effect for the weak encoding and retrieval cue condition (W-W). This sensitization to strong associates suggests that encoding specificity may have occurred only when an already existent semantic memory association was reinforced and subsequently cued. Encoding specificity did not occur when a new associate had to be formed. In other words, when the association re-established remote learning, it was facilitating, but when it necessitated that the patient cognitively reorganize his or her semantic network for purposes of retaining an episodic event, the outcome was abysmal.

This finding of effective cueing of amnesic patients' retrieval only when previously established semantic associates were activated had been anticipated by Winocur and Weiskrantz (1976) and by Warrington and Weiskrantz (1978). These investigators noted that whenever amnesic patients were given a cue that automatically facilitated the "regeneration" of a response, the patient tended to declare that the response was appropriate. However, when such regeneration did not lead directly to the desired response (as with weak cues), a correct answer was rarely elicited from the patients. This meant that amnesic patients might be cued successfully under conditions that automatically regenerated a correct response, but might fail to produce that same word immediately thereafter when given a cue that did not automatically generate the desired response.

To directly test this hypothesis, Cermak and Stiassny (1982) conducted a generation-recognition experiment (Tulving & Thomson, 1973). The procedure was the same as the encoding specificity paradigm except that after two lists utilizing the W-W condition were given, the retention test was changed on the next trial. Following a third list that had also been presented with weak cues, each patient was given 12 "strong" associate cues of each TBR word (i.e., an unexpected W-S condition). This time, the patient was also given *four* blank spaces in which to write down the first four words that the cue brought to mind. Then, the patient was asked to circle those words which he or she thought might have appeared on the most recent list that had been presented. As expected, the amnesic Korsakoff patients' performance was significantly below normal on the W-W cueing tasks. however, their performance on the generation-recognition phase of the experiment exceeded our expectations in two ways: First, Korsakoff patients generated as many critical TBR words as did normal and alcoholic controls. Second, they circled (recognized) as many of these critical words as did the controls.

Although this outcome was dramatic, it was apparent that the Korsakoff's impressive generation-recognition performance could have been due to activation of their semantic memory system (Kinsbourne & Wood, 1975; Cermak, Reale, & Baker, 1978). That is, the patients may have generated the critical words to the strong associative cues quite independently of the experimental events preceding such generation. Then they may have circled the strongest associate of each cue word merely on the basis of associative familiarity. To test this possibility, the same Korsakoff patients were given a form 2 months later that contained precisely the same strong-associative cues received previously.

They were also given the same generation-recognition instructions as before. The number of critical (TBR) words that the Korsakoff patients generated in response to the strong associates at this time was the same as it had been on the initial task. In addition, they "recognized" as many of these critical words as they had previously. The only difference between the initial generation-recognition task and the one performed months later was that the critical word was more frequently generated as the first word on the initial task. Apparently, the recent presentation of an item temporarily strengthened that item's representation in the semantic memory hierarchy enough to produce it sooner than ordinarily would be the case.

This finding of a temporary strengthening of an item's semantic memory representation had been previously demonstrated by Gardner, Boller, Moreines, and Butters (1973), who dubbed the elicitation of this response the *out of the blue* phenomenon. They found that amnesic patients provided category exemplars that were not ordinarily strong associates of a particular category whenever that exemplar had occurred in a prior task. Because this same effect has also been replicated by Graf, Shimamura, and Squire (1985), it can be concluded that amnesic patients' semantic memory hierarchy can be temporarily altered through activation to produce apparent retention, even when the patient is not aware of this activation.

Why is it that amnesic patients cannot *utilize* these temporarily activated, non-primary associates as retrieval cues during a usual paired-associate task? Interestingly, this question continuously resurfaces in every discussion of amnesics' inability to retain new information. It could be that these patients do not utilize nonprimary associations between words because the relationship is not detected at the time of input. Or, it could be that the patient realizes the association at input but cannot reconstruct the association at retrieval because primary associates to the cue compete and appear to be more familiar to the patient. Warrington and Weiskrantz (1982) arrived at this latter conclusion when they observed that amnesic patients are impaired on those memory tasks in which the stored benefits of cognitive mediation are important, but are unimpaired when cognitive mediation is unnecessary for retention, as in those instances where previously acquired associations have been activated and cued. In other words, amnesics realize the relationship between two words (analysis) but can't use this realization to store (encode) or to reconstruct the relationship at retrieval. However, when the relationship merely restipulates an already established link, such reactivation will facilitate retrieval.

Encoding theorists could still hold to their first viewpoint (i.e., that patients fail to analyze), but these theorists now had to account for the fact that the patients must have had to detect a relation during acquisition in order for the relation to become activated in semantic memory. In other words, patients have to be able to analyze information on some level in order for activation to occur at all. To assimilate this fact, acquisition deficits needed to be subdivided into "analysis" and then the "encoding" of this analysis. Encoding had to be redefined as a stage, following initial perceptual analysis, in which the subject cognitively manipulates analyzed features of the information to permit differential storage of that material based on these features. The encoding deficit theory then had to define amnesia as an inability on the part of the patient to *profit* from his analysis of information, rather than an inability to perform it at all. Some amnesics (Korsakoffs) may indeed have faulty analytic skills, but many others are amnesic because they fail to cognitively manipulate their analysis for purposes of storage. Warrington and Weiskrantz' amnesic patients have normal analytic abilities, yet do not profit from these analyses. Cermak's (1976; Cermak and O'Connor, 1983) densely amnesic post-encephalitic patient, S.S., seems able to analyze the most sophisticated semantic features of verbal information, yet has no memory for the desired material nor for how he analyzed it. Lhermitte and Signoret (1972) presented similar findings for a group of post-encephalitc patients, and Squire (1982a) proposed that his ECT patients have no analytic deficits, yet still fail to consolidate new material into memory. Thus, it appears that *analytic* deficits are not critical to all amnesic disorders, but *encoding* deficits, when defined as the inability to perform the cognitive manipulations necessary for storage of information, are critical to all amnesic disorders.

This conceptualization of encoding deficits as an explanation of amnesia has received unexpected support from Graf, Shimamura, and Squire (1985), who stated recently that even though activation of previously acquired material can occur for amnesic patients, "they lack the ability to elaborate, organize and consciously recollect information learned since the onset of amnesia" (p. 394). All of these recent proposals converge on the possibility that anterograde amnesia results from the patient's inability to "encode" his or her analysis. This view of encoding as manipulation and organization of features of information into a more permanent memory achieves the distinction of bringing encoding deficit theories, consolidation deficit theories, and retrieval deficit theories of amnesia into general agreement. It also takes the emphasis of encoding theory off the initial attention-to-features level and admits that some patients can automatically detect these features and still be amnesic. What the patient does with his or her analysis subsequently determines the probability of his or her retrieval.

RELATIONSHIP TO OTHER THEORIES OF AMNESIA

This redefinition of encoding deficit theory is by no means the only new approach to amnesia that has emerged during the last decade. Another approach that has been highly visible is one that divides memory into its procedural and declarative components (Cohen & Squire, 1980) and then suggests that amnesic patients can perform procedural tasks (e.g., mirror-writing, maze learning) normally, but fail on declarative (recall, recognition) tasks. The amnesic patient seems to "know how" to perform a particular task, but does not "know that" he or she has learned it.

Another theory that differentiates amnesics' preserved memory abilities from their deficiencies is one based on Tulving's (1972, 1983) episodic/semantic memory distinction. Kinsbourne and Wood (1975) initially proposed that amnesics have an intact semantic memory in the absence of any episodic memory. Their proposal stemmed from the clinical observation that patients could describe an object such as a railroad ticket but could not describe a single instance or episode in which they had used that object. Cermak, Reale, and Baker (1978) made a further assessment of amnesics' semantic memory organization and found that Korsakoff patients were unimpaired in their lexical search "rate" but were impaired in the "rate" at which they searched conceptual semantic memory, even though they arrived at a correct answer to questions as often as normals. Consequently, they concluded that amnesics' semantic memory probably does retain its normal organization even though the ease with which certain features can be accessed may be affected. Recently, Cermak, Talbot, Chandler, and Wolbarst (1985) and Tulving (1985) have pointed out that the episodic/semantic and the procedural/declarative models of amnesia need not be viewed as being opposed to one another. Instead, the episodic/semantic distinction can be conceived of as being a subdivision of the declarative distinction. Both episodic and semantic memory tasks seem to require that the patient "declare" that he or she knows about specific information. Thus, the two theories are predicting amnesics' deficits on different levels.

Yet one more distinction between amnesics' abilities and inabilities has been forwarded by Jacoby (1984). He has suggested that a form of episodic memory of which the patient is unaware might exist for amnesic patients even though their aware memory is deficient. Jacoby suggested that whereas memory with awareness is involved in the recognition of an episode, memory without awareness need only be demonstrated by the effect that a specific episode has on subsequent behavior. Interestingly, proponents of each of the three dichotomies presented thus far (procedural/declarative, episodic/semantic, and aware/unaware) all cite Jacoby's results (faster identification of previously presented words even when patients do not remember these words) as support for their point of view. Cohen and Squire feel that this effect of perceptual priming is an example of procedural learning. Cermak feels that it represents an "activation" of semantic memory. Jacoby believes that it is memory without awareness of the event that produced the effect.

SEMANTIC ACTIVATION VERSUS EPISODIC RETENTION BY AMNESICS

Cermak et al. (1985) have attempted to untangle these various explanations of the priming phenomena by devising a priming procedure that used pseudowords in contrast to real words. These investigators proposed that if semantic activation alone produced a priming phenomenon for amnesics, then the presentation of pseudowords would not enhance their perceptual identification of these stimuli on a subsequent threshold task. Because the results confirmed this prediction with Korsakoff patients, Cermak et al. suggested that exposure to pseudowords had not activated any pre-existing representations (a conclusion also proposed by Diamond & Rozin, 1984), and without such activation, amnesic patients could not be primed.

It is entirely possible, however, that some patients with memory disorders (other than Korsakoffs) may be capable of sufficient learning to support "unaware" episodic retention of new material. Evidence for this possibility has been provided by Graf and Schacter (1985), who reported that some patients with memory problems can be primed for word-stem completion by the presence of a previously learned associative cue word over and above the level of stem completion that occurs when no associative cue is present. This implies that some implicit associative learning must have occurred for these patients. Although this effect could not be produced with Korsakoff patients (Cermak et al., 1985), it did exist for S.S., our post-encephalitic patient (Cermak, Blackford, O'Connor, & Bleich, in press). Apparently, a very temporary new learning effect can exist for some amnesics on a level that is sufficient to support unaware episodic memory (see also Moscovitch, Winocur, and McLachlan, 1986). Schacter and Graf (1986) feel that this effect occurs for moderate, but not severe, amnesics. Our results with S.S. suggest that another explanation may also be possible. It may be that patients who suffer deficits at the analytic level of information processing (Korsakoff patients) have no ability to learn on an unaware level, whereas patients who can perform such analysis obtain sufficient learning to support unaware memory of an episode.

Further evidence for this possibility came from other demonstrations that S.S.'s implicit retention is superior to that of alcoholic Korsakoff patients (Cermak et al., in press). His perceptual identification of novel (pseudoword) material can be primed; he can utilize previously presented low frequency words to complete word stems, and his spelling of an ambiguous word can be biased in a direction opposite his preferred spelling. On all of these tasks, he demonstrates that a dense amnesic can learn new information on a level sufficient to support implicit retention. However, this effect is limited to the facilitation of single words and isolated items of information, and it does not extend to conceptual learning.

S.S.'s implicit memory capacity sharply distinguishes his amnesic disorder from that of alcoholic Korsakoff patients. These latter patients have consistently demonstrated that activation of previously acquired information totally accounts for any success they appear to achieve on priming and/or biasing tasks (Cermak et al., 1985; in press). They prime for recently presented words and can be biased to spell a word in a particular way only when the critical material is available to them prior to the onset of their amnesia. Korsakoff patients do not seem able to achieve a level of *new* learning sufficient to support implicit retention. Thus, a qualitative difference in learning ability exists between the forms of amnesia exemplified by S.S. and that seen in Korsakoff's Syndrome.

S.S.'s performance is consistent with theories proposing that there are two abilities involved in the retention of an episode. Graf and Schacter (1985) preferred to define these abilities according to the tasks that are utilized to measure them (i.e., explicit or implicit). However, Jacoby (1984), has suggested that these abilities might be defined along a dimension of awareness. As described previously, Jacoby distinguished between memory with awareness, which allows the individual to freely recall or recognize that a word has been presented in a particular context, and memory without awareness, which supports the priming or biasing of subsequent performance. Our findings suggest that S.S. is capable of achieving memory without awareness and that this type of memory *is* sufficient to support his implicit performance.

The reason why S.S. can achieve a sufficient level of unaware memory to support implicit retention, whereas Korsakoff patients cannot, may reside in S.S.'s previously documented analytic abilities, which also differentiate him from Korsakoff patients (Cermak, 1975; Cermak & O'Connor, 1983). It is possible that these superior analytic skills provide a level of learning that is sufficient to support implicit retention of new information. This hypothesis contradicts Jacoby's (1984) proviso that differential levels of analysis do *not* influence unaware memory abilities. However, debate on this issue must be withheld until we are certain that this factor is, in fact, the underlying contributor to S.S.'s success on these implicit tasks. What can be concluded is that the severity of one's amnesia does not necessarily determine ability to demonstrate new learning on implicit tasks.

CORE AMNESIA

A casualty of the separation of amnesias into subtypes as determined by the locus of their processing deficit along an input continuum (and perhaps an output continuum as well) is that the logic of a "core" amnesia dissipates. Schacter (1987) has argued persuasively against this concept, pointing out correctly that the notion stemmed from neuroscientists' desire to "localize" all primary behavioral abilities. In order to do such localizing, the concept of what represents the "core" of amnesia has been seen as necessary (Squire, 1982b; Weiskantz, 1985). However, if amnesia is defined as an end product that can occur as a result of disconnection anywhere along a processing continuum, then a concept such as core amnesia becomes unnecessary.

Herein lies the true distinction between the cognitive psychologist and the traditional neuroscientist. The cognitive psychologist is content to discuss processes, the neuroscientist wants something more tangible to localize. This distinction poses a great difficulty for those of us who straddle the fence between the two disciplines. On the one hand, we are eager to discover the underlying neuroanatomy and neurochemistry of amnesia and, on the other hand, we are forced to admit that memory and amnesia are not entities in and of themselves but rather the consequences of processing functions. These differences between the disciplines would become even more apparent if scientists were ever persuaded to acknowledge the existence of the next topic of this chapter, namely synergistic ecphory. Suppose neuroanatomists felt compelled to search for its location. Although this image may promote derision among both cognitive and neuroscientists, acceptance of the stance taken by this chapter and by Schacter's (1987) treatise on frontal amnesia suggests that this may be the direction we are headed.

SYNERGISTIC ECPHORY

Tulving (1983) has defined ecphoric information as the product of the encoding process and the retrieval cue. The "coming together" of this information during the retrieval process is a rather dynamic process that he termed *synergy*. The power of this synergy seems to provide the recaller with a sensation of confidence in his or her retrieval decision. The absence of such ecphoric synergy is clearly a characteristic of the amnesic patient. For whatever reason, the amnesic patient never puts the initial processing and the cue together, thus, never experiences the sensation of knowing that an episode occurred. In fact, the ecphoric end product upon which to base his or her retrieval never even seems to exist. I have argued here that it may not occur for a variety of reasons largely related to the encoding process. However, others have argued that it does not occur because of difficulties during the retrieval processes. Nonetheless, all seem to agree that ecphoric information does not develop for amnesics during the process of attempting to learn and remember information and consequently the sensation, or synergy, to know when one is correct never exists.

Although this characterization of amnesia may be one upon which many theorists could concur, it still leaves open the arguments of where in the process the breakdown occurs, and whether it occurs at the same point for all patient populations. At first glance, then, the description seems to have nothing new to offer. However, because it does place strong emphasis on the belief that memory is a process that is initiated during the first moment of attention to a stimulus and culminates when the individual realizes the match between cue and his or her reconstruction of the episode, it provides a term for describing the relationship between encoding and retrieval. If we can agree that ecphoric information is determined by the confluence of encoding and retrieval conditions, then we have a term for what it is that is lost in amnesia and we can proceed from there to investigate the contributing conditions to this apparent vacuum of ecphoric information in the amnesic patient.

REFERENCES

Cermak, L. S. (1972). *Human memory: Research and theory.* New York: Ronald Press.

Cermak, L. S. (1975). Imagery as an aid to retrieval for Korsakoff patients. *Cortex, 11,* 163–169.

Cermak, L. S. (1976). The encoding capacity of a patient with amnesia due to encephalitis. *Neuropsychologia, 14,* 311–326.

Cermak, L. S. (1979). Amnesic patients' level of processing. In L. S. Cermak & F. I. M. Craik (Eds.), *Levels of processing in human memory,* (pp. 119–139). Hillsdale, NJ: Lawrence Erlbaum Associates.

Cermak, L. S. (In press). Encoding and retrieval deficits of amnesic patients. In E. Perecmon (Ed.), Integrating Theory and Practice in Clinical Neuropsychology. New York: IRBN Press.

Cermak, L. S., Blackford, S. P., O'Connor, M., & Bleich, R. P. (In press). The implicit memory abilities of a patient with amnesia due to encephalitis. *Brain and Cognition.*

Cermak, L. S., & Butters, N. (1972). The role on interference and encoding in the short-term memory deficits of Korsakoff patients. *Neuropsychologia, 10,* 89–96.

Cermak, L. S., Butters, N., & Gerrein, J. (1973). The extent of the verbal encoding ability of Korsakoff patients. *Neuropsychologia, 11,* 85–94.

Cermak, L. S., Butters, N., & Moreines, J. (1974). Some analyses of the verbal encoding deficit of alcoholic Korsakoff patients. *Brain and Language, 1,* 141–150.

Cermak, L. S., Naus, M. J., & Reale, L. (1976). Rehearsal and organizational strategies of alcoholic Korsakoff patients. *Brain and Language, 3,* 375–385.

Cermak, L. S., & O'Connor, M. (1983). The anterograde and retrograde retrieval ability of a patient with amnesia due to encephalitis. *Neuropsychologia, 21,* 213–234.

Cermak, L. S., Reale, L., & Baker, E. (1978). Alcoholic Korsakoff patients' retrieval from semantic memory. *Brain and Language, 5,* 215–226.

Cermak, L. S., & Stiassny, D. (1982). Recall failure following successful generation and recognition of responses by alcoholic Korsakoff patients. *Brain and Cognition, 1,* 165–176.

Cermak, L. S., Talbot, N., Chandler, K., & Wolbarst, L. R. (1985). The perceptual priming phenomenon in amnesia. *Neuropsychologia, 23,* 615–622.

Cermak, L. S., Uhly, B., & Reale, L. (1980). Encoding specificity in the alcoholic Korsakoff patient. *Brain and Language, 11,* 119–127.

Cohen, N. J. & Squire, L. R. (1980). Preserved learning and retention of pattern analyzing skill in amnesia: Dissociation of knowing how and knowing that. *Science, 210,* 207–209.

Diamond, R., & Rozin, P. (1984). Activation of existing memories in anterograde amnesia. *Journal of Abnormal Psychology, 93,* 98–105.

Gardner, H., Boller, F., Moreines, J., & Butters, N. (1973). Retrieving information from Korsakoff patients: Effects of categorical cues and reference to the task. *Cortex, 9,* 165–175.

Graf, P., & Schacter, D. L. (1985). Implicit and explicit memory for new associations in normal and amnesic subjects. *Journal of Experimental Psychology: Learning, Memory, and Cognition, 11,* 501–518.

Graf, P., Shimamura, A. P., & Squire, L. R. (1985). Priming across modalities and priming across category levels: Extending the domain of preserved function in amnesia. *Journal of Experimental Psychology: Learning, Memory, and Cognition, 11,* 386–396.

Jacoby, L. L. (1984). Incidental vs. intentional retrieval: Remembering and awareness as separate issues. In L. R. Squire & N. Butters (Eds.), *The neuropsychology of memory* (pp. 145–156). New York: Guilford Press.

Kinsbourne, M., & Wood, F. (1975). Short-term memory processes and the amnesic syndrome. In D. Deutsch & J. A. Deutsch (Eds.), *Short-term memory* (pp. 257–291). New York: Academic Press.

Lhermitte, F., & Signoret, J. L. (1972). Neurological analysis and differentiation of amnesic syndromes. *Revue Neurologique, 126,* 161–178.

Moscovitch, M., Winocur, G., & McLachlan, D. (1986). Memory as assessed by recognition and reading time in normal memory-impaired people with Alzheimer's Disease and other neurological disorders. *Journal of Experimental Psychology: General, 115,* 331–347.

Schacter, D. L. (1987). Memory, amnesia, and frontal lobe dysfunction. *Psychobiology, 15,* 21–36.

Schacter, D. L., & Graf, P. (1986). Effects of elaborative processing on implicit and explicit memory for new associations. *Journal of Experimental Psychology: Learning, Memory, and Cognition, 12,* 432–444.

Squire, L. R. (1982a). Comparisons between forms of amnesia: Some deficits are unique to Korsakoff's syndrome. *Journal of Experimental Psychology, 8,* 560–571.

Squire, L. R. (1982b). The neuropsychology of human memory. *Annual Review of Neuroscience, 5,* 241–273.

Thomson, D. M., & Tulving, E. (1970). Associative encoding and retrieval: Weak and strong cues. *Journal of Experimental Psychology, 86,* 255–262.

Tulving, E. (1972). Episodic and semantic memory. In E. Tulving & W. Donaldson (Eds.), *Organization of Memory* (pp. 381–403). New York: Academic Press.

Tulving, E. (1983). *Elements of episodic memory.* Oxford: Clarendon Press.

Tulving, E. (1985). How many memory systems are there? *American Psychologist, 40,* 385–398.

Tulving, E., & Thomson, D. M. (1973). Encoding specificity and retrieval processes in episodic memory. *Psychological Review, 80,* 352–373.

Warrington, E. K., & Weiskrantz, L. (1978). Further analysis of the prior learning effect in amnesic patients. *Neuropsychologia, 16,* 169–177.

Warrington, E. K., & Weiskrantz, L., (1982). Amnesia: A disconnection syndrome? *Neuropsychologia, 20,* 233–248.

Weiskrantz, L., (1985). On issues and theories of the human amnesic syndrome. In N. M. Weinberger, J. L. McGaugh, & G. Lynch (Eds.), *Memory systems of the brain* (pp. 380–415). New York: Guilford Press.

Wickens, D. D. (1970) Encoding strategies of words: An empirical approach to meaning. *Psychology Review, 22,* 1–15.

Winocur, G., & Weiskrantz, L. (1976). An investigation of paired-associate learning in amnesic patients. *Neuropsychologia, 14,* 97–110.

Confabulation and the Frontal Systems: Strategic versus Associative retrieval in Neuropsychological Theories of Memory

8

Morris Moscovitch
Department of Psychology
Erindale College,
University of Toronto,
and Unit for Memory Disorders

It would be pleasant to record that Endel Tulving's theories of memory sparked my interest in confabulation, but the truth is that I became interested in the topic because of a patient at Baycrest Hospital in Toronto. At first, I merely listened to his confabulating stories with fascination; then I tried to elicit them when they did not occur spontaneously, and finally I began to investigate the syndrome more systematically in an attempt to understand it. I learned quickly that studying single cases is much more difficult than I had anticipated. As a consequence, my study of the confabulating patient consists more of a series of observations than of controlled experiments. Nonetheless, the observations suggest some interesting hypotheses about the nature of the phenomenon and its relevance to theories of memory.

Confabulation can be defined as "honest lying." The confabulating patient provides information that is patently false and sometimes self-contradictory without intending to lie. In fact, the patient is often unaware of the falsehoods, and even when confronted with the truth, may cling to his or her own version of it, no matter how preposterously fantastic that version may be. Talland (1965) and Berlyne (1972) restrict confabulation to verbal statements, but I think this is not correct. Our own patient's attempt to leave the hospital for home every evening because he mistook his hospital room for his office suggests that his actions can convey the same type of information as his verbal denials that he is in a hospital.

Talland (1965) correctly argued against the claim that confabulations are usually "gratuitously invented, fabricated, rather they are erroneously reproduced or reconstructed from actual data" (p. 42). Similarly, he did not believe that the core of a confabulation is produced "to oblige the listener, or to fill in gaps in their knowledge of facts" (p. 42), though "secondary" confabulations may arise to explain (away) the internal inconsistencies of the primary confabulations that are sometimes apparent even to the patient.

In the end, Talland (1965) proposed the following as characteristic of all confabulations:

> (a) Typically, but not exclusively, an account, more or less coherent and internally consistent, concerning the patient. (b) This account is false in the context named and often false in details within its own context. (c) Its content is drawn fully or principally from the patient's recollection of his actual experiences, including his thoughts in the past. (d) Confabulation reconstructs this context, modifies and recombines its elements, employing the mechanisms of normal remembering. (e) This method is presented without awareness of its distortions or of its inappropriateness, and (f) serves no other purpose, is motivated in no other way than factual information based on data. (pp. 49–50)

To these I add two additional points: (g) The readiness to confabulate may be determined by the patient's "personality structure, his traits evolved in dealing with the environment and in monitoring his self image" (Talland, 1965; p. 44). As Gainotti (1975) observed, patients with a premorbid pattern of denial or rationalization of illness and with a need for prestige and domination in interpersonal relations were two to three times more likely to confabulate than patients who did not have these traits; and (h) All confabulating patients seem to suffer from anasagnosia, an unawareness of their memory deficit or, at best, a profound lack of concern and lack of appreciation of its severity and extent (McGlynn & Schacter, in press).

Patient HW

HW is a 61-year-old right-handed man who underwent surgery in 1984 to have a subarachnoid hemorrhage clipped. Clipping near the anterior communicating artery (ACoA) was followed by widespread bilateral frontal ischemia and infarction. The CAT scan shows massive bilateral frontal damage extending somewhat more superiorly in the right, than in the left. Because of visual artifacts caused by the clip, it is difficult to determine exactly which structures in the basal forebrain were damaged. Significantly, there is little or no damage to the temporal lobes either mesially or laterally.

HW was 1 of 12 children born to an observant Catholic family. He received a traditional Catholic school education and continues to be a practicing Catholic. Shortly after graduating from high school, he moved to Ontario, where he held a variety of jobs including one at a lumber mill. He had been working at H., his current place of employment since 1955 and had advanced to the position of personnel manager in 1975, the job he held at the time of his operation. In 1951, he married Martha M. and had four children who were 34, 32, 31, and 27 years old when we tested their father in 1987. When the children were young, HW was involved in organizing sport leagues and seemed to take an active interest in sports himself. He played golf regularly and was quite knowledgeable about sports in general.

On being interviewed, HW was friendly and cooperative, almost jocular. He had little insight into his condition, often attributing his stay in the hospital to a bowel operation that he had for cancer in 1961. In fact, he was disoriented in time and place but not confused. He was also not upset when confronted with the truth of his condition. Although disoriented, he got to know the hospital routine and negotiated his way easily around the ward. The only time he was agitated, and sometimes abusive, was in the evenings when he would routinely begin to pack his bags to go home after what he considered to be the end of his day at work. He became quite upset with the attending staff who prevailed on him to stay. Aside from this, the only other behavioral problem he presented to the staff was that he was incontinent of urine and slovenly in his dress. With the help of a behavior modification program, he learned to control his bladder, modify his dressing habits, and reduce the frequency of his attempts to leave the hospital. Although he also had a history of alcohol abuse, there was no evidence of it after he entered the hospital.

Interview

HM: Do you know where you are right now?

HW: This is the H. building.

HM: This is the H. building, not the hospital that you're in?

HW: No.

HM: What floor in the H. building?

HW: Fourth floor (the correct floor of the hospital).

HM: Do you usually have beds in your room in the H. building?

HW: No.

HM: So why do you have beds here?

HW: They just put them in there since we ran into this epidemic.

HM: What epidemic is that? (no answer). Let me set you straight a bit. Let me give you a hint, it's Bay . . .

HW: . . .crest.

HM: Correct. It's not the H. building, let's get that straight. Do you know how long you have been here?

HW: Just since yesterday.

HM: What date is that?

HW: The 30th of September.

HM: What year?

HW: 1987.

HM: It's now May of 1987. You jumped a little bit ahead. Can you just tell me a little bit about yourself? How old are you?

HW: I'm 40, 42, pardon me, 62.

HM: Are you married or single?

HW: Married.

HM: How long have you been married?

HW: About 4 months.

HM: What's your wife's name?

HW: Martha.

HM: How many children do you have?

HW: Four. (He laughs.) Not bad for 4 months.

HM: How old are your children?

HW: The eldest is 32, his name is Bob, and the youngest is 22, his name is Joe.

HM: (He laughs again.) How did you get these children in 4 months?

HW: They're adopted.

HM: Who adopted them?

HW: Martha and I.

HM: Immediately after you got married you wanted to adopt these older children?

HW: Before we were married we adopted one of them, two of them. The eldest girl Brenda and Bob, and Joe and Dina since we were married.

HM: Does it all sound a little strange to you, what you are saying?

HW: (He laughs.) I think it is a little strange.

HM: I think when I looked at your record it said that you've been married for over 30 years. Does that sound more reasonable to you if I told you that?

HW: No.

HM: Do you really believe that you have been married for 4 months?

HW: Yes.

HM: You have been married for a long time to the same woman, for over 30 years. Do you find that strange?

HW: Very strange.

HM: Do you remember your wedding well?

HW: No, not particularly. (In other interviews he is able to describe his wedding in some detail.)

HM: Were your parents at the wedding?

HW: Yes.

HM: How old were they?

HW: My father is 95–96. My mother is 10 years younger so she is 85–86. (In fact, they had died quite a few years ago when they were in their 70s.)

HM: So you got married for the first time when you were 61 years old? You weren't married when you were younger?

HW: This is my second marriage. The first woman was 2 years ago.

HM: That would make you how old when you got married the first time?

HW: 50.

HM: What happened to your first wife?
HW: Not a thing.
HM: Did you get divorced?
HW: Yes.
HM: Are you Protestant or Catholic?
HW: (He laughs.) I'm Catholic.
HM: That would make it pretty difficult wouldn't it?
HW: Yes, the first one was invalid.
HM: So the first marriage was annulled. Do you know what the name of your first wife was?
HW: Yes. Her name was Martha also. (He is now referring to an old girlfriend whose name was also Martha whom he dated before he married his wife.)

COMMENTS ON LITERATURE REVIEW
AND PATIENT

The confabulation that Talland described is typically associated with the acute phase of Wernicke-Korsakoff syndrome. This type of confabulation usually subsides and eventually disappears as the patient settles into the chronic amnesic phase of Korsakoff's syndrome. Some patients' confabulation never clears. The occurrence of confabulations and its persistence have little to do with the severity of the memory disorder, suggesting that different mechanisms are involved in producing amnesia and confabulation.

Whereas amnesia is caused by bilateral damage to limbic structures, such as the hippocampus, mammillary bodies, or dorsomedial nucleus of the thalamus, confabulation is linked to lesions of the frontal lobes and related structures that include the basal forebrain, the cingulate gyrus, cingulum, septum, and anterior hypothalamus all of which are fed by the ACoA (Alexander & Freedman, 1984). Stuss, Alexander, Lieberman, and Levine (1978), Kapur and Coughlan (1980), and Baddeley and Wilson (1986) noted that confirmed or suspected frontal-lobe damage or dysfunction was a common feature of confabulation; in the case reported by Kapur and Coughlan, confabulation cleared as frontal functions returned. Lhermitte and Signoret (1976) and Luria (1976), however, believe that confabulation is associated with damage to the cingulate and to the basal forebrain and hypothalamus, respectively. Although it is probably the case that damage restricted to the frontal lobes is not sufficient to produce confabulation, it is not known whether frontal dysfunction, in combination with damage to related structures, is a necessary condition for confabulation. For convenience, therefore, I refer to the frontal lobes and the related structures served by the ACoA as *the frontal system*.

HW, like the other cases, had extensive frontal system damage. Although he had a history of alcohol abuse, the immediate cause of his disorder was infraction of the frontal lobes and related structures that resulted from clipping the ACoA.

The implication of the frontal system in confabulation is consistent with two of the most common functional explanations of confabulation. One is that confabulation arises from "the disruption of [the patient's] temporal frame of reference" (Talland, 1965, p. 56), Van Der Holst, 1932, cited in Williams & Rupp, 1938) and the other is that it is a deliberate, but clumsy and ineffectual, attempt to cover up lapses of memory or fill in gaps of knowledge, as much to oblige a listener as to satisfy the patient's own needs. The latter, in short, is a confabulation of exigency or embarrassment (Bonhoffer, 1901; cited in Talland, 1965). Support for both explanations can be found in the interview. HW's gross underestimation of the length of his marriage can be attributed to a disordered time sense, whereas his claim that he adopted four grown children can be seen as an attempt to reconcile obviously discrepant beliefs.

These two need not be rival explanations, as they are often presented in the literature, but can be complementary instead. I would go so far as to say that they are negative and positive signs of the same underlying frontal disorder. According to the temporal explanation, the memories are intact (more or less) but their chronology is wrong. Information from events that are related but are widely separated in time and place become fused or are misattributed to another context. Confronted with the flagrantly inconsistent accounts that such a process will sometimes produce, the patient counters with an explanation that is sometimes even more preposterous (and laughable) than the inconsistencies it was meant to reconcile.

It is tempting to consider as primary those confabulations that are caused by disorders in temporal sequencing. All other forms of confabulations are secondary or reactive. Such an interpretation is consistent with evidence that temporal memory judgments are impaired after frontal lobe lesions (Milner, 1974, 1982) as, perhaps, are all attributions of temporal or spatial context to any event (Smith & Milner, 1984; Schacter, 1987). Confabulation is source amnesia (Schacter, Harbluk, & McLachlan, 1984) magnified and extended to include an entire lifetime of experience. Were the confabulations of exigency plausible, one might go along with this view of things. Yet they are often so farfetched that they demand a deeper explanation than one that merely states that confabulations of exigency are reactive, the normal response to conflicting beliefs. Moreover, a temporal disorder interpretation would fail to account for fantastic confabulations that cannot be described as true events that are merely displaced in time, but rather are honest and fabulous inventions. To identify the temporal disorder as the primary source of confabulations is to mistake a symptom of the disorder for its cause.

Before speculating about the true cause of confabulation and its relevance to theories of memory, more information is needed about the disorder itself and the other cognitive deficits that are associated with it. From all accounts, it would seem that the memory deficit that typically accompanies confabulation is one of retrieval more than of encoding, consolidation, or storage (Lhermitte & Signoret, 1976); "of the ability to 'ekphoria' than of engram formulation" (Williams & Rupp, 1938; p. 403). Memory for the content of an event is relatively preserved, but memory for its spatial or temporal context is impaired.

Even non-Korsakoff confabulators, such as HW, suffer from severe memory disorders that make them appear to be amnesic on casual observation. Yet unlike true amnesics, confabulating patients perform unusually well on some explicit memory tests. Case 4 of Stuss et al.'s (1978) series improved his score on the Wechsler Memory Scale from 87 to 112, but his confabulation continued unabated. Kapur and Coughlan (1980) reported that their confabulating patient performed normally on tests of recognition that would stump amnesic patients, yet the same patient scored zero on the tests of recall. Is this pattern of performance on memory tests typical of confabulating patients whose memory disorder is not caused primarily by limbic system damage but rather by frontal system damage? If so, HW should perform similarly to those patients both on a standard battery of neuropsychological tests of intelligence and memory, and on a number of tests that are sensitive to frontal lobe damage. HW's results are reported in the next section.

Neuropsychological Testing

The results of standard neuropsychological tests appear in Table 8.1. His full-scale IQ is in the low average range. The verbal subtests revealed an unremarkable pattern except that his score on General Information was low. The slight drop in his full-scale IQ from his estimated premorbid level of functioning is probably the result of his impulsive, poorly organized, and idiosyncratic approach on many of the performance tests. For example, he tended to accept the presented order of cards in the Picture Arrangement subtest and provided idiosyncratic stories based on that incorrect sequence. This type of performance is consistent with radiological and behavioral evidence of frontal lobe damage. It should be noted, however, that HW did not perform poorly on all tests that are sensitive to frontal damage. Although he could not achieve more than a single correct category on the WCST, he produced the normal number of words on the FAS test of verbal fluency, suggesting that at least the left orbito-frontal region may have been spared.

His performance on tests of memory shows marked impairment in recall, scoring zero whenever a substantial delay is introduced. Significantly, however, his recognition scores were in the normal range.

No formal tests of language function were administered because his linguistic skills seemed perfectly adequate.

TABLE 8.1
Neuropsychological Test Results for Patient HW

Test	Score
WAIS-R Full Scale IQ	89
Verbal IQ	94
Performance IQ	83
Wechsler Memory Scale MQ	76
Logical Memory Immediate	2.5/23
delayed	0/23
Paired associate: easy: immediate	6.5/9
delayed	5/6
hard: immediate	0/12
delayed	0/4
Visual reproduction: immediate recall	2/14
delayed recall	1/14
recognition	14/14
California Verbal Learn Test	
Recall immediate (trials 1–5)	24/80
short delay	0/16
long delay	1/16
delayed recognition	12/16
Rey Osterieth Drawing	
Copy	20/36
Immediate recall	0/36
FAS Test of Verbal Fluency	37
Wisconsin Card Sorting Test	0 categories
(Test stopped after 45 cards, 39 perseverative errors)	

COMMENT ON NEUROPSYCHOLOGICAL TESTS

Dissociation Between Recognition and Recall:
The role of the Frontal Lobes

There is a strong resemblance between HW and Kapur and Coughlan's patient. Although HW was not as intelligent, both patients performed similarly on tests of recall and recognition. Recognition was surprisingly well preserved, given how abysmally HW performed on tests of delayed call. The discrepancy between recall and recognition is so striking that is deserves additional comment. Although clever experimenters can contrive to make recall better than recognition (Tulving & Thomson, 1973), the reverse is typically the case. The relative superiority of recognition over recall, however, remains fairly constant both within a population and even across populations that differ in type of brain damage that includes patients with anoxia, closed head injury, Alzheimer's Disease, and encephalitis. One can even predict the level of recognition from performance on tests of recall if the same tests are administered to all patients. The major exception to this rule are patients with ACoA aneurysms whose performance on recognition far exceeds the predicted level (Schacter, Moscovitch, & Tulving, unpublished observations).

Having been alerted to this phenomenon, I was reminded of two similar observations in the literature. Both examples concerned patients with bilateral frontal-lobe signs or with damage to structures that are intimately related to the frontal lobes. Hirst, Johnson, Kim, Phelps, Reese, and Volpe (1986) reported that patients with Korsakoff's syndrome who were matched with normal control subjects on recognition, nonetheless scored almost zero on delayed recall. Another group of patients who showed a comparable discrepancy were patients with Parkinson's Disease. In many PD patients the head of the caudate nucleus, an area sending primary projections to the frontal lobes, is dysfunctional. In a recent study, Huberman, Freedman and Moscovitch (1988) found that a subset of non-demented Parkinson's patients scored at the level of mildly demented Alzheimer's patients on immediate verbal recall, that is, they performed at the floor, getting no more than 3 out of 16 items correct. Their performance on 4-item forced choice delayed recognition, however, was 14/16 correct, a score that was at least as good as that of matched controls and much better than that of Alzheimer patients.

The discovery of a large discrepancy between performance on implicit and explicit tests of memory in amnesic patients, a discrepancy as large as the one between recognition and recall in some confabulating patients, has been offered as evidence in support of the idea that performance on implicit and explicit tests is mediated by independent memory systems. If I were a proponent of such a position, I would be forced to consider seriously the proposition that recognition and recall are also mediated by different systems. If one adds the evidence of functional independence between recognition and recall, then only the outcomes of tests of stochastic independence stand in the way of such a conclusion. In some circumstances, however, the dependent relationship that is observed is sufficiently small that it sometimes is only a matter of faith whether one chooses to interpret the results as favoring a multiple memory system hypothesis or refuting it.

Because I do not wish to be drawn into this debate again, let me return to the interpretation advanced by Williams and Rupp (1938), which is that retrieval, rather than retention, is impaired in patients whose memory disorder is of frontal origin. I will go a bit further and specify the type of retrieval process that is impaired. Tulving has long argued that retrieval is necessary for both recognition and recall, and I do not think that the present finding need challenge his argument. Rather, it is necessary to distinguish between two types or components of retrieval. Retrieval processes have both a *strategic or organizational* and a *associative* component (Lockhart, Craik, & Jacoby, 1975). Working from minimal cues, processes that comprise the strategic or organizational component are largely self-initiated and goal-oriented (Craik, 1983). They are concerned with reinstating the temporal and spatial context in which the target is embedded and, having reinstated it, they coordinate the various other retrieval processes that utilize general knowledge as well as episodic cues to home in on the target. The process can be likened to one that occurs when solving problems. A general problem is set up and relevant knowledge is recruited to constrain it further until local routines can be applied to arrive at a solution. Once you figure out that, say, a solution requires that you divide x by y, the operation of division, the local routine, is easily executed. The homologue in memory to the local routine is associative retrieval. It is a retrieval process that is mediated by local, or proximal, cues whose relation to the target is more direct and specific than the general, quite distal cues that initiate strategic retrieval. At the extreme, the associative component deals with that information that was encoded as a unit with the target.

One might presume from this discussion that associative retrieval always follows strategic. Although that might be typical of free recall, it need not always be that way. The two processes are interactive, but somewhat independent of each other. One can easily imagine the situation in which the target is retrieved associatively with the aid of a highly distinctive cue and then, using this knowledge, the individual retrieves strategically the context in which the target was embedded. Again, the analogy from problem solving is instructive. In those cases in which one cannot even frame the problem properly, being provided with the answer allows one to work backwards to derive the steps leading to it.

It is apparent from this discussion that I believe that the strategic component of retrieval is selectively impaired in patients who confabulate but who show relatively preserved recognition. The strategic component is mediated by frontal system structures. Before I speculate further about the role of the frontal system in this process, I wish to present some additional observations concerning HW's confabulation and memory. In particular, the way I have formulated my hypothesis of impaired strategic retrieval suggests that it would apply equally to remote as well as to recent and newly acquired memories, to semantic as much as to episodic memories, and perhaps to any problem, mnemonic or otherwise, that requires a deliberate, organized, and sequential search. Similar proposals have been advanced by a number of other investigators (Baddeley & Wilson, 1986; Goldberg & Bilder, 1986; Goldberg & Costa, 1986; Lhermitte & Signoret, 1972, 1976; Luria, 1976; Mercer, Wapner, Gardner & Benson, 1977; Rozin, 1976; Schacter, 1987; Shapiro, Alexander, Gardner, & Mercer, 1981; Stuss & Benson, 1986, among others). The following observations and experiments generally confirm these predictions.

ADDITIONAL OBSERVATIONS

Crovitz (1973) Test: Critique and Data

Beginning with Kinsbourne and Woods (1975), a number of investigators have used this test to see whether amnesic patients can retrieve episodic memories in response to a word cue, such as "flag." The object of the test is to describe in detail a specific episode that the word conjures up. Kinsbourne and Woods' patients typically gave general answers (eg., I see flags at parades) rather than specific episodes, and this was taken as evidence that episodic, but not semantic, memory was impaired in these patients (see Robinson, 1976, and Rubin, 1986, for other studies using the Crovitz technique).

The conclusion is not warranted for two reasons. First, no comparably difficult test was administered that tapped semantic memory. For example, it is conceivable, indeed highly likely, that had some patients been asked to describe a remote historical event in which a "flag" or "gun" figured prominently, they would have been as much at a loss as they were in describing a specific episode. Both episodic and semantic answers demand strategic retrieval, a process that the patients being Korsakoff amnesics with probable frontal dysfunction, would fail (see Goldberg & Bilder, 1986; Goldberg & Costa, 1986, for similar ideas concerning generic and singular memories).

Second, performance should not be uniformly poor. Sometimes, the cue word may have a strong associative link to a memory and that memory, if it is highly unitized, would emerge in rich detail.

Robin Green and I administered the Crovitz test twice to HW. The first time, he retrieved only 2 memories to 12 of the same prompts used by Baddeley and Wilson (1986); the second time, he retrieved an additional 3. Here is an example: In response to the word "game" he said, after a long silence, "I didn't start playing golf until about 5 years ago and that's a little late; you should start playing when you're younger. [He stopped and had to be prompted to produce a particular episode]. I can remember playing in a tournament. [He then described the rules of tournament play and had to be reminded again that we were after a specific episode]. I'm always reluctant to play first, but this time I got caught and went first. There were a lot of people waiting to hit and a fair group that was watching. I set my ball up. There was a bit of chatter going around. It didn't bother me but the starter told them all to quiet down. They all quieted down and they were looking at me. I'm normally a nervous person anyway. So I swung and missed the ball. What if I missed it again? Finally I hit the ball, a beautiful one, better than 200 yards."

I admit that with a confabulating patient it is difficult to know whether the story is true. He did, however, tell a very similar story the second time we tested him a few days later. The only significant detail that changed concerned his membership in the club where the tournament was held.

The story may also be part of one's "personal folklores" (Cermak, 1984; Cermak & O'Connor, 1983). These stories are so well rehearsed that they lose their episodic, personal character and assume the status of a folktale. We have no way of judging whether this is the case except to say that he was able, when questioned, to supply additional incidental details about the event he recounted such as who was in the crowd, what kind of day it was, and what time of year the tournament was held.

HW's failures on the Crovitz test are as informative as his successes. In response to the words "letter" and "find," HW just remained silent. In response to prompts, he admitted writing and receiving letters and having found something, but could get no further than that. To the word "dog," he smiled and said, "There used to be a dog," but then required prompts to supply each additional bit of information concerning the color of the dog, its home, and where he saw it. Even with these prompts, HW could not recall a single episode involving the dog, but only generic information about him. "A black dog that my brothers and I used to see in our neighborhood." In part, this was because our prompts invited that type of information. Not having access to his episodic memory, we had no idea what prompts would serve as good associative cues to an episode. Happily, when we asked whether he had ever been bitten by a dog, he was able to supply somewhat more detailed episodic information about one of his own dogs who had bitten him on the leg because he teased the dog by prodding him with a stick.

HW's performance on the Crovitz test is consistent with the hypothesis that strategic retrieval is impaired in confabulating patients. Unless the target or later prompts triggered an episodic memory, HW seemed incapable of searching his memory systematically to find an appropriate episode. Given the nature of the deficit, my guess was that HW would experience similar difficulties when his semantic memory was probed.

The reader will recall that HW's lowest score on the verbal scale of the WAIS-R was in the information subtest where he had a scaled score of 6, which is 3 points lower than his next lowest score. When questioned about recent or remote historical events, he sometimes was way off the mark; he believed, for example, that the Magna Carta was signed by the Americans and Germans in 1400. More typically, his answers are in the right ball park, but the details are vague or incorrect. Thus, he knew that the first atomic bomb was dropped by the US on Hiroshima, but was not sure exactly what effect it had on World War II. He knew that Queen Elizabeth I and Queen Victoria both ruled England in the remote past, but could not supply the dates nor any significant events that occurred during their reigns.

Like many Canadians, his knowledge of hockey was somewhat better than that of English history; here, too, he had the same difficulties as he had on episodic memory tasks. When asked how many Canadian teams were in the National Hockey League he answered two, Montreal and Toronto. This was the number in the league before the late 1970s, when the league expanded and took in 5 additional Canadian teams. When I told him that there were more, he refused to believe it. When I asked him to try to figure out which cities might have teams he had no strategy for attacking the problem. I then asked him to name major Canadian cities and decide if they had teams or not. Although he could generate some appropriate cities, he still denied that they had teams. When, however, I would say, "The name of the team is the Vancouver?", he would supply the correct name to the team when I paused after saying the city's name. Nevertheless, he protested that his answers were just wild guesses.

INDUCING CONFABULATION:
DATES, PLACES AND PROCEDURES

HW's performance on tests of both semantic and episodic memory is consistent with the hypothesis that strategic retrieval is impaired, whereas associative retrieval is better preserved. Confabulation seems to occur when a memory, be it episodic or semantic, can be associatively retrieved but because strategic retrieval is impaired, it cannot be placed in the proper temporal or spatial context. For example, a retrieval cue, whether self-generated or provided by an external source, can conjure up any number of memories that may be linked associatively to it. HW's answers to the question "What did you do yesterday?" are determined by those memories that were habitually linked to the query in the past. He says he went to work or, if he believes it was a holiday, he says he went to church. Having impaired strategic retrieval processes, he cannot edit or suppress the associatively retrieved memories and, consequently, accepts them as valid (Mercer et al., 1977; Shapiro et al., 1981). *Confabulation, therefore, is a function both of the accessibility of associatively retrieved memories and of the dependence of the act of remembering on strategic retrieval. This principal applies equally to semantic as to episodic memories.* Our observation of confabulation for dates, places, and procedures is consistent with this hypothesis.

Dates

Reports of confabulating patients suggest that temporal ordering and dating may be especially dependent on strategic retrieval. Many writers have commented on the temporal disorientation of the patient, which they considered to be either a sufficient or necessary condition for confabulation (for review see Berlyne, 1972; Talland, 1965). The temporal disorder prevents the patient from establishing a point of reference in time about which he or she can order the sequence of events in his or her life. Implicit in these explanations is that confabulation is restricted to the patient's personal experiences or what he or she takes to be his or her personal experiences. According to them, the material for confabulation is episodic, not semantic, memory. I argue, however, that the temporal disorder that is characteristic of confabulation affects semantic as much as episodic memory, at least in patient HW. The evidence I present supports the claim I made earlier that temporal disorientation is a symptom, rather than the cause, of confabulation.

I asked HW to give the dates of 10 events in his own life, such as the date of his birth, wedding, high school graduation, and birth of his first child, and the date of 15 well-known historical events. Five were events that he had experienced: the beginning and end of World War II, the Korean War, the Vietnam War, and the Canada War Measures Act. The other 10 were events from the remote past, which included the date of the French Revolution, the American Declaration of Independence, and the Battle of the Plains of Abraham.

HW performed similarly regardless of whether the events were autobiographical or historical, recent or remote. Except for identifying the date of his own and Jesus' birth and the year America was discovered, HW did not get any of the answers correct. His errors were illuminating. He placed the events he experienced, whether personal or historical, in the time since his birth, whereas he assigned remote historical events to the distant past. His estimate of the dates and even order of the events were often wildly off the mark and inconsistent. For example, according to HW, World War II began sometime between 1940 and 1976 and ended as early as 1954 and as late as 1979. Sometimes he believed that it preceded the Korean War and sometimes that it followed it, and the Vietnam War, as well. After having said that America was discovered in 1492, he then claimed that the American Declaration of Independence was signed in 1400. When I called his attention to this anomoly, he gave an embarrassed giggle and changed his answer to 1500. As the initial excerpt from his interview indicates, he fared no better in dealing with personal events.

HW's performance is consistent with the hypothesis that accurate recovery of temporal information involves strategic, rather than associative, retrieval processes. The quality of the deficit was nicely captured in a temporal version of Shallice and Evans' (1978) cognitive estimation test. Shallice asked subjects to estimate the probable distance between two locations, the heights of some buildings, the weight or cost of different objects, and so on (see also Smith & Milner, 1984). HW, like other frontal patients, was obviously impaired on these tests. Not only were some of his estimates off by an order of magnitude (he thought the distance between Toronto and Vancouver was 400 miles), but the ordering was also off (he estimated the distance between Vancouver and Halifax as 250 miles). In the temporal version, I asked HW to guess the approximate date at which the following events occurred: the introduction of TV, VCRs, Xeroxing, personal computers, and satellites. I chose these events because dating them almost always induces deliberate, strategic retrieval in normal people. For each, he claimed he did not know but was willing to play along. The dates given for the above items were 1935, 1940, 1968, 1962, and 1963 respectively. When I asked him how he arrived at this answer, he said simply that he guessed. If I tried to get him to adopt a search strategy to inform and refine his guesses, he could neither initiate the strategy that involved relating the events to known landmarks, nor benefit from it when it was initiated for him.

Places

Confabulation about place is less readily elicited than about time because associative retrieval cues are less likely to be misleading for spatial information than for temporal information. Consider the difference between these two questions that I put to HW: "How long have you been married?" and "Where were you married?" He confabulates about the first, but not about the second. The answer to the first question, however, changes with time, whereas the answer to the second is constant. Even in our own experience, we often have the sense that some events in the distant past seem to have occurred only yesterday. Our sense of the location of the events, however, is relatively fixed. To acknowledge the passage of time requires the suppression of some feelings of immediacy and the recruitment of strategic retrieval strategies. It is significant that when HW erred, he usually placed events that he experienced closer to the present. For historical dates, the ready availability of year numbers and some knowledge of the historical period in which the event occurred, was enough to elicit a confabulatory response to a recognizable event.

Although less frequent, confabulation about place, when it does occur, is probably caused by the same processes as confabulation about time. Confabulation about place, as about time, should be the same for information derived from semantic, as from episodic, memory. By and large, our observations are consistent with this prediction.

In the episodic task, HW attempted to identify a number of locations in Toronto, and for the semantic task, the capitals of 15 countries. In both conditions, some items were highly familiar and easy for HW to identify, such as the location of his house and the CN Tower or the capital of Canada or the United States; some that were less familiar, but still recognizable, such as the capital of Germany and of Switzerland or, in Toronto, the location of the YMCA and the Columbus Centre; and some that were unfamiliar and probably impossible for HW to identify, such as the capital of Borneo and Nepal or the location of the mayor's house and of an obscure church.

HW performed as predicted on the Toronto locations, getting the easy landmarks correct, admitting that he had no idea about the location of the unfamiliar landmarks, and confabulating about the less familiar, but still recognizable landmarks. On the semantic test, however, HW insisted that he did not know the capital of any country, even of Canada, although he was able to pick Ottawa from among four alternatives.

Does this mean that for places, unlike dates, confabulation occurs only for episodically derived information? I think not. A more likely explanation is that none of the countries' names triggered a city's name as an associative response to queries about capitals. When the response items were more readily available, such as providing the continents in which each country belonged, HW behaved as predicted. He answered correctly for the European countries, but gave Asia as a response to both Brazil and Morocco. For historical dates, the ready availability of year numbers and some vague knowledge of the historical period in which an event occurred, was enough to elicit a confabulatory response to a recognizable event. The same holds true for recognizable locations where "place" responses are readily available. To queries about unfamiliar events and locations, however, HW would simply deny he had heard of either rather than confabulate or guess.

Procedures

Our hypothesis suggests that confabulation should virtually be absent for HW's knowledge about procedures or skills. In most cases, it is improbable that a strategic search is involved in figuring out whether one does or does not know how to carry out some tasks. To test this idea, we asked HW whether he could carry out some ordinary repairs that any householder might know and some specialized repairs that he conceivably might know but in fact did not. The "ordinary" repairs included changing a light bulb, installing a light socket, or changing a tire. The "specialized" repairs included fixing a typewriter, a computer, a camera, a Xerox machine. He answered "yes" to all the ordinary repair questions and was then able to give a pretty good, although not perfectly accurate, description of how to conduct the task (Tulving, Schacter, McLachlan, & Moscovitch, 1988). He answered "no" to all the specialized repair questions and would not budge from his answers even though I tried to lead him to believe that he might be able to carry them out. When he said he could not fix a typewriter, I suggested that surely he must have fixed some broken ones at work. He denied ever fixing one but was willing to say that he might see what he could do if a key got stuck.

For procedures, the query seems associatively linked to the correct response and, if the procedure is well rehearsed or highly structured, HW's description of it will be accurate. Although he confabulated about the jobs he held, mixing up the jobs with the places in which he held them, HW was nonetheless able to give an accurate description of the duties associated with each job. About his last job he said "I administered wages and salaries by evaluating each person's job. That includes their job knowledge, the education or pertinent product background, the mental requirements to perform the job, direction of others with their supervisory positions and physical requirements. In the supervisory jobs, there is also another heading, the direction of others, which is responsibility for leading and guiding the people. In my absence or sickness it would be up to the general manager to appoint one guy to look after it. In some cases the top foreman would take over and he knew enough people and enough about the job that he could either do it himself or assign it to someone else."

Given the appropriate conditions, it is conceivable that HW might confabulate about his knowledge of some procedures just as he would about time and place. For example, he might confabulate if the procedure is one that he once attempted but never quite succeeded in mastering, or that he always wanted to execute but never did. Here, the query might elicit a positive response that could be rejected only after a strategic search that evaluates whether he had, in fact, executed the task correctly. Little children, whose frontal lobes are not fully developed, are often caught in such "lies" when they talk about their abilities or plans.

THE FRONTAL SYSTEM AND MEMORY: A CASE FOR STRATEGIC RETRIEVAL

In his book, *Elements of Episodic Memory,* Tulving (1983) referred to a patient described by Luria (1976) who suffered from a severe amnesia following the rupture of an aneurysm of the ACoA. In many respects, that patient resembled HW. Tulving (1983) was impressed by the patient's ability to learn unrelated picture–word pairs and retain them for a few days despite not being able to describe the learning episode moments after it had occurred. He remarked, "The contents of the episode—individual pairs of associations—had become functionally separated from the episodic system" (p. 114), and referred to such decontextualized bits of information as "free radicals."

The concept of free radicals was to undergo some rapid, major modification. There is a clear line of development from Tulving's ideas about free radicals to Schacter's studies on source amnesia (e.g., Schacter et al., 1984) and to his subsequent proposal that the frontal lobes embody a mechanism necessary for ascribing spatio-temporal context to episodic memory (Schacter, 1987). Once attributed to amnesia, the existence of free radicals and source amnesia is now associated with frontal-lobe damage. Schacter favors the hypothesis, initially advanced by Pribram and Tubbs (1967), that the frontal lobes play a major role in contextual chunking, that is "the segmentation and organization of ongoing experience into distinctive units that are discriminable from one another" (Schacter, 1987, p. 32). The existence of free radicals and source amnesia is interpreted as symptomatic of an impairment in contextual chunking. Using evidence from studies on memory for frequency of occurrence, temporal order, and spatial location (e.g., Hasher & Zacks, 1979), Schacter proposed that contextual chunking is a relatively automatic process. Memory for spatial-temporal information does not depend on effortful, strategic processing.

On the face of it, this proposal seems to be at odds with my own hypothesis that front-system damage is associated with deficits in strategic retrieval. The two hypotheses differ not only with regard to the automaticity of the processes involved but also with the stage at which they are presumed to occur. Although not stated explicitly, the contextual chunking hypothesis applies primarily to encoding, whereas mine applies primarily to retrieval (but see Schacter, this volume).

The two hypotheses need not compete with each other. Only a subset of patients with frontal-lobe lesions and amnesia confabulate. It is the behavior of this subset that the strategic retrieval deficit hypothesis was meant to explain. The contextual chunking hypothesis, on the other hand, attempts to account for the observed effects of circumscribed frontal lesions in nonconfabulating humans and in animals. Of the two hypotheses, the strategic retrieval one accounts best for HW's impairment in ascribing spatio-temporal context to remote, premorbidly acquired memories. Whether confabulating patients also have a contextual chunking deficit at encoding is not known.

At this point, I think it is important to call attention to the possibility that what is typically taken to be a deficit in encoding may, in fact, be a deficit in retrieval. Consider the finding that judgments of temporal recency (Milner 1974; 1982) and frequency of occurrence (Smith & Milner, 1988) are impaired following frontal-lobe lesions. It is as likely that the effects depend on faulty retrieval of properly encoded information as the other way around. Indeed, as a subject in a frequency estimation study, I found that the real work came at retrieval when I had to review in my mind the events that I experienced and estimate, on the basis of different kinds of information that I brought to mind, what a good answer might be. In short, the tasks required the kind of strategic retrieval process that I believe is impaired in patients who confabulate and that may also be impaired, but to a lesser extent, in many patients with circumscribed, unilateral frontal-lobe lesions.

The same argument applies to the issue of automaticity. I do not wish to dispute the evidence that spatio-temporal context is encoded with little effort. It does not follow, however, that the deficit that frontal patients have in ascribing spatio-temporal context is the result of impaired automaticity. The context may still be encoded automatically, but frontal patients may have difficulty in retrieving that information strategically.

By arguing for frontal-lobe involvement at retrieval, I do not preclude the possibility that the frontal lobes are also involved at encoding. The two hypotheses are not incompatible. I wish to emphasize, however, that the type of processing in which the frontal lobes are involved, at both encoding and retrieval, would be similar; it would be effortful and strategic, rather than automatic. At encoding, the frontal lobes may be critical for developing or acting on expectancies, organizing encoding strategies, making inferences, and even segregating the flow of events into discrete chunks, but not automatically. (For recent evidence that encoding of frequency of occurrence is not always automatic, see Fisk & Schneider, 1984; Green, 1988; Hanson & Hirst, 1988; Naveh-Benjamin & Jonides, 1986; Rowe, 1974; but see Hasher & Zacks, 1984, for a rejoinder.)

As for frontal-lobe involvement at retrieval, it is appropriate at this point to consider exactly what aspect of the retrieval process is strategic. According to Tulving (1983), if the subject is in a retrieval mode and retrieval information is available, "the obligatory elements of the retrieval process consist of ecphory, ecphoric information, recollective experience, conversion of ecphoric information, and memory performance" (p. 169). For those of you who have not committed the definition of ecphory to memory, let me remind you that "it is the process by which retrieval information is brought into interaction with stored information."[1] That interaction makes ecphoric information available, which forms the basis of the subject's recollective experience. Conversion is the process by which ecphoric information and recollective experience is translated into observable behavior.

Of all these processes, only ecphory and the availability of ecphoric information is presumed to be automatic "in the sense that once the subject is in the retrieval mode and the retrieval information and the engram are available the subject has little control over the product of the ecphoric process" (p. 190). All other aspects of retrieval are, to a greater or lesser extent, under the subject's control. This is most obvious in dealing with a post-ecphoric process, such as conversion. Poor ecphoric information may be adequate for recognition because it is based on familiarity, but it may not be adequate for recall, which requires detailed ecphoric information to support a verbal or nonverbal description of the to-be-remembered event. Even if the ecphoric information is detailed, as it sometimes is in confabulating patients, it may not be appropriate given the demands of the task, or it may be inconsistent with other knowledge, or it may be too varied, in the sense that a particular cue may give rise to ecphoric information from more than one event. In each of these cases, the subject must initiate additional processes whose outcomes will determine his or her performance on a particular task.

Let me illustrate with an example that we have all probably experienced at least once, if not often. In dating a check in the new year, there is a tendency to put the date of the previous year on the check. Our ability to correct this error, when in fact we do correct it, is based on a control process that evaluates the ecphoric information with other knowledge so that we do not immediately accept the first available answer. Or, consider your response to the query "what did you do two weekends ago?" Two different, and incompatible, events may come to mind: You were out of town at a conference, and you spent the weekend at home entertaining friends. Or the question may, for some reason, revive the memory of

---

[1]Many people complained that they found the meaning of "ecphory" elusive and suggested I find a substitute whose meaning is more apparent. Unfortunately, no single, common word captures the same meaning. Perhaps "contact and recovery" or simply "memory fetch" conveys the appropriate sense of an automatic memory process involving cue-engram interaction as opposed to "memory search" which is more strategic. In deference to Tulving, however, I will continue to use "ecphory" in this paper, though the troubled reader is free to substitute one of the suggested terms for it.

a particularly wonderful weekend you spent skiing with a friend in college. Your choice of the correct answer will depend on initiating a set of processes, both semantic and episodic, inferential and deductive, that will finally enable you to choose among the alternatives. When all alternatives but one are obviously wrong, the process is almost instantaneous and seemingly effortless. When the alternatives are plausible, the process is prolonged and labored. It is these strategic retrieval processes that are likely to be impaired in confabulating amnesics. Ecphoric information is offered without evaluation. When the responses are inconsistent or contradictory, the confabulating patient, although he or she may have the presence of mind to appreciate blatant errors, lacks the resources to undo them and substitutes one preposterous tale with another.

Even the adoption of a retrieval mode and the selection of retrieval information is an effortful, strategic process. In recognition, the process is not so obvious because a copy cue is given; but in free and cued recall, the information supplied by the tester is minimal. The subject must use this information to initiate an ecphoric process whose products become the retrieval information for the next ecphoric process, and so on, until the subject is satisfied that the ecphoric information and the recollective experience is suitable for the task at hand. This description of the recall process indicates that both pre- and post-ecphoric retrieval processes may be impaired in confabulating patients.

A NEUROPSYCHOLOGICAL MODEL
OF MEMORY BASED ON EVIDENCE
FROM AMNESIA AND CONFABULATION

The model I propose borrows heavily from Endel Tulving's ideas of encoding-specificity, ecphory, and retrieval. Amnesia, I still believe, is characterized by the following four dissociations, in which the first function is relatively well preserved and the second is impaired: (a) dissociation of intelligence from memory, (b) of primary from secondary memory, (c) of pre-morbid from post-morbid memory, and (d) of memory without awareness from conscious recollection (Moscovitch, 1982b). In the years since I proposed these dissociations, it has become clear that there are patients with severe memory disorders for whom some of these dissociations do not apply. In particular, patients have been reported whose memory loss extends as far back as childhood (e.g., Butters & Cermak, 1986; Squire & Cohen, 1982; Tulving et al., 1988), and patients whose performance on some tests of memory without awareness is as severely compromised, if not more so, as their performance on tests of conscious recollection (Martone, Butters, Payne, Becker, & Sax, 1984; Shimamura, Salmon, Squire, & Butters, 1987). Nonetheless, I propose a model that accounts for the four dissociations and then indicate what other types of memory disorders can occur if structures designated by the model to mediate different processes are damaged.

Amnesia is defined as loss of conscious recollection of post-morbid events. Since Milner and Scoville's (1957) description of amnesia caused by surgical resection of the mesial temporal lobes and hippocampus in HM, it has been assumed that these structures are critical for conscious recollection of post-morbid memories. The precise function of these structures has been debated ever since. Milner (1966) and others have proposed that they are critical for consolidation; Butters and Cermak and their colleagues (1980) have championed the role of these structures at encoding; Warrington and Weiskrantz (1973) have been the principal proponents of the view that the structures are critical for retrieval.

Although I favored a modified version of the consolidation hypothesis (Moscovitch, 1982b), there were elements of it that made me uneasy. In particular, the hypothesis has always remained primarily a physiological or biochemical hypothesis for me rather than a psychological one, despite Squire, Cohen, and Nadel's (1984) efforts to translate it into psychological terms. Here are some further thoughts on the matter.

The hippocampus is necessary for making memories of recently experienced events available to consciousness, be they episodic or semantic (Moscovitch, Winocur, & McLachlan, 1986). If we consider this statement in terms of Tulving's theories, it implies that the hippocampus is the mechanism that mediates the ecphoric process whose product forms the basis of conscious recollective experience. If the encoding specificity principle is correct, namely that a necessary condition for effective retrieval is that the retrieval cue–target relation be established at the time of storage, then it strongly suggests that the hippocampus is also involved in encoding of information in long-term or secondary memory (see Cermak, Uhly, & Reale, 1980, Schacter, 1985, L. Tulving, 1981,[2] for evidence that the encoding specificity principle is not consistently upheld in amnesia). It is this process that underlies consolidation of an event and the subsequent reinstatement of the event at retrieval. The process is depicted in Fig. 8.1.

According to the model, an event occurs that is picked up by perceptual modules whose output, but not operation, is available to conscious awareness (see Moscovitch & Umilta, in preparation; Chapter 18 of this volume; and Schacter, McAndrews, & Moscovitch, 1988, for a discussion of the dissociation of the output of specific modules from conscious awareness). The information is then organized, and what is available to conscious experience is then collated by the hippocampus with the activity (or information) in the modules that gave rise to that experience. At retrieval, the cue information made available to the hippocampus interacts with the stored engram in the modules to produce the ecphoric information that is available to consciousness. With time, or recollective experi-

---

[2]Linda Tulving is Endel's daughter. It seems appropriate to provide this information in a Festschrift for Professor Tulving.

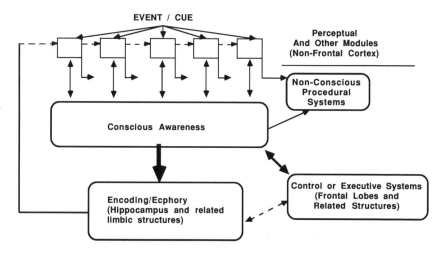

FIG. 8.1. A neuropsychological model of memory. The dashed lines indicate that the interaction is optional. The cortical modules that interact with the hippocampal system will vary depending on the information about the event that is available to consciousness when the event is initially experienced and when it is being remembered (see text for details).

ence, the ecphoric process for a particular event ceases to be mediated by the hippocampus. Instead, alternate access routes to the engram become established (see Squire et al., 1984; and Teyler & Di Scenna, 1986, for a similar proposal). What those alternate routes are is unknown, but presumably the ecphoric process must be similar to the one mediated by the hippocampus to give rise to a true consciously recollected experience, an experience of having lived an event rather than merely knowing about it.

I should point out that this model of memory is neutral with regard to the hippocampus' role in storing information. Some theorists believe that without hippocampal involvement, the engram decays rapidly, whereas others believe that engram storage is dependent only on intramodular interactions, the hippocampus being involved only in providing access to them.

If the ecphoric process is automatic, as Tulving has suggested, it implies that the process is modular in much the same way that some perceptual processes are modular (Fodor, 1983). The hippocampus can be considered a module whose input is the encoding and retrieval of information available to conscious awareness and whose output is ecphoric information (see Moscovitch & Umilta, in preparation, for an extended discussion). It is this modular aspect of hippocampal function that forms the basis for the gross errors committed by confabulators. Like all other modules, the hippocampus "lacks intelligence". Its operation is triggered by retrieval information and its output is automatic and shallow. The "intelligent" memory work is done by the system involved in conscious awareness in conjunction with a control system. For the system to operate efficiently, a control process is needed that can make appropriate encoding and retrieval information available to the hippocampus and that can organize and evaluate the ecphoric information that is its output. These control processes are mediated by the frontal lobes and its related structures.

Judging from the performance of memory-disordered people, or even normal people, memory is often fragmented. One aspect of an event may be remembered separately from another. The subject may remember the semantic attributes of an item, but not its sensory properties; the content of an event, but not its setting; the elements but not their order; and for all these examples, the reverse may also occur. Different retrieval information may be necessary to retrieve one aspect of the trace rather than another, suggesting that the information may also have been encoded differently. The foregoing indicates that the ecphoric information delivered to conscious awareness is piecemeal and not necessarily well organized or even delivered in a sequence that reproduces the initial experience. The ecphoric information is only as good as that specified by the retrieval cue. That memories often appear to be organized may be as much a function of pre- and post-ecphoric processes mediated by the frontal lobes as of ecphoric ones that are mediated by the hippocampus. Sometimes the environmental cue is sufficient to elicit the correct content and setting; sometimes only one of the two will be elicited, the other requiring additional queries that are self-generated.

The essentially irrational, shallow, and fragmented output of the hippocampally mediated system is most obvious in the confabulating patient, HW. Having severely damaged the frontal system, HW haphazardly combines information from disparate events, jumbles their sequence, and essentially accepts as veridical whatever the ecphoric process delivers to consciousness. The minimal organization that his memories show is dependent on loose rules of plausibility and association rather than on systematic strategies aimed at recovering additional ecphoric information. In cases of fantastic confabulation (e.g., Berlyne, 1972; Stuss et al., 1978), retrieval information interacts with whatever information is currently active in the perceptual and semantic modules to deliver ecphoric information that reflects recent thoughts, perceptions, or fantasies rather than relevant past experiences. Prior to concluding my interview with HW, I had a conversation about his golfing buddy and office mate, MG. Before saying goodbye, I asked HW whether he remembered who I was. Without hesitation he replied "Sure, you're MG". More dramatic examples are recounted by Stuss et al. (1978).

IMPLICIT VERSUS EXPLICIT TESTS OF MEMORY

My remarks throughout have been addressed to issues regarding conscious recollection as reflected in explicit tests of memory. Memory may also be tested implicitly. According to my model, performance on implicit tests is dependent on non-ecphoric activation of the engram whose output may enter consciousness or may inform and control non-conscious procedural systems. Thus, in tests of speeded reading, perceptual identification, or word completion, prior exposure allows the subsequent test stimulus to reactivate the engram directly and to deliver its output more quickly, efficiently, or with a higher probability, to consciousness or to the relevant non-conscious system. Depending on the demands of the task and the nature of the retrieval information, performance on two implicit tests of memory may be dependent or independent of each other (Witherspoon & Moscovitch, 1989). It follows that performance on one type of implicit tests of memory should be dissociable from that on another in patients whose damage affects the output of perceptual modules to non-conscious operating systems. Recent evidence supports this prediction (Heindel, Salmon, Butters, & Shutts, 1987; Martone et al., 1984). In addition, whether the frontal systems are engaged in such implicit tests depends on the level of organization that the test requires. On tests such as learning the Tower of London or Toronto (Shallice, 1982; Saint Cyr, Tylor & Lang, 1988), where planning and sequencing is critical, patients with frontal-lobe dysfunction have great difficulty acquiring the skill, although their memory for the learning episode is intact. Where the task and cue are highly structured, performance on implicit tests may be normal even in patients with frontal dysfunction (Heindel et al, 1987; Huberman et al., 1988).

PROVISO AND CONCLUSION

Although single-case studies are in vogue, I am somewhat suspicious of them. I agree with the arguments that Weiskrantz presents in this volume (chapter 6) that we learn most about the functional organization of the brain from studies of dissociation. My interpretation of HW's disorder is based as much on symptoms that were associated one with another as those that were dissociated from each other. I do not know to what extent these associated symptoms such as temporal disorders for semantic and episodic information, or retrieval of detailed semantic and episodic information on the Crovitz test, are obligatory in patients who confabulate or, for that matter, in any amnesic patient. Nor is it certain that damage to regions within the frontal lobe is responsible for confabulation and its related memory disorder. If it were, the ventromedial frontal cortex would be a likely candidate (Mishkin & Appenzeller, 1987). The critical lesion, however, may involve related, but nonfrontal, structures that comprise the territory of the ACoA.

Finally, I do not wish to leave the reader with the impression that the frontal lobes are a single, uniform structure. There is ample evidence from both animal and human research for dissociation of function between regions of the frontal lobes. The confabulating patient may show the cluster of symptoms because so much of the frontal system is dysfunctional. Nonetheless, there is something romantic in trying to find unity or at least a family resemblance (Teuber, 1972) among the variety of memory deficits observed after frontal system damage. I end, then, by restating my belief that pre- and post-ecphoric strategic retrieval functions are mediated by the frontal lobes and related structures. Receiving as it does input from all major association cortices, the hippocampal system, and subcortical motivational systems, as well as being closely allied to motor output structures, the frontal lobes are ideally situated to guide, organize, and evaluate the essentially modular, ecphoric processes mediated by the hippocampus and its related limbic structures.

ACKNOWLEDGMENTS

I thank Morris Freedman for referring the patient to me, Lee C. Smith for administering the neuropsychological test battery and for helping me interpret the nature of HW's confabulations, Robin Green for assisting me in collecting my data, Gus Craik for commenting on a previous draft of this paper, and Maureen Patchett for preparing the manuscript. The research was supported by an MRC of Canada grant.

REFERENCES

Alexander, M. P. & Freedman, M. (1984). Amnesia after anterior communicating artery aneurysm rupture. *Neurology, 34,* 752–757.
Baddeley, A., & Wilson, B. (1986). Amnesia, autobiographical memory, and confabulation. In D. C. Rubin (ed.), *Autobiographical memory* (pp. 225–252). Cambridge: Cambridge University Press.
Berlyne, N. (1972). Confabulation. *British Journal of Psychiatry, 120,* 31–39.
Butters, N., & Cermak, L. S. (1980). *Alcoholic Korsakoff's syndrome: An information processing approach to amnesia.* New York: Academic Press.
Butters, N., & Cermak, L. S. (1986). A case study of the forgetting of autobiographical knowledge: Implications for the study of retrograde amnesia. In D. C. Rubin (Ed.), *Autobiographical memory* (pp. 254–272). Cambridge: Cambridge University Press.
Cermak, L. S. (1984). The episodic–semantic distinction in amnesia. In L. R. Squire & N. Butters (Eds.), *Neuropsychology of memory* (pp. 55–62). New York: Guilford Press.
Cermak, L. S., & O'Connor, M. (1983). The retrieval capacity of a patient with amnesia due to encephalitis. *Neuropsychologia, 21,* 213–234.
Cermak, L. S., Uhly, B., & Reale, L. (1980). Encoding specificity in the alcoholic Korsakoff patient. *Brain & Language, 11,* 119–127.
Craik, F. I. M. (1983). On the transfer of information from temporary to permanent memory. *Philosophical Transactions of the Royal Society of London. B302,* 341–359.
Crovitz, H. (1973, November). *Unconstrained search in long-term memory.* Paper presented at the meeting of the Psychonomic Society, St. Louis, MO.
Fisk, A. D., & Schneider, W. (1984). Memory as a function of attention, level of processing, and automatization. *Journal of Experimental Psychology: Learning, Memory, and Cognition, 10,* 181–197.

Fodor, J. (1983). *The modularity of mind.* Cambridge, MA: The MIT Press.

Gainotti, G. (1975). Confabulation of denial in senile dementia. *Psychiatria Clinica, 8,* 99–108.

Goldberg, E., & Bilder, R. M. (1986). Neuropsychological perspectives: Retrograde amnesia and executive deficits. In L. W. Poon (Ed.), *Clinical memory assessment of older adults* (pp. 55–68). Washington, DC: APA Press.

Goldberg, E., & Costa, L. D. (1986). Quantitative indices in neursychological assessment: an extension of Luria's approach to executive deficit following prefrontal lesions. In I. G. Grant & K. A. Adams (Eds.). *Neuropsychological Assessment of Neuropsychiatric Disorders* (pp. 48–64). New York: Oxford University Press.

Green, R. L. (1988). Generation effects in frequency judgment.*Journal of Experimental Psychology: Learning, Memory, and Cognition, 14,* 298–304.

Hanson, C., & Hirst, W. (1988). Frequency encoding of token and type information. *Journal of Experimental Psychology: Learning, Memory, and Cognition, 14,* 289–297.

Hasher, L., & Zacks, R. T. (1979). Automatic and effortful processes in memory. *Journal of Experimental Psychology: General, 108,* 356–388.

Hasher, L., & Zacks, R. T. (1984). Automatic processing of fundamental information: the case of frequency of occurrence. *American Psychologist, 39,* 1372–1388.

Heindel, W., Salmon, D., Butters, N., & Shults, L. (1988). Implicit memory in patients with Parkinson's disease (abstract). *Journal of Clinical and Experimental Neuropsychology, 10,* 54.

Hirst, W., Johnson, M. K., Kim, J. K., Phelps, E. A., Risse, G., & Volpe, B. T. (1986). Recognition and recall in amnesics. *Journal of Experimental Psychology: Learning, Memory & Cognition, 12,* 445–451.

Huberman, M., Freedman, M., & Moscovitch, M. (1988, June). *Performance on implicit and explicit tests of memory in patients with Parkinson's and Alzheimer's Disease.* Paper presented at the meeting of the International Society for the Study of Parkinson's Disease, Jerusalem, Israel.

Kapur, N., & Coughlan, A. K. (1980). Confabulation and frontal lobe dysfunction. *Journal of Neurology, Neurosurgery, and Psychiatry, 43,* 461–463.

Kinsbourne, M., & Wood, F. (1975). Short-term memory processes and the amnesic syndrome. In J. A. Deutsch & D. Deutsch (Eds.), *Short-term memory.* New York: Academic Press.

Lhermitte, F., & Signoret, J. L. (1972). Analyse neuropsychologique et differenciation des syndromes amnesiques. *Revue Neurologique, 126,* 161–178.

Lhermitte, F., & Signoret, J.-L. (1976). The amnesic syndromes and the hippocampalmammillary system. In M. R. Rosenzweig & E. L. Bennett (Eds.), *Neural mechanisms of learning and memory* (pp. 44–56). Cambridge, MA:MIT Press.

Lockhart, R. S., Craik, F. I. M. & Jacoby, L. L. (1975). Depth of processing in recognition and recall: Some aspects of a general memory system. In J. Brown (Ed.), *Recognition and recall* (pp. 75–102). London: Wiley.

Luria, A. (1976). *The neuropsychology of memory.* New York: Wiley.

Martone, M., Butters, N., Payne, M. Becker, J. T., & Sax, D. S. (1984). Dissociation between skill learning and verbal recognition in amnesia and dementia. *Archives of Neurology, 41,* 965–970.

McGlynn, S. M., & Schacter, D. L. (in press). Unawareness of deficit in neuropsychological syndromes. *Journal of Clinical and Experimental Neuropsychology.*

Mercer, B., Wapner, W., Gardner, H., & Benson, D. F. (1977). A study of confabulation. *Archives of Neurology, 34,* 429–433.

Milner, B. (1966). Amnesia following operation on the temporal lobe. In C. W. M. Whitty & O. L. Zangwill (Eds.), *Amnesia* (pp. 109–133). London: Butterworth & Co.

Milner, B. (1974). Hemispheric specialization: Scope and limits. In F. O. Schmitt & F. G. Worden (Eds.), *The neurosciences: Third research program* (pp. 75–89). Cambridge, MA: MIT Press.

Milner, B., (1982). Some cognitive effects of frontal lobe lesions in man. *Philosophical Transactions of the Royal Society of London, 298,* 211–226.

Milner, B., & Scoville, W. B. (1957). Loss of recent memory after bilateral hippocampal lesions. *Journal of Neurology, Neurosurgery, and Psychiatry, 20,* 11–21.

Mishkin, M., & Appenzeller, T. (1987). The anatomy of memory. *Scientific American, 256,* 80–89.

Moscovitch, M. (1982a). A neuropsychological approach to perception and memory in normal and pathological aging. In F. I. M. Craik & S. Trehub (Eds.), *Aging and cognitive processes* (pp. 55–78). New York: Plenum.

Moscovitch, M. (1982b). Multiple dissociations of function in amnesia. In L. S. Cermak (Ed.), *Human memory and amnesia* (pp. 337–370). Hillsdale, NJ: Lawrence Erlbaum Associates.

Moscovitch, M., & Umilta, C. (in preparation). *Modularity and neuropsychology.*

Moscovitch, M., Winocur, G., & McLachlan, D. (1986). Memory as assessed by recognition and reading time in normal and memory impaired people with Alzheimer's disease and other neurological disorders. *Journal of Experimental Psychology: General 115,* 331–347.

Naveh-Benjamin, M., & Jonides, J. (1986). On the automaticity of frequency encoding: Effects of competing task loads, encoding strategy, and intention. *Journal of Experimental Psychology: Learning, Memory, and Cognition, 12,* 378–386.

Pribram, K. H., & Tubbs, W. E. (1967). Short term memory, parsing, and the primate frontal cortex. *Science, 156,* 1765–1767.

Robinson, J. A. (1976). Sampling autobiographical memory. *Cognitive Psychology, 8,* 578–595.

Rowe, E. J. (1974). Depth of processing in a frequency judgment task. *Journal of Verbal Learning and Verbal Behavior, 13,* 638–643.

Rozin, P. (1976). The psychobiological approach to human memory. In R. M. Rosenzweig & E. L. Bennett (Eds.), *Neural mechanisms of learning and memory* (pp. 3–48). Cambridge, MA: MIT Press.

Rubin, D. C. (Ed.) (1986). *Autobiographical memory.* Cambridge, Eng.: Cambridge University Press.

Saint-Cyr, J. A., Taylor, A. E., & Lang, A. E. (1988). Procedural learning and neostriatal dysfunction in man. *Brain, 111,* 941–959.

Schacter, D. L. (1985). Priming of old and new knowledge in amnesic patients and normal subjects. *Annals of the New York Academy of Sciences, 444,* 41–53.

Schacter, D. L. (1987). Memory, amnesia, and frontal lobe dysfunction. *Psychobiology, 15,* 21–36.

Schacter, D. L., Harbluk, J. L., & McLachlan, D. R. (1984). Retrieval without recollection: An experimental analysis of source amnesia. *Journal of Verbal Learning and Verbal Behavior, 23,* 593–611.

Schacter, D. L., McAndrews, M. P., & Moscovitch, M. (1988). Access to consciousness: Dissociations between implicit and explicit knowledge in neuropsychological syndromes. In L. Weiskrantz (Ed.), *Thought without language* (pp. 242–278). Oxford: Oxford University Press.

Shallice T. (1982). Specific impairments of planning. *Philosophical Transactions of the Royal Society of London.* B298, 199–209.

Shallice, T., & Evans, B. (1978). The involvement of the frontal lobes in cognitive estimation. *Cortex, 14,* 294–303.

Shapiro, B. E., Alexander, M. P., Gardner, H., & Mercer, B. (1981). Mechanisms of confabulation. *Neurology, 31,* 1070–1076.

Shimamura, A. P., Salmon, D. P., Squire, L. R., & Butters, N. (1987). Memory dysfunction and word priming in dementia and amnesia. *Behavioral Neuroscience, 101,* 347–351.

Smith, M. L., & Milner, B., (1984). Differential effects of frontal lobe lesions on cognitive estimation and spatial memory. *Neuropsychologia, 22,* 697–705.

Smith, M. L., & Milner, B. (1988). Estimation of frequency of occurrence of abstract designs after frontal or temporal lobectomy. *Neuropsychologia, 26,* 297–306.

Squire, L. R., & Cohen, N. (1982). Remote memory, retrograde amnesia, and the neuropsychology of memory. In L. S. Cermak (Ed.), *Human memory and amnesia* (pp. 275–303. Hillsdale, NJ: Lawrence Erlbaum Associates.

Squire, L. R., Cohen, N. J., & Nadel, L. (1984). The medial temporal region and memory consolidation: A new hypothesis. In H. Weingartner & E. Parker (Eds.), *Memory consolidation: Towards a psychobiology of cognition* (pp. 185–210). Hillsdale, NJ: Lawrence Erlbaum Associates.

Stuss, D. T., & Benson, D. F. (1986). The frontal lobes and control of cognition and memory. In E. Perecman (Ed.), *The frontal lobes revisited* (pp. 141–158). New York: The IRBN Press.

Stuss, D. T., Alexander, M. D., Lieberman, A., & Levine, H. (1978). An extraordinary form of confabulation. *Neurology, 28,* 1166–1172.

Talland, G. A. (1965). *Deranged memory.* New York: Academic Press.

Teuber, H.-L. (1972). Unity and diversity of frontal lobe functions. *Acta Neurologica Experimentalis, 32,* 615–656.

Teyler, T. J., & Di Scenna, P. (1986). The hippocampal memory indexing theory. *Behavioral Neuroscience, 100,* 147–154.

Tulving, E. (1983). *Elements of episodic memory.* Oxford: Clarendon Press.

Tulving, E., Schacter, D. L., McLachlan, D., & Moscovitch, M. (1988). Priming of semantic autobiographical knowledge: A case study of retrograde amnesia. *Brain & Cognition, 8,* 3–20.

Tulving, E., & Thomson, D. M. (1973). Encoding specificity and retrieval processes in episodic memory. *Psychological Review, 80,* 352–373.

Tulving, L. (1981). *Interaction of encoding and retrieval factors in amnesia.* Unpublished master's thesis, University of Toronto.

Warrington, E. K., & Weiskrantz, L. (1973). Analysis of short-term and long-term memory defects in man. In J. A. Deutsch (Ed.), *The physiological basis of memory* (pp. 365–396). New York: Academic Press.

Williams, H. W., & Rupp, C. (1938). Observation on confabulation. *American Journal of Psychiatry, 95,* 395–405.

Witherspoon, D., & Moscovitch, M. (1989). Stochastic independence between two implicit memory tasks. *Journal of Experimental Psychology: Learning Memory & Cognition, 15,* 22–30.

Inferring Psychological Dissociations from Experimental Dissociations: The Temporal Context of Episodic Memory

9

David S. Olton
The Johns Hopkins University

In my conversations with Endel Tulving, I have always come away wiser and more knowledgeable: wiser because I have learned something about the logic of analysis; more knowledgeable because I have learned some more information about the organization of memory. This chapter reflects both of his contributions.

The first part concerns the classification problem in learning and memory (Tulving, 1985) and asks the question, "How many memory systems are there?" (Tulving, 1985b). It discusses the types of empirical dissociations that are necessary to make strong inferences (Platt, 1964) about functional dissociations of psychological processes and neural mechanisms, and suggests that our experimental designs are not yet sufficient to demonstrate qualitative, all-or-none distinctions that separate memory into two different categories (see also chapters 1, 6, and 13, this volume). More broadly, these data suggest that a dimensional view of memory is preferable to a dichotomous one.

The second part concerns the elements of episodic memory (Tulving, 1983), particularly the neural systems that are involved in temporal discriminations. It focuses on the frontal cortex and the hippocampus, both of which have been implicated in temporal processes associated with memory (Milner, Petrides, & Smith, 1985; Rawlins, 1985), and shows that these subserve complementary functions in temporal discriminations.

DIMENSIONS, DICHOTOMIES, AND DISSOCIATIONS

Dissociations to the memory researcher are what fruit flies are to the geneticist: a convenient medium through which the phenomena and processes of interest can be explored and elucidated (adapted from Tulving, 1983, p. 146). As emphasized by Fodor (1985), the Handsome Cognitivist has been seeking dissociations among different cognitive processes, that can be defined psychologically as well as neurally. Certainly, we have every reason to believe that the brain is not a homogeneous mess of porridge, and that the mind is not a homogeneous mixture of associations. Functions are localized, both neurally and psychologically. But what criteria are necessary to move beyond an empirical demonstration of a dissociation in a particular experimental procedure to infer a functional dissociation of different cognitive or neural processes? The taxonomy of memory is a topic that has often been addressed by Tulving (1984a, 1985a, 1985b).

The use of empirically observed dissociations to make implications about the independence of underlying psychological processes has been discussed in detail by G. Loftus (1978) and by others in this volume (see chapters 1, 6, and 13). Many dissociations of empirical results may not indicate dissociations of underlying psychological processes (Olton, in press).

In neuropsychological experiments, the double dissociation has often been used as evidence of functional dissociations and dichotomies. The results are presented schematically in Fig. 9.1. The vertical axis presents choice accuracy ranging from impaired to normal. The horizontal axis indicates two different tasks (A and B), each of which measures a specific psychological functions.

Lesions are made in one of two different structures in a between-groups

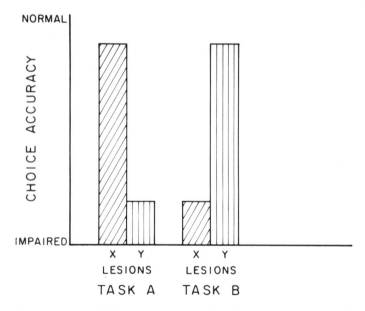

Fig. 9.1   A schematic presentation of a double dissociation. A lesion of structure Y impairs choice accuracy in task A but not task B, whereas a lesion of structure X impairs choice accuracy in task B but not Y. For further discussion, see the text.

design. One group has a lesion in structure X, the other group has a lesion in structure Y. In a real experiment, of course, appropriate control groups are included. In order to simplify the analysis, however, I have chosen to consider the results of the lesion groups *relative* to those of the control groups. Thus, *normal* choice accuracy is as accurate as that of controls (whatever that baseline might be), and *impaired* choice accuracy is less accurate than that of controls. This simplified analysis ignores at least two very important factors influencing the interpretation of behavior following lesions: (a) the choice accuracy of the control group, and (b) the magnitude of the impairment produced by the lesion. However, the analysis presented here is important in its own right, and can proceed independently of consideration of these other two factors. In short, an understanding of the issues presented here is necessary for correct categorization (and deserves exposition), but it is not sufficient (and other topics must also be addressed).

The double dissociation is indicated in the schematic results; a lesion of structure X has no effect on choice accuracy in task A, but severely impairs it in task B, whereas a lesion of structure Y produces the opposite pattern of results, a severe impairment in task A, but not in task B. The neural dissociations (different lesions have different behavioral effects in the same task) indicate functional localization within the brain so that not all structures participate equally in the two tasks. The behavioral dissociations (different tasks show different behavioral effects from the same lesion) indicate that the structure in question is not equally involved in all tasks. If the two tasks measure different types of memory, then this pattern of results is taken to indicate that structure Y participates in the memory that is special to task A, whereas structure X participates in the memory that is specific to task B. A dichotomy between types of memory follows, with the neuropsychological data suggesting a psychological and neural dichotomy. This reasoning can be seen in many different theories of memory (including my own), so in order to avoid difficulties from pointing a finger at any one theory, I have chosen no special theory to illustrate this analysis.

The empirical dissociation described here certainly is accurate for the experimental parameters used in these experiments. The question is whether the empirical dissociation can be used to indicate a functional dichotomy for psychological processes, behavioral tasks, or neural systems.

Unfortunately, data from a double dissociation with a single set of parameters are not capable of proving a dichotomy at any level of analysis. This point is illustrated in Fig. 9.2, which presents some possible outcomes of a parametric analysis. Again, the vertical axis presents choice accuracy ranging from impaired to normal. The horizontal axis presents the task demand for each task (task A on left, task B on the right), ranging from low to high. The term "task demand" indicates a parametric manipulation of a particular component of the task that requires greater activation of a particular psychological process. For example, in delayed conditional discriminations, the task demand for recent memory is often

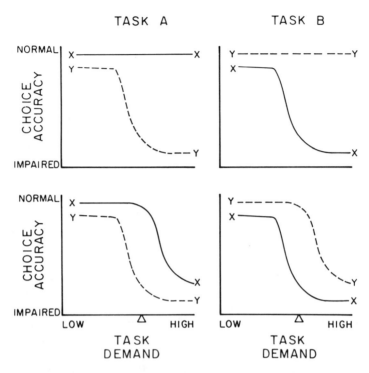

Fig. 9.2 Schematic presentations of two possible outcomes from parametric manipulations of the task demand in task A and task B. The vertical axis on each graph presents choice accuracy, ranging from impaired to normal. The horizontal axis on each graph presents the task demand, ranging from low to high for task A (left side) and task B (right side). The setting of the parameters to obtain the double dissociation illustrated in Fig. 9.1 is indicated by the arrow on the horizontal axis for each task. See text for further discussion.

manipulated by varying the amount of information presented at the beginning of the trial and the delay interval during which that information must be remembered. Choice accuracy (even in normal individuals) decreases with increasing task demand. Thus, a task demand is changed by manipulating a discrete experimental variable that should in turn alter a specific psychological function (but see comments in chapter 6 that no task is specific). The arrow at the bottom of the graph indicates the parametric setting of the task demand that produces the double dissociation illustrated in Fig. 9.1. At that level of task demand, in task A, lesion Y produces impaired choice accuracy, whereas lesion X does not. Just the opposite pattern of results occurs in task B with that level of task demand; lesion X produces impaired choice accuracy at that point along the horizontal axis, whereas lesion Y does not.

The top pair of graphs presents one possible outcome of the parametric manipulation of task demand for task A and task B. With a minimal task demand, lesion Y produces no impairment of choice accuracy. As task demand increases, however, lesion Y produces a steady decrease in choice accuracy until it is severely impaired. Lesion X produces a different pattern of results in this task. Like lesion Y, it leaves choice accuracy intact at low levels of task demand (left side of horizontal axis). Unlike lesion Y, it has no effect on choice accuracy as task demand increases. Even with the greatest task demand (right side of horizontal axis), choice accuracy is normal. This lack of effect on task demand following lesion Y strongly suggests that all of the cognitive processes activated by manipulation of this task demand are unaffected by the lesion of structure Y.

The complementary pattern of results and interpretations occurs with manipulations of task demand in task B. Following lesion X, increased task demand produces monotonically decreasing choice accuracy, from normal choice accuracy with a minimal task demand (left side of horizontal axis) to impaired choice accuracy with a substantial task demand (right side of horizontal axis). Following lesion Y, increased task demand has no effect on choice accuracy; it remains normal at all levels, producing a horizontal line.

This pattern of results provides strong support for a dichotomous division between the two different types of memories and between the functions of the brain structures. The results indicate that even with a substantial demand for the type of memory in task A, lesions in structure X have no effect on choice accuracy (left graph), and with a similar high demand for the type of memory involved in task B, lesions of structure Y have no effect on choice accuracy (right graph). Stated differently, the individual in the experiment is able to solve even the most difficult version of task A without structure X, and the most difficult version of task B without structure Y.

Unfortunately, this pattern of results is not the only one that can be obtained from an empirical dissociation such as that observed in Fig. 9.1. A different pattern is illustrated in the bottom two graphs of Fig. 9.2, and these suggest that there is no qualitative dissociation between the effects of lesions in structures X and Y on tasks A and B. Importantly, the results presented in Fig. 9.1 do not eliminate the possibility of the pattern observed in these two lower graphs. Consider task A first. Lesion Y produces impaired choice accuracy as task demand increases. With minimal task demand (left side of horizontal axis), choice accuracy is normal, indicating that all the basic sensory, motor, motivational, and cognitive skills necessary for performance in this task are adequate for normal choice accuracy. As task demand increases, however, choice accuracy monotonically decreases; this negative correlation between task demand and choice accuracy strongly suggests that the empirically observed behavioral impairment at a high task demand is due to the specific cognitive process manipulated by this demand. Because all the other variables are the same when choice accuracy is normal (with low task demand) and when it is impaired (with high task demand), these variables are unlikely to be responsible for the impairment. Rather, the critical variables must be those associated with the manipulation of task demand.

The double dissociation of Fig. 9.1 is still present in these lower graphs at the task demands indicated by the arrowhead on the horizontal axis. In task A, a lesion of structure Y has a greater effect on choice accuracy than a lesion of structure X. In task B, a lesion of structure X has a greater effect on choice accuracy than a lesion of structure Y.

However, the effects of these lesions are obviously not qualitatively different. Consider the results of two experiments with different memory demands. With very low task demand, in both tasks, no dissociation follows the two lesions because the individuals perform well in both tasks. Likewise, with very high task demand for both tasks, no dissociations follow the lesions because the individuals perform poorly in both tasks. A dissociation that appears and disappears with parametric settings is a very slippery phenomenon, and one that must be interpreted with great care.

Some of the experiments examining the role of brain mechanisms in memory have made parametric manipulations in tasks using one type of memory. These experiments have consistently demonstrated that the magnitude of the impairment following a neural manipulation is strongly dependent on the task demand for that kind of memory. This pattern of results demonstrates that the magnitude of the impairment produced by the lesion depends on the manipulation of a particular variable, with the implication that the variable being manipulated is responsible for the impairment in the task. Unfortunately, parametric manipulations are rarely made of the other type of memory, the one that is thought not to involve the structure in question. Thus, the data do not help to address the issue of interest here, the extent to which two memory systems are functionally dissociated as a dichotomy. For this analysis, the task demands for *both* types of memory must be manipulated in a parametric fashion.

For example, consider the following experimental design, which is a variation of ones often used to support dichotomous descriptions of memory processes. One task is delayed match-to-sample (DMS), a procedure that assesses recent memory. At the beginning of each trial, a sample stimulus is presented, and then removed. Following a delay interval, the sample stimulus and another stimulus are presented; the correct response is to choose the sample. The task demand can be increased by a variety of manipulations: increasing the delay interval, increasing the number of sample stimuli presented prior to a choice, decreasing the intertrial interval, and restricting the number of stimuli used in the experiment. All these manipulations decrease choice accuracy in normal animals and normal people. The second task is a two-choice simultaneous discrimination (SD). Two stimuli are presented for each trial. One stimulus is correct, the other is incorrect. Many types of lesions produce the following pattern of results: (a) in DMS with a minimal task demand, choice accuracy is normal (the same as that of controls);

(b) in DMS with a maximal task demand, choice accuracy is impaired (worse than that of controls); and (c) in two-choice simultaneous discrimination, choice accuracy is normal.

This pattern of results is usually interpreted as follows: (a) the normal performance in DMS with a minimal task demand indicates that many nonmnemonic processes (perception, motivation, motor control) are sufficiently intact to support normal performance; (b) the increasing impairment in DMS with increasing task demand indicates that at least one mnemonic process necessary for recent memory in this task is disrupted by the lesion; and (c) the normal performance in the two-choice simultaneous discrimination indicates that the type of memory required for this task is normal.

The present discussion focuses on the third conclusion. With only a single setting for the task demand in the two-choice simultaneous discrimination, this conclusion is either risky or wrong. It is at least risky; a manipulation of task demand may produce two different outcomes, each of which leads to a different interpretation. It may be wrong; the manipulation of task demand may produce a curvilinear function similar to that in the bottom of Fig. 9.2.

This discussion has used examples of experiments with lesions. However, the problems are endemic to all experimental designs that seek to make inferences about functional (rather than empirical) dissociations. They include all other neural manipulations that disrupt brain functions: drugs, naturally occurring changes such as aging, and degenerative diseases such as Alzheimer's disease. Likewise, these same issues extend beyond procedures that compromise the functioning of the nervous system, and include recordings of activity of the normal nervous system. The presence of significant behavioral or mnemonic correlates of neural activity in one task and the absence of those correlates in another task can not be used to demonstrate dissociations of function unless task demands have been manipulated in both tasks. In short, the absence of proof (the failure to conduct to a parametric manipulation in both tasks) is not proof of absence (an independence of psychological functions).

The currently available data all support the conclusion that when task demand is manipulated, choice accuracy varies. These parametric functions are so ubiquitous that they deserve our attention. We may develop the logic to explain why these parametric functions are consistent with theories that emphasize qualitative differences in the types of memory. Certainly, smooth parametric functions can indicate separate underlying processes (Cooper, Bloom, & Roth, 1986, p. 97; Gage, Armstrong, & Thompson, 1980; chapter 6, this volume). However, this conclusion demands more sophisticated reasoning than that currently used to support the various divisions of memory. Alternatively, we may reconsider our theories of memory, and decide to develop ones that emphasize dimensions rather than dichotomies. These types of theories can have several advantages. First, they relate more easily to the actual data obtained from our experiments. Second, they permit easier computational modelling, with parametric manipulations of variables rather than all-or-none states. Third, they are more consistent with the types of analyses that have been conducted in other fields.

In summary, Tulving has made valuable contributions discussing the logic of the analysis to be used to classify the memory (Tulving, 1984a; 1985a, 1985b). My discussion here continues this examination. What criteria are we going to use to decide whether or not memory systems are dissociated from each other? More generally, should we assume that there are different types of memory systems, reflected in different boxes in our models and different sets of characteristics in our tables (Tulving, 1983, p. 35)? If the dichotomous classifications require independence irrespective of parametric settings, but our experiments do not manipulate these parameters, then we forever delude ourselves into thinking that we have qualitative dissociations when we do not. Likewise, if we do not consider carefully the types of empirical dissociations that are necessary to provide strong inference (Platt, 1964) to test our theories about cognitive dissociations, then our cognitive theories will always stand the risk of being perpetuated without critical tests. These difficulties hold for every qualitative dichotomy that has been proposed to date. Thus, I raise the following two questions. First, if the behavioral effects are all quantitative ones dependent on parameters, is not a dimensional view of memory more appropriate than a dichotomous one? Second, if the qualitative, dichotomous classification scheme is to be maintained, what experimental designs are necessary to prove that the dissociations are really qualitative ones, rather than idiosyncratic outcomes of parametric settings (G. Loftus, 1978)?

Personally, I think we will make more progress if we give up the attempt to divide memory into different elements, and pursue the leads given to us by parametric experimental designs like the ones discussed here. At the worst, this approach will clarify the types of data that are necessary to support our current ideas about the organization of memory. At the best, it might lead us to reconsider our current theories and replace them with better ones. (Other views concerning this topic are presented in chapters 1, 6, and 13.)

TEMPORAL CODING OF MEMORIES

Every event that we remember happened at a specific time. For some types of problems, the temporal context of the event must be associated with that event in order for that memory to be useful and influence behavior adaptively. The importance of temporal context is seen in many different situations: humans recalling past experiences, animals foraging in natural habitats, and individuals (both humans and animals) solving certain kinds of discrimination tasks in the laboratory. Each of these situations will be discussed in turn.

Episodic memory is memory that includes temporal context (Tulving, 1983). Although differences in the "strength" of different memories could be used as a means to code the relative recency of events, this type of coding can not be the only one used, and it is unlikely to have much value even in the limited cases of its applicability (e.g., Peterson, Johnson, & Coatney, 1969). For example, consider the analysis offered by Tulving and Madigan (1970):

> In our opinion, the strength hypothesis is a product of desperation. It is entirely possible that in absence of any other relevant information the subject may, correctly or incorrectly, reason that of the two items the one appearing more familiar may look so because it occurred more recently, but this does not mean that the subject has no access to more direct information about the temporal code of an item in many other situations.
>
> We suggest the following simple experiment to those who believe in the strength hypothesis. Present to the subject a series of items, one of which is the subject's own name and some other very conspicuous item. Test many subjects for recall of all the items from such series. All subjects will remember seeing their own name. Hence, the trace strength of the name must be very high, possibly higher than that of any other item. Then ask the subjects to estimate the recency of various items, including the name. If the subjects say that the name was the last item in the series, please write to us, and to Science and Nature. If the subjects are reasonably accurate in their recency judgments about the name, do some more thinking about the strength hypothesis. Clearly, some kind of active cognitive process must provide the information that leads to accurate judgments about the temporal context of an event. (pp. 463–464)

The nature of this active cognitive process remains to be explored. Certainly, the relative order of the to-be-remembered (TBR) item with respect to other similar items is one means of coding this information (Loftus & Marburger, 1983; Thompson, 1982). Other variables affecting the accuracy of judgments about the time that an event occurred include the physical context in which that event was learned (Neisser, 1987; Smith, 1982), rehearsal (Thompson, 1982), the spacing of the items (D'Amato, 1973; Winograd & Soloway, 1985), and the general associational context of the TBR items (Tzeng & Cotton, 1980; Tzeng, Lee, & Wetzel, 1979; Yntema & Trask, 1963).

Animals in natural habitats are faced with many situations in which remembering the temporal context of an event will provide an adaptive advantage to the animal who remembers that context, as compared to an animal who doesn't. Many resources in the environment occur in specific and repeated temporal patterns. Consequently, an optimal foraging strategy requires the animal to engage in specific behaviors at specific times, a strategy that can be facilitated by remembering the temporal pattern of the previous events (see review in Kamil & Sargent, 1981; Krebs, 1978; Olton, 1985).

Many nectar-feeding insects and birds have a renewable resource that is depleted by the animal on each visit. Until the visited resource is renewed, the optimal strategy for the animal is to visit other locations that have more resources available. For example, the Hawaiian honeycreeper *(Loxops virens)* obtains nectar from the flowers of the mamane tree. During each visit to a flower, the bird depletes the nectar, and the flower requires approximately 4 hours to regenerate it. The optimal strategy during the 4-hour period of regeneration is to visit other flowers that have not been visited within the past 4 hours, and then return to the previously visited flowers. The honeycreeper is not perfect in following this strategy, but it is substantially better than expected by chance (Kamil, 1978).

Other animals horde food in a cache, which is then subsequently depleted following a visit to it. When given a supply of seeds, the marsh tit takes them individually and stores each one in a different cache. The optimal strategy for the bird is to return to each cache once and only once in order to obtain the seed hidden there. Like the honeycreeper, the marsh tit is not perfect, but it is very good, and much better than expected by chance (Shettleworth & Krebs, 1982).

Many laboratory tests emphasize memory for the temporal context of an event. Delayed conditional discriminations are tasks in which the response that is correct at the end of a trial depends (is conditional) on stimuli that were present only at the beginning of that trial. For some delayed conditional discriminations, the stimuli presented at the beginning of a trial come from a limited set of familiar stimuli that are often repeated during the experiment. Consequently, in order to choose correctly at the end of the trial, the animal must associate a particular stimulus with its temporal context, the current trial. This association of a stimulus with its temporal context may occur in many different laboratory tasks (Rawlins, 1985; Thomas 1984).

If time and memory are interrelated in fundamental ways, then the brain mechanisms involved in memory may also be involved in temporal discriminations. The series of experiments described here was designed to test this idea. It makes two obvious assumptions. First, the brain and the mind are interrelated in such a way that understanding the functional organization of the brain also tells us something about the functional organization of the mind. Second, rats and humans have enough in common (both neurally and psychologically) that information obtained from each species can be related to the other.

The functional descriptions of both the frontal and the hippocampal system, which are closely related through neuroanatomical connections, have often included some reference to both time and memory (Milner et al., 1985; Rawlins, 1985). Empirical data support a conjoint role of these two systems. Single unit activity during some tasks was very similar in both the frontal cortex and the hippocampus (Fuster, 1973; Niki & Watanabe, 1976; Rolls, Miyashita, Cahusac, & Kesner, 1985; Sakuri, 1985; Watanabe & Niki, 1985), and lesions in the two areas produced similar impairments in some tasks (Petrides & Milner, 1982; see reviews by Kolb, 1984; Olton, Becker, & Handelmann, 1979). These analyses indicate that both the frontal and hippocampal systems must be involved in the temporal aspects of memory. However, the exact nature of that involvement has not been specified clearly enough to provide obvious experimental tests of the proposed functions for these systems. (See also Passingham, 1985; Rosenkilde, Rosvold, & Mishkin 1981; and Shallice 1982; for related discussions.)

The experiments used operant procedures (Roberts, 1981) and a series of probe trials that were variations of a signalled fixed interval (FI) schedule of reinforcement (Meck, Church, & Olton, 1984; Church, Wenk, & Olton, 1987; Olton, Meck, & Church, 1987; Olton, Wenk, Church, & Meck, 1988). Each rat was tested in a standard operant box. Stimuli were a light and a sound. Responses were made on a lever. Reinforcement was provided by a pellet feeder, which delivered a food pellet to a cup in the operant box. Each rat was first shaped to press the lever to get food, and then given a variety of different types of trials, counterbalanced across rats, test sessions, and stimuli. In order to summarize the conclusions concisely, the following sections are organized to emphasize each of the major conclusions, rather than the temporal progression of the experiment. Full details of the procedures are available in the relevant articles.

Training

Each rat was trained in a signalled fixed interval (FI) schedule of reinforcement. At the start of each trial, the signal was turned on. After the FI ended, the first bar press produced reinforcement and turned off the stimulus. Thus, the optimal strategy for the rat was to press the lever as soon as possible after the FI had ended, and not press it at any other time.

At the beginning of training, the rat's responses were distributed randomly throughout the test session. After approximately 30 days of testing, the rat's response rate was relatively low when the signal was first turned on; it steadily increased until the end of the FI when a lever press produced food and the rat stopped pressing the lever to eat the food pellet. The response rate remained low for the duration of the intertrial interval. Thus, although the rats did not perform perfectly (a single response right at the end of the FI), they did learn about the temporal contingencies, and increased their response rate as reinforcement became available at the end of the FI.

Reference Memory for the Duration of an Ongoing Stimulus: Probe Trials

In the FI training procedure just described, the rat had two cues to indicate when the FI had ended: Food was delivered, and the stimulus was turned off. Probe trials removed both of these cues: No food was given for any response, and the signal remained on for at least twice as long as the usual FI. Because these probe trials had no explicit information to indicate when the FI had ended, they could measure the time when rats expected reinforcement. During these probe trials, the response rate increased after the signal was turned on, reached a peak at the end of the FI (when food would have been delivered in a training trial), and then decreased to baseline levels. The *peak time* was defined as the time at which the response rate function reached its maximum.

For normal rats, the peak time was centered at the time when reinforcement was usually received (40 seconds after the onset of the signal), indicating that

TABLE 9.1
Peak Time in Probe Trials

Time (seconds)	30	35	40	45	50
Peak Time		FF	CON	FC	

these rats had an accurate expectation of the time of reinforcement (Table 9.1). For rats with lesions of the frontal cortex (FC), the peak time was later (shifted to the right), indicating that these rats expected reinforcement later than it actually occurred. For rats with lesions of the fimbria-fornix (FF), which disrupted projections to and from the hippocampus, the peak time was earlier (shifted to the left), indicating that these rats expected reinforcement earlier than it actually occurred in the FI schedule (Meck et al., 1987).

A shift in the peak time could occur for a variety of reasons. Subsequent analysis focused on a distinction between a change in the speed of the internal clock, and a change in the remembered time of reinforcement, a reference memory for the time at which previous events occurred (Meck, 1983). A change in the clock speed and a change in reference memory can be distinguished by the way in which the peak time changes following experimental manipulations. If a manipulation alters clock speed but not memory, peak time should shift immediately and then return to normal with additional trials. In contrast, if a manipulation selectively alters the ability to encode the time when an event occurs, peak time should be normal during the next trial (because both the clock and the previous memory are correct), and gradually shift during subsequent trials (because although the clock is correct, the memory becomes increasingly incorrect)[1].

---

[1] If these predictions are not immediately obvious, consider the following example. Each morning, at 7 a.m., you set your watch (correctly) to the correct time. During the day, you look at your watch and leave the office so that you arrive at your favorite restaurant at 12:00 noon, when it opens for lunch. Usually, this system works well; when you reach the doors of the restaurant, it is noon and the doors open for you. One day, however, your clock's mechanism is altered so that it gains 1 minute in each hour. As a result, you arrive at the restaurant at 11:55 a.m. and have to wait 5 minutes before the door opens. If the error of your watch is consistent, gaining 1 minute in each hour, you make this same mistake for several days in a row, and you remember the relationship between the time on your watch and the opening of the restaurant, you will gradually adjust your behavior so that you plan to arrive at the restaurant when your watch says 12:05, which is really noon. Thus, a change in a clock speed results in an immediate error on the first trial after the change, but a gradual adjustment to correct behavior (assuming that clock speed is consistent and memory is intact).

Just the opposite pattern occurs if there is a failure to encode the time of an event correctly. Assume that you remember events as occurring earlier than they really do. The first day you visit the restaurant on time because all the memories of previous visits are intact. However, on each of the subsequent days, your temporal encoding mechanism stores incorrect information and the influence of this incorrect information gradually overpowers the influence of the previously correct information. As a result, you begin arriving at the restaurant earlier and earlier. Thus, a change in the ability to encode temporal information produces the complementary pattern of results; correct timing on the very first trial, and gradual disruption with continued experience.

The performance of the rats with lesions indicated that the shift in peak time was due to a change in reference memory rather than clock speed. Immediately after the lesions, the peak time in the probe trials was normal. This normal position of the peak time indicates that clock speed (and all other aspects of timing) were unaffected by the lesion. However, with continued testing, the peak time in the probe trials gradually moved leftward for the rats with FF lesions and rightward for the rats with FC lesions, eventually reaching a stable asymptote after about 10 sessions.

Working Memory for the Duration of a Previous Stimulus: Gap Trials

For the probe trials just described, the stimulus remained on for the duration of the trial so that the rat always performed in the presence of the stimulus. A within-trial memory component (to be distinguished from the between-trial memory component of the probe trials) was imposed by placing a gap in the duration of the signal. As in the probe trials, the signal remained on for more than twice the length of time in the FI trials, and no food was available. In these gap trials, however, the stimulus was turned off for a short gap (.5 to 10 sec) after it had been on for a short time (0.5 sec to 10 sec).

During gap trials, the peak time of normal rats shifted rightward by an amount equal to the duration of the gap. These rats followed a *stop rule*. They stopped timing during the gap, remembered the duration of the signal prior to the gap, and when the signal began again following the gap, added this value to the duration of the continuing signal.

Rats with FC lesions performed in the same manner as normal rats. Rats with FF lesions showed a shift in the peak time equal to the duration of the gap in the stimulus *plus* the duration of the signal prior to the gap. These rats followed a *reset rule*. When the gap occurred, they stopped timing; when the stimulus began again following the gap, they began timing from the beginning. This behavior suggests that the rats had no working memory for the duration of the stimulus prior to the gap.

Divided Attention for the Duration of Two Ongoing Stimuli: Compound Probe Trials

In all the preceding procedures, only one stimulus was presented at a time. In compound probe trials, two stimuli were presented simultaneously. The long stimulus was 20 sec, the short stimulus was 10 sec. Each rat was first trained in the usual FI training trials and probe trials with each stimulus alone. Then, compound trials were given with both stimuli. The long stimulus was presented, and at a variable interval ranging from 0 sec to 10 sec later, the short stimulus was presented. Compound FI trials and compound probe trials were given as described before.

With compound probe trials, normal rats showed two peak times; one was appropriate for the short stimulus, the other was appropriate for the long stimulus. Consequently, these rats timed both stimuli simultaneously.

Rats with FF lesions performed similarly. Rats with FC lesions also had two peak times, one of which was appropriate for the short stimulus. However, the peak for the long stimulus was displaced rightward by 10 sec, the value of the short stimulus. The FC rats were able to time each stimulus individually, but had a specific deficit in timing both stimuli simultaneously. When the second (short) stimulus was presented, they stopped timing the first stimulus and timed only the second one. When the second one ended, they remembered the previous duration of the first stimulus and started timing again, resulting in the rightward shift of the peak time by a value equal to the duration of the short stimulus.

The results from the timing experiments show three empirical dissociations:

1. In probe trials, FF lesions produced a leftward shift of the peak time while FC lesions produced a rightward shift. These results demonstrate that both the frontal and hippocampal systems are involved in the reference memory for the duration of time, but in complementary ways.

2. In gap trials, FF lesions produced resetting, while FC lesions had no effect. These results suggest that the hippocampal system, but not the frontal system, is necessary for within-trial, temporary, working memory.

3. In compound probe trials, FC lesions produced a failure to time simultaneously, while FF lesions had no effect. These results suggest that the frontal system, but not the hippocampal system, is involved in attentional mechanisms allowing divided attention to simultaneous events.

As mentioned in the introduction, the importance of time and memory has been a theme of Tulving's work. This theme has been most prominent in his discussion of episodic memory and the temporal components that are involved in distinguishing one episode from another. The results from the experiments discussed here begin to provide more information about the influence of temporal factors on memory, and begin to describe some of its neuroanatomical underpinnings, emphasizing frontal cortex and hippocampus.

CONCLUSIONS

Descriptions of frontal and hippocampal function often refer to temporal and mnemonic processes, suggesting that both of these structures importantly participate in both time and memory. If the functional interrelationship among brain structures is reflected in a similar functional relationship among the cognitive processes that they subserve, then the cognitive modules of time and memory must share some important common elements. However, a comparison of the two sections of this chapter indicates that I have yet to practice what I preach about the analysis of dissociations. The dissociations in the operant experiments were obtained with only a few settings of the relevant experimental parameters. The results certainly demonstrate the utility of this approach to examine timing and related cognitive processes. Additional experiments are obviously necessary to determine the extent to which these dissociations are stable when confronted with parametric manipulations.

Thus, I hope I have reciprocated Endel's contributions, and left the reader wiser and more knowledgeable: Wiser about the logic that is necessary to make inferences about psychological dissociations from empirical dissociations, and more knowledgeable about the ways in which one can test cognitive processes in animals, and use neuropsychological investigations to examine the relationships between time and memory.

ACKNOWLEDGMENTS

The author thanks E. Tulving for knowledge, wisdom, and a great deal of hospitality; B. Crowder, J. Neely, R. Roediger, and L. Weiskrantz for comments on the chapter; F. Craick and R. Roediger for an invitation to attend this conference; R. Church and W. Meck for a series of productive and delightful collaborations; and D. Harris for preparation of the manuscript.

REFERENCES

Cooper, J. R., Bloom, F. E., & Roth, R. H. (1986). *The biochemical basis of neuropharmacology*, Fifth Edition. New York: Oxford University Press.

D'Amato, M. R. (1973). Delayed matching and short-term memory in monkeys. In G. H. Bower (Ed.), *The psychology of learning and motivation* (Vol. 7). Hillsdale, NJ: Lawrence Erlbaum Associates.

Fodor, J. A. (1985). Precis of the modularity of mind. *The Behavioral and Brain Sciences, 8,* 1–42.

Fuster, J. M. (1973). Unit activity in prefrontal cortex during delayed response performance: Neural correlates of transient memory. *Journal of Neurophysiology, 36,* 61–78.

Gage, R. H., Armstrong, D. R., & Thompson, R. G. (1980) Behavioral kinetics: a method for deriving qualitative and quantitative changes in sensory responsiveness following septal nuclei damage. *Physiology and Behavior, 24,* 479–484.

Kamil, A. C. (1978). Systematic foraging by a nectar-feeding birds, the amakihi (Loxops virens). *J. comp. Physiol. Psych., 92,* 388–396.

Kamil, A. C., & Sargent, T. C. (Eds.) (1981). *Foraging behavior: Ecological, ethological, and psychological approaches.* New York: Garland STPM Press.

Kolb, B. 1984. Functions of the frontal cortex of the rat: A comparative review. *Brain Research, 8,* 65–98.

Krebs, J. R. (1978). Optimal foraging: Decision rules for predators. In J. R. Krebs & N. B. Davies (Eds.), *Behavioural ecology: An evolutionary approach* (pp. 23–63). Oxford: Blackwell Scientific Publications.

Loftus, G. R. (1978). On interpretation of interactions. *Memory & Cognition, 6,* 312–319.

Loftus, E. F., & Marburger, W. (1983). Since the eruption of Mt. St. Helens, has anyone beaten you up? Improving the accuracy of retrospective reports with landmark events. *Memory and Cognition, 11,* 114–120.

Meck, W. H. (1983). Selective adjustment of the speed of internal clock and memory processes. *Journal of Experimental Psychology: Animal Behavior Processes, 9*(2), 171–201.

Meck, W. H., Church, R. M., & Olton, D. S. (1984). Hippocampus, time, and memory. *Behavioral Neuroscience, 98,* 3–22.

Meck, W. H., Church, R. M., Wenk, G. L., & Olton, D. S. (1987). Nucleus basalis magnocellularis and medial septal area lesions differentially impair temporal memory. *Journal of Neuroscience, 7,* 3505–3511.

Milner, B., Petrides, M., & Smith, M. L. (1985). Frontal lobes and the temporal organization of memory. *Human Neurobiology, 4,* 137–142.

Niki, H., & Watanabe, M. (1976). Prefrontal unit activity and delayed response: Relation to cue location versus direction of response. *Brain Research, 105,* 79–88.

Olton, D. S. (1985). The temporal context of spatial memory. In L. Weiskrantz (Ed.), *Animal intelligence* (pp. 79–85). Oxford: Clarendon Press.

Olton, D. S. (in press). Dimensional mnemonics. In G. H. Bower (Ed.), *The Psychology of Learning and Motivation: Advances in Research and Theory,* Vol 23. New York: Academic Press.

Olton, D. S., Becker, J. T., & Handelmann, G. E. (1979). Hippocampus, space and memory. *The Behavioral and Brain Sciences, 2,* 313–365.

Olton, D. S., Meck, W. H., & Church, R. M. (1987). Separation of hippocampal and amygdaloid involvement in temporal memory dysfunctions. *Brain Research, 404,* 180–188.

Olton, D. S., Wenk, G. L., Church, R. M., & Meck, W. H. (1988). Attention and the frontal cortex as examined by simultaneous temporal processing and lesions of the basal forebrain cholinergic system. *Neuropsychologia, 26,* 307–318.

Passingham, R. E. (1985). Memory of monkeys (Mucaca mulatta) with lesions in the prefrontal cortex. *Behavioral Neuroscience, 99,* 3–21.

Peterson, L. R., Johnson, S. T., & Coatney, R. (1969). The effect of repeated occurrences on judgments of recency. *Journal of Verbal Learning and Verbal Behavior, 8,* 591–596.

Petrides, M., & Milner, B. (1985). Deficits on subject-ordered tasks after frontal and temporal-lobe lesions in man. *Neuropsychologia, 23,* 601–614.

Platt, J. R. (1964). Strong inference. *Science, 146*(3642), 247–353.

Rawlins, J. N. P. (1985). Association across time: The hippocampus as a temporary memory store. *Behavioral Brain Sciences, 8,* 479–496.

Roberts, S. (1981). Isolation of an internal clock. *Journal of Experimental Psychology: Animal Behavior Processes, 7,* 242–268.

Rolls, E. T., Miyashita, Y., Cahusac, P., & Kesner, R. P. (1985). The response of single neurons in the primate hippocampus related to the performance of memory tasks. *Society for Neuroscience Abstracts, 11,* 525.

Rosenkilde, C. E., Rosvold, H. E., & Mishkin, M. (1981). Time discrimination with positional responses after selective prefrontal lesions in monkeys. *Brain Research, 210,* 375–394.

Sakurai, Y. (1985). Neuronal activity of prefrontal cortex and dorsomedial thalamus during a continuous nonmatching-to-sample task in the rat. *Society for Neuroscience Abstracts, 11,* 516.

Shallice, T. (1982). Specific impairments of planning. *Philosophical Transactions of the Royal Society of London, B298,* 199–209.

Shettleworth, S. J., & Krebs, J. R. (1982). How marsh tits find their hoards: The roles of site preference and spatial memory. *Journal of Experimental Psychology: Animal Behavior Processes, 8,* 354–375.

Smith, S. M. (1982). Enhancement of recall using multiple environmental contexts during learning. *Memory & Cognition, 10*(3), 405–412.

Thomas, G. J. (1984). Memory: Time binding in organisms. In L. R. Squire & Butters (Eds.), *Neuropsychology of memory* (pp. 374–384). New York, NY: The Guilford Press.

Thompson, C. P. (1982). Memory for unique personal events: The roommate study. *Memory & Cognition, 10*(4), 324–332.

Tulving, E. (1983). *Elements of episodic memory*. Oxford: Oxford University Press.

Tulving, E. (1984a). Multiple learning and memory systems. In K. M. J. Lagerpetz & P. Neimi (Eds.), *Psychology in the 1900s* (pp. 163–184). North Holland, Elsevier Science Publishers B.V.

Tulving, E. (1984b). Precis of elements of episodic memory. *Behavioral and Brain Sciences, 7,* 223–268.

Tulving, E. (1985a). On the classification problem in learning and memory. In L.-G. Nilsson & T. Archer (Eds.), *Perspectives on learning and memory* (pp. 67–91). Hillsdale, NJ: Lawrence Erlbaum Associates.

Tulving, E. (1985b). How many memory systems are there? *American Psychologist, 40,* 385–398.

Tulving, E., & Madigan, S. A. (1970). Memory and verbal learning. *Annual Review of Psychology, 21,* 437–384.

Tzeng, O. J. L., & Cotton, B. (1980). A study-phase retrieval model of temporal coding. *Journal of Experimental Psychology: Human Learning and Memory, 6*(6), 705–716.

Tzeng, O. J. L., Lee, A. T., & Wetzel, C.D. (1979). Temporal coding in verbal information processing. *Journal of Experimental Psychology: Human Learning and Memory, 5*(1), 52–64.

Watanabe, T., & Niki, H. (1985). Hippocampal unit activity and delayed response in the monkey. *Brain Research, 325,* 241–254.

Winograd, E., & Soloway, R. M. (1985). Reminding as a basis for temporal judgments. *Journal of Experimental Psychology, 11*(2), 262–271.

Yntema, D. B., & Trask, F. P. (1963). Recall as a search process. *Journal of Verbal Learning and Verbal Behavior, 2,* 64–74.

10

The Boundaries of Episodic Remembering: Comments on the Second Section

Marcel Kinsbourne
Eunice Kennedy Shriver Center
Harvard Medical School

THE DISTINCTIVE STATUS OF EPISODIC REMEMBERING

Endel Tulving has placed an indelible imprint on memory research. He has raised issues that no one had thought were issues, and challenged explicit or implicit assumptions thought to be too obvious to test. Given the generally nonprogressive nature of behavioral science (Tulving, 1983)), it is not immediately obvious which of a near infinity of possible questions is the most worth asking. Tulving has a flair for choosing topics for research that redirect the attention of memory investigators everywhere.

Tulving's latest enterprise in scientific navigation is a change in course on the unity of the construct of memory itself. Although he listed in his book (1983) numerous previously proposed dichotomies in the memory domain, memory investigators had ignored these proposals, and studied memory in the same general way, regardless of what was being remembered, and how. This was so, despite the fact that neuropsychologists, in their then separate domain, had long been persuaded (through phenomena of double dissociation) that there are separable memory mechanisms in the brain. Tulving's force of conviction and strength of personality has compelled cognitive psychologists to take account of neuropsychological findings, and brought neuropsychologists closer to the cognitive mainstream. His initiative is already visibly connecting these naturally very compatible fields.

The key question that directs effort in current neuropsychological memory research is the one posed by Tulving (1983): How many memory systems are there? As is always the case with Professor Tulving's influential thought, there is

179

a reason why this question has fired his imagination. I can best explain my opinion about this by amending the question to: Is there one or are there more? The crux of the matter is not a count on systems, but Tulving's effort to differentiate a particular one from the rest—the memory system that involves conscious experience.

The form of remembering termed *episodic* by Tulving (1972) typically takes the form of a partial reexperiencing of a previously experienced event. Episodic recollection necessarily involves awareness. Other learned behaviors need not. We have emphasized that episodic memory is not simply responding biased by what transpired during the episode. Remembering without awareness is not episodic remembering, even if it is based on a specific event (Jacoby & Witherspoon, 1982). It is remembering based on a conscious recapitulation of some of the actual experience that characterized the episode (Kinsbourne & Wood, 1975, 1982). What divides those who subscribe to Tulving's two memory systems (namely episodic versus the rest) from those who do not is whether they consider the presence or absence of awareness to be a promising organizing principle for distinguishing between brain systems. For those who, like Professor Tulving, take consciousness to be the central problem in psychology, classifying by awareness is at least plausible and potentially important. For those who would banish awareness from their ostensibly objective science, it is counterintuitive if not revisionist. They would be more apt to assert the unity of memory (e.g., McKoon, Ratcliff, & Dell, 1986) or dichotomize it in some other manner (Squire & Cohen, 1982).

The extent to which awareness participates in a mental operation may be subjectively obvious, but resist quantification. A superior way of demonstrating its role is to identify patients who have lost the ability to reexperience the past— that is, have lost episodic memory. Amnesics appear to be such people (Kinsbourne & Wood, 1975). Here I focus on experiments with amnesics that help delineate the boundaries of episodic memory, both laterally (relative to other modes of remembering) and vertically, with respect to the transition between the present and the previous episode.

The interpretative logic relies on the double dissociation, which is authoritatively explained by Weiskrantz (chapter 6, this volume). The other limb of the dissociation—preserved episodic but impaired semantic memory—rests precariously on a single case report (DeRenzi, Liotti, & Nichelli, 1987). The limitations inherent in dissociation logic have been analyzed by Dunn and Kirsner (1988). But Olton (chapter 9, this volume), in the context of his elegant animal studies of temporal memory relative to focal experimental brain lesions, questions, if not the logic, at least its usual application. He argues that the two presumptively dissociated parameters have to be varied, each along some dimension of task difficulty. This is because at a suitable difficulty level, both parameters might be revealed as influenced by the same manipulation. If so, Olton would dismiss the dissociation as spurious (see also Dunn & Kirsner's 1988 attempt at a refinement of the dissociation logic).

This recommendation makes an unwarranted assumption: that adjusting task difficulty leaves the nature of the task unchanged. In fact, the opposite is often clearly true. Curtailing visual exposure time may change a task from one that is limited by rate of identification to one in which the performance-limiting operation (Kinsbourne, 1971) is pattern detection. Accelerating a sequence of speech sounds for immediate recall may change the performance-limiting operation from ability to chunk to ability to decode. Olton's (1985) own device of varying task difficulty by increasing the number of arms of a maze from two to eight does not hold constant the nature of demands on memory. To remember one's actions on the previous trial might call for an act of episodic remembering that is trivially easy (and therefore not performance-limiting) when there are two limits only. When I discuss an as yet unpublished time estimation experiment (later in this chapter), I point out how this study, too, would be misinterpreted from Olton's perspective. In brief, parametric variation is treacherous and should only be used if positive grounds exist for believing that the nature of the task has not been changed or complicated.

With amnesics, one can readily demonstrate the dissociated loss of explicit autobiographical memories, with retention of skill acquisition (see Korsakoff's [1889] original description of alcoholic amnesia). More elegantly, one can show how, whereas the experience of an episode cannot be recaptured, it may systematically bias existing response predispositions. This is currently labelled "priming". It is the methodology that Tulving favors, and many others have followed suit.

PRIMING

George Talland (1967) called amnesia "a world without continuity." Amnesia research is perhaps also such a world. For instance, the current chief focus of amnesia research interest, preserved priming, was first experimentally demonstrated by Schneider (1912). He gave Korsakoff patients a series of tasks, each given repeatedly across successive sessions (e.g., recognizing cue-depleted figures, assembling fragments to form familiar objects). He found learning without recollection. The subjects benefited from the prior experience, but could not remember that they had had it.

At the time, theoretical interests were centered elsewhere, and Schneider's discovery was not followed up. But when Warrington and Weiskrantz (1974) reported "word stem completion" in the absence of recognition, they found a more receptive audience. The amnesic patient became the preferred means for demonstrating the dissociability of recollection from the reshaping of response disposition (Kinsbourne & Wood, 1975). Perhaps the most dramatic example of this dissociation has been best studied in Tulving's laboratory. This is *source amnesia* (Evans & Thorn, 1966, Schacter, Harbluck, & McLachlan, 1984). The patient is told a "fact". Soon after, he or she can respond to questioning with the gist of that fact, but has no recollection of when or from whom he or she learned it. That this factual knowledge is no free floating fragment (Tulving, 1983) but has been incorporated into the patient's knowledge structure, can be easily demonstrated. For instance: "The Golden Gate bridge has 100 tons of rust scraped off it each year" (pseudofact). Subsequently: Q.–"Do you know anything about bridges and the weather?" A.–"Well, a bridge made of metal may rust"—and so on.

I view priming not as indicative of a separate memory system, nor as a fringe phenomenon of little generality, but as a window on the acquisition of knowledge. Priming may be a means by which we consolidate our convictions—or amend them. That is, an imbalance in response predispositions may increase, or conversely, may reverse. The growth of human knowledge can be viewed as cumulative response differentiation.

This view of priming can be presented in a weak or a strong form (Schacter & Graf, 1986). According to the weak form, priming can only modify response probabilities within an existing response repertoire. The stronger claim would be that all knowledge arises in the same way. According to this view, complete absence of response to a stimulus, however unfamiliar, is too atypical to consider. Instead, even the unknown elicits response, although the response may be relatively nonspecific. A mechanism akin to priming shapes the response so as to render it more adaptive.

MULTIPLE OPERATIONS OF REMEMBERING, NOT MULTIPLE STORES FOR MEMORIES

The preceding formulation acknowledges no fundamental distinction between two hypothesized variants of memory—declarative and procedural (Squire & Cohen, 1982). Both, when perfected, can be elicited without mediation of conscious recollection—knowing that and knowing how. Yet they seem, on the face of it, different: knowing the name of the President, or how to shoot baskets. On closer scrutiny, the distinction loses some of its appeal.

In many cases, the distinction is moot. Does one know *what* a word is, or *how* to read it; how to count, or what the numbers are; how to play chess, or what is a good move; how to solve a problem, or what the answer is? When one considers learning, things get worse. Ryle (1949) said of the "intelligent reasoner": "the rules that he observes have become his way of thinking" (p. 48). Knowing that yields to knowing how. Initially, deliberate explicit knowledge-based action becomes automatized, and unconscious in its detailed maneuverings. The acquisition of motor skills is usually taken to be the most self-evident instance of pure knowing how. Yet skill learning is initially based on knowing a set of rules, and pursued by knowing the results of each component act (feedback). In knowing how, there is an implicit history of knowing that.

As Weiskrantz remarks (chapter 6, this volume), few tasks in neuropsychology are functionally (or factorially) pure. When retrieving a partially learned fact, one may assist oneself by recollecting previous encounters with the subject matter. Retrieving semantic information is assisted by episodic recollection. Conversely, an episodic task, recognition, may be partly supported by a semantic mechanism, priming (Hirst et al., 1986). While acquiring a problem-solving skill, one may with advantage recollect the outcome of previous attempts at solution. The absence of episodic memory does not usually preclude the acquisition of knowledge or skill, but it does slow it down. For instance, our amnesic subjects did manage to learn (and retain) the mathematical Fibonacci principle, but more slowly than controls (Kinsbourne & Wood, 1975). Proportionately, the amnesic patients do better in learning than in recollection, which they cannot accomplish at all. But it is questionable whether they learn at a normal rate. Apparent demonstration of normal rates of acquisition may be confounded by ceiling effects (e.g., mirror-reading performance, as in Cohen & Squire, 1980). In contrast, primed responding of the relevant episode, without awareness of the relevant episode, is preserved.

The patient who responds based on knowledge alone will first produce the dominant response within the category. "Name the President"—the question asks for an instance of a category, presidents, within a temporal context, now. The patient produces the name that is highest in his response category—say, Kennedy (unqualified by temporal context). Does he therefore take himself currently to be living in the sixties? Not at all. Does he know presidents since Kennedy? Yes, and he can list them. The incumbent's name is produced as an item in the list. When in time does the amnesic consider himself to be living? That depends on when, and under what ongoing conditions, one asks him the question. If one cannot retrieve episodes, one cannot use their temporal ordering to establish the sequence of events in past experience (Talland, 1965).

Whether amnesics can correctly produce facts depends on the fact. If the answer is overlearned or unique, yes. If it calls for selection from a response list, usually not.

THE DURATION OF THE EPISODE

The time frame of a reexperienced episode is usually demarcated by shifts in the pattern of activity. But suppose the subject continues to do the same thing and the context does not change? By such means, can an episode be extended indefinitely in time?

Recent data (Kinsbourne & Hicks, in press) may speak on this issue. Korsakoff amnesics and two contrast groups were asked to advance a sequence of single-digit displays by moving a lever at a one-per-second rate. After a predetermined interval, the subject was stopped. The three groups did not differ in their estimates of *present* time as inferred from the rate at which they advanced the display. The amnesics' semantic (''declarative'') knowledge of the length of a second was unimpaired. At the end of each trial, they were asked to estimate how long they had been engaged in the task. For durations up to about 30 seconds, amnesics' estimates did not differ significantly from those of the contrast groups. All three groups showed a parallel decline in the ratio of estimated to clock time past. Beyond 30 seconds, this ratio stabilized for the contrast groups, but continued to decline for the amnesics. We argue that within a 30-second period, subjects can directly process the temporal aspect of a single episode, that information still being available to direct awareness (although diminishingly). Further increments in time seemed only a little longer to the amnesics. It was as if they were processing a moving window of the present (an episode), with minimal ability to recollect that anything had transpired before then—that is, during the previous episode. Incidentally, although their judgments were nominally prospective, they could not take advantage of the use of a temporal counter or register, as they forgot that they would be asked to estimate temporal duration, which rendered their estimates effectively retrospective. Note that we cannot equate short and long intervals with easy and difficult judgments, because subjects were asked to let their time judgments reflect their subjective experience. They were not asked to infer clock time. As we have seen, once short-term memory has expired, the nature of the mental operations called for by the task changes.

On this view, the amnesic is tied to the episode that happens to be. How does that limit him in real life, as distinct from the laboratory?

IMPLICATIONS OF AMNESIA FOR ADAPTATION

Consider Claparede's (1911) famous observation. The clinician's handshake concealed a sharp object, which hurt the patient's hand. Later, the patient would not shake hands with the clinician. ''People may have sharp objects in their hands, which might hurt you''. Lacking episodic memory, she overgeneralized what she had learned. Instead of selectively avoiding one person's handshake, her formulation incriminated them all. (Claparede's observation was incomplete; did his patient also avoid handshakes with others?)

To generalize, the here and now of mental set and stimulus context will sometimes not suffice to elicit the most adaptive response. A previous episode harbors the necessary discriminative stimulus. Episodic remembering recovers the bygone episode and thus the needed information.

Episodic remembering calls for the ability to focus attention selectively on specific cues and replace present experience temporarily with recollected experience triggered by these cues. By such means, a predator can uncover its prey hiding (not for the first time) behind a particular bush, or a memory researcher can recall previous work that makes sense of his or her present findings.

When an episode is successfully reexperienced, subjects typically feel confident of their recollections. Even when amnesics respond correctly in an explicit memory task, based only on their fund of knowledge, they may still be uncertain. Intact people, having recovered an episode, exhibit the confidence that accompanies direct experience. Conversely, amnesics lack normals' uncertainty with a questionable memory. More importantly, they lack the cognitive machinery for assigning a confidence level to a recollection (Talland, 1967). Behavior controlled by response predispositions is statistically based. A given response within a set of alternatives may be assigned the greatest relative subjective probability, but there is no mechanism for assigning it certainty.

In an imaginative case study, Moscovitch (chapter 8, this volume) explored the mechanism of confabulation, in a patient with bilateral frontal lesions. He found that the patient is apt to confabulate under specific conditions, as follows: (a) the question is one that arouses an association, which is an incorrect answer. (b) the correct solution calls for strategic retrieval, which is no longer available to the patient. He made the good point that defective strategic retrieval can handicap the eliciting of memories from general knowledge as well as from person experience. this appears to correspond to what Pribram (1969) called *context-bound retrieval:* "Rather than identify an item, the organism must fit the present event in a "context of prior occurrences, only some of which relate directly to the situation at hand" (p. 136). Why is this difficult? In our terms (e.g., Kinsbourne & Wood, 1975), this is, in both cases, a consequence of the patients' (frontal or Korsakoff) difficulty in escaping from the influence of existing mental states and stimulus circumstances. I would add to the list the demand characteristics of the situation—the motive of the question, the fact that the question is asked. The demeanor of the questioner: "Do you remember that trip by night through the African jungle, when natives attacked the train?" (in animated tones). The Korsakoff patient remembered. Later, "Did you *really* remember taking such a train trip?" (skeptical tone). "Well I suppose I must have taken it, because you said I did, and you are the doctor".

The "frontal" component of Korsakoff symptomatology certainly impairs strategic retrieval, and Moscovitch has given an insightful account of how confabulation might result. It contributes to, but in itself does not suffice to account for, the severity of the amnesic's episodic memory loss.

Tulving (1983) has thoroughly considered the adaptive implications of the ability to reexperience a previous event that is relevant to the existing situation. Considerations such as the aforementioned support his conclusions (see also Kinsbourne & Wood, 1975; Sherry & Schacter, 1987). The episodic memory system is seen to be coherent in evolutionary as well as neuropsychological perspective.

A MODEL FOR AMNESIA
IN NORMAL REMEMBERING?

Normal subjects were asked to render either prospective or retrospective time estimations for the duration of a set task (Kinsbourne & Hicks, in press). The task, inspection of a tartan fabric with a view to judging its complexity and aesthetic qualities, was deliberately chosen to be featureless and devoid of distinctive elements that could act as substrate for a retrospective reconstruction of time past (Hicks, Miller, & Kinsbourne, 1976). For periods of up to about 30 seconds, prospective and retrospective time judgments were approximately equal; a result consistent with the outcome of the previously mentioned experiment involving Korsakoff as well as normal subjects. For longer durations, increments in clock time resulted in only very modest increments in estimated time when the judgment was retrospective; that is, when subjects had no occasion to activate a counter or temporal register at the initiation of the trial. The period of time prior to the last 30 seconds (i.e., prior to the present episode) appears largely to have been forgotten.

The "amnesic" effect in these normal subjects arises from the fact that they did not experience any distinctive events within the trial period, that might subsequently have served as cues for time past. Such undifferentiated activity is barely remembered, even with respect to its duration. Not only the content of time, but the time itself, is forgotten. I suspect that this captures the essence of the Korsakoff amnesic's subjective experience. The amnesic does not experience long stretches of time past filled with shadowy, intangible, unidentifiable events. He experiences little or no time past at all.

As we were able to show, within the confines of the present episode, Korsakoff amnesics were able to have judgments on the number of events (stimuli, responses), although other studies (e.g., of running span—Talland, 1965) show that they would have difficulty in identifying distinctive events retrospectively. Outside the episode, the patients can barely tell that anything at all happened, let alone what. For them, most—if not all—successive activity is, in a respect crucial for remembering, effectively undifferentiated. The mechanism of this phenomenon addresses issues raised by Cermak (chapter 7, this volume).

THE LOCUS OF
KORSAKOFF AMNESIC FORGETTING

Cermak and his colleagues have evaluated the hypothesis that deficient encoding is responsible for amnesia in an extensive and consistent research program. As he reviewed this work, he found it revealing of much that is of interest in Korsakoff information processing, but he did not identify any deficit commensurate in scale with the extreme memory problem that these patients often exhibit. He is nevertheless loath to abandon the notion that Korsakoff amnesics are impaired in their registration of information, and postulates that "they fail to cognitively manipulate their analysis for purposes of storage". In support, he cited Graf, Shimamura, and Squire (1985), according to whom amnesics "lack the ability to elaborate, organize and consciously recollect information" (p. 385). Unfortunately, there are no data in the latter publication to support such a conclusion. Mandler (1980) convicted amnesics of deficiency in "elaborative" processing. A specific view of "organization" was taken by Hirst et al. (1986) when they proposed that amnesics lack the "glue" that holds individual events together and creates the larger picture. However, beyond lack of empirical support for these proposals, it is hard to conceive of how such purely cognitive refinements could account for dramatic failures to recognize (as well as recall) people and things after they have been encountered many times. How much organization or relational glue is needed to recognize one's doctor after dozens of recent meetings? Also, organizational activity seems too controlled (deliberate) to account for the major difficulty amnesics have with incidental learning (Talland, 1965). Finally, organizational processes do not readily address the striking *persistence* of experiences in Korsakoff amnesics, as indicated by the perseverative way in which they respond to situations (Talland, 1965) and the effect of prior response patterns in blocking the acquisitions of modified responses (Kinsbourne & Winocur, 1980, Winocur & Kinsbourne, 1978, Winocur & Weiskrantz, 1976).

Nonetheless, dissatisfaction with specific proposals does not compel rejection of the time-honored concept that Korsakoff patients have an impairment in the way that they register information. I would trace the problem back to an undue reliance on variables of current interest in normative memory research. Looking toward organizational or elaborative variables may be like looking for a coin, not in the dark where it was lost, but under a lamp post, because that is where there is light. I would advocate the processing, not of *relations* between stimuli or events, but differences between them, that is, their *distinctive* attributes. Nor need we be bound by the traditional tussle between encoding and retrieval theorists, but instead, with ourselves (Kinsbourne & Wood, 1982) and Cermak (chapter 7, this volume), invoke a disordered mental operation that is involved at both these stages. At registration, the memorandum should be processed as distinct from what surrounds it in space and time, at retrieval, from what is currently the case. After all, it is the distinctive aspect of an event that renders the event episodically recollectable (Moscovitch & Craik, 1976), not what it has in common with other like events.

NOVELTY AND TERMINATION OF MENTAL SETS

Judging an event distinctive takes cognizance both of its identity and that of adjacent events. Distinctiveness is a relational concept. Processing of distinctiveness is more than emitting different responses in succession. One may respond differentially to successive inputs, and yet not respond discriminatively to the fact of their distinctiveness. The orienting reaction to novelty, which is norepinephrinergically mediated (Foote & Bloom, 1979), may be deficient in Korsakoff psychosis (Mair & McEntee, 1983) or more broadly in the diencephalic subtype of amnesia, while the responses themselves proceed in the ordinary way. Norepinephrine agonists may improve Korsakoff memory (Mair & McEntee, 1986). Conversely, reducing norepinephrine production impairs the memory of normals. (Furth et al, 1987). Talland (1965), among others, remarked on how insensitive Korsakoff amnesics are to novel stimuli, and also how they are apt to leave their own mutually contradictory responses uncorrected. Error detection may be akin to novelty responding, in that it involves an unexpected mismatch between what was anticipated and what is the case. It is, at any rate, relational, in that it addresses neither the question per se, nor the response, but the relation between them. The proposal that Korsakoff amnesics fail to respond to novelty fits nicely with the results of a class of experiments that illustrate amnesics' failure to shift categorical set even though they have changed the category of their responses.

The failure of Korsakoff amnesics to exhibit release from proactive inhibition (PI release), discovered by Cermak and Butters (1972), is a case in point. Over successive interference trials for memoranda within a category, the Korsakoff patients showed the expected decline in short-term memory performance. But when, on the "release trial", the category of the memoranda was abruptly switched, they, unlike normals, failed to improve their performance (i.e., exhibit PI release). Curiously, they responded within the new category, but at a level of performance appropriate to the old category. This dissociation shows that PI release is not an automatic consequence of a shift in category of response, but reflects the activity of a brain system that is ordinarily triggered by the shift (and not so triggered in Korsakoff amnesics). In the patients, the existing mental set does yield, but only over multiple trials (Kinsbourne & Wood, 1975), or repeated category shifts (Winocur, Kinsbourne & Moscovitch, 1981). Alternatively, if the shift is grossly salient, or attended by a striking contextual change, the prior mental set is terminated, and release from PI does occur (Winocur & Kinsbourne, 1978, Kinsbourne & Winocur, 1980).

Generalizing from such findings, I suggest that Korsakoff amnesics fail to code successive events as distinctive, and instead maintain a uniform—even perseverative—response set across situations. This processing deficit is maladaptive in its own right, quite apart from its role in impairing the ability to recollect. At retrieval, this persistence of response set is also detrimental, in that one can only recapture a previous experience if one detaches attention from the present one. These registration and retrieval failures are two sides of the same coin.

An additional consequence of this deficit is referable to "anticipatory memory"—the projection of expectations into the future. As the White Queen remarked to Alice, "it is poor sort of memory which only works backwards". The inability of amnesics to envisage future possibilities (Tulving, 1985) can hardly be explained by conventional encoding or retrieval theories. It is compatible, however, with a problem in escaping from the control of the current brain state.

Tulving's selection of the episode as a topic for inquiry has born fruit. The session that I have been discussing attests to the impact of his research perspective on the deciphering of neuropsychological phenomena and its utility in clarifying the workings of the mind.

ACKNOWLEDGEMENT

The author acknowledges helpful discussion with Robert E. Hicks during the preparation of this chapter.

REFERENCES

Cermak, L. S., & Butters, N. (1972). The role of interference and encoding in the short-term memory deficits of Korsakoff patients. *Neuropsychologia, 10,* 86–89.

Claparede, E. (1911). Recognition et moiite. *Archives de Psychologie, Geneve, 11,* 79–90.

Cohen, N. J., & Squire, R. L. (1980). Preserved learning and retention of pattern-analyzing skill in amnesia: Dissociation of "knowing how" and "knowing that". *Science, 210,* 207–210.

DeRenzi, E., Liotti, M., & Nichelli, P. (1987). Semantic amnesia with preservation of autobiographical memory. A case report. *Cortex, 23,* 575–597.

Dunn, J. C., & Kirsner, K. (1988). Discovering functionally independent mental processes: The principle of reversed association. *Psychological Review, 95,* 91–101.

Evans, F. J., & Thorn, W. A. F. (1966). Two types of post hypnotic amnesia: Recall amnesia and source amnesia. *International Journal of Clinical and Experimental Hypnosis, 14,* 162–179.

Foote, S. L., & Bloom, F. E. (1979). Activity of norepinephrine-containing locus ceruleus neurons in unanesthetized squirrel monkey. In E. Usdin, I. J. Kopin, & J. Barchas (Eds.), *Catecholamines: Basic and clinical frontiers.* New York: Pergamon.

Furth, C., Dowdy, J., Ferrier, J. & Crow, T. J. (1987). Selective impairment of paired associate learning after administration of alpha 2 adrenergic agonist (clonidine). *Psychopharmacology, 87,* 490–493.

Graf, P., Shimamura, A. P., & Squire, L. R. (1985). Priming across modalities and priming across category levels: Extending the domain of preserved function in amnesia. *Journal of Experimental Psychology: Learning, Memory and Cognition, 11,* 385–395.

Hicks, R. E., & Kinsbourne, M. (in prep). *Effect of episodic memory loss in Korsakoff psychosis on time judgments.* Manuscript submitted for publication.

Hicks, R. E., Miller, G. W., & Kinsbourne, M. (1976). Prospective and retrospective judgments of time as a function of amount of information processed. *American Journal of Psychology, 89,* 719–730.

Hirst, W., Johnson, M. K., Kim, J. K., Phelps, E. A., Risse, G., & Volpe, B. T. (1986). Recognition and recall in amnesics. *Journal of Experimental Psychology: Learning, Memory and Cognition, 12,* 445–451.

Jacoby, L. L., & Witherspoon, D. (1982). Remembering without awareness. *Canadian Journal of Psychology, 36,* 300–324.

Kinsbourne, M. (1971). Cognitive deficit: Experimental analysis. In J. McGaugh (Ed.), *Psychobiology* (pp. 285–348). New York: Academic Press.

Kinsbourne, M., & Hicks, R. E. (in press). The extended present: Evidence from time estimation by amnesics and normals. In G. Vallar & T. Shallice (Eds.), *Neuropsychological impairments of short-term memory.* London: Cambridge University Press.

Kinsbourne, M., & Winocur, G. (1980). Response competition and interference effects in paired-associate learning by Korsakoff amnesics. *Neuropsychologia, 18,* 541–548.

Kinsbourne, M., & Wood, F. (1975). Short-term memory processes and the amnesic syndrome. In J. A. Deutsch (Ed.), *Short term memory* (pp. 258–291). New York: Academic Press.

Kinsbourne, M., & Wood, F. (1982). Theoretical considerations regarding the episodic-semantic distinction. In L. Cermak (Ed.), *Human memory and amnesia* (pp. 195–218.Hillsdale, NJ: Lawrence Erlbaum Associates.

Korsakoff, S. S. (1889). Uber eine besondere Form psychischer Storung, combiniert mit multiplen Neuritis. *Archiv für die Psychiatrie, 21,* 669–704.

Mair, R. G., & McEntee, W. J. (1983). Korsakoff psychosis: Noradrenergic symptoms and cognitive impairment. *Behavior and Brain Research, 9,* 1–32.

Mair, R. G., & McEntee, W. J. (1986). Cognitive enhancement in Korsakoff psychosis by clonidine: A comparison with L-dopa and ephedrine. *Psychopharmacology, 88,* 374–380.

Mandler, G. (1980). Recognizing: The judgment of previous occurrence. *Psychological Review, 87,* 252–271.

McKoon, G., Ratcliffe, K., & Dell, G. (1986). A critical evaluation of the semantic–episodic distinction. *Journal of Experimental Psychology: Learning, Memory and Cognition, 12,* 295–306.

Moscovitch, M., & Craik, F. I. M. (1976). Depth of processing, retrieval cues, and uniqueness of encoding as factors in recall. *Journal of Verbal Learning and Verbal Behavior, 15,* 447–458.

Olton, D. S. (1985). Strategies for the development of animal models of human memory impairments. In D. S. Olton, E. Gamzu, & S. Corkin (Eds.), *Memory dysfunctions. Annals of the New York Academy of Sciences, 30,* 113–121.

Pribram, K. H. (1969). The amnestic syndromes: Disturbances in coding. In G. A. Taland & N. C. Waugh (Eds.), *The pathology of memory.* New York: Academic Press.

Ryle, G. (1949). *The concept of mind.* New York: Barnes and Noble.

Schacter, D. L., & Graf, P. (1986). Preserved learning in amnesic patients: Perspectives from Experimental Neuropsychology, 8, 727–743.

Schacter, D. L., Harbluck, J. L., & McLachlan, P. R. (1984). Retrieval without recollection: An experimental analysis of source amnesia. *Journal of Verbal Learning and Verbal Behavior, 23,* 593–611.

Schneider, K. (1912). Uber einige klinisch-pathologische Untersuchungsmethoden und ihre Ergebnisse, Zugleich ein Beitrag zur Psychopathologie der Korsakowschen Psychose. *Zeitschrift fur Neurologie und Psychiatrie, 8,* 553–616.

Sherry, D. F., & Schacter, L. L. (1987). The evolution of multiple memory systems. *Psychological Review, 94,* 439–454.

Squire, L. R., & Cohen, N. J. (1982). Remote memory, retrograde amnesia, and the neuropsychology of memory. In L. S. Cermak (Ed.), *Human memory and amnesia* (pp. 275–304. Hillsdale, NJ: Lawrence Erlbaum Associates.

Talland, G. (1965). *Deranged memory.* New York: Academic Press.

Talland, G. (1967). Amnesia: A world without continuity. In *Readings in psychology today* (pp. 268–275). Del Mar, California: CRM Books.

Tulving, E. (1972). Episodic and semantic memory. In W. Donaldson & E. Tulving (Eds.), *Organization of memory.* New York: Academic Press.

Tulving, E. (1983). *Elements of episodic memory*. London: Oxford University Press.

Tulving, E. (1985). Memory and consciousness. *Canadian Psychologist, 26*, 1–12.

Warrington, E. K., & Weiskrantz, L. (1974). The effect of prior learning on subsequent retention in amnesic patients. *Neuropsychologia, 12*, 419–428.

Winocur, G., & Kinsbourne, M. (1978). Contextual cueing as an aid to Korsakoff amnesics. *Neuropsychologia, 16*, 671–682.

Winocur, G., Kinsbourne, M., & Moscovitch, M. (1981). The effect of cueing on release from proactive interference in Korsakoff amnesic patients. *Journal of Experimental Psychology: Human Learning and Memory, 7*, 56–65.

Winocur, G., & Weiskrantz, L. (1976). An analysis of paired-associate learning in amnesic patients. *Neuropsychologia, 14*, 97–110.

III CLASSIFICATION SYSTEMS FOR MEMORY

11 A Rational Analysis of Human Memory

John R. Anderson
Carnegie-Mellon University

My approach to human memory has been to search for mechanisms to explain the observed phenomena; this has probably been the dominant approach in the field. It has had its notable successes but also its notable failures. High among the list of such failures has been the inability to resolve the many theoretical dichotomies, such as the status of short-term memory (Crowder, 1982; Wickelgren, 1973), parallel versus serial processing (Townsend, 1974), semantic versus episodic memory (Tulving, 1983), and imaginal versus propositional representations (Anderson, 1978; Kosslyn, 1980; Pylyshyn, 1981). One gets the impression that mechanistic theories of memory involve a precision in theoretical specification that cannot be supported by behavioral data. Without repudiating the mechanistic approach, this chapter is devoted to exploring an alternative way of casting a theory of memory. This alternative formulation starts with the following principle about human memory:

Principle of Rationality: Human memory behaves as an optimal solution to the information-retrieval problems facing humans.

It is called a principle of rationality and it is like the rational man hypothesis in economics. Just as economic behavior is supposedly predictable on the assumption that humans are rational and act to optimize their economic interests, so this principle asserts that human memory is rationally designed to produce optimal performance in human information-retrieval tasks. But how could one entertain for more than a moment the proposition that memory behaves optimally? Aren't we always failing to retrieve the memory we want? Taking long periods to do retrievals that computers do instantaneously? Misremembering what it was that

195

we experienced? If memory were rationally designed, surely it would deliver to us instantaneously and exactly the memories we want. However, such anti-rationality arguments make two unreasonable assumptions:

1. Memory can know what fact we want before memory has retrieved and tested that fact. This assumption is much too strong. The cues that the environment provides for us are only probabilistic. Until we retrieve and carefully test a fact, we cannot determine if it is relevant to the current needs. The best that one can assume is that memory can make some best guesses as to what facts out of our great storehouse we want and offer these first for judgment.

2. Things can be done instantaneously. This assumption is clearly wrong— there must be some time costs to the acts of memory. In particular, there has to be a cost associated with testing a retrieved memory and determining if it is relevant.

Basically, the point is that memory cannot be omniscient or omnipotent. The principle of rationality only requires that it be optimal.

To apply the principle of rationality to human memory, it is necessary to have some way of framing the information-retrieval problem faced by humans that embodies the two preceding constraints. Framing the optimization problem is where the real theory lies in a rational analysis. For instance, much of the current debate about the rational analysis in economics is not whether human economic behavior is rational, but rather how to frame human economic behavior so that it will be rational. In proposing a rational analysis of human memory, it seems reasonable to start with a framing of the information-retrieval problem that is as simple and bland as possible. Only if that proves inadequate should we go to a more complex framing.

AN ANALYSIS OF INFORMATION RETRIEVAL

There already exists an analysis of information retrieval in the subfield of computer science called, curiously enough, "information retrieval" (Salton & McGill, 1983). The generic information-retrieval system has a data base of stored items and must respond with an ordered subset of these given a query that consists of some key words. Perhaps our most frequent use of such systems in academia is in library searches where we provide some content words and the system responds with a list of possible books and their abstracts. Like human memory, computer information-retrieval systems cannot know what the user really wants. They can only make wise guesses. Secondly, there are real costs in a system associated with mistaken guesses. As with human memory, the system may fail to retrieve the desired items, which clearly is a costly error. However, there is also a cost associated with retrieving an inappropriate item—which is the user's cost in considering it and rejecting it. Thus, the information-retrieval system cannot just deal with the problem of undergeneration by retrieving everything. In the field of information retrieval, the problem of generating the desired items is called *recall* and the problem of not generating irrelevant items is called *precision*. We can now specify the basic information-retrieval problem for computers—given a query, provide an ordered list of items that provides a maximal combination of recall and precision. I postpone defining "maximal combination" until I come to considering the human situation.

This is the information-retrieval problem as it is conventionally conceived of in computer science. Now let's consider how this maps onto human information retrieval:

1. The items to be retrieved are units of human memory. I refer to these as *structures,* neglecting the issue of whether these units are propositions, productions, images, associations, schemata, or whatever your favorite flavor of cognitive chunk. The important feature of a structure is that it consists of a number of *terms.* Figure 11.1 illustrates some structures that I carry around in my memory. I have a memory of stepping out of the elevator on the 22nd floor of the Waikiki Beachcomber and seeing a sign announcing the ESP floor. There is a memory structure, B, in Fig. 11.1 encoding this memory with terms "22nd floor," "elevator," "Waikiki Beachcomber," "ESP," "sign," and possibly others. Also shown in Fig. 11.1 are memory structures A, relating the terms Tulving and ESP, and C, relating Waikiki Beachcomber, Hawaii, and hotel. It is a further assumption that all the items that were ever recorded as memory structures are still there to be retrieved. Whether this assumption is literally true, or human memory just behaves as if it were, is irrelevant to this rational analysis.

2. The query that prompts our memory is a set of terms that we encode from the current context. Thus, if I am asked, "How does Endel Tulving remind you of Hawaii?", among the terms that would be part of my current memory query would be, "Endel Tulving" and "Hawaii." However, the total query set consists of anything attended to. So it would presumably also include the person asking the question and perhaps other contextual elements.

3. At any point in time, there is a subset of my memory structures that are the targets. They are structures that will help me answer my current information-retrieval demands. For instance, given the example query in the preceding paragraph (2.), a sufficient set of structures would be A, B, and C. In an explicit memory test, the information-processing demands being placed on us may seem pretty clear, but presumably, all throughout life we have to retrieve information to respond to the demands of the current situation.

4. There is a cost associated with failing to retrieve the necessary information. There is also a cost associated with our system retrieving an irrelevant item,

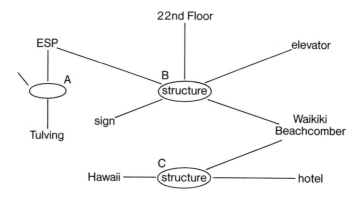

Query

How does Endel Tulving remind you of Hawaii ?

Targets

Structures sufficient to allow you to calculate an
answer to the current problem — A, B & C above.

FIG. 11.1.   Files and terms.

which we then have to process and reject (by "process," nothing is implied
about whether that processing is available to consciousness). Let us denote the
cost associated with a failed recall as C_R for recall failure cost, and the cost
associated with processing an irrelevant item as C_P for lack of precision cost.
These costs are somewhat analogous to Type 1 and Type 2 errors in statistics.
The nature of the recall failure cost should be apparent. I think of the lack of
precision cost as largely coming from the wasted effort in testing and rejecting
irrelevant memories.

Now we are in the position to define the optimization problem for human
memory. Let $p[A]$ be an estimated probability that memory structure A is relevant—that is, a target. A rationally designed information-retrieval system would
retrieve memory structures ordered by their probabilities $p[A]$ and stop retrieving
when a structure A was encountered such that:

$$p[A]C_R < (1-p[A])C_P \qquad (1)$$

That is, the system should stop retrieving when the probabilities are so low
that the expected loss due to failing to recall a target item is less than the expected

loss due to retrieving an irrelevant item. Presumably, in most situations, C_R is much larger than C_P so that this inequality will only hold for very small $p[A]$, but considering the number of structures in memory, most would have very small probabilities of being relevant. It should also be noted that in a particular situation, 0, 1, or more memory structures might be relevant. Thus, the $p[A]$ are not constrained to sum to 1. To be able to predict speed and accuracy of recall, we need to inquire as to what factors memory can use to estimate $p[A]$, and our prediction will be that these factors determine memory performance.

This discussion of the optimization problem is framed in serial and conscious terms—first the subject considers one target structure, then another, and so on. However, clearly, the subject need not be aware of the consideration of memory structures. It should also be clear, given our knowledge of the parallel-serial equivalence (Townsend, 1974), that the serial terminology is nothing more than an expository convenience. Indeed, I think of this all as being implemented in the parallel pattern-matching machinery of ACT* (Anderson, 1983). In ACT*, the system can assign resources to the structures it is processing according to their plausibility, and the system can effectively ignore structures below some threshold of plausibility. Thus, whether parallel or serial, the critical feature is that knowledge structures are consulted in order of plausibility until they become too implausible to consider. It is not the goal of this chapter to inquire as to the mechanisms that achieve this ordering, only to inquire whether we can predict memory performance assuming that memory does achieve this ordering.

ESTIMATION OF LIKELIHOODS OF MEMORY STRUCTURES

We are now one big step from having a theory that specifies the behavior of memory from purely rational considerations. That one big step is to specify the $p[A]$ in the preceding discussion.

One solution to the estimation of $p[A]$ that appears in the computer information retrieval literature (Bookstein & Swanson, 1974, 1975) is to use Bayesian estimation procedures. The two obvious pieces of information for evaluating whether a memory structure will be relevant is its past history and the terms in the query. Thus, each structure A has some history H_A of being relevant in the past. The current context consists of a set of terms that I call *cues* and denote by indices i. I denote the set of cues as Q, for query. In doing Bayesian estimation, we are trying to calculate the posteriori probabilities, giving us the following equation:

$$\frac{p(A|H_A\&Q)}{p(\bar{A}|H_A\&Q)} = \frac{p(A|H_A)}{p(\bar{A}|H_A)} \times \prod_{i \in Q} \frac{p(i|A)}{p(i|\bar{A})} \qquad (2)$$

That is, the odds ratio for item A is the product of the odds ratio for item A given history H_A times the product of the ratios of the conditional probabilities for each cue i in the context. This equation assumes that all the cues and history are independent. This is a strong assumption, but one that is typically made in the computer information-retrieval literature for purposes of tractability.[1] The first item, $p(A|H_A)/p(\bar{A}|H_A)$, is basically a prior odds ratio for the item, given its frequency and recency of occurrence. The other quantities, the $p(i|A)/p(i|\bar{A})$, are the odds ratios of the conditional probabilities of the cues, given that the structure is relevant versus not relevant. These ratios can be thought of as associative strengths. One can imagine a great matrix giving these values for each combination of cue and memory structure. Indeed, if we were to listen to connectionists, this is just what we would believe is in the head. However, these implementation details are not really relevant to the goal of this chapter. Our concern is with what factors should rationally influence the cue strengths and the prior history factor.

The basic behavioral assumption is that memory performance is monotonically related to the preceding ratio, which will be called structure A's likelihood ratio. It would be possible to develop a mapping of likelihood ratio into probability of recall and latency measures in memory research. However, this would be unnecessary detail for the purposes of this chapter. The assumption of a monotonic relationship is good enough to make the points that we are concerned with. The purposes of this chapter are to determine the factors that rationally should determine the history factor or the cue strengths, determine the qualitative predictions of these factors, and ascertain whether these predictions are in fact correct. I deal only with the most basic memory effects—all of which embody ordinal relationships only. It would be of interest to try to map likelihood into probability of recall and latency and see if we can reproduce exact numbers, but that is another paper.

THE HISTORY FACTOR

To address the history factor, we need to determine how the past history of a structure's usage predicts its current usage. To determine this in the most valid way, we would have to follow people about in their daily lives, keeping a complete record of when they use various facts. Such an objective study of human information use is close to impossible. What is possible is to look at records from nonhuman information-retrieval systems that can be objectively studied. For instance, such studies have been done of borrowing from libraries (Burrell, 1980; Burrell & Cane, 1982) and access to computer files (Stritter, 1977). Both systems tend to yield rather similar statistics. If we believe that the

---

[1]Human memory may not be so constrained and it is interesting to inquire as to which of our predictions might be upset by nonindependence.

statistics of human memory information retrieval mirror the statistics of these nonhuman systems, we are in a position to make predictions about how the human should estimate need probabilities, given past history.

Burrell has developed a mathematical theory of usage for information-retrieval systems such as libraries (a very similar model appears in Stritter, 1977 for file usage). His theory involves two layers of assumptions. First, Burrell assumes that the items (books, files, memory structures) in an information retrieval system vary in terms of their desirability. He assumes that they vary as a gamma distribution with parameter b and index v (i.e., if $v=1$ this is an exponential with parameter b). Such a distribution will produce mean desirability values of v/b and variances v/b^2. Second, given an item with desirability λ the time to next use is an exponential process with mean $1/\lambda$.

If we assume that this model describes the statistics of usage in the human memory system, we are in position to calculate the historical component of the need function. Suppose we observe a particular memory structure that was introduced t time units ago and has been used n times since its introduction. What we have to do in calculating the need function is to determine the probability that this item will be used in the next time unit. We denote this probability by $RF(t,n)$ and it is given by the following formula:

$$RF(t,n) = 1 - \left[\frac{t+b}{t+b+1} \right]^{v+n} \tag{3}$$

If $t + b$ is much larger (eg., 10 times) than $v + n$, Equation 3 is approximated by the following expression:

$$RF(t,n) \approx \frac{v+n}{t+b} \tag{3'}$$

We can always guarantee this approximation by using small enough time units. Or said otherwise, if the interval that we are predicting for is small enough, this approximation will be close.

Equation 3′ can be simplified in various ways to address some of the basic memory variables. Let us consider the retention function where we wait t seconds after an item was studied and first test it. In this case, n is zero. The equation now takes the form $v/(t + b)$. A function of this form would give a very good mimicry of human retention functions that are typically described by power functions. Newell & Rosenbloom (1981) concluded that it was basically impossible to distinguish hyperbolic functions such as the one implied by Burrell's model from power functions. If we assume that the human information-retrieval system faces a distribution of demands similar to the objectively observable distributions for retrieval systems like libraries or file systems, then the principle of rationality would predict the observed human retention function. This is the first success for the rational analysis.

We can also examine what this function implies about the effect of n, which is the number of times the structure has been practiced holding t constant. The reader will observe that it implies that need probability has a linear relationship to practice with a positive, non-zero intercept. (Because we are working with small time intervals and low need probabilities, we don't have to worry about non-linearity as the probability approaches one). What this implies about the learning function depends on how need probability is mapped into observable measures. It turns out, for instance, that ACT* (Anderson, 1983) assumed a linear growth in strength of just this form and did a nice job of predicting learning curves. The ability to predict the learning curve is the second success for the rational analysis.

According to Burrell's model, it does not matter what the spacing of these n presentations is. All that matters in Burrell's model is the total number of presentations (n) and the total elapsed time (t). This lack of sensitivity to spacing is a consequence of the ahistorical character of the exponential process that characterizes the intervals between uses of an item. The question arises whether Burrell's model correctly describes the likelihood function. Is it the case that in information retrieval systems there is no massing of need? Burrell's model implies that the n presentations should be uniformly spaced over the t interval. In fact, Burrell's model is not descriptively accurate here, as one might expect. For instance, in Carnegie-Mellon's library system, there are very definite clusterings of borrowings and one can reject the hypothesis of uniform distribution of the borrowings of a book over a fixed time interval. There are lots of reasons for such massings, such as a book being relevant to a course taught in only one semester. Stritter (1977) noted such deviations from uniformity, but chose to ignore them in developing his model of file systems. It is fairly intuitive that the same is true of human memory, although it is hard to verify the human likelihood function objectively.

If some use is massed and some is not, then the intervals between successive uses should predict the probability of the item being needed now. Thus, compare one item that has been used fairly uniformly n times over the year and another item whose n uses all occurred in a 3-month period 6 months ago. Clearly, the first is more likely to be needed now. We would therefore predict better memory for spaced items, as long as we are not comparing to a massing of study that has just occurred. It seems then that the spacing effect is a third success for the rationality analysis. However, we have no formal model for the clustering that does occur in information retrievals. Thus, we can do more than make the prediction that after sufficient delay, human memory should show better performance for those items whose studies are widely distributed.

CUE STRENGTH

The preceding analysis has been concerned with analyzing the history factor that was the first term in Equation 2. Now we turn to calculating the remaining quantities, $p\ (i|\text{A})/p(i|\bar{\text{A}})$, which are the cue strengths. We assume that the way the system assesses these probabilities is by comparing the cue terms against the terms that occur in the structure. Thus, the system might compare the cue term "Tulving" against the memory term "ESP." Intuitively, the cue strengths should increase as the cue terms are more related to the terms in the memory trace. The formal definition of relatedness that I use is taken whole cloth out of the text on information retrieval by Salton & McGill (1983).

Basically, two terms are regarded as related to the degree that they appear in the same memory structures. Let t_{ik} be defined as 1 if term i occurs in memory structure k, and 0 otherwise. Then we can define the relatedness between terms i and j as follows:

$$r_{ij} = \frac{\sum_k t_{i,k} t_{j,k}}{\sum_k t_{i,k} + \sum_k t_{j,k} - \sum_k t_{i,k} t_{j,k}} \qquad (4)$$

where the sums are over all structures in memory. The basic intuition is that if i and j are highly related, one is likely to want a structure involving j if one sees i, or vice versa. However, it will take a fair bit of mathematics to relate this basic intuition to our Bayesian framework[2]. Let A be a structure containing e terms. We define the average relatedness between A and i as:

$$R[A,i] = (\sum_j r_{ij})/e \qquad (5)$$

where the sum is over the terms in structure A and e is the number of such terms. We can define the proportion association between A and i, or normalized relatedness, as

$$N[A,i] = R[A,i]/ (\sum_j R[A,j]) \qquad (6)$$

where the sum is over all possible terms. The final quantity we need to know is what the association is between structures other than A and i. It is given by the following formula:

$$N[\bar{A},i] = \sum_{X \neq A} N(X,i)/(M - 1) \qquad (7)$$

where M is the total number of structures.

These quantities figure in the calculation of the cue strengths, $P(i \mid A)/P(i \mid \bar{A})$. We first focus on calculating $P(i \mid A)$. The basic assumption is that the probability of a cue being present is a function of the normalized relatedness of that cue to

---

[2]The mathematics also strikes me as a bit arbitrary. However, I believe any reasonable mapping of the quantities r_{ij} onto $P(i \mid A)/P(i \mid \bar{A})$ will preserve the qualitative results.

larger structures—i.e., the N(A,i). However, there are complications. One complication is that we have to keep separate the cases where the cue is actually relevant and the cases where it is not. That is, some of the cues in the environment will be just "noise" and have no relationship to our current information-retrieval needs. We assume that, on average, the environment provides X relevant cues and Y irrelevant cues. With this in mind, we break up the calculation of $P(i \mid A)$ into three parts corresponding to the three ways that i might appear as a cue if A is relevant:

1. There is the possibility that i is a potential cue for A. However, this does not mean that it will occur as a cue because the potential cues might exceed the X slots for relevant cues. We assume that if there are X relevant cues and T target structures, then each structure gets on average X/T cues. The probability that i is one of these cues should be its proportion relatedness to A times the mean number of cues per structure. In other words, the probability in this case is:

$N[A,i] * (X/T)$

2. There is the possibility that i is a cue for some other target structure than A. The average probability of this happening should be a product of the mean number of cues per target, (X/T), the average proportion relatedness between a term i and structures other than A, $(N[\bar{A},i])$, and the number of structures i could be cueing, $(T - 1)$. So the average probability in this case is:

$(T-1) * N[\bar{A},i] * (X/T)$

3. The third possibility is that i is not a relevant cue for any structure but is just noise. The probability of this happening is a function of the ratio of noise cues to total number of cues. Thus, this probability is:

Y/m

where m is the total number of possible cues—the sum of all terms (as distinct from structures whose sum is M) in the data base. Combining 1., 2., and 3. we get:

$$P(i \mid A) = N[A,i]*(X/T) + (T-1)*N[\bar{A},i]*(X/T) + Y/m \qquad (8)$$

The calculation of $P(i \mid \bar{A})$ can be broken into two cases.

1. Cue i is one of the relevant cues. The probability of this being true is basically the product of the average relevance of cue i to structures other than A $(N[\bar{A},i])$ and the number of cues (X). Thus:
   $X * N[\bar{A},i]$

2. The cue is an irrelevant cue. In this case, as before, the probability is:
   Y/m

Combining 1. and 2. we get:

$$P(i \mid \bar{A})/ = N[A,i]*X + Y/m \qquad (9)$$

Finally, we can derive the formula for cue strength:

$$P(i \mid A) / P(i \mid \bar{A}) = 1 + (N[A,i] - N[\bar{A},i])/K \qquad (10)$$

$$\text{where } K = T(N[\bar{A},i] + Y/Xm)$$

A cue strength of greater than 1 increases the likelihood ratio of A, whereas a cue strength less than 1 decreases the likelihood ratio. Thus, the likelihood ratio of A will be increased just in case the relatedness of i and A is greater than average. In a typical data base like human memory, a cue will have above-average relatedness to a few structures and slightly below-average relatedness to most structures. The average relatedness should also be relatively close to zero.

This analysis of cue strength can be directly related to the priming literature if we make an identification between association norms and cue relatedness, r_{ij}. It predicts that words like *dog* will prime judgments of related words like *cat*. The r_{ij} values between such words will be high. Therefore, the N[A,i] values between one word, like *dog,* and memory structures involving another word, like the structure encoding the spelling of *cat,* will be high. Thus, access to these structures will be facilitated. The mathematics we have gone through should not be allowed to obscure the basic rationality of this prediction. The basic prediction is that information such as the spelling of *dog* is made more available in the presence of related words like *cat* because in fact the subject is more likely to need such information in these contexts.

This analysis also predicts inhibitory effects, something my own theory, ACT*, cannot do. Irrelevant cues will have slightly less than average N[A,i] values to the target structure and so lower the odds ratio that defines the structure's likelihood. That is, for instance, a prime like *lip* should make knowledge about *dog* less available because *lip* is seldom present when knowledge about dog is required.

Finally, this analysis can predict another startling result that ACT* failed to handle. This is the observation that one cannot seem to get second-order priming. DeGroot (1983—see also Balota & Lorch, 1986; Ratcliff & McKoon, 1987) used triplets of words like bull–cow–milk where there is a strong association between the first and second and between the second and third but not between the first and third. The first did not prime the third as would be predicted by a spreading activation model in which activation would spread from the first to the second and hence to the third. However, on the preceding analysis, the first and third terms would have low relatedness. This is in fact the rational thing to do: If milk is never processed in the presence of bull, one should not prime structures involving milk when bull appears.

Thus, we see that this rational approach predicts three additional properties of human memory—raising our a priori prediction rate to 6 out of 6. Again, to remind the reader, these predictions are being made on the assumption that probability correct and reaction times are monotonically related to the probability that a structure is needed. These need probabilities are the $p[A]$ from Equation 1 or the $p(A \mid H_A$ & $Q)$ from Equation 2.

FACT RETRIEVAL AND FAN EFFECTS

Much of my experimental life has been spent studying how subjects retrieve sentences that they have learned (Anderson, 1983). My favorite manipulation has been one where I have varied the number of facts that a particular concept appeared in. The present relatedness analysis can be extended to apply to these experiments.

To show how the fan effect falls out of this relatedness analysis, I will work with a particularly idealized situation where we assume that each term in the data base has a fan of f (that is, it occurs in f structures), each structure has e elements in it, and no two terms co-occur in more than one structure. These uniformity assumptions facilitate mathematical analysis, but the same points come through in more complicated ways if we assume that the memory is not so uniformly organized with respect to fan.

The relatedness between any term and itself is 1. The relatedness between a term and another term that occurs in the same proposition is $1/(2f-1)$. With all other terms, the relatedness is 0. Thus, we have:

$r_{ij} = 1$ if $i = j$
$\quad = 1/(2f-1)$ if i and j occur in the same structure
$\quad = 0$ otherwise.

The average relatedness between a structure and a term that appears in it is $(2f + e - 2)/e(2f-1)$. The average relatedness between a structure and a term that occurs with one of the structure's terms in another structure is $1/e(2f-1)$. Thus,

$R[A,i] = (2f + e - 2)/e(2f - 1)$ if i occurs in A
$\quad = 1/e(2f - 1)$ if i and some term j in A co-occur in another structure
$\quad = 0$ otherwise

We can now calculate the quantities $N[A,i]$ and $N[\bar{A},i]$, which go directly into calculating the ratio $P(i/A)/P(i/\bar{A})$:

$$N[A,i] = \frac{2f + e - 2}{e[e(f + 1) - 1]}$$

$$N[\bar{A},i] = \frac{(f - 1)[f(e + 1) + e - 2]}{[M - 1)e[e(f + 1) - 1]}$$

where M is the number of structures in the data base. $N[A,i]$ varies from 1 when $f = 1$ to 0 when $f = \infty$. $N[\bar{A},i]$ varies from 0 when $f = 1$ to $1/M-1$ when $f = \infty$. Thus, the difference between the two decreases with increasing fan and so the ratio $P(i \mid A)/P(i \mid \bar{A})$ decreases.

Increasing the fan has another effect besides lowering the cue strength of a particular structure. It also increases the number of structures to which the cue has non-zero relatedness. This can have an effect in two situations. First, when the subjects are in a situation where they have to exhaust all related structures, they should be slowed down. This is the situation when a subject must reject a foil in a typical fact-retrieval experiment. Thus, we predict the fan effect for foils, although on a different basis than the fan effect for targets.

Also, subjects are sometimes in situations where they can respond on the basis of any of a number of structures. In this case, the higher the fan, the more relevant structures there are, and the faster they should respond. This is basically a base rate effect in a Bayesian framework. This is the situation in the experiments (Reder & Ross, 1983; Reder & Wible, 1984) that have allowed subjects to respond if they studied anything thematically consistent with the query. Here, a "negative fan effect" is found. The more things the subjects have studied that are consistent with the theme, the faster they are to respond.

There are many interactions involving the fan effect. However, to address interactions rather than main effects, I would have to define a mapping from the likelihood ratio to the dependent measures of reaction time and probability. This mapping is necessary so we can determine which things are going to be additive and which are not. As already announced, this is not the task of the present chapter, so I have to be content with picking up three more predictive successes from this a priori analysis to get my total up to 9 out of 9.

ENCODING SPECIFICITY

It is only reasonable that my tenth predictive success should be the encoding specificity phenomenon (Tulving & Thomson, 1973), which Tulving used to haunt my previous theories. Consider the basic demonstration: Subjects study "train–black" and are later asked to recognize black in the presence of train (the best condition), alone (the next best condition), or in the presence of white (the worst condition). This result follows directly from the present analysis of cue strength. If a cue like "train" is part of the target trace, it will have greater similarity ($N[A,i]$) to the target trace and so will increase the likelihood ratio for the target trace. If there was nothing studied with the target, the interitem similarities r_{ij} will not be affected and so the cue will have a base similarity to the trace. If a different cue was present at study, the similarity between the test cue and trace will be reduced due to the normalization in the calculation of N[A,i] (Equation 6) and so the likelihood ratio for the target trace will be lowered.

RELATIONSHIP TO GILLUND & SHIFFRIN

It is worth commenting on the similarity between this proposal for cue combination and the SAM (Gilland & Shiffrin, 1984) model. Both models share the following components:

1. The idea that the cues combine multiplicatively (Equation 2 in this chapter).
2. The idea that the critical intervening variable is strength of associations between items and memory structures (Equation 5 in this chapter).
3. The idea that strength of associations should be normalized against competing associations (Equation 6 in this chapter).

The actual mathematics by which the two theories achieve their predictions are quite different, but it is hard to appreciate the significance of these differences. There is one fundamental conceptual difference, however. In the SAM model, the associations between the terms and the structures (N[A,i] in this chapter) are conceived of as reflecting the amount of time which A and i were together in the buffer. In the present model, they are based on the measure of co-occurrence relatedness, r_{ij}, taken from the information retrieval literature.

In typical information-retrieval systems, the concept of a time in the buffer together has no meaning and so one could not derive a measure like that in SAM. However, I suspect that even if it were available, it would be judged inadequate. One cannot count on having all relevant item-structure pairs co-occur together in the past to yield stable estimates of the probability of a structure given the item as a cue (or vice versa). Even in the scheme proposed here, it is something of a leap of faith to go from interitem relatedness to such a probability, but at least one is aggregating over more experiences and not insisting that the item and the structure be part of the same experience. Thus, rationally the model presented here is to be preferred.

CONCLUSIONS

At least ten of the basic phenomena that memory researchers have labored long to document can be predicted by the principle of rationality. I submit that this is a rather startling outcome. However, it should be acknowledged that the principle of rationality cannot apply to memory (or any other human domain, including economic behavior) without a framing of what the problem is. Conceivably, one might frame the problem of human memory differently and come up with different predictions. I would be less than honest if I did not admit that my knowledge of human memory influenced my framing of the basic memory problem. However, I think the framing is quite reasonable.

One of the reasons why I have stuck with ordinal predictions and refrained from mapping this analysis onto interval predictions about time and probability is that I cannot see an equally plausible way of further framing the problem to make that mapping. Thus, if we are going to take this rational analysis of memory beyond these ten first-order predictions, the major agenda item is study of the task facing human memory—that is, the task that the system has evolved to handle. Perhaps we can gather evidence for some way of further specifying the memory task.

Although the present results are preliminary, they do support the hypothesis that we can predict the phenomena of human memory from the assumption that it operates rationally. What are we to make of this result if it continues to hold up under further analyses? One might take the attitude that the experimental study of memory is unnecessary because its behavior can be deduced from a priori premises. I do not think this is the correct conclusion. It ignores the fact that it is not certain a priori how to frame the problem faced by human memory so that we can propose a rational solution. The experimental research provides guidance here. Moreover, the rationality hypothesis, even with a framing, is just a scientific claim and still requires experimental test. However, I do think that the hypothesis throws an amazing light on the years of experimental research into human memory. It seems that these experiments may have been telling us that human memory was designed rationally.

ACKNOWLEDGMENTS

I should acknowledge Lynne Reder's invaluable contribution to this paper. If she had not got me reading and thinking about the work in information retrieval, I would never have discovered the framing of the memory problem that I have presented. Lynne also went through the manuscript with me to help assure that I got it right. I am also grateful for the comments of Bob Bjork, Gus Craik, and Roger Ratcliff. This research was supported by grant BNS 8705811 from the National Science Foundation.

REFERENCES

Anderson, J. R. (1978). Arguments concerning representations for mental imagery. *Psychological Review, 85*, 249–277.

Anderson, J. R. (1983). *The architecture of cognition.* Cambridge, MA: Harvard University Press.

Balota, D., & Lorch, R. (1986). Depth of automatic spreading activation: Mediated priming effects in pronunciation but not in lexical decision. *Journal of Experimental Psychology: Learning, Memory, & Cognition, 12,* 336–345.

Bookstein, A., & Swanson, D. R. (1974). Probabilistic models for automatic indexing. *Journal of the ASIS, 25,* 312–318.

Bookstein, A., & Swanson, D. R. (1975). A decision theoretic foundation for indexing. *Journal of the ASIS, 26,* 45–50.

Burrell, Q. L. (1980). A simple stochastic model for library loans. *Journal of Documentation, 36,* 115–132.

Burrell, Q. L., & Cane, V. R. (1982). The analysis of library data. *Journal of the Royal Statistical Society, Series A*(145), 439–471.

Crowder, R. G. (1982). *The psychology of reading: An introduction.* New York: Oxford University Press.

DeGroot, A. (1983). The range of automatic spreading activation in word priming. *Journal of Verbal Learning and Verbal Behavior, 22,* 417–436.

Gillund, G., & Shiffrin, R. M. (1984). A retrieval model for both recognition and recall. *Psychological Review, 91,* 1–67.

Kosslyn, S. M. (1980). *Image and mind.* Cambridge, MA: Harvard University Press.

Newell, A., & Rosenbloom, P. (1981). Mechanisms of skill acquisition and the law of practice. In J. R. Anderson (Ed.), *Cognitive skills and their acquisition* (pp. 1–55). Hillsdale, NJ: Lawrence Erlbaum Associates.

Pylyshyn, Z. W. (1981). The imagery debate: Analogue media versus tacit knowledge. *Psychological Review, 88,* 1–24.

Ratcliff, R. & McKoon, G. 1988). A retrieval theory of priming in memory. Psychological Review, *95,* 385–408.

Reder, L. M., & Ross, B. H. (1983). Integrated knowledge in different tasks: The role of retrieval strategy on fan effects. *Journal of Experimental Psychology: Learning, memory, and cognition, 9,* 55–72.

Reder, L. M., & Wible, C. (1984). Strategy use in question answering: Memory strength and task constraints on fan effects. *Memory & Cognition, 12,* 411–419.

Salton, G., & McGill, M. J. (1983). *Introduction to modern information retrieval.* New York: McGraw-Hill.

Stritter, E. (1977). *File migration.* Unpublished doctoral dissertation, Stanford University.

Townsend, J. T. (1974). Issues and models concerning the processing of a finite number of inputs. In B. H. Kantowitz (Ed.), *Human information processing: Tutorials in performance and cognition* (pp. 133–185). Hillsdale, NJ: Lawrence Erlbaum Associates.

Tulving, E. (1983). *Elements of episodic memory.* London: Oxford University Press.

Tulving, E., & Thomson, D. M. (1973). Encoding specificity and retrieval processes in episodic memory. *Psychological Review, 80,* 352–373.

Wickelgren, W. A. (1973). The long and short of memory. *Psychological Bulletin, 80,* 425–438.

12 Lasting Representations and Temporary Processes

Donald Broadbent
University of Oxford

THE TECHNIQUE OF INTERFERENCE

Of the many possible ways of classifying memory, this chapter uses only one; the effects on memory of interference from other events that happen to the person. We can find types of memory that are impaired by event A but not by B, whereas a different class of memories may show impairment by B but not by A. Consequently, there must be something different about the changes in the nervous system that hold the representations of each type. The two types need not, of course, be physically distinct, in location in the brain or in the type of physiological coding used. They are, however, computationally distinct; they do different things. As we shall see, a classification based on this approach may well parallel classifications of other types, and does not exclude them.

In traditional experiments on interference, A and B might correspond to different types of material. A task in which an event A occurs may affect memory for earlier material that also includes A, but not for memory that only includes B. Nowadays, I expect, many of us, influenced by Endel Tulving, would say that A and B are cues that have each formed a separate and specific code with the items that are to be remembered. The intervening task damages one kind of memory, and not the other, because it affects only retrieval of the code that is elicited through cue A. The fact that recall and recognition show different effects of interference becomes very reasonable. It does not now disturb us, although it used to be a matter of great concern.

By using interference in this way, we could, if we wished to do so, classify memories as those that depend on A and those that depend on B. There would be little interest in doing so, when A and B are cues idiosyncratic to one experiment.

It is more interesting to examine cases in which the interfering task does not involve the same content as the original task. Such cases often arise in temporary or working memory, where it is notorious that the same item need not recur in the memory material and in the interfering task. What does matter, however, is the modality of input, or that of output, or sometimes simply the amount of general processing that happens in the intervening task. Many of the phenomena have been reviewed by Baddeley (1986).

REPRESENTATION AND PROCESS

Let us start with some very familiar results, on the modality of input. The difference between written and spoken input shows up clearly in interference experiments; free recall of spoken words may be unimpaired by visual tasks that are performed between learning and recall, whereas visual memory is damaged by such tasks (Martin & Jones, 1979). On the other hand, an auditory interfering task will impair memory for spoken words more than it will for visual material. Even an irrelevant spoken input, requiring no action, will show more interference with memory for spoken words than it does for visual ones (Conrad & Hull, 1968; Crowder & Morton, 1969). These results favor a distinction between two kinds of initial encoding of the memory material; spoken inputs disturb something that written ones do not.

Considering the input alone, however, is not enough. When you read some written words, you may say them to yourself; or you may not. If it is made actively difficult for you to talk to yourself, perhaps because you are asked to repeat a nonsense phrase over and over, you will recall less well. Even holding a pencil in your mouth may have this effect (Barlow, 1928). Nevertheless, there will be some memory even for these unarticulated items. There are therefore two kinds of representation that can arise from written material, the articulated and the nonarticulated. We know the two kinds of representation are different, because most conveniently there is an effect on recall from the length of words that have been articulated, but not of those that have not. So, if you stop a person articulating while reading written words, memory for short words suffers more than memory for long ones (Baddeley, Thomson, & Buchanan, 1975).

At this point, let me introduce a key distinction between brief events located at some particular moment in time, and lasting states of the system. The latter may not be permanent, but at least they persist for a matter of seconds or minutes. In temporary memory, if I say the digits 297, you may continue to read a longish passage of written prose and still be able to recall the spoken digits on demand. There is some state of the person that endures throughout the interval, and that is different from the state of any person who is not holding such information. On the other hand, the arrival of the sounds at your ears, or your response, are each events happening at one point in time. The distinction matters to me, because the event of recalling a memory may have effects different from that of simply retaining it.

I call the enduring states *representations,* and the relatively brief transitions *processes;* those words are used in other senses by other people, but perhaps that is unimportant as long as we are clear on what is meant here. The borderline between representation and process is also hazy, rather like the decision whether a man has a beard or not when he looks a bit bristly. That need not stop us using the distinction for practical purposes; the key point I want to discuss is that a representation may exist for a period, then be transformed (by some process) into a corresponding representation of a different type, and then persist for a further period in the new form.

In these terms, must the process of articulation take place when the original input arrives; is it merely what happens in the original encoding? Some of the recent work of Baddeley and his colleagues (Baddeley, Lewis, & Vallar, 1984) shows that articulation can happen at a later time. For words that are spoken rather than written, the word-length effect continues to be present even if one suppresses articulation during the arrival of the input. This was for a time a puzzle, because there is some evidence that the special form of representation for speech inputs does not seem to be affected by word length (Watkins, 1972; Watkins & Watkins, 1973). However, it now appears that the word-length effect can indeed be abolished by articulatory suppression, provided that one stops the person articulating, not merely while listening; but also for the whole time until recall has occurred (Baddeley, et al., 1984). For written items, the process of articulation must occur soon after input; but for spoken items, it can be delayed until after presentation. To summarize, there is some special kind of representation for spoken inputs, that endures longer than any corresponding one for written inputs. From either of them, the process of articulation can create a third kind. It is particularly neat that the difference between spoken and written shows more clearly if the person is occupied with something else during the event of presentation, so that the visual input cannot be transformed into another form (Routh, 1976).

The suppression of articulation is certainly, therefore, interfering with a process, because the time at which it happens is important. Suppose, however, that written material is allowed to arrive freely and thus to be transferred into the articulated form; does it then become immune to any later irrelevant articulation? No; the suppression does not have to be imposed at a particular time to be effective. It can be delayed until after the visual input has all arrived, and be confined to the retention interval. (Gillie & Broadbent, in preparation) Thus, in this case, irrelevant speech is disturbing a lasting representation, whereas in the Baddeley, Lewis, and Vallar case, it is preventing a temporary event of recoding the input; both effects are possible.

The whole classification of representations used thus far is the same as that put forward earlier by Broadbent (1984), under the name of the "Maltese

Cross''. The notion was that there are broadly four main classes of representation, those interfered with by sensory events, those disturbed by output events, those suffering no interference from fresh events as such but only from changes in the mapping of associations; and a last, somewhat debatable, class that is disturbed by fresh events regardless of their sensory or motor character. An item in any one class of representation can be shifted to one of the others by optional processes; hence the ''cross'', because the four classes are linked by processes that can access any of them, and deliver the information to any other.

In this chapter, I extend this classification in two ways. The first point considers more closely the nature of the output or motor store. Some of the results we have considered already show that it is not simply an alternative form of initial encoding, because it can be created, and interfered with, at a time after presentation. One can go further; because it is disturbed by output, it is more plausibly described as a buffer containing output motor commands, rather than as a store closely similar to an input. But these motor commands need not issue in overt response; the first point I emphasize is that information can be held in one output buffer for a time, and then be brought back for output by some other mode.

The second point I make examines the question of changes in the processing system itself. An inexperienced person may transfer information between representations in a different way from an experienced one. This is an effect of experience, but not one that itself creates a memory of a past event. As we shall see, such procedural knowledge appears under rather different conditions from the creation of representations in the other four categories.

NEW LIGHT ON THE OUTPUT BUFFER

In an earlier section, the difference between articulated and nonarticulated material was used to illustrate the fact that memory might become recoded after input. Once recoded, some of it seems to be kept in some output mechanism. It thus suffers interference when the mechanism is employed for another purpose. That interpretation is supported by a result of FitzGerald and Broadbent 1985a), who required subjects to prefix recall of one memory list by output of another list. Unsurprisingly, this prefix activity damaged recall of the main list, as has been found many times previously. (Conrad, 1958; Baddeley & Hull, 1979). FitzGerald and Broadbent confirmed that the prefix was still damaging even if it was always the same, and if the subjects had experienced a number of trials. Thus, perfectly predictable outputs seem to reduce the chances of retention for some of the main-list items. This again is consistent with the notion that some of the main-list material is held in an *output buffer* and lost by irrelevant output.

The same notion can explain a finding that appears when two simultaneous lists are presented and then later recalled successively. From the view put forward already, we would expect the output of the first list to disrupt retention for any items of the second list that were held in the output system. Indeed, there is an effect of recall order; the second list recalled does show lower performance than the first. Now if the person is told to give special priority to one of the lists, the effect of recall order is larger for that list. (Bryden, 1971; FitzGerald & Broadbent, 1985b; FitzGerald, Tattersall, & Broadbent, in press; Martin, 1978, 1980). This implies that the proportion of items in the output buffer is greater for the high-priority list than it is for the low-priority list. That in turn is reasonable if we are dealing with an intelligent memory system, which uses its options of recoding and transfer from one representation to another in order to hold as many of the high-priority items as possible. Such a system would reasonably put more of the high-priority list into the output buffer, and gamble that the experimenter will ask for their recall first rather than second. In the same way, the high-priority list shows a larger effect of irrelevant articulation; people articulate the list that they are told is important, and let the other one take its chance.

However, there was another result of FitzGerald and Broadbent (1985a) that was much more puzzling. The effect of output interference was just as great when there was articulatory suppression as when articulation was allowed. This will *not* fit the idea that articulation transfers a proportion of items into an output buffer; from which they are ejected by output of any other material. If that were true, then suppressing articulation ought to reduce output interference. The best explanation FitzGerald and Broadbent could suggest was that there is a generalized output buffer, separate from the articulatory code, and that this retains items as well as internal speech does.

Light has now dawned: FitzGerald and Broadbent used written responses in their experiment. What their results show, therefore, is that *writing* a prefix list has just as big an effect on *writing* the main list, whether or not the person has been allowed to articulate. If we take the Maltese Cross seriously however, the articulatory buffer is likely to be a set of commands to the muscles of the throat and mouth, not to those of the hand and arm. Writing and talking would, in that case, be subsets of the output store, just as visual and speech codes are subsets of the input store. Twenty years ago, Margrain (1967) showed that output by writing and by speaking had different effects on later recall; indeed, FitzGerald and Broadbent quoted those results. Perhaps, therefore, information held by internal speech is different to, and separate from, that held by internal writing. If so, FitzGerald and Broadbent used the wrong way of recording the output from their subjects.

Tattersall (1987) has now confirmed that this analysis is correct. He carried out essentially the same experiment as FitzGerald and Broadbent, but with spoken responses rather than written. The results are then quite different; subjects whose articulation is suppressed *do* show a smaller amount of output interference. Even for written responses, stopping articulation means that people can remember less, because it removes one of the possible codes in which material can be held. But it does not remove the code that is disturbed by writing some other material. Internal speech is not the same kind of code as internal writing is.

Tattersall (1987) has another and particularly striking result that makes the same point. Suppose a subject sees a list of letters and a list of digits, and knows in advance that one list is to be recalled before the other, and also that one list is to be written and one spoken. Knowing before presentation which list is to be written, but not the order, is less disturbing than knowing the order, but not the mode of response. To encode the input as a string of motor commands while it is arriving allows it to be held while the other list is being processed. If the code of output is not known, however, then it is dangerous to use internal speech to retain, say, the letters; because the digits may need to be spoken and so to disrupt the letters.

This view, in turn, implies the importance of the encoding at the time of arrival of visual information that is to be remembered. As far as possible, the person must encode it at that time, already in a form that is suitable for response; because any other coding will waste some of the available means of retention. Consistent with that view is the fact that successive presentation of two lists gives slightly different results from simultaneous presentation. As we saw earlier, there is a larger effect of output interference for the higher priority list of two arriving simultaneously. If the lists are successive, output interference becomes independent of the priority of the lists (FitzGerald, Tattersall, & Broadbent, 1988). What does matter is their order of arrival; the more recent list to arrive is the one that shows a larger output interference effect.

The intelligent memory system, that we found it necessary earlier to postulate, takes its decisions during the arrival of the information; only if it has two competing sets of material coming in at once does it share the output system between the lists. Otherwise, it codes each list in turn into the output mode; and thus the most recent list shows the larger output interference. If there is a good deal of information in play at the time of presentation, the choice of a code at the time of presentation has to be selective. Hence, there is no sharp difference between the areas of psychology traditionally called "memory" and those traditionally called "attention".

AN OVERVIEW OF THE SYSTEM

These various experiments on the nature of output coding emphasize some important points about the whole system:

1. They show the recycling of information from one representation to another. This is implied by the separation of internal speech and internal writing, combined with our older knowledge that internal speech does assist recall by

writing. Work on the various forms of original encoding does not need such an assumption.

2. Thus, representations can be transferred from one temporary store to another while preserving their identity. Such a system allows a "look-ahead" form of computation on a model of the world, and such a computation can result in successful construction of novel representations that have not occurred in experience. If we say to ourselves that John is taller than David, and see that David is taller than Mary, the two representations can be combined to produce the spoken output that John is taller than Mary.

3. The use of representations in this way goes further than the minimum needed to explain traditional memory experiments, and it means that we must distinguish two senses of "representation". Although a person who knows the response "1492" to the input "Christopher Columbus" has a representation that is denied to those without that knowledge, it could represent only a procedure of saying those digits in the presence of that input. A rather different kind of "declarative" representation is needed to allow replies to questions never previously encountered, such as "Is the date of Columbus before or after the death of Richard III of England?" To perform such a task requires a representation that can be used as a manipulable counter in a series of internal operations; not simply one single operation.

4. These results also show that memory for an event depends on processes that occur at input; as indeed we have known from much earlier work (Craik & Lockhart, 1972; Tulving & Thomson, 1973). The present results make it particularly clear that the action taken at the time of learning depends on the conditions then current; if there are two lists, encode in one way, but if one list, encode in a different way. The person is showing the operation of condition-action rules in the fashion shown by production system models of cognition (Anderson, 1983). The transient processes, as well as the lasting representations, are important for successful recall. The memorizer operates in a way that suggests the consultation of a "look-up table" that prescribes the action to be taken in each of a variety of situations.

SIGNS AND SYMBOLS

We thus need to distinguish between manipulable representations and those that are not manipulable. The manipulable were often called "symbols" in the past, and the nonmanipulable "signs" (see e.g., Morris, 1946, and Yerkes, 1943). Recently, the terms have appeared again, in the writings of Rasmussen (1983, 1987). The distinction has been forced on his attention by the problems of human error in power stations, process control, and similar complex situations. The controllers of such systems may make some errors that are simply due to lack of motor skill, but those are of decreasing importance as technology advances. More important are errors of two other kinds, at the levels of rule-based and of knowledge-based performance. Since Three Mile Island, the operators of US nuclear power plants have to have higher academic qualifications. This makes sure that they have a background of symbolic knowledge from which they may work out in their heads a viable solution to problems that are new and never previously encountered. Because we cannot specify what may go wrong in a power station, such knowledge is vital, and the operators cannot be left merely to apply rules worked out in advance. On the other hand, symbolic knowledge is not enough; the operator faced with an emergency must categorize it correctly, and thus must respond to the signs that distinguish one kind of emergency from another. Without the correct rule-based operations, the symbolic knowledge will not be manipulated correctly. In the laboratory, an example is provided by Lewis and Anderson (1985), studying the solution of geometric problems such as the congruity of triangles. Such problems obviously depend on symbolic, manipulable knowledge of geometry. The solver needs to decide, however, whether the problem can be solved using two sides and the included angle; or two angles and the included side. If the problem is miscategorized, the symbolic knowledge will be useless; for the same reason, many academic physicists might be quite dangerous in control of a nuclear power station. Possession of declarative or symbolic knowledge is important; so also is the procedural knowledge of the signs that indicate the correct operations to perform on symbolic knowledge.

The interesting question then arises, whether rule-based knowledge starts from symbolic knowledge that is gradually "compiled" into standard routine and invariant procedures. Alternatively, can one learn procedures and their corresponding signs without symbolic knowledge, only later constructing an edifice of manipulable information on the basis of one's own procedures? Anderson (e.g., 1983) has considered both possibilities, but Lewis and Anderson concluded that declarative knowledge was prior. Their reason was that learning of geometric problem solving is more effective if people report explicit symbolic hypotheses guiding their solutions. In the rest of this chapter, I argue in favor of the opposite view, that one can acquire procedures before the corresponding symbolic knowledge. In some cases, it may be that symbolic knowledge *never* develops.

The main technique we discuss is again that of interference. Symbolic representations move around between the various forms of working memory; but each of those forms is limited in some way. The articulatory output store can cope only with an amount that could be spoken in a fixed time (Vallar & Baddeley, 1982), the speech input store can cope only with speech that is not followed by other speech (Crowder & Morton, 1969), and whatever the mechanism of "abstract working memory", it appears to hold a fixed number of items (Broadbent, 1981). The information held in symbolic representations must therefore be selective. It cannot represent everything that has been experienced, only a part. If we apply some other task while the procedures of learning or performance are taking place, then we may impair the operation of symbolic knowledge without necessarily damaging procedural knowledge.

VERBAL REPORT AND SECONDARY TASKS

Let us start with some studies by Porter (1986) on the learning and performance of a computer game. The game is complex, requiring control of the movements of a whale, which moves about on a screen containing a number of icebergs. The player has to consider a number of input variables, in order to pursue two main goals. On the one hand, from time to time kayaks steered by Eskimos appear and move towards the whale; if they hit it, the whale suffers harpooning and this is to be avoided. The answer is to go around the far side of an iceberg, so that the kayak proceeding straight towards the whale will run into the obstacle and be sunk. The other purpose held by the whale is to eat, and this involves moving into the same spot as an area of plankton that moves semirandomly about the screen. Unlike most laboratory tasks, this one is actively enjoyed by the subjects.

Porter measured performance with and without various secondary tasks such as articulatory suppression, the holding in memory of various numbers of items, and the random generation of sequences of digits. Each of these had serious effects on the efficiency with which the whale ate plankton; but the effects on the dodging of kayaks were relatively small and often absent altogether. This seems odd, because the process of dodging kayaks is fairly complex and was rated as such by the subjects. The eating of plankton, on the other hand, is simple and obvious, apparently a matter only of visuo-motor skill.

However, there are other very suggestive differences between dodging and eating. From the introspections of people who play the game, one can formulate various verbal propositions about the way to succeed; and one can determine how many subjects agree with each of these propositions. In the case of eating plankton, people are likely to believe that it is useful to stay in the part of the screen close to the plankton, to turn towards the plankton if one is not already in contact with it, and so on. The relative merits of these verbal statements can be checked objectively, by running correlations between the way the whale moves and success at eating plankton. The principles that are most important by this objective criterion are also the ones that subjects are most likely to believe; verbally expressible knowledge about the plankton task is fairly accurate. Correspondingly, an interfering verbal task impairs performance at eating plankton.

Dodging kayaks is another matter. Subjects are likely to believe that one should turn away from kayaks; or that one should not bump into icebergs (which destroys them and thus reduces the number of hiding places). Objectively, the second of these principles is unrelated to success; and the first is actually the wrong way around. Declarative knowledge about the kayak-dodging is therefore poor. Yet the subjects have learned something from their practice at the task. They do better on the kayaks at the end of the session than at the beginning. They have therefore learned what to do, but cannot (or at least do not) say what it is.

Correspondingly, it does their kayak-dodging little harm to interfere with their verbal working memory. So, the parts of the task for which there is good verbal knowledge are also those that suffer from an interfering verbal task. There are other examples of the same effect. For instance, Berry (1984; Berry & Broadbent, 1988) has developed two tasks that are closely similar to each other in performance but differ in the degree to which people have verbal knowledge about the system they are controlling. Hayes (1987; Hayes & Broadbent, 1988) took these same two tasks and found that performance on the version with good verbal knowledge was slowed down by simultaneous performance of a verbal randomising task whereas the version without verbal knowledge was not.

Again, Reber (1967) asked people to learn sequences of letters, which, without the subjects' attention being drawn to it, in fact obeyed the rules of an artificial "grammar". Experienced subjects could subsequently discriminate fresh examples that obeyed the rules from examples that did not; but did not verbalize the correct rules. Reber (1976) contrasted this indirect or "implicit" learning situation with one in which people were asked explicitly to learn rules, and found that explicit learning was actually inferior to implicit learning. Hayes (1987, in press) repeated the contrast of explicit and implicit instructions, but added a simultaneous verbal task. Learning was impaired for the explicit instructions, but not for the implicit ones. We have, therefore, three cases in which tasks with a dissociation between verbal knowledge and performance are also tasks that are only slightly impaired by a simultaneous verbal task.

SALIENT AND NONSALIENT TASKS

The last of the three examples raises the question of *why* some tasks give rise to verbal, explicit, or "conscious" knowledge about one's own performance, whereas other tasks do not. It would be trivial if all verbal tasks showed interference from articulatory suppression whereas all nonverbal ones did not. In fact, for each of the three examples, the overt inputs and outputs were both verbal or nonverbal to the same degree. The differences lay in other factors.

Reber's two tasks both involved letter strings, and the overt responses were the same in both cases; the difference lay in the instructions. Yet Hayes found one of them vulnerable to a secondary task and the other was not. Incidentally, it has been suggested by Dulany, Carlson, & Dewey (1984) that the performance of Reber's implicit group was nevertheless due to verbally expressible rules rather than to some form of knowledge that is inaccessible to speech. Their argument was that behavior based on the imperfect hypotheses reported by the subjects would in fact have given rise to above-chance performance. The results of Hayes appear to damage that argument quite severely. If both tasks were performed by consulting verbal rules, it is odd that only one is impaired by a simultaneous verbal task. We appear to need some other factor in the performance of the implicit group.

Reber himself argued that a key feature of implicit learning lies in the "salience" of the key features of the task. Thus (Reber, Kassin, Lewis, & Cantor, 1980), explicit instructions are positively helpful to subjects who receive letter strings in groups, so arranged that examples illustrating the same rules are adjacent. The advantage for implicit learning depends on the examples being mixed up unsystematically. If the subject were trying to learn by adopting an explicit hypothesis and then testing it observationally, the grouped examples would be more likely to give rise to the correct hypothesis.

Let us define "salience" more generally. The learning of any task may be performed *either* by unselective learning of many aspects of the task, *or* alternatively by selective examination of some small subset of the events in the task. "Salience" of the crucial features of a task will be increased by any factor that will favor selective encoding of the crucial features rather than of incorrect and irrelevant features. Reber's grouped examples would be salient because they favored a selective encoding of the input, in which emphasis would lie on those features of the examples that were indeed key features. In the ungrouped case, however, any selective encoding would be unlikely to pick the crucial features; correspondingly, the verbal hypotheses reported by the subjects were not the ones designed into the material by the experimenter.

The same principle of salience explains the other pairs of tasks. Porter's plankton and kayak tasks both involved spatial inputs and finger-press responses, and neither of them required the verbal system overtly. The two tasks differed however; the plankton task had only few features, and a selective verbal encoding would be likely to pick the correct ones. The kayak task had many different aspects and characteristics, so that selective encoding might well pick the wrong features to encode.

Berry's two tasks, that Hayes later showed to be differentially vulnerable to a secondary task, both involved verbal inputs and outputs. They were, in fact, simulations of a personal interaction, in which the human subject was asked to bring a computer-simulated person to a particular degree of intimacy. This was done by the human picking an adjective describing a degree of intimacy, to indicate their own behavior. This adjective was fed into the machine, which then responded with another adjective. The human made a further choice, and so on for a number of trials. For tasks of this general type, it was repeatedly found by Berry and Broadbent (1984) that people might show good performance at securing a desired behavior from the computer, with little ability to answer questions about the rules governing the interaction. In such a task there are, of course, many possible hypotheses and potential key factors in the situation, any of which might be chosen by a selective encoding of what is present.

Berry (1984; Berry & Broadbent, 1988) managed to produce a version of the task that did show good verbalizable understanding of the situation; she did it by programming the computer-person to respond always two steps of intimacy below the level that the human subject had chosen. This relationship is obvious, likely to be chosen by any selective encoding, and correspondingly, the subjects who had learned to perform it were able to answer successfully questions about the interaction. If a relationship of the same simplicity were used, but with the computer-person basing its response on the last-but-one behavior of the human subject, then question-answering was poor. Again, any system attempting to encode a selected part of the situation would be unlikely to pick that particular part. These two tasks, the salient and the nonsalient, are the ones that Hayes used to show differential effects of secondary tasks.

A number of other tasks in the literature confirm the principle that salient tasks will show an association of verbal knowledge and performance, whereas nonsalient ones do not; even though they have not been used with secondary tasks. (Berry & Broadbent, 1987; Broadbent, Fitzgerald, & Broadbent, 1986).

QUANTITY OF INFORMATION

One way in which selection of key variables can be made more difficult is sheer increase in the amount of irrelevant information. Hayes (1987; Hayes & Broadbent, in preparation) used a task in which the subject saw information about a series of people. The task was to learn, from this information, which of three cities was the home of each person. Each of the people in the series was described by a set of sentences, and only one of these sentences was unique to that person (and thus indicated the city). The task was, in fact, very similar to the classic concept formation task using one crucial stimulus dimension (Hull, 1920), except that the response was three-choice rather than being simply a binary Yes–No choice.

In such a task, one can measure level of performance, and also verbal knowledge about the task. Hayes used several measures of verbal knowledge, including the number of times that a subject recognized a sentence as unique and also could identify verbally the city that it indicated. This sounds just like the task itself, but in fact it isn't, because in the test of verbal knowledge the sentence is presented on its own, rather than in the company of other sentences. Might this give rise to a context effect dependent on encoding specificity? No, because Hayes found that if the other sentences gave absolutely no information about the correct answer, the test of verbal knowledge was not significantly different from actual performance. But, it was also possible to arrange that the non-unique sentences did give some information of relevance for performance. If there were three such sentences, and if each occurred equally often with each of the three cities, nevertheless the particular combination of "irrelevant" sentences might be unique to the correct answer. When that is done, performance in the task is significantly better than verbal knowledge would predict.

There are two key features to this result. First, by its nature, it cannot happen if there are only two sentences attached to each problem. In Hayes' data, it happens when there are four, one of which is unique, and the others form a unique combination. With this quantity of relevant and irrelevant information, a selective encoding of the input has a low probability of picking the unique sentence and thus of giving rise to a successful verbal hypothesis. When only two sentences appear on each display, there is a good chance that selective encoding will pick the correct feature of the display; the task is automatically salient rather than nonsalient.

When there is much information presented in the task, in other words, the person establishes a procedure of launching the correct action in the presence of a pattern of input conditions; while still not possessing the manipulable representation that would produce correct question-answering.

The second key feature of Hayes' results bears on the question raised by Lewis and Anderson (1985). Their evidence was that successful learning of procedures was associated with explicit verbal knowledge. This favored the notion that procedures result from the compiling of earlier declarative knowledge into a less explicit form. In Hayes' results, however, the state of verbal knowledge was tested at two stages of practice: when performance was at the level of two-thirds correct decisions (with a chance level of one third), and when 100% correct had been reached. Performance only exceeded verbal knowledge at the earlier stage of learning. If the same subjects, or fresh groups, reached 100% correct performance, then the differences between performance and verbal knowledge tended to disappear. When performance is perfect, then people have the declarative knowledge as well. In Hayes' situation, one can develop the successful procedures before the verbally expressible knowledge, and then apparently acquire the latter by analysis of one's own performance.

Why, then, did Lewis and Anderson obtain the contrary result? A plausible possibility is because they used geometrical problems in which there were only two alternative strategies that might be successful. The task of the subjects was to learn the appropriate strategy to apply, given the information in the problem. With two alternatives, there is a good chance that selective encoding will pick the correct variables; the task of Lewis and Anderson may well have been a salient one.

CONCLUSIONS

From these results, the following points may be made about the classification of memory systems.

1. There are several broad types of coding for representations, as the Maltese Cross model supposed; these include alternative output codes as well as input codes. Coding for output may be advantageous at the time of input.

2. The information in these codes is manipulable, meaning that it can pass from one form to another after the time of original arrival. It is also "declarative" information, in that it can be reported by verbal or other propositional forms of output.

3. It is therefore distinguishable from another kind of knowledge that can be acquired through practice, but that does not allow people to answer questions about what they know. This will, for example, apply to the procedures that decide where any particular information is to go when passing from one code to another.

4. This latter kind of knowledge seems to be favored by tasks in which much information is presented, and in which the key factors are not obvious, so that selective encoding of some aspects of the task would be unlikely to pick the key ones.

5. Once this procedural type of knowledge has been acquired, declarative knowledge may arise from it, as well as vice versa.

As was said at the beginning of this chapter, this classification bears on a number of others. Given the occasion, it is particularly interesting to align it with classifications that have been produced by Tulving (1983, 1984). He too distinguishes declarative from procedural knowledge, being himself more interested in the former. In his terms, the experiments on input and output interference are all concerned with episodic memory, whereas those on controlling complex systems and on the learning of concepts are concerned with semantic memory. He has long emphasized the importance for episodic memory of the coding adopted at input, and the results discussed in this chapter reinforce and extend his views on that point. One important line of extension is the manipulability of declarative knowledge, and the changes of coding after presentation. The evidence on that point links his major contribution to the long tradition of work in reasoning and problem solving.

Perhaps the major uncertainty concerns the relationship between semantic memory and procedural knowledge. He has rightly pointed out that semantic memory can be expressed in propositions, and is not to be identified with procedural knowledge. Thus, Tulving (1984) has distinguished three classes, and explained memory unaffected by elaboration of processing (Jacoby & Dallas 1981) as being semantic but still not procedural. The discussion after Tulving's paper showed some unease about this distinction. Tulving, Schacter, and Stark (1982) did, in fact, suggest that priming effects are due to a further, and still unanalyzed, form of memory; so there is some uncertainty about the best division.

In our results, subjects can sometimes state declarative knowledge about the systems they are controlling. In some conditions, however, they know the correct procedures but not the propositions. Can one suggest that semantic memory, unlike episodic, may be either declarative or procedural? Remember Christopher

Columbus; general and manipulable propositions can grow out of rote-learned procedures.

Whatever the solution to this particular problem, it is clear that this field of work will be forever indebted to the insights of Endel Tulving.

REFERENCES

Anderson, J. (1983). *The architecture of cognition.* Cambridge, MA: Harvard University Press.

Baddeley, A. D. (1986). *Working memory.* Oxford University Press.

Baddeley, A. D., & Hull, A. (1979). Prefix and suffix effects: Do they have a common basis? *Journal of Verbal Learning and Verbal Behavior, 18,* 129–140.

Baddeley, A. D., Lewis, V. J., & Vallar, G. (1984). Exploring the articulatory loop. *Quarterly Journal of Experimental Psychology, 36,* 233–252.

Baddeley, A. D., Thomson, N., & Buchanan, M. (1975). Word length and the structure of short-term memory. *Journal of Verbal Learning and Verbal Behavior, 14,* 575–589.

Barlow, M. C. (1928). The role of articulation in memorising. *Journal of Experimental Psychology, 11,* 306–312.

Berry, D. (1984). *Implicit and explicit knowledge in the control of complex systems.* Unpublished doctoral dissertation, University of Oxford.

Berry, D. C., & Broadbent, D. E. (1984). On the relationship between task performance and associated verbalizable knowledge. *Quarterly Journal of Experimental Psychology, 36A,* 209–231.

Berry, D., & Broadbent, D. E. (1987). The combination of explicit and implicit learning processes in task control. *Psychological Research, 49,* 7–15.

Berry, D., & Broadbent, D. E. (1988). Interactive tasks and the implicit–explicit distinction. *British Journal of Psychology. 79,* 251–272.

Broadbent, D. E. (1981). From the percept to the cognitive structure. In A. D. Baddeley & J. Long (Eds.), *Attention and performance IX* (pp. 1–24). Hillsdale, NJ: Lawrence Erlbaum Associates.

Broadbent, D. E. (1984). The Maltese cross: A new simplistic model for memory. *The Behavioral and Brain Sciences, 7,* 55–94.

Broadbent, D. E., FitzGerald, P., & Broadbent, M. H. P. (1986). Implicit and explicit knowledge in the control of complex systems. *British Journal of Psychology, 77,* 33–50.

Bryden, M. P. (1971). Attentional strategies and short-term memory in dichotic listening. *Cognitive Psychology, 2,* 99–116.

Conrad, R. (1958). Accuracy of recall using keyset and telephone dial, and the effect of a prefix digit. *Journal of Applied Psychology, 42,* 285–288.

Conrad, R., & Hull, A. J. (1968). Input modality and the serial position effect in short-term memory. *Psychonomic Science, 10,* 135–136.

Craik, F. I. M., & Lockhart, R. S. (1972). Levels of processing: A framework for memory research. *Journal of Verbal Learning and Verbal Behavior, 11,* 671–684.

Crowder, R. G., & Morton, J. (1969). Precategorical acoustic storage (PAS). *Perception and Psychophysics, 5,* 365–373.

Dulany, D. E., Carlson, R. A., & Dewey, G. I. (1984). A case of syntactical learning and judgment: How conscious and how abstract? *Journal of Experimental Psychology: General, 113,* 541–555.

FitzGerald, P., & Broadbent, D. E. (1985a). Order of report and the structure of temporary memory. *Journal of Experimental Psychology: Learning, Memory, and Cognition, 11,* 217–228.

FitzGerald, P., & Broadbent, D. E. (1985b). Memory for attended and unattended visual stimuli. *Quarterly Journal of Experimental Psychology, 37A,* 339–365.

FitzGerald, P., Tattersall, A., & Broadbent, D. E. (1988). Separating central mechanisms by POCs: Evidence for an input–output buffer. *Quarterly Journal of Experimental Psychology.* 40A, 109–134.

Gillie, A., & Broadbent, D. E. (in preparation). *Effects of irrelevant speech and articulatory suppression during encoding and retention.*

Hayes, N. (1987). *Systems of explicit and implicit learning.* Unpublished doctoral dissertation, University of Oxford.

Hayes, N. (in press). Consciousness cannot explain syntactical judgment: A rebuttal of Dulany, Carlson, & Dewey. *Memory and Cognition.*

Hayes, N., & Broadbent, D. E. (1988). Two modes of learning for interactive tasks. *Cognition.* 28, 249–276.

Hayes, N., & Broadbent, D. E. (in preparation). *Two modes of learning for attribute identification.*

Hull, C. L. (1920). Quantitative aspects of the evolution of concepts. *Psychological Monographs, 28,* (1, Whole No. 123).

Jacoby, L. L., & Dallas, M. (1981). On the relationship between autobiographical memory and perceptual learning. *Journal of Experimental Psychology: General, 110,* 306–340.

Lewis, M. W., & Anderson, J. R. (1985). Discrimination of operator schemata in problem solving: Learning from examples. *Cognitive Psychology, 17,* 26–65.

Margrain, S. A. (1967). Short-term memory as a function of input modality. *Quarterly Journal of Experimental Psychology, 19,* 109–114.

Martin, M. (1978). Retention of attended and unattended auditorily and visually presented material. *Quarterly Journal of Experimental Psychology, 30,* 187–200.

Martin, M. (1980). Effect of list length on recall after dichotomous visual presentation. *Acta Psychologica, 44,* 245–252.

Martin, M., & Jones, G. V. (1979). Modality dependency of loss of recency in free recall. *Psychological Research, 40,* 273–289.

Morris, C. (1946). *Signs, language, and behavior.* New York: Prentice-Hall.

Porter, D. B. (1986). *A functional examination of intermediate cognitive processes.* Unpublished doctoral dissertation, University of Oxford.

Rasmussen, J. R. (1983). Skills, rules, and knowledge; signals, signs, and symbols, and other distinctions in human performance models. *IEEE Transaction on Systems, Man, and Cybernetics, SMC-13,* 257–266.

Rasmussen, J. (1987). Cognitive control and human error mechanisms. In J. Rasmussen, K. Duncan, & J. Leplat (Eds.), *New technology and human error* (pp. 53–61). New York: Wiley.

Reber, A. S. (1967). Implicit learning of artificial grammars. *Journal of Verbal Learning and Verbal Behavior, 5,* 855–863.

Reber, A. S. (1976). Implicit learning of synthetic languages: The role of instructional set. *Journal of Experimental Psychology: Human Learning and Memory, 2,* 88–94.

Reber, A. S., Kassin, S. M., Lewis, S., & Cantor, G. (1980). On the relationship between implicit and explicit modes of learning a complex rule structure. *Journal of Experimental Psychology: Human Learning and Memory, 6,* 492–502.

Routh, D. (1976). An "across-the-board" modality effect in immediate serial recall. *Quarterly Journal of Experimental Psychology, 28,* 285–304.

Tattersall, A. (1987). *Divided attention and the structure of temporary memory.* Unpublished doctoral dissertation, University of Oxford.

Tulving, E. (1983). *Elements of episodic memory.* Oxford: Oxford University Press.

Tulving, E. (1984). Precis of *Elements of Episodic Memory Behavioral and Brain Sciences, 7,* 223–268.

Tulving, E., Schacter, D. L., & Stark, H. A. (1982). Priming effects in word-fragment completion are independent of recognition memory. *Journal of Experimental Psychology: Learning, Memory, and Cognition, 8,* 336–342.

Tulving, E., & Thomson, D. M. (1973). Encoding specificity and retrieval processes in episodic memory. *Psychological Review, 80,* 352–373.

Vallar, G., & Baddeley, A. D. (1982). Short-term forgetting and the articulatory loop. *Quarterly Journal of Experimental Psychology, 34,* 53–60.

Watkins, M. J. (1972). Locus of the modality effect in free recall. *Journal of Verbal Learning and Verbal Behavior, 11,* 644–648.

Watkins, M. J., & Watkins, O. C. (1973). The post-categorical status of the modality effect in serial recall. *Journal of Experimental Psychology, 99,* 226–230.

Yerkes, R. M. (1943). *Chimpanzees: A laboratory colony.* New Haven: Yale University Press.

13 Experimental Dissociations and the Episodic/Semantic Memory Distinction

James H. Neely
State University of New York at Albany

Endel Tulving has made many significant and seminal contributions to the theoretical and empirical study of human memory. They include his research on organizational processes (e.g., Tulving, 1962), the efficacy of retrieval cues (e.g., Tulving & Osler, 1968; Tulving & Pearlstone, 1966; Tulving & Psotka, 1971), the encoding specificity principle (e.g., Tulving & Thomson, 1973), and the relationship between recall and recognition (e.g., Flexser & Tulving, 1978; Tulving, 1976, Tulving & Thomson, 1973; Tulving & Wiseman, 1975). However, as important as these contributions have been for mainstream memory researchers, Tulving is probably most well known (particularly to "outsiders" such as linguists, philosophers, and social psychologists) for the distinction he has made between episodic and semantic memory (e.g., Tulving, 1972, 1984, 1985).

In this chapter, I provide a conceptual and methodological analysis of the experimental methods and results that one can use to support the distinction between episodic and semantic memory and/or other memory systems. In particular, I focus on the procedures and logic that constitute the experimental dissociation paradigm with nonamnesic human subjects. In so doing, I highlight my points by selectively citing the literature and by emphasizing recent research from my laboratory. I justify this selectivity on the basis of there already being several extensive reviews of the many empirical studies relevant to the episodic/semantic memory distinction (e.g., Anderson & Ross, 1980; McKoon, Ratcliff, & Dell, 1986; Richardson-Klavehn & Bjork, 1988; Shoben, 1984; Tulving, 1983, 1984).

In Section 1 of this essay, I begin by briefly reviewing Tulving's episodic/semantic memory distinction and how the experimental dissociation paradigm has been used to provide support for that distinction. I then give prescriptions for equating the procedures employed in episodic and semantic memory tests in the experimental dissociation paradigm. In Section 2, I describe experiments from my laboratory that have followed most of these prescriptions and I discuss how their results both support and challenge some of Tulving's (1983, 1984) claims concerning the nature of episodic and semantic memory.

In Section 3, I discuss the broader conceptual issues involved when one claims support for the episodic/semantic memory distinction on the basis of experimental dissociations obtained in experiments that procedurally equate their episodic and semantic memory tests. To anticipate, I make the three following arguments:

1. As Dunn and Kirsner (1988) have noted, a dissociation must take a specific form if it is to provide strong evidence for the operation of functionally distinct memory systems.

2. Although this specific form of dissociation is a necessary condition for inferring functionally distinct mnemonic processes, it is not a sufficient condition for inferring that they are rooted in the episodic/semantic memory distinction. To achieve sufficiency, the episodic/semantic distinction must be precisely enough delineated to predict the exact conditions under which dissociations will be present or absent. The converging operations (cf. Garner, Hake, & Eriksen, 1956) of using several different episodic and semantic memory tasks (cf., Roediger, 1984) should then be used to verify these predictions.

3. Even if the necessary and sufficient conditions for establishing the psychological validity of the episodic/semantic memory distinction are met, it cannot be determined whether this distinction is rooted in storage or retrieval processes or both.

THE EPISODIC/SEMANTIC
MEMORY DISTINCTION
AND DISSOCIATION LOGIC

Tulving (1972) originally made a procedural and heuristic distinction between episodic and semantic memory tests. According to Tulving, episodic memory tests require that the subject consciously recollect the temporal-spatial context in which he or she previously experienced some event. For example, subjects might study a list of words and later be asked to recall or recognize the words that had appeared in that particular study list. Or they might be asked what they were doing when they first heard about John Kennedy's having been shot. Semantic memory tests, on the other hand, require the retrieval of information concerning the graphological, phonological, and semantic properties of words and other symbols and/or the retrieval of the subject's general world knowledge without requiring that the subject retrieve the temporal-spatial context in which that information or knowledge was acquired. For example, subjects might be asked to determine if a letter string is an English word or to verify if the sentence "John Kennedy died from gunshot wounds" is true or false.

More recently, Tulving (1983, 1984) has metamorphosed his original tax-onomic task distinction into a psychological distinction by arguing that these different procedures for testing memory actually invoke the operation of func-tionally distinct memory systems. Specifically, Tulving (1983) considers epi-sodic and semantic memory to be two subsystems of propositional (declarative) memory, which is distinct from procedural memory. According to Tulving, declarative memory contains propositional information about which assertions of truth or falsity can be readily verbalized (e.g., "It is true that Ronald Reagan is President of the U.S." or "It is false that I believe I studied the word *tree* in this experiment"). Procedural memory, on the other hand, contains difficult-to-ver-balize "how to" knowledge, which in and of itself is neither true nor false (e.g., the set of operations necessary to perform some complex motor skill). Tulving (1985) has also argued that these three memory systems are associated with different states of consciousness.

Most memory researchers accept the functional psychological distinction be-tween propositional and procedural memory as well as the *heuristic* utility of the episodic/semantic task distinction as a device for stimulating empirical research. However, because considerable controversy surrounds the issue of whether the episodic/semantic memory distinction is *psychologically* valid (e.g., see the commentaries on Tulving's, 1984, *Brain and Behavioral Sciences* article), one needs to devise paradigms that can test this issue empirically. In this chapter, I focus on the experimental dissociation paradigm, which is widely accepted as the best available paradigm for assessing the psychological reality of the epi-sodic/semantic memory distinction.

According to experimental dissociation logic, evidence that episodic and se-mantic memory represent functionally distinct memory systems comes from the observation that a variable differentially affects performance in episodic and semantic memory tests[1]. However, as Neely and Payne (1983) have noted, a necessary (but not sufficient) condition for this logic being valid is that the two types of memory test be procedurally equated on all variables other than the instructions the subjects receive as to the nature (episodic vs. semantic) of the information they must retrieve in order to perform the two types of tests. If this is not done, the dissociative effect that an experimental variable has on perfor-

---

[1]Although I couch my arguments in terms of the episodic/semantic memory distinction, they apply to any case in which one uses an experimental dissociation as evidence for the operation of two functionally distinct memory systems, whether they be episodic versus semantic memory, explicit versus implicit memory (e.g., Graf & Schacter, 1985; Schacter, 1987), intentional versus incidental memory (Jacoby, 1984) or procedural versus declarative memory (e.g., Anderson, 1983).

mance in the two types of test could be due either to (a) the effects of that variable being different in the two types of test (a genuine episodic/semantic dissociation) or (b) the effects of that variable interacting with the effects of some extraneous variable that was not held constant across the two types of test (an artifactual episodic/semantic dissociation).

Although the foregoing point seems obvious, most dissociation experiments have not equated the two types of memory tests on all variables other than the instructions necessary to differentiate them. Because of this unfortunate state of affairs, Table 13.1 provides a list of prescriptions for how one should equate several variables that can easily be confounded across episodic and semantic memory tests. Table 13.1 also gives cases of when each of these prescriptions is most likely not to be followed and indicates whether the failure to follow each particular prescription poses problems for interpreting the presence of a dissociation, the absence of a dissociation, or both.

1.1. Equate the General Nature of the Materials

Episodic memory tests have often employed individual words, whereas semantic memory tests have often employed sentential materials (e.g., in a sentence verification task in which subjects must decide whether it is true or false that "Napoleon Bonaparte owned an Edsel"). Because of this, one should be sure that the effects of the type of material are not confounded with the effects of the type of memory test when one makes across-experiment comparisons of the effects of some variable in the two types of memory tests. Of course, one can easily avoid this confounding. For example, in addition to testing subjects' semantic memories concerning the truth value of sentences after they have been memorized, one can test their episodic memories for them (e.g., Shoben, Wescourt, & Smith, 1978). Conversely, in addition to testing subjects' episodic memories for words, one can have subjects memorize words and later ask them to make a semantic decision about whether a test word represents a concrete object (Wood, Taylor, Penny, & Stump, 1980), is a member of a particular semantic category (e.g., Herrmann & Harwood, 1980), or when intermixed with nonwords is indeed a word (e.g., Caroll & Kirsner, 1982; Duchek & Neely, in press; Durgunoğlu & Neely, 1987; McKoon & Ratcliff, 1979; Neely & Durgunoğlu, 1985). Obviously, the failure to equate materials in episodic and semantic memory tests poses interpretive problems regardless of whether the variable of interest does or does not produce a dissociative effect in the two types of tests.

1.2. Equate Prior Study of Some of the Test Items

In laboratory experiments, a subject must study to-be-remembered episodes prior to receiving an episodic memory test. Thus, to equate the two types of memory tests, the analogous semantic memory test should also be preceded by these same

TABLE 13.1
Summary of Prescriptions for Proper Experimental Design in Dissociation Experiments

Prescription	Typical Violations	Interpretive Problem Avoided[a]
1. Equate materials.	Across experiment comparisons.	P & A
2. Equate prior study of some test items.	Almost all studies not involving direct explicit/implicit memory comparisons.	P & A
3. Equate encoding for previously studied items, using *both* incidental and intentional orienting instructions.	Almost all studies not involving direct explicit/implicit memory comparisons, which themselves do not use *both* instructions.	P & A[b]
4. Use identical test lists.	When "yes" and "no" test items in the semantic memory test must be different as in sentence verification and lexical decision experiments.	P & A[c]
5. Equate test stimulus presentation parameters.	In comparisons of episodic recognition and recall with perceptual identification and word-fragment completion tests.	P & A[c]
6. Equate response modality and number of response alternatives.	In comparisons of episodic recognition and recall with perceptual identification and word-fragment completion tests.	P & A[c]
7. Make the to-be-retrieved episodic and semantic information uncorrelated.	When "yes" and "no" test items in the semantic memory test must be different as in sentence verification and lexical decision experiments.	P & A[c]
8. Randomly pre-cue each test item with the type of test query.	All known experiments.	P[d]

[a]P means the interpretation of the *presence* of a dissociation is undermined if the prescription is not followed; A means the *absence*. [b]Available data suggest it may not be important to follow this prescription. See text. [c]Available data suggest it is important to follow this prescription. See text. [d]Following this prescription could make it more likely one would fail to observe a dissociation. See text.

study episodes. This is important because of the existence of long-term repetition priming effects in semantic memory tests. Repetition priming is the finding that relative to items not previously studied, prior study of an item typically facilitates the speed and/or accuracy of responding to that item when it subsequently appears in a semantic memory test. These repetition priming effects can occur even when there are relatively long delays between that prior study and the semantic memory test (e.g., Graf & Schacter, 1985; Jacoby & Dallas, 1981; Mitchell & Brown, 1988; Roediger & Blaxton, 1987; Sloman, Hayman, Ohta, Law, & Tulving, 1988; Tulving, Schacter, & Stark, 1982).

Consider the typical case (e.g., Shoben et al., 1978) in which test items are studied prior to the episodic memory test, as they must be, but are not studied prior to the semantic memory test. In this typical case, a variable's effect for *nonstudied* items in the semantic memory test is compared with its effects for *studied* items in the episodic memory test. If that variable's effects interact with long-term repetition priming effects in the semantic memory test, either the presence or absence of a dissociation effect for that variable would be ambiguous. That is, the dissociative effect of that variable might disappear or appear if one compared its effects for *previously studied* test items for both the semantic and episodic memory tests.

1.3. Use Both Intentional and Incidental Orienting Instructions for the Encoding Done During Prior Study of the Test Items

If the to-be-dissociated variable's effects are modulated by encoding differences during prior study of the test items, and if encoding differences are induced by the type of subsequent memory test subjects expect (cf., Balota & Neely, 1980), subjects should receive identical encoding instructions for the study episodes given prior to both types of memory tests. Furthermore, these identical instructions should be intentional memory instructions for some subjects and incidental memory instructions for others. Intentional memory instructions forewarn subjects that they will receive an episodic memory test for the studied items. Incidental memory instructions provide no forewarning about any kind of test being given following the encoding of the studied items. Subjects are merely led to believe that their performance on the task that they perform on the study items (e.g., rating them for their pleasantness) is the only variable of interest to the experimenter.

The use of both intentional and incidental memory instructions helps to rule out the possibility that a variable's dissociative effects in episodic and semantic memory tests are due to that variable's effects interacting with the effects of motivational differences during retrieval. This possibility is particularly problematic when only intentional memory instructions are used. That is, after having been given intentional memory instructions, subjects who received an episodic memory test might be well motivated because they were receiving the expected type of memory test, whereas subjects receiving the semantic memory test might be miffed and poorly motivated because they were receiving an unexpected type of memory test. (Such a motivational difference would also undermine the interpretation of the absence of a dissociation, because a dissociation might have occurred if the motivation during retrieval had been equated for the two types of tests.)

The obvious solution to this problem would be to give incidental memory instructions in which subjects are not led to expect any kind of memory test at all. However, only a very few experiments have included identical study episodes for which subjects received identical incidental encoding instructions prior to the administration of both their episodic and semantic memory tests. These experiments have examined how the type of incidental encoding instruction affects subsequent performance on previously studied items when these items are tested in (a) word-stem completion and on episodic cued-recall tests (Graf & Mandler, 1984; Graf, Mandler, & Haden, 1982; Squire, Shimamura, & Graf, 1987), (b) perceptual identification and episodic recognition tests (Jacoby & Dallas, 1981), and (c) lexical decision and episodic recognition tests (Duchek & Neely, in press). However, there are also potential problems associated with using *only* incidental encoding instructions. Specifically, relative to subjects who receive the semantic memory test, subjects who receive the episodic memory test might feel more deceived (and hence be less motivated during their memory test). They might feel more deceived because they are explicitly being asked to remember items that they had been implicitly instructed to not remember when they studied them.

The way out of these two dilemmas is to use a Y (levels on the to-be-dissociated varible Y) x 2 (type of test: episodic vs. semantic) x 2 (encoding instructions for study: intentional vs. incidental) design. Such a design permits one to determine if motivational differences at retrieval were responsible for Y's dissociative effect when the episodic and semantic memory tests were given following only intentional or only incidental memory instructions. That is, if motivational differences between the two types of test were responsible for the dissociation, one should observe a statistically significant Y x Type of Test x Encoding Instructions interaction. Specifically, the dissociative Y x Test Type interaction observed when the two types of tests follow the same encoding instructions (either intentional or incidental) should not be as strong when they follow different encoding instructions. (This is so because when the two types of tests follow the different encoding instructions, one has better equated the two tests' expectancy values and hence has better equated the motivational levels they engender. That is, episodic and semantic memory tests are more "expected" after intentional and incidental encoding instructions, respectively, whereas episodic and semantic memory tests are more "unexpected" after incidental and intentional encoding instructions, respectively.) If, on the other hand, the dissociated variable's differential effect is due to the type of memory test and not to motivational differences at retrieval, one should obtain a Y x Type of Test interaction that is not qualified by its higher order interaction with encoding instructions.

As far as I know, only one experiment (Roediger, Weldon & Stadler, 1987) has used both incidental and intentional memory instructions in a single experiment that directly compares the effects of a variable (in this case, levels-of-processing) in episodic and semantic memory tests. In both types of tests, subjects received either word-stems or word-fragments as retrieval cues. In the episodic tests, they were to use these cues to help them retrieve a previously studied word; in the semantic memory tests, they were to give the first word that each of these cues brought to mind. For present purposes, the major finding was that deeper levels of processing on the studied words increased episodic recall but had no effect in the two semantic memory tests, and this was so whether or not subjects knew at the time of study that they were going to receive an episodic memory test. Thus, this demonstrates that the previously obtained dissociative effect of levels of processing in episodic cued recall and "semantic" word-stem completion tests (Graf & Mandler, 1984; Graf et al., 1982; but see Squire et al., 1987) was not due to the levels-of-processing effect interacting with the effects of motivational differences during retrieval induced by subjects receiving expected versus unexpected memory tests.

Roediger et al.'s (1987) demonstration that the dissociative effect of levels-of-processing in episodic and semantic memory tests was the same whether subjects received intentional or incidental memory instructions for the study list suggests that one probably need not be concerned about a variable's dissociative effect in episodic and semantic memory tests being due to motivational differences at retrieval. This conclusion is further supported by Weiner's (1966) literature review, which indicated that between-subject manipulations of retrieval motivation have little effect on episodic memory performance. Nevertheless, it might be useful to demonstrate that motivational differences are not producing episodic/semantic dissociations with variables other than the levels-of-processing variable that Roediger et al. (1987) examined.

1.4. Use Identical Test Lists

The test lists should be identical in the two types of test, because of considerable evidence that the manner in which a variable influences performance on a particular trial in a semantic or episodic memory test depends on the nature of other test trials in which that particular trial is embedded. (See also section 1.8.) The following findings demonstrate such list context effects.

1. The magnitude of word-frequency effects on lexical decision times depends on the proportion of high- and low-frequency words in the test list (e.g., Glanzer & Ehrenreich, 1979; Gordon, 1983; Neely, 1980) and the nature of the nonword distractors (James, 1975).

2. For a particular critical set of episodically or semantically related prime-target pairs in a lexical decision test, the qualitative nature or magnitude of the priming observed depends on (a) the nature of the prime-target relationship instantiated in other trials in the test list (Becker, 1980; den Heyer, Briand, & Smith, 1985; Durgunoğlu & Neely, 1987; Lorch, Balota, & Stamm, 1986; Snow & Neely, 1987); (b) the number of related word-prime/word-target pairs (den Heyer, Briand, & Dannenbring, 1983; Neely, Keefe, & Ross, in press; Tweedy, Lapinski, & Schvaneveldt, 1977) and word-prime/nonword-target pairs (Neely et al., in press) that occur on other trials in the test list; (c) the nature of the nonword distractors (Shulman & Davison, 1977); and (d) the stimulus onset asynchronies between the prime and target that occur on other trials in the test list (Durgunoğlu & Neely, 1987; Neely, Fisk, & Ross, 1983).

3. Episodic recognition performance (Neely, Schmidt, & Roediger, 1983) and retrieval of a word from semantic memory (Blaxton & Neely, 1983; Brown, 1981) depends on the number of prior test items that are members of the same semantic category as the critical test item.

4. In episodic recognition memory for sentences, the effects of the number of predicates fanning from a subject term on reaction times to a studied sentence depends on the nature of the nonstudied distractor items that appear on other trials in the test (see Reder, 1982, p. 275; Reder & Anderson, 1980).

Because of these list context effects, the items used in the episodic and semantic memory tests should be identical. The fact that this was not so in an experiment reported by Shoben et al. (1978) potentially undermines the validity of the dissociation they obtained. (See also McCloskey & Santee, 1981.)

The prescription that identical items constitute the two types of test is sometimes not followed when the lexical decision task, which must include nonwords, is the semantic memory task used in a dissociation design. In this case, nonwords are sometimes not included in the analogous episodic recognition test (e.g., McKoon & Ratcliff, 1979), although sometimes they are (e.g., Carroll & Kirsner, 1982; Neely & Durgunoğlu, 1985). (See also section 1.7.)

In summary, the test items must be identical in the two types of tests to rule out the possibility that the presence or absence of a dissociation for episodic and semantic memory tests is not due to a List Context x Variable Y interaction artifactually producing the observed Y x Episodic/Semantic Test interaction or to its masking a genuine Y x Episodic/Semantic test interaction.

1.5. Equate the Parameters of Test Stimulus Presentation

In episodic/semantic comparisons, the stimulus conditions for the two types of test have often been different. For example, in some semantic memory tests, an item is briefly presented and masked (in a perceptual identification task) or is presented in fragmented form (in word-fragment or word-stem completion), whereas in episodic memory tests, the test items are clearly presented (in episodic recognition) or not presented at all (in free recall). It is important that the stimulus parameters of test-item presentation be equated in the two types of memory tests. Otherwise, one can very easily argue that the episodic/semantic memory differences are due to the two different stimulus presentation conditions encouraging different amounts of data-driven versus conceptually driven processing in the episodic and semantic memory tests (cf., Jacoby, 1983; Roediger & Blaxton, 1987; and chapter 1 of this book). The failure to equate stimulus presentation conditions for the two types of tests also undermines the interpretation of the absence of a dissociation effect. It could be that a dissociation would have occurred had the same stimulus presentation conditions been used in both tests.

1.6. Equate Response Modality
and Number of Response Alternatives

If this is not done, the dissociative effects of variable Y in the two types of memory test could be attributed to a Variable Y x Response Modality (or Number of Response Alternatives) interaction rather than to a Variable Y x Episodic/Semantic Test interaction. Because response modality and number of alternative responses have typically been confounded, I hereafter treat differences in response modality and/or number of response alternatives as a single variable, which I for brevity's sake call *response modality*. Evidence that the concern about response modality is legitimate would come from evidence that response modality modulates a variable's effect *within* episodic or semantic tests. Such evidence exists for both types of test.

The clearest evidence that subtle differences in response modality can have effects on episodic memory performance comes from an experiment described by Tulving (1983, Table 14.2). He and Judith Sutcliffe used identical test items (i.e., identical retrieval cues) but had subjects respond differently to these test items in a direct comparison of "recall" and recognition. In "recall", subjects wrote beside each test item a studied word of which that test item reminded them. If the test item did not remind them of a studied word, they wrote an X beside it. In recognition, on the other hand, subjects wrote "yes" beside the test item if they remembered having studied it and "no" if they did not, along with a confidence rating of the accuracy of their response. There were two kinds of test items of interest: the studied item itself or an associate of a studied item. For the studied items, performance was worse in recall than in recognition; for the associates, in recognition the probability of incorrectly responding that the test item had been studied increased across retention interval, whereas in recall the effectiveness of that test item as a retrieval cue for its studied associate decreased across retention interval. If, as Tulving (1983) claimed, the dissociative effect of retention interval *within* these two types of *episodic* memory tests was indeed due to differences in response modality in the two tests, then response modality should be equated in establishing dissociation effects in episodic versus semantic memory tests.

There is also strong evidence that response modality can modulate a variable's effect on performance within semantic memory tests. Referring back to section 1.4, the effects of test list context (a) on word-frequency effects (Forster, 1981) and (b) on semantic priming effects (Lorch et al., 1986; Seidenberg, Waters, Sanders, & Langer, 1984) do not occur when subjects must pronounce the test items rather than indicate their lexical decisions to them by pressing a "word" or a "nonword" key. Furthermore, priming from backward associations, from mediated associations, from syntactic associations, and from non-associative semantic relations sometimes differ in lexical decision and pronunciation tasks (Balota & Lorch, 1986; Lupker, 1984; Seidenberg et al., 1984).[2]

The existence of these dissociation effects *within* an episodic or semantic memory test when it employs different response modalities demonstrates the necessity of equating response modalities across episodic and semantic memory tests. Because differences in response modality might mask the genuine dissociation effect that would have occurred had response modality been equated for the two types of tests, the failure to equate response modality in the two types of tests poses problems for interpreting either the presence or absence of a variable's dissociative effect.

1.7. The Episodic and Semantic Information That Must Be Retrieved in the Two Tests Should Not Be Correlated

If this prescription is not followed, one decreases the likelihood that a dissociation effect will be obtained. To understand this, consider a situation in which subjects study only true sentences prior to either a semantic memory sentence verification task or its analogous episodic recognition memory test. In such a circumstance, subjects in the verification task could use information about a test item's study status to aid their "true" responses in the sentence verification task. Specifically, because they studied only true sentences, if they recognize a test sentence as having been studied, they know that it is true. This might encourage them to turn the nominal semantic memory test into a functional episodic memory test, and this would reduce the likelihood that one would obtain a dissociation

---

[2]It is possible that these different results in the lexical decision and pronunciation tasks are due not to response modality per se but rather to the inclusion of nonwords in the lexical decision task but not in the pronunciation task. However, Neely, Blackwell, and Campbell (1988) have obtained differences in episodic and semantic priming effects in lexical decision and pronunciation tasks when both included nonwords.

effect. Contrariwise, semantic information could be useful in the episodic analog of the sentence verification task. Because false sentences would be included in the sentence verification test, they should also appear in the analogous episodic recognition memory test. Thus, in the episodic test, subjects could use information about the test item's falseness to aid their decision that the test sentence had not been studied. A similar problem exists in a lexical decision test (which must include nonwords) and an episodic recognition test given after a study list that includes only words. In the episodic recognition memory test, knowing that a test item is a word provides evidence that it was studied; in the lexical decision test knowing that the item was studied provides evidence that it is a word.

Table 13.2 provides an example of how, in principle, the foregoing problem can be avoided in a sentence verification test and an episodic recognition test. Basically, the problem is avoided if the study list given prior to the two tests contains equal numbers of true and false sentences and if the test list contains equal numbers of studied and nonstudied "true" and "false" sentences. As shown by the correct responses required in the two types of tests in Table 13.2, under these conditions, knowledge of an item's study status provides no information about its semantic status or vice versa. Thus, subjects cannot use episodic information to aid their performance in the sentence verification task nor can they use semantic information to help them in the episodic recognition test. The effects of the to-be-dissociated variable should then be compared for studied "true" sentences (which require "yes" responses in both tests) and for non-studied "false" sentences (which require "no" responses in both tests). Similar logic dictates that when dissociation effects are to be demonstrated in lexical decision and episodic recognition tests, half of the words and the nonwords in the test list should have been previously studied and half not studied (e.g., Carroll & Kirsner, 1982; Neely & Durgunoğlu, 1985). Dissociation effects should then be

TABLE 13.2
An Example Study and Test List in Which There is
No Correlation Between a Test Item's Study Status and
Its Semantic Status (i.e., Truth Value)

Study Sentences		
(1) Gerald Ford pardoned Richard Nixon.		
(2) Hubert Humphrey was a ballet dancer.		
	correct test response in	
Test Sentences	EPIS RGN	SENT VER
(1) Gerald Ford pardoned Richard Nixon.	Yes	Yes
(2) Hubert Humprey was a ballet dancer.	Yes	No
(3) Endel Tulving is a memory researcher.	No	Yes
(4) Jimmy Carter was born in Toronto.	No	No

Note. EPIS RGN = episodic recognition test; SENT VER = sentence verification test.

examined for studied words (which require "yes" responses in both tests) and for nonstudied nonwords (which require "no" responses in both tests).

Unfortunately, the foregoing procedures will not totally eliminate the problem if episodic memorability is different for the items to which different responses are required in the semantic memory test. To make this point clear for the lexical decision test, assume that following their study, episodic memory for words is perfect and for nonwords is nonexistent. In this case, even though an equal number of word and nonword test items had been studied and nonstudied, if an item in the lexical decision test is remembered as having been studied, then it is certainly a word; if it is remembered as nonstudied, the odds are 2 : 1 that it is a nonword. Thus, subjects could use episodic memory to aid their lexical decisions, thereby rendering the lexical decision task a less pure instance of a semantic memory task. A similar problem exists if previously studied "true" and "false" sentences in a sentence verification test are not equally memorable, as seems likely. (Of course, if the episodic recognition data demonstrated equivalent recognition scores for the words and nonwords and for the "true" and "false" sentences, no problem would exist.)

In the foregoing examples, it was necessary to use different test items in the conditions for which "yes" and "no" are the correct responses in the semantic memory tests. As just outlined, this is problematic if these different items are not equivalent in their episodic memorabilities. Obviously, this problem could be avoided by devising a semantic memory test in which exactly the same test items could serve in the conditions for which "yes" and "no" are the correct responses. One such task would be as follows: Have subjects study a list of exemplars from different semantic categories and then give them a semantic memory test in which a category name is followed by a category exemplar. The subject's task would be to respond "yes" to the category exemplar if it is a member of the semantic category represented by the preceding category name and "no" if it is not. In this procedure, exactly the same item (e.g., *cat*) could require a "yes" response (when preceded by *ANIMAL*) or a "no" response (when preceded by *FRUIT*). Furthermore, this item could have been previously studied or not studied. To equate the contexts in which the test item *cat* appears in the two types of memory tests, the analogous episodic memory test would also present a category name prior to each test item. One could then compare across the two tests a variable's effect on (a) correct "yes" responses to *cat* when it had been studied and followed the category *ANIMAL* at test or (b) correct "no" responses to *cat* when it had not been studied and followed the category *FRUIT* at test. Although this is probably the best that one can do, even these procedures are not foolproof. If episodic memory for *cat* is better following *ANIMAL* than following *FRUIT*, better episodic memory would be correlated with a "yes" response in the semantic memory test. But once again, this could be checked by comparing episodic recognition for *cat* following *ANIMAL* and following *FRUIT*.

In conclusion, it is important to note that the failure to make episodic and semantic information totally independent in the two types of memory tests is problematic only if one *fails* to obtain a dissociation effect. With such a failure, one could conclude that the subjects had actually used episodic (semantic) information in performing the semantic (episodic) task, thereby rendering the nominally different tasks functionally equivalent. However, if a dissociation is obtained when the episodic and semantic information are correlated, its validity is strengthed rather than undermined by this correlation.

1.8. Randomly Pre-Cue Each Test Item With the Type of Test Query (Episodic vs. Semantic) that Must Be answered for That Test Item.

To understand why this is important, consider the nth item in an episodic or semantic memory test, where n is not equal to 1. If Variable Y produces dissociative effects on performance on this item, it could be due to its interactive effect with (a) the effects of the particular kind of memory query made for that item or (b) the effects of the n-1 episodic versus semantic test trials that preceded it. Evidence that performance on a critical trial can be affected by the episodic versus semantic nature of the query answered about previous test items is provided by Lewandowsky (1986). In an episodic recognition test, he found that the priming produced by an item semantically related to a critical, nonstudied lure depended on whether a semantic or episodic memory query was answered about the priming item. When the query was semantic, inhibitory priming occurred; when the query was episodic, facilitatory priming occurred.

Lewandowsky (1986) interpreted his very interesting finding as supporting the episodic/semantic memory distinction, and at one level it does. That is, it shows that the episodic versus semantic nature of the information retrieved about an item affects the type of priming that item produces for a subsequently presented nonstudied critical item about which a negative *episodic* recognition judgment is to be made. However, if a similar effect were obtained when a negative *semantic* judgment is made about the critical test item, the data would tend to undermine the distinction. That is, one could argue that (a) episodic processing is difficult whereas semantic processing is easy, (b) whenever processing of a semantically related prime is difficult, that prime produces the aforementioned facilitatory priming effect whereas when its processing is easy it produces the aforementioned inhibitory priming effect, and (c) these two types of priming effects are independent of the critical test item's processing difficulty. Clearly, such an explanation appeals to there being a difference in episodic and semantic processing. However, because this difference is quantitative rather than qualitative, it would not strongly support the episodic/semantic memory distinction.

The foregoing analysis suggests that in a dissociation design, the episodic (semantic) test on a particular item should be preceded by exactly the same pattern of prior episodic and semantic tests. This can be achieved by pre-cuing the type of query (episodic vs. semantic) that must be answered for each test item and equating the pattern of the queries that precede the critical target item for which half the subjects will answer an episodic query and half a semantic query. Under these conditions, any dissociation effect of Variable Y must be due to the episodic versus semantic nature of the query given for that particular critical test item and not to the effects of Variable Y interacting with the effects of the type of test queries that were interposed between that item's study and test presentations.

As far as I know, no experiments have abided by this prescription, though some have come close. For example, Feustel, Shiffrin, and Salasoo (1983) and Johnston, Dark, and Jacoby (1985) compared performance in episodic and semantic memory tests that were equated in terms of the episodic and semantic memory tests that occurred on previous trials. They accomplished this as follows: On each test trial, a test item was presented and masked, with the presentation duration cyclically increasing until subjects could identify the item. This was the semantic memory (perceptual identification) task. Immediately following identification, subjects were asked whether or not they had previously studied that item, the episodic memory test. Although this controls for the proactive effects of the episodic and semantic memory tests given on the preceding trials, because the semantic memory test was always given before the episodic memory test, it does not control for this *within* a trial.

A failure to equate proactive effects from prior tests by randomly pre-cuing the episodic and semantic memory tests poses interpretive problems for either the presence or absence of a dissociation. That is, a dissociation might be eliminated (or might appear) if the proactive effects from prior tests had been equated. There are, however, two potential dangers associated with using the pre-cuing procedure. First, if episodic and semantic information are correlated (see section 1.7), subjects might be more likely to discover this correlation if they received both episodic and semantic memory tests. Second, in receiving both kinds of tests, subjects might adopt a *single* retrieval strategy that would permit them to avoid the onerous task of selecting and mobilizing the optimal test-specific retrieval strategy for each test trial. Obviously, if the pre-cuing procedure did induce subjects to use a single retrieval strategy, it would make it less likely that a dissociation effect could be observed.[3]

---

[3]The problem of the random pre-cuing procedure inducing a single retrieval strategy is particularly severe when one examines dissociations in explicit versus implicit memory. In an implicit memory test, the experimenter wants subjects to respond to a test item, such as a word-fragment, without reference to the contents of a study list that preceded that test. Thus, the experimenter wants to disguise the fact that some of the correct answers to the test fragments appeared in the study list. This ruse would be unmasked if the random pre-cuing procedure were used. That is, in the analogous explicit memory tests, subjects would be told to use the word-fragments to retrieve a word from the study list. If such trials were randomly intermixed with the implicit memory tests, subjects would be

Summary

Under *ideal* conditions, the eight foregoing prescriptions for equating episodic and semantic memory tests on various variables should *all* be met if one is to draw unambiguous conclusions that a variable has dissociative effects on performance in episodic and semantic memory tests. However, as we all know, it is much too costly to control all potential extraneous variables in every single experiment. Because of this, the pragmatics of experimentation require that experiments be conducted to determine which of the aforementioned eight variables need not be controlled because they do not have an interactive effect with the to-be-dissociated variable's effect on performance in the episodic and semantic tests of interest. Until these additional experiments are conducted, we must interpret with extreme caution any dissociation obtained in an experiment that has not equated its episodic and semantic memory tests on *all* potentially important variables other than instructions as to the nature (episodic vs. semantic) of the information that subjects must retrieve in them. With this in mind, we can turn to a consideration of results obtained in three different experimental dissociation designs conducted in my laboratory.

2. THREE ILLUSTRATIVE EXPERIMENTAL DISSOCIATION PARADIGMS

In the three experimental dissociation designs from my laboratory that I report here, we failed to follow prescriptions 1.3 and 1.8 (from section 1). Specifically, we did not use both incidental and intentional encoding instructions for the study episodes that preceded the administration of the two types of memory tests. As was discussed in section 1.3, this could have produced motivational differences in the subjects who received our episodic and semantic memory tests. However, as was also discussed in section 1.3, the scant data that are relevant to this issue suggest that even if such motivational differences existed, they would be unlikely to influence our results (e.g., Roediger et al., 1987; Weiner, 1966). We also did not pre-cue randomly the type of memory query, episodic versus semantic, that subjects were to answer for a particular test item. Thus, the presence or absence of dissociations in our experiments could have been due to differential proactive effects of the prior episodic versus semantic memory tests that preceded the

---

likely to first try to retrieve words from the study list even if they were cued that on the present trial they should respond with the first item that comes to mind. This would serve to destroy the explicit versus implicit memory manipulation. Of course, if one still found a dissociative effect of some variable in explicit and implicit memory tests that used the random pre-cuing procedure, that dissociation would provide very strong support for the distinction (assuming that the two types of tests were equated on the other variables I have discussed here).

244

episodic versus semantic memory tests, respectively, from which we report our data. Despite these flaws, our experiments were well controlled relative to other experimental dissociation experiments relevant to the episodic/semantic memory distinction. (The only experiment that I know about that is better controlled than the experiments I report here is the Roediger et al., 1987, experiment. It failed to follow only prescription 1.8. However, as discussed in footnote 3, this is not problematic.)

2.1. A Word-Frequency x Levels-of-Processing Dissociation in Episodic and Semantic Memory Tests

Duchek and Neely (in press) compared the combined effects of word frequency and levels-of-processing in speeded episodic recognition and lexical decision tests[4]. In the study phase, subjects answered rhyme questions (*Does the item rhyme with bat?*) or semantic questions (*Does it provide an appropriate completion to "The blank chased the mouse?"*) about words and pronounceable nonwords. With the exception of the semantic questions about nonwords (to which the correct answer was always "no"), on half of the word and nonword trials the correct answer was "yes" and on the other half it was "no". After this study phase, subjects given each type of test received a test list containing exactly the same set of word and pronounceable nonword items, with half of each type of item having been previously studied or nonstudied.

Table 13.3 displays the main results, which come from the words for which "yes" had been the correct response to the semantic or rhyme question answered during the prior study phase. These data were selected because Craik and Tulving (1975) have shown that levels-of-processing effects in episodic recognition are greatly attenuated when "no" is the correct response to the semantic or rhyme question answered during the study phase. Because error rates showed the same pattern of results as the reaction times (RTs), only the RT data are presented. The first main result for these RTs was that word frequency had an opposite effect on performance in the two types of tests, replicating previous confounded across-experiment comparisons for episodic recognition (e.g., Balota & Neely, 1980; Glanzer & Adams, 1985) and lexical decisions (e.g., Norris, 1984; Scarborough, Cortese, & Scarborough, 1977). Specifically, as can be seen in the first two columns of the rows labelled WFE in Table 13.3, when averaged across the

---

[4]Because Tulving argues that semantic and episodic memory are both declarative memories, it is important that lexical memory be declarative, rather than procedural, if one is using the lexical decision task to provide a dissociation supporting the episodic/semantic memory distinction. Although it is controversial whether lexical memory is procedural or declarative (see Tulving, 1983, pp. 69–71), I am biased to believe that it is declarative. If it is, the lexical decision task can be used as a semantic memory task and the dissociations it yields are relevant to the episodic/semantic memory distinction. If, on the other hand, lexical memory is procedural, the dissociations that come from lexical decision and episodic recognition tasks may be construed as supporting the declarative/ procedural memory distinction.

TABLE 13.3
Duchek and Neely's (in press) Word-Frequency
× Levels-of-Processing Dissociation in Episodic
Recognition (ERGN) and Lexical Decision (LD) Tasks

Task	Type of Study Encoding		
	Semantic	Rhyme	LOPE
ERGN			
HF	1101	1219	+118
LF	996	1146	+150
WFE	−105	−73	+32
LD			
HF	600	648	+48
LF	714	719	+5
WFE	+114	+71	−43

Note. The data entries are the means of median reaction times (RTs) in msec. LOPE = levels-of-processing effect computed by subtracting semantic RTs from Rhyme RTs; HF = high-frequency words; LF = low-frequency words; WFE = word-frequency effect computed by subtracting HF RTs from LF RTs.

semantic and rhyme encoding conditions, RTs to low-frequency words were 89 msec faster than RTs to high-frequency words in episodic recognition, whereas in the lexical decision test they were 92 msec slower. However, the finding of opposite effects of word frequency in episodic recognition and lexical decision tests is not compelling support for the episodic/semantic distinction; it also occurs in episodic recognition versus episodic recall tests (Balota & Neely, 1980; Gregg, 1976).

For present purposes, Duchek and Neely's (in press) most interesting finding was that the Word-Frequency x Levels-of-Processing interaction was qualitatively different in the two types of memory tests. Specifically, as shown in the LOPE column in the WFE rows in Table 13.3, in episodic recognition the levels-of-processing effect was 32 msec larger for low- than for high-frequency words, whereas in the lexical decision task it was 43 msec smaller. This crossover dissociation effect could be construed as supporting Tulving's episodic/semantic memory distinction. Furthermore, it calls into question Forster and Davis' (1984) claim that *episodic* memory produces the word-frequency-attenuation-through-repetition effect in the lexical decision test, which is the observation that the typical word-frequency effect (superior performance on high-frequency words relative to low-frequency words) is reduced in magnitude for previously studied, i.e., repeated, words (Forster & Davis, 1984; Scarborough et al., 1977). This effect, hereafter called *the word-frequency attenuation effect,* occurs because long-term repetition priming effects are greater for low than for high-frequency words (cf., Jacoby & Dallas, 1981). Indeed, this word-frequency attenuation effect occurred in Duchek and Neely's (in press) experiment. Specifically, as shown in the last column in Table 13.4, for nonstudied words, RTs to low-frequency words were 183 msec slower than RTs to high-frequency words. However, for previously studied words, these standard word-frequency effects were attenuated by 75 msec—the average of the WFAE entries for the semantic and rhyme encoding conditions in Table 13.4—to yield word-frequency effects of 108 msec for previously studied words. This word-frequency attenuation effect occurred because, as shown in Table 13.4, repetition priming—averaged across the semantic and rhyme encoding conditions—was 75 msec greater for studied low-frequency words than for studied high-frequency words (107 msec vs. 32 msec, respectively).

Forster and Davis (1984) argued that the word-frequency attenuation effect is being mediated by differences in *episodic* memory for the high- and low-frequency words' first presentations, which is known to be better for low- than for high-frequency words. This argument is undermined by Duchek and Neely's (in press) results. Specifically, they found that in episodic recognition, the facilitation from prior semantic processing relative to prior rhyme processing was 32 msec greater for low-frequency words than for high-frequency words. (See LOPE column in the first WFE row in Table 13.3.) According to Forster and Davis' analysis, because a deeper level of semantic processing enhanced *episodic* memory for low-frequency words relative to high-frequency words, it should have produced a larger word-frequency attenuation effect in the lexical decision task; but this

TABLE 13.4

Repetition Priming and Word-Frequency Attenuation Effects for Studied Words and Word-Frequency Effects for Nonstudied Words in Duchek and Neely's (in press) Lexical Decision Task

	Type of Study Encoding		
	Semantic	Rhyme	Nonstudied
HF	+41	+23	641
LF	+110	+105	824
WFAE	+69	+82	WFE +183

Note. The data entries are the means of median reaction times (RTs) in msec. HF = high-frequency words; LF = low-frequency words. For the semantic and rhyme encoding conditions, the entries are repetition priming effects computed by subtracting the RTs for studied words from the RTs for nonstudied words; WFAE = word-frequency attenuation effect, which is the amount by which repetition priming reduced the word-frequency effect for studied words relative to the word-frequency effect obtained for nonstudied words; WFE = word-frequency effect, which was computed by subtracting HF RTs from LF RTs.

was not so. In Duchek and Neely's lexical decision task, deeper semantic processing *reduced* the word-frequency attenuation effect by 43 msec. rather than enhancing it. Thus, contrary to Forster and Davis' analysis, the word-frequency attenuation effect in Duchek and Neely's lexical decision task was not being mediated solely by differential episodic memory for high- and low-frequency words.

The foregoing conclusion is important vis à vis the episodic/semantic memory distinction. That is, it suggests that although a test item's prior occurrence as an episodic input leads to a long-term repetition priming effect in a semantic memory task, this repetition priming effect in *semantic memory* is not due to repetition's having incremented that item's *episodic* familiarity. It is due to some other mechanism. This has implications for theories (e.g., Balota & Chumbley, 1984) that assume that the word-frequency effect in the lexical decision task is, for the most part, being mediated by the test item's familiarity having an impact on the decision stage of processing rather than on speed of lexical access per se. The implication is that if familiarity is indeed influencing the decision stage in the lexical decision task, it is a type of familiarity other than the *episodic* familiarity that mediates recognition memory performance.

2.2. Are Episodic and Semantic Memory Differentially Context-Dependent?

Tulving (1984, see his Table 1) has claimed that episodic memory is more context-dependent than semantic memory. We have collected data that are relevant to this claim in two different experimental paradigms. One of these paradigms has yielded data challenging the claim (Neely & Payne, 1983), the other supporting it (Durgunoğlu & Neely, 1987; Neely & Durgunoğlu, 1985). I first consider the data challenging the claim.

Recognition Failure of Recallable Famous Names. David Payne and I (Neely & Payne, 1983) followed up a very interesting experiment reported by Muter (1978). Muter used a semantic memory test to examine the phenomenon of recognition failure of recallable information, a phenomenon that has been well established in episodic memory (e.g., Tulving & Thomson, 1973; Tulving & Wiseman, 1975). In episodic memory, after studying a pair such as *grasp BABY*, subjects fail to recognize *BABY* in a recognition test, even though they are later able to recall *BABY* when given the cue *grasp*. This recognition failure effect demonstrates a strong context-dependency in episodic memory retrieval. That is, subjects can sometimes recall an item in the presence of a cue that reinstates the study context, even though they fail to recognize that recallable item when it is presented in the recognition test isolated from its study context. Moreover, Tulving and Wiseman (1975) have shown that the probability of failing to recognize an item that is recallable is, across many experiments, very well predicted by a quadratic equation based on the overall probability of recognition. (See Nilsson, Law, & Tulving, 1988, for an update.)

Muter (1978) showed that recognition failure also occurs in a semantic memory test with famous names. That is, subjects sometimes failed to recognize *ROSS* as the surname of a famous person even though they were able to recall *ROSS* to the cue *Maker of U.S. flag: Betsy*. Of even greater interest was the finding that the rate of recognition failure was well predicted by the very same quadratic equation used to predict recognition failure in episodic memory! If recognition failure is taken as a measure of context dependency in retrieval, then one is left with the conclusion that episodic and semantic memory retrieval are equally context-dependent. Clearly, this runs counter to Tulving's claim and undermines the episodic/semantic memory distinction.

As clever as Muter's (1978) experiment was, and as clear as his results were, there are two potential problems associated with Muter's research. Both problems stem from the fact that he did not directly compare recognition failure rates for famous names in both episodic and semantic memory tests that were equated according to the prescriptions given in section 1. It could be that even though the Tulving-Wiseman function does an excellent job of predicting recognition failure of famous names in semantic memory, it might not do so for the same materials in episodic memory. This is possible because recognition failure is not well predicted by the Tulving-Wiseman function for every single episodic memory experiment. (See Nilsson et al., 1988, for the few exceptions to the Tulving-Wiseman function.) If *episodic* recognition failure of famous names turned out to be higher than that predicted by the Tulving-Wiseman function, the data would support Tulving's conclusion that episodic memory is more context-dependent than is semantic memory (as evidenced by a higher than expected rate of recognition failure in episodic memory but not in semantic memory).

However, even if the Tulving-Wiseman function accurately predicted recognition failure rates for studied famous names in episodic memory and for non-studied famous names in semantic memory, a second potential problem would still remain. The problem is that recognition failure rates for famous names in a semantic memory test could be higher than that predicted by the Tulving-Wiseman function, if these famous names have received recent episodic input. This would show that semantic memory retrieval is more context-dependent when the to-be-retrieved information has been recently episodically encoded, which would be somewhat congruent with Tulving's claim.

Neely and Payne (1983) avoided these two problems by directly comparing recognition failure rates for famous names in episodic and semantic memory tests that included equal numbers of previously studied and nonstudied famous and nonfamous names. As shown in the last two columns of the first row of Table 13.5, they found that episodic recognition failure rates for nonfamous names were lower than predicted by the Tulving-Wiseman function. This provides partial justification for the fear that *episodic* recognition failure rates for *names*

TABLE 13.5

Neely and Payne's (1983) Recognition Failure Results for Episodic
Recognition (ERGN) and Semantic Fame Recognition (SFR) Tests

Test & Item Type	Recognition Hit Rate	Correct Cued Recall	Observed RF	Predicted RF
ERGN				
NF studied	.71	.12	.05*	.19
F studied	.77	.60	.15	.14
SFR				
F nonstudied	.43	.52	.41	.44
F studied	.68	.66	.20	.21

Note. NF = nonfamous name; F = famous name.
* = observed different from predicted, $p < .05$.

might not be well predicted by the Tulving-Wiseman function. However, this justification is only partial, in that episodic recognition failure rates for famous names was well predicted by the Tulving-Wiseman function. (See the last two columns in the second row of Table 13.5.) Although prior study of a famous name increased overall recognition of that name as being famous (compare recognition hits in rows 4 and 3 of Table 13.5; see also chapter 19, this volume), it did not affect the excellent accuracy of the predictions of the Tulving-Wiseman function. (See the last two columns of rows 4 and 3 in Table 13.5.)

Because Neely and Payne's (1983) results confirm Muter's (1978) findings, one can safely conclude that neither recent episodic input nor the nature of the memory query affects the amount of context dependency observed in the retrieval of famous names. This finding runs counter to Tulving's claim that episodic memory is more context-dependent than semantic memory. That recognition failure in semantic memory was equally well predicted by the Tulving-Wiseman function for nonstudied items as for studied items is also evidence against Flexser and Tulving's (1978) claim that recognition failure is mediated by the ''goodness'' of a recent *episodic* encoding.

Episodic and Semantic Priming Effects in Episodic and Semantic Memory Tasks. Although the recognition failure data show that episodic and semantic memory are similarly context dependent, data from an experiment by Neely and Durgunoğlu (1985) call this into question. Their experiment was based on earlier experiments by McKoon and Ratcliff (1979) and Carroll and Kirsner (1982). In McKoon and Ratcliff's (1979) experiments, subjects first learned paired associates between weakly related pairs such as *penny SMALL, garden WATER, sacred CHURCH,* and *bullet FAST.* Following this paired-associate learning, they were given a test in which they made either an episodic recognition judgment or a lexical decision to a target item. The target item could be either a previously studied response term or a nonstudied item. McKoon and Ratcliff (1979) were interested in how RTs to a target item would be affected by the relation between that target item and the immediately preceding test item, which was called the prime. In a baseline control condition, the prime had served as a stimulus term during paired-associate learning and was totally unrelated to the target item, in that it had not been studied in the same pair as the target and was not related to the target in semantic memory. (For the study list given earlier, in the baseline control *bullet* would serve as the prime for the studied target *CHURCH* or as the prime for the nonstudied target *STUDY*).

For present purposes, there were two priming conditions of interest in McKoon and Ratcliff's experiment: (a) the episodic priming condition, in which the prime and target had been studied in the same pair (e.g., *penny SMALL*) and (b) the semantic priming condition, in which the nonstudied prime and target were strongly related (e.g., *green GRASS*). McKoon and Ratcliff found significant priming effects in both of these conditions in both of their tests. Because they found a significant episodic priming effect in their lexical decision task and a significant semantic priming effect in their episodic recognition test, McKoon and Ratcliff concluded that there was transfer between the two memory systems. They further argued that this transfer across the two memory systems undermines Tulving's episodic/semantic distinction. However, there are potential problems with this conclusion. First, their two memory tests were not equated on several variables (more on this later). Second, the semantic priming effects they found in the two types of test were opposite—facilitatory for lexical decisions and inhibitory for episodic recognition. Third, Carroll and Kirsner (1982), using somewhat different procedures, failed to find an episodic priming effect in a lexical decision task.

Aydin Durgunoğlu and I (Neely & Durgunoğlu, 1985) investigated these issues by following paired-associate learning with lexical decision and episodic recognition tests that were equated according to all but prescriptions 1.3 and 1.8. Under these conditions, we found dissociative episodic and semantic priming effects in the two types of tests. Specifically, as shown in Table 13.6, in episodic recognition we found facilitatory episodic priming and inhibitory semantic priming in episodic recognition, replicating McKoon and Ratcliff's (1979) results; however, in the lexical decision test, we found no evidence of episodic priming, thereby replicating Carroll and Kirsner's (1982) results, nor did we find evidence of semantic priming[5].

---

[5]The semantic priming effects in Table 13.6 come from a condition in which the semantically related primes had appeared as stimulus terms in the paired-associate study lists. In McKoon and Ratcliff's (1979) experiments, the semantically related primes had not been previously studied. However, Neely and Durgunoğlu (1985; Durgunoğlu and Neely, 1987) also included nonstudied semantically related primes in some of their lexical decision experiments and found only very small and inconsistent semantic priming effects for them as well.

TABLE 13.6
Episodic and Semantic Priming Effects in Episodic Recognition
(ERGN) and Lexical Decision (LD) Tasks in Neely and
Durgunoğlu's (1985) Experiment 2

Test & SOA	Episodic Priming	Semantic Priming
ERGN		
150 ms	+76*	−29
950 ms	+117*	−55*
LD		
150 ms	−10	+1
950 ms	+14	−7

Note. The data entries are the mean priming effects (in msec), computed relative to an unrelated word-prime baseline. SOA = stimulus onset asynchrony between the prime and target.
* = p < .05.

In subsequent research (Durgunoğlu & Neely, 1987), we tried to determine why McKoon and Ratcliff (1979) had obtained episodic priming for lexical decisions, whereas Caroll and Kirsner (1982) and Neely and Durgunoğlu (1985) had not. We found that episodic priming was greatest when (a) no nonwords had been studied, (b) the primes in the semantic priming condition had not been studied (see footnote 5), and (c) the time interval between the prime and target was always long (i.e., 950 msec). All three of these conditions were satisfied in McKoon and Ratcliff's (1979) Experiment 1, which was the lexical decision experiment most comparable to their episodic recognition experiment (Experiment 4).

McKoon and Ratcliff (1979) were clearly aware that when nonwords are not studied, subjects might use episodic information to aid their word/nonword decisions, and that this utilization of episodic information might cause episodic priming to be obtained in a lexical decision task. Indeed, in consideration of this possibility, they included nonwords in the study list of their Experiment 2 and still obtained episodic priming in the lexical decision task. However, as noted in point 1.7, if nonwords are not as well episodically remembered as words (which cannot be determined, because McKoon & Ratcliff did not include nonwords in their episodic memory test), subjects could still use episodic information in making their lexical decisions even when both words and nonwords have been studied. Furthermore, unlike their Experiment 1, McKoon and Ratcliff's Experiment 2 also emphasized episodic information, in that it included only episodic priming conditions and no semantic priming conditions in the lexical decision test list. Thus, it could be that McKoon and Ratcliff (1979) failed to find a dissociative episodic priming effect because their Experiment 1 lexical decision task gave subjects the opportunity to use episodic information in making their lexical decisions[6].

In summary, in experiments using the paired-associate priming paradigm in which the effects of extraneous variables were carefully controlled in the episodic and semantic memory tests, Neely and Durgunoğlu's data supported Tulving's (1984) claim that retrieval from episodic memory is more context dependent than retrieval from semantic memory. Their data supported this by showing that the context produced by episodic and semantic primes had an effect in episodic recognition but not in a lexical decision task. Clearly, this conclusion is discrepant from the one drawn from data obtained using Muter's (1978) and Neely and Payne's (1983) recognition failure paradigm. As elaborated on in section 3.2, such discrepancies point to the need for obtaining converging evidence from more than one experimental paradigm when one collects empirical evidence relevant to the episodic/semantic memory distinction.

2.3. Is Semantic Memory Retrieval Automatic Whereas Episodic Memory Retrieval is Deliberate?

Although Tulving (1984, see his Table 1) has answered this question in the affirmative (see also Neely, 1977, p. 251, for a similar incorrect point of view), there are data suggesting that episodically based priming effects can, under certain conditions, satisfy three of Posner and Snyder's (1975) criteria for a

---

[6]Two other points should be made concerning the possibility that episodic priming occurred in McKoon and Ratcliff's (1979) Experiment 1 lexical decision task, because nonwords were not included in the study lists. First, McKoon and Ratcliff's (1979) Experiment 2 included nonwords in the study lists and still yielded episodic priming for lexical decisions. Thus, it is clear that the exclusion of nonwords from the study list is not a *necessary* condition for obtaining an episodic priming effect in the lexical decision task (at least when the semantic priming condition is not instantiated in the tests lists, as was so in McKoon and Ratcliff's Experiment 2.) However, it is just as clear from Durgunoğlu and Neely's (1987) results that when a semantic priming condition is included in the test list, episodic priming for lexical decisions is much greater in magnitude when nonwords are excluded from the study list. Because McKoon and Ratcliff included semantic primes in the lexical decision task they used as the analog of their episodic recognition task, it is possible that episodic priming in that lexical decision task occurred because nonwords did not appear in the study list. The second point is that because episodic recognition RTs are typically much longer than lexical decision RTs, one might argue that subjects would be unable to use episodic information to aid their lexical decisions, even though it were logically available for such a use. However, it is very likely that RTs in episodic recognition tests are much longer than the time it takes for episodic information sufficient to discriminate studied from nonstudied items to become available in the memory system. Specifically, after this discriminative episodic information becomes available, considerable additional time could be consumed by (a) an effortful conscious decision as to which response is indicated by this activated episodic information and (b) response selection and execution. These two time-consuming operations need not be performed in order for episodic information to influence lexical decision times.

priming effect being automatic. According to Posner and Snyder, three necessary conditions for establishing the automaticity of a priming effect produced by a particular relation between a prime and a target are that the priming effect (a) occur at a short ($<$ 200 msec) prime-target stimulus onset asynchrony (SOA); (b) produce facilitation in a related priming condition relative to both a neutral and an unrelated priming condition; and (c) be unaccompanied by inhibition in the unrelated priming condition relative to the neutral priming condition.

When an episodic recognition judgment is being made to the target, episodic priming effects satisfying these criteria have been obtained (Ratcliff & McKoon, 1981a, 1981b). These automatic episodic priming effects in episodic recognition tests refute Tulving's blanket claim that episodic memory retrieval is deliberate, that is, nonautomatic. However, in fairness to Tulving, it should also be noted that episodic priming effects in episodic recognition tests do not always satisfy Posner and Snyder's three criteria for automaticity. That is, although Neely and Durgunoğlu (1985) obtained episodic priming in episodic recognition at a short 150 msec SOA (see Table 13.6), this priming effect was mostly due to inhibition in the unrelated priming condition rather than to facilitation in the episodic priming condition. (However, their neutral priming condition, a string of XXXs, differed from the one used by Ratcliff & McKoon, 1981a, 1981b, which was a single repeated string of random letters.)

Although episodic priming effects often satisfy Posner and Snyder's three criteria for automaticity when episodic recognition judgments are being made about the target, one can ask whether an episodic relation between the prime and target can produce an automatic priming effect when a semantic memory test is given for the target. To answer this question, McKoon and Ratcliff (1986) used a lexical decision test on the target and obtained evidence for automatic episodic priming effects. However, subsequent research by Durgunoğlu and me (Durgunoğlu & Neely, 1987) has indicated that automatic episodic priming effects occur in a lexical decision test only under a rather circumscribed set of conditions. (See den Heyer, 1986, for more evidence that automatic episodic priming effects are not obtained in a lexical decision task.) Specifically, we obtained episodic priming effects satisfying Posner and Snyder's (1975) three criteria for automaticity only when all word targets were studied, all nonword targets were nonstudied, and no semantically related prime-target pairs appeared in the test list. Obviously, these conditions maximized the likelihood that subjects could use episodic information to aid their lexical decisions.

In short, then, the data all converge to indicate that automatic episodic priming effects occur in episodic recognition tests but not in ''pure'' semantic memory tests. That episodic priming effects occur in episodic but not semantic memory tests supports Tulving's views concerning the distinction between episodic and semantic memory. However, that these episodic priming effects are automatic in nature runs contrary to his views (as well as to Neely's, 1977, p. 271, related views) that episodic memory retrieval is deliberate (nonautomatic), whereas semantic memory retrieval is automatic. In fact, the data concerning whether semantic memory retrieval is automatic are also in seeming conflict—for example, see Henik, Friedrich, and Kellogg (1983), M. C. Smith (1979), M. C. Smith, Theodor, and Franklin (1983), and Snow and Neely (1987) versus Favreau and Segalowitz (1983) and Neely (1977). However, it is beyond the scope of this chapter to provide a detailed analysis of the extensive literature on semantic priming effects and of the controversial concept of automaticity (e.g., see Logan, 1985).

3. PRESCRIPTIONS FOR INTERPRETING DISSOCIATION EFFECTS FROM WELL-CONTROLLED EXPERIMENTS

Section 1 outlined some prescriptions for conducting well-controlled experiments using the experimental dissociation paradigm. Section 2 discussed some dissociations obtained in my laboratory and showed that previous conclusions concerning the presence or absence of experimental dissociations changed when the effects of extraneous variables were carefully controlled. For example, when subjects can use episodic information in a semantic (lexical decision) memory test, one fails to find dissociative episodic priming effects (McKoon & Ratcliff, 1979), whereas when they cannot use such episodic information, a dissociative episodic priming effect does occur (Carroll & Kirsner, 1982; Neely & Durgunoğlu, 1985). However, even if an experimental dissociation is obtained in a well-controlled experiment, problems of interpretation still remain vis à vis the episodic/semantic memory distinction. In this section, I provide additional prescriptions for avoiding some of these problems.

3.1. Focus on Dissociations that Represent Interpretable Interactions

In a statistical, analysis-of-variance sense, the simplest type of dissociation represents a Memory Task (episodic vs. semantic) x Variable Y interaction. In discussing which, if any, forms of a Memory Task x Variable Y interaction can provide compelling evidence for the operation of two functionally distinct memory systems, I follow the lead of most memory theories and merely assume (a) that the observed dependent variable in each memory test is some unspecified monotonic mapping function of the unobservable memory process of interest, and (b) that these mapping functions are weakly monotonic in that they can have any number of plateaus in them. (If the mapping functions for the two types of tests are nonmonotonic, the following arguments do not apply. As far as I know, for this more complex case it would not be possible to use a Memory Task x Variable Y interaction to infer two functionally distinct memory systems.)

As G. Loftus (1978) has noted, under the assumption of unspecified weak monotonicity, a dissociation is not interpretable when a variable has similar effects in the two types of memory tests, with the magnitude of the effect being statistically larger in one task than in the other. Such an interaction could be an artifact of scaling, because it can be eliminated when an appropriate monotonic transformation is applied to the dependent variable. Nor is an interaction interpretable when a variable has *no* effect in one task and a statistically significant effect in the other. This is so, even if the statistical power is high enough to rule out a Type II error for the task in which the variable had no effect. As Dunn and Kirsner (1988) have noted, this type of single dissociation interaction would occur if the two levels of the manipulated variable were in a plateau region for one test and a non-plateau region in the other test. Furthermore, Dunn and Kirsner (1988) noted that this same reasoning applies to the case of an uncrossed double dissociation, which is the observation that Variable Y influences Task A but not Task B, whereas the opposite is so for Variable Z. (See chapter 9 of this book for a similar point.) Clearly, this line of reasoning undermines the claim that Neely and Durgunoğlu's (1985) dissociative episodic and semantic priming effects (see Table 13.6) support the episodic/semantic memory distinction.

What is typically taken as the most convincing type of dissociation is what Dunn and Kirsner (1988) called the *crossed double dissociation:* As Variable Y changes from Level 1 to Level 2, performance becomes better in Task A and worse in Task B. However, Dunn and Kirsner argued that even the crossed double dissociation does not provide compelling evidence for the operation of two functionally distinct memory processes. Specifically, they argued that such a dissociation would occur if (a) only one process were operating, and (b) performance in the two memory tests were negatively correlated. This argument is certainly logically correct. However, in the absence of a plausible uniprocess theory that precisely explains why performance in the two memory tests should be negatively correlated, the psychologically more plausible interpretation would seem to be that if performance in two memory tests is negatively correlated, then these two memory tests tap functionally distinct processes.

But even if a two-process interpretation of a crossover double dissociation is typically more plausible than a uniprocess, negative-task-correlation account, Dunn and Kirsner (1988) provided an additional reason for eschewing the crossover double dissociation as an evidentiary tool for inferring functionally distinct memory processes. Their additional reason is that, to be logically correct, such inferences demand that the dissociated variable(s) must selectively influence only one process, and that each of these selectively influenced processes selectively influence performance in only one of the two types of memory tasks. When the assumption of selective influence of the variables on the processes is violated (which, as Dunn and Kirsner correctly noted, is likely to be most of the time), one will fail to obtain a crossover double dissociation, even though two functionally distinct processes are operating in the two types of tasks. In those few cases in which the assumption of selective influence of the variables on the processes is not violated, one will correctly infer from a crossover double dissociation that two functionally distinct processes are at work. However, in this case, one cannot determine whether (a) one of the two processes is selectively influencing one task and the other process is selectively influencing the other task, or (b) only one of the two processes is selectively influencing one task, whereas the other process is influencing both tasks. (See Dunn & Kirsner, 1988, pp. 96–97, for details.)

Fortunately, Dunn and Kirsner (1988) provided a solution to all of the interpretive problems associated with using a crossover double dissociation as support for two functionally distinct memory processes. They called their solution reversed *as*sociation logic. Like crossover double dissociation logic, reversed association logic assumes weak monontonicity, and cannot be applied to cases in which the mapping functions between task performance and the operation of a memory process is nonmonotonic. However, unlike a crossover double dissociation, a reversed association logically demands the postulation of two distinct memory processes and its interpretation does not depend on the assumption of selective influence.

To observe a reversed association, one plots performance in one memory task as a function of performance in the other memory task for the different experimental conditions common to both tasks. If this Task-A-performance/Task-B-performance function is nonmonotonic (which requires that one plot at least three points, i.e., data from three experimental conditions common to both tasks), then a reversed association has occurred. Because performance levels in the two tasks are *nonmonotically* related, a reversed association rules out the possibility that one process is operating and that performance in the two tasks is negatively (but monontonically) correlated. As noted earlier, it is just this possibility that cannot logically be ruled out by a crossover double dissociation. Thus, a reversed association provides the strongest possible support for the operation of two functionally different memory processes.

Two considerations concerning a reversed association are noteworthy. First, a reversed association is a special case of a crossover double dissociation. Thus, all Test Type x Variable Y interactions that yield a reversed association will also yield a crossover double dissociation. However, the converse is not true. Indeed, most crossover double dissociations will not yield a reversed association, because most crossover double dissociation designs employ a 2 (Test Type) x 2 (Levels on Variable Y) design. To obtain a reversed association, there must be at least three levels on Variable Y (or if there are only two levels on Variable Y the design must be a Test Type x Variable Y x Variable Z design). Indeed, Dunn and Kirsner (1988) cited only one example of a reversed association, which comes from a study by Graf and Schacter (1985). For present purposes, it is interesting that Graf and Schacter's (1985) reversed association effect is eliminated if one excludes the data for their amnesic subjects. (See Fig. 6 of Dunn & Kirsner, 1988).

Although I have by no means done an extensive literature review to determine the frequency with which reversed associations have occurred with nonamnesic subjects, I do know of two such reversed association effects. One of these reversed association effects was obtained in Duchek and Neely (in press). The data are taken from the present Table 13.3 and are displayed in Fig. 13.1. Clearly, there was a nonmonotonicity in performance in Duchek and Neely's lexical decision and episodic recognition tests for the semantically encoded high-frequency words, the rhyme-encoded high-frequency words, and the rhyme-encoded low-frequency words. The other reversed association effect with non-amnesic subjects was obtained in Roediger et al.'s (1987) implicit and explicit word-fragment completion tests for their graphemically encoded words, "graph-emically"-encoded pictures, and their semantically encoded words.

The second point is that although a reversed association logically compels one

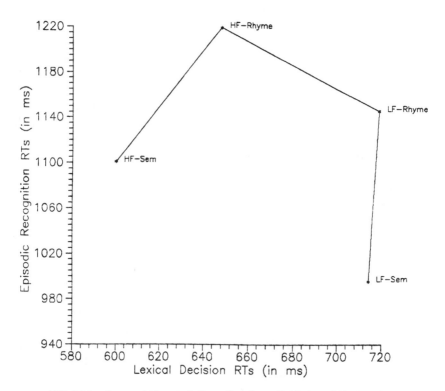

FIG. 13.1.   A reversed association effect from Duchek and Neely's (in press) episodic recognition and lexical decision tasks.

to posit the operation of two processes, it does not by itself constrain what the exact nature of these two processes is. Thus, a reversed association effect for a particular episodic and semantic memory test does not conclusively show that the two distinct processes that produced the reversed association are rooted in the episodic/semantic memory distinction. For a more conclusive demonstration, one needs to show that a variable produces a similar reversed association effect across multiple episodic and semantic memory tasks. It is to this issue that I now turn.

3.2. Use More than One Episodic and Semantic Memory Test and Look for Higher Order Dissociations

The suggestion to use multiple episodic and semantic memory tests has been made by Blaxton (1985), Roediger (1984), and Roediger and Blaxton (1987). The rationale for this suggestion is that a dissociation (a term hereafter used generically to include a reversed association) that occurs *across* episodic and semantic memory tests cannot be taken as support for the episodic/semantic memory distinction if that same dissociation also occurs for two tests *within* a memory system. Following the lead of Jacoby (1983), Blaxton (1985) has argued that episodic versus semantic memory differences per se are not responsible for dissociations that occur for (a) the effects that an item's prior presentation has on episodic memory for that prior presentation, and (b) the repetition priming effects that prior presentation produces in semantic memory tests such as word-fragment completion and perceptual identification (e.g., Challis & Roediger, 1987; Durgunoğlu & Roediger, 1987; Graf et al., 1982; Graf & Mandler, 1984; Jacoby & Dallas, 1981; Jacoby, 1983; Roediger & Blaxton, 1987).

According to Blaxton (1985), these types of dissociations occur because the particular episodic and semantic memory tests emphasize different kinds of processing during retrieval. Specifically, Blaxton claimed that the episodic memory tests evoked the retrieval of conceptual/associative information associated with the test stimulus (so-called conceptually driven processing, e.g., did I study an item having this meaning and/or is this test item episodically associated with some other item I know I studied?), whereas the semantic memory tests emphasized extraction of information from the visual/orthographic information in the test stimulus (so-called data-driven processing). In an elegant set of experiments, Blaxton (1985) showed that a dissociation that occurred for a conceptually driven episodic memory test and a data-driven semantic memory test could be replicated when one compared conceptually driven and data-driven *episodic* memory tests and conceptually driven and data-driven *semantic* memory tests. She therefore concluded that it was more parsimonious to explain these dissociations using a unitary transfer-appropriate processing account (cf., McDaniel, Friedman, & Bourne, 1978; Morris, Bransford, & Franks, 1977) than by using a two-factor episodic/semantic memory account.

For present purposes, there are two interesting features of Blaxton's (1985) analysis. First, although the amount of data-driven versus conceptually driven processing varies with the nature of the test stimulus presentation parameters (with brief masked presentations and word-fragment presentations invoking a heavier emphasis on data-driven processing), it can also vary for identical test stimulus presentations *within* episodic and semantic memory tests as a function of the nature of the information the subject must retrieve in order to utilize the test stimulus as a retrieval cue. Because of this, one cannot rule out Blaxton's transfer-appropriate processing explanation for an episodic/semantic memory task dissociation by merely equating the stimulus presentation parameters for the test items in the two types of test[7].

Clearly, before a dissociation can be used to support the episodic/semantic memory distinction (as opposed to the data-driven/conceptually driven processing distinction), one must equate the episodic and semantic memory tests on the amounts of data-driven and conceptually driven processing they require. Although Roediger et al. (chapter 1 of this book) have developed an independent criterion for determining if a task is predominantly conceptually driven (it yields a generation effect; cf. Slamecka & Graf, 1978) or predominantly data-driven (it yields a reverse generation effect), they have not developed procedures that permit one to equate two tests on *both* the amounts of data-driven and conceptually driven processing they require. Without such procedures, one cannot know if an obtained dissociation supports the episodic/semantic distinction or is due to the episodic and semantic memory tests not having been equated on both the amounts of data-driven and conceptually driven processing they require.

The second point of interest concerning Blaxton's (1985) analysis is that although it holds up nicely for the tasks she used, it does not necessarily provide a general account of episodic/semantic memory dissociations. It would do so only if it could be shown that (a) *all* such dissociations come from episodic and semantic memory tasks that have been confounded by differences in either the amounts of data-driven or conceptually driven processing they invoke, and (b) the nature of the dissociations obtained is what one would expect based on these confounded differences. However, to show this, one would need to solve the difficult problem of developing a means of precisely and independently measuring the amounts of data-driven and conceptually driven processing a particular test invokes.

---

[7]Recent data from Weldon, Roediger, and Challis (in press) suggests that when word stems or word fragments serve as retrieval cues, subjects are likely to use data-driven retrieval strategies, even when they are given episodic memory instructions. This suggests that the stimulus presentation parameters play a stronger role than retrieval instructions in inducing data-driven versus conceptually driven processing. However, when a semantic cue was presented along with the word stems or word fragments, evidence for conceptually driven processing was obtained only if subjects were given episodic memory instructions. This suggests that retrieval instructions can play some role in determining whether test processing will be data-driven or conceptually driven.

Blaxton's (1985) and Roediger and Blaxton's (1987) demonstrations provide us with a sobering note. Even when episodic and semantic memory tests are perfectly equated on all variables other than the instructions concerning the information that subjects must retrieve, these tests may induce differences in retrieval strategies that have nothing to do with the episodic versus semantic nature of the information being retrieved (cf. Reder & Ross, 1983). This greatly complicates things, because now one must not only equate the episodic and semantic tasks on all observable variables, but also on hidden variables that can have different levels when the directly observable conditions are identical.

Shoben and Ross (1986) have suggested one way out of this problem. They suggested that, in addition to using multiple episodic and semantic memory tests to test for episodic/semantic dissociations, one should also use multiple independent variables, so as to provide the opportunity for observing higher-order dissociative interactions among their effects. If no higher-order dissociations are observed across episodic versus semantic memory tests when multiple independent variables and multiple tasks are used, one becomes more convinced that their absence is not due to one having merely chosen variables that affect "peripheral" processes (e.g., encoding and response preparation) that are not inherently tied to differences in episodic versus semantic processing. Also, if similar higher-order dissociations are observed across several episodic versus semantic memory tests, it becomes less likely that they are merely due to retrieval strategies induced by the particular episodic and semantic memory tests chosen. But even if higher-order dissociations are obtained in several different episodic and semantic memory tests, it is difficult to know what episodic/semantic dissociations mean in the absence of a well-specified theory. It is to this final point that I now turn.

3.3. Develop a Well-Specified Theory of Episodic Versus Semantic Memory Mechanisms

Even if experimental dissociations are obtained for episodic versus semantic memory tests when the eight prescriptions given in Section 1 and prescriptions 3.1 and 3.2 are followed, it is not entirely clear exactly what these dissociations imply. At the most general level, reversed association effects imply that *something* is psychologically different when subjects perform tasks in which they are required to retrieve episodic information and when they perform tasks in which they are required to retrieve semantic information. But this is hardly news. Clearly, the experimenter has intended that different psychological operations be performed, and introspectively it seems as though we are doing very different things when we try to retrieve a specific episode versus when we do not.

As several people have pointed out (e.g., Durgunoğlu & Neely, 1987; Hintzman, 1984; McKoon, et al., 1986; Neely & Durgunoğlu, 1985; Roediger, 1984; Shoben, 1984; Shoben & Ross, 1986), what Tulving and other proponents of the episodic/semantic memory distinction have not done adequately is to specify the nature of the mechanisms responsible for this apparent psychological difference. Without such specification, it is difficult to know which variables one should manipulate in order to produce a dissociation effect and to predict the exact form that the dissociation will take. Heretofore, the logic has too often been that the mere existence of an experimental dissociation supports the episodic/semantic memory distinction, regardless of its exact form.

There are two reasons that it is important that episodic/semantic theory be developed to the point of being able to predict when dissociations will or will not occur and if they do occur, the exact form that they will take. First, for any subset of episodic/semantic dissociations, one can develop an alternative account for the exact dissociation that has occurred. A good example of this is Roediger and Blaxton's (1987) transfer-appropriate processing account, which I just discussed. One needs to be able to derive contrasting predictions from episodic/semantic theory and the transfer-appropriate processing account to determine which account is better. This will require the development of a principled theoretical analysis of episodic versus semantic memory structures and processes (and probably a sharpening of the data-driven versus conceptually driven processing account as well).

A second reason for needing a detailed episodic/semantic theory is that Tulving (1984) has recently argued that episodic memory is embedded in semantic memory. (Without further specification, it is difficult to know how this view differs from Anderson & Bower's, 1973, and Anderson & Ross', 1980, view that episodic information is represented as temporal-spatial tags associated with the nodes and pathways of semantic memory.) This embeddedness view requires considerable theoretical specification to account for certain kinds of dissociations. To understand this, consider the generate-recognize theory of recall and recognition (e.g., Anderson & Bower, 1972, 1974; Kintsch, 1970, 1974). In this theory, the recognition process that mediates performance in an episodic recognition test is the same recognition process that serves as the second stage in episodic recall, the first stage of which involves the generation of the to-be-recognized items.

As Neely and Balota (1981) have pointed out, it is easy for generate-recognize theory to account for a variable having an effect in recall but not recognition. It can do so by arguing that the variable affects the generation stage of recall but not recognition. However, complexities arise when one uses such a theory to account for a variable affecting recognition but not recall or for a crossover interaction. To do so, one must argue that the variable is having an effect in one direction for the generation process and an offsetting opposite effect on the subsequent recognition process. To predict whether the result would be a null-effect-in-recall or a crossover interaction would require rather precise quantification of the variable's effect on each of the two processes embedded in recall. (See Dunn & Kirsner, 1988, for a more detailed analysis of this issue.) If episodic memory is embedded in semantic memory, just as recognition is embedded in recall, a similar complexity would need to be met by a similar theoretical precision to account for a variable's having an effect in a semantic memory task and no effect or an opposite effect in an analogous episodic memory test.[8].

A final comment concerning theoretical interpretations of genuine episodic/semantic dissociations relates to determining whether they are produced by different storage systems or different retrieval processes operating on a unified storage system. The problems encountered in disentangling these two possibilities are similar to those encountered in trying to determine if tasks that require the retrieval of imaginal versus propositional information involve accessing functionally distinct storage systems or involve the retrieval of differentially activated features within the same storage system. As Anderson (1978) has argued, it is impossible to distinguish between these two possibilities on the basis of behavioral data. The problem is that if the data disconfirm the predictions of a theory based on its assumptions about there being only unimodal propositional or imaginal representations, one can always retain the unimodal representational assumptions and accommodate the data by changing one's assumptions about the manner in which retrieval mechanisms extract information from that single representational format.

The same general argument seemingly applies to trying to determine if a genuine episodic/semantic dissociation is due to the episodic and semantic memory tests tapping different storage systems or is due to these tests invoking different kinds of procedures for retrieving information from a unimodal storage format. Although most people seem to believe that a retrieval difference is not as important as a storage difference, I believe that retrieval and storage differences are equally important. Furthermore, the distinction between retrieval and storage mechanisms has become somewhat blurred in recent connectionist (e.g., McClelland & Rumelhart, 1986) and proceduralist (e.g., Kolers & Roediger, 1984) models of memory. Thus, I do not see the retrieval/storage indeterminancy problem as seriously undermining properly obtained experimental dissociations as evidence for a functional episodic/semantic memory distinction.

---

[8]It is interesting that the short-term/long-term memory distinction has many conceptual parallels to the episodic/semantic distinction (cf., Wolters, 1984). For example, experimental dissociations were first taken as evidence for a structural distinction between short-term and long-term memory (see Crowder, 1976, for a review). However, some (e.g., Shulman, 1971) have argued that short-term and long-term memory tasks emphasized the retrieval of different kinds of information from the same storage system, and more recent formulations (e.g., Shiffrin & Schneider, 1977) treat short-term memory as being embedded in long-term memory—that is, as the activated subset long-term memory. In fact, Crowder (1982, see also chapter 14 of this volume) argues that many of the experimental dissociations originally taken as evidence for the short-term/long-term memory distinction can be reinterpreted within the framework of a unifactor theory of temporal discriminability (cf., Glenberg, 1987). It will be interesting to see if the episodic/semantic distinction continues down a parallel path, with episodic/semantic accounts of dissociations being replaced by a unifactor explanation.

IV. SUMMARY

The proper use of experimental dissociations as evidence supporting or undermining Tulving's (1972, 1983, 1984) episodic/semantic memory distinction demands both methodological and theoretical rigor. In terms of methodological rigor, one must use a host of procedural safeguards for controlling extraneous variables across episodic and semantic memory tests, as well as employ rather complicated factorial designs in which the effects of multiple independent variables are assessed in multiple episodic and semantic memory tests. Furthermore, to provide compelling support for the episodic/semantic memory distinction the experimental dissociations obtained with these complex procedural safeguards should take the form of what Dunn and Kirsner (1988) called a *reversed association effect*. In terms of theoretical rigor, detailed analyses must be provided concerning how episodic and semantic memory mechanisms differ so that one can ultimately predict the conditions under which dissociations will or will not occur, and the exact form such dissociations will take.

Given that very few extant experimental dissociations have come from experiments that have achieved the methodological rigor prescribed here, it may be unreasonable to ask proponents of the episodic/semantic memory distinction to provide us with detailed deductions from well-formulated theoretical principles. Perhaps the proper view of the status of the episodic/semantic distinction is that we are still in the inductive phase of the science. This view does not seem overly pessimistic. Although the episodic/semantic memory distinction has been around in some form or another at least since Bergson (1911), it has been the object of direct empirical scrutiny for fewer than the 15 years since Tulving (1972) resurrected it.

Regardless of whether the current emphasis should be placed on theoretical development, additional empirical work, or both, I want to close by endorsing Shoben and Ross' (1986) position. (See chapter 9 of this book for a similar point of view.) These authors argue that even though it is a demanding task to execute them properly and to interpret their results properly, experimental dissociation designs remain an important and useful tool for furthering our understanding of functionally distinct memory mechanisms. This is so whether these mechanisms turn out to be based on episodic/semantic differences, data-driven versus conceptually driven processing differences, or some other difference altogether. My hope is that adherence to the prescriptions that I have outlined here will facilitate the proper use of this important tool and thereby accelerate our acquisition of uncontaminated information concerning whether the heuristically useful distinction that Tulving has given us has psychological validity as well.

ACKNOWLEDGMENT

Preparation of this manuscript was supported by Grant RO1 HD15054 from the National Institute of Child Health and Human Development.

REFERENCES

Anderson, J. R. (1978). Arguments concerning representations for mental imagery. *Psychological Review, 85,* 249–277.

Anderson, J. R. (1983). *The architecture of cognition.* Cambridge, MA: Harvard University Press.

Anderson, J. R., & Bower, G. H. (1972). Recognition and retrieval processes in free recall. *Psychological Review, 79,* 97–123.

Anderson, J. R., & Bower, G. H. (1973). *Human associative memory.* Washington, D.C.: Winston.

Anderson, J. R., & Bower, G. H. (1974). A propositional theory of recognition memory. *Memory & Cognition, 2,* 406–412.

Anderson, J. R., & Ross, B. H. (1980). Evidence against a semantic–episodic distinction. *Journal of Experimental Psychology: Human Learning and Memory, 6,* 441–466.

Balota, D. A., & Chumbley, J. I. (1984). Are lexical decisions a good measure of lexical access? The role of word frequency in the neglected decision stage. *Journal of Experimental Psychology: Human Perception and Performance, 10,* 340–357.

Balota, D. A., & Lorch, R. F. (1986). Depth of automatic spreading activation: Mediated priming effects in pronunciation but not in lexical decision. *Journal of Experimental Psychology: Learning, Memory, and Cognition, 12,* 336–345.

Balota, D. A., & Neely, J. H. (1980). Test-expectancy and word-frequency effects in recall and recognition. *Journal of Experimental Psychology: Human Learning and Memory, 6,* 576–587.

Becker, C. A. (1980). Semantic context effects in visual word recognition: An analysis of semantic strategies. *Memory & Cognition, 8,* 493–512.

Bergson, H. (1911). *Matter and memory.* London: Allen & Unwin.

Blaxton, T. A. (1985). *Examining theoretical accounts of dissociations among memory measures.* Unpublished doctoral dissertation, Purdue University.

Blaxton, T. A., & Neely, J. H. (1983). Inhibition from semantically related primes: Evidence of a category-specific retrieval inhibition. *Memory & Cognition, 11,* 500–510.

Brown, A. S. (1981). Inhibition in cued retrieval. *Journal of Experimental Psychology: Human Learning and Memory, 7,* 204–215.

Carroll, M., & Kirsner, K. (1982). Context and repetition effects in lexical decision and recognition memory. *Journal of Verbal Learning and Verbal Behavior, 21,* 55–69.

Challis, B. H., & Roediger, H. L. (1987, May). *Effects of identity repetition and conceptual repetition on performance in free recall and word fragment completion.* Paper presented at the meeting of the Midwestern Psychological Association, Chicago, IL.

Craik, F. I. M., & Tulving, E. (1975). Depth of processing and the retention of words in episodic memory. *Journal of Experimental Psychology: General, 104,* 268–294.

Crowder, R. G. (1976). *Principles of learning and memory.* Hillsdale, NJ: Lawrence Erlbaum Associates.

Crowder, R. G. (1982). The demise of short-term memory. *Acta Psychologica, 50,* 291–323.

den Heyer, K. (1986). Manipulating attention-induced priming in a lexical decision task by means of repeated prime-target presentations. *Journal of Memory and Language, 25,* 19–42.

den Heyer, K., Briand, K., & Dannenbring, G. L. (1983). Strategic factors in a lexical decision task: Evidence for automatic and attention-driven processes. *Memory & Cognition, 11,* 374–381.

den Heyer, K., Briand, K., & Smith, L. C. (1985). Automatic and strategic effects in semantic priming: An examination of Becker's verification model. *Memory & Cognition, 11,* 374–381.

Duchek, J., & Neely, J. H. (in press). A dissociative word-frequency x levels-of-processing interaction in episodic recognition and lexical decision tasks. *Memory & Cognition, 17.*

Dunn, J. C., & Kirsner, K. (1988). Discovering functionally independent mental processes: The principle of reversed association. *Psychological Review, 95,* 91–101.

Durgunoğlu, A. Y., & Neely, J. H. (1987). On obtaining episodic priming in a lexical decision task following paired-associate learning. *Journal of Experimental Psychology: Learning, Memory, and Cognition, 13,* 206–222.

Durgunoğlu, A. Y., & Roediger, H. L. (1987). Test differences in accessing bilingual memory. *Journal of Memory and Language, 26,* 377–391.

Favreau, M., & Segalowitz, N. S. (1983). Automatic and controlled processes in the first- and second-language reading of fluent bilinguals. *Memory & Cognition, 11,* 565–574.

Feustel, T. C., Shiffrin, R. M., & Salasoo, A. (1983). Episodic and lexical contributions to the repetition effect in word identification. *Journal of Experimental Psychology: General, 112,* 309–346.

Flexser, A. J., & Tulving, E. (1978). Retrieval independence and recall. *Psychological Review, 85,* 153–171.

Forster, K. I. (1981). Frequency blocking and lexical access: One mental lexicon or two? *Journal of Verbal Learning and Verbal Behavior, 20,* 190–203.

Forster, K. I., & Davis, C. (1984). Repetition priming and frequency attenuation in lexical access. *Journal of Experimental Psychology: Learning, Memory, and Cognition, 10,* 680–698.

Garner, W. R., Hake, H., & Eriksen, C. W. (1956). Operationism and the concepts of perception. *Psychological Review, 63,* 149–159.

Glanzer, M., & Adams, J. K. (1985). The mirror effect in recognition memory. *Memory & Cognition, 13,* 8–20.

Glanzer, M., & Ehrenreich, S. L. (1979). Structure and search of the internal lexicon. *Journal of Verbal Learning and Verbal Behavior, 18,* 381–398.

Glenberg, A. M. (1987). Temporal context and memory. In D. S. Gorfein & R. R. Hoffman (Eds.), *Memory and cognitive processes: The Ebbinghaus Centennial Conference* (pp. 173–190). Hillsdale, NJ: Lawrence Erlbaum Associates.

Gordon, B. (1983). Lexical access and lexical decision: Mechanisms of frequency sensitivity. *Journal of Verbal Learning and Verbal Behavior, 22,* 24–44.

Graf, P., & Mandler, G. (1984). Activation makes words more accessible, but not necessarily more retrievable. *Journal of Verbal Learning and Verbal Behavior, 23,* 553–568.

Graf, P., Mandler, G., & Haden, P. (1982). Simulating amnesic symptoms in normal subjects. *Science, 218,* 1243–1244.

Graf, P., & Schacter, D. L. (1985). Implicit and explicit memory for new associations in normal and amnesic subjects. *Journal of Experimental Psychology: Learning, Memory, and Cognition, 11,* 501–518.

Gregg, V. (1976). Word frequency, recognition and recall. In J. Brown (Ed.), *Recall and recognition* (pp. 183–216). New York: Wiley.

Henik, A., Friedrich, F. J., & Kellogg, W. A. (1983). The dependence of semantic relatedness effects upon prime processing. *Memory & Cognition, 11,* 366–373.

Herrmann, D. J., & Harwood, J. R. (1980). More evidence for the existence of separate semantic and episodic stores in long term memory. *Journal of Experimental Psychology: Human Learning and Memory, 6,* 467–478.

Hintzman, D. L. (1984). Episodic vs. semantic memory: A distinction whose time has come—and gone? *The Behavioral and Brain Sciences, 7,* 240–241.

Jacoby, L. L. (1983). Remembering the data: Analyzing interactive processes in reading. *Journal of Verbal Learning and Verbal Behavior, 22,* 485–508.

Jacoby, L. L. (1984). Incidental vs. intentional retrieval: Remembering and awareness as separate issues. In N. Butters & L.R. Squire (Eds.), *The neuropsychology of memory* (pp. 145–156). New York: Guilford Press.

Jacoby, L. L., & Dallas, M. (1981). On the relationship between autobiographical memory and perceptual learning. *Journal of Experimental Psychology: General, 110,* 306–340.

James, C. T. (1975). The role of semantic information in lexical decisions. *Journal of Experimental Psychology: Human Perception and Performance, 1,* 130–136.

Johnston, W. A., Dark, V. J., & Jacoby, L. L. (1985). Perceptual fluency and recognition judgments. *Journal of Experimental Psychology: Learning, Memory, and Cognition, 11,* 3–11.

Kintsch, W. (1970). Models for free recall and recognition. In D. A. Norman (Ed.), *Models of human memory* (pp. 333–373). New York: Academic Press.

Kintsch, W. (1974). *The representation of meaning in memory.* Hillsdale, NJ: Lawrence Erlbaum Associates.

Kolers, P. A., & Roediger, H. L. (1984).Procedures of mind. *Journal of Verbal Learning and Verbal Behavior, 23,* 425–449.

Lewandowsky, S. (1986). Priming in recognition memory for categorized lists. *Journal of Experimental Psychology: Learning, Memory, and Cognition, 12,* 562–574.

Loftus, G. R. (1978). On interpretation of interactions. *Memory & Cognition, 6,* 312–319.

Logan, G. D. (1985). Skill and automaticity: Relations, implications, and future directions. *Canadian Journal of Psychology, 39,* 367–386.

Lorch, R. F., Balota, D. A., & Stamm, E. G. (1986). Locus of inhibition effects in the priming of lexical decisions: Pre- or post-lexical access? *Memory & Cognition, 14,* 95–103.

Lupker, S. J. (1984). Semantic priming without association: A second look. *Journal of Verbal Learning and Verbal Behavior, 23,* 709–733.

McClelland, J. L., & Rumelhart, D. E. (1986). A distributed model of human learning and memory. In J. L. McClelland, D.E. Rumelhart, & the PDP Research Group (Eds.), *Parallel distributed processing: Explorations in the microstructure of cognition, Vol. 2: Psychological and biological models* (pp. 170–215). Cambridge, MA: MIT Press.

McCloskey, M., & Santee, J. (1981). Are semantic memory and episodic memory distinct systems? *Journal of Experimental Psychology: Human Learning and Memory, 7,* 66–71.

McDaniel, M. A., Friedman, A., & Bourne, L. E. (1978). Remembering the levels of information in words. *Memory & Cognition, 6,* 156–164.

McKoon, G. & Ratcliff, R. (1979). Priming in episodic and semantic memory. *Journal of Verbal Learning and Verbal Behavior, 18,* 463–480.

McKoon, G., & Ratcliff, R. (1986). Automatic activation of episodic information in a semantic memory task. *Journal of Experimental Psychology: Learning, Memory, & Cognition, 12,* 108–115.

McKoon, G., Ratcliff, R., & Dell, G. S. (1986). A critical evaluation of the semantic/episodic distinction. *Journal of Experimental Psychology: Learning, Memory, and Cognition, 12,* 295–306.

Mitchell, D. B., & Brown, A. S. (1988). Persistent repetition priming in picture naming and its dissociation from recognition memory. *Journal of Experimental Psychology: Learning, Memory, and Cognition, 14,* 213–222.

Morris, C. D., Bransford, J. D., & Franks, J. J. (1977). Levels of processing versus transfer appropriate processing. *Journal of Verbal Learning and Verbal Behavior, 16,* 519–533.

Muter, P. (1978). Recognition failure of recallable words in semantic memory. *Memory & Cognition, 6,* 9–12.

Neely, J. H. (1977). Semantic priming and retrieval from lexical memory: Roles of inhibitionless spreading activation and limited-capacity attention. *Journal of Experimental Psychology: General, 106,* 226–254.

Neely, J. H. (1980, May). *The role of expectancy in the word-frequency effect in a lexical decision task.* Paper presented at the meeting of the Midwestern Psychological Association, Chicago, IL.

Neely, J. H., & Balota, D. A. (1981). Test-expectancy and semantic-organization effects in recall and recognition. *Memory & Cognition, 9,* 283–300.

Neely, J. H., Blackwell, P., & Campbell, K. (1988, November). Episodic and semantic priming in lexical decision and pronunciation tasks. Paper presented at the meeting of the Psychonomic Society, Chicago, IL.

Neely, J. H., & Durgunoğlu, A. (1985). Dissociative episodic and semantic priming effects in episodic recognition and lexical decision tasks. *Journal of Memory and Language, 24*, 466–489.

Neely, J. H., Fisk, W. J., & Ross, K. L. (1983, November). *On obtaining facilitatory and inhibitory priming effects at short SOAs.* Paper presented at the meeting of the Psychonomic Society, San Diego, CA.

Neely, J. H., Keefe, D. E., & Ross, K. L. (in press). Semantic priming in the lexical decision task: Roles of prospective prime-generated expectancies and retrospective semantic matching. *Journal of Experimental Psychology: Learning, Memory, and Cognition, 15.*

Neely, J. H., & Payne, D. G. (1983). A direct comparison of recognition failure rates for recallable names in episodic and semantic memory tests. *Memory & Cognition, 11*, 161–171.

Neely, J. H., Schmidt, S. R., & Roediger, H. L. (1983). Inhibition from related primes in recognition memory. *Journal of Experimental Psychology: Learning, Memory, and Cognition,9*, 196–211.

Nilsson, L. G., Law, J., & Tulving, E. (1988). Recognition failure of recallable unique names. *Journal of Experimental Psychology: Learning, Memory, & Cognition, 14*, 266–277.

Norris, D. (1984). The effects of frequency, repetition and stimulus quality in visual word recognition. *Quarterly Journal of Experimental Psychology, 36A*, 507–518.

Posner, M. I., & Snyder, C. R. R. (1975). Attention and cognitive control. In R. L. Solso (Ed.), *Information processing and cognition: The Loyola symposium* (pp. 55–85). Hillsdale, NJ: Lawrence Erlbaum Associates.

Ratcliff, R., & McKoon, G. (1981a). Automatic and strategic priming in recognition. *Journal of Verbal Learning and Verbal Behavior, 20*, 204–215.

Ratcliff, R., & McKoon, G. (1981b). Does activation really spread? *Psychological Review, 88*, 454–462.

Reder, L. M. (1982). Plausibility judgments versus fact retrieval: Alternative strategies for sentence verification. *Psychological Review, 89*, 250–280.

Reder, L. M., & Anderson, J. R. (1980). A partial resolution of the paradox of interference: The role of integrating knowledge. *Cognitive Psychology, 12*, 447–472.

Reder, L. M., & Ross, B. H. (1983). Integrated knowledge in different tasks: The role of retrieval strategy on fan effects. *Journal of Experimental Psychology: Learning, Memory, and Cognition, 9*, 55–72.

Richardson-Klavehn, A., & Bjork, R. A. (1988). Measures of memory. *Annual Review of Psychology, 39*, 475–544.

Roediger, H. L. (1984). Does current evidence from dissociation experiments favor the episodic/semantic distinction? *The Behavioral and Brain Sciences, 7*, 252–254.

Roediger, H. L., & Blaxton, T. A. (1987). Retrieval modes produce dissociations in memory for surface information. In D. S. Gorfein & R. R. Hoffman (Eds.), *Memory and cognitive processes: The Ebbinghaus Centennial Conference* (pp. 349–379). Hillsdale, NJ: Lawrence Erlbaum Associates.

Roediger, H. L., Weldon, M. S., & Stadler, M. (1987, November). *Direct comparison of two implicit measures of retention.* Paper presented at the meeting of the Psychonomic Society, Seattle, WA.

Scarborough, D. L., Cortese, C., & Scarborough, H.S. (1977). Frequency and repetition effects in lexical memory. *Journal of Experimental Psychology: Human Perception and Performance, 3*, 1–17.

Schacter, D. L. (1987). Implicit memory: History and current status. *Journal of Experimental Psychology: Learning, Memory, & Cognition, 13*, 501–518.

Seidenberg, M., Waters, G., Sanders, M., & Langer, P. (1984). Pre- and post-lexical loci of contextual effects on word recognition. *Memory & Cognition, 12*, 315–328.

Shiffrin, R. M., & Schneider, W. (1977). Controlled and automatic human information processing II: Perceptual learning, automatic attending, and a general theory. *Psychological Review, 84*, 127–190.

Shoben, E. J. (1984). Semantic and episodic memory. In R. S. Wyer, Jr., & T. K. Srull (Eds.), *Handbook of social cognition, Vol. 2* (pp. 213–231). Hillsdale, NJ: Lawrence Erlbaum Associates.

Shoben, E. J., & Ross, B. H. (1986). The crucial role of dissociations. *The Behavioral and Brain Sciences, 9,* 568–570.

Shoben, E. J., Wescourt, K. T., & Smith, E. E. (1978). Sentence verification, sentence recognition, and the semantic–episodic distinction. *Journal of Experimental Psychology: Human Learning and Memory, 4,* 304–317.

Shulman, H. G. (1971). Similarity effects in short-term memory. *Psychological Bulletin, 75,* 399–415.

Shulman, H. G., & Davison, T. C. B. (1977). Control properties of semantic coding in a lexical decision task. *Journal of Verbal Learning and Verbal Behavior, 16,* 92–98.

Slamecka, N. J., & Graf, P. (1978). The generation effect: Delineation of a phenomenon. *Journal of Experimental Psychology: Human Learning and Memory, 4,* 592–604.

Sloman, S. A., Hayman, G. C. A., Ohta, N., Law, J., & Tulving, E. (1988). Forgetting in primed fragment completion. *Journal of Experimental Psychology: Learning, Memory, & Cognition, 14,* 223–239.

Smith, M. C. (1979). Contextual facilitation in a letter search task depends on how the prime is processed. *Journal of Experimental Psychology: Human Perception and Performance, 5,* 239–251.

Smith, M. C., Theodor, L., & Franklin, P. E. (1983). On the relationship between contextual facilitation and depth of processing. *Journal of Experimental Psychology: Learning, Memory, and Cognition, 9,* 697–712.

Snow, N., & Neely, J. H. (1987, November). *Reduction of semantic priming from inclusion of physically or nominally related prime-target pairs.* Paper presented at the meeting of the Psychonomics Society, Seattle, WA.

Squire, L. R., Shimamura, A. P., & Graf, P. (1987). Strength and duration of priming effects in normal subjects and amnesic patients. *Neuropsychologia, 25,* 195–210.

Tulving, E. (1962). Subjective organization in recall of "unrelated" words. *Psychological Review, 69,* 344–354.

Tulving, E. (1972). Episodic and semantic memory. In E. Tulving & W. Donaldson (Eds.), *Organization of memory* (pp. 381–403). New York: Academic Press.

Tulving, E. (1976). Ecphoric processes in recall and recognition. In J. Brown (Ed.), *Recall and recognition* (pp. 37–73). London: Wiley.

Tulving, E. (1983). *Elements of episodic memory.* New York: Oxford University Press.

Tulving, E. (1984). Precis of *Elements of episodic memory. The Behavioral and Brain Sciences, 7,* 223–238.

Tulving, E. (1985). How many memory systems are there? *American Psychologist, 40,* 385–398.

Tulving, E., & Osler, S. (1968). Effectiveness of retrieval cues in memory for words. *Journal of Experimental Psychology, 77,* 593–601.

Tulving, E., & Pearlstone, Z. (1966). Availability vs. accessibility of information in memory for words. *Journal of Verbal Learning and Verbal Behavior, 5,* 381–391.

Tulving, E., & Psotka, J. (1971). Retroactive inhibition in free recall: Inaccessibility of information available in the memory store. *Journal of Experimental Psychology, 87,* 1–8.

Tulving, E., Schacter, D. L., & Stark, H. A. (1982). Priming effects in word-fragment completion are independent of recognition memory. *Journal of Experimental Psychology: Learning, Memory, and Cognition, 8,* 336–342.

Tulving, E., & Thomson, D. M. (1973). Encoding specificity and retrieval processes in episodic memory. *Psychological Review, 80,* 352–373.

Tulving, E., & Wiseman, S. (1975). Relation between recognition and recognition failure of recallable words. *Bulletin of the Psychonomic Society, 6,* 79–82.

Tweedy, J. R., Lapinski, R. H., & Schvaneveldt, R. W. (1977). Semantic-context effects on word recognition: Influence of varying the proportion of items presented in an appropriate context. *Memory & Cognition, 5,* 84–99.

Weiner, B. (1966). Effects of motivation on the availability of and retrieval of memory traces. *Psychological Bulletin, 65,* 24–37.

Weldon, M. S., Roediger, H. L., & Challis, B. H. (in press). The properties of retrieval cues constrain the picture superiority effect. *Memory & Cognition, 17.*

Wolters, G. (1984). Memory: Two systems or one system with many subsystems? *The Behavioral and Brain Sciences, 7,* 256–257.

Wood, F., Taylor, B., Penny, R., & Stump, D. (1980). Regional cerebral blood flow response to recognition memory vs. semantic classification tasks. *Brain and Language, 9,* 113–122.

14 Modularity and Dissociations in Memory Systems

Robert G. Crowder
Yale University

A cynical attitude toward progress in psychology is that we simply move back and forth between well-defined polarities, on pendulum swings, without really getting anywhere. Personally, I much prefer the model of a helix, in which we can recognize steady progress in one direction while not denying oscillations of perspective on certain other issues. One unmistakable trend that has been sweeping across the behavioral and cognitive sciences is the advancement of genetic explanations over environmental explanations. This is easy to find in such diverse fields as linguistics, intelligence, personality, and mental health, to say nothing of medicine. My grandparents were staunch believers in genetic causation, too, but I like to think we now have better reasons for our attitudes than they did.

A different trend back to earlier ideas is becoming evident in the reappearance of *faculty psychology* in cognition, generally, and in the analysis of memory, in particular. Publication of Fodor's *Modularity of Mind* (Fodor, 1983) only celebrates this newest cycle. The histories of such topics as localization of function in the brain and the interpretation of intelligence put the trend in perspective. The impulse to subdivide memory into isolated subsystems should be appreciated as a manifestation of Fodor's views, with modularity itself manifesting a historical rhythm that governs our approach to many of the great issues.

TWO SORTS OF MODULARITY IN MEMORY

In this first section of the chapter, I identify two very different interpretations of what *modularity* could mean in memory, one that may well be generally accepted as conventional wisdom and the other controversial. These correspond, I think, to Fodor's "horizontal" and "vertical" modularity, and to Jackendoff's (1987) "representation-based modules" and "fundamental principles," but I call them, less abstractly, *coding modularity* and *process modularity*. In later sections, I take the dissociation of short-term storage (STS) and long-term storage (LTS) as a case in point, raising caution about concluding in favor of separate memory systems. I show that belief in Hebbian consolidation is quite general in the animal field, just as the STS/LTS distinction has been among students of human memory. I conclude that the evidence is equally fragile in both cases. Finally, the status of empirical dissociations is discussed in general, including the cases of recognition and recall and of declarative and procedural memory.

Coding Modularity

Any attitude toward information processing must acknowledge that different kinds of information use different parts of the brain. Trivially, the auditory and visual systems engage distinct input pathways and cortical projections, as do the so-called minor senses. The specialization of the left hemisphere for language processing has been more tantalizing for the cognitive psychologist, perhaps only because it gives tangible reality to the concept of language.

As students of memory, many of us have blandly recognized this left–right specialization and yet, at the same time, we have held to a sort of Lashley position about learning and memory—that they depend on having *something* between the ears, but it is all-purpose machinery (some say oatmeal) to be found there. Such reliance on all-purpose equipment causes no one to lose sleep, provided learning and memory are themselves considered specialized functions of the mind. This assumption is dubious, however.

The growing identification of perception and information processing as being synonymous with learning, or memorization (Craik & Lockhart, 1972; Crowder & Morton, 1969; Kolers, 1975), led many of us to change our attitudes in an important way: Once memory is regarded as a by-product of information processing, the implicit concept of all-purpose memory storage dissolves. To me, a comfortable language to describe this attitude is to say that *memory is not a storage process as such; it is simply the property of information processing that extends in time afterwards.*

In much the same way, the neutrinos detected at several international observatories starting on February 24, 1987, were not a sort of time capsule, laid down by Supernova 1987A for our benefit. These neutrinos represent part of that original event itself, in a galaxy called the Large Magellenic Cloud—an event that occurred 163,000 years ago and a billion billion miles away from here. These neutrinos *are* the event, observed at a remote context. And so it is with at least some kinds of memories. The retention is just an aspect of the original episode itself, manifest at some temporal remove. To me, this attitude is the essence of proceduralism.

This attitude makes notions like *memory stores,* specialized to hold information over time, superfluous. If the memory is, in some sense, an aspect of the original event, then the memory resides wherever in the nervous system the event did. The Proustian mechanism of redintegration based on olfactory/gustatory cues must then reside in the brain structures specialized for olfactory/gustatory processing, and of course the connections of these structures with others. Recognition memory for a kaleidoscope slide, for a snowflake, for a musical timbre, or perhaps for a spatial layout, would activate the participating units from their own respective information-processing episodes. Presumably, in these cases the processing, and therefore the memory residue, would have been scarcely verbalized. And when the information processing of interest consists, all along, of linguistic manipulations, the success or failure of retrieval efforts will depend on whether the originally active systems get reactivated by the cues at hand. I consider this view of episodic memory to be faithful to Tulving's (see Tulving, 1983) *encoding specificity principle.* It is also profoundly compatible with Hebb's (1949) ideas on cell assemblies and phase sequences as the agencies of memory. Related ideas in the animal-physiological approach to memory are found in Squire (1987, chapters 5 & 8).

Process Modularity

So, coding modularity in memory is the inevitable consequence of (a) brain specialization in cognition and (b) proceduralism in memory. What Fodor called *horizontal modularity,* which I call *processing modularity,* is quite another story. In this case, the separate subsystems cut across information formats (coding, or vertical modularity) in favor of common processes. An example that now seems rather crude, and which was cited derisively by Fodor (1983, p. 13–14), would be to propose distinct short- and long-term memory subsystems in which all sorts of memories would belong to one system up until some number of seconds had elapsed, and then to another system afterwards. Another case of process modularity is the distinction between procedural and declarative memory, increasingly popular in the 1980s. The same original experience, according to this last distinction, gets entered into distinct memory systems, one procedural, accessible to implicit memory tests, and intact in the amnesic, the other declarative, accessible to explicit probes of memory and seriously compromised in the amnesic.

What does it mean to propose distinct memory systems? Perhaps an analogy with visual information processing is instructive: It is now conventional to separate visual processing pathways, and their associated cortical relay sites, into two broad classes, some concerned with the identification of objects and others with their location in space (see, for example, Squire, 1987, p. 69). In addition, the same sort of distinction might cover sound localization and pitch perception, where the same stimuli might undergo processing in the two systems, for different purposes.

In the remainder of this chapter, I try to examine the evidence and arguments that once made us embrace the distinction between short- and long-term storage. The case was grounded in solid empirical dissociations. I conclude, as I have before (Crowder, 1982), that the case for two memory systems is weak, even when the distinction is broadened to cover the Hebbian consolidation theory of memory.

On the basis of empirical dissociations between implicit and explicit memory tests, some are now urging us to make a distinction between another processing dichotomy, procedural and declarative memory (Squire, 1987, chapter 11; Tulving, 1987). These systems of memory would constitute processing modules of just the sort that Fodor and others have warned against. We can see in both the dual-trace approach to memory storage (STS/LTS), and also in the more recent procedural/declarative distinction, that empirical demonstrations of *dissociation* are central to the arguments. Why have the dissociations of the 1960s come on hard times? What does this tell us about the usefulness of empirical dissociations in proposing memory subsystems? I argue that Tulving (1987) is too eager to make this inferential leap from processing dissociations to separate subsystems. Before going on, however, I should affirm that I attach the highest importance for theory to dissociations between and among memory variables. I take that importance to be beyond argument. The only question is whether they are sufficient to differentiate memory systems.

THE CASE OF SHORT-TERM STORAGE

I have reviewed elsewhere (Crowder, 1982) my revisionist interpretations of the concept of short-term storage (primary memory), and so I need not go into detail here. In a few words, I will try to point out how the evidence relied on empirical dissociations. I pause to do that because the term *dissociation* was not popular in mainstream cognition until the exciting work on amnesics enriched our language with this particularly medical connotation.

Review of Evidence

Recency. The traditional association of the recency effect in free recall with some transient memory has now been discredited by the work of Bjork and Whitten (1974; Whitten & Bjork, 1972, see also Baddeley & Hitch, 1977; Greene, 1986; Tzeng, 1973; Watkins & Peynircioglu, 1983). They showed that a post-list period of distraction, sufficient by itself to disrupt normal recency, does not eliminate recency if the items were spaced sufficiently from one another during presentation. If the distractor eliminates short-term memory, then this long-term recency effect must not be caused by short-term storage. Maybe the "normal" recency effect is not caused by it either.

I fully appreciate that this inference is not universal: For example, Schneider and Detweiler (1987) preferred to associate the short-term and long-term recency effects with different underlying mechanisms. Although I agree that parsimony is not a serious virtue in the theory of cognition, still, I think the burden of evidence must lie with those who wish to impose a complicated theoretical interpretation on a simple data pattern. If two creatures both look like goldfish and both act like goldfish, we should be prepared to accept that they are, in fact, *not* both goldfish, but the job of proving the distinction belongs to whomever believes in it.

Brown-Peterson Forgetting.   The second signature of the short-term storage system was the slope of the Brown-Peterson forgetting curve. Again, I have detailed elsewhere (Crowder 1976) how this evidence was handled by the two-store theory, and the argument is quite standard. Whether one's theory of loss in the Brown-Peterson task is an appeal to temporal decay, to displacement, or to perturbation of ordered rehearsal cycles, it *overpredicts* forgetting, specifically on the first trial of the experiment. That is, these mechanisms say nothing about proactive inhibition. There is nothing in these theories about why decay, displacement, and perturbation, respectively, do not occur or have only negligible effects on the first trial of an experimental session. Far less do they anticipate that a change in the meaning category of the stimulus items would make decay, displacement, or perturbation suddenly become ineffective; nor why allowing a long intertrial interval would nullify these three mechanisms.

Broadly, then, a theory of Brown-Peterson forgetting has to be a theory of how proactive inhibition works in this task (see Crowder & Greene, 1987a). Theories of proactive inhibition tend to fall into two main categories: First, some assume that the essence of proactive inhibition is really negative transfer— subsequent items never get learned as well as the items presented on the very first trial. Besides the studies reviewed in Crowder (1982), a recent application of this second idea can be found in Schneider and Detweiler (1987). Second, some theories assume that proactive inhibition represents a problem of recency discrimination among traces that are widely available: We must always remember which stored items were those that appeared on only the most recent trial. This latter hypothesis is particularly well equipped to handle the findings listed heretofore, as Gorfein (1987) has explained and as I assert again later. Notice that neither hypothesis for proactive inhibition has anything to do with special-purpose mechanisms of short-term storage. Both are well-understood principles of memory, plain and simple.

But recency and the Brown-Peterson slope were originally considered evidence for STS mainly because of *dissociations.* Recency recall and prerecency recall were sensitive to different variables. Recency depended on distraction, but recall from early and middle positions did not. The asymptote depended on such factors as word frequency, rate of presentation, and age of the subjects, but the recency effect did not.

The analysis of Brown-Peterson forgetting depended on the *theoretical* dissociation first advanced by Waugh and Norman (1965) between the asymptote and slope of forgetting functions. But this assumption never had much in the way of an experimental test because experimenters never had the patience to collect enough data points to allow separate estimates of these two performance parameters. This effort would have required curve-fitting based on tests of many different retention intervals within the same experiment.

Alternative Account Using Temporal Coding

Both the recency effect and the Brown-Peterson slope were dissociated from other performance measures in the same task (prerecency recall and the Brown-Peterson asymptote, respectively). There is a good case that both were originally misinterpreted. Furthermore, both results can now be explained in essentially the same way. They may depend on retrieval by means of the temporal context.

Recency has periodically been described in terms of "temporal" coding (e.g., Murdock, 1960). Recently, a temporal-discriminability approach to recency has been suggested by Glenberg (1987; Glenberg & Swanson, 1986).[1] The reasoning is that events that just happened are more distinctive with regard to their time of occurrence than are events from the more distant past. If time of occurrence were to be a retrieval cue, the recency advantage would result. Bjork and Whitten (1974) evoked a principle of "temporal perspective" in which an evenly spaced list of items was approached, for purposes of recall, from the recency direction, much as a line of evenly spaced telephone poles could be seen in spatial perspective from the near end. They assumed that the temporal discriminability of the recency items would be better than that of earlier items to the extent that the items were themselves spaced widely in time. Recall might depend on a sort of Weber-fraction, expressing (a) distance of the observer from the most recent event, as a proportion of (b) the spacing between events. The ratio would be increased either by recalling promptly after occurrence of the most recent item, or alternatively, by increasing the interitem spacing. The rule seems to predict recall well (Glenberg, Bradley, Kraus, & Benzaglia, 1983; Glenberg, Bradley, Stevenson, Kraus, Tkachuk, Gretz, Fish, & Turpin, 1980; Hitch, 1985). In a general sense, then, recency and temporal coding seem to have been joined in a coherent and quite general principle of human memory. Such a theory is able to address with one voice the long- and short-term recency effects, unlike the dual-trace position. As such, it must be taken seriously as a possible explanation of why people remember recent experiences better than distant ones.

It is not hard to imagine that factors such as word frequency, intelligence, presentation rate, and age would have minimal effects on temporal coding, and

---

[1]Crowder and Greene (1987a,b) have commented on a possible error in conceptualizing the *modality effect* in this way, but my concern here is with the general idea that recency results from temporal discriminability of items at the end of a series.

hence be ineffective in controlling recency. These variables would, however, continue to exert their familiar positive effects on degree of learning, and so affect performance where temporal coding has little impact, on the pre-recency segments of the serial position curve. Thus, the empirical dissociations on which the case for two stores was based are equally plausible by the alternative account.

One approach to the Brown-Peterson task, one that dispenses with talk of separate short-term memory systems, also stresses temporal coding. Bennett (1975) and Gorfein (1987) have advanced specific versions of this approach. They assume that subjects always face the problem of distinguishing the most recent memory items from those that occurred on earlier trials. On the first trial, these most recent memories are the only ones eligible and so the "discrimination problem" disappears and there is no forgetting. After the first trial, the difficulty in making the recency discrimination depends on several factors. One is the retention interval: Even if there are many competing items from earlier trials, if the most recent one has just been presented, with no interpolated material, it is still in the foreground of the temporal context. Lengthening the retention interval destroys the special foreground privilege of the most recent item, perhaps in conformity with Glenberg's (1987) "ratio rule" for recency in general. This accounts qualitatively for why there is no forgetting on the first trial of a Brown-Peterson experiment and for why forgetting increases with retention interval after the first trial. Gorfein's position also easily accounts for data on shifts in taxonomic category of the memory items and data showing sensitivity of Brown-Peterson forgetting to the interval elapsing between trials.

I cannot guarantee that this sort of approach will carry the day, in the end, for the Brown-Peterson task. But the account is very good now, and so the burden of evidence must now fall on those who believe in some mechanism of short-term storage, such as a limited-capacity buffer, decay, or the perturbation principle. The detailed facts of forgetting in Brown-Peterson experiments do not demand any such extra principle, so these advocates must find other sorts of evidence to support them. Furthermore, these principles all make one crucial prediction for which evidence is weak: They expect that there should be memory loss on the very first trial of a Brown-Peterson experiment. Nothing in perturbation, limited capacity, or buffer principles says that "all bets are off" during the first experimental trial. Indeed, our lives are full of "first trial" situations, with the varieties of experiences outside, as opposed to inside, the laboratory. So, the first trial is not an exceptional circumstance, to be set aside as a fluke; it is ecologically central to our task as theorists. Let us examine first-trial forgetting for a moment:

Forgetting Without PI? A Survey of the Literature

A crucial question for theory is therefore whether, after all, people forget on trial one of a Brown-Peterson experiment. I have been amazed that this question is not stressed more, given the quality and quantity of evidence available and given the importance for theory of the question. Baddeley and Scott (1971) deliberately sought good evidence on the point, explicitly appreciating its importance. (Part of the problem with investigating this issue is that a subject is wasted after his or her first few trials in an experiment, a matter of a few minutes, and must then be sent home.) Baddeley and Scott combined individual studies by Baddeley and his associates in which a single trial had been given, in order to amass sufficient observations to trace first-trial forgetting curves in detail. The total n was an impressive 922. The combined result showed a reliable decline over the first 5 seconds, but the function was not monotonic, showing improvement in performance between 6 and 9 seconds. So this ambitious effort leaves some readers unsatisfied and in need of additional evidence.

Most of the many remaining experiments published on proactive inhibition set a fixed retention interval, often 20 seconds, and examined build-up and release as a function of other variables. As Baddeley and Scott (1971) said, of the data permitting estimation of trial-one performance, some are furthermore uninterpretable owing to ceiling effects on the first-trial—notably the famous and frequently reprinted data of Keppel and Underwood (1962) themselves.

Among the few adequate studies, Loess (1964) showed no loss on the first trial in two independent experiments. In the first, performance was near the ceiling at some intervals (scores of.958, .875, and .958, respectively, for intervals of 9, 18, and 27 seconds). In Loess's second experiment, the first-trial scores were .79, .75, and .79 for intervals of 3, 9, and 18 seconds. In both experiments, there were 24 observations per data point. Noyd (1965; see Fuchs & Melton, 1974) tested independent groups of 27 subjects on either two-, three-, or five-word items following delays of either 4, 8, or 24 seconds of digit reading. The two-word items were at ceiling. Performance on the three-word items was .927 at each interval, perhaps also uncomfortably close to the performance limit. Corresponding results for the five-word items were .676, .630, and .638, respectively. The decline between 4 and 8 seconds with the five-word items corresponds to 23% of a word and was not reliable, and so in this experiment there was no loss over time in the absence of proactive inhibition. Cofer and Davidson (1968) tested 18 subjects each at 3 or 18 seconds of counting backwards on three-consonant syllables and obtained perfect recall rates of .78 and .83, respectively. This gain as a function of retention interval was nonsignificant. Wright (1967) tested 240 people, 80 each at 3, 9, and 18 seconds of counting backwards and obtained correct recall proportions of .93, .90, and .96, respectively. These proportions are close to the performance ceiling, but the number of observations per data point is commanding and what trend might be evident in the data is not a declining one. Turvey, Brick, & Osborn (1970) tested subgroups of 40 subjects on three-consonant items at 5, 10, 15, 20, or 25 sec, obtaining recall probabilities of .87, .85, .93, and .95. Finally, an experiment by Gorfein and Viviani (data given in Gorfein, 1987) showed off-ceiling performance that did not deteriorate with retention interval.

So, what should we conclude about forgetting on the first trial of a Brown-Peterson experiment? Perhaps the most conservative conclusion is that there are some inconsistencies in the literature but that first-trial forgetting is the exception rather than the rule. At best, the role of any additional short-term storage or primary memory mechanism, over and above the principles responsible for pro-active inhibition, is *empirically slight* in relation to observed performance losses in the Brown-Peterson task. This task can therefore no longer be exhibited as the showcase for short-term storage. Only with faith and enormous effort can evidence for short-term storage be coaxed from this task.

New Sources of Evidence?

So much for the techniques once thought to bring short-term storage into the laboratory, recency and Brown-Peterson forgetting slopes. What new kinds of task are cited for the concept nowadays? In a recent review of the evidence for buffer storage, Schneider and Detweiler (1987) cited a third phenomenon, the *span effect*. The reference is to the fact that immediate ordered recall is limited to about a handful or two of items, depending in well-understood ways on what the memory items are. But the early hypothesis that this performance represents a fundamental constant in cognitive capacity (e.g., Miller, 1956) has not aged well. Watkins (1977) has demonstrated different forms of coding for the early and late serial positions of an eight-item memory-span list. Others have dissociated age effects on the primacy and recency segments (Cohen & Sandberg, 1977; Huttenlocher & Burke, 1976; Samuel, 1978). A more plausible candidate for memory span may be that achieved with running-memory-span tests (Crowder, 1969; Pollack, Johnson, & Knaff, 1959), but its size is more on the order of 2 or 3 items than 7 ± 2 (Glanzer, 1972). Such a miniscule memory span is unattractive to those who would like to give short-term storage a role in other cognitive tasks. As we shall see, the working memory system of Baddeley and Hitch (1974; Baddeley, 1983) does have informative things to say about memory span, but more that it results from a highly specialized trick—the articulatory loop—than that it is a fundamental manifestation of an all-purpose capacity to buffer information.

To my knowledge, new candidates for *epitomizing* short-term memory within an explicit testing format have not received widespread acceptance, the way the recency and distractor techniques were accepted in the past. Rather, the newer orientation is to see short-term retention as a participant in integrated cognitive functioning, as *working memory,* to which attitude we now turn.

Working Memory

One commendable development in the academic study of memory has been its integration with ongoing cognitive tasks that are not, in themselves, memory tests. This began with the early computer models of associative memory (Anderson's FRAN, etc.) and has continued, for example, with models of reading (Daneman & Carpenter, 1983) and reasoning (Case, Kurland, & Goldberg, 1982). The introduction of the term *working memory* by Baddeley & Hitch (1974; see Baddeley, 1986) has underlined this increased ecological perspective on memory. From relatively simple beginnings, the model of working memory has been elaborated steadily, and now stands as our most comprehensive theory of short-term memory (Baddeley, 1983, 1986). The evidence from experiments that functionally distinguish among components such as the articulatory loop and visuo-spatial scratchpad is convincing. Notice that these distinctions are largely based on coding differences rather than storage-time differences; they exemplify coding modularity and not process modularity.[2]

Working memory does not, for me, merely reorient the older concept of STS in a new dressing. In its most fully articulated components, it is more like a *bag of tricks,* each a modular coding format in the sense discussed earlier in this chapter. The tight connection between the articulatory loop and specific motor codes (Baddeley, Thomson, & Buchanan, 1975; Ellis & Hennelly, 1980) illus- trates this point admirably. So does the experiment of Reisberg, Rappaport, & O'Shaughnessy (1984), in which people were taught to use a simple, thought- less, finger-tapping "loop" to hold an additional item or two for memory span, beyond what they could otherwise handle. This form of "buffer storage" is fundamentally procedural, highly code-specific, and not at all representative of a "memory system" to be distinguished from LTS.

Necessity of Buffer Memory for Cognition?

The utility of talking about working memory is that it stresses that people re- quire—without any possible argument—to remember small packages of infor- mation briefly in order to succeed in any complex thinking task. But is this an argument for the necessity of memory per se in human cognition, or is it rather an argument for a separate memory subsystem that is different in structure or func- tion from "regular" memory, whatever that is? Here, I think we drift off from issues on which evidence has been brought to bear. *Evidence for (a distinct subsystem of) short-term storage is not at all the same as evidence that people need to store things over the short term.* No quarrel is possible with the assertion that people need memory for the recent past in order to engage in language comprehension, written or spoken, in problem solving, in musical cognition, in playing bridge, or in almost any reasoning or language activity. Perhaps the truest sense in which we need a working memory mechanism is that we need a memory system that works. Distinguishing theoretically the operating principles

---

[2]I say "largely" with cause: Salamé and Baddeley (1982) have subdivided the articulatory loop into storage and processing components, which are examples of processing modularity within a form of coding.

of (a) memory for recent events from (b) memory for remote events is a much stiffer assignment, and one that I find relatively neglected these days.

Why, then, does it seem so intuitively *correct* that we attribute working or immediate memory phenomena to a different system than passive, long-term memories? Part of the answer is that some proposed subsystems, such as the articulatory loop, do indeed have integrity as separate forms of information processing. Because these codes are especially useful in the short term, we are fooled into thinking that they are distinctive because of their short-term properties, rather than because of their coding format.

The assumption of process modularity—horizontally distinct memory subsystems—must make a much stronger claim, namely that short- and long-term storage are different *within a common coding format*. Otherwise, if coding format and short- versus long-term status are confounded, there may be no need for the latter distinction. What evidence is there that a phonetic memory code used in digit span is different in kind than a phonetic memory code used in word encoding experiments like those of Fisher and Craik (1977), where words were cued by phonetic hints some 5 minutes after learning? I believe there is none.

Historically, the theoretical confounding of coding and process modularity probably arose in the following way: The early workers stressed mainly the coding distinctions in the belief that they were subdividing short-term storage. In other words, the lesson of coding diversity was first appreciated with short-term storage. As evidence accumulated that traditional memory—long-term storage—was comparably subdivided into coding modules, the implicit responsibility arose for distinguishing which type of modularity—coding or process—was the more important. That is the central issue faced in this essay, and the answer I give is obviously that coding modularity is well supported, but process modularity is not.

In answer to our question of why primary memory seems so distinctive, I can only appeal to language so often quoted from William James (1890) on the nature of primary memory. With virtually unchanged internal and external context, information from the immediate past *seems* still to belong to the psychological present, in the sense of Tulving's (1983) "recollective experience." Memory and forgetting do not demonstrably obey different principles, provided that we equate for their coding format. That is, what marks *semantic coding in memory* is the same whether testing occurs without appreciable delay (which may be rare) or quite a bit later. What marks phonetic coding is likewise continuous between short and long testing delays, the same for olfactory coding and for visual-imagery. These different forms of coding may be more or less durable, perhaps because of the density of interference that occurs after learning, but different laws do not suddenly come into play with long retention intervals. The difference between long and short intervals is, in all cases, that the immediate test occurs with little contextual change, and therefore the system of time perception registers almost no change, whereas at longer intervals the change has been considerable.

Thus, the same dissociations that led us to distinguish STS and LTS need not imply two separate memory stores, as we once thought. The coding (vertical) modularity proves to be the more valuable principle than process (horizontal) modularity, in memory theory as Fodor (1983) claimed for cognition in general. In the next section, I examine a closely related aspect of memory theory, consolidation, in order to trace parallels with the dual-store ideas.

Where Did STS Come From? The Case of Consolidation

I recently had occasion to review some work in the neuropsychological theory of memory. I was reminded that we cognitive psychologists should not be possessive of STS, as if we had invented it, via such workers as Broadbent (1958), Brown (1958), and Peterson and Peterson (1959). Neuropsychologists believe that the concept is legitimately theirs, and indeed their case is a good one: The history of thinking on *consolidation theory* over recent decades is instructive when we consider dissociations and the evidence for a separable state of short-term storage. To my surprise, I found the same bankruptcy in the original concept of consolidation as I have in the concept of STS. As we shall see, a new conception of consolidation has emerged.

Hebb & Gerard

Hebb's (1949; see also Gerard, 1949) neuropsychological theory was the landmark in the modern history of consolidation theory. His statement had a wide influence in what we now call the neurosciences, as well as its influence in psychology, anticipating as it did the popular dual-trace (STS/LTS) distinction. According to Hebb's version of the dual-trace hypothesis, experience is first recorded in the form of labile, reverberating, organized patterns of firing among neural units, which, if allowed to remain active long enough in concert, lead to the formation of structural changes in the nervous system, the basis of long-term memory. Notice how congenial Hebb's formulation is with the famous lines of William James that characterized primary memory as the persistence of (active) attention and secondary memory as memory proper. We see Hebb's ideas honored even more in the modern two-process theory of Estes (1972; Lee & Estes, 1981),about reverberatory cycles of ordered information giving way, with rehearsal, to structural representations of serial order.

The continued debate on the idea of memory consolidation has centered on several research areas. Of these, the two most prominent are (a) animal memory and (b) human clinical amnesia. As Weingartner (1984) said, the concept of memory consolidation, central as it was to many developments in the modern psychobiology of learning and memory ". . . was either ignored or rejected by investigators of cognitive processes in unimpaired human subjects" (p. 204).

Exceptions to Weingartner's observation are few: Interest continues sporadically in *sleep* as a factor in retention (Ekstrand, 1972). No doubt seems to exist that retention is better following an interval containing sleep than following one that does not (see also Hockey, Davies, & Gray, 1972). The theoretical weight of this fact is not easily measured, however. Subjects in conditions calling for sleep almost immediately after learning must be irresistably drawn to rehearsal while they are "drifting off" to sleep. But Ekstrand (1972) cited evidence that memory is a reliable function of whether or not, during sleep, there has been rapid eye movement (REM) activity. REM activity indicates the presence of dreaming during deep sleep. One outcome reported by Ekstrand is that memory performance is better following periods without REM activity than following REM episodes. But other reports (Empson & Clarke, 1970) have selectively deprived people of REM sleep with resulting *damage* to recall performance (see Jones, 1979, for discussion and more citations on this point.) Comparing sleep with and without REM activity is obviously better than comparing sleep versus wakefulness, but the content of REM dreaming itself might provide interference (or sources of reinstatement of the learning activity).

Another use of the consolidation idea in research on normal human subjects is due to Landauer (1974; 1977). Essentially, Landauer's experiments show that a given amount of high-similarity interference, in short-term paired-associate learning, has a larger effect if it comes right after acquisition than if it comes after a delay. Landauer's (1974, 1977) results are consistent with consolidation theory in that perseveratory activity specifically promoting consolidation of an item is more likely to be broken apart by highly similar items than by items sharing little with the original learning. Relatively speaking only, low-similarity interference may be said to correspond to sleep. If so, the earlier perseveratory activity is disrupted, the more its consolidation for the long run should be compromised. But that result is also consistent with other ideas about memory, and so it does not uniquely favor consolidation theory. For example, both the acid-bath theory of Posner and Konick (1966) and Estes' stimulus perturbation models (Estes, 1972) predict just this result. At any rate, we do not need to resort to perseveration-consolidation to explain the especially damaging effects of prompt, as opposed to delayed, interference. Now, the alternative explanations for this pattern of results may eventually boil down to formal equivalence with consolidation theory once consolidation theory is worked out in detail. For the moment, the evidence about consolidation from conventional experimentation is not nearly so powerful as the clinical evidence.

Wickelgren (1977, 1979) is the leading advocate of consolidation theory who is not *primarily* identified with research on amnesia. Wickelgren's treatment of consolidation (1977) distinguishes between two possibilities for what changes when perseveration is allowed to run its course. An hypothesis based on *unitary strength* would assume that the memory trace just gets stronger and stronger following learning. If this were true, reminiscence would be the rule rather than a delicate and elusive phenomenon. Alternatively, (a) the beneficial influence of consolidation following learning and (b) the detrimental influence of decay could be rationalized with some version of the STS/LTS distinction. However, it would be preposterous to assign the STS mechanism a role lasting up to several *decades,* and the data on ECT do indeed provide evidence that the consolidatory process extends over decades (Squire, Slater, & Chace, 1975).

Wickelgren's own formulation of consolidation theory, based on these rational considerations and on the study of amnesia, is called the *decreased fragility hypothesis.* This idea is a single-trace-strength hypothesis about memory representation, but it has a two-factor account of trace dynamics over time. As traces age, they undergo decay. But at the same time, they "grow in resistance to decay;" they decrease in fragility. Decay, for Wickelgren, need not be simple disuse with the passage of time. Resistance to decay (decreased fragility) is assumed to grow indefinitely as the memory trace gets older and older, but with diminishing returns, so that the first moments after learning are the most important ones.

Two historical "laws" of memory anticipate Wickelgren's notion of trace fragility. Ribot (1881) deserves priority in this: His *law of regression* states that the vulnerability of memories to disruption lessens with their age. Ribot derived this generalization from a survey of amnesia cases produced by head injury. As now, the evidence for this important proposition then came from the clinic more than from the laboratory. Jost's second law (1897; see Woodworth, 1938; McGeoch, 1942) says that *if two associations are of equal strength but different age, the older one diminishes less with time.* Jost had been interested in a related idea as manifested in experimental studies of distribution of practice.

Wickelgren showed (see summary in Wickelgren, 1977) that the detailed analysis of forgetting curves was consistent with a mathematical model including separate trace strength and trace fragility expressions. However, the main evidence was clinical, from amnesia cases, including the Squire, Slater, & Chace (1975) study of ECT. This study, and data on head injury seem to show that recent memory is disrupted according to a temporal gradient by a traumatic event. The "lost memories" are very definitely "still there", however, because (a) *before* an ECT session, subjects are fine at remembering material from the most recent decades (which is unavailable just after ECT), and (b) as Russell & Nathan (1946) pointed out for head injury cases, the memories spontaneously recover with the passage of time since the injury (that is, the amnesic material comes back in reverse order to its age).

The modern version of consolidation theory takes these facts seriously, and the rest of us should quit ignoring them. That is one lesson of this section. The other lesson is that Hebbian consolidation, the dual-trace theory, which was so congenial to STS/LTS distinctions, now has little to recommend it as a general theory, for the same two reasons just examined, as well as others. And what of research evidence from animals?

Evidence From Animal Experiments.   One of the most persuasive reasons for experimentation on animals, rather than humans, is that radical manipulations comparable to the trauma of head injury can be produced at will with animals but not, ethically, with humans. Accordingly, the truly experimental analysis of consolidation has belonged to the animal laboratory for many years. With animals, the investigator is free to introduce some electrical or chemical agency that might block organized perseveration in the brain and the resulting consolidation. The time course of consolidation can then be studied by manipulating the delay between learning and the administration of such an amnesic agency.

Skipping over much history, we can focus on the experiment in which rats are taught to step down from a platform to escape shock to their feet. In experimental conditions, electroconvulsive shock (ECS) is administered at various delays after a single step-down trial. The question is whether it impairs storage of the remembered footshock. The results of the Chorover and Schiller (1965) experiment and other subsequent ones did indeed show amnesic effects of an ECS treatment following one-trial punishment training, but only when the time between initial acquisition and ECS was less than 10 seconds. A temporal gradient occurred in that ECS delays of more than 10 seconds gave results like control conditions without ECS. Hilgard and Bower (1975) have written a thorough review of subsequent developments in the animal ECS experiments. For now, the important point is that an experimental amnesia, with a temporal gradient, can be produced in rats. This observation supports the Hebbian consolidation theory of memory, but even this support has not been unequivocal in light of further reports:

1.   Experiments on different species (for example, mice) or even different strains of rat, or experiments using slightly different task details have turned in wildly variable time constants for consolidation, even using the Chorover-Schiller experimental logic (Chorover, 1976; McGaugh & Gold, 1974). At the least, consolidation time estimates frustrate those who would have hoped for a single "magic number" for such a fundamental brain process as consolidation.

2.   Memories impaired by ECS just after learning can be recovered spontaneously just by a lapse in time before testing, as Russell and Nathan, (1946) documented long ago for head injury cases in humans. Miller and Springer (1973) reviewed some of the evidence for recovery in the animal studies. If the temporal gradient of lost memories shrinks with the passage of time before testing, we cannot say for sure that materials "forgotten" in a test are necessarily unavailable. It is always possible that waiting a little longer would show recovery.

3.   The effects of ECS can be reversed, or largely reversed, if a "reminder" is given during the interval before testing. In one situation, rats were given a simple footshock outside the training and test apparatus. This apparently (R. Miller & Springer, 1973) reinstated the training contingency between stepping

off the platform and footshock. If the memory could be reinstated by such a reminder, it must have been laid down after all, and not obliterated by disruption of the consolidation process.

For these and other reasons, some workers have chosen to regard the induction of retrograde amnesia in animals, by ECS, as compromising primarily the *retrieval process* and not the consolidation process as originally thought (Gold & McGaugh, 1984; McGaugh & Gold, 1974; Miller & Marlin, 1984; Zechmeister & Nyberg, 1982). Miller and Marlin (1984) are especially emphatic in rejecting the consolidation interpretation of amnesia as it was originally intended by Müller and Pilzecker, suggesting that: "To define all retrograde disruption of acquired information as consolidation failure and then cite retrograde disruption of acquired information as evidence of consolidation failure is circular and does not add to knowledge . . ." (pp. 86–87).

Hebbian Theory as an Article of Faith

However, these same authors (Miller & Marlin, 1984) endorsed Hebbian memory consolidation almost on logical grounds: The very first moments following an experience must, they said, carry that experience in some form of activity trace. Nobody would maintain that a structural brain change occurs instantaneously. But a structural brain change must happen sometime, for it is unreasonable to assume that all memory is an activity pattern even years later. Therefore, they said, there must be a transition between the two forms of storage, as Hebb proposed. Miller and Marlin reported some analyses that suggest that such consolidation can take place as rapidly as within 500 milliseconds following an experience.[3] Once this reasoning is accepted, so then is the consolidation hypothesis of memory. Whether consolidation is a concept that explains any *observable behavior* is altogether another question, however. If the reversibility of ECT amnesia and the recovery of memories lost to retrograde amnesia argue against disruption of consolidation in humans, now we find that little or no evidence can be cited for this hypothesis in animals, either.

Consolidation Reinterpreted

Renewed interest in consolidation, now reinterpreted in terms of Ribot's Law, can determine whether this is just a different way of talking about familiar mechanisms (rehearsal, test events, and so on) or whether we have been missing out on important discoveries. More to the point for present purposes, the status of consolidation, as that idea was originally understood, turns out to be quite like

---

[3]Others (Hilgard & Bower, 1975, p. 508–516) have reviewed essentially the same literature and reached the conclusion that consolidation is the concept.

that of short-term storage: Workers seem disposed to trust the idea, almost on sheer faith, without clear evidence that can be cited as uniquely favoring it.

Taking stock of the arguments presented here, we note that the discussion of consolidation theory has pertained most directly to the bankruptcy of the concept of short-term storage. Beyond this, one may well wonder whether I am not proposing to substitute one form of processing modularity for another, by revising what interpretation of consolidation is tenable in light of the evidence. This question, in turn, depends on whether consolidatory changes could one day be understood in terms of coding modularity. So far as I know, the issue has not been addressed. With agencies such as ECT and memories of human beings for information from the recent and remote past, changes in coding might well be important. With lower species, such reasoning appears fanciful. Currently, we must restrict ourselves to the more conservative point that the theory of consolidation does nothing to limit the generality of my earlier conclusions about short-term storage.

DISSOCIATING RECALL AND RECOGNITION

It would have been a mistake, as I believe I have shown, to accept dissociations as grounds for distinguishing short- and long-term storage systems. Let us take still another example, briefly: If empirical dissociation were the criterion for differentiating memory systems, our field of memory might soon become a taxonomic science resembling botany. Then, surely, not only STS and LTS would have remained processing modules, but also recall and recognition would have. I have organized the dissociating evidence for recall and recognition elsewhere (Crowder, 1976), but the best known factors are word frequency, intentional versus incidental learning, and semantic organization. The effects of these variables on recall are either opposite to their effects in recognition, a pattern called *crossed double dissociation* by Dunn and Kirsner (1987), or there are null effects in the case of one measure and positive effects in the case of the other (*simple dissociation*).

The recall/recognition dissociations are important theoretically. They serve to falsify single-process theories like strength, which might claim that recognition is only a more sensitive measure of the underlying trace than recall (a point first made by Anderson & Bower, 1972). By the same token, the dissociations advance the case for theories that assume more than one underlying process in retrieval (generate-recognition theories, for example, or Mandler's [1980] familiarity-plus-retrieval theory). But nowadays, recognition and recall are considered as belonging to declarative memory, tested explicitly, and requiring deliberate recollection of the encoding episode. Evidence we used formerly to distinguish them is still valid for just that, but we would not maintain that they represent different systems of memory, in the sense of process modularity.

Dunn and Kirsner (1987) have argued that crossed double dissociations can be expected even from single-process models whenever there are two performance measures that are necessarily reciprocal to each other. In the Anderson and Bower (1972) theory of recognition and recall, two separate processes are postulated in order to account for the dissociations mentioned in the last paragraph, pathway tagging and context associations. The dissociation data are indeed consistent with this two-process theory. But they are also consistent with the view that one of these factors is just what is left over after the other is used. Anything that then increases one of the factors would necessarily have to reduce the other. If going from incidental to intentional learning increases pathway tagging, for example, it would have to reduce the importance of what remains, perhaps context associations, without affecting this latter factor directly. Single dissociations, according to Dunn and Kirsner, are even more easily dismissed. If a common single factor is included in two tasks, its effective range of action might be more suited to one than another. In the limit, if this factor affects one task reliably, it could fail to affect another because, within the context of this second task, it is at floor or ceiling. For example, the experimental factor of retention interval seems to have different effective ranges of action on primed fragment completion than it does on explicit recall and recognition (Sloman, Hayman, Ohta, Law, & Tulving, 1988).

In summary, then, the empirical dissociations of the past have not been sufficient for postulating multiple memory systems. I have included information about short-term storage, about consolidation theory, and about recall/ recognition differences, to make this point. Now what of the dissociations that are popular today?

THE PROCEDURAL/DECLARATIVE DISTINCTION

We read much evidence, these days, for multiple memory systems based on dissociations between the relation of different tasks and different independent variables (Squire, 1987; Tulving, 1987). The particularly dramatic reports are of dissociations between explicit and implicit memory in amnesics (Cohen & Squire, 1980; Graf & Schacter, 1985; see chapters in Squire & Butters, 1984). The same two systems have also been dissociated in normal subjects as a function of experimental operations (e.g., Jacoby, 1983). Nobody doubts that these dissociations have exciting implications for theory; the only question is the legitimacy of concluding that dissociations show the existence of *different memory systems* (Dunn & Kirsner, 1987; Jacoby, 1983; Roediger, 1984, Chapter 1, this volume). In this section, I argue that such a conclusion is risky at best. I do not attempt to review the growing evidence on implicit and explicit tests of memory, however, because I think no such review is needed.

Dissociations Within Implicit and Explicit Memory. Besides repeating the cautions I have already mentioned about interpreting empirical dissociations, I pause here to cite a particularly sobering context for the procedural/declarative (or perhaps implicit/explicit) subsystem distinction: Roediger and Blaxton (1987) have shown that we should not be so quick to declare that a dissociation of one memory measure from another heralds a distinction between systems of memory. They have found that striking empirical dissociations occur when several testing procedures for implicit memory are compared in response to the same independent variable. In the end, a dissociation is a particularly well-behaved and replicable *interaction* (Tulving, 1987), in which one set of tasks responds to a manipulation and another does not, or vice versa. We are all used to getting theoretical mileage from interactions, of course, but additional arguments are needed to defend a distinction between memory systems in the sense of processing modularity.

Dunn and Kirsner (1987) maintain that dissociations, and even double dissociations, are not logically acceptable grounds for distinguishing mental processes. They have suggested the method of "reversed association" as a more defensible pattern on which to distinguish process. A reversed association is essentially a nonmonotonic relationship between two tasks across conditions and subjects.

At the least, the preceding review of two-process memory theory should have made clear that proposing distinct processing on the basis of even orderly empirical dissociations is premature. Now we are seeing strong and fascinating empirical dissociations between implicit and explicit tests of memory. As we seek to interpret these, perhaps we should be cautious in suggesting two underlying memory systems, such as procedural and declarative memory.

Two Systems or a Modular Component? In relation to procedural and declarative memory, we talk as if two systems have been isolated, but really there is only one element—the declarative encoding of temporal context—that is separate from all the other diverse procedural formats. Each of the latter is "stored" in its processing locus in the brain. Procedural memory is really an umbrella term for processing residues of all sorts, depending on the mode of original information processing. The structure of Schneider and Detweiler's (1987) recent "connectionist/control" model seems to recognize some of these attitudes: They propose processing modules assorted by principles of vertical modularity, that is, assorted by processing formats—coding modules—such as visual, auditory, phonetic, semantic, lexical, and so on. Among these is a module representing context. In on-line processing, the connections between this context module and other processing centers constitutes attention. Although I disagree with Schneider and Detweiler on the necessity of special assumptions for a system of buffer storage, the survival of contextual connections in the short-

and long-term will very plausibly comment on two of our concerns in this chapter. First, the uninterrupted pace of contextual change could provide the constancy that gives "primary memory" its Jamesian recollective experience of belonging to the conscious present. Second, the source of classical amnesia may be understood by virtue of a special vulnerability, or fragility in the sense of neo-consolidation theory, of the contextual connections with other aspects of the processing system. The argument that amnesia could not be a disturbance of consciousness is a well-understood proviso in the theory of amnesia—amnesics show no obvious signs of not being aware of the world around them as they go about their lives. It is the survival of traces connecting this awareness with the processing systems used in the past that may be disturbed.

This does not sound to me like a distinction between procedural and declarative memory as two systems, as such. It sounds like one element of normal memory—the knowledge that *that* processing occurred in *that* context—is compromised. On the other hand, if we have a model of memory that is vertically modular, each of quite a few coding formats distinct from the others, then loss of context connections would be just the loss of information of one among many specialized codes.

ACKNOWLEDGMENTS

I greatly appreciate the comments of my colleagues Donald Broadbent, Fergus Craik, and Michael Watkins on an earlier version of this chapter, whose preparation was also supported by Grant BNS 86 08344 from the National Science Foundation.

REFERENCES

Anderson, J. R., & Bower, G. H. (1972). Recognition and retrieval processes in free recall. *Psychological Review, 79,* 97–123.

Baddeley, A. D. (1983). Working memory. *Philosophical Transactions of the Royal Society of London, B, 382,* 311–324.

Baddeley, A. D. (1986). *Working memory.* New York: Oxford University Press.

Baddeley, A. D., & Hitch, G. J. (1974). Working memory. In G. H. Bower (Ed.), *The psychology of learning and motivation,* (Vol. 8), (pp. 47–89). New York: Academic Press.

Baddeley, A. D., & Hitch G. J. (1977). Recency revisited. In S. Dornic (Ed.), *Attention and Performance 6* (pp. 647–667). Hillsdale, NJ: Lawrence Erlbaum Associates.

Baddeley, A. D., & Scott, D. (1971). Short-term forgetting in the absence of proactive inhibition. *Quarterly Journal of Experimental Psychology, 23,* 275–283.

Baddeley, A. D., Thomson, N., & Buchanan, M. (1975). Word length and the structure of short-term memory. *Journal of Verbal Learning and Verbal Behavior, 14,* 575–589.

Bennett, R. W. (1975). Proactive interference in short-term memory: Fundamental forgetting processes. *Journal of Verbal Learning and Verbal Behavior, 14,* 123–144.

Bjork, R. A., & Whitten, W. B. (1974). Recency-sensitive retrieval processes in long-term free recall. *Cognitive Psychology, 6,* 173–189.

Broadbent, D. E. (1958). *Perception and communication.* New York: Pergamon.

Brown, J. (1958). Some tests of the decay theory of immediate memory. *Quarterly Journal of Experimental Psychology, 10,* 12–21.

Case, R., Kurland, M. D., & Goldberg, J. (1982). Operational efficiency and the growth of short-term memory span. *Journal of Experimental Child Psychology, 33,* 386–404.

Chorover, S. L. (1976). An experimental critique of the "consolidation studies" and an alternative "model systems" approach to the biophysiology of memory. In M. R. Rosenzweig & E. L. Bennett (Eds.), *Neural mechanisms of learning and memory* (pp. 561–582). Cambridge, MA: MIT Press.

Chorover, S. L., & Schiller, P. H. (1965). Short-term retrograde amnesia in rats. *Journal of Comparative and Physiological Psychology, 59,* 73–78.

Cofer, C. N., & Davidson, E. H. (1968). Proactive interference in STM for consonant units of two sizes. *Journal of Verbal Learning and Verbal Behavior, 7,* 268–270.

Cohen, N. J., & Squire, L. R. (1980). Preserved learning and retention of pattern-analysing skill in amnesia: Dissociation of knowing how and knowing that. *Science 210,* 207–210.

Cohen, R. L., & Sandberg, T. (1977). Relations between intelligence and short-term memory. *Cognitive Psychology, 9,* 534–554.

Craik, F. I. M., & Lockhart, R. S. (1972). Levels of processing; a framework for memory research. *Journal of Verbal Learning and Verbal Behavior, 11,* 671–684.

Crowder, R. G. (1969). Behavioral strategies in immediate memory. *Journal of Verbal Learning and Verbal Behavior, 8,* 524–528.

Crowder, R.G. (1976). *Principles of learning and memory.* Hillsdale, NJ: Lawrence Erlbaum Associates.

Crowder, R. G. (1982). The demise of short-term memory. *Acta Psychologica, 50,* 291–323.

Crowder, R. G., & Greene, R. L. (1987a). The context of remembering. In D. S. Gorfein & R. R. Hoffman (Eds.), *Memory and learning: The Ebbinghaus centennial conference* (pp. 191–199). Hillsdale, NJ: Lawrence Erlbaum Associates.

Crowder, R. G., & Greene, R. L. (1987b). On the remembrance of times past: The irregular technique. *Journal of Experimental Psychology: General, 116,* 265–278.

Crowder, R. G., & Morton, J. (1969). Precategorical acoustic storage (PAS). *Perception and Psychophysics, 5,* 365–373.

Daneman, M., & Carpenter, P. A. (1983). Individual differences in working memory and reading. *Journal of Verbal Learning and Verbal Behavior, 19,* 450–466.

Dunn, J. C., & Kirsner, K. (1987). *Discovering functionally independent mental processes: The principle of reversed association.* Unpublished manuscript.

Ekstrand, B. R. (1972). To sleep, perchance to dream (about why we forget). In C. P. Duncan, L. Sechrest, & A. W. Melton (Eds.), *Human memory: Festschrift for Benton J. Underwood* (pp. 59–82). New York: Appleton Century Crofts.

Ellis, N. C., & Hennelly, R. A. (1980). A bilingual word-length effect: Implications for intelligence testing and the relative ease of mental calculation in Welsh and English. *British Journal of Psychology, 71,* 43–52.

Empson, J. A. C., & Clarke, P. R. E. (1970). Rapid eye movement and remembering. *Nature, 227,* 287–288.

Estes, W. K. (1972). An associative basis for coding and organization in memory. In A. W. Melton & E. Martin (Eds.), *Coding processes in human memory* (pp. 161–190). Washington, DC: Winston & Sons.

Fisher, R. P., & Craik, F. I. M. (1977). Interaction between encoding and retrieval operations in cued recall. *Journal of Experimental Psychology: Human Learning and Memory, 3,* 701–711.

Fodor, J. A. (1983). *Modularity of mind.* Cambridge, MA: MIT Press.

Fuchs, A. H., & Melton, A. W. (1974). Effects of frequency of presentation and stimulus length on retention in the Brown-Peterson paradigm. *Journal of Experimental Psychology, 103,* 629–637.

Gerard, R. W. (1949). Physiology and psychiatry. *American Journal of Psychiatry, 105,* 161–173.

Glanzer, M. (1972). Storage mechanisms in recall. In G. H. Bower & J. T. Spence (Eds.), *The psychology of learning and motivation, Volume 5* (pp. 129–193). New York: Academic Press.

Glenberg, A. M. (1987). Temporal context and memory. In D. S. Gorfein & R. R. Hoffman (Eds.), *Memory and learning: The Ebbinghaus centennial conference* (pp. 173–190). Hillsdale, NJ: Lawrence Erlbaum Associates.

Glenberg, A. M., Bradley, M. M., Kraus, T. A., & Benzaglia, G. J. (1983). Studies of the long-term recency effect: Support for a contextually guided retrieval theory. *Journal of Experimental Psychology: Learning, Memory, and Cognition, 9,* 231–255.

Glenberg, A. M., Bradley, M. M., Stevenson, J. A., Kraus, T. A., Tkachuk, M. J., Gretz, A. L., Fish, J. F., & Turpin, B. A. M. (1980). A two-process account of long-term serial position effects. *Journal of Experimental Psychology: Human Learning and Memory, 6,* 355–369.

Glenberg, A. M., & Swanson, N.   (1986). A temporal distinctiveness theory of recency and modality effects. *Journal of Experimental Psychology: Learning, Memory, and Cognition, 12,* 3–24.

Gold, P. E., & McGaugh, J. L. (1984). Endogenous processes in memory consolidation. In H. Weingartner & E. S. Parkers (Eds.), *Memory consolidation: Psychobiology of cognition* (pp. 65–84). Hillsdale, NJ: Lawrence Erlbaum Associates.

Gorfein, D. S. (1987). Explaining context effects on short-term memory. In D. S. Gorfein & R. R. Hoffman (Eds.), *Memory and learning: The Ebbinghaus centennial conference* (pp. 153–172. Hillsdale, NJ: Lawrence Erlbaum Associates.

Graf, P., & Schacter, D. L. (1985). Implicit and explicit memory for new associations in normal and amnesic subjects. *Journal of Experimental Psychology: Learning, Memory, and Cognition, 11,* 501–518.

Greene, R. L. (1986). Sources of recency effects in free recall. *Psychological Bulletin, 99,*221–228.

Hebb, D. O. (1949). *Organization of behavior.* New York: Wiley.

Hilgard, E. R., & Bower, G. H. (1975). *Theories of learning* (4th ed.). Englewood Cliffs, NJ: Prentice-Hall.

Hitch, G. J. (1985). Short-term memory and information processing in humans and animals: Towards an integrative framework. In L. G. Nilsson & T. Archer (Eds.), *Perspectives on learning and memory.* Hillsdale, NJ: Lawrence Erlbaum Associates.

Hockey, G. R. J., Davies, S., & Gray, M. W. (1972). Forgetting as a function of sleep at different times of day. *Quarterly Journal of Experimental Psychology, 24,* 386–393.

Huttenlocher, J., & Burke, D. (1976). Why does memory span increase with age? *Cognitive Psychology, 8,* 1–31.

Jackendoff, R. (1987). *Consciousness and the computational mind.* (Chapter 12). Cambridge, MA: Bradford/MIT.

Jacoby, L. L. (1983). Remembering the data: Analysing interactive processing in reading. *Journal of Verbal Learning and Verbal Behavior, 22,* 485–508.

James, W. (1890). *Principles of psychology.* New York: Holt.

Jones, D. M. (1979). Stress and memory. In M. M. Gruneberg & P. E. Morris (Eds.), *Applied problems in memory* (pp. 185–214). London: Academic Press.

Jost, A. (1897). Die Associazionfestigkeit in ihrer Abhangigkeit von der Verteilung der Weiderholungen. *Zeitschrift fur Psychologie, 14,*436–472.

Keppel, G., & Underwood, B. J. (1962). Proactive inhibition in the short-term retention of single items. *Journal of Verbal Learning and Verbal Behavior, 1,* 153–161.

Kolers, P. (1975). Specificity of operations in sentence recognition. *Cognitive Psychology, 7,* 289–306.

Landauer, T. K. (1974). Consolidation in human memory: Retrograde amnestic effects of confusable items in paired-associate learning. *Journal of Verbal Learning and Verbal Behavior, 12,* 119–131.

Landauer, T. K. (1977). Remarks on the detection and analysis of memory deficits. In E. M. Birnbaum & E. S. Parker (Eds.), *Alcohol and human memory* (pp. 23–42). Hillsdale, NJ: Lawrence Erlbaum Associates.

Lee, C. L., & Estes, W. K. (1981). Item and order information in short-term memory: Evidence for multilevel perturbation processes. *Journal of Experimental Psychology: Human Learning and Memory, 7,* 149–169.

Loess, H. (1964). Proactive inhibition in short-term memory. *Journal of Verbal Learning and Verbal Behavior, 3,* 362–368.

Mandler, G. (1980). Recognition: The judgment of previous occurrence. *Psychological Review, 87,* 252–271.

McGaugh, J. L., & Gold, P. E. (1974). Conceptual and neurobiological issues in studies of treatments affecting memory storage. In. G. H. Bower (Ed.), *The psychology of learning and motivation* (Vol. 8) (pp. 233–264). New York: Academic Press.

McGeoch, J. A. (1942). *The psychology of human learning.* New York, NY: Longmans Green & Co.

Miller, G. A. (1956). The magical number seven plus or minus two: Some limits on our capacity for processing information. *Psychological Review, 63,* 81–97.

Miller, R. R., & Marlin, N. A. (1984). The physiology and semantics of consolidation. In H. Weingartner & E. S. Parkers (Eds.), *Memory consolidation: Psychobiology of cognition* (pp. 85–110). Hillsdale, NJ: Lawrence Erlbaum Associates.

Miller, R. R., & Springer, A. D. (1973). Amnesia, consolidation, and retrieval. *Psychological Review, 80,* 69–79.

Murdock, B. B., Jr. (1960). The distinctiveness of stimuli. *Psychological Review, 67,* 16–31.

Noyd, D. E. (1965, June). *Proactive and intra stimulus interference in short-term memory for two-, three-, and five-word stimuli.* Paper presented at meeting of the Western Psychological Association, Honolulu.

Peterson, L. R., & Peterson, M. J. (1959). Short-term retention of individual items. *Journal of Experimental Psychology, 61,* 12–21.

Pollack, I., Johnson, I. B., & Knaff, P. R. (1959). Running memory span. *Journal of Experimental Psychology, 57,* 137–146.

Posner, M. I., & Konick, A. W. (1966). On the role of interference in short-term retention. *Journal of Experimental Psychology, 72,* 221–231.

Reisberg, D., Rappaport, I., & O'Shaughnessy, M. (1984). Limits of working memory: The digit digit-span. *Journal of Experimental Psychology: Learning, Memory, & Cognition, 10,* 203–221.

Ribot, T. (1881). *Les maladies de la memoire.* Paris: Germer Baillere.

Roediger, H. L., III (1984). Does current evidence from dissociation experiments favor the episodic/semantic distinction? *Behavioral and Brain Sciences, 7,* 252–254.

Roediger, H. L., III, & Blaxton, T. A. (1987). Retrieval modes produce dissociations in memory for surface information. In D. S. Gorfein & R. R. Hoffman (Eds.), *Memory and learning: The Ebbinghaus centennial conference* (pp. 349–379). Hillsdale, NJ: Lawrence Erlbaum Associates.

Russell, W. R., & Nathan, P. W. (1946). Traumatic amnesia. *Brain, 69,* 280–300.

Salamé, P., & Baddeley, A. D. (1982). Disruption of short-term memory by unattended speech: Implications for the structure of working memory. *Journal of Verbal Learning and Verbal Behavior, 21,* 150–164.

Samuel, A. G. (1978). Organization versus retrieval factors in the development of digit span. *Journal of Experimental Child Psychology, 26,* 308–319.

Schneider, W., & Detweiler, M. (1987). A connectionist/control architecture for working memory. In G. H. Bower (Ed.), *The psychology of learning and memory, Volume 21* (pp. 53–119). New York: Academic Press.

Sloman, S. A., Hayman, C. A. G., Ohta, N., Law, J., & Tulving, E. (in press). Forgetting in primed fragment completion. *Journal of Experimental Psychology: Learning, Memory, and Cognition.*

Squire, L. R. (1987). *Memory and brain.* New York: Oxford University Press.

Squire, L. R., & Butters, N. (Eds.). (1984). *Neuropsychology of memory.* New York: Guilford Press.

Squire, L. R., Slater, P. C., & Chace, P. M. (1975). Retrograde amnesia: Temporal gradient in very long-term memory following electroconvulsive therapy. *Science, 187,* 77–79.

Tulving, E. (1983). *Elements of episodic memory.* New York: Oxford University Press.

Tulving, E. (1987). Introduction: Multiple memory systems and consciousness. *Human Neurobiology, 6,* 67–80.

Turvey, M. T., Brick, P., & Osborn, J. (1970). Proactive interference in short-term memory as a function of prior-item retention interval. *Quarterly Journal of Experimental Psychology, 22,* 142–147.

Tzeng, O. J. L. (1973). Positive recency effect in delayed free recall. *Journal of Verbal Learning and Verbal Behavior, 12,* 436–439.

Watkins, M. J. (1977). The intricacy of memory span. *Memory & Cognition, 5,* 529–534.

Watkins, M. J., & Peynircioglu, Z. F. (1983). Three recency effects at the same time. *Journal of Verbal Learning and Verbal Behavior, 22,* 375–384.

Waugh, N. C., & Norman, D. A. (1965). Primary memory. *Psychological Review, 72,* 89–104.

Weingartner, H. (1984). Psychobiological determinants of memory failures. In L. R. Squire & N. Butters (Eds.), *Neuropsychology of memory* (pp. 205–212). New York: Guilford Press.

Whitten, W. B., & Bjork, R. A. (1972 April). *Test events as learning trials: The importance of being imperfect.* Paper presented at the Midwestern Mathematical Psychological meeting, Bloomington, IN.

Wickelgren, W. A. (1977). *Learning and memory.* Englewood Cliffs, NJ: Prentice-Hall.

Wickelgren, W. A. (1979). Chunking and consolidation. A theoretical synthesis of semantic networks, configuring in conditioning, S-R versus cognitive learning, normal forgetting, the amnesic syndrome, and the hippocampal arousal system. *Psychological Review, 86,* 44–60.

Woodworth, R. S. (1938). *Experimental psychology.* New York: Holt.

Wright, J. H. (1967). Effects of formal interitem similarity and length of retention interval on proactive inhibition in short-term memory. *Journal of Experimental Psychology, 75,* 366–395.

Zechmeister, E. B., & Nyberg, S. E. (1982). *Human memory: An introduction to research and theory.* Monterey, CA: Brooks/Cole.

15 Classification of Human Memory: Comments on the Third Section

Lars-Göran Nilsson
University of Umeå, Sweden

Classification is crucial to any science, and the science of memory is no exception. Notable reasons for a classificatory enterprise in learning and memory have been pointed out and discussed by Tulving (1985a). The paper by Tulving does not yet seem to be known to a large research community; a brief review of some of the main issues might therefore be in order as a point of departure for the present discussion of the four chapters presented under the rubric of Classificatory Systems for Memory.

Tulving (1985a) has claimed two general functions of classification—one pragmatic and the other theoretical. Facilitation of communication is the cardinal aspect of the pragmatic function. The existence of a generally accepted classificatory system in a research field means an increased economy of concepts and therefore, an improved quality of communication in that field. Few would probably disagree with this implication, but there are probably also very few who would regard this to be the critical reason for deriving and suggesting a classificatory system for any field.

The theoretical function is more fundamental and it has many facets. One is that a valid classificatory system enhances comprehensive understanding of the subject matter. By means of an accepted classificatory system one is more likely to arrive at a general picture of the subject matter. In this sense, classification would allow a manifestation of general regularity of theory and data in the field. Other theoretical facets include the provision of guidelines for generalizations of empirical findings and for facilitating the determination of the fit between empirical findings and the sought-for generalized regularity. Still another facet is that a classificatory system may contribute to the establishment and improvement of the nomenclature of the field. The lack of terminological clarity is a problem

295

of long standing in many areas of psychological research and, again, the scientific understanding of memory constitutes no exception. Those involved in research in this field are deeply aware of the problem, but radical attempts to improve this state of affairs have been notable only by their absence. Tulving's (1985a) argument that the construction of a classificatory system for memory should change these matters is interesting and ought to be taken seriously.

For obvious reasons, empirical facts must play a primary role in the establishment of a classificatory system for memory. This is also the view taken in those chapters of the present section that are addressed to this issue. However, in the paper cited, Tulving (1985a) argued that the construction of a classificatory system for memory simply on the basis of observations of memory performance is unlikely to be successful. The critical complement to behavioral evidence is the requirement that the classification be based on what is known about brain activity in learning and memory. In determining the degree of relatedness or unrelatedness of memory phenomena, we should try to establish whether these phenomena are based on the same or on different underlying brain mechanisms. In agreement with Olton (1985), Tulving referred to this approach as the *neuropsychological criterion*.

None of the four chapters presented in this section explicitly makes contact with these issues discussed by Tulving. An obvious consequence of this state of affairs is that the issue of classification is treated in very different ways. Apparently, the notion of classificatory systems for memory has quite different meanings for the four authors who were invited to contribute to this section. This, in itself, may be a reflection of an immature field of research—at least with respect to the issue of nomenclature.

PRINCIPLE OF RATIONALITY

The principle of rationality, proposed by Anderson (chapter 11), has generally very little to do with classificatory systems. This principle states that "human memory behaves as an optimal solution to the information retrieval problems facing humans." Anderson implicitly solved the problem of classification by denying that it exists. He proposed one large unitary memory entity that is responsible for all different kinds of analyses of information. This memory entity is conceived of as an inference system whose main function is to test hypotheses about the world. Anderson evinced no real interest in studying the nature of this general mechanism and expressed no concern about determining whether there are subprocesses or submechanisms on the basis of which the general inference system operates.

Existing principles of rationality in any science are based on axioms of a logical system, for example, if $A > B$ and $B > C$, then $A > C$. A certain solution that does not show $A > C$ is a case of irrationality. This type of reasoning is also the basis for Anderson's rationality principle. Inferences are made on the basis of expectation such that a given set of information is evaluated with respect to its agreement with or deviation from expectation. The brain, according to Anderson, is a sophisticated device for minimizing chi-square.

Because Anderson's principle of rationality can predict ten of the most basic phenomena in memory research, his theory must be regarded as a sophisticated product of a most impressive nature. I suspect, though, that it may strike at least some readers as somewhat bleak with respect to the psychological dynamics of memory. More important, however, is the fact that the theory is incomplete in the same way as all theories of optimal solutions are incomplete. In all such theories there is a general process that causes an optimal solution, but those potential subprocesses on which the general process is based need not themselves be optimal, and it is in this respect that such theories are incompletely developed. The theory of evolution in terms of the "survival-of-the-fittest" notion provides a reasonably good example of this point. Whereas the large evolutionary process causes an optimal solution in terms of the survival of the fittest, single sub-processes of the evolution need not be optimal. There might be robust single solutions that are not even approximately optimal.

The reverse case is also problematic. That is, there might be single sub-processes leading to optimal solutions in each case, without any optimal solution for the general process. The classical example is that of the "Prisoners' Dilemma" process of negotiations according to game theory. An optimal solution for the group and the individual can be found, but this solution is not stable with respect to the negotiation pre se; the optimal solution has to be complemented by some kind of social agreement in order to reach stability. Anderson did concede that the results of his conceptualization are preliminary, and this may be interpreted as reflecting the incompleteness in development of theories that are based on optimal solutions.

The principle of optimal solutions may also be regarded as unnecessarily restrictive. The search for an optimal solution may cause the rejection of many alternative and potentially fruitful ideas. In this regard, a theory of optimal solutions is a paradox. An optimal *development* of theories of memory is not possible if there is only one optimal solution available.

REPRESENTATION AND PROCESS

The classificatory system for memory discussed by Broadbent (chapter 12) is based on the "Maltese Cross" (Broadbent, 1984), and an extension is presented for the first time in the present volume. The Maltese Cross notion is that of four classes of representation, namely "those interfered with by sensory events, those disturbed by output events, those suffering no interference from fresh events as such but only from changes in the mapping of associations and . . . [those that are] . . . disturbed by fresh events regardless of their sensory or motor character.'' The extension of this classificatory system concerns, first, a buffer containing output motor commands and, second, changes in the processing system itself.

Much of the message on classificatory systems for memory in Broadbent's chapter relates to the fractionation of short-term memory by various aspects of modality of presentation (e.g., Murdock & Walker, 1969). There is no doubt that Broadbent's proposals give a more satisfactory account of the modality effect than those in vogue 20 years ago. However, with respect to the specific issue of classificatory systems under scrutiny here, Broadbent's account is clearly reminiscent of previous conceptualizations.

The modality effect refers to the reliable phenomenon showing a superior recall of auditorily as opposed to visually presented words in short-term memory experiments, (e.g., Craik, 1969; Nilsson, 1973; Penney, 1975; Rönnberg & Ohlsson, 1980). At least three general types of theories have been proposed to account for this effect. (In retrospect, these theories can be regarded as being related to the issue of memory systems). According to one of these theories (Craik, 1969), there is one single short-term memory store. Auditorily presented information can be processed directly and efficiently by this store because of its acoustic-articulatory nature. Visually presented information, however, must be translated into an acoustic-articulatory form in order to be stored for later recall. Owing to the need for such translation, less capacity is left over for pure memory processes, and, as a consequence, recall of visually presented information is inferior to that of auditorily presented information. Another theoretical account of the modality effect is that of modality-specific short-term stores varying in capacity (e.g., Murdock & Walker, 1969; Nilsson, 1974). A larger capacity for the auditory store is assumed to be responsible for the auditory superiority. A third view is that proposed by Crowder and Morton (1969). According to this view, there is one short-term store only, but the modality effect is assumed to occur because of the pre-categorical acoustic store favoring the auditory modality.

About 20 years ago, the modality effect was a phenomenon of intense study. However, the demise of short-term memory (Crowder, 1982) made many researchers turn to what were regarded as more fashionable aspects of memory. During the last few years, there has been a renewed interest in the modality effect (Crowder, 1986; Glenberg & Swanson, 1986; Metcalfe & Sharpe, 1985; Rönnberg & Nilsson, 1987). Broadbent's chapter (chapter 12) in the present volume under the rubric of classificatory systems is a further manifestation of this development.

Although the relations to various aspects of the modality effect have been emphasized here, it should be stressed that Broadbent's chapter is richer than that. Most importantly in this context, Broadbent's current view relates to the distinction between procedural and declarative memory and to the trichotomy advocated by Tulving (1983, 1984, 1985b, 1987): procedural, semantic, and episodic memory. In terms of the concern mentioned initially about the role of classificatory systems in facilitating communication and improving nomenclature, it is of interest to note that the experiments on input and output interference discussed by Broadbent can be conceptualized as reflecting episodic memory. In the same vein, the experiments on the learning of concepts and control of complex systems are explicitly concerned with semantic memory. However, as a reminder that the scientific understanding of memory is still meager, Broadbent pointed out that there is uncertainty about the relationship between semantic memory and procedural knowledge. A possible solution suggested by Broadbent is that semantic memory, unlike episodic memory, may be either declarative or procedural.

MODULARITY AND DISSOCIATION

In chapter 14, on modularity and dissociations of memory systems, Crowder commented on the return of a pendulum towards faculty psychology in cognition in general and in the analysis of memory in particular.

Crowder took note of the return of some basic issues in memory research from the 1960s. Students of memory at that time were considering the possibility of separate memory systems, and this is still the topic of the day. According to Crowder, not very much has changed—the dichotomy during the 1960s was that of short-term and long-term memory; today it is procedural and declarative memory, or the trichotomy of procedural, semantic, and episodic memory. As before, empirical dissociations play a cardinal role in providing evidence for the distinctions between subsystems of memory. So, not very much is new, according to Crowder. Possibly, what is new is that we know now that the dichotomy between short-term and long-term memory is not tenable. The dissociations demonstrated were not enough, according to Crowder, to demonstrate that there are separate short-term and long-term memory systems. We should learn this lesson, Crowder reminds us, and refrain from arguing for different memory systems today too. Crowder argues that it is risky—at best—to think that existing empirical dissociations constitute evidence for separate memory systems. However, Crowder seemed to suggest that dissociations do have theoretical importance; not as criteria for establishing memory systems, but rather as criteria for memory variables. For example, he argued that dissociations between recall and recognition are theoretically important for the purpose of falsifying single-process theories like the strength theory.

Although the notion of the neuropsychological criterion (Olton, 1985; Tulving, 1985a) was not touched on by Crowder, his own thinking differs from that characterizing the 1960s in that his ambition apparently is to anchor his discussion to the neuropsychological data on amnesia. Crowder's speculations about the source of classical amnesia in this context are provocative. His reasoning centers on evidence that the source of classical amnesia cannot be a disturbance of consciousness, because the amnesics seem to be well aware of various aspects of the world. It is more reasonable, according to Crowder, to conceive of amnesia as a "special vulnerability or fragility in the sense of a neo-consolidation theory of contextual connections with other aspects of the processing system." He suggested that these ideas should not be taken to indicate the existence of separate procedural and declarative systems. Crowder argued that his view means one normal memory (i.e., the knowledge that processing occurred in a given context), which, in his terminology, is vertically modular (cf. Fodor, 1983). Each one of a large number of coding formats is different from the others, and the loss of context connections is "just the loss of information of one among many, or several, specialized codes."

EXPERIMENTAL METHODS

In chapter 13, Neely provided a thorough analysis of the experimental methods used for supporting the distinction between episodic and semantic memory.

Neely's analysis is both methodological and conceptual and, in principle, it seems to hold for other types of distinctions between memory systems as well. Explicitly, Neely set out to prescribe some basic procedural safeguards for equating the procedures employed in episodic and semantic memory tests. He also reported a number of experiments from his own laboratory that are based on paradigms that satisfy these safeguards. The results from some of these experiments support the episodic-semantic distinction, whereas others do not.

After lengthy analysis, Neely arrived at the conclusion that dissociation experiments are complicated and demanding to conduct and their results are often difficult to interpret. Despite these difficulties, he stated his belief that dissociations will remain an important and useful tool for distinguishing between various systems or mechanisms. It is noteworthy that Neely arrived at this conclusion without even considering the neuropsychological criterion that others (e.g., Olton, 1985; Tulving, 1985a) regard as fundamental in evaluating evidence in the classification of memory systems.

In most respects, Neely's chapter constitutes a complete coverage of issues to be considered when evaluating the distinction between episodic and semantic memory. Most issues are non-controversial and need hardly be commented on. However, there is one aspect that should not pass without notice, namely the role of context dependency in evaluating the distinction. Neely took a claim by Tulving (1984) as a point of departure for a discussion of this issue. The claim in question is that episodic memory is more context-dependent than semantic memory. Neely himself has collected data that both challenge (Neely & Payne, 1983) and support (Durgunoğlu & Neely, 1987; Neely & Durgunoğlu, 1985) the claim by Tulving (1984). These two sets of data are based on different paradigms, and the issue I raise here is task analysis—in my opinion a much-neglected topic in memory research. It is true that Neely compared various aspects of the two paradigms leading to different conclusions about the role of context in episodic and semantic memory, and these comparisons are clearly necessary first steps towards a task analysis. However, we need to approach this issue more thoroughly, and this is true for most research on memory, not only for the case that Neely discussed.

TASK ANALYSIS

I argue that task analysis, or an analysis of the demands of the immediately surrounding environment, constitutes an inevitable prerequisite for understanding memory and remembering. The essence of the argument is that memory structures and memory processes have evolved into their present form through a long historical process of interactions with various demands of the environment. A full understanding of memory therefore requires that we understand the environmental demands with which the subjects are confronted in memory experiments. A reasonable first step in this regard would seem to be to identify and describe these factors.

Several attempts to analyze and categorize experimental memory tasks were made in the early years of modern research on human learning and memory (e.g., McGeoch & Irion, 1965; Melton, 1964). Later, as the information-processing theories of memory grew in popularity, such attempts were regarded as less fruitful; the focus of interest turned to hypothetical memory structures and processes. For example, when the short-term and long-term memory distinction was the fashion of the day, little emphasis was placed on uncovering the nature of the task. Whenever the task as such was discussed, it was seen merely as an independent variable. There was little theoretical emphasis given to the task or to the interaction between the task and memory. Experimental outcomes were typically explained in terms of the hypothetical properties of short-term and long-term memory. The task per se was rarely seen as a part of the explanation of the results, and the same held true for the many observed interactions between the task and memory. The general attitude was that these interactions constituted something that had to be explained. The possibility that they *were* the explanations was not considered. As a reaction towards the traditional short-term memory models, Craik and Lockhart (1972) proposed the levels of processing approach. In retrospect, it is easy to see that this view entailed a renewal of interest in task–memory interactions. The levels-of-processing view held that semantic orienting tasks led to deep processing, whereas phonemic and orthographic tasks caused the subject to engage in a more shallow processing (e.g., Craik & Tulving, 1975). At that time, however, little was done to elaborate theoretically the implications of the nature of the task. The emphasis was clearly on the characteristics of memory processing.

In relation to the notion of memory systems, Tulving (1985a) pointed out the need to take the task into account more directly. Such an enterprise was seen as necessary and important, but no suggestions were made on how to go about analyzing tasks.

A thorough analysis of tasks requires, first, a broad classification of tasks. Such a classification might start by grouping the tasks used in memory experiments into separate categories. A possible principle for this grouping might be to consider what the tasks afford the person who performs the tasks (cf. Gibson, 1979). On the basis of this grouping, the next step is to make sure that the tasks grouped in the same category can be described in a multidimensional space (e.g., Rönnberg & Ohlsson, 1985). The next step is to measure how the subject reacts to tasks classified in each category, thereby trying to determine the validity of the task classification made. Ideally, the tasks classified into a given category should produce similar reactions in some basic parameters, and tasks classified into different categories should produce differences in data patterns.

At our present stage of knowledge, a particularly informative criterion for assessing the validity of the classification of tasks is the neuropsychological criterion mentioned earlier (Olton, 1985; Tulving, 1985a). Several new technological inventions are suitable for such measurements; scalp-recorded event-related potentials (see e.g., Halgren & Smith, 1987) and regional cerebral blood flow (see e.g., Wood, 1987) are two such techniques that would produce rich enough data on brain activity for an analytical comparison of tasks. The rationale is that tasks that produce similarities in brain activity pattern are to be classified as belonging to the same category. Conversely, tasks that have been classified into different categories should produce differences in brain activity patterns. Qualitative evaluations of such patterns might constitute a first step towards determining the validity of the classification made on the basis of the conceptual analyses of the tasks. However, quantitative evaluations of these multidimensional brain activity data could also be made in various ways; for example, in terms of principal component analysis (e.g., Ståhle & Wold, 1986).

Thus, on the basis of the interplay between conceptual classification of tasks and empirical validation by means of measured brain activity, a classificatory system for the task–brain interaction could be developed. No such system has yet been accomplished. Speculatively, one might arrive at a classificatory system that reveals different brain activity patterns for declarative memory tasks and procedural memory tasks (cf. Cohen & Squire, 1980). It might also be possible to differentiate episodic and semantic memory tasks from each other (Kinsbourne & Wood, 1982) and from procedural memory tasks in a way that would reflect the classificatory system suggested by Tulving (1983, 1984, 1985b, 1987). In the same way as a dichotomy between episodic and semantic memory tasks would constitute a differentiation of declarative memory tasks, it might also be possible to detect a further division of tasks categorized as procedural memory tasks. For example, it might be possible to differentiate between one subcategory of associative memory tasks and one subcategory of priming tasks that would reflect the distinction made by Weiskrantz (1987) between associative memory and priming within procedural memory.

Because no empirical test of this type of reasoning has yet been undertaken, there is little point in taking these speculations further at present. One point to be made though, is that analyses of task–brain interactions like the one proposed here may suggest a finer and more detailed classification of memory systems than exists at present (cf. Tulving, 1987).

The next step in this kind of research activity would therefore be the study of memory performance in various groups of patients for different but systematically related tasks, and to evaluate the performance for each group in relation to groups of normal control subjects tested with the same set of tasks. On the basis of what is already known about the basic characteristics of each task and the neurological damage of each patient group, it should be possible to predict the qualitative and quantitative nature of the dissociations expected. Knowledge about the basic characteristics of the tasks employed would serve as the background for predicting memory performance for each well-defined group of patients. This knowledge about tasks together with knowledge abut particular brain dysfunctions for various groups of patients would then be the basis for making differential predictions of dissociations across groups. The main thrust of this reasoning is that it is not until such predictions have been supported by empirical data that inferences about *memory systems* can be made.

The understanding of memory is a complicated matter, and it may still be too early to propose separate memory systems. I have argued here that careful analyses of memory tasks and of interactions between tasks and brain activity must be undertaken before we can reach a stage where we can make inferences about such systems. The argument that human memory can be understood in terms of interactions between tasks and brain activity patterns is not to say that everything interacts with everything else and that lawfulness and regularity cannot be accomplished in this field of research. On the contrary, it is claimed that the understanding of such interactions constitutes a necessary prerequisite for the formulation of general laws in the science of memory (Nilsson, Law, & Tulving, 1988).

ACKNOWLEDGMENTS

The author's research is supported by the Swedish Council for Research in the Social Sciences and the Humanities and by the Bank of Sweden Tercentenary Foundation. The author is indebted to Åke E. Andersson for discussions of rationality and optimal solutions.

REFERENCES

Broadbent, D. E. (1984). The Maltese cross: A new simplistic model for memory. *Behavioral and Brain Sciences, 7,* 55–94.

Cohen, N. J., & Squire, L. R. (1980). Preserved learning and retention of pattern analyzing skill in amnesia: Dissociation of knowing how and knowing that. *Science, 210,* 207–209.

Craik, F. I. M. (1969). Modality effects in short-term storage. *Journal of Verbal Learning and Verbal Behavior, 8,* 658–664.

Craik, F. I. M., & Lockhart, R. S. (1972). Levels of processing: A framework for memory research. *Journal of Verbal Learning and Verbal Behavior, 11,* 671–684.

Craik, F. I. M., & Tulving, E. (1975). Depth of processing and the retention of words in episodic memory. *Journal of Experimental Psychology: General, 104,* 268–294.

Crowder, R. G. (1982). The demise of short-term memory. *Acta Psychologica, 50,* 291–323.

Crowder, R. G. (1986). Auditory and temporal factors in the modality effect. *Journal of Experimental Psychology: Learning, Memory and Cognition, 12,* 268–278.

Crowder, R. G., & Morton, J. (1969). Precategorical acoustic storage (PAS). *Perception & Psychophysics, 5,* 365–373.

Durgunoğlu, A. Y., & Neely, J. H. (1987). On obtaining episodic priming in a lexical decision task following paired-associate learning. *Journal of Experiment Psychology: Learning, Memory and Cognition, 13,* 206–222.

Fodor, J. A. (1983). *Modularity of mind.* Cambridge, MA: MIT Press.

Glenberg, A. M., & Swanson, N. G. (1986). A temporal distinctiveness theory of recency and modality effects. *Journal of Experimental Psychology: Learning, Memory and Cognition, 12,* 3–15.

Gibson, J. J. (1979). *The ecological approach to visual perception.* Boston: Houghton Mifflin.

Halgren, E., & Smith, M. E. (1987). Cognitive evoked potentials as modulatory processes in human memory formation and retrieval. *Human Neurobiology, 6,* 129–139.

Kinsbourne, M., & Wood, F. (1982). Theoretical considerations regarding the episodic–semantic memory distinction. In L. S. Cermak (Ed.), *Human memory and amnesia* (pp. 195–217). Hillsdale, NJ: Lawrence Erlbaum Associates.

McGeoch, J. A., & Irion, A. L. (1965). *The psychology of human learning.* New York: David McKay.

Melton, A. W. (1964). *Categories of human learning.* New York: Academic Press.

Metcalfe, J., & Sharpe, D. (1985). Ordering and reordering in the auditory and visual modalities. *Memory & Cognition, 13,* 435–441.

Murdock, B. B., Jr., & Walker, K. D. (1969). Modality effects in free recall. *Journal of Verbal Learning and Verbal Behavior, 8,* 665–676.

Neely, J. H., & Durgunoğlu, A. (1985). Dissociative episodic and semantic priming effects in episodic recognition and lexical decision tasks. *Journal of Memory and Language, 24,* 466–489.

Neely, J. H., & Payne, D. G. (1983). A direct comparison of recognition failure rates for recallable names in episodic and semantic memory tests. *Memory & Cognition, 11,* 161–171.

Nilsson, L.-G. (1973). Organization by modality in short-term memory. *Journal of Experimental Psychology, 100,* 246–253.

Nilsson, L.-G. (1974). Further evidence for organization by modality in immediate free recall. *Journal of Experimental Psychology, 103,* 948–957.

Nilsson, L.-G., Law, J., & Tulving, E. (1988). Recognition failure of recallable unique names: Evidence for an empirical law of memory and learning. *Journal of Experimental Psychology: Learning, Memory and Cognition, 14,* 266–277.

Olton, D. S. (1985). Memory: Neuropsychological and ethopsychological approaches to its classification. In L.-G. Nilsson & T. Archer (Eds.), *Perspectives on learning and memory* (pp. 95–113). Hillsdale, NJ: Lawrence Erlbaum Associates.

Penney, C. G. (1975). Modality effects in short-term verbal memory. *Psychological Bulletin, 82,* 68–84.

Rönnberg, J., & Nilsson, L.-G. (1987). The modality effect, sensory handicap, and compensatory functions. *Acta Psychologica, 65,* 263–283.

Rönnberg, J., & Ohlsson, K. (1980). Channel capacity and processing of modality specific information. *Acta Psychologica, 44,* 253–267.

Rönnberg, J., & Ohlsson, K. (1985). The challenge of integrating animal learning and human memory research. In L.-G. Nilsson & T. Archer (Eds.), *Perspectives on learning and memory* (pp. 293–324). Hillsdale, NJ: Lawrence Erlbaum Associates.

Ståhle, L., & Wold, S. (1986). On the use of some multivariate statistical methods in pharmacological research. *Journal of Pharmacological Methods, 16,* 91–110.

Tulving, E. (1983). *Elements of episodic memory.* New York: Oxford University Press.

Tulving, E. (1984). Relations among components and process of memory. *Behavioral and Brain Sciences, 7,* 257–268.

Tulving, E. (1985a). On the classification problem in learning and memory. L.-G. Nilsson & T. Archer (Eds.), *Perspectives on learning and memory* (pp. 67–94). Hillsdale, NJ: Lawrence Erlbaum Associates.

Tulving, E. (1985b). How many memory systems are there? *American Psychologist, 40,* 385–398.

Tulving, E. (1987). Multiple memory systems and consciousness. *Human Neurobiology, 6,* 67–80.

Weiskrantz, L. (1987). Neuroanatomy of memory and amnesia: A case for multiple memory systems. *Human Neurobiology, 6,* 93–105.

Wood, F. (1987). Focal and diffuse memory activation assessed by localized indicators of CNS metabolism: The semantic–episodic memory distinction. *Human Neurobiology, 6,* 141–151.

IV CONSCIOUSNESS, EMOTION, AND MEMORY

16 Retrieval Inhibition as an Adaptive Mechanism in Human Memory

Robert A. Bjork
University of California, Los Angeles

It is argued herein that inhibition plays an important role in higher-order as well as lower-order cognitive processes. One such form of inhibition for which there is accumulating evidence is retrieval inhibition, characterized by a loss of access to certain items that are, in fact, stored in memory. Some of that evidence is summarized in this chapter, and the possible adaptive role played by retrieval inhibition in the updating of human memory, in the ability of higher-order units in memory to act as units, and in the long-term retention of order information is outlined.

Because the word *inhibition* is used in a number of ways in the literature—often simply as a descriptor for empirical effects that are the opposite of *facilitation*—it is important to emphasize that "inhibition" is used here in the strong sense, as in *suppression;* that is, as the opposite of *excitation*. The distinction is important because effects labelled as "inhibitory" are often the consequence of strengthening or activating incompatible or alternative responses, rather than the consequence of directly suppressing or inhibiting the response of interest. Such distinctions are discussed more fully in the final section of this essay.

INHIBITORY MECHANISMS AS EXPLANATORY CONSTRUCTS

In the broadest sense, we know that inhibitory processes are as important as excitatory processes in human information processing. At the neural level, inhibitory and excitatory processes work together to convey sensory information. In the ontogeny of brain development the later-developing (higher order) brain structures inhibit, via descending fibers, the earlier-developing (lower order) structures, which permits the organism to override simple reflexes, then fixed-action patterns, then instrumental behaviors, and, eventually, to operate on internalized representations.

In our theories of human memory, however, inhibitory processes have played little or no role. There are two reasons for that, in my opinion. First, notions of inhibition or suppression in human memory have an unappealing association to certain poorly understood clinical phenomena, such as repression. Second, the information-processing approach to the study of human memory, grounded as it is in the computer metaphor, leads us to think in terms of processes like storing, scanning, grouping, erasing, and so forth. Notions like inhibition, suppression, unlearning, and spontaneous recovery are not easily compatible with the computer metaphor. It is my belief, however, that inhibitory processes *do* play a major role in higher cognitive processes, such as memory.

It is interesting that Endel Tulving, the man in whose honor this essay is written, has had so little to say—in his written work—about inhibitory mechanisms (a clear exception being Tulving & Hastie, 1972, which deals with inhibition of the blocking type that is discussed later in this essay). For the last quarter of a century, Endel Tulving has been a key player and often the prime mover in many of the important developments in the study of human memory. The fact that he has written so little on inhibitory processes illustrates the minor role the inhibition construct has played in our theorizing. In presenting Endel Tulving as a kind of case study, however, I must add that he has, in his informal comments to myself and others over the years, expressed with his typical vigor the need for theories of memory to incorporate inhibitory mechanisms—because, he has argued, memory phenomena are ultimately the product of the living brain, not the product of an information-processing architecture analogous to that in the typical computer.

At the current stage of research on human memory, we are poorly served by the computer metaphor. Thirty years ago, as an alternative to the stimulus–response approach, the information-processing approach was invaluable. It led us to distinguish between control processes (software) and structural features (hardware), and it opened the black box to theoretical speculations about the number and nature of the processing stages inside. We have come to realize, however, that in virtually every important respect, the human information processor is functionally nothing like the standard digital computer. From the standpoint of a computer scientist, there appears to be considerable value in drawing upon modern neuroscience and cognitive science to reconfigure the processing architecture of the next generation of computers. From the standpoint of a cognitive psychologist, there is no remaining value in the standard computer metaphor.

Let me illustrate the foregoing points with an example from my own research. Some years back, we looked at the directed-forgetting manipulation in the context of Sternberg's (1966, 1969) memory-scanning paradigm (Bjork, Abramo-witz, & Krantz, 1970). On each trial, subjects were presented a string of 0, 1, 2, 3, or 4 digits in one color (Color A) at a 0.67 sec rate before a switch to 1, 2, 3, or 4 digits presented in another color (Color B). A change in color served to cue subjects to forget the first set of digits (the TBF digits); the second set of digits defined the positive or to-be-remembered (TBR) set for that trial. At the end of the string of digits, a single-digit probe was presented in white, and the subjects were required to respond "yes" or "no" (with a button push) as quickly as possible depending on whether the probe was or was not in the TBR set of digits on that trial. Thus, there were two types of negative probes: those that were presented on that trial but in the TBF rather than in the TBR set (F-NOs), and those that were not presented at all on that trial (N-NOs). It should be noted that a digit was never repeated from the TBF or the TBR set in the same trial.

One further procedural detail is important. Subjects could not ignore the digits presented in the first color because on 33% of the trials there was no change of color, which meant that the TBR or positive search set was the Color A digits. On such trials, then, the procedure was the same as the standard Sternberg paradigm. Furthermore, because there was no way for the subject to know on any given trial whether there would be a color change until that change actually occurred, the subject had to try to remember Color A items on all trials.

This experiment produced stunning results. Those results were never pub-lished, however, because they seemed to defy interpretation. The principle ques-tions of interest, in advance, were the following: (a) would YES reaction times depend on the size of the TBF set; (b) would reaction times for F-NO and N-NO responses differ; and (c) would F-NO reaction times differ as a function of the size of the TBF set?

The answer to the second question is shown in Fig. 16.1, where reaction time is plotted as a function of the size of the TBR set, averaged across the size of the TBF set. All three types of responses bear the standard linear relationship to the size of the TBR (positive) set, with F-NO responses being slower than N-NO responses by a relatively constant amount.

The answers to the other two questions are shown in Fig. 16.2, in which the reaction times are plotted as a function of the size of the TBF set, averaged over the size of the TBR set. None of the three response types vary as a function of the size of the TBF set.

At the time that we obtained these results, they defied description by any of the single-process (serial-parallel) search models then available. How could YES responses have shown no effect of the TBF set whatsoever when, at the same time, F-NO responses were slower than N-NO responses? If subjects could limit their search to the TBR set (as indicated by the YES results), why should it matter whether a negative probe was presented in the TBF set or not? And, as it did matter (F-NO responses were slower than N-NO responses), how can F-NO reaction times *not* depend on the size of the TBF set?

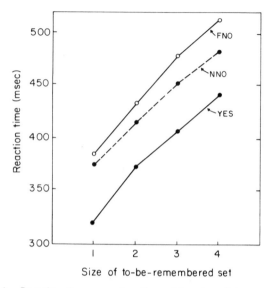

FIG. 16.1. Reaction times as a function of the size of the second (to-be-remembered) set on a given trial. YES and NO probes denote test items that did or did not appear in the TBR set; F-NO and N-NO probes differ in whether they did or did not appear in the first (to-be-forgotten) set. (After Bjork et al., 1970.)

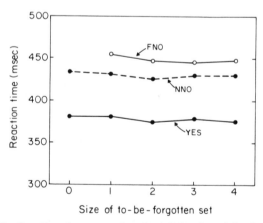

FIG. 16.2. Reaction times as a function of the size of the first (to-be-forgotten) set on a given trial. YES and NO probes denote test items that did or did not appear in the second (to-be-remembered) set; F-NO and N-NO probes differ in whether they did or did not appear in the to-be-forgotten set. (After Bjork et al., 1970.)

Dual-process models of memory scanning, as formulated by Atkinson and Juola (e.g., 1974) and their co-workers (e.g., Juola, Fischler, Wood, & Atkinson, 1971) shortly after the data in Figs. 16.1 and 16.2 were collected, also seemed unable to account for the results. The basic idea underlying such models is that a YES–NO decision can be based either on an initial familiarity judgment or on a systematic search of the type proposed by Sternberg (1966). Test probes whose familiarity is below some low threshold or above some high threshold trigger a rapid NO or YES response, respectively, whereas probes of intermediate familiarity require a slower search process. Response latencies of the former type are presumed to be independent of the size of the search set, whereas response latencies of the latter type are presumed to increase linearly with search set size.

The data in Figs. 16.1 and 16.2 pose two types of problems for such models. First and foremost, given the kind of procedure employed by Bjork et al. (1970) (TBF and TBR sets drawn from the digits 0–9 on every trial), the dual-process model is presumed by Atkinson and Juola (1974) to reduce to a Sternberg-type single-process search model. All items in the set of digits are presented repeatedly across trials, which, according to Atkinson and Juola, renders familiarity judgments essentially useless in distinguishing targets from distractors. Such an assumption enables the dual-process model to account for the greater slopes of response-time functions when items from a small pool of items are reused across trials when compared to the slopes of response-time functions obtained when items from a large pool are used without replacement across trials.

If one attempts to ignore such considerations in an effort to apply the unique-set version of the dual-process model to the present data, a second type of problem emerges. To account for the results in Figs. 16.1 and 16.2, one would like to assume that the prior presentation of F-NO probes in the TBF set increases the familiarity level of such items independent of the TBF and TBR set size on a given trial—resulting in a fixed increment in the likelihood that a search (rather than a rapid NO response) would have to be executed. It could then be assumed that the increased response times for F-NOs (and possibly the greater slope of the response-time function) are a function of the increased likelihood of search for such items. Assuming that such an increment in search likelihood is independent of TBF and TBR set size is, however, completely implausible. As there was no temporal break between the TBF and TBR sets, an F-NO probe on a trial with a small TBR set may be temporally more recent (and, hence, more familiar) than a YES probe on a trial with a larger TBR set. Conversely, with a large TBF set and a large TBR set, a given F-NO probe may have been presented further back in time (in terms of intervening items) than an N-NO probe on a trial when the TBF and TBR sets were small. That is, given that the items used on successive trials were independent samples from the pool of digits, it was frequently the case that an N-NO probe item was presented on the preceding trial as a TBF, TBR, or probe item, and under some conditions that prior presentation may have been quite recent.

There may well be an elaboration of the dual-process model that gives a reasonable account of the data in Figs. 16.1 and 16.2. The point of resurrecting those data, however, is not to argue about alternative scanning models. Rather, the point is the following: We never even entertained an interpretation that is not only entirely consistent with the results, but also consistent with Sternberg's characterization of what slope differences and intercept differences are supposed to reflect. Suppose that TBF items are inhibited by the forget instruction, and that one consequence of that inhibition is to slow down the encoding of those items when they are presented as probes. Once such probes are encoded, suppose further that the subsequent scanning processes are no different from those that follow N-NO probes. Everything in Figs. 16.1 and 16.2 then falls into place: Subjects can limit their search to the TBR set, but F-NO probes take longer to encode, which accounts for the difference in intercept between F-NO and N-NO reaction times.

The present issue is not whether that inhibition-based explanation of the Bjork et al. data is adequate or inadequate when held up to other existing or potential results. In fact, I doubt that such an explanation would hold up in the face of additional experimentation. The point is that we could not, 18 years ago, even generate such an explanation. We exhausted the possible explanations based on computer-type search/scanning/decision processes, but we were unable to even entertain an explanation based on an inhibitory mechanism.

INHIBITION IN DIRECTED FORGETTING

The kind of explanatory bias just illustrated characterized the early work of myself and others on directed forgetting (exceptions being the work of Roediger & Crowder, 1972; Weiner, 1968; and Weiner & Reed, 1969). The effects of a cue to subjects that they can forget the items presented prior to the cue—items that they had been trying, prior to the cue, to learn—are dramatic. Interference owing to the TBF items in the recall of the post-cue TBR items is typically eliminated, and intrusions of TBF items into the recall of TBR items is negligible. It is as if the TBF items had not been presented, although tests of recognition demonstrate that they exist in memory at essentially the same strength as comparable TBR items (although they are nowhere near as recallable). As of 9 or 10 years ago, however, it seemed that all such effects of instructing subjects to forget could be explained in terms of positive actions on the part of the subject— focusing post-cue rehearsal and other mnemonic activities on the TBR items and (somehow) segregating the TBR items in memory in a way that differentiated them from the earlier TBF items.

Those of us working on directed forgetting in that early period (with the exceptions noted previously) were accused by Erdelyi and Goldberg (1979) of having "ignored or brushed aside" (p. 382) the relationships of our work to repression and posthypnotic amnesia. In my own case, I was so convinced that directed-forgetting phenomena had nothing to do with inhibition or repression or posthypnotic amnesia that I would typically start off colloquia with a disclaimer to that effect (sometimes, as a consequence, losing selected members of my audience). Evidence began to accumulate, however, that there was a "missing mechanism" in our explanation of directed-forgetting phenomena (see Bjork, 1978, and Bjork & Geiselman, 1978), and we became convinced, as a consequence of the work reported by Geiselman, Bjork, and Fishman (1983), that the missing mechanism was retrieval inhibition.

Geiselman et al. presented subjects with a list of two different types of items: items subjects were asked to learn and items subjects were asked to judge on a pleasantness scale (incidental items) rather than learn. The two item types were perfectly interleaved in the list (i.e., they were presented in strict alternation). Midway through the list there was an instruction: either that the to-be-learned words presented thus far were practice and should be forgotten, or that the to-be-learned words presented thus far were the first half of the list and should be remembered. After a list of either type, the subjects were asked to free-recall *all* the words they could remember from the list, *judge* words as well as *learn* words, and first-list-half words as well as second-list-half words.

The results of the first of the Geiselman et al. experiments are shown in Fig. 16.3. The learn words show a standard pattern: A cue to forget, compared to a cue to remember, results in lowered recall of the pre-cue (TBF) items (left panel) and enhanced recall of the post-cue (TBR) items (right panel). The important result in Fig. 16.3 is that the incidental (judge) items exhibit the same pattern. For the

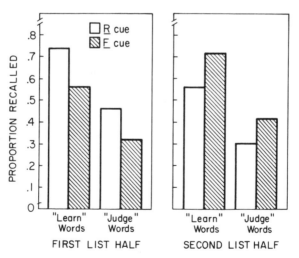

FIG. 16.3.   Proportion correct recall as a function of list half and type of midlist cue; R = remember and F = forget. (After Geiselman et al., 1983.)

intentional items, the pattern of results can be explained in terms of differential rehearsal and/or grouping of the second-list-half learn words following the forget cue. The effects of the forget cue on the judge words, however, cannot be explained in those terms. The subjects were not trying to learn or rehearse those items, and, in fact, the forget (or remember) cue was not "aimed" at the judge words. It appears that the judge words, by virtue of their being interlaced with the learn words, are inhibited by the forget cue. They are in the wrong place at the wrong time, so to speak.

The results in Fig. 16.3 can be given two alternative interpretations: (a) that subjects lost track of what items were learn words and what items were judge words, and/or (b) that the pattern in Fig. 16.3 is attributable to differential output interference owing to TBR items being recalled before TBF items. In subsequent experiments, Geiselman et al. were able to rule out those alternatives. They found that subjects were able, with high accuracy, to sort the words they recalled into judge and learn categories. They also found that when the potential for confusion between learn and judge words was eliminated by drawing those words from different categories, the same pattern of results (shown in Fig. 16.3) was obtained. With respect to the possible contributions of differential output interference, Geiselman et al. found that controlling order of output did not change the basic pattern of results.

The inhibition of to-be-forgotten items appears to take the form of retrieval inhibition. When Geiselman et al. tested yes–no recognition rather than recall, none of the variables that make such a difference in Fig. 16.3 mattered at all. The recognition results are shown in Fig. 16.4. The to-be-forgotten learn (or judge) words are as well recognized as the to-be-remembered learn (or judge) words. Although not particularly germane to the present issue, the lack of an overall difference between learn and judge words in recognition is also interesting, given that learn words were better recalled than judge words (see Fig. 16.3). It seems plausible to assume that the two item types may not have differed substantially in depth of processing, but that the learn words—because they were to-be-learned and recalled—received cumulative inter-item associative processing across the list presentation. The effects of any such inter-item processing on recall should be clearly larger than the effects, if any, on recognition.

It is worth commenting that the results obtained by Geiselman et al. do not rule out list differentiation as an important mechanism in directed forgetting. That is, some kind of list or item differentiation is a precondition for TBF items to be selectively suppressed or inhibited. Such an observation is by no means new. Crowder (1976), for example, in his discussion of interference theory, made a similar point in contrasting the response-set suppression (Postman, Stark, & Fraser, 1968) and list-differentiation (Underwood & Ekstrand, 1966, 1967) hypotheses.

It is also important to emphasize, however, that list differentiation alone is not sufficient to explain the present results. Without additional assumptions (such as

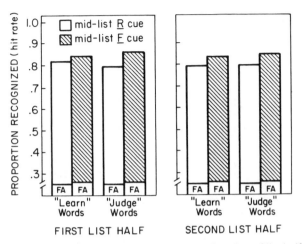

FIG. 16.4. Proportion correct recognition as a function of list half and type of midlist cue; R = remember, F = forget, and FA = false-alarm rate. (After Geiselman et al., 1983.)

retrieval inhibition) there is no reason to expect that recall of the first list half in the F-cue condition would be impaired simply by virtue of those items being well differentiated in memory from second-list-half items. In the case of learn words, one can argue that cumulative processing of learn words in the first list half was carried over into the second list half given a midlist R-cue, but that no such carry over occurred given a midlist F-cue. Such "carried over" processing would enhance recall of learn words from the first list half and impair recall of words from the second list half (producing the pattern shown in Fig. 16.3). As stated earlier, however, no such argument can be made to explain the similar pattern observed for the incidental judge words.

RELEASE OF INHIBITION IN DIRECTED FORGETTING

The recognition results shown in Fig. 16.4, and earlier results also showing unimpaired recognition of to-be-forgotten items, indicate that simply presenting the TBF item restores that item to full "strength," as measured by a recognition test. Studies of repetition effects (e.g., Geiselman & Bagheri, 1985), in which TBF items are later represented as TBR items (e.g., in another list), also indicate that TBF items can be readily brought back to full strength—in fact, to approximately the level of items presented twice as TBR items.

Research by Bjork, Bjork, and Glenberg (1973) and Bjork, Bjork, and White (1984) suggests that the absence of interference from TBF items in the recall of TBR items can be changed to interference under certain conditions. Two aspects

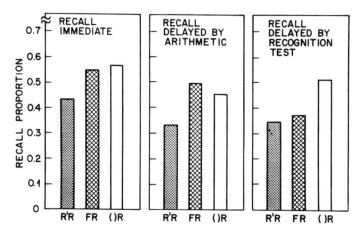

FIG. 16.5.   Recall performance on the second sublist of 16 words as a function of list type and test condition; FR and R'R denote lists in which the first sublist of 16 words was to be forgotten and to be remembered, respectively, and (-)R denotes lists where there was no first sublist of words. (After E. Bjork et al., 1973.)

of such reinstatement of interference merit comment. First of all, the simple presence of TBF-item foils on a test of TBR-item recognition causes interference, even though a test of TBR-item recall administered at that same point would not show such interference. Apparently, it is not the case that the lack of interference owing to TBF items in the recall of TBR items is attributable to the subject being able to identify TBF items in memory as TBF items. Rather, it appears that TBF items do not interfere because they are not "encountered" in the recall process—were they to be encountered, they would intrude into and interfere with the recall of the TBR items.

The second way in which the interference owing to TBF items can be reinstated is illustrated by the results shown in Fig. 16.5. E. Bjork et al. (1973) presented subjects with three types of word lists: lists with a midlist cue to forget the first half of the list (FR lists), lists with a midlist cue to remember the first half of the list (R'R lists), and lists without a first half (a shape-judgment task took the place of the words that would have been in the first list half)—(-)R lists. There were 16 words in each list half.

Immediate recall of the words in the second list half is shown in the left panel of Fig. 16.5. Delayed recall of those same words is shown in the middle and right panels, where recall was delayed by an intervening arithmetic task and an intervening recognition test (for second-list-half words), respectively. In the FR and (-)R conditions, subjects were asked to free-recall the words in the second list half; in the R'R condition, they were asked to free-recall all the words in the list. Immediate recall and recall delayed by arithmetic show the same pattern: Recall of second-list-half words is as good in the forget condition as it is in the condition without any first-list-half words, and it is significantly better than recall of those words in the remember condition. When recall is delayed by a recognition test, however, the pattern changes. The forget condition and remember condition are now equivalent, and significantly worse than the condition where there were no first-list-half words.

The recognition test consisted of eight forced-choice tests, four of which paired a TBR word with a TBF word and four of which paired a TBR word with a new word. The recall of the second-list-half items that did not appear on the recognition test is plotted in the right-hand panel. It appears that the exposure of only 4 of the 16 TBF items, in the context of the decision processes involved on the recognition test, was enough to reinstate the interference owing to the entire set of TBF items.

The later results of E. Bjork et al. (1984) add to the results shown in Fig. 16.5 in two important ways. First, they replicate exactly the pattern of results shown in the first and third panels of Fig. 16.5. Second, they demonstrate that it is a necessary condition for the reinstatement of F-item interference that F-items are re-exposed on the recognition test. When recall was delayed via a recognition test that did not include first-list foils, the results were similar to that shown in the middle panel of Fig. 16.5; that is, there was no recovery of the proactive interference owing to F-items.

NECESSARY CONDITIONS FOR RETRIEVAL INHIBITION IN DIRECTED FORGETTING

We have known for some time (see Bjork, 1970) that a cue to forget prior items is much more effective if it precedes the presentation of the to-be-remembered items. If the cue is delayed until after the TBR items are presented (but before they are recalled), the effects of the cue are minimal, no matter how well the TBF and TBR sets are segregated in time and by item type. There is little, if any, reduction in the proactive interference owing to the TBF items on the recall of the TBR items, and the subsequent recall of the TBF items themselves, when requested, is largely unimpaired (in contrast to the near-zero level of recall of those items when the forget cue precedes the presentation of the TBR items).

What we do not know is how to interpret the foregoing pattern of results. It could mean that TBF items are inhibited as a consequence of learning the subsequent TBR items (that is, of starting the learning process over again). It could also mean, however, that retrieval inhibition is a direct consequence of being instructed to forget, but that such instructions can be delivered too late to be effective (owing, perhaps, to consolidation-type processes that would stabilize the representation of TBF items in memory).

Gelfand and Bjork (1985) set out to address that issue by means of the

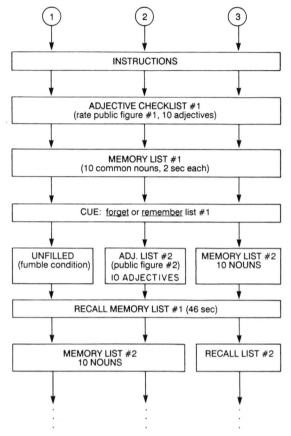

FIG. 16.6. Sequence of events for groups of subjects that differed in whether they were cued to forget or remember a first list of nouns and in the nature of the activity interpolated between that cue and a test of their ability to recall those nouns. (After Gelfand & Bjork, 1985.)

experiment diagrammed in Fig. 16.6. The subjects knew that they were going to be presented two types of 10-word lists: lists of 10 adjectives, about which they were to say whether each adjective in turn was or was not descriptive of a certain public figure (e.g., Ronald Reagan), and lists of 10 nouns, which they were to try to remember. After going through a first adjective check list, and being presented a first list of nouns to learn, half of the subjects were then cued to forget the first list of nouns ("what you have done so far is practice . . .") and the remaining subjects were cued to remember the first list of nouns. The critical manipulation, as shown in Fig. 16.6, is what happened next. One group of subjects did nothing (while the experimenter fumbled around killing time), another group was presented a second adjective check list, and the third group

TABLE 16.1
Proportion List-1 Words Recalled as a Function of the Post-List-1
Cue and the Activity Interpolated Prior to the Recall of List 1
(after Gelfand & Bjork, 1985)

Cue re memory list 1	Interpolated Activity		
	Unfilled	Adjective Checklist	Memory List 2
Forget	.58	.53	.37
Remember	.61	.55	.54

learned a second list of nouns. After that intervening activity, all groups were tested for their recall of the first list of nouns. Groups 1 and 2 were then presented a second list of nouns to learn, whereas group 3, which had already been presented a second list of nouns, was asked to recall that second list. The subsequent events in the design are not relevant to the present issues.

The proportions of list-1 words recalled in the various conditions are shown in Table 16.1. The pattern of results in Table 16.1 seems to argue strongly that the retrieval of TBF items is inhibited as a by-product of new learning. Compared to the remember-cue conditions, there was only minor loss of list-1 recall owing to the forget cue in the unfilled and adjective-check-list conditions (.58 vs. .61 and .53 vs. .55, respectively). When the second to-be-memorized list was interpolated, however, there was substantial loss of access to list 1 (.37 vs. .54). Were the forget cue to operate as a kind of magic wand, inhibiting the TBF items as a direct consequence of the instruction itself, there should be no interaction of the type shown in Table 16.1. That is, it is the resetting of the learning process initiated by the presentation of a new list of to-be-remembered items that is necessary for the prior to-be-forgotten items to be inhibited.

An additional result, consistent with the results of E. Bjork et al. (1973, 1984), deserves mention. In the F-cue condition, the effort by subjects to recall the first list reinstated the interference owing to those items in the recall of the second list. In the third column of Fig. 16.6, the levels of recall of list 2 (following the effort to recall list 1) were .48 and .46 in the F-cue and R-cue conditions, respectively.

RETRIEVAL INHIBITION IN THE BROADER CONTEXT

Updating

The layperson tends to think that the singular problem in using one's memory effectively is to remember things. Efficient use of our memories, however, also requires that we update the system effectively. When we need to remember our current phone number, the current married name of a female acquaintance, the trump suit on this hand, and where we left the car today, it does not help us to remember our old phone numbers, our friend's maiden name, the trump suit on the last hand, and where we left the car yesterday. That is, we need some means to suppress, set aside, destroy, or discriminate out-of-date information in memory in order to remember current information effectively.

The updating process in computers is brutal but effective: When a new value of some variable is entered, the old value is destroyed. There are clear drawbacks to such a system, however, should the old value become pertinent once again in some way. Retrieval inhibition, as an updating mechanism, is a more sophisticated system with the following adaptive properties: (a) Because the old material becomes nonretrievable (by virtue of learning the new material), that material also becomes non-interfering in the recall of the new material; (b) the old material, however, remains in memory, is apparently at full strength from a recognition standpoint, and is, therefore, familiar and identifiable when it reoccurs; and (c) the old material is not only recognizable but also, apparently, relearnable in the sense that it becomes fully accessible in memory when presented again as to-be-learned material.[1]

Unitization

A recent dissertation by Hirshman (1988) suggests that retrieval inhibition may play an adaptive role in another context. In a large number of experiments, Hirshman explored a paradoxical effect of semantic relatedness. When subjects were asked to study a list of word pairs differing in associative strength (some strongly related, like TABLE–CHAIR, some weakly related, like GLUE–CHAIR), their ability to free recall the response words was actually better for the weakly related pairs. Such a result is paradoxical on several grounds. First, cued recall, not surprisingly, shows a large advantage for strongly related pairs. Second, free recall of the response component of a pair is often going to be mediated by recall of the stimulus component, and such mediation should clearly be more effective the stronger the associative relationship between the stimulus and the response terms. Finally, the advantage of weakly related pairs in free recall goes

---

[1]Donald Broadbent (personal communication) has pointed out that, in some respects, computers are not as different from human memory as this passage suggests. In typical file management systems, an instruction to erase a file does not destroy the information in that file, but, rather, changes entries in a directory; the locations where that file was stored become available for later storage. Until those locations are overwritten, the "erased" file can be retrieved by special means—but *only* by special means, which Broadbent argues may be analogous to a kind of retrieval inhibition. Even when an updated (revised) version of a given file is stored, the old version may or may not be destroyed, depending on the design of the system. What can be said with some confidence, Broadbent's interesting arguments notwithstanding, is that the write process in a computer is fundamentally destructive in a way that the write process in humans is probably not.

TABLE 16.2
Proportion of Response Words Recalled as a Function of
Type of Test and Associative Strength (after Hirshman,
1988, Experiment 1)

Type of Test	Strongly Related Pairs	Weakly Related Pairs
Free recall	.23	.34
Cued recall	.93	.73

against a strong generalization in verbal learning: that learning is positively related to meaningfulness. The kind of results obtained by Hirshman are shown in Table 16.2.

Based on substantial empirical support, Hirshman isolated encoding and retrieval processes that he believes give rise to such paradoxical effects of semantic relatedness. My own less-well-supported view of his research is that such effects illustrate a fundamental associative principle that characterizes human memory (and the development of expertise): as items become associated to the point that they become unitized, independent access to those items becomes inhibited. The ability to operate in higher-order units composed of components that were once separate units (in children, e.g., going from letters as units to words as units) is critical to the development of intelligence and skills. Apparently, inhibiting access to the separate components of a higher-order unit is adaptive in the sense that it is part and parcel of those components acting as one chunk in memory.

A colleague in my department at UCLA (Wendell Jeffrey) mentioned an anecdote that is probably a good everyday example of the unitization effect. After ordering an item from a catalog by phone, he was asked for his name and address by the operator. As he was starting to give what for him, and for most of us, is a fairly unitized sequence, the operator said she needed his zip code first. He momentarily was unable to retrieve that overlearned item and had to go through the sequence to get it. When he apologized to the operator, she said "that happens all the time; I don't know why the computer wants it that way."

Memory for Serial Order

The difficulty that Wendell Jeffrey experienced in attempting to go directly to the last component of his address, also illustrates the possible role of inhibition in the retention of order information—as postulated by Estes (1972). Estes assumes that for the items in a sequence to be output properly ". . . the individual must inhibit response tendencies to later items in the sequence until the responses to earlier items have been emitted" (p. 183). As a consequence of rehearsal and practice, in his theory, "the inhibitory tendencies required to properly shape the response output become established in memory and account for the long-term preservation of order information'' (p. 183). More specifically, he assumes that when the higher-order ''control element'' that stands for the sequence in memory is activated, excitation flows to all elements in the sequence. However, the responses associated with later elements in the sequence are inhibited, owing to the inhibitory connections that have been established from each earlier item to each later item. Upon the actual output of an earlier item, Estes assumes, the inhibitory input from the item to later items ceases.

Another role that must be played by some kind of inhibitory mechanism in the output of an ordered sequence is the inhibition of items in the sequence that have already been generated. That is a particularly vexing problem conceptually, because—as is discussed in the next section—generating an item makes that item more accessible in memory and may block access to related items in memory.

TYPES OF RETRIEVAL INHIBITION

As mentioned at the outset, the word *inhibition* is used in a number of ways. I have focused on inhibition as a suppression-type process directed at the to-be-inhibited information for some adaptive purpose. I assume that the target of such suppression is information that already resides in memory, hence, the term *retrieval* inhibition. Such a usage is close to inhibition in the classic sense of *repression* (cf. Freud, 1914), or the class of processes Osgood (1953) refers to as ''motivated forgetting.''[2] I refer to the ''classic sense'' of repression because, in more recent times, repression is often defined as an unconscious defense mechanism, whereas retrieval inhibition of the type referred to here would, typically, be characterized by a conscious intent to suppress. In their very thorough discussion of the meaning of repression, however, Erdelyi and Goldberg (1979) point out that Freud himself viewed repression as typically intentional and ''from his earliest psychological writings to his last . . . uses 'suppression' and 'repression' interchangeably'' (p. 366).

It is retrieval inhibition in the foregoing sense that has played little role in our recent theories of memory. Another type of ''retrieval inhibition''—when retrieval of target information from memory is blocked temporarily by the retrieval

---

[2]With respect to my earlier point that the computer metaphor is partly responsible for our not appealing to inhibitory processes as explanatory constructs, it is of historical interest to note that the handbooks of experimental psychology written by Osgood (1953) and by Woodworth and Scholsberg (1954) cover ''motivated forgetting'' in some detail. Those thorough and highly rigorous books were written prior to the onset of the information-processing approach in the late 1950s and its accompanying computer metaphor. The stimulus–response approach was still dominant in the early 1950s, and notions of inhibition, suppression, unlearning, and so forth were more compatible with that approach.

of related non-target information—has played a much more frequent role in our theorizing (see, e.g., Bjork & Geiselman, 1978; Blaxton & Neely, 1983; A. Brown, 1981; J. Brown, 1968; Kato, 1985; Nickerson, 1984; Roediger, 1974, 1978; Roediger & Neely, 1982; Rundus, 1973; Tulving & Hastie, 1972; and Watkins, 1975). Such inhibition or blocking comes about, presumably, because there is a kind of capacity limitation on retrieval: As some items in a category are activated in the sense of being made more accessible in memory—via their being presented or recalled—the access to other items is slowed down or blocked. There may be good reasons that such retrieval blocking is a more frequent construct in our theories, but its more frequent use may be attributable, in part, to its being more compatible with the computer metaphor. Retrieval inhibition/suppression and retrieval inhibition/blocking share the basic properties that access to some target information in memory is impaired, and that such impairment is temporary, but differ in most other important respects.

Retrieval Inhibition/Suppression

Inhibition in the sense of suppression would seem to have the following characteristics: It is directed at the to-be-inhibited information, and it is initiated to achieve some goal (such as the reduction of proactive interference, or the avoidance of painful recollection). In addition to some of the examples discussed previously, the *response-set suppression* hypothesis of Postman et al. (1968) is a perfect example of an inhibitory process with those properties. According to Postman et al., when a second to-be-learned list is similar to a first (e.g., in the A-B, A-D paradigm), retroactive interference is, in part, attributable to subjects suppressing first-list responses during second-list learning. Such suppression supposedly facilitates second-list learning by blocking the covert or overt intrusions of first-list responses during second-list learning, but it also leads to worsened performance on list 1, should that list be tested after list-2 learning is completed. Such suppression is directed at the to-be-suppressed items, and it is adaptive in the sense that it facilitates list-2 learning.

Retrieval Inhibition/Blocking

Inhibition in the sense of blocking, on the other hand, is a by-product of the activation of other items in memory, and may not be adaptive—at least on the short term. Consider the kind of retrieval blocking demonstrated by J. Brown (1968): Subjects who spent 5 minutes studying the names of 25 of the 50 states later recalled more of those 25 states but fewer of the other 25 states than did subjects in a control group that spent those 5 minutes doing light reading. It was not the goal of the experimental subjects to inhibit the 25 names of states they did not study, nor was such inhibition adaptive in terms of the goal of recalling all 50 states, nor were the pre-recall activities of those subjects directed at those 25 names, but, rather, at the 25 names they *did* study. (For a review of the variety of such part-list cuing procedures, and the negative effects of such procedures on the recall of uncued items, see Nickerson, 1984).

Complications and Gray Areas

In principle, the properties of inhibition as suppression and inhibition as blocking seem fairly well defined and non-overlapping. In practice, however, it is easy to cite phenomena and theories that illustrate that those two types of retrieval inhibition are neither exhaustive nor mutually exclusive. Consider, for example, the Gelfand and Bjork (1985) results shown in Table 16.1. As discussed earlier, those results seem to be strong evidence that the to-be-forgotten list is inhibited as a by-product of learning the new list—not simply as a consequence of the forget instruction itself. That sounds like inhibition/blocking is the operative mechanism, but then one might have expected the middle condition in Fig. 16.6, in which ten adjectives were "studied" prior to list-1 recall, to have resulted in some inhibition of the to-be-forgotten words as well. It could be that both the intent to update the system (that is, to forget some prior information) and the process of storing/activating new information are necessary conditions for retrieval inhibition. Without the ongoing list-2 learning, for example, the suppression of list-1 responses (as in the response-set suppression hypothesis of Postman et al., 1968) may not be possible. Even repression, in the psychoanalytic sense, might be accomplished by people activating more pleasant memories rather than directly suppressing the offending memory.

The *unlearning hypothesis* put forth by Melton and Irwin (1940) as a factor in retroactive interference seems like a similar ambiguous case. Is one "unlearning" a specific list-1 response to a given stimulus during list-2 learning by suppressing that response or by storing a new response that blocks access to the list-1 response? Once again, both the intent to suppress and the opportunity to store a new association may be necessary.

The possible role of retrieval inhibition in unitization and the retention of serial order illustrates another problem. The inhibition of direct access to individual elements in a well-learned sequence may be adaptive, as argued previously, but it is difficult to characterize the process leading to such inhibition as intentional on the part of the subject. Such inhibition, which seems more like suppression than blocking, also seems more like an automatic by-product of other associative activities in the brain, rather than a process over which the organism has control.

What is adaptive and is not adaptive, on the short term and on the long term, is also not so easy to judge. In the J. Brown (1968) example cited earlier, the blocking of later retrieval of the non-studied states by the studied states did not seem adaptive, and was not intentional on the subjects' part. Overall, however, retrieval blocking may be an adaptive component in updating the system—that is, in facilitating access to current information. Information that is accessed in memory becomes more accessible (a new home phone number, e.g.), and information that is not accessed, even if perfectly accessible at some earlier point in time (an old home phone number, e.g.), gradually becomes less accessible. In general, such a system will result in information that is more pertinent to the present state of affairs being more accessible in memory owing to its having been retrieved more often in the recent past. Information that is less pertinent, or completely out of date, will be non-retrievable and, hence, non-interfering. (For a more detailed argument regarding the adaptive side of retrieval failure in autobiographical memory, see Bjork & Bjork, 1988).

Finally, there are a variety of recent phenomena that can be interpreted either in terms of retrieval/blocking mechanisms or in terms of retrieval/suppression mechanisms. Blaxton and Neely (1983), for example, in discussing inhibition in the cued recall of category exemplars owing to the prior generation of other exemplars (measured in terms of reaction times), outline two theoretical alternatives, a retrieval/blocking interpretation derived from the Raaijmakers and Shiffrin (1981) model (SAM), and a retrieval/suppression interpretation derived from the Keele and Neill (1978) model of attention.

"Retrieval" Inhibition at Encoding

This chapter has focused on inhibition in the retrieval of information from memory. I have not addressed the formidable array of evidence for inhibition in sensory and perceptual processes, in attention, in lexical decision tasks, and in recognition tasks. On the surface, at least, such inhibition would seem to impair an encoding and/or judgment process—not a retrieval process. The encoding/retrieval distinction is not an entirely clean one, however, as my earlier discussion of the Bjork, Abramowitz, and Krantz (1970) results indicates (Figs. 16.1 and 16.2). The inhibition-based interpretation of those results assumes that the encoding of a negative probe is slowed down (inhibited) when that probe has appeared earlier in the to-be-forgotten set. In that interpretation, the slowed encoding of the probe is attributed to the retrieval inhibition effected by the forget cue. Similarly, Neely and Durgunoğlu (1985) account for inhibited (slowed) episodic recognition of words following a semantically related prime in terms of a suppression-type retrieval inhibition. They assume that "subjects actively tried to suppress the prime's semantic associates in the episodic recognition task because the retrieval of such associates was irrelevant to the task— namely, knowing that a target is semantically related to its prime does not provide information as to its study status" (p. 485).

These two examples, as well as others that could be cited (e.g., Dosher, 1984), illustrate that retrieval inhibition may impair a subject's ability to encode or recognize or judge the lexical status of an inhibited item. Those examples also suggest that inhibition on the input side may be more active/volitional than is often thought to be the case. An additional striking example that underscores that point comes from research by Allport, Tipper, and Chmiel (1985). They presented subjects with trials consisting of a prime stimulus followed by a probe stimulus. Both stimuli consisted of a red letter and a green letter on top of each other (the prime might be a red A and a green B, for example, and the probe might be a red C and a green D). At the end of a trial, subjects were asked first to name the red letter in the probe stimulus and then to recall the red letter from the prime stimulus. On the trials where the green (to-be-ignored) letter in the prime stimulus was repeated as the red (to-be-named) stimulus in the probe stimulus, there was an inhibitory effect: The subjects were slowed down in their ability to name that letter. On the final trial of the experiment, subjects—rather than being presented a probe stimulus—were asked to recall the green (to-be-ignored) letter from the preceding prime stimulus. The fact that few subjects could do so indicates that a kind of active retrieval inhibition was responsible for the slowed encoding observed by Allport et al. (1985).

CONCLUDING COMMENT

In all likelihood, the general thesis in this chapter—that inhibitory processes play a critical role in the overall functioning of human memory—will seem uncontestable in the near future, possibly even by the time this chapter appears in print. A new metaphor has emerged to influence the thinking of memory researchers: the brain metaphor. As other chapters in this volume attest, our ideas about memory are being shaped by the accelerating knowledge of the possible functions of certain brain structures in human memory. In addition, the neural/connectionist approach to the simulation of cognitive processes is being pursued with enthusiasm and high expectations. In contrast to the computer metaphor, which tended to lead us away from explanations based on inhibitory processes, the brain metaphor, if anything, will push us towards such explanations.

ACKNOWLEDGMENTS

Preparation of this essay was aided by a grant from the Academic Senate of the University of California. The author thanks James Neely, Larry Jacoby, Elizabeth Bjork, and Tom Minor for useful comments and criticisms, and Henry Roediger for his unsparing efforts to edit this chapter.

REFERENCES

Allport, D. A., Tipper, S. P., & Chmiel, N. R. J. (1985). Perceptual integration and postcategorical filtering. In M. I. Posner & O. S. I. Marin (Eds.), *Attention and performance, XI* (pp. 107–132). Hillsdale, NJ: Lawrence Erlbaum Associates.

Atkinson, R. C., & Juola, J. F. (1974). Search and decision processes in recognition memory. In D. H. Krantz, R. C. Atkinson, R. D. Luce, & P. Suppes (Eds.), *Contemporary developments in mathematical psychology* (pp. 243–293). San Francisco: Freeman.

Bjork, E. L., & Bjork, R. A. (1988). On the adaptive aspects of retrieval failure in autobiographical memory. In M. M. Gruneberg, P. E. Morris, & R. N. Sykes (Eds.), *Practical aspects of memory: Current research and issues: Vol. 1: Memory in everyday life* (pp. 283–288). London: Wiley.

Bjork, E. L., Bjork, R. A., & Glenberg, A. (1973, November). *Reinstatement of interference owing to to-be-forgotten items.* Paper presented at the meeting of the Psychonomic Society, St. Louis, MO.

Bjork, E. L., Bjork, R.A., & White, S. (1984, November). *On the induced recovery of proactive interference.* Paper presented at the meeting of the Psychonomic Society, San Antonio, TX.

Bjork, R. A. (1970). Positive forgetting: The noninterference of items intentionally forgotten. *Journal of Verbal Learning and Verbal Behavior, 9,* 255–268.

Bjork, R. A. (1978). The updating of human memory. In G. H. Bower (Ed.), *The psychology of learning and motivation,* (Vol. 12, pp. 235–259). New York: Academic Press.

Bjork, R. A., Abramowitz, R. L., & Krantz, D. H. (1970, April). *Selective high-speed scanning of item-sets in memory.* Paper presented at the Midwest Mathematical Psychology Meetings, Bloomington, IN.

Bjork, R. A., & Geiselman, R. E. (1978). Constituent processes in the differentiation of items in memory. *Journal of Experimental Psychology: Human Learning and Memory, 4,* 344–361.

Blaxton, T. A., & Neely, J. H. (1983). Inhibition from semantically related primes: Evidence of a category-specific inhibition. *Memory & Cognition, 11,* 500–510.

Brown, A. S. (1981). Inhibition in cued retrieval. *Journal of Experimental Psychology: Human Learning and Memory, 7,* 204–215.

Brown, J. (1968). Reciprocal facilitation and impairment of free recall. *Psychonomic Science, 10,* 41–42.

Crowder, R. G (1976). *Principles of learning and memory.* Hillsdale, NJ: Lawrence Erlbaum Associates.

Dosher, B. A. (1984). Discriminating preexperimental (semantic) from learned (episodic) associations: A speed–accuracy study. *Cognitive Psychology, 16,* 519–555.

Erdelyi, M. H., & Goldberg, B. (1979). Let's not sweep repression under the rug: Toward a cognitive psychology of repression. In J. F. Kihlstrom & F. J. Evans (Eds.), *Functional disorders of memory* (pp. 355–402). Hillsdale, NJ: Lawrence Erlbaum Associates.

Estes, W. K. (1972). An associative basis for coding and organization in memory. In A. W. Melton & E. Martin (Eds.), *Coding processes in human memory.* Washington, DC: Winston.

Freud, S. (1914). *Psychopathology of everyday life.* New York: Macmillan.

Geiselman, R. E., & Bagheri, B. (1985). Repetition effects in directed forgetting: Evidence for retrieval inhibition. *Memory & Cognition, 13,* 57–62.

Geiselman, R. E., Bjork, R. A., & Fishman, D. (1983). Disrupted retrieval in directed forgetting: A link with posthypnotic amnesia. *Journal of Experimental Psychology: General, 112,* 58–72.

Gelfand, H., & Bjork, R. A. (1985, November). *On the locus of retrieval inhibition in directed forgetting.* Paper presented at the meeting of the Psychonomic Society, Boston, MA.

Hirshman, E. L. (1988). The expectation–violation effect: Paradoxical effects of semantic relatedness. *Journal of Memory and Language, 27,* 40–58.

Juola, J. F., Fischler, I., Wood, C. T., & Atkinson, R. C. (1971). Recognition time for information stored in long term memory. *Perception & Psychophysics, 10,* 8–14.

Kato, T. (1985). Semantic-memory sources of episodic retrieval failure. *Memory & Cognition, 13,* 442–452.

Keele, S. W., & Neill, W. T. (1978). Mechanisms of attention. In E. C. Carterette & M. P. Friedman (Eds.), *Handbook of perception,* (Vol. 9, pp. 3–47). New York: Academic Press.

Melton, A. W., & Irwin, J. M. (1940). The influence of degree of interpolated learning on retroactive inhibition and the overt transfer of specific responses. *American Journal of Psychology, 53*, 173–203.

Neely, J. H., & Durgunoğlu, A. Y. (1985). Dissociative episodic and semantic priming effects in episodic recognition and lexical decision tasks. *Journal of Memory and Language, 24*, 466–489.

Nickerson, R. S. (1984). Retrieval inhibition from part-list cuing: A persistent enigma in memory research. *Memory & Cognition, 12*, 531–552.

Osgood, C. E. (1953). *Method and theory in experimental psychology.* New York: Oxford.

Postman, L., Stark, K., & Fraser, J. (1968). Temporal changes in interference. *Journal of Verbal Learning and Verbal Behavior, 7*, 672–694.

Raaijmakers, J. G., & Shiffrin, R. M. (1981). Search of associative memory. *Psychological Review, 88*, 93–134.

Roediger, H. L. (1974). Inhibiting effects of recall. *Memory & Cognition, 2*, 261–296.

Roediger, H. L. (1978). Recall as a self-limiting process. *Memory & Cognition, 6*, 54–63.

Roediger, H. L., & Crowder, R. G. (1972). Instructed forgetting: Rehearsal control or retrieval inhibition (repression)? *Cognitive Psychology, 3*, 255–267.

Roediger, H. L., & Neely, J. H. (1982). Retrieval blocks in episodic and semantic memory. *Canadian Journal of Psychology, 36*, 213–242.

Rundus, D. (1973). Negative effects of using list items as recall cues. *Journal of Verbal Learning and Verbal Behavior, 12*, 43–50.

Sternberg, S. (1966). High-speed scanning in human memory. *Science, 153*, 652–654.

Sternberg, S. (1969). Memory scanning: Mental processes revealed by reaction-time experiments. *American Scientist, 57*, 421–457.

Tulving, E., & Hastie, R. (1972). Inhibition effects of intralist repetition in free recall. *Journal of Experimental Psychology, 92*, 297–304.

Underwood, B. J., & Ekstrand, B. R. (1966). An analysis of some shortcomings of the interference theory of forgetting. *Psychological Review, 73*, 540–549.

Underwood, B. J., & Ekstrand, B. R. (1967). Studies of distributed practice, XXIV: Differentiation and proactive inhibition. *Journal of Experimental Psychology, 74*, 574–580.

Watkins, M. J. (1975). Inhibition in recall with extralist "cues." *Journal of Verbal Learning and Verbal Behavior, 14*, 294–303.

Weiner, B. (1968). Motivated forgetting and the study of repression. *Journal of Personality, 36*, 213–234.

Weiner, B., & Reed, H. (1969). Effects on the instructional sets to remember and to forget on short-term retention: Studies of rehearsal control and retrieval inhibition (repression). *Journal of Experimental Psychology, 79*, 226–232.

Woodworth, R. S., & Scholsberg, H. (1954). *Experimental psychology.* New York: Holt.

17 Theoretical Issues in State Dependent Memory

Eric Eich
University of British Columbia

The idea that what has been learned in a certain state of mind or brain is best remembered in that state is an old and familiar one in psychology. The credit for this concept—one that I refer to as *state dependent memory*—goes to an astute French aristocrat, the Marquis de Puységur (Chastenet de Puységur, 1809; Ellenberger, 1970). In 1784, Puységur discovered that although a person might appear, upon awakening, to be amnesic for events that had occurred during hypnosis, memory for these events returned once the individual reentered a state of "magnetic sleep"—Puységur's term for hypnosis. Decades later, a French physician named Azam (1876) related a strikingly similar observation in connection with the case of a young woman who suffered sudden attacks of hysterical somnambulism, or "pathological sleep," as the disorder was then known. And in an article published in 1910, Morton Prince conjectured that the reason most people have difficulty remembering their dreams is not because they do not *want* to remember—as Freud (1953) and other psychodynamicists of the day were claiming—but rather, because they *cannot* remember, owing to the dissimilarity between the states of "natural sleep" and ordinary wakefulness.

Like psychology itself, the concept of state dependent memory has a long past, but a short history as a subject of scientific study. Indeed, the earliest experimental demonstrations of human state dependence date only to the late 1960s (see Eich, 1977; Weingartner, 1978), and of the 100-plus empirically oriented articles of the subject that have appeared since then, approximately 70% have been published within the last 10 years.

During the first decade of research on human state dependent memory, from about 1967 to 1976, almost all experiments dealt with drug-defined differences in state. This type of experiment is exemplified by the work of Goodwin, Powell,

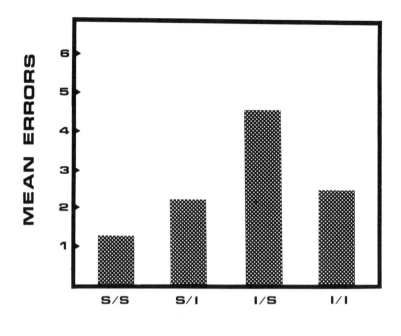

FIG. 17.1.   Mean number of errors of associative recall as a function of study/test states. *Source:* Goodwin et al., 1969.

Bremer, Hoine, and Stern (1969). Their experiment entailed two sessions, which I will call *study* and *test*. In the study session, medical students were administered an assortment of cognitive tasks, one of which was to produce verbal associations to verbal stimuli. These tasks were completed after the students had consumed either a soft drink or a cocktail containing, on average, about 10 ounces of 80-proof vodka—the equivalent of a rather potent dose of 1.5 milliliters of absolute alcohol per kilogram of body weight. A second set of tasks, which included an assessment of associative recall, was administered one day later, in the test session. The students performed this second set of tasks either in the same drug state—sobriety or intoxication—that they had experienced the day before or in the contrasting pharmacologic context.

The results of the experiment, in the form of mean errors of associative recall, are illustrated in Fig. 17.1. Inspection of the figure reveals that fewer errors were made when the students' study and test states were the same than when they differed. It is this interaction of states at study and at test that operationally defines the occurrence of state dependent memory.

During the second decade of research, from 1977 to the present, attention has

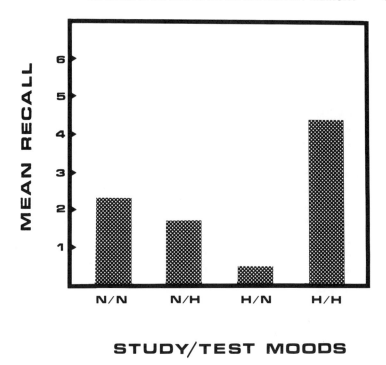

STUDY/TEST MOODS

FIG. 17.2.   Mean number of words recalled as a function of study/test moods. *Source:* Bartlett & Santrock, 1979.

gradually shifted away from the state dependent effects of drugs on human memory to those associated with alterations of affect or mood. Representative of this new direction in research is a study by Bartlett and Santrock (1979). In principle, what these investigators intended was for preschoolers to internalize the mood suggested by a series of either happy or sad stories, and for the children to recall the contents of these stories after they had internalized the affect implied by a collection of either happy or sad pictures. In practice, what Bartlett and Santrock found was that although the children did indeed feel happy after they had heard happy stories or viewed happy pictures, they seldom felt sad following exposure to sad stimuli—perhaps the children were just too cheery by nature for these stimuli to have much impact. Whatever the reason, the important point is that the key contrast in Bartlett and Santrock's study is between a happy mood and neutral mood, rather than between happiness and sadness.

Figure 17.2 shows the mean number of story items that were recalled. For now, the one aspect of the figure that I want to accentuate is that recall was better when the childrens' moods at study and at test matched than when they mismatched—a crossover pattern of results similar to the one shown in Fig. 17.1, which was derived from Goodwin et al.'s (1969) study of alcohol state dependence in adults. Later on, I discuss a second, more subtle aspect of the data depicted in both Fig. 17.1 and Fig. 17.2.

Although recent in origin, research on human state dependent memory has proven useful in at least three respects. First, studies of state dependence have aided the development of what Tulving (1979) has termed an "interactive" view of remembering. To clarify, it is worth noting that until the mid 1970s, the chief concern of most memory theorists was with how knowledge is acquired and retained, or how information is encoded and stored. There was generally little interest in how memorial knowledge affects conscious awareness, or how information is utilized or retrieved. Owing in large measure to Tulving's influential articles on encoding specificity (e.g., Tulving & Thomson, 1971; 1973), the current situation is different. Today, most theorists assume that how well something is remembered depends not only on what that something is, or how it was encoded, but also on the circumstances that surround its retrieval. Accordingly, remembering is now conceptualized as the joint product or interaction between information that has been stored in the past and information that is present in the cognitive environment of the remember (Tulving, 1976; 1979; 1983). Studies showing that memory performance depends on the similarity or match between drug or mood states at encoding and retrieval thus square with this interactive view of remembering, and thereby strengthen its appeal.

Second, recent research on human state dependence has suggested some new ways of thinking about the memory impairments that accompany certain clinical conditions, such as depression. As Reus, Weingartner, and Post (1979) have remarked, severely depressed patients frequently find it difficult to recall or elaborate on earlier periods of well being. Reus and his associates argue that this difficulty may be due not to a psychodynamic process of denial, but instead, to a mismatch between the positive affect that is attached to memories of prior pleasant experiences, on the one hand, and the negative affect that pervades the patients' present state, on the other. In addition to depression, state dependent memory has been implicated in such diverse disorders as epilepsy (Eich, 1986), hyperactivity (Swanson & Kinsbourne, 1976), multiple personality (Ludwig, Brandsma, Wilbur, Bendtfeldt, & Jameson, 1972), and myofascial pain (Eich, Reeves, Jaeger, & Graff-Radford, 1985).

Third, studies such as those by Bartlett and Santrock (1979), Goodwin et al. (1969), and others have illuminated an array of issues that have implications for theories of state dependence in particular and human memory in general. Three of these issues are the subjects of discussion in the remainder of this chapter. One has to do with whether memory deficits caused by a change of state are selective rather than spread uniformly across all types of stimulus materials, encoding tasks, or retrieval conditions. A second issue is whether the transition from a normal or "prototypical" state of mind or brain to an abnormal or "variant" state has a less detrimental effect on memory than does a shift in the reverse direction. And a third issue is whether memory impairments incurred in the transition from one pharmacological state to another, or from one physical setting to a different setting, are mediated by alterations of affect or mood. I will discuss the issue of *selectivity* first, and then turn to the topics of *asymmetry* and *mood mediation*.

SELECTIVITY OF STATE DEPENDENT MEMORY

Evidence from several sources suggests that state dependent effects in human memory are selective rather than pervasive in nature. As an example, Eich and Birnbaum (1982) observed a stronger state dependent effect of alcohol in the recall of once-presented as opposed to repeatedly presented words. Also, Petersen (1977) found that following a shift from alcoholic intoxication to sobriety, abstract nouns were more often forgotten than were concrete nouns. And numerous investigations involving alcohol, drugs, or moods have shown that state dependent effects are more likely to emerge when retention is assessed by means of a nominally noncued procedure, such as free recall, than by a test of either cued recall or recognition memory (Bower, 1981; Eich, 1980).

Still another respect in which state dependent memory may be selective is suggested by recent research is the area of affect and cognition. One thing that this research makes plain is that experimental manipulations of mood produce powerful effects on the performance of some—but not all—types of tasks. Among the tasks that seem most sensitive to mood manipulations are word association, narrative construction, and interpersonal assessment (see Blaney, 1986; Bower, 1981; Isen, 1984; Teasdale, 1983). Thus, for example, angry people produce angry associations, tell hostile stories, and tend to find fault in others (Bower & Cohen, 1982). Among the least sensitive tasks are Stroop interference, speech shadowing, and perceptual identification (Blaney, 1986; Bower, 1985). By way of illustration, Gerrig and Bower (1982) failed to find a reliable effect of hypnotically induced elation or anger on tachistoscopic thresholds for naming pleasant versus unpleasant words.

One plausible interpretation of this pattern of results is that the tasks that are not particularly sensitive to experimental modifications of mood are those that place a premium on the automatic or data-driven perception of *external* events. In contrast, the tasks that are especially sensitive are ones that involve the *internal* production of what Johnson and Raye (1981) call "cotemporal thought"— "the sort of elaborative and associative processes that augment, bridge, or embellish ongoing perceptual experience but that are not necessarily part of the veridical representation of perceptual experience" (p. 70). If this interpretation is valid, then there should be implications for memory. Specifically, a shift from one mood state to another—from happiness to sadness, for instance—should produce a greater impairment of memory for items that had been generated internally than for those that had been given externally.

To find out whether mood dependent effects are indeed more pronounced for internal than for external events, Janet Metcalfe and I (Eich & Metcalfe, in press) performed four experiments that relied on procedures developed by Slamecka and Graf (1978). In particular, participants in our research either read a target item, such as VANILLA, that was paired with a category name and a related exemplar (e.g., milkshake flavors: chocolate–VANILLA), or generated (with a very high probability) the same item when primed with its initial letter, in combination with the category name and exemplar cues (e.g., milkshake flavors: chocolate–V). In this manner, memory for one and same target item could be assessed in relation to its source: either internal (the generate condition) or external (the read condition).

During the encoding phase of our first experiment, every subject generated 16 target items and read 16 others. (To avoid item-selection artifacts, any item that was generated by one subject was read by another.) Half of the subjects completed the encoding task while happy, and half did so while sad. During the retrieval session, which was held two days after encoding, all subjects received an unexpected test of free recall of all of the target items. The subjects completed this test either in the same mood in which they had generated or read the targets, or in the alternative affective state. Thus, the experiment conformed to a 2 × 2 × 2 mixed design, with both encoding mood (happy vs. sad) and retrieval mood (happy vs. sad) as between-subject factors, and item type (generate vs. read) as a within-subject variable. Each of the four combinations of encoding and retrieval moods was represented by 12 subjects, all of whom were tested individually throughout the course of the experiment.

To manipulate mood, we played the subjects various selections of either "happy" or "sad" music. As they listened, the subjects were asked to muse about pleasant or unpleasant incidents from their personal past.

Just before the music began, and every 5 minutes thereafter, the subjects rated their current level of mood on a 9-point scale ranging from +4 (extremely happy) through 0 (neutral) to −4 (extremely sad), and they also rated their current level of arousal on an analogous 9-point scale. Unbeknownst to the subjects, we required that a "critical" level of mood be reached before the encoding (generate/read) or retrieval (free recall) tests could begin. For purposes of happy encoding or happy retrieval, this critical level was defined as a mood rating of +3 or higher (very or extremely happy); for purposes of sad encoding or sad retrieval, the requisite rating was −3 or lower (very or extremely sad). Thus, subjects assigned to the different mood conditions of the experiment (encode happy/retrieve sad or encode sad/retrieve happy) experienced an absolute change of at least 6 points on the 9-point mood scale, whereas subjects representing the same mood conditions (encode happy/retrieve happy or encode sad/retrieve sad) experienced an absolute change in mood of, at most, 1 point. The intent here was to insure that the different mood conditions of the experiment were indeed different, and that the same mood conditions were truly the same.

Results of the experiment, in the form of mean proportions of generate and

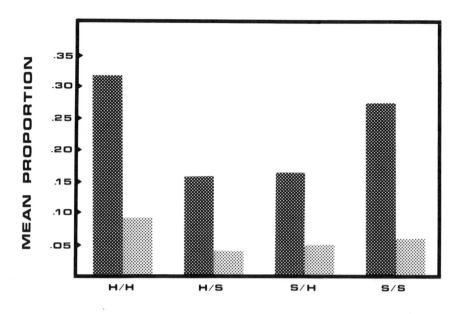

ENCODING/RETRIEVAL MOODS

FIG. 17.3. Mean proportions of generate and read items recalled (dark and light bars, respectively) as a function of encoding/retrieval moods. *Source:* Eich & Metcalfe, in press/Experiment 1.

read items recalled, appear in Fig. 17.3 in relation to encoding and retrieval moods. Replicating the oft-reported "generation effect" (Slamecka & Graf, 1978), analysis of these results revealed a significant simple effect of item type, such that generate items were more likely to be recalled than were read items. In addition, analysis revealed a significant triple interaction among encoding mood, retrieval mood, and item type. As is evident in Fig. 17.3, the advantage in recall of same over different mood conditions was greater for generate items [means of .30 vs. .17; $t(46) = 3.88$, $p < .01$] than for read items [means of .08 vs. .05; $t(46) = 2.02$, $p < .05$].

In three subsequent experiments, Metcalfe and I found results that were generally, although not completely, consistent with those of the first. In Experiment 2, for example, we endeavored to reduce, and perhaps even reverse, the generation effect by giving subjects three opportunities to read certain target items, but only one opportunity to generate certain others. Although the probability of recall, averaged across encoding/retrieval conditions, was in fact higher for thrice-read than for once-generated items, only the latter type of target showed significant mood dependence. In Experiment 3, however, a shift in mood state resulted in an equivalent reduction in the accessibility of thrice-read and thrice-generated items. Finally, in Experiment 4, a reliable mood dependent effect was evident in the recall of both once- and thrice-generated items, but not in the recall of either once- or thrice-read items. Interestingly, in all four experiments, subjects who shifted from one mood to another without appreciably affecting their level of arousal tended to recall more targets than did subjects who experienced a marked alteration in both mood and arousal. This finding is compatible with the claim made by Clark and her colleagues (Clark, 1982; Clark, Milberg, & Ross, 1983) that arousal can act as a cue for the retrieval of arousal-related material from memory.

Taken together, the results just reviewed indicate that, in the main, generate items are relatively less likely to be recalled than read items following a shift in mood state. This observation is significant in two respects: first, it suggests a new way in which state dependent effects are selective, and second, it affords new insight into why many researchers have had difficulty demonstrating these effects experimentally (see Blaney, 1986; Bower, 1985). To elaborate on the latter point, it is interesting to note that apart from a study by Weingartner, Miller, and Murphy (1977)—who found that affectively disturbed patients who had generated verbal associations during an episode of mania recalled 97% more of these items when tested in a manic than in a normal mood state—all earlier experiments on mood dependence, of which I am aware, have examined memory for external rather than internal events. Whereas Weingartner and his associates apparently succeeded in showing mood dependence, many other investigators have failed, and the reason may relate to the ideas sketched earlier: namely, that events that are generated through internal processes such as reasoning, imagination, and thought are more closely connected to or colored by one's current mood than are those that derive from external sources, and as a consequence, internal events are more apt to be rendered inaccessible for retrieval in the transition from one mood state to another than are external events.

Although the notion that internally generated events are especially susceptible to mood dependence seems promising, it is far from being proven. It remains to be seen, for instance, whether mood dependent effects are stronger for generate than for read items even when the items are meaningless letter strings, rather than legitimate words. Another open issue is whether results paralleling those summarized heretofore would obtain if one manipulated arousal, rather than mood, in a direct and deliberate manner (see Clark et al., 1983). As new information becomes available on these and related issues, the relations between mood dependence and memory for internal versus external events are bound to become more intricate, but perhaps more interesting as well.

ASYMMETRY OF STATE DEPENDENT MEMORY

Intuitively, it seems reasonable to suppose that a shift in state from, say, sobriety to alcoholic intoxication should impair memory performance by the same margin as a shift from intoxication to sobriety. Though such a *symmetric* pattern of memory impairments has occasionally been observed (e.g., Lowe, 1981; Petersen, 1977), the more common—and counterintuitive—finding has been one of *asymmetric* state dependence: Memory performance appears to be more impaired by a shift from intoxication to sobriety than by a shift in the reverse direction (see Overton, 1984; Ryback, 1971).

Figure 17.1, which reflects the results of the associative recall task reported by Goodwin et al. (1969), gives a good example of asymmetric state dependence. Inspection of this figure suggests that associations that had been generated during intoxication were significantly more likely to be recalled in an intoxicated than in a sober state (means error rates of 2.50 vs. 4.58). In contrast, associations generated during sobriety were only marginally more recallable under alcohol-absent than alcohol-present conditions (mean error rates of 1.25 vs. 2.25). A similar pattern of results emerged in an experiment by Eich, Weingartner, Stillman, and Gillin (1975), which examined the state dependent effects of marijuana on the free recall of conceptually categorized words. In that experiment, the difference in mean word recall between the study intoxicated/test intoxicated and study intoxicated/test sober conditions (.22 − .14 = .08) was more than double the difference between the sober/sober and sober/intoxicated conditions (.24 − .21 = .03).

Demonstrations of asymmetric state dependence are not restricted to studies involving centrally acting depressants, such as alcohol and marijuana. Peters and McGee (1982), for example, showed that the free recall of high imagery nouns is asymmetrically state dependent for nicotine—a psychomotor stimulant. What is more, asymmetry may be an attribute not only of drug dependent memory, but of mood dependent memory as well. This point is underscored by Bartlett and Santrock's (1979) finding, illustrated in Fig. 17.2, that whereas the reinduction of a happy mood was crucial for the recall of words that children had learned while they were happy, a neutral mood at recall conferred little, if any, advantage on the recall of words studied during a prior neutral state.

The case of Jonah, a multiple personality patient examined by Ludwig et al. (1972), provides a particularly intriguing instance of asymmetric state dependence. Jonah, a 27-year-old Vietnam veteran, was described by Ludwig et al. as being shy, polite, passive, and highly conventional. While being interviewed, Jonah manifested all of these characteristics, and he sometimes seemed scared and confused as well. It was difficult to get Jonah to give other than vague, noncommittal responses, and when pressed on sensitive issues, he would react in an emotionally shallow manner.

Jonah may be regarded as the core or primary personality, inasmuch as it was he who was "out there," interacting with the world most of the time. Occasionally, however, Jonah would surrender control over consciousness and behavior to one of three alternate or secondary personalities, each of whom embodied different emotions, experiences, and traits. These three secondary personalities were (a) King Young: a charming, gregarious, pleasure-oriented ladies' man who could not take no for an answer, (b) Sammy: a rational, purely intellectual individual who enjoyed twisting words, engaging in debates, and accumulating knowledge for knowledge's sake, and (c) Usoffa Abdulla: alias Son of Omega, a sullen, sulfurous, physically powerful figure whose duty was to protect Jonah from danger.

Ludwig et al. had Jonah and his secondary selves perform a variety of clinical, psychophysiological, and cognitive tasks. One of the latter was a "paired words" task. The materials for this task consisted of four separate lists, each containing ten stem words paired with five difficult and five easy words in association value. One of these lists was presented to one personality until the associations were learned to a criterion of three errorless recalls. Afterwards, according to the authors, "the same list of ten stem words was read to each of the three other personalities in turn who were required to respond quickly with the 'correct' association. As a check against spontaneous memory loss, this same list of ten stem words was presented again to the original personality who was asked to give his associations to each"[1] (p. 302).

This same procedure was repeated with a different list for each personality. In this manner, the extent to which all of the personalities shared memory for associations studied by any one personality could be assessed. Thus, the paired words task conformed to a 4 × 4 (study personality × test personality) within-subject design, in the truest sense of the term.

Figure 17.4 displays the number of errors made by each personality in recalling his own and the others' associations. Looking first at the leftmost panel of the figure, it can be seen that associations studied by the secondary personality King Young were well remembered by King Young, but were much less accessible to either the primary personality, Jonah, or to the other secondary selves, Sammy and Usoffa Abdulla. Similarly, whereas Sammy did well recalling Sammy's associations, the other personalities did poorly. In the case of Usoffa Abdulla, the dissociation of memory is complete: no one but Usoffa could recall any of Usoffa's associations, and his recall was perfect.

Data appearing in the rightmost panel of Fig. 17.4 present a different picture. As these data indicate, Jonah's recall of Jonah's associations was neither better nor worse than that of any of the three secondary personalities.

---

[1] Just what is meant by the terms "correct association" and "his associations" is unclear. One interpretation is "the association that either your or another personality studied earlier," which would imply that each personality was given an *explicit* test of memory for paired associates learned by the same or a different personality. An alternative interpretation is "whatever association comes to mind," in which case the test would have tapped one personality's *implicit* memory for his own or another personality's associations. Although the latter view is consistent with Ludwig et al.'s reference to the paired words task as a form of free association (p. 306), the issue cannot be completely resolved. The problem here is that Ludwig et al. did not distinguish between explicit and implicit memory tests—a distinction that is now considered central in understanding phenomena of amnesia (see Schacter 1987; Schacter & Kihlstrom, in press). As a result, the recall requirements of the paired word task are rather ambiguous.

STUDY PERSONALITY

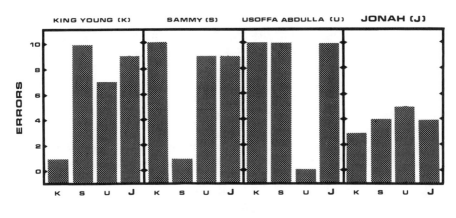

FIG. 17.4. Number of errors of associative recall as a function of study and test personalities. *Source:* Ludwig et al., 1972.

What conclusions can be drawn from the case of Jonah, and from the other studies cited earlier in this section? To me, the main message is that information transfers more poorly in the direction of an abnormal or special state of consciousness to a normal or standard state than it does in the reverse direction. Thus, I would argue that Jonah is the personality counterpart to sobriety or a neutral mood, whereas alcohol intoxication and happiness represent pharmacologic and affective analogues of, say, Sammy and King Young. I would also argue that the results of Eich and Metcalfe's (in press) first experiment, showing a *symmetric* mood dependent effect in the free recall of internally generated items (see Fig. 17.3) does not discredit the current position, because in that experiment, items were generated and recalled in either the same abnormal state (viz. a very happy or a very sad mood) or in different abnormal states. Had we contrasted a more typical, neutral mood with an atypical affect, such as intense happiness, it is possible—I think probable—that evidence of asymmetric mood dependence would have emerged.

How is asymmetric state dependence to be explained? This is a difficult question, not only because the effect is counterintuitive, but also because it is at odds with some deep-seated theoretical assumptions that originated in the early 1960s, when research on drug dependent memory in animals began in earnest. As Overton (1984) has observed, most early experimenters expected that the transition from a no-drug (N) to a drug (D) state would prove just as detrimental to memory as a shift in the opposite order, because a response learned by an animal was thought to be contingent on specific cues that occur only in the N state (e.g., cues associated with the injection of saline), whereas a response acquired under D conditions was contingent on a unique constellation of D cues (Belleville, 1964; Otis, 1964). In addition, D cues produced by the administration of a drug were assumed to displace or overshadow pre-existing N cues, so that an animal could not experience both kinds of cues concurrently (Overton, 1984; Overton, Merkle, & Hayes, 1983). Because these assumptions argue for symmetry, evidence suggestive of asymmetric drug dependence (e.g., Barnhart & Abbott, 1967; Berger & Stein, 1969) was dismissed as artifactual, epiphenomenal, or unreliable (Deutsch & Roll, 1973; Overton, 1974).

Recent years have witnessed the development of a different conception of the consequences of N versus D learning. According to this new account, internal stimuli associated with the D state do serve as retrieval cues required for the performance of responses learned in that state, resulting in a loss of memory following a D to N state shift. The N state, however, is not considered to have significant cuing properties in its own right. Rather, the performance of N state responses is assumed to be contingent on apparatus cues and interoceptive stimuli, such as hunger or fear, that are present during both D and N test sessions; as a result, responses learned in the N state are expected to generalize, with little or no decrement, to the D state. Thus, whereas the original hypothesis held that animals learn to discriminate drug cues from no-drug cues, the more modern idea is that animals learn to discriminate the presence of particular drug cues from their absence. In other words, animals discriminate drug cues from no cues, rather than drug cues from no-drug cues (Overton, 1984; Overton et al., 1983; see also Barry, 1978; Boyd & Caul, 1979; Colpaert, 1978; Shannon & Holtzman, 1977).

Among contemporary animal-learning theorists, one of the first to argue for a "no cue" interpretation of the N state was Barry (1978). His premise is that internal stimuli associated with infrequently occurring states of drug intoxication are especially noticeable, novel, or "abnormal," whereas those associated with the sober state are seen as "normal" and therefore do not attract much attention. By Barry's reasoning, an animal is apt to attend to the salient and unique internal stimuli that it experiences while drugged, and to associate these stimuli with other ongoing activities, thus allowing drug-produced stimuli to act as potent cues for the retrieval of responses that had been acquired in the D state. In contrast, no salient or unique internal stimuli will be associated with responses learned in the N state, and hence, no particular interoceptive cues will be required to effect retrieval of these responses. The implication, then, is that drug dependent effects in animals should be asymmetric in form: Responses acquired in the N state should generalize to a variety of D states, but those acquired in a particular D state should be performable only in that state.

In a recent appraisal of Barry's argument, Overton (1984) stated that it is reasonable to assume that the novelty of drug-produced stimuli should diminish with repeated exposures to the drug. If so, then Barry's hypothesis would seem to predict that pre-exposure to a drug will reduce its ability to acquire discriminative control over responding during subsequent D versus N training. According to Overton (1984), however, this prediction has not been borne out in most studies designed to test for it (e.g., Overton, 1972; 1974).

Despite this setback, Barry's (1978) hypothesis does provide a plausible account of asymmetric drug dependent memory, and it therefore deserves continued consideration. Parenthetically, it is interesting to note that Barry's "no cue" hypothesis, which is geared towards *animal* learning and memory, bears a striking conceptual resemblance to Watkins' (1979) "cue-overload" theory, which relates directly to *human* cognition. As Watkins (1979) has commented, "Cue-overload theory is the simple idea that recall is mediated by cues and that these cues are subject to overload. In other words, as a memory cue comes to subsume more and more events, its probability of effecting recall of any particular event declines" (p. 364). One can imagine, then, that in comparison with the D state, the N state not only offers fewer salient or unique cues (a la Barry), but those that it does provide are associated with so many different events that the N state is, for all practical purposes, a useless overloaded cue (a la Watkins).

Promising though Barry's and Watkins' proposals may be as explanations of asymmetric state dependent memory, other possibilities should be explored. One such possibility is suggested by Tversky's set-theoretic approach to the analysis of similarity relations (Tversky, 1977; also see Gati & Tversky, 1984; Tversky & Gati, 1978). Taking this approach, Tversky has developed a model in which objects are represented as collections of features, and the similarity between objects is described as a linear combination, or contrast, of measures of their common and distinctive features.

For present purposes, the most important aspect of Tversky's analysis is that similarity is not necessarily a symmetric relation. In his well-known 1977 article, Tversky pointed out that when people make similarity statements of the form "*a* is like *b*," they tend to select the more common or familiar stimulus (the "prototype") as the referent of the comparison, and the less common or familiar stimulus (the "variant") as the subject. Thus, people say "an ellipse is like a circle," not "a circle is like an ellipse." Tversky also showed that this asymmetry in the *choice* of similarity statements is associated with asymmetry in *judgments* of similarity, such that people perceive the variant as being more similar to the prototype than the prototype is similar to the variant. Thus, the judged similarity of an ellipse to a circle exceeds the judged similarity of a circle to an ellipse.

In an effort to extend Tversky's analysis of similarity relations beyond physical objects, and into the realm of psychological states, suppose we think of, say, sobriety as the prototypical state, and of alcoholic intoxication as the variant state. If an individual encodes an event while sober and attempts to retrieve it while intoxicated, he or she may perceive the psychological similarity between the two states as being greater than if encoding had occurred during intoxication, and retrieval during sobriety. Now, if it is also true that the probability of retrieval is directly related to the perceived psychological similarity between encoding and retrieval states, then drug dependent effects in memory would be expected to materialize in an asymmetric form.

Admittedly, these are big "ifs." Still, asking subjects to rate, at the time of retrieval, how similar they feel now relative to how they felt at encoding should result in higher ratings under conditions of sober encoding and intoxicated retrieval than under the reverse conditions. By the same token, substituting a neutral affect and, for instance, intense happiness for sobriety and intoxication should produce the same result. Thus, the ideas just introduced, though purely speculative at present, make specific predictions that merit future testing.

Before leaving the issue of asymmetry aside, there is one last point to pursue. Throughout this section, the term "normal state" has been variously identified with a condition of sobriety, a neutral mood, or a primary personality (viz. Jonah), whereas "abnormal state" has been used in reference to alcohol intoxication, intense happiness, and a secondary personality (e.g., Sammy). The point to be made is that normal and abnormal are relative, not absolute, terms, and that what is an abnormal state for one person may be normal for another.

To clarify, consider the conjecture that whereas sobriety is normal, and intoxication abnormal, for a social drinker, the difference between these states may be less prominent, and possibly even reversed, for a chronic alcoholic. It follows from this conjecture that social drinkers should be more likely than chronic alcoholics to show signs of asymmetric state dependence, with memory impairments being more pronounced after a shift from intoxication to sobriety than from sobriety to intoxication. Indeed, it is conceivable that alcoholics would display asymmetric state dependence, but in a direction opposite to that demonstrated by nonalcoholics.

Data relevant to these considerations have been reported by Weingartner and Faillace (1971/Experiment 2). Subjects in that experiment were five alcoholics, with documented histories of long-term alcohol abuse, and five nonalcoholics, matched with respect to age, education, and other demographic variables. During the study session, subjects memorized, and then immediately recalled, a list of random words. During the test session, held 2 days later, subjects completed a second, delayed test of free recall of the same word list. In addition to subject group, the experiment incorporated two within-subject variables: study session state (sober vs. intoxicated) and test session state (again, sober vs. intoxicated). The dose of alcohol administered, 1.6 ml/kg, was the same for all subjects.

Results of the experiment, in the form of mean proportions of words recalled immediately (during the study session) that were also recalled after a 2-day delay (during the test session), are depicted in Fig. 17.5 as a function of study state, test state, and subject group. As can be seen in the figure, evidence of asymmetric state dependent memory was obtained from both the alcoholics and the

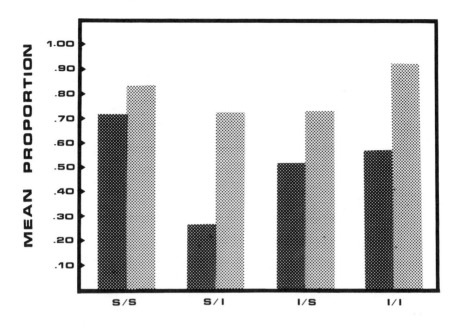

FIG. 17.5. Mean proportion of words produced in immediate (study session) recall that were also produced in delayed (test session) recall by alcoholic and nonalcoholic subjects (dark and light bars, respectively) as a function of study/test states. *Source:* Weingartner & Faillace, 1971/Experiment 2.

nonalcoholics, but the direction of the asymmetry was opposite in the two groups. Specifically, whereas the difference in delayed recall between the study intoxicated/test intoxicated and the study intoxicated/test sober conditions was greater among the nonalcoholics than among the alcoholics (.18 vs. .07), the difference in delayed recall between the sober/sober and sober/intoxicated conditions was greater for alcoholic than for control subjects (.44 vs. .12). As such, these results provide a measure of support for the speculations stated earlier, and they raise some interesting issues for research. One might ask, for example, whether chronically depressed patients have more difficulty remembering events that transpired during a passing period of well-being than they do remembering depression-related experiences during a nondepressed episode. An investigation of this issue, using ECT or tricyclic drugs to lift depression, could have important implications both for clinical research and for cognitive theory.

MOOD AS A MEDIATOR OF DRUG DEPENDENT AND PLACE DEPENDENT MEMORY

We turn now to a third issue of theoretical interest, and that is whether impairments of memory incurred in the transition from one *pharmacological* environment to another, or from one *physical* environment to a different one, are mediated by alterations of affect or mood. Let us consider the concept of mood mediation in relations to drugs first, and places second.

The idea that drugs engender their state dependent effects on memory by virtue of their effects on mood was originally offered by Overton (1973) for two reasons: First, the potential of a drug to acquire discriminative control over behavior was believed to be strongly associated with the drug's potential for abuse; second, drug abuse was thought to be caused by the positive affective consequences of drug self-administration. Although the first of these assumptions now appears doubtful—data compiled by Overton and Batta (1977) from numerous animal studies suggest that the correlation between drug discriminability and abuse liability is modest at best—the concept of mood-mediated state dependent memory can be defended on other grounds.

In the first place, human research reviewed by Eich (1980) indicates that reliable drug dependent effects are seldom seen unless the dose of drug administered is high enough to produce overt symptoms of intoxication, such as uncoordinated movement or slurred speech. Such symptoms are likely to occur in conjunction with covert changes in one's subjective state of pleasure, arousal, or more generally, one's mood.

Of related interest is a study by Weingartner (1978), in which depressed patients generated verbal associations while under the influence of amphetamine, and were asked to reproduce these associations 4 days later, while drug free. On each occasion, the patients rated various aspects of their present subjective state, including their levels of activation and euphoria. Weingartner found that the greater the subjective change in state between the generation and reproduction phases of the study, the greater the number of associations forgotten ($r = .89$)— a finding that fits well with the mood mediation theory of drug dependent memory.

In his 1978 essay, Weingartner reported a second successful demonstration of drug dependence, this one involving normal subjects treated with the anticholinesterase agent physostigmine. According to Bower (1981), this finding conflicts with the mood mediation theory, because physostigmine "seems to have little emotional effect beyond some elevation in 'arousal' " (p. 146). However, given Clark et al.'s (1983) claim that changes in arousal per se can produce state dependent effects on memory, and in view of Russell's (1980) argument that arousal is one of the two chief components of affective experience (the other being pleasure), Weingartner's demonstration of physostigmine dependent memory may actually add to, rather than detract from, the plausibility of the mood mediation theory.

Although the results reviewed in this section, in addition to those described elsewhere (see Overton, 1978), suggest that shifts in mood are correlated with the occurrence of drug dependent memory, they do not constitute evidence of a causal connection between the affective and state dependent properties of drugs. In an effort to secure such evidence, Isabel Birnbaum and I (Eich & Birnbaum, 1988) conducted an experiment in which 24 male undergraduates studied, and then immediately recalled, a conceptually categorized word list after they had consumed a small amount of alcohol (approximately 0.6 ml/kg). The subjects' level of intoxication was assessed both subjectively (via a subject-supplied rating on a 4-point scale ranging from "not at all intoxicated" [0] to "extremely intoxicated" [3]) and objectively (via a Breathalizer test, which measures blood alcohol concentration). Just before the subjects studied the list, their mean subjective rating of intoxication was 2.1, and their mean blood alcohol concentration was 40 mg%. On the test of immediate free recall, the mean proportion of words remembered was .37.

The test session of the experiment was held 1 week later. Depending on the particular *expectancy condition* to which he had been randomly assigned, each subject was told that he would receive either (a) a drink containing tonic water only, or (b) a drink containing the same mixture of vodka and tonic that had been served the week before. In the *expect-tonic condition,* the subject watched as an assistant filled a glass with tonic water from a newly opened bottle. In the *expect-alcohol condition,* the subject looked on as the assistant mixed what appeared to be a drink containing one part vodka to four parts tonic. Although the subject did not know it, the original contents of the vodka bottle had been replaced with tonic water. To give the "cocktail" the true scent of alcohol, the assistant discretely swabbed the rim of the glass with a little real vodka.

Shortly after the subjects had finished their drinks, they rated their current level of subjective intoxication, and then took another Breathalizer test. In the expect-alcohol condition, the Breathalizer machine had been rigged to produce a reading of 40 mg%—the reading one would expect had the subject actually received the same dose of alcohol he had taken during the study session—and the subject was shown this bogus reading. In the expect-tonic condition, the Breathalizer registered an accurate reading of 0 mg%, which the subject was allowed to see.

Once subjective and objective measures of intoxication had been recorded, the subjects were asked to freely recall all of the words they remembered having studied 1 week earlier. On completing this unanticipated test of delayed recall, the subjects were debriefed.

Although the methods just summarized may seem rather involved, the reasoning behind them was straightforward. Specifically, we hypothesized that if performance on the delayed test depends not on the objective or pharmacological similarity between study and test states (i.e., on whether or not the subjects have alcohol in their blood and brains), but rather on the subjective or psychological similarity between study/test states (i.e., on whether the subjects act, think, and most important, feel as though they are drunk during recall), then expect-alcohol subjects should outperform their expect-tonic counterparts.

Such was not the case: The mean proportion of words recalled on the delayed test, conditionalized on recall of the same words in the immediate test, was slightly *lower* among expect-alcohol than among expect-tonic subjects (.54 vs. .55). Although this null result may mean that our reasoning was flawed, it may instead reflect the fact that our expectancy manipulation was not very strong. Analysis of the subjective intoxication ratings showed that subjects in the expect-alcohol condition did not feel nearly as "high" during the test session as they had during the study session (mean ratings of 0.6 vs. 2.0). Thus, the expect-alcohol treatment did not return the subjects to their original subjective state; it only made the psychological disparity between study and test states somewhat smaller than it would have been had the subjects known for a fact that they were drinking pure tonic. Given the weakness of the expectancy manipulation, the absence of an advantage in delayed recall of expect-alcohol over expect-tonic treatments is not surprising.

Although our expectancy experiment did not reveal evidence of a causal relation between the subjective and state dependent effects of alcohol, it did produce a curious piece of correlational data. When we correlated the probability of delayed word recall (again conditionalized on immediate recall) with the absolute difference between study and test ratings of subjective intoxication, the resulting coefficient was marginally significant [$r(22) = -.39, p < .10$]. Thus, memory performance depended to some degree on the subjective similarity between study and test states, even though these states were objectively dissimilar. This observation must, however, be regarded as tenuous. To assess its validity, one would need to gain greater control over the subjective similarity between study/test states than was achieved in the current expectancy experiment. How might this need be met?

One possibility is to try the expectancy experiment again, this time relying on more elaborate techniques, such as those developed by Sher (1985), to bias subjects' beliefs about the alcoholic contents of their drinks. Alternatively, it might be better to replace alcohol with a drug, such as nitrous oxide (N_2O), whose physical and psychological effects may be more malleable, and hence more susceptible to expectancy manipulations. Three factors favoring nitrous oxide are (a) N_2O, being a colorless and faintly scented gas (see Wynne, 1985), cannot be easily discriminated from pure oxygen, making it well suited for expectancy manipulations, (b) N_2O, when administered in safe, subanesthetic concentrations, has a marked impact on mood (Steinberg, 1956), and (c) whereas many people drink alcohol recreationally, and know how the drug affects them subjectively and physiologically, few individuals have experienced nitrous ox-ide; thus, prospective subjects may be particularly responsive to suggestions concerning the presence or absence of N_2O in their systems.

Experimental manipulations of expectancy represent one of several tacts that might be taken in researching the role of mood shifts in drug dependent memory. A different strategy is suggested by the finding that alcohol has a biphasic influence on mood, such that positive affects (pleasantness, relaxation) arise mainly during the absorption phase, whereas negative affects (depression, drowsiness) predominate during the elimination phase (Persson, Sjoberg, & Svensson, 1980). If the state dependent effects of alcohol on memory are medi-ated by shifts in mood, then it should be possible to show that information transfers more completely between corresponding phases of the absorption/elim-ination cycle than between contrasting phases, even under conditions where blood alcohol concentration remains constant across phases. Still another ap-proach to the mood mediation issue is implied by Smith's (1979) finding that memory impairments caused by a change of environmental context can be elimi-nated by instructing subjects to reconstruct cognitively the room in which learn-ing took place. By extension, it may be possible to eliminate, or at least reduce, the retrieval deficit that results from a shift from alcoholic intoxication to so-briety by instructing subjects to undertake retrieval in an imaginary state of inebriation.

To this point in the discussion, the central issue has been whether changes in mood mediate the state dependent effects of drugs on memory. Recently, I have speculated that alterations of affect may also be responsible for memory failures that follow from a change in physical setting or environmental context (Eich, 1985; Eich & Birnbaum, 1988). This speculation stems, in part, from the results of an experiment by Godden and Baddeley (1975). Subjects in their experiment studied a list of words in one of two natural environments—on land or under-water—and were subsequently tested for free recall in either the same or the alternative environment. Relative to subjects whose study and test environments were held constant, those who experienced a change of context recalled, on average, almost one-third fewer words.

To what is this deficit due? The obvious answer is that the world *looks* different when viewed from beneath than from above the sea, and that it is the loss of important visual cues that leads to the observed loss of memory. But it is also obvious that being underwater *feels* different from being on land, and thus it may be that what the deficit really reflects is a change in experiential instead of environmental context. Put differently, and more generally, it is possible that how well information transfers from one environment to another depends more on how similar the environments are to each other affectively rather than perceptually.

The idea that place dependent memory represents a special case of mood dependent memory is approachable from a number of different experimental angles. One way to test the idea might be collect normative data on both the affective and the perceptual similarity between various pairs of environments—a church during a wedding and the same church during a funeral, for instance—and then use these data to select four particular pairs that represent the factorial combination of two variables: type of interpair similarity (affective vs. perceptual) and degree of interpair similarity (high vs. low). One member of each pair could then serve as the environment in which target items are encoded, and the other member as the environment in which retrieval of the targets it tested. If it is indeed the case that the effects of environmental context changes on memory are mediated by changes in mood, then test performance should depend primarily on the degree of affective, rather than perceptual, similarity between encoding/retrieval environments.

If supported by studies such as the one just proposed, the mood mediation hypothesis might shed *some* light on why previous research on place dependent memory has produced inconsistent results (e.g., Metzger, Boschee, Haugen, & Schnobrich, 1979; Saufley, Otaka, & Bavaresco, 1985). I stress the word "some" because it is likely that processes in addition to, or perhaps other than, mood mediation play a pivotal role in the emergence of place dependent effects. Fernandez and Glenberg (1985), for example, have conjectured that in order to establish an association between an event and the environment in which it occurs, contiguity alone between the event and the environment may not be sufficient. Rather, it may be necessary that a person perceives the environment as causing or enabling the event to happen, for only then will a change in the environment cause the event to be forgotten. This conjecture, which is reminiscent of Thorndike's (1932) concept of causal belongingness, has been extended by Bower (1985) to encompass moods. By Bower's account, evidence of mood dependent memory is unlikely to materialize unless subjects are convinced that their current emotions are caused by the events that they will later be asked to remember. Analogously, it is possible that drug dependent effects in memory are more apt to obtain if subjects believe in a causal connection between the events to be remembered and their current pharmacological state. Just how real or remote this possibility is remains to be seen, but for now, it seems wise to keep an open mind about the contributions of both affect change and causal belongingness to the occurrence of drug, mood, and place dependent memory.

CLOSING COMMENTS

Earlier it was remarked that research on human state dependence has illuminated a broad range of issues that have implications for theories of state dependence in particular and human memory in general. The three that have been considered in this chapter—selectivity, asymmetry, and mood mediation—are representative of such issues. But more than that, the three addressed here are, in my opinion, among the more empirically manageable and theoretically meaningful issues that have yet taken shape. As such, their investigation may be expected to enhance our understanding of both the circumstances under which state dependent effects occur, and the memory mechanisms that enable their emergence.

ACKNOWLEDGMENTS

This chapter was prepared with the aid of NSERC grant U0298, and it profited from the cogent comments and criticisms offered by Bob Bjork, Jennifer Campbell, Peter Graf, Roddy Roediger, Jim Russell, and Dan Schacter.

REFERENCES

Azam, M. (1876). Periodical amnesia; or, double consciousness. *Journal of Nervous and Mental Disease, 3,* 584–612.

Barnhart, S. S., & Abbott, D. W. (1967). Dissociation of learning and meprobamate. *Psychological Reports, 20,* 520–522.

Barry, H. (1978). Stimulus attributes of drugs. In H. Anisman & G. Bignami (Eds.), *Psychopharmacology of aversively motivated behavior* (pp. 455–485). New York: Plenum Press.

Bartlett, J. C., & Santrock, J. W. (1979). Affect-dependent episodic memory in young children. *Child Development, 50,* 513–518.

Belleville, R. E. (1964). Control over behavior by drug-produced internal stimuli. *Psychopharmacologia, 5,* 95–105.

Berger, B. D., & Stein, L. (1969). Asymmetrical dissociation of learning between scopolamine and Wy 4036, a new benzodiazepine tranquilizer. *Psychopharmacologia, 14,* 351–358.

Blaney, P. H. (1986). Affect and memory: A review. *Psychological Bulletin, 99,* 229–246.

Bower, G. H. (1981). Mood and memory. *American Psychologist, 36,* 129–148.

Bower, G. H. (1985). *Review of research on mood and memory.* Paper presented at the Symposium on Affect and Cognition, British Psychological Society, Oxford, England.

Bower, G. H., & Cohen, P. R. (1982). Emotional influences in memory and thinking: Data and theory. In M. S. Clark & S. T. Fiske (Eds.), *Affect and cognition: The seventeenth annual Carnegie symposium on cognition* (pp. 291–331). Hillsdale, NJ: Lawrence Erlbaum Associates.

Boyd, S. C., & Caul, W. F. (1979). Evidence of state dependent learning of brightness discrimination in hypothermic mice. *Physiology & Behavior, 23,* 147–153.

Chastenet de Puységur, A. M. J. (1809). *Mémoires pour servir à l'historie et à l'establissement du magnétisme animal* (2nd ed.). Paris: Cellot.

Clark, M. S. (1982). A role for arousal in the link between feeling states, judgments and behavior. In M. S. Clark & S. T. Fiske (Eds.), *Affect and cognition: The seventeenth annual Carnegie symposium on cognition* (pp. 263–289). Hillsdale, NJ: Lawrence Erlbaum Associates.

Clark, M. S., Milberg, S., & Ross, J. (1983). Arousal cues arousal-related material in memory: Implications for understanding effects of mood on memory. *Journal of Verbal Learning and Verbal Behavior, 22,* 633–649.

Colpaert, F. C. (1978). Discriminative stimulus properties of narcotic analgesic drugs. *Pharmacology, Biochemistry and Behavior, 9,* 863–887.

Deutsch, J. A., & Roll, S. K. (1973). Alcohol and asymmetrical state dependency: A possible explanation. *Behavioral Biology, 8,* 273–278.

Eich, E. (1985). Context, memory, and integrated item/context imagery. *Journal of Experimental Psychology: Learning, Memory, and Cognition, 11*, 764–770.

Eich, E. (1986). Epilepsy and state specific memory. *Acta Neurologica Scandinavica, 74*, 15–21.

Eich, E., & Birnbaum, I. M. (1982). Repetition, cuing, and state dependent memory. *Memory & Cognition, 10*, 103–114.

Eich, E., & Birnbaum, I. M. (1988). On the relationship between the dissociative and affective properties of drugs. In G. M. Davies & D. M. Thomson (Eds.), *Memory in context: Context in memory* (pp. 81–93). Sussex, England: John Wiley.

Eich, E., & Metcalfe, J. (in press). Mood dependent memory for internal versus external events. *Journal of Experimental Psychology: Learning, Memory, and Cognition.*

Eich, E., Reeves, J. L., Jaeger, B., & Graff-Radford, S. B. (1985). Memory for pain: Relation between past and present pain intensity. *Pain, 23*, 375–379.

Eich, J. E. (1977). State-dependent retrieval of information in human episodic memory. In I. M. Birnbaum & E. S. Parker (Eds.), *Alcohol and human memory* (pp. 141–157). Hillsdale, NJ: Lawrence Erlbaum Associates.

Eich, J. E. (1980). The cue-dependent nature of state-dependent retrieval. *Memory & Cognition, 8*, 157–173.

Eich, J. E., Weingartner, H., Stillman, R. C., & Gillin, J. C. (1975). State-dependent accessibility of retrieval cues in the retention of a categorized list. *Journal of Verbal Learning and Verbal Behavior, 14*, 408–417.

Ellenberger, H. F. (1970). *The discovery of the unconscious.* New York: Basic Books.

Fernandez, A., & Glenberg, A. M. (1985). Changing environmental context does not reliably affect memory. *Memory & Cognition, 13*, 333–345.

Freud, S. (1953). The interpretation of dreams. In J. Strachey (Ed.), *The standard edition of the complete psychological works of Sigmund Freud* (vols. 4 & 5). London: Hogarth Press. (Originally published in 1900.)

Gati, I., & Tversky, A. (1984). Weighting common and distinctive features in perceptual and conceptual judgments. *Cognitive Psychology, 16*, 341–370.

Gerrig, R. J., & Bower, G. H. (1982). Emotional influences on word recognition. *Bulletin of the Psychonomic Society, 19*, 197–200.

Godden, D. R., & Baddeley, A. D. (1975). Context-dependent memory in two natural environments: On land and underwater. *British Journal of Psychology, 66*, 325–331.

Goodwin, D. W., Powell, B., Bremer, D., Hoine, H., & Stern, J. (1969). Alcohol and recall: State dependent effects in man. *Science, 163*, 1358–1360.

Isen, A. M. (1984). Toward understanding the role of affect in cognition. In R. S. Wyer & T. K. Srull (Eds.), *Handbook of social cognition* (vol. 3, pp. 179–230). Hillsdale, NJ: Lawrence Erlbaum Associates.

Johnson, M. K., & Raye, C. L. (1981). Reality monitoring. *Psychological Review, 88*, 67–85.

Lowe, G. (1981). State-dependent recall decrements with moderate doses of alcohol. *Current Psychological Research, 1*, 3–8.

Ludwig, A. M., Brandsma, J. M., Wilbur, C. B., Bendtfeldt, F., & Jameson, D. H. (1972). The objective study of a multiple personality. *Archives of General Psychiatry, 26*, 298–310.

Metzger, R. L., Boschee, P. F., Haugen, T., & Schnobrich, B. L. (1979). The classroom as learning context: Changing rooms affects performance. *Journal of Educational Psychology, 71*, 440–442.

Otis, L. S. (1964). Dissociation and recovery of a response learned under the influence of chlorpromazine or saline. *Science, 143*, 1347–1348.

Overton, D. A. (1972). State-dependent learning produced by alcohol and its relevance to alcoholism. In B. Kissen & H. Begleiter (Eds.), *The biology of alcoholism. volume II: Physiology and behavior* (pp. 193–217). New York: Plenum Press.

Overton, D. A. (1973). State-dependent learning produced by addicting drugs. In S. Fisher & A. M. Freedman (Eds.), *Opiate addiction: Origins and treatment* (pp. 61–75). Washington, DC: V. H. Winston.

Overton, D. A. (1974). Experimental methods for the study of state-dependent learning. *Federation Proceedings, 33,* 1800–1813.

Overton, D. A. (1978). Major theories of state dependent learning. In B. T. Ho, D. W. Richards, & D. L. Chute (Eds.), *Drug discrimination and state dependent learning* (pp. 283–318). New York: Academic Press.

Overton, D. A. (1984). State dependent learning and drug discriminations. In L. L. Iverson, S. D. Iverson, & S. H. Synder (Eds.), *Handbook of psychopharmacology* (vol. 18, pp. 59–127). New York: Plenum Press.

Overton, D. A., & Batta, S. K. (1977). Relationship between the abuse liability of drugs and their degree of discriminability in the rat. In T. Thompson & K. Unna (Eds.), *Predicting dependence liability of stimulant and depressant drugs* (pp. 125–135). Baltimore: University Park Press.

Overton, D. A., Merkle, D. A., & Hayes, M. L. (1983). Are "no-drug" cues discriminated during drug-discrimination training? *Animal Learning and Behavior, 11,* 295–301.

Persson, L. O., Sjoberg, L., & Svensson, E. (1980). Mood effects of alcohol. *Psychopharmacology, 68,* 295–299.

Peters, R., & McGee, R. (1982). Cigarette smoking and state-dependent memory. *Psychopharmacology, 76,* 232–235.

Petersen, R. C. (1977). Retrieval failures in alcohol state-dependent learning. *Psychopharmacology, 55,* 141–146.

Prince, M. (1910). The mechanism and interpretation of dreams. *Journal of Abnormal Psychology, 5,* 139–195.

Reus, V. I., Weingartner, H., & Post, R. M. (1979). Clinical implications of state-dependent learning. *American Journal of Psychiatry, 136,* 927–931.

Russell, J. A. (1980). A circumplex model of affect. *Journal of Personality and Social Psychology, 39,* 1161–1178.

Ryback, R. S. (1971). The continuum and specificity of the effects of alcohol on memory. *Quarterly Journal of Studies on Alcohol, 32,* 995–998.

Saufley, W. H., Otaka, S. R., & Bavaresco, J. L. (1985). Context effects: Classroom tests and context independence. *Memory & Cognition, 13,* 522–528.

Schacter, D. L. (1987). Implicit memory: History and current status. *Journal of Experimental Psychology: Learning, Memory, and Cognition, 13,* 501–518.

Schacter, D. L., & Kihlstrom, J. F. (in press). Functional amnesia. In. F. Boller & J. Grafman (Eds.), *Handbook of neuropsychology.* Amsterdam: Elsevier.

Shannon, H. E., & Holtzman, S. G. (1977). Further evaluation of the discriminative effects of morphine in the rat. *Journal of Pharmacology and Experimental Therapeutics, 201,* 55–66.

Sher, K. J. (1985). Subjective effects of alcohol: The influence of setting and individual differences in alcohol expectancies. *Journal of Studies on Alcohol, 46,* 137–146.

Slamecka, N. J., & Graf, P. (1978). The generation effect: Delineation of a phenomenon. *Journal of Experimental Psychology: Human Learning and Memory, 4,* 592–604.

Smith, S. M. (1979). Remembering in and out of context. *Journal of Experimental Psychology: Human Learning and Memory, 5,* 460–471.

Steinberg, H. (1956). "Abnormal behaviour" induced by nitrous oxide. *British Journal of Psychology, 47,* 183–194.

Swanson, J. M., & Kinsbourne, M. (1976). Stimulant-related state-dependent learning in hyperactive children. *Science, 192,* 1354–1357.

Teasdale, J. D. (1983). Negative thinking in depression: Cause, effect or reciprocal relationship? *Advances in Behaviour Research and Therapy, 5,* 3–25.

Thorndike, E. L. (1932). *The fundamentals of learning.* New York: Teachers College.

Tulving, E. (1976). Ecphoric processes in recall and recognition. In J. Brown (Ed.), *Recall and recognition* (pp. 37–73). London: John Wiley.

Tulving, E. (1979). Relation between encoding specificity and levels of processing. In L. S. Cermak & F. I. M. Craik (Eds.), *Levels of processing in human memory* (pp. 405–428). Hillsdale, NJ: Lawrence Erlbaum Associates.

Tulving, E. (1983). *Elements of episodic memory*. Oxford: Oxford University Press.

Tulving, E., & Thomson, D. M. (1971). Retrieval processes in recognition memory: Effects of associative context. *Journal of Experimental Psychology, 87,* 116–124.

Tulving, E., & Thomson, D. M. (1973). Encoding specificity and retrieval processes in episodic memory. *Psychological Review, 80,* 353–373.

Tversky, A. (1977). Features of similarity. *Psychological Review, 84,* 327–352.

Tversky. A., & Gati, I. (1978). Studies of similarity. In E. Rosch & B. Lloyd (Eds.), *Cognition and categorization* (pp. 79–98). Hillsdale, NJ: Lawrence Erlbaum Associates.

Watkins, M. J. (1979). Engrams as cuegrams and forgetting as cue overload: A cuing approach to the structure of memory. In C. R. Puff (Ed.), *Memory organization and structure* (pp. 347–372). New York: Academic Press.

Weingartner, H. (1978). Human state dependent learning. In B. T. Ho, D. W. Richards, & D. L. Chute (Eds.), *Drug discrimination and state dependent learning* (pp. 361–382). New York: Academic Press.

Weingartner, H., & Faillace, L. A. (1971). Alcohol state-dependent learning in man. *Journal of Nervous and Mental Disease, 153,* 395–406.

Weingartner, H., Miller, H., & Murphy, D. L. (1977). Mood-state-dependent retrieval of verbal associations. *Journal of Abnormal Psychology, 86,* 276–284.

Wynne, J. M. (1985). Physics, chemistry, and manufacture of nitrous oxide. In E. I. Eger (Ed.), *Nitrous oxide/N$_2$O* (pp. 23–39). New York: Elsevier.

18

On the Relation Between Memory and Consciousness: Dissociable Interactions and Conscious Experience

Daniel L. Schacter
University of Arizona

Understanding the relation between memory and consciousness would appear to be an essential task for both cognitive and neuropsychological theories of memory. Yet, as Tulving (1985b) has argued, modern memory researchers have taken surprisingly few steps toward such an understanding:

> One can read article after article on memory, or consult book after book, without encountering the term 'consciousness.' Such a state of affairs must be regarded as rather curious. One might think that memory should have something to do with remembering, and remembering *is* a conscious experience. . . Nevertheless, through most of its history, including the current heyday of cognitive psychology, the psychological study of memory has largely proceeded without reference to the existence of conscious awareness in remembering. (p. 11)

One would be hard pressed to argue convincingly against the thrust of Tulving's claim: The relation between memory and consciousness has certainly not been near the top of, or even on, the agenda of most memory researchers. As Tulving (1985b) pointed out, this circumstance is not entirely surprising in view of the historical neglect of consciousness in many sectors of psychology.

In recent years, however, the "benign neglect" (Tulving, 1985b, p. 1) accorded the memory and consciousness issue has been replaced by growing interest. A good deal of this interest has been sparked by demonstrations of striking dissociations between memory and consciousness in normal subjects and amnesic patients: Performance on various tasks can be facilitated by recent experiences even though subjects may lack any conscious awareness or recollection of those experiences. The major purpose of the present chapter is to sketch a framework for conceptualizing the relation between memory and consciousness. The framework draws on, and attempts to integrate, findings and ideas from cognitive, neuropsychological, and neurophysiological studies of both memory and consciousness.

Before proceeding further, some discussion of terminology is necessary. It comes as no surprise to state that "consciousness" is one of the most ephemeral, difficult-to-define terms in all of psychology, and no formal definition is attempted here. It is possible, however, to provide guidelines concerning how the term is used. In this chapter, the terms "conscious" and "consciousness" are used interchangeably with terms such as "phenomenal awareness," to refer to what Dimond (1976) called "the running span of subjective experience" (p. 377). Thus, I do not use consciousness in reference to generalized states of arousal or alertness (e.g., sleep, coma, waking), but rather in reference to a person's ongoing awareness of specific mental activity.

The terms *implicit memory* and *explicit memory* (Graf & Schacter, 1985; Schacter, 1987) are also used frequently throughout the chapter. Explicit memory refers to intentional recollection of previous experiences as revealed on standard laboratory tests of recall and recognition. Explicit memory is roughly equivalent to "memory with consciousness" or "memory with awareness." Implicit memory, on the other hand, refers to situations in which previous experiences facilitate performance on tests that do not require intentional or deliberate remembering, such as word stem and fragment completion, word identification, and lexical decision. Implicit memory, as revealed by priming effects on such tests, need not and often does not involve any conscious memory for a prior experience. However, it is important to distinguish between two senses of "conscious memory" or "conscious recollection" that are often used interchangeably. On the one hand, conscious recollection can refer to the manner in which retrieval is *initiated*. When a subject intentionally attempts to "think back" to a prior experience, as required on standard recall and recognition tests, this voluntary and deliberate initiation of retrieval can be described as "conscious." On the other hand, conscious recollection can refer to a phenomenological quality of the *product* of the retrieval process—the presence of what Tulving (1983) has called "recollective experience" or "sense of pastness." It is this aspect of the memory/consciousness relation that is of primary interest here. To keep the foregoing distinction clear, I use the terms intentional/unintentional or voluntary/involuntary to refer to the manner in which retrieval is initiated, and only use the terms "conscious recollection" or "conscious remembering" to refer to subjects' recollective experience once the retrieval process has been completed (for further discussion, see Schacter, Bowers, & Booker, in press).

IMPLICIT MEMORY AND THE MEMORY/CONSCIOUSNESS RELATION: A BRIEF SURVEY

Research on implicit memory indicates that the effects of previous experiences can be revealed in the absence of conscious recollection. I have reviewed implicit memory research in some detail elsewhere (Schacter, 1987) and only highlight some key points here.

Consider first observations concerning patients with organic amnesia. As discussed by Weiskrantz and Cermak in chapters 6 and 7, such patients have severe difficulties remembering recent experiences and learning many different kinds of new information despite normal intelligence, perception, and linguistic function (for review, see Cermak, 1982; Hirst, 1982; Squire & Cohen, 1984; Weiskrantz, 1985). However, beginning in the middle 19th century (e.g., Dunn, 1845; Korsakoff, 1889), numerous investigators have reported that amnesic patients show implicit memory for experiences that they cannot recollect consciously. Thus, it has been demonstrated repeatedly that even profoundly amnesic patients, such as the well-known case H. M., can show normal or near-normal learning of various perceptual and motor skills without any conscious memory for the experiences of learning (e.g., Brooks & Baddeley, 1976; Cohen & Squire, 1980; Eslinger & Damasio, 1985; Milner, Corkin, & Teuber, 1968; Moscovitch, 1982; Nissen & Bullemer, 1987).

It has also been established firmly that, following a single exposure to an item, amnesic patients show intact priming effects on various implicit memory tests, including stem completion, word identification, free association, and lexical decision, despite the fact that they are frequently unable to recall or recognize the items on explicit memory tests (e.g., Cermak, Talbot, Chandler, & Wolbarst, 1985; Graf, Shimamura, & Squire, 1985; Graf, Squire, & Mandler, 1984; Moscovitch, Winocur, & McLachlan, 1986; Schacter, 1985; Schacter & Graf, 1986b; Shimamura & Squire, 1984; Warrington & Weiskrantz, 1968, 1974; for more extensive review, see Schacter, 1987, Shimamura, 1986). Priming in the foregoing studies was observed when patients studied old, familiar items that have pre-existing, unitized representations in memory, such as words, common idioms, and highly related paired associates. Priming of such familiar items in amnesic patients appears to be a relatively transient phenomenon, lasting only a couple of hours (Diamond & Rozin, 1984; Graf et al., 1984; Squire et al., 1987). In addition, several studies have found that amnesic patients do not show priming of pseudowords, which have no pre-existing memory representations (Cermak et al., 1985; Diamond & Rozin, 1984), thereby suggesting that priming may be attributable to temporary activation of pre-existing representations (e.g., Cermak et al., 1985; Diamond & Rozin, 1984; Graf et al., 1984). In contrast, several studies have recently shown that some amnesic patients can show implicit memory for novel information that does not have any pre-existing, unitized representation in memory. Thus, Graf and Schacter (1985) reported that amnesic patients showed implicit memory for a newly acquired association between normatively unrelated words on a stem completion task. However, Schacter and Graf (1986b) found that this associative effect was observed only in mildly amnesic patients. Cermak and his colleagues (Cermak, Blackford, O'Connor, & Bleich, in press; Cermak, Bleich & Blackford, 1988) found that Korsakoff patients did not show implicit memory for new associations on the stem completion test, whereas a severely amnesic encephalitic patient (S.S.) did. Moscovitch et al. (1986) observed that even severely amnesic patients showed normal implicit memory for new associations between unrelated words on a test that involved reading degraded word pairs. McAndrews, Glisky, and Schacter (1987) showed patients sentences that were difficult to understand (e.g., "The notes were sour because the seams split") and provided a critical word that rendered the sentence comprehensible (e.g., *bagpipes*) when patients could not generate the word themselves. Sentences were re-presented after retention intervals of up to 1 week. Although severely amnesic patients did not explicitly recognize any of the old sentences, they showed a marked facilitation in generating the critical words even after a 1-week retention interval, thereby indicating that patients had implicit memory for these novel sentences. These kinds of observations suggest that some priming effects in amnesics may reflect the influence of newly established episodic representations.

Amnesic patients have shown implicit memory for recent experiences, together with a reduction or absence of conscious memory for those experiences, in numerous other tasks and situations that are only noted briefly here. These include classical conditioning (Weiskrantz & Warrington, 1979), learning of new facts (Schacter, Harbluk, & McLachlan, 1984), stories (Luria, 1976), and complex computer commands (Glisky & Schacter, 1987, in press; Glisky, Schacter, & Tulving, 1986), acquisition of preferences (Johnson, Kim, & Risse, 1985), and detection of hidden figures (Crovitz, Harvey, & McLanahan, 1979). Of course, patients' performance is not entirely normal on all of these implicit tasks. The point to be stressed at this stage, however, is that amnesic patients have shown *some* implicit memory for just about every kind of experimental material that one could imagine.

There has also been a great deal of recent research on implicit memory in normal subjects, particularly within the domain of repetition priming. Although I will not undertake a detailed review of this work (see Schacter, 1987), it should be noted that

1. Normal subjects, like amnesic patients, have shown implicit memory on a variety of tests.

2. Implicit and explicit memory have been dissociated experimentally (e.g., Graf & Mandler, 1984; Graf & Schacter, 1987; Jacoby & Dallas, 1981; Roediger & Blaxton, 1987; Schacter & Graf, 1986a; Sloman, Hayman, Ohta, & Tulving, 1988; Tulving, Schacter, & Stark, 1982).

3. Implicit memory has been observed both for items that have integrated or unitized pre-existing memory representations, such as familiar words and idioms, and for new associations that were established for the first time during a study trial (e.g., Graf & Schacter, 1985, 1987; McKoon & Ratcliff, 1979, 1986; Schacter & Graf, 1986a).

4. Some implicit effects are relatively short lived (e.g., Forster & Davis, 1984; Graf et al., 1984), whereas others persist for days, weeks, and months (e.g., Jacoby & Dallas, 1981; Schacter & Graf, 1986a; Tulving et al., 1982).

Although studies of amnesic patients demonstrate clearly that robust implicit memory can be observed without any conscious recollection of a prior experience, the data concerning normal subjects are not as clear cut. As argued elsewhere (Schacter, 1987), it appears that normal subjects can show implicit memory without any conscious recollective experience when they are prevented, at the time of study, from encoding target material in an elaborative manner. This can be accomplished by presenting the target on an unattended channel (Eich, 1984), giving extremely brief stimulus exposures that attenuate or eliminate conscious perception (Bargh & Pietromonaco, 1982; Kunst-Wilson & Zajonc, 1980; Mandler, Nakamura, & Van Zandt, 1987), or requiring subjects to perform non-semantic orienting tasks (Graf & Mandler, 1984). Under these conditions, robust implicit memory has been observed even though recall and recognition are at or near chance levels, thereby suggesting that subjects possess little or no conscious experience of remembering the information that is expressed on an implicit memory test. However, when subjects are given elaborative study tasks, recall and recognition performance are generally quite high, indicating that the kind of information necessary for conscious remembering is potentially available to subjects when they are performing an implicit memory task. Of course, the fact that subjects *can* consciously remember target material on an explicit test does not necessarily mean that they do so when performing an implicit test (Schacter, 1987; Schacter et al., in press). It does suggest, however, that if elaborative study tasks are used, caution must be exercised when making inferences about whether normal subjects lack a conscious experience of remembering on an implicit memory test.

A recent study conducted in collaboration with Jeffrey Bowers (see Schacter et al., in press) provides some pertinent information. Subjects in that study were shown a list of common words, some under semantic encoding conditions (e.g., rating the pleasantness of a word) and some under non-semantic encoding conditions (e.g., counting vowels and consonants). The experimental group most relevant to the present concerns was told that the purpose of the experiment was to examine perception of words and other materials; no mention was made of a later memory test. A series of filler tasks was then given (e.g., generating names of countries and cities), followed by a stem completion test, which was presented as another filler task. Subjects were instructed to complete the stem with the first word that came to mind; they were not told that some of the stems could be completed with words from the earlier encoding task. Following the completion test, subjects were given a detailed questionnaire that probed whether they were aware that any of the completions represented previously studied items.

Analysis of the questionnaire responses revealed that even those subjects who expressed no awareness that any test stems had been completed with previously studied items showed robust implicit memory. Twenty subjects were classified as unaware (they responded negatively to all questionnaire items), and 20 subjects were classified as aware (they responded positively to at least one questionnaire item). Overall level of implicit memory in aware (33%) and unaware (31%) subjects did not differ significantly. Following non-semantic encoding, aware subjects completed 23% of stems with study-list items, whereas unaware subjects completed 28% (baseline completion rate was 12%). Following semantic encoding, aware subjects completed more stems with list items (43%) than did unaware subjects (33%). The critical point, however, is that unaware subjects showed substantial implicit memory following semantic encoding. Because it seems reasonable to infer that these subjects did not consciously remember having studied any of the items that they provided as completions, these data would appear to indicate that normal subjects can show implicit memory, devoid of conscious recollective experience, even for items that have been encoded in a semantic or elaborative manner.

In summary, several types of implicit memory phenomena have been observed in amnesic and normal subjects: gradual acquisition of perceptual, motor, and cognitive skills; transient activation of pre-existing memory representations; and long-lasting effects of newly established episodic representations. Various theoretical ideas have been put forward to account for these manifestations of implicit memory, but none successfully accommodates all of them (see Schacter, 1987). I consider some of these ideas later and attempt to integrate them into a general framework. Before turning to the theoretical issues, however, it is necessary to consider a series of phenomena that, in my view, provide key clues concerning the nature of the relation between memory and consciousness.

IMPLICIT/EXPLICIT DISSOCIATIONS
IN NEUROPSYCHOLOGICAL SYNDROMES

Recent studies of brain-damaged patients with specific perceptual and cognitive deficits have shown that patients have access to knowledge that they are not aware that they possess and cannot express consciously. Just as amnesic patients show implicit memory for information that they do not consciously remember, these patients show implicit knowledge of stimuli that, depending on the exact nature of their impairment, they either cannot perceive, identify, recognize, or understand consciously. The evidence for such dissociations has been reviewed and discussed in detail elsewhere (Schacter, McAndrews, & Moscovitch, 1988). For the present purposes, it suffices to present a few illustrative examples and then delineate their theoretical implications.

Consider first the phenomenon of prosopagnosia. Prosopagnosic patients have serious difficulties recognizing familiar faces, usually because of bilateral lesions to occipito-temporal cortex (e.g., Damasio, 1985). Such patients typically report no familiarity with the faces of family, relatives, and friends. Despite the absence of any conscious experience that a face is familiar, recent data indicate that patients do have implicit knowledge of facial familiarity. In a psychophysiological study, Tranel and Damasio (1985) found that a severely prosopagnosic patient showed larger skin conductance responses to familiar than to unfamiliar faces—yet none of the faces seemed familiar to the patient. Also using the skin conductance response, Bauer (1984) reported a similar phenomenon in another prosopagnosic patient. De Haan, Young, and Newcombe (1987) reported data from various behavioral measures that dovetail nicely with the psychophysiological evidence. Their patient was entirely unable to distinguish consciously between familiar and unfamiliar faces. Yet on a matching task that entailed same–different judgments about two simultaneously exposed faces, this patient, like control subjects, was faster to respond when a judgment was made about familiar than unfamiliar faces. In addition, the patient was subject to interference from familiar faces—even though he did not recognize them—on a Stroop-like naming task. De Haan et al. concluded that their patient had access to much the same information about familiarity that control subjects did; the critical difference was that the patient could not express it consciously (see also, Young, 1988).

Results like those obtained with prosopagnosics have been reported in other neuropsychological syndromes. A great deal of experimental work has been directed at the phenomenon of *blindsight* (Weiskrantz, 1986). Patients with lesions to striate cortex typically lack conscious perceptual experiences within their scotoma. Yet it has been consistently demonstrated that, when required to "guess," such patients can make above-chance forced-choice judgments concerning stimulus attributes (e.g., location) that they do not consciously "see" (e.g., Richards, 1973; Weiskrantz, 1977, 1980, 1896; Zihl, 1980). Although some aspects of the blindsight phenomenon have been disputed and are subject to alternative interpretations (Campion, Latto, & Smith, 1983), there are good reasons to believe that these patients can gain access implicitly to information that does not inform conscious visual experience (Schacter et al., 1988; Weiskrantz, 1986). Similar dissociations have been observed in the syndrome of alexia without agraphia. Alexic patients cannot read visually presented words unless they resort to a letter-by-letter decoding strategy. However, when words are presented at brief tachistoscopic exposures that prevent letter-by-letter decoding, such patients can make above-chance lexical decisions, semantic categorizations, and other judgments about words that they are unable to identify consciously (Coslett, 1986; Landis, Regard, & Serrat, 1980; Shallice & Saffran, 1986).

Implicit knowledge of information that is not accessible to consciousness has also been observed in patients with visual object agnosia (Margolin, Friedrich, & Carlson, 1983; Warrington, 1975), Broca's and Wernicke's aphasia (Andrewsky

& Seron, 1975; Blumstein, Milberg, & Schrier, 1982; Milberg & Blumstein, 1981; Milberg, Blumstein, & Dworetzky, in press), and in studies of inter-hemispheric transfer in split-brain patients (Holtzman, Sidtis, Volpe, Wilson, & Gazzaniga, 1981; Sergent, 1987). This corpus of dissociations raises a number of conceptual and interpretive issues that have been dealt with elsewhere (Schacter et al., 1988). For the present purposes, however, two key points need to be stressed. The first concerns the *generality* and *diversity* of the dissociations: Similar patterns of results have been observed across different patient groups, experimental tasks, types of information, and perceptual/cognitive processes. This observation complements and extends the previously noted diversity of implicit memory phenomena. Second, the failures to gain access to con-sciousness observed in the various neuropsychological syndromes are selective or *domain specific*. By *domain specific,* I mean that patients do not have difficul-ties gaining conscious access to information outside the domain of their specific impairment. Thus, for example, prosopagnosic patients do not have the difficul-ties consciously reading words that alexic patients do, whereas alexic patients do not have the difficulties consciously recognizing familiar faces that prosopag-nosic patients do. Similarly, amnesic patients do not have problems consciously perceiving visual stimuli, and blindsight patients are not characterized by diffi-culties in conscious recollection. The striking disruptions of conscious processes observed in these and other patients occur largely in the circumscribed bandwidth of cognition that is defined by their specific deficit. By the present view, the diversity and domain-specificity of these phenomena provide clues concerning the relation between memory and consciousness.

DISSOCIABLE INTERACTIONS
AND CONSCIOUS EXPERIENCE

The dissociations discussed thus far indicate clearly that memory for recent experiences can be revealed in performance without any conscious experience of remembering, and also indicate that various kinds of knowledge can be ex-pressed in the absence of conscious experiences of perceiving, identifying, or knowing. It is possible, of course, that the resemblance among these phenomena is entirely superficial, and that each dissociation demands a separate theoretical treatment. By this view, it would be uninformative and possibly misleading to approach the memory and consciousness issue in the context of the phenomena discussed in the previous section. Such a possibility cannot be ruled out with any certainty. However, I believe that it is worth exploring the idea that there is a theoretically significant relation among the dissociations. This belief is based in part on several of Tulving's admonitions concerning the proper approach to psychological issues that are highly familiar to his students and colleagues. First, the self-correcting nature of the scientific enterprise insures us that nothing much will be lost if the ideas put forward here turn out to be wrong (this can also be read as an excuse for speculation). Second, broad conceptual approaches are currently needed instead of premature formalism (I take this as an excuse for vagueness). Third, falsifiability is not the only criterion for a useful scientific idea (in other words, circularity can be excused). Fourth, all current ideas in psychology are wrong anyway, so why not give it a shot?

In conformity with the foregoing, I use the observations of implicit/explicit dissociations in various neuropsychological syndromes to motivate a general framework for understanding the memory/consciousness relation. The main usefulness of the framework, in my view, is that it brings together a variety of phenomena and ideas that might not otherwise be related. The spirit of the present proposal is similar to Tulving's (1983) GAPS framework (General Abstract Processing System), which organizes and interrelates diverse phenomena via a small number of ideas, but does not offer detailed explanations or quantitative predictions. And just as the acronym GAPS reflected Tulving's acute awareness that his model was incomplete, I have chosen an acronym for the present approach—DICE—that reflects my awareness that attempting to relate diverse phenomena to one another is a gamble that involves considerable risk. In addition, as should become clear shortly, some of the central ideas to be put forward are captured in the words that the acronym represents: Dissociable Interactions and Conscious Experience. DICE draws on and attempts to integrate ideas that have been proposed by Baars (1983), Dimond (1976), Johnson-Laird (1983), Kihlstrom (1984), Marcel (1983), Mesulam (1981), Norman and Shallice (1986), Squire and Cohen (1984), Tulving (1985a,b), and Weiskrantz (1977, 1980), among others.

DICE is built on a half-dozen or so main ideas:

1. Conscious experiences of remembering, perceiving, and knowing all depend on the involvement of a specific mechanism or system.

2. This system is normally activated by the outputs of various processing and memory modules, and the resulting *interaction* between a particular module and the conscious system defines a particular kind of conscious experience.

3. In some cases of neuropsychological impairment, specific processing and memory modules are *selectively disconnected* from the conscious system, thereby resulting in a domain-specific deficit of conscious experience.

4. Information that does not have access to the conscious system can still affect verbal/motor response systems.

5. The conscious system functions as a gateway to executive control systems.

6. Procedural knowledge does not normally have access to the conscious system.

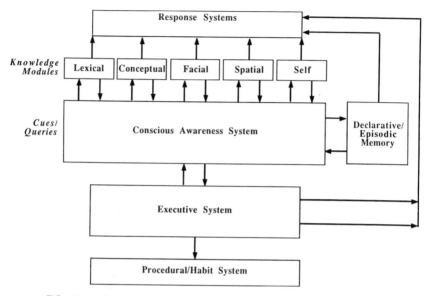

FIG. 18.1. A schematic depiction of DICE. Knowledge modules represent various types of overlearned information; declarative/episodic memory subserves remembering of recent events and information; the procedural/habit system is involved in perceptual/motor skill learning. Phenomenal awareness of specific types of information depends on intact connections between the conscious awareness system and individual knowledge modules or declarative/episodic memory. The procedural/habit system does not have any connections with the conscious awareness system. The conscious awareness system serves as the gateway to the executive system, which is involved in initiation of voluntary activities.

I first flesh out these notions in a bit more detail, and then discuss evidence that suggests a neurophysiological basis for the various components of DICE. To aid the reader's understanding of the model, Fig. 18.1 displays a schematic of its components and the relations among them.

Central to the present approach is the idea that conscious experiences of remembering, knowing, and so forth all depend on the functioning of a specific mechanism or system that is distinct from, but interacts with, modular mechanisms that process and represent various types of information. I refer to this system simply as the Conscious Awareness System (CAS). By the present view, activation at the modular level—in a particular perceptual or memory system, for example—is not sufficient to produce conscious awareness of the activated representation. Such awareness depends on the activation of CAS by the output of perceptual or memory modules. Thus, activation of CAS is held to occur at a relatively late stage in processing, only after information has been elaborated extensively at the modular level. However, activation of CAS represents just one output route from a particular module. It is also possible for information represented in a particular module to be expressed via output routes to verbal or motor response systems that do not involve CAS. When modular outputs affect response systems without activation of CAS, knowledge is expressed implicitly, in the absence of any phenomenal awareness or subjective experience of perceiving, remembering, or knowing. In the present scheme, CAS serves three functions. First, as implied previously, its activation is necessary for the subjective sense that one "remembers," "knows," or "perceives" something. Second, CAS can be viewed as a "global data base" (Baars, 1983) that integrates the output of modular processes. Such an integrative mechanism is crucial in any modular system in which processing and representation of different types of information is handled in parallel by separate modules (Allport, 1979; Baars, 1983; Johnson-Laird, 1983). Third, it is hypothesized that CAS sends outputs to an *executive system* that is involved in regulation of attention and initiation of such voluntary activities as memory search, planning, and so forth. Whereas CAS can be activated by inputs from various sources (i.e., modules), its major output is to the executive control system. Thus, CAS is not itself an executive system, but it outputs the kind of information that can be used by executive systems (cf. Baars, 1983). The distinction between CAS and the executive system is central to the present view, and I attempt to justify it on neuropsychological grounds later in the chapter.

DICE incorporates a distinction between procedural and declarative memory systems, and also accepts a further distinction between types of declarative memory that is similar but not identical to Tulving's (1972, 1983) episodic/semantic distinction. I use the procedural/declarative distinction in the manner of Anderson (1976) and Winograd (1975), who were among the first to apply it to psychological issues—procedural memory entails "knowing how," and is involved primarily in various kinds of incremental skill learning, whereas declarative memory entails "knowing that," and involves primarily memory for words, events, facts, and so on (for a somewhat different use of the procedural/declarative distinction, see Squire, 1987). "Procedural" is used here in a sense that is roughly equivalent to the notion of "habit" proposed by Mishkin and his colleagues (e.g., Mishkin, Malamut, & Bachevalier, 1984), and so I refer to the system held to be involved in incremental skill learning as the procedural/habit system. An important postulate of DICE is that this system does not send input to CAS under *any* circumstances. It is frequently acknowledged that people do not have conscious access to psychological processes or procedures (e.g., Johnson-Laird, 1983; Kihlstrom, 1984; Kinsbourne & Wood, 1982; Nisbett & Wilson, 1977), and it seems reasonable to argue that people do not have conscious access to *modifications* of these processes (e.g., Cohen, 1984; Squire, 1986). The notion that the procedural/habit system does not have an input link to CAS, however, does not mean that this system is totally isolated. Clearly, it is possible to voluntarily *initiate* various acquired skills or procedures, and some procedural learning may require the allocation of attention (cf. Nissen & Bullemer, 1987). Accordingly, DICE postulates that the executive system has an output link to procedural memory that permits the voluntary initiation of skills that depend on procedural systems. The critical point, however, is that the actual running off of a procedure, skill, or habit does not constitute input to CAS. The implication of this idea is that all manifestations of the procedural/habit system are implicit. With respect to the finding of normal skill learning in amnesic patients who do not explicitly remember learning any skills, the present account is much the same as that of Cohen and Squire (1980) or Mishkin et al. (1984): The procedural/habit system is assumed to be spared in organic amnesia.

If the data indicated that only perceptual and motor skills could be expressed without conscious awareness of remembering, it would be possible to argue that conscious memory is a property of the declarative memory system, and that whenever declarative memory is involved in task performance, remembering will be characterized by conscious recollective experience. However, it appears that implicit memory phenomena can be observed in tasks that involve memory for what many people would describe as declarative (i.e., representational) information—words, sentences, paired associates, facts, and so on. How can implicit memory for declarative information occur? By the present view, the answer to this question is to be found in the relation between CAS and declarative memory structures. CAS is assumed to have connections with two dissociable types of declarative memory. The first resembles what Tulving (1972) has termed *episodic* memory, in the sense that it is responsible for storing and retrieving *new* information. In the present scheme, however, this memory system is responsible for representing various types of new information (e.g., facts, associations, context, etc.), whereas Tulving (1983) restricts episodic memory to auto-biographical information. In DICE, explicit remembering of a recent event depends on an *interaction* between the declarative/episodic system and CAS. Activation of a representation in declarative/episodic memory is not itself a sufficient condition for explicit remembering of a recent event. For explicit remembering to occur, the output of declarative/episodic memory must be able to gain access to CAS. If such access does not occur, an episodic representation may still affect verbal or motor response systems via alternative output routes that do not involve CAS. Under these conditions, however, information from declarative/episodic memory will affect performance implicitly, without any conscious experience of remembering.

The second class of declarative memory structures with access to CAS are those that represent highly overlearned and unitized information of various kinds—lexical, conceptual, autobiographical, spatial, visual, and so forth. These structures could be viewed either as a subset of declarative memory or as a distinct *semantic* memory system (Tulving, 1983). For the present purposes, the critical point is that "semantic memory" appears to be composed of different modules that represent various types of information (e.g., Allport & Funnell,

1981; Johnson-Laird, 1983; Warrington & Shallice, 1984). For descriptive purposes, I refer to these as "knowledge modules" or "semantic memory modules." Although no firm assumptions are made here regarding the specific nature of these modules, it is hypothesized that explicit knowledge of words, concepts, familiar faces, and so forth depends on an *interaction* between the appropriate knowledge module and CAS. Mere activation of a semantic memory representation is not sufficient to yield a conscious experience of knowing or identifying. The route from a particular module to CAS must also be functional in order for activated information to produce a conscious experience of knowing. If information represented in a specific module cannot gain access to CAS, it is postulated that the activated information can still affect verbal or motor response systems through routes that bypass CAS. When such routes are used, however, the output of a specific module will be expressed implicitly, without a conscious experience of knowing or identifying.

Whereas CAS can be activated by an "upstream" flow of input from knowledge modules or declarative/episodic memory, voluntary or deliberate access to information represented by a particular memory module depends on the executive system, which is assumed to have unidirectional "downstream" links to memory structures. The executive system can thus query various memory structures regarding the accessibility of sought-after information, a process that corresponds to the initiation of search or voluntary retrieval. If the sought-after information is activated, it can gain access to CAS and produce a conscious experience of remembering or knowing.

Within the context of the foregoing ideas, there are two ways in which implicit memory for declarative information can occur: (a) through transient activation of pre-existing representations in semantic memory modules, and (b) through the establishment of new declarative/episodic representations that are expressed through retrieval routes that do not involve CAS. Consider first the role of activation. Following relatively short retention intervals, a pre-existing representation that had been activated at the time of study may gain access to CAS when an appropriate cue is provided on an implicit memory test (e.g., a word stem), thereby resulting in the conscious experience of a familiar word "popping into mind." However, access of an activated representation to CAS does not provide any contextual information about the occurrence of a recent event, and therefore does not provide a basis for explicit remembering. For explicit remembering to occur, CAS must receive input from declarative/episodic memory. In normal subjects, this can happen when test instructions call for explicit remembering (e.g., Graf & Mandler, 1984; Schacter & Graf, 1986a), thereby initiating a "query" from the executive system to declarative/episodic memory that can produce an input to CAS. When appropriate information is available (i.e., following elaborative encoding), CAS will be activated, and remembering of the prior occurrence of a word in a study list will occur; however, when appropriate information is not available (i.e., following non-semantic encoding), CAS will not be activated, and thus explicit remembering will not occur.

This formulation can also be applied to the finding of normal priming of old or pre-existing knowledge in amnesic patients. Amnesic patients generally do not have difficulty gaining conscious access to highly overlearned information such as words and concepts. Therefore, it is reasonable to posit that such information can be activated normally and can gain access to CAS. However, amnesic patients do not remember explicitly the prior occurrence of an activated word. One possible reason for this is that amnesic patients do not store or retain new declarative information about an event, information whose retrieval is necessary for conscious recollection to occur. A second possibility, which is advocated here, is that at least some amnesic patients can "store" new declarative information, but such information is unable to gain access to conscious awareness. Why should one favor this notion over the idea that the declarative/episodic representations are simply unavailable? The main reason stems from the various demonstrations that some amnesic patients can show implicit memory for new, contextually specific information, such as unrelated paired associates (Cermak et al., in press; Graf & Schacter, 1985; Moscovitch et al., 1986; Schacter & Graf, 1986b), sentence puzzles (McAndrews et al., 1987), repeated spatio-temporal patterns (Nissen & Bullemer, 1987), and some kinds of factual information (Glisky et al., 1986; Schacter et al., 1984). By the present view, such newly acquired declarative/episodic information can affect motor and verbal response systems via routes that bypass CAS. The fact that this newly learned information is not always retrieved *normally* in amnesic patients (e.g., Schacter et al., 1984; Squire, 1986) can be accommodated by postulating some damage to the declarative/episodic system itself as well as disconnection from CAS.

The foregoing constitutes an overview of DICE and illustrates how some of its main ideas can be applied to various implicit/explicit dissociations. To evaluate the plausibility of this framework, however, it is necessary to examine in greater detail the nature of and empirical basis for these ideas. In the following section, I first discuss further the evidence for CAS, followed by consideration of the neuropsychology of the executive system and its relation to CAS. I then elaborate my view of modularity and the issue of multiple memory systems. Finally, I compare the present approach to other views of the memory/consciousness issue and then outline several predictions that are made by DICE.

CONCEPTIONS OF CAS

Although a great many psychological and neurophysiological theories concerning the nature of conscious awareness have been advanced, two broad approaches to the problem can be distinguished. One has a *global* emphasis: Consciousness is identified with the sum total of all information processing activities or as an emergent property of diffuse brain or cognitive systems (e.g., Karmiloff-Smith, 1986; Neisser, 1976; Sperry, 1969). The other has a *local* emphasis: Consciousness is identified with the activity of a specific psychological/neurological mechanism or system (e.g., Baars, 1983; Dimond, 1976; Hilgard, 1977; Johnson-Laird, 1983; Kihlstrom, 1984; Posner, 1978, 1980). As described in the previous section, the present approach has a decidedly, although not exclusively, local emphasis. Any attempt to identify conscious awareness with a specific mechanism or system immediately raises two interrelated problems. First, it is all too easy to endow such a system with homunculus-like properties that enable it to perform a host of activities that are casually grouped together under the heading of *conscious*. Part of the problem here is that the term *conscious* is often used to refer to a variety of psychological functions, including phenomenal awareness of mental activity, voluntary or intentional initiation of action, selection of stimuli for attention, and control of processing activity. To postulate a conscious mechanism and blithely assign it all of the foregoing capacities is not terribly helpful. Thus, to escape or at least minimize the homunculus charge, one must be quite specific about the properties and functions of any alleged conscious mechanism. I have attempted to do so by identifying CAS with one particular function: phenomenal awareness of ongoing mental activity. CAS is held to be activated by input from various modular processors, and to represent such information in a way that it can be output to executive systems. The present conception of CAS is close in spirit to Baars' (1983) notion that consciousness is a "global data base" that represents in an integrated manner the output of parallel modular systems. Of course, it could be argued that restricting one's conception of CAS in such a manner merely shifts the homunculus to the executive system. Although there may be some truth to this, there are also reasonably strong neuropsychological grounds for distinguishing between CAS and executive systems, as is argued in this and the next section.

The second main problem in attempting to identify conscious awareness with a specific mechanism or system is that this *description* could be mistakenly viewed as an *explanation*. Clearly, to postulate that conscious awareness depends on a specific mechanism in no way explains how consciousness is achieved or exactly what it is. Accordingly, one must guard against any tendency to reify the hypothetical conscious system or to imagine that the problem has been "solved" merely by postulating the existence of such a system. In the present formulation, the notion of CAS can be viewed as a convenient shorthand for the idea that conscious awareness of a specific bit of information requires processing beyond the modular level. Even if postulation of a conscious system amounts to no more than redefining the problem, this is not without value when the redefinition is useful (White, 1982)—that is, when it suggests a fruitful line of approach to the phenomenon and raises questions that might not be investigated otherwise. If we hypothesize the existence of a system such as CAS, we are led to ask questions concerning the reasons for supposing its existence, how it interacts with other systems, the areas of the brain that are involved in CAS, what happens when these areas are damaged, and so forth. These questions are quite different than those that would be posed if consciousness were viewed as a global, emergent property of brain organization, and the next section addresses some of them.

THE NEUROANATOMY
AND NEUROPSYCHOLOGY OF CAS

If the notion of CAS is to be more than just a fanciful speculation that is invoked *post-hoc* to describe various implicit/explicit dissociations, it ought to be possible to cite evidence of its existence independently of the phenomena that led to the initial postulation of it. I believe that there are empirical grounds for inferring the existence of a system akin to CAS. More specifically, both neuroanatomical and neuropsychological evidence suggest that a posterior region of the cortex, critically involving the inferior parietal lobes, constitutes part of a circuit or system subserving conscious awareness (e.g., Dimond, 1976; Mountcastle, 1978).

Consider first the neuroanatomical basis for suggesting the involvement of posterior parietal cortex in conscious awareness. Two characteristics of CAS delineated earlier are that it is activated at a relatively late stage in the processing of a particular stimulus, and that it serves to integrate the output of various modules. A neural system that fits this description would be one with (a) access to information that has already been analyzed extensively at earlier stages of processing, and (b) access to highly processed information from a variety of sources (i.e., modules). Recent neuroanatomical evidence indicates that certain areas of the parietal lobes meet both of these criteria. For example, Mesulam and his colleagues (Mesulam, Van Hoesen, Pandya, & Geschwind, 1977) showed that the inferior parietal lobule in rhesus monkeys is uniquely characterized by the convergence of projections from all multimodal or higher-order association areas of the cortex, as well as from the limbic system. By contrast, the inferior parietal region receives relatively few projections from unimodal or low-level sensory areas. What this means is that the inferior parietal region takes as its input information which already has been processed to high levels in association areas, and it gets such input from multiple sources. As Mesulam (1985) stated, the inferior parietal lobule ". . . could be considered an association area for high-order association areas" (p. 152). He noted further that "We have examined the connectivity of many other cortical areas . . . but we have not yet found an area that receives sensory input which is this extensively preprocessed" (1983, p. 395). Although some caution must be exercised when making inferences regarding human cortical organization from monkey data, the foregoing observations suggest that regions of parietal cortex have precisely the pattern of interconnections that would be necessary if they constituted part of a larger system with the hypothesized properties and functions of CAS.

The idea that parietal lobes form part of a system that underlies conscious awareness was noted and discussed in an important but little cited article by Dimond (1976). He proposed the existence of a "consciousness circuit" extending across a posterior section of the cortex, with the parietal lobes representing the lateral endpoints of the circuit. Other key neural structures that Dimond hypothesized to be part of this system include the posterior regions of the corpus callosum, particularly the cingulate area in the splenium of the callosum. If the circuit proposed by Dimond is even a rough approximation of the neuroanatomical substrate of CAS, it would be expected that lesions to the various components of the system should produce disorders of conscious awareness. Neuropsychological observations are consistent with this idea. Discussing literature on split-brain patients, Dimond noted that disturbances of awareness that are sometimes observed in such patients are found only following sectioning of the posterior third of the callosum—the part that links the parietal lobes and is thus an important component of the consciousness circuit. Patients in whom the anterior two thirds is sectioned and the posterior third is preserved do not show any disturbances of awareness (Gordon, Bogen, & Sperry, 1971). Dimond also noted that severe disturbances of consciousness have been observed following lesions in the cingulate area, which also forms part of the bridge that links the parietal lobes. For example, the phenomenon of akinetic mutism has been observed in patients with cingulate lesions: They are unresponsive to external stimuli, apathetic, and do not voluntarily speak or move, although they are "awake" (i.e., eyes are open and reflexes are intact) and not considered to be comatose (e.g., Barris & Schuman, 1953; Nielsen & Jacobs, 1951). Cingulate lesions have also been associated with confusional states, which are characterized by disordered thought, severe disorientation, and a breakdown of selective attention—in short, a global disorder of conscious awareness (Amyes & Nielsen, 1955; Whitty & Lewin, 1960).

Several lines of evidence indicate that lesions to certain regions of the parietal lobes can produce disorders of conscious awareness. First, global confusional states have been reported in right parietal patients (Geschwind, 1982; Mesulam & Geschwind, 1978; Mesulam, Waxman, Geschwind, & Sabin, 1976). Second, the syndrome of anosognosia—unawareness and denial of a neuropsychological deficit—is often associated with parietal damage (e.g., Bisiach, Vallar, Perani, Papagno, & Berti, 1986; Critchley, 1953; Frederiks, 1985; Koehler, Endtz, Tevelde, & Hekster, 1986; Warrington, 1962; for review, see McGlynn & Schacter, in press). Anosognosic patients may be unaware of motor deficits (e.g., hemiplegia), perceptual deficits (e.g., hemianopia and blindness), or cognitive deficits (e.g., jargon aphasia), and complete unawareness can be observed even when the primary deficit is severe (i.e., total blindness). Patients' subjective sense that their deficient function is normal can be extraordinarily compelling, and they often deny a deficit in the face of contrary evidence, resorting to rationalizations and confabulations. This dramatic disorder of awareness in parietal lobe patients implies a disruption of CAS.

Further relevant evidence is provided by the phenomenon of unilateral neglect. A large body of neuropsychological observations indicates that unilateral damage to the inferior parietal lobe, particularly in the right hemisphere, produces a striking disorder of attention or awareness (e.g., Bisiach, Luzzati, & Perani, 1979; Brain, 1941; Critchley, 1953; Mesulam, 1985; Vallar & Perani, 1986): Neglect patients appear entirely unaware of the existence of the internal and external world contralateral to their lesion, even though basic sensory/perceptual function is intact. Such patients may fail to shave, wash, or dress the neglected side of the body, constantly bump into objects on the side of space contralateral to their lesion, and even fail to report the content of internally generated images from the contralateral side (Bisiach & Luzzati, 1978; Bisiach et al., 1979). The apparent reason for this disorder is that patients are unable to shift attention away from the field ipsilateral to their lesion (Posner, Inhoff, Friedrich, & Cohen, 1987). Thus, it is possible that neglect ought not to be viewed as a disruption of CAS in the same way that such phenomena as confusional states, anosognosia, and akinetic mutism are. The disruption may be at the level of the output of CAS to attentional control systems. However, Dimond (1976) has suggested a way of conceptualizing neglect as a deficit of consciousness. He proposed that:

> . . . the patient with parietal lobe damage is deficient in the capacity for the production of consciousness. We believe that the cerebral disorder is such as to seriously restrict that which the patient can accommodate in consciousness; the individual now possesses only a narrowed and restricted channel through which the stuff of consciousness can pass with the result that much fails to enter. He is in other words deprived of one arm of the system for consciousness and like any one-armed individual is seriously restricted in what he an do. (p. 387)

It is also worth noting that lesions of the inferior parietal lobule in monkeys produce an inattention syndrome that is, in several respects, similar to neglect in humans (Lynch, 1980; Mountcastle, 1978). Noting the convergence from human and animal data, Mountcastle (1978) offered an interpretation similar to Dimond's (1976): "A patient with a parietal lobe lesion has a defect of conscious awareness, for he no longer has the capacity to attend to the contralateral world; for him it no longer exists. And the withdrawn self-isolation of a monkey after bilateral parietal lobe lesions suggests a reduction in his level of conscious awareness" (p. 48).

Taken together, the foregoing considerations provide reasonable grounds for postulating a neural circuit or system that corresponds to CAS. It must be emphasized, however, that the existing evidence can be regarded as no more than suggestive. For example, there are only a few empirical observations linking posterior regions of the corpus callosum—the heart of the consciousness circuit postulated by Dimond (1976)—with disorders of conscious awareness. Likewise, damage to inferior parietal regions, which constitute the lateral end-points of Dimond's system, does not inevitably result in a disruption of awareness, and in some instances produces other kinds of neuropsychological disturbances (e.g., Critchley, 1953; Frederiks, 1985). Nevertheless, the existing empirical clues are suggestive enough to merit serious consideration.

It should also be noted that some of the phenomena observed in conjunction with parietal lesions, such as neglect and anosognosia, have been observed in connection with frontal damage (see Stuss & Benson, 1986). Although it is not clear whether the parietal and frontal manifestations of these phenomena are identical (McGlynn & Schacter, in press; Stuss & Benson, 1986), such observations have led to the suggestion that frontal lobes are critically involved in self-awareness (Stuss & Benson, 1986). It is possible that the posterior-based CAS described here interacts with frontal regions and thus forms part of a larger network concerned with various kinds of awareness (see Mesulam, 1981, for a similar idea with respect to selective attention). The fact that there are strong reciprocal links between parietal and frontal lobes (e.g., Mesulam, 1981; Nauta, 1971) lends neuroanatomical plausibility to this suggestion. However, as described in the next section, the present approach emphasizes the involvement of frontal lobes in the closely related domain of executive formation and intentional retrieval.

EXECUTIVE SYSTEM
AND INTENTIONAL RETRIEVAL

I have distinguished several times between two ways in which the concept of consciousness has been used with respect to memory: to indicate phenomenal awareness of remembering or "recollective experience" on the one hand, or to refer to deliberate or intentional initiation of retrieval on the other. In outlining DICE, the latter activity was assigned an executive system that is distinct from CAS. In addition, it was suggested that when an activated representation gains access to CAS, it is made available to the executive system and can thus be used in intentional actions and behaviors that are controlled by the executive. By contrast, it was hypothesized that activated representations that do not gain access to CAS cannot be used by the executive. Such representations can only affect output systems involved in relatively automatic responding.

Recent ideas advanced by Norman and Shallice (1986; Shallice, 1982) provide a basis for sharpening these suggestions and linking them to neuropsychological observations. Norman and Shallice described two mechanisms for the control of action. The first, referred to as *contention scheduling,* involves relatively automatic triggering of highly activated schemas by appropriate environmental information. This mechanism supports the execution of routine behaviors that run off without voluntary control and are determined solely by which schema is most strongly activated by an environmental trigger. Although it is an efficient means of controlling action, contention scheduling breaks down when non-routine behaviors are demanded; an organism operating on the basis of contention schedule alone is susceptible to perseverative responding and involuntary "slips of action." For example, an intended action may not be performed because a strong, although inappropriate, schema is activated and "captures" response systems (e.g., a person walks through his back porch to get his car, and ends up putting on a jacket and boots for gardening; Reason, 1979). In view of the shortcomings of contention scheduling, Norman and Shallice postulated a second mechanism, referred to as the Supervisory Attentional System (SAS), which is involved in intentional or deliberate control of action. SAS "contains the general programming or planning systems that can operate on schemas in every domain" (Shallice, 1982, p. 20). It functions to bias the contention scheduling mechanism by adding additional activation to appropriate schemas and inhibiting inappropriate ones. SAS is thus crucial for various kinds of voluntary, non-routine behaviors.

What I have described as the executive system corresponds roughly to Norman and Shallice's SAS. As has been pointed out by Norman and Shallice and others (e.g., Luria, 1966; Milner, 1982; Stuss & Benson, 1986), neuropsychological observations support the existence of such a system and tie it closely to prefrontal cortex. Beginning with the classic observations of Luria (1966), it has been reported repeatedly that patients with frontal lesions have difficulties in the programming, planning, and monitoring of behavior. Such patients can perform routine, stimulus-driven tasks well, but are impaired when a task requires self-initiated responses, active planning, sequential organization, or response monitoring (Milner, 1982). These are all activities that can be roughly described as "executive functions."

The critical point of the foregoing is to suggest that there are reasonable grounds for distinguishing between intentional and unintentional control of behavior and action. In DICE, intentional initiation of retrieval is handled by the executive. In addition, only those activated representations that gain access to CAS can be used by the executive system and thus influence voluntary activities. Activated information that does not gain access to CAS can still influence response systems, along the lines suggested by Norman and Shallice in their discussion of contention scheduling. However, such implicitly expressed information cannot serve as a basis for formulating plans or other kinds of voluntary action. Consider, for example, an amnesic patient who has no conscious recollection of a recent experience, yet demonstrates retention of that experience via priming effects on an implicit memory test. Such a patient would likely be unable to use the information acquired during the episode as a basis for formulating future plans or strategies, although such information might affect the patient's automatic response in the presence of an appropriate environmental trigger. Thus, an amnesic patient in whom CAS is disconnected from declarative/episodic memory would have no "memory for the future" (Tulving, 1985b), because recently acquired information is unavailable to the executive system. It is interesting to note in this regard that Marcel (1986) reported a similar observation in the case of a blindsight patient:

> Cortically blind patients who have no phenomenal experience of an object in the blind field will nonetheless preadjust their hands appropriately to size, shape, orientation and 3-D location of that object in the blind field when forced to attempt to grasp it . . . Yet such patients will make no spontaneous attempt to grasp a glass of water in their blind field even when thirsty. Voluntary actions often depend upon conscious perception. (p. 41)

MODULARITY, MEMORY SYSTEMS, AND CAS

In outlining the basic ideas of DICE, I suggested that CAS could be activated by input from different modules, and distinguished between declarative/episodic memory on the one hand and semantic memory on the other. I also argued that the procedural/habit system does not send input to CAS under any circumstances. It is now time to examine the ideas of modularity and multiple memory systems more closely.

Consider first the notion of modularity. A large number of investigators have recently adopted the general idea that processing of different kinds of information is handled by distinct modules (e.g., Fodor, 1983; Gardner, 1983; Gazzaniga, 1985; Marshall, 1984; Mountcastle, 1979; Shallice, 1981). Although the various conceptions of modularity differ from one another (compare, for example, Mountcastle, 1979 and Fodor, 1983), the general point of agreement is that modules perform domain-specific computations and operate largely independently of one another. With respect to memory, it has been proposed that the various cortical areas (i.e., modules) that analyze different types of declarative information are also the storage sites of the particular kinds of information that they process (e.g., Mishkin, 1982; Squire, 1987). If this notion is accepted, it follows quite naturally that each module could have its own input link to CAS, a link that could be selectively disrupted by a specific kind of brain damage. Consider, for example, the implicit/explicit dissociation in prosopagnosia discussed earlier. There are reasons to postulate a specific module for analyzing and storing the information necessary for facial recognition (Bruce & Young, 1986). If the output of this module were selectively disconnected from CAS, we would expect the kind of implicit or covert "recognition" of faces, without any phenomenal awareness of familiarity, that has been found in prosopagnosia (Bauer, 1984; de Haan et al., 1987; Tranel & Damasio, 1985; Young, 1988). This same line of reasoning could be applied to several of the other dissociations discussed earlier, where lexical, conceptual, and other kinds of knowledge that may be represented in distinct modules appear to be selectively disconnected from CAS. The key problem at this stage is that we have only the foggiest notions concerning precisely what functions to ascribe to hypothetical modules, and this severely limits the kinds of statements that can be made concerning the relation between CAS and a particular module. All that can be said is that the general hypothesis that specific input pathways from individual modules to CAS can be disrupted selectively appears promising enough to pursue further.

Does the idea that distinct modules or cortical regions participate in the representation of different kinds of information imply the existence of multiple independent memory systems? It all depends on how one defines such notions as "memory system" and "multiple memory systems." In a recent article, Sherry and Schacter (1987) defined a memory system as an interaction among acquisition, retention, and retrieval mechanisms that is characterized by certain rules of operation, and suggested that the notion of *multiple memory systems* should be invoked only when two putative systems are characterized by fundamentally different rules of operation. It was argued further than the existence of distinct modules that represent domain-specific information need not imply multiple memory systems, because each of the modules could be operating according to similar rules—that is, using the same basic mechanisms of storage and retrieval. Psychological students of memory have long accepted the idea that memories are composed of multiple "attributes" or "components" (e.g., Bower, 1967; Underwood, 1969). One could think of individual modules as being the source of the various attributes of a memory, without subscribing to a "multiple memory systems" view in the sense outlined by Sherry and Schacter. However, Sherry and Schacter did argue that neurobiological, neuropsychological, and evolutionary considerations all pointed toward a distinction between memory systems roughly equivalent to the declarative/procedural (Cohen & Squire, 1980) or the habit/memory (Mishkin et al., 1984) dichotomies. Neuropsychological data have demonstrated a double dissociation between skill learning and declarative remembering (e.g., Butters, 1987; Heindel, Butters, & Salmon, 1988), and both these results and findings from animal lesion studies (e.g., Mishkin et al., 1984) suggest that the basal ganglia play a critical role in the procedural/habit system. As noted earlier, in the present framework the declarative system has input links with CAS, whereas the procedural/habit system does not.

An important and as yet unresolved question concerns whether further distinctions among memory systems need to be made within the realm of declarative memory. As noted previously, the existence of domain-specific modules that represent different types of declarative information need not imply multiple systems in the sense of Sherry and Schacter (1987), that is, systems that operate according to different rules. The best known attempt to distinguish memory systems within the declarative realm is of course Tulving's (1972, 1983) episodic/semantic distinction, where episodic memory is identified with recollection of specific personal experiences and semantic memory is identified with general knowledge of the world. This is not the place to debate the merits and drawbacks of the episodic/semantic distinction, but it should be noted that the evidence for it from studies of both normal and amnesic subjects is equivocal (e.g., McKoon, Ratcliff, & Dell, 1986; Tulving, 1984, 1986).

Although the episodic/semantic distinction may be problematic, there does seem to be a need to distinguish in some manner between newly acquired declarative information and old or overlearned declarative information. One important reason for this is the dissociation observed in many amnesic patients between access to old and newly acquired information. Amnesics are generally able to gain conscious access to various kinds of overlearned semantic information acquired well before their illness (e.g., vocabulary, job-related knowledge), and in cases of restricted medial temporal damage like H. M. (Corkin, 1984) and R. B. (Zola-Morgan, Squire, & Amaral, 1986), patients can retrieve autobiographical episodes that predate their illness by more than a few years. Similarly, studies of retrograde amnesia in ECT patients have reported evidence of a temporal gradient: Access to information acquired during the 2–3 years prior to the onset of amnesia is severely impaired, whereas access to information acquired in the more remote past is preserved (Squire, Slater, & Chace, 1975).

These kinds of observations suggest that old or overlearned information (both autobiographical and non-autobiographical) has a different representational status than does newly acquired information. In order to avoid creating new terminology, I use the terms "knowledge modules" or "semantic memory modules" to refer to the representation of the various types of old, overlearned information and "declarative/episodic memory" to refer to the representation of newly acquired information. However, the distinction adopted here differs from Tulving's insofar as it does not subscribe to the idea that the critical difference between "episodic" and "semantic" memory is the autobiographical/non-autobiographical nature of the target information.

One promising account of the observed differences is accessibility of old and new information in amnesic patients has been offered by Squire, Cohen, and Nadel (1984). They argued that the hippocampus (and medial temporal region more generally) interacts with cortical areas where information is stored for some time—perhaps up to several years—after learning. As suggested by Teyler and DiScenna (1986), who have put forward similar ideas, ". . . each experiential event is represented in a unique spatio-temporal array of neocortical modules," and "The role of the hippocampus is to store a map or index of those cortical modules activated by the experiential event" (p. 149). By this view, the hippocampal–cortical interaction is necessary for newly acquired information to achieve coherence and stability. When such stability is achieved, the medial temporal region is no longer needed to maintain the cortically based representation, and the now consolidated information exists independently of the medial temporal area. What I have referred to as "declarative/episodic memory" roughly corresponds to the various representations (e.g., new facts, specific personal experiences) that are dependent on the hippocampus and medial temporal region. By contrast, when I speak of "knowledge modules" or "semantic memory modules" I am referring to the cortical modules that represent various types of information independently of the medial temporal region. However, the present view of the functional role of the medial temporal region differs somewhat from the view of Squire et al. and Teyler and DiScenna. Rather than—or perhaps in addition to—consolidating or organizing the representation itself, I suggest that the medial temporal region provides a temporary access route to CAS while a more "permanent" route is being built from the cortical modules that represent the new memory to CAS (see Moscovitch et al., 1986, for a similar idea). That is, a new declarative representation is dependent on the hippocampus to gain access to CAS until a direct access route to CAS is established. Whether or not such a direct or permanent route to CAS is built would probably depend on a variety of factors, such as the salience of a recent experience, the frequency with which it is retrieved, and so forth. Thus, whereas conscious recollection of a recent experience is initially dependent on the participation of the medial temporal region, if that experience is subsequently brought to mind often enough, a direct route from cortical sites that represent the oft-retrieved experience to CAS will be constructed. As Teyler and DiScenna (1986) suggested, ". . . continual reactivation of a particular hippocampal index would have a slowly incrementing effect on the cortical circuitry it indexes. If this is the case, the hippocampal index would, with time, result in the ability of the cortex alone to match to the pattern of experientially activated cortical modules" (p. 150). They further speculated that ". . . an often reaccessed index would become cortically based at a faster rate than one rarely indexed" (p. 150).

With respect to amnesic patients, if a direct route from the cortical modules that represent an experience to CAS has been established, so that conscious access no longer depends on the hippocampus, patients should be able to show conscious recollection of that experience. However, retrieval of such an experience would entail access to what has been called "semantic autobiographical knowledge" (e.g., Butters & Cermak, 1986; Tulving, Schacter, McLachlan, & Moscovitch, 1988)—frequently repeated and thus overlearned information about personal experiences. It has been noted that the "episodic" memories that amnesic patients do retrieve are typically oft-repeated bits of "family folklore" (Cermak & O'Connor, 1983) that predate the onset of amnesia by many years. According to the present view, these are the only kinds of personal experiences that severely amnesic patients should have conscious access to, because in these cases a route to CAS was established before the medial temporal region was damaged. (For purposes of expositional clarity, I am referring only to cases of "pure" medial temporal amnesia. When cortical areas are damaged, thereby presumably disrupting or degrading the representations themselves, different patterns will be observed.) Most memories from just prior to the onset of amnesia ought to be consciously inaccessible, because these would be dependent on a medial temporal route to CAS. And, of course, conscious recollection of new experiences will be severely compromised for the same reason.

This latter point brings us back to the major reason for suggesting that the medial temporal region may serve as an access route to CAS—namely, that some aspects of new experiences can be expressed implicitly by amnesic patients, thereby indicating that they are represented at some level in the system. As suggested earlier, newly acquired information can gain access to verbal and motor response systems through routes that do not involve CAS. Thus, amnesic patients may be able to spew forth bits and pieces of recently acquired information, and in some cases, show priming effects that depend on the establishment of new associations. But the expression of such information lacks any sense of familiarity or recollective experience. By the present view, this is because new representations are dependent on the medial temporal region to gain access to CAS. A further observation that is consistent with this view is that in cases of ECT-induced retrograde amnesia, which is thought to result from disruption of the medial temporal region (Squire, 1987), many memories from 1–2 years prior to ECT that are subject to retrograde amnesia are eventually recovered (Squire et al., 1975; Squire, Slater, & Miller, 1981). Although some memories from just prior to ECT appear to be lost permanently (Squire, 1987), the fact that a significant proportion of them recover indicates that ECT-induced retrograde amnesia cannot be just a "wiping out" of representations (see also chapter 14, this volume); a temporary loss of access to awareness is also involved.

ALTERNATIVE VIEWS
OF MEMORY AND CONSCIOUSNESS

It was noted at the beginning of the chapter that few investigators have addressed the memory and consciousness issue. However, some ideas have been put forward, and it is instructive to compare them to the present view. Tulving (1985a, 1985b) has argued that different memory systems are ". . . characterized by different kinds of consciousness" (1985a, p. 388)—procedural memory is associated with "anoetic" (non-knowing) consciousness, semantic memory with "noetic" (knowing) consciousness, and episodic memory with "autonoetic" (self-knowing) consciousness. The main difference between Tulving's approach and the present one is that he argued that the various kinds of consciousness are *properties* of specific memory systems: "Noetic (knowing) consciousness is an aspect of the semantic memory system . . . Autonoetic (self-knowing) consciousness is a necessary correlate of episodic memory" (1985a, p. 388). By contrast, I have suggested that conscious experiences of knowing and remembering depend on the interaction between specific memory modules or systems and a separate awareness system. Although the informational output of a particular memory system will determine the content of awareness, the system itself has no particular "awareness" as an integral feature of it. One advantage of the present view is that it allows for, and can make sense of, implicit memory for episodic information. In Tulving's scheme, episodic information is by definition explicit and consciously accessible, so the demonstration of implicit memory for episodic information necessitates the postulation of yet another memory system (e.g., the "QM" system; Tulving, 1983), one that is not endowed with the property of consciousness. It remains to be determined whether such a system exists.

The idea that awareness of remembering is not an integral feature of a specific memory system has been advocated by Jacoby (1984). He argued that awareness of remembering depends on the active use of a *fluency heuristic* that enables one to attribute "pastness" to a particular mental event. Lockhart (1984) has also advocated this idea. Although it is similar in some respects to the present view, one problem with the attribution view is that it implies that amnesic patients have lost the ability to make appropriate inferences or attributions, and I know of no evidence to this effect. Similarly, it is not clear how this attribution idea could be applied to the implicit/explicit dissociations in various neuropsychological syndromes that are crucial to the present view.

Another approach to memory and consciousness is found in Johnson's (1983) MEM model. Johnson distinguished between reflection, perceptual, and sensory subsystems, each of which handles and stores different kinds of information. She noted that each of the subsystems interacts with attentional mechanisms in different ways. The outputs of the reflection and perceptual subsystems are accessible to awareness, and are thus involved in conscious remembering. However, Johnson pointed out that these systems can influence performance without gaining access to awareness. In addition, Johnson's sensory subsystem, a procedural-like system that is largely involved in perceptual and motor learning, normally does not have access to awareness (1983, p. 89). Thus, Johnson's ideas are clearly similar in spirit to those put forward here.

CONCLUDING COMMENTS:
THREE PREDICTIONS

The ideas put forward in this chapter are rather general, and they probably raise more questions than they answer. A good deal more effort will have to be put into specifying the nature of the various systems that comprise DICE, the mechanisms by which they interact, and the conditions under which they become disconnected. For example, it would be desirable to specify the rules or mechanisms that regulate priority of access to the conscious system—that is, the means of determining which modular outputs gain access to CAS and which do not. Similarly, it is necessary to describe in greater detail the retrieval routes involved when information is expressed in the absence of conscious remembering. It is also important to delineate criteria for determining which amnesic patients suffer from disconnection between CAS and declarative/episodic memory, and which suffer from damage to the memory system itself. These and other problems will have to be addressed in order to enhance both the descriptive and explanatory power of the set of ideas that have been discussed.

Despite the rather general nature of the present framework, it does provide a basis for making predictions, and I conclude by noting three of them. First, DICE predicts that it should be possible to demonstrate implicit memory for the contextual features of newly acquired information in amnesic patients with "pure" disconnection of declarative/episodic memory from CAS. As noted earlier, some of the data on implicit memory for new associations are suggestive of such an outcome. However, they do not demonstrate it conclusively. In most existing instances of implicit memory for new information in amnesic patients, the kind of information that is expressed implicitly differs from the kind of information that cannot be expressed explicitly. Therefore, these observations can be interpreted as indicating that the kind of contextual information necessary for explicit, conscious remembering is either not encoded or not retained by amnesic patients. According to the present ideas, however, this information is available, in the sense that it can influence verbal and motor response systems via routes that do not involve CAS, but cannot be brought to the level of conscious awareness in "disconnected" amnesic patients. Accordingly, it should be possible to demonstrate implicit memory for global context (e.g., time and space) in at least some amnesic patients.

A second, related prediction is that it should be possible to demonstrate some implicit memory for information acquired by an amnesic patient in the several years prior to the onset of amnesia. As stated earlier, patients typically cannot consciously recall experiences from this period; according to DICE, this is because such experiences still require the hippocampal system in order to gain access to CAS. But if the appropriate implicit memory test could be devised, it should be possible to show that these experiences can be primed and thus affect verbal or motor response systems independently of any recollective experience on the part of the patient. In fact, we have recently reported suggestive observations along these lines (Tulving et al., 1988). A related prediction concerns the phenomenon of shrinking retrograde amnesia, briefly alluded to earlier when noting that memories subject to retrograde amnesia are often recovered. In some cases, shrinkage of retrograde amnesia follows a temporal pattern in which older memories are recovered before more recent ones (e.g., Benson & Geschwind, 1967). By the present view, recovery of memories subject to retrograde amnesia reflects the gradual re-establishment of an access route to CAS. Accordingly, if appropriate implicit measures of remote memory could be devised, the temporal pattern of shrinkage apparent on explicit measures should not be observed.

Third, DICE makes predictions regrading the kinds of double dissociations that should be possible in cases of neuropsychological impairment. For example, the procedural system, which in the present scheme subserves habit or skill learning, is held to be separate from declarative memory structures and independent of CAS. Accordingly, it should be possible to find patients who have deficits in skill learning but have no difficulty with conscious remembering. Recent evidence indicates that patients with Huntington's disease partly fit this description (Butters, 1987; Heindel et al., 1988). DICE also predicts that another kind of double dissociation ought to occur—it should be possible to find patients who fail to show implicit memory for words, sentences, and other kinds of declarative information (i.e., priming effects) but have normal explicit memory for that information. Such a pattern of performance would occur if the output of a particular memory module were disconnected from verbal/motor response systems, but the route from that module to CAS remained intact (see Fig. 18.1). As far as I know, no results of this kind have been reported. It has been documented that some Alzheimer patients do not show priming effects (Shimamura et al., 1987), but these patients also have deficits in explicit remembering; their priming failure likely reflects a degradation of cortical representations rather than a disconnection (Shimamura et al., 1987). The idea that it ought to be possible to find patients who show explicit but not implicit memory for declarative information represents a novel prediction of DICE, and could lead to empirical discoveries that might not otherwise have been made.

If the foregoing predictions are not confirmed, there would be grounds for rejecting the basic tenets of DICE. In so doing, however, valuable clues could be provided concerning the nature of the relation between memory and consciousness.

ACKNOWLEDGMENTS

This chapter was supported by a Special Research Program Grant from the Connaught Fund, University of Toronto, by Grant No. U0361 from the Natural Sciences and Engineering Research Council of Canada, and by a Biomedical Research Support Grant from the University of Arizona. I am grateful to Laird Cermak, Peter Graf, Larry Jacoby, John Kihlstrom, Bob Lockhart, Mary Pat McAndrews, Susan McGlynn, Morris Moscovitch, Lynn Nadel, Roddy Roediger, and Endel Tulving for helpful comments and discussion concerning many of the ideas presented in this chapter.

REFERENCES

Allport, D. A. (1979). Conscious and unconscious cognition: A computational metaphor for the mechanism of attention and integration. In L.-G. Nilsson (Ed.), *Perspectives on memory research*, (pp. 61–82). Hillsdale, NJ: Lawrence Erlbaum Associates.

Allport, D. A., & Funnell, E. (1981). Components of the mental lexicon. *Philosophical Transactions of the Royal Society of London, B 295*, 397–410.

Amyes, E. W., & Nielsen, J. M. (1955). Clinicopathologic study of vascular lesions of the anterior cingulate region. *Bulletin of the Los Angeles Neurological Society, 20*, 112–130.

Anderson, J. R. (1976). *Language, memory, and thought*. Hillsdale, NJ: Lawrence Erlbaum Associates.

Andrewsky, E. L., & Seron, X. (1975). Implicit processing of grammatical rules in a classical case of agrammatism. *Cortex, 11*, 379–390.

Baars, B. J. (1983). Conscious contents provide the nervous system with coherent, global information. In R. J. Davidson, G. E. Schwartz, & D. Shapiro (Eds.), *Consciousness and self-regulation* (vol. 3, pp. 41–79). New York: Plenum.

Bargh, J. A., & Pietromonaco, P. (1982). Automatic information processing and social perception: The influence of trait information presented outside of conscious awareness on impression formation. *Journal of Personality and Social Psychology, 43,* 437–449.

Barris, R. W., & Schuman, H. R. (1953). Bilateral anterior cingulate gyrus lesions. *Neurology, 3,* 44–52.

Bauer, R. M. (1984). Autonomic recognition of names and faces in prosopagnosia: A neuropsychological application of the guilty knowledge test. *Neuropsychologia, 22,* 457–469.

Benson, D. F., & Geschwind, N. (1967). Shrinking retrograde amnesia. *Journal of Neurology, Neurosurgery, and Psychiatry, 30,* 539–544.

Bisiach, E., & Luzzati, C. (1978). Unilateral neglect of representational space. *Cortex, 14,* 129–133.

Bisiach, E., Luzzati, C., & Perani, D. (1979). Unilateral neglect, representational schema and consciousness. *Brain, 102,* 609–618.

Bisiach, E., Vallar, G., Perani, D., Papagno, C., & Berti, A. (1986). Unawareness of disease following lesions of the right hemisphere: Anosognosia for hemiplegia and anosognosia for hemianopia. *Neuropsychologia, 24,* 471–482.

Blumstein, S. E., Milberg, W., & Shrier, R. (1982). Semantic processing in aphasia: Evidence from an auditory lexical decision task. *Brain and Language, 17,* 301–315.

Bower, G. H. (1967). A multicomponent theory of the memory trace. In K. W. Spence & J. T. Spence (Eds.), *The psychology of learning and memory* (vol. 1, pp. 229–325). New York: Academic Press.

Brain, W. R. (1941). Visual disorientation with special reference to lesions of the right cerebral hemisphere. *Brain, 64,* 244–272.

Brooks, D. N., & Baddeley, A. D. (1976). What can amnesic patients learn? *Neuropsychologia, 14,* 111–122.

Bruce, V., & Young, A. W. (1986). Understanding face recognition. *British Journal of Psychology, 77,* 305–327.

Butters, N. (1987, February). *Procedural learning in dementia: A double dissociation between Alzheimer and Huntington's disease patients on verbal priming and motor skill learning.* Paper presented to International Neuropsychological Society, Washington.

Butters, N., & Cermak, L. S. (1986). A case study of the forgetting of autobiographical knowledge: Implications for the study of retrograde amnesia. In D. C. Rubin (Ed.), *Autobiographical memory* (pp. 257–282). Cambridge: Cambridge University Press.

Campion, J., Latto, R., & Smith, Y. M. (1983). Is blindsight an effect of scattered light, spared cortex, and near-threshold vision? *The Behavioral and Brain Sciences, 6,* 423–486.

Cermak, L. S. (Ed.). (1982). *Human memory and amnesia.* Hillsdale, NJ: Lawrence Erlbaum Associates.

Cermak, L. S., Blackford, S. P., O'Connor, M., & Bleich, R. P. (in press). The implicit memory ability of a patient with amnesia due to encephalitis, *Brain Cognition.*

Cermak, L. S., Bleich, & Blackford, S. P. (1988). Deficits in the implicit retention of new associations by alcoholic Korsakoff patients, *Brain Cognition, 7,* 312–323.

Cermak, L.S., & O'Conner, M. (1983). The retrieval capacity of a patient with amnesia due to encephalitis. *Neuropsychologia, 21,* 213–234.

Cermak, L. S., Talbot, N., Chandler, K., & Wolbarst, L. R. (1985). The perceptual priming phenomenon in amnesia. *Neuropsychologia, 23,* 615–622.

Cohen, N. J. (1984). Preserved learning capacity in amnesia: Evidence for multiple memory systems. In L. R. Squire & N. Butters (Eds.), *Neuropsychology of memory* (pp. 83–103). New York: Guilford Press.

Cohen, N. J., & Squire, L. R. (1980). Preserved learning and retention of pattern-analyzing skill in amnesia: Dissociation of "knowing how" and "knowing that." *Science, 210,* 207–209.

Corkin, S. (1984). Lasting consequences of bilateral medial temporal lobectomy: Clinical course and experimental findings in H.M. *Seminars in Neurology, 4,* 249–259.

Coslett, H. B. (1986, June). *Preservation of lexical access in alexia without agraphia.* Paper presented at the 9th European Conference of the International Neuropsychological Society, Veldhoven, The Netherlands.

Critchley, M. (1953). *The parietal lobes.* New York: Hafner Publishing Company.

Crovitz, H. F., Harvey, M. T., & McLanahan, S. (1979). Hidden memory: A rapid method for the study of amnesia using perceptual learning. *Cortex, 17,* 273–278.

Damasio, A. R. (1985). Disorders of complex visual processing: Agnosias, achromatopsia, Balint's syndrome, and related difficulties of orientation and construction. In M. M. Mesulam (Ed.), *Principles of behavioral neurology* (pp. 259–288). Philadelphia: F. A. Davis.

deHaan, E. H. F., Young, A., & Newcombe, F. (1987). Face recognition without awareness. *Cognitive Neuropsychology, 4,* 385–415.

Diamond, R., & Rozin, P. (1984). Activation of existing memories in the amnesic syndrome. *Journal of Abnormal Psychology, 93,* 98–105.

Dimond, S. J. (1976). Brain circuits for consciousness. *Brain, Behaviour and Evolution, 13,* 376–395.

Dunn, R. (1845). Case of suspension of the mental faculties. *Lancet, 2,* 588–590.

Eich, J. E. (1984). Memory for unattended events: Remembering with and without awareness. *Memory & Cognition, 12,* 105–111.

Eslinger, P. J., & Damasio, A. R. (1985). Preserved motor learning in Alzheimer's disease, *Journal of Neuroscience, 6,* 3006–3009.

Fodor, J. A. (1983). *The modularity of mind.* Cambridge, MA: MIT Press.

Forster, K. I., & Davis, C. (1984). Repetition priming and frequency attenuation in lexical access. *Journal of Experimental Psychology: Learning, Memory, and Cognition, 10,* 680–698.

Frederiks, J. A. M. (1985). Disorders of the body schema. In J. A. M. Frederiks (Ed.), *Handbook of clinical neurology* (vol. 1, pp. 373–393). Holland: Elsevier.

Gardner, H. (1983). *Frames of mind.* New York: Basic Books.

Gazzaniga, M. S. (1985). *The social brain.* New York: Basic Books.

Geschwind, N. (1982). Disorders of attention: A frontier in neuropsychology. *Philosophical Transactions of the Royal Society of London, B298,* 173–185.

Glisky, E. L., Schacter, D. L., & Tulving, E. (1986). Computer learning by memory-impaired patients: Acquisition and retention of complex knowledge. *Neuropsychologia, 24,* 313–328.

Glisky, E. L., & Schacter, D. L. (1987). Acquisition of domain-specific knowledge in organic amnesia: training for computer-related work. *Neuropsychologia, 25,* 893–906.

Glisky, E. L., & Schacter, D. L. (in press). Extending the limits of complex learning in organic amnesia: computer training in a vocational domain. *Neuropsychologica.*

Gordon, H. W., Bogen, J. E., & Sperry, R. W. (1971). Absence of deconnexion syndromes in two patients with partial section of the neocommissures. *Brain, 94,* 327–336.

Graf, P., & Mandler, G. (1984). Activation makes words more accessible, but not necessarily more retrievable. *Journal of Verbal Learning and Verbal Behavior, 23,* 553–568.

Graf, P., & Schacter, D. L. (1985). Implicit and explicit memory for new associations in normal and amnesic subjects. *Journal of Experimental Psychology: Learning, Memory, and Cognition, 11,* 501–518.

Graf, P., & Schacter, D. L. (1987). Selective effects of interference on implicit and explicit memory for new associations. *Journal of Experimental Psychology: Learning, Memory, and Cognition, 12,* 45–53.

Graf, P., Shimamura, A. P., & Squire, L. R. (1985). Priming across modalities and priming across category levels: Extending the domain of preserved function in amnesia. *Journal of Experimental Psychology: Learning, Memory, and Cognition, 11*, 385–395.

Graf, P., Squire, L. R., & Mandler, G. (1984). The information that amnesic patients do not forget. *Journal of Experimental Psychology: Learning, Memory, & Cognition, 10*, 164–178.

Heindel, W. C., Butters, N., & Salmon, D. P. (1988). Impaired learning of a motor skill in patients with Huntington's disease. *Behavioral Neuroscience, 102*, 141–147.

Hilgard, E. R. (1977). *Divided consciousness.* New York: Wiley.

Hirst, W. (1982). The amnesic syndrome: Descriptions and explanations. *Psychological Bulletin, 91*, 435–460.

Holtzman, J. D., Sidtis, J. J., Volpe, B. T., Wilson, D. H., & Gazzaniga, M. S. (1981). Dissociation of spatial information for stimulus localization and the control of attention. *Brain, 104*, 861–872.

Jacoby, L. L. (1984). Incidental versus intentional retrieval: Remembering and awareness as separate issues. In L. R. Squire & N. Butters (Eds.), *Neuropsychology of memory* (pp. 145–156). New York: Guilford Press.

Jacoby, L. L., & Dallas, M. (1981). On the relationship between autobiographical memory and perceptual learning. *Journal of Experimental Psychology: General, 110*, 306–340.

Johnson, M. (1983). A multiple-entry, modular memory system. In G. H. Bower (Ed.), *The psychology of learning and motivation* (vol. 17, pp. 81–123). New York: Academic Press.

Johnson, M. K., Kim, J. K., & Risse, G. (1985). Do alcoholic Korsakoff's syndrome patients acquire affective reactions? *Journal of Experimental Psychology: Learning, Memory, and Cognition, 11*, 27–36.

Johnson-Laird, P. (1983). *Mental models.* Cambridge: Harvard University Press.

Karmiloff-Smith, A. (1986). From meta-processes to conscious access: Evidence from children's metalinguistic and repair data. *Cognition, 23*, 95–147.

Kihlstrom, J. F. (1984). Conscious, subconscious, unconscious: A cognitive perspective. In K. S. Bowers & D. Meichenbaum (Eds.), *The unconscious reconsidered* (pp. 149–211). New York: Wiley.

Kinsbourne, M., & Wood, F. (1982). Theoretical considerations regarding the episodic–semantic memory distinction. In L. S. Cermak (Ed.), *Human memory and amnesia* (pp. 195–217). Hillsdale, NJ: Lawrence Erlbaum Associates.

Koehler, P. J., Endtz, L. J., Te Velde, J., & Hekster, R. E. M. (1986). Aware or non-aware. On the significance of awareness for the localization of the lesion responsible for homonymous hemianopia. *Journal of the Neurological Sciences, 75*, 255–262.

Korsakoff, S. S. (1889). Etude médico-psychologique sur une forme des maladies de la mémoire. *Revue Philosophique, 28*, 501–530.

Kunst-Wilson, W. R., & Zajonc, R. B. (1980). Affective discrimination of stimuli that cannot be recognized. *Science, 207*, 557–558.

Landis, T., Regard, M., & Serrant, A. (1980). Iconic reading in a case of alexia without agraphia caused by a brain tumor: A tachistoscopic study. *Brain and Language, 11*, 45–53.

Lockhart, R. S. (1984). What do infants remember? In M. Moscovitch (Ed.), *Infant memory* (pp. 131–143). New York: Plenum.

Luria, A. R. (1966). *Higher cortical functions in man.* London: Tavistock.

Luria, A. R. (1976). *The neuropsychology of memory.* Washington: V. H. Winston.

Lynch, J. C. (1980). The functional organization of posterior parietal association cortex. *The Behavioral and Brain Sciences, 3*, 485–534.

Mandler, G., Nakamura, Y., Van Zandt, B. J. S. (1987). Nonspecific effects of exposure on stimuli that cannot be recognized. *Journal of Experimental Psychology: Learning, Memory, and Cognition,13*, 646–649.

Marcel, A. J. (1983). Conscious and unconscious perception: Experiments on visual masking and word recognition. *Cognitive Psychology, 15*, 197–237.

Marcel, A. J. (1986). Consciousness and processing: Choosing and testing a null hypothesis. *The Brain and Behavioral Sciences, 9*, 40–41.

Margolin, D., Friedrich, F., & Carlson, N. (1983). Visual agnosia and optic aphasia: A continuum of visual-semantic dissociation. *Neurology, 33*, 242.

Marshall, J. C. (1984). Multiple perspectives on modularity. *Cognition, 17*, 209–242.

McAndrews, M. P., Glisky, E. L., & Schacter, D. L. (1987). When priming persists: Long-lasting implicit memory for a single episode in amnesic patients. *Neuropsychologia, 25*, 497–506.

McGlynn, S. M., & Schacter, D. L. (in press). Unawareness of deficits in neuropsychological syndromes. *Journal of Clinical and Experimental Neuropsychology*.

McKoon, G., & Ratcliff, R. (1979). Priming in episodic and semantic memory. *Journal of Verbal Learning and Verbal Behavior, 18*, 463–480.

McKoon, G., & Ratcliff, R. (1986). Automatic activation of episodic information in a semantic memory task. *Journal of Experimental Psychology: Learning, Memory, and Cognition, 12*, 108–115.

McKoon, G., Ratcliff, R., & Dell, G. (1986). A critical evaluation of the semantic/episodic distinction. *Journal of Experimental Psychology: Learning, Memory, and Cognition, 12*, 295–306.

Mesulam, M.-M. (1981). A cortical network of directed attention and unilateral neglect. *Annals of Neurology, 10*, 309–325.

Mesulam, M.-M. (1983). The functional anatomy and hemispheric specialization for directed attention—the role of the parietal lobe and its connectivity. *Trends in Neuroscience, 6*, 384–387.

Mesulam, M.-M. (1985). Attention, confusional states, and neglect. In M.-M. Mesulam (Ed.), *Principles of behavioral neurology* (pp. 125–168). Philadelphia: F. A. Davis Co.

Mesulam, M.-M., & Geschwind, N. (1978). On the possible role of neocortex and its limbic connections in the process of attention and schizophrenia: Clinical cases of inattention in man and experimental anatomy in monkey. *Journal of Psychiatric Research, 14*, 249–259.

Mesulam, M.-M., Van Hoesen, G. W., Pandya, D. N., & Geschwind, N. (1977). Limbic and sensory connections of the inferior parietal lobule (area PG) in the rhesus monkey: A study with a new method for horseradish peroxidase histochemistry. *Brain Research, 136*, 393–414.

Mesulam, M.-M., Waxman, S. G., Geschwind, N., & Sabin, T. D. (1976). Acute confusional states with right middle cerebral artery infarctions. *Journal of Neurology, Neurosurgery, and Psychiatry, 39*, 84–89.

Milberg, W., & Blumstein, S. E. (1981). Lexical decision and aphasia: Evidence for semantic processing. *Brain and Language, 14*, 371–385.

Milberg, W., Blumstein, S. E., & Dworetzky, B. (in press). Processing of lexical ambiguities in aphasia. *Brain and Language*.

Milner, B. (1982). Some cognitive effects of frontal lobe lesions in man. In D. E. Broadbent & L. Weiskrantz (Eds.), *The neuropsychology of cognitive function* (pp. 211–226). London: The Royal Society.

Milner, B., Corkin, S., & Teuber, H. L. (1968). Further analysis of the hippocampal amnesic syndrome: 14 year follow-up study of H.M. *Neuropsychologia, 6*, 215–234.

Mishkin, M. (1982). A memory system in the monkey. *Philosophical Transactions of the Royal Society of London [Biology], 298*, 85–95.

Mishkin, M., Malamut, B., & Bachevalier, J. (1984). Memories and habits: Two neural systems. In J. L. McGaugh, G. Lynch, & N. M. Weinberger (Eds.), *Neurobiology of learning and memory* (pp. 69–77). New York: Guilford Press.

Moscovitch, M. (1982). Multiple dissociations of function in amnesia. In L. S. Cermak (Ed.), *Human memory and amnesia* (pp. 337–370). Hillsdale, NJ: Lawrence Erlbaum Associates.

Moscovitch, M., Winocur, G., & McLachlan, D. (1986). Memory as assessed by recognition and reading time in normal and memory-impaired people with Alzheimer's disease and other neurological disorders. *Journal of Experimental Psychology: General, 115*, 331–347.

Mountcastle, V. B. (1978). Some neural mechanisms for directed attention. In P. A. Buser & A.

Rougeul-Buser (Eds.), *Cerebral correlates of conscious experience*, INSERM Symposium No. 6 (pp. 37–51). Amsterdam: North-Holland.

Mountcastle, V. B. (1979). An organizing principle for cerebral function: The unit module and the distributed system. In F. O. Schmitt & F. G. Worden (Eds.), *The neurosciences fourth study program* (pp. 21–42). Cambridge, MA: MIT Press.

Nauta, W. J. H. (1971). The problem of the frontal lobe: A reinterpretation. *Journal of Psychiatric Research, 8,* 167–187.

Neisser, U. (1976). *Cognition and reality: Principles and implications of cognitive psychology.* San Francisco: Freeman.

Nielsen, J. M., & Jacobs, L. J. (1951). Bilateral lesions of the anterior cingulate gyri. *Bulletin of the Los Angeles Neurological Society, 16,* 231–234.

Nisbett, R. E., & Wilson, T. D. (1977). Telling more than we can know: Verbal reports on mental processes. *Psycholgical Review, 84,* 231–259.

Nissen, M. J., & Bullemer, P. (1987). Attentional requirements of learning: Evidence from performance measures. *Cognitive Psychology, 19,* 1–32.

Norman, D. A., & Shallice, T. (1986). Attention to action. Willed and automatic control of behavior. In R. J. Davidson, G. E. Schwartz, & D. Shapiro (Eds.), *Consciousness and self-regulation* (vol. 4, pp. 1–18). New York: Plenum Press.

Posner, M. I. (1978). *Chronometric explorations of mind.* Hillsdale, NJ: Lawrence Erlbaum Associates.

Posner, M. I. (1980). Mental chronometry and the problem of consciousness. In P. W. Jusczyk & R. M. Klein (Eds.), *The nature of thought* (pp. 95–113). Hillsdale, NJ: Lawrence Erlbaum Associates.

Posner, M. I., Inhoff, A. W., Friedrich, F. J., & Cohen, A. (1987). Isolating attentional systems: A cognitive-anatomical analysis. *Psychobiology, 15,* 107–121.

Reason, J. T. (1979). Actions not as planned. In G. Underwood & R. Stevens (Eds.), *Aspects of consciousness,* (pp. 67–89). London: Academic Press.

Richards, W. (1973). Visual processing in scotomata. *Experimental Brain Research, 17,* 333–347.

Roediger, H. L. III, & Blaxton, T. A. (1987). Retrieval modes produce dissociations in memory for surface information. In D. S. Gorfien & R. R. Hoffman (Eds.), *Memory and cognitive processes: The Ebbinghaus centennial conference* (pp. 349–379). Hillsdale, NJ: Lawrence Erlbaum Associates.

Schacter, D. L. (1985). Priming of old and new knowledge in amnesic patients and normal subjects. *Annals of the New York Academy of Sciences, 444,* 41–53.

Schacter, D. L. (1987). Implicit memory: History and current status. *Journal of Experimental Psychology: Learning, Memory, and Cognition, 13,* 501–518.

Schacter, D. L., Bowers, J., & Booker, J. (in press). Intention, awareness, and implicit memory: The retrieval intentionality criterion. In S. Lewandowsky, K. Kirsner, & J. Dunn (Eds.), *Implicit memory: theoretical issues.* Hillsdale, NJ: Lawrence Erlbaum Associates.

Schacter, D. L., & Graf, P. (1986a). Effects of elaborative processing on implicit and explicit memory for new associations. *Journal of Experimental Psychology: Learning, Memory, and Cognition, 12,* 432–444.

Schacter, D. L., & Graf, P. (1986b). Preserved learning in amnesic patients: Perspectives from research on direct priming. *Journal of Clinical and Experimental Neuropsychology, 8,* 727–743.

Schacter, D. L., Harbluk, J. L., & McLachlan, D. R. (1984). Retrieval without recollection: An experimental analysis of source amnesia. *Journal of Verbal Learning and Verbal Behavior, 23,* 593–611.

Schacter, D. L., McAndrews, M. P., & Moscovitch, M. (1988). Access to consciousness: Dissociations between implicit and explicit knowledge in neuropsychological syndromes. In L. Weiskrantz (Ed.), *Thought without language* (pp. 242–278). Oxford: Oxford University Press.

Sergent, J. (1987). A new look at the human split brain. *Brain, 110,* 1375–1392.

Shallice, T. (1981). Neurological impairment of cognitive processes. *British Medical Bulletin, 37,* 187–192.

Shallice, T. (1982). Specific impairments of planning. In D. E. Broadbent & L. Weiskrantz (Eds.), *The neuropsychology of cognitive function* (pp. 199–209). London: The Royal Society.

Shallice, T., & Saffran, E. (1986). Lexical processing in the absence of explicit word identification: Evidence from a letter-by-letter reader. *Cognitive Neuropsychology, 3,* 429–458.

Sherry, D. F., & Schacter, D. L. (1987). The evolution of multiple memory systems. *Psychological Review, 94,* 439–454.

Shimamura, A. P. (1986). Priming effects in amnesia: Evidence for a dissociable memory function. *Quarterly Journal of Experimental Psychology, 38A,* 619–644.

Shimamura, A. P., & Squire, L. R. (1984). Paired-associate learning and priming effects in amnesia: A neuropsychological study. *Journal of Experimental Psychology: General, 113,* 556–570.

Shimamura, A. P., Salmon, D., Squire, L., & Butters, N. (1987). Memory dysfunction and word priming in dementia and amnesia. *Behavioral Neuroscience, 101,* 347–351.

Sloman, S. A., Hayman, C. A. G., Ohta, N., & Tulving, E. (1988). Forgetting and interference in fragment completion. *Journal of Experimental Psychology: Learning, Memory, and Cognition, 14,* 223–239.

Sperry, R. W. (1969). A modified concept of consciousness. *Psychological Review, 76,* 532–536.

Squire, L. R. (1986). Mechanisms of memory. *Science, 232,* 1612–1619.

Squire, L. R. (1987). *Memory and brain.* New York: Oxford University Press.

Squire, L. R., & Cohen, N. J. (1984). Human memory and amnesia. In J. McGaugh, G. Lynch, & N. Weinberger (Eds.), *Proceedings of the conference on the neurobiology of learning and memory* (pp. 3–64). New York: Guilford Press.

Squire, L. R., Cohen, N. J., & Nadel, L. (1984). The medial temporal region and memory consolidation: A new hypothesis. In H. Weingartner & E. Parker (Eds.), *Memory consolidation* (pp. 185–210). Hillsdale, NJ: Lawrence Erlbaum Associates.

Squire, L. R., Shimamura, A. P., & Graf, P. (1987). Strength and duration of priming effects in normal subjects and amnesic patients. *Neuropsychologia, 25,* 195–210.

Squire, L. R., Slater, P. C., & Chace, P. M. (1975). Retrograde amnesia: Temporal gradient in very long-term memory following electroconvulsive therapy. *Science, 187,* 77–79.

Squire, L. R., Slater, P. C., & Miller, P. M. (1981). Retrograde amnesia following ECT: Long-term follow-up studies. *Archives of General Psychiatry, 38,* 89–95.

Stuss, D. T., & Benson, D. F. (1986). *The frontal lobes.* New York: Raven Press.

Teyler, T. J., & DiScenna, P. (1986). The hippocampal memory indexing theory. *Behavioral Neuroscience, 100,* 147–154.

Tranel, D., & Damasio, A. R. (1985). Knowledge without awareness: An autonomic index of facial recognition by prosopagnosics. *Science, 228,* 1453–1454.

Tulving, E. (1972). Episodic and semantic memory. In E. Tulving & W. Donaldson (Eds.), *Organization of memory* (pp. 381–403). New York: Academic Press.

Tulving, E. (1983). *Elements of episodic memory.* Oxford: The Clarendon Press.

Tulving, E. (1984). Multiple learning and memory systems. In K. M. J. Lagerspetz & P. Niemi (Eds.), *Psychology in the 1990's* (pp. 163–184). North-Holland: Elsevier Science Publishers B. V.

Tulving, E. (1985a). Ebbinghaus's memory: What did he learn and remember? *Journal of Experimental Psychology: Learning, Memory, and Cognition, 11,* 485–490.

Tulving, E. (1985b). How many memory systems are there? *American Psychologist, 40,* 385–398.

Tulving, E. (1986). What kind of a hypothesis is the distinction between episodic and semantic memory? *Journal of Experimental Psychology: Learning, Memory, and Cognition, 12,* 307–311.

Tulving, E., Schacter, D. L., McLachlan, D. R., & Moscovitch, M. (1988). Priming of semantic autobiographical knowledge: A case study of retrograde amnesia. *Brain and Cognition,* 3–20.

Tulving, E., Schacter, D. L., & Stark, H. A. (1982). Priming effects in word-fragment completion are independent of recognition memory. *Journal of Experimental Psychology: Learning, Memory, and Cognition, 8,* 336–342.

Underwood, B. J. (1969). Attributes of memory. *Psychological Review, 76,* 559–573.

Vallar, G., & Perani, D. (1986). The anatomy of unilateral neglect after right-hemisphere stroke lesions. A clinical/CT-scan correlation study in man. *Neuropsychologia, 24,* 609–622.

Warrington, E. K. (1962). The completion of visual forms across hemianopic field defects. *Journal of Neurosurgery and Psychiatry, 25,* 208–217.

Warrington, E. K. (1975). The selective impairment of semantic memory. *Quarterly Journal of Experimental Psychology, 27,* 635–657.

Warrington, E. K., & Shallice, T. (1984). Category specific semantic impairments. *Brain, 107,* 829–954.

Warrington, E. K., & Weiskrantz, L. (1968). New method of testing long-term retention with special reference to amnesic patients. *Nature, 217,* 972–974.

Warrington, E. K., & Weiskrantz, L. (1974). The effect of prior learning on subsequent retention in amnesic patients. *Neuropsychologia, 12,* 419–428.

Warrington, E. K., & Weiskrantz, L. (1982). Amnesia: A disconnection syndrome? *Neuropsychologia, 20,* 233–248.

Weiskrantz, L. (1977). Trying to bridge some neuropsychological gaps between monkey and man. *British Journal of Psychology, 68,* 431–445.

Weiskrantz, L. (1980). Varieties of residual experience. *Quarterly Journal of Experimental Psychology, 32,* 365–386.

Weiskrantz, L. (1985). On issues and theories of the human amnesic syndrome. In N. Weinberger, J. McGaugh, & G. Lynch (Eds.), *Memory systems of the brain: Animal and human cognitive processes* (pp. 380–415). New York: Guilford Press.

Weiskrantz, L. (1986). *Blindsight.* New York: Oxford University Press.

Weiskrantz, L., & Warrington, E. K. (1979). Conditioning in amnesic patients. *Neuropsychologia, 17,* 187–194.

White, P. (1982). Beliefs about conscious experience. In G. Underwood (Ed.), *Aspects of consciousness* (pp. 1–25). London: Academic Press.

Whitty, C. W. M., & Lewin, W. (1960). A Korsakoff syndrome in the post-cingulectomy confusional state. *Brain, 83,* 648–653.

Winograd, T. (1975). Understanding natural language. In D. Bobrow & A. Collins (Eds.), *Representation and understanding* (pp. 185–210). New York: Academic Press.

Young, A. W. (1988). Functional organisation of visual recognition. In L. Weiskrantz (Ed.), *Thought without language* (pp. 78–107). London: Oxford University Press.

Zihl, J. (1980). 'Blindsight': Improvement of visually guided eye movements by systematic practice in patients with cerebral blindness. *Neuropsychologia, 18,* 71–77.

Zola-Morgan, S., Squire, L. R., & Amaral, D. (1986). Human amnesia and the medial temporal region: Enduring memory impairment following a bilateral lesion limited to the CA1 field of the hippocampus. *Journal of Neuroscience, 6,* 2950–2967.

19 Memory Attributions

Larry L. Jacoby
McMaster University

Colleen M. Kelley
Williams College

Jane Dywan
McMaster University

What word comes to mind as a completion for the following fragment: L—ST? A social psychologist with a Freudian bent might treat the fragment as a projective test, revealing enduring dispositions, particularly if the completion fits with Freudian concerns as in the case of LUST. A perception psychologist may focus on the constraints provided by the particular letters given, or the frequency of the completion word, as Broadbent (Broadbent & Broadbent, 1975) has done. A memory theorist may see the fragment as an indirect memory test and assume that the completion word was recently encountered, even if the circumstances of that encounter are not remembered. In this case, a completion such as LIST might be readily attributed to recent discussions of memory experiments. The attribution of a completion to the effects of memory, perception, or personality is probably sometimes justified. We suggest that not only do psychologists attribute observed effects to a source, but experimental subjects in an experiment do the same thing. A subject's claim that he or she remembers is an attribution of a response to a particular cause; that is, to the past. The subject differs from the experimenter, however, in that the subject has access to fewer control conditions than does the experimenter. Consequently, the subject's attributions will more often be in error. The particular word completion might be primarily due to the influence of memory but may be misattributed to some other source. We focus on misattributions of memory later. First, we argue for the necessity of an attributional analysis of remembering, and then provide a general framework for that approach.

We write this chapter to honor Endel Tulving for his contribution to our understanding of human memory. Tulving has a great talent for picking an important issue, and then taking a controversial position on it. In doing so, he focuses the attention of the field on a topic that might otherwise have been neglected. We emulate that style by making claims that are likely to be controversial. We also hope to honor Endel by our focus on an issue that he has found important.

Recently, Tulving has emphasized the importance of the subjective experience of remembering (e.g., Tulving, 1983). Differences in subjective experience may be the quality that most clearly differentiates amnesics from people with normally functioning memories. As noted in many of the chapters in this volume, amnesics often show evidence of memory in their objective performance of a task although they deny having the subjective experience of remembering. Tulving accounts for this dissociation by proposing that remembering relies on an episodic memory system that is separate from the memory system that produces effects of prior experience on performance. The separate memory systems are assumed to differ in terms of representations. Episodic memory preserves the details of a particular event, whereas other memory systems preserve more general information. In contrast, we argue that the subjective experience of remembering is not a direct manifestation of a particular kind of representation. Using a memory representation is neither necessary nor sufficient for the subjective experience of remembering. Rather, we claim that subjective experience involves an attribution or unconscious inference that is as much a function of the present as a record of the past.

The Need for An Attributional Analysis of Remembering

People often use memory of a prior experience to help accomplish a present task without consciously remembering the prior experience. We (Jacoby & Kelley, 1987) have thought about the separability of the use of memory and conscious recollection in terms of Polanyi's (1958) distinction between using a tool versus inspecting it as an object. When using a hammer to pound in a nail, we attend to the nail; the hammer is treated as a tool. In contrast, we can attend to the hammer as a thing in itself, and focus on its weight and appearance. In both cases, the hammer is the same object, but we treat it differently. Similarly, memory is a tool when we solve problems, write papers, perceive and comprehend events, and so on. When memory is a tool, the focus of attention is not on the memory as such but on the present task. However, the same memory can be the object of attention, and it will then be experienced consciously. When memory is an object, the focus of attention is on the past.

However, an analysis in terms of retrieval processes or focus of attention is incomplete. What is missing from such an analysis is the subjective experience of remembering, and it is subjective experience that is the hallmark of remembering. Many others (e.g., James, 1892; Lockhart, 1984; Titchener, 1928; Tulving, 1983) have noted that remembering is more than reviving a copy of an original event. The subjective experience of remembering also involves a feeling of familiarity or "pastness," a reference of the present to the past. Without such a feeling of familiarity, we do not claim to *remember,* as such. To illustrate, suppose you were confronted with incontestable evidence that you said or did something. Even so, you could comfortably insist that you did not remember making the statement or committing the act. Although the objective record must be accepted, it does not substitute for the subjective experience of remembering. Whereas researchers have concentrated on the objective validity of memory claims, it is the subjective experience of remembering that seems most fundamental to the rememberer. In this chapter, our focus is on the subjective experience of remembering, its basis, and its antecedents.

The subjective experience of remembering is a compelling and distinctive feeling of familiarity. It may cause people to believe that they are using a different "faculty" when they are remembering than when they are perceiving, imagining, thinking, or solving problems. The feeling of familiarity is experienced as an unlearned primitive quality of the memory system in operation. A logical possibility is that the feeling of familiarity totally reflects properties of the memory trace so that having and using a memory trace is necessary and sufficient to produce a subjective experience of remembering. If so, the subjective experience of remembering would be closely tied to representation. An inability to experience remembering would be readily understood as the absence of a corresponding representation. For example, an amnesic incapable of experiencing remembering may lack the ability to represent particular aspects of episodes, such as time and place.

However, the tie between representation and subjective experience is actually a loose one. Amnesics who do not experience remembering nonetheless have memory representations that they can use to interpret homophones (Jacoby & Witherspoon, 1982), complete word stems (Warrington & Weiskrantz, 1974), or answer questions (Schacter, Harbluk, & McLachlan, 1984). A contrasting case is the experience of remembering without a corresponding memory representation, that is, confabulation. Amnesics are sometimes convinced of the validity of their answers to questions about the past even when they are wrong (Mercer, Wapner, Gardner, & Benson, 1977). Bowers and Hilgard (1986) provided further examples to show that the subjective experience of remembering can be uncoupled from the presence or absence of a memory representation that corresponds to it for normal people as well as for amnesics.

The lack of correspondence between subjective experience and a veridical memory representation can be dramatic as in cryptomnesia or unconscious plagiarism (Reed, 1974). A famous case of cryptomnesia involved Helen Keller (Bowers & Hilgard, 1986). When she was 11 years old, she wrote a short story that was published. Readers found the story to be very similar in theme and even wording to a story published earlier by another writer. She denied copying the story and had no memory of having "heard" it before writing her story. However, a family friend remembered telling it to her via sign language 3 years earlier. Helen apparently used the memory for the story as a tool in her own writing, without consciously remembering it. That is, it came to mind without an accompanying feeling of familiarity. Mark Twain came to her defense by claiming that most of literature is plagiarized, unintentionally and otherwise. Much the same can be said for science.

Disputes about what actually happened are common. Sutton (1984) described the conflicting memories of two physicists who won the Nobel Prize in 1957 for their discovery that the radioactive decay of many atomic nuclei is not completely symmetric with respect to space and time. Their accounts of the events leading up to their discovery are also not symmetric. Chen Ning Yang's account of their work in his *Collected Papers* so distressed his partner Tsung Dao Lee that he felt compelled to produce his own account of the events in question. The accounts differ in points such as who said what in a crucial meeting in a restaurant in New York, whether Yang and Lee both met with Einstein in his office, or only Yang, and whether Enrico Fermi influenced their thinking or did not. Apparently, both Lee and Yang have reconstructed plausible accounts of their collaboration and have invested these reconstructions with the status of remembering. Both experience a compelling feeling of remembering for the events they are reporting, although at least one of the two must be in error. Neisser (1982) pointed to similar examples in John Dean's memories reported during his testimony in the Watergate hearings, memories that Nixon's tapes later proved were false, although Dean's confidence led many to believe that his memory was excellent.

The feeling of familiarity is not to be found residing in a memory representation. Mismatches between subjective experience and memory representations imply that the subjective experience of remembering is an attribution or inference. We think of such inferences as unconscious, analogous to Helmholtz's notion of unconscious inferences in perception. Lockhart (1984) also argued that remembering is an inference about the past, and cited William James as an ally in reaching this conclusion. If familiarity is an inference, the absence of familiarity in amnesia is not necessarily due to the absence of a memory representation. Although representations obviously play a role in remembering, the presence of a memory representation is neither a necessary nor a sufficient condition for the subjective experience of remembering. To understand remembering, it is necessary to view the feeling of familiarity as the result of an inference or an attribution, and attempt to gain some understanding of the bases for making that particular attribution.

If we identify the *feeling* of familiarity as similar to an emotion, we could then apply an attributional analysis similar to that used to understand other emotions (e.g., Schachter & Singer, 1962). Although there has been recent interest in memory for emotional events and the effects of emotions on memory (e.g., Bower, 1981), the feeling of familiarity has not been generally regarded as itself being a type of affective experience. In this chapter, we illustrate the attributional analysis of emotional experience in normal subjects and apply a similar analysis to the feeling of familiarity.

According to Schachter (e.g., Schachter & Singer, 1962), an emotional state is the result of the interaction between nonspecific physiological arousal and a cognition about the arousing situation. Physiological arousal determines the intensity of an emotion, but not the particular emotion. Cognition about the cause of the arousal determines the particular emotion, if any, that is experienced. The cognitive processes involved are assumed to occur very rapidly and to be unavailable to conscious introspection.

To reveal the contribution of cognition to the experience of emotions, experimental situations are arranged such that emotional experience is actually a *misattribution* of arousal. Schachter and Singer (1962) injected subjects with adrenalin in conditions that could be interpreted as either frustrating or pleasurable. Subjects experienced the adrenalin-induced arousal as either anger or happiness, depending on the contextual cues. Those particular results have been criticized (see Reisenzein, 1983), but when subjects are aroused by exercising and then enter an emotional situation, they also experience intensified emotions (Zillmann, 1978), in line with an attributional theory of emotion.

For us, the important point taken from Schachter's theory of emotion is that some nonspecific experience is attributed to a particular cause, and so experienced as a particular emotion. In an attributional analysis of the feeling of familiarity, the ease with which an idea comes to mind or the relative fluency of accomplishing a task might serve a role similar to physiological arousal in Schachter's analysis of emotions. Titchener (1928) may have had such fluency in mind when he stated: "If we take . . . the pattern of consciousness in recollection, we find what may be figuratively described as a reconstruction along the line of least resistance" (p. 414). Similarly, Baddeley (1982a) suggested that the ease with which ideas "pop into mind" can be taken as evidence that one is remembering. We (e.g., Jacoby & Dallas, 1981) have suggested that perceptual fluency can serve as a basis for the feeling of familiarity in recognition memory decisions. Items that were read during study were perceptually identified more readily at the time of test than were "new" items, and this difference in identification may underlie the feeling of familiarity. The claim is in accord with subjects' reports that the old items seem to "jump out" on a test of recognition memory.

As in Schachter's account of emotion, an inference regarding the cause of fluency is important for the experience of remembering. The question "Do you remember?" directs us to attribute to the past those ideas that come to mind readily, and so experience remembering. However, if remembering is an attribution, it should be possible to produce misattributions by arranging it so that something other than the past is the most salient cause of an idea coming to mind. For example, when we are writing, old ideas that come to mind may not be attributed to the past, but may instead be experienced as new ideas and perhaps as particularly good ones because of the authority with which they present themselves. The result would be the use of memory as a tool without the subjective experience of remembering—unintentional plagiarism. In later sections we provide evidence of misattributions of this sort as well as showing that the subjective experience of remembering can be produced without a corresponding veridical memory representation. First, however, we provide a general framework for our treatment of memory as an attribution. By doing so, we mean to emphasize the points that we think are most important.

Toward a General Framework for Remembering as Attribution

Remembering is an Attribution of Effects on Performance to the Past

In other investigations of familiarity and memory, familiarity has had the role of explanatory construct and has not itself been analyzed (c.f., Atkinson & Juola, 1974; Mandler, 1980). In contrast, we propose that the feeling of familiarity is not a given for theories of memory. Familiarity cannot be considered a necessary outcome of using a memory representation, nor is using a representation sufficient to produce the feeling of familiarity. Instead, we propose that there are processes that give rise to the subjective experience of remembering, and we outline our speculations about those processes.

We begin our speculation about the underpinnings of that subjective experience by looking to the larger class of effects of past performance. In the tradition of learning theory, we know that past experience on a task influences present performance from research across innumerable tasks, a variety of species, and the whole range of development. There is an old term in learning theories for such effects of the past on present performance—transfer effects. Positive transfer refers to cases in which past experience enhances present performance, allowing the present task to be performed more quickly, efficiently, fluently, or with greater accuracy. The past can also have a detrimental effect on present performance, and those effects are termed negative transfer.

We think differences in performance of the sort produced by transfer could serve as the basis for the subjective experience of remembering. People might learn to interpret variations in the fluency of their performance on current tasks as a sign that they are using the past. If transfer effects are quite specific rather than general, then those effects would be diagnostic of specific past experiences. Such specificity of transfer effects would make them both suitable and likely as an underpinning for the subjective experience of remembering. The subjective experience of remembering would depend on detecting very specific transfer effects, and learning to attribute them to the past. We should actually use the term "transfer-like effects", because people would really be learning to detect changes in performance of the sort that *could* be due to past experience. Such effects, whether really due to transfer from past experience or to some other factor such as general difficulty of a task, carry no guaranteed mark of their origin.

Recent work in memory development suggests that early experiences do show transfer effects of extreme specificity. Rovee-Collier (in press) tested infants' memory by conditioning them to kick in the presence of a particular crib mobile. (The kicking makes the mobile spin, which appears to be really rewarding for a 6-month-old). Rovee-Collier and her colleagues assessed the infants' memory for this experience by returning up to 2 weeks later, attaching the mobile to the crib, and observing their subjects' rate of kicking. Her subjects showed much better memory than was previously credited to infants. Most interesting to us is the extraordinary specificity of their "memories." Changing even small features of the mobile wiped out transfer of the kicking response to the new mobile. Effectively, the infants were behaving as if they recognized the old mobile and could discriminate it from very similar foils. Although we can't tell whether or not the infants in Rovee-Collier's studies experienced remembering, they exhibited a specificity of transfer that is diagnostic of past events, and so could serve as the basis for the experience of remembering. The acquisition of remembering would depend on learning to interpret these transfer effects as remembering. Changes in one's own performance would be cues that one has experienced something similar before.

Our analysis is similar to Brunswik's (1956) ecological approach to perception. By his lens model of perception, people search for cues in the environment that could serve as a basis for inferences. These inferences produce perceptual experiences, such as depth perception and size constancy. In contrast, in our analysis of remembering, the cues that signal prior experiences are more likely to be internal aspects of one's performance, such as fluency, rather than cues in the environment.

Correctly attributing transfer effects in one's own performance to their source in the past places one in the role of intuitive scientist (Kelley, 1973). It may be useful to first consider whether the task of correctly attributing transfer effects can be done by *any* scientist. That is, are cues in performance sufficiently diagnostic of the past? Imagine that you are an experimenter trying to assess whether a subject has ever learned to read French, but are not allowed to ask directly. You could easily give the subject some sentences in French to read and use his or her performance as an indicator of past experience. Next, you might try to assess whether he or she has read a particular sentence before. You could give the subject a number of sentences of equal difficulty and test whether any sentence is read more fluently than the other. Relative fluency would be the basis for inferences of particular past experiences. We think subjects as well as experimenters can use relative fluency to infer particular past experiences. However, subjects don't have access to the same control conditions that an experimenter can arrange. The subject observing his or her own performance on a set of sentences cannot differentiate between fluent performance on a particular sentence that is due to the past and fluency due to the relative difficulty of that sentence. As we will see, such limitations on the subject's inferences regarding the cause of fluency can lead to memory illusions that are analogous to perceptual illusions.

Transfer effects can occur at any level of activity—reading a word more fluently, solving a problem more easily, or even generating a train of ideas more readily. Although most of our experiments have measured perceptual fluency (Johnston, Dark, & Jacoby, 1985; Kelley, Jacoby, & Hollingshead, 1988), the notion of fluency as the basis for an attribution of familiarity is not restricted to the perceptual level of analysis. The familiarity of arguments, ideas, and other meaningful activities can also stem from an attribution of fluency. The most common reason for accepting an idea as a memory when we are trying to recall is the authority with which the idea presents itself. If an idea immediately comes to mind in response to a query, it is likely to be accepted as the answer. However, if fluency of an idea coming to mind is not sufficiently diagnostic of the past for remembering, people can engage in additional activities and assess the fluency of their processing on these new levels of analysis. For example, consider trying to answer a question such as "Did you eat dinner at La Casa a few weeks ago?". An image of sitting at a table in a restaurant might readily come to mind, but that image may not be sufficient to specify a particular visit to the restaurant. You then might elaborate on that train of thought until your elaborations narrowly specify an event. An additional detail might come to mind, such as "oh yes, we were discussing the election results" that would allow you to infer that you were truly "remembering" a specific event from several weeks ago. However, we take this experience of remembering as an attribution. An image is fluently generated, and that image includes specific details that are diagnostic of a particular prior experience. The transfer is assumed to occur between the actual event several weeks before and later fluent imagining of the event. But even the fluent generation of details can be open to error, as in the case of confabulation and errors of reconstruction. We discuss confabulation and manipulations that make people more likely to accept incorrect details that come to mind as memories in a later section on illusions of memory.

If transfer effects such as fluency are relatively specific to details of previous occurrence rather than widely generalizable, then its attribution to a source is typically correct. It is this specificity of fluency that makes it a useful heuristic for remembering. Part of the development of remembering may be learning to set ourselves cognitive tasks during retrieval that will be likely to show transfer from past experiences and rule out competing sources as explanations of our performance. Of course, we also have to engage in processing at the time of events that will lead to specific transfer effects later. Here, Tulving's emphasis on encoding specificity and distinctive processing also are important for determining transfer effects in an attributional analysis of remembering.

Although transfer can be correctly attributed to the past to produce remembering, other factors can also influence performance in ways that are indistinguishable from the effects of prior events, as illustrated by our example of completing the fragment L—ST. A particular idea may come to mind because the task is so tightly constrained that no other response is possible. Even very specific details that come to mind while attempting to remember an event do not guarantee that one is "really remembering." The details can represent the easy exercise of imagination, rather than transfer from past experience of an event. Errors of the opposite sort can also occur. Fluency that actually is a transfer effect of past experience can be misattributed to other sources, as in the case of cryptomnesia. The subjects' misattribution of fluency probably depends on their goal in a particular situation, as when they are solving a problem or writing a paper rather than remembering.

Attributions are Influenced by Goals and Contexts.   The major factor directing the attribution process is the goal set by subjects. If their goal is remembering, subjects will correctly attribute fluency to the past. If their goal is judging temporal duration, the difficulty of a problem, or the flow of a paper, fluency resulting from the past is likely to be misattributed to goal-relevant aspects of the situation. The goals may be quite explicit, or implicitly derived from the context in which fluency occurs. Of course, the subject's goal does not totally determine the course of attributions. People do sometimes spontaneously remember even when they are directed toward another task.

The importance of the goal in the experience of remembering is also relevant to the notion of remembering as an affective response. Goal-directed action is an important cause of emotions. For example, obtaining a goal creates happiness and satisfaction, whereas being blocked from a goal can produce anger or frustration. Similarly, familiarity and other affective aspects of remembering may increase when one's goal is remembering.

Our discussion of goals is relevant to descriptions of amnesia accompanied by frontal lobe damage, a deficit in the ability to form and pursue goals (Stuss & Benson, 1986). A goal directs processing and influences the attribution of effects on performance to a particular source. Remembering can be seen as setting successively more exacting goals designed to limit irrelevant sources of effects on performance and so allow more accurate attribution of familiarity. A failure to elaborate on the cues provided at the time of test restricts the opportunity for transfer to be experienced on various levels—conceptual as well as perceptual or motor. An inability to form and pursue the goal of remembering limits the opportunity for the subjective experience of remembering.

Implications for Dissociation of Remembering and Transfer Effects on Performance. How does our analysis of remembering as an attribution relate to various dissociations of transfer effects in performance and recognition? By other accounts, dissociations between remembering and transfer reflect the operation of different memory systems (e.g., Cermak, 1984; Cohen & Squire, 1980; Tulving, 1985). In contrast, we argue that "pastness" cannot be found in a memory trace but, rather, reflects an attribution of transfer in performance. Dissociation occurs when recognition is based on a different level of analysis than is the measure of transfer. For example, a dissociation will be seen if the experimenter measures transfer on the level of perceptual identification but the subject uses ease of generating context as a basis for recognition. However, if the experimenter measures transfer on the same level of analysis that the subject employs as a basis for remembering (e.g., perceptual identification and recognition based on perceptual fluency), dependence between transfer and remembering will be observed.

Our view emphasizes dependence between transfer and remembering, rather than emphasizing the dissociation of the two. By a memory-systems view, dissociations are important as evidence of separate memory systems. By our view, dissociations are easily obtained, but dependence can be even more revealing. The trick is the match between the transfer that is measured by the experimenter and the transfer used by the subject as a basis for an attribution of remembering. Dependence can reveal the cues and processes that underlie the subjective experience of remembering.

People Act on the Basis of Their Subjective Experience of Remembering. Most investigations of memory focus on the objective accuracy of performance. Such a focus may run contrary to the subjective experience of an individual. To illustrate, consider a behaviorist's objective definition of aggression as one person, perhaps a child, hitting another. The definition may be very unsatisfactory to the child. Upon being reprimanded for fighting, children often rightfully object that they were only playing. An act must be interpreted in a larger context rather than in isolation. Similarly, the subjective experience of remembering involves the interpretation of an act in the context of ongoing activity.

Why should we be concerned with subjective experience rather than being content to talk about objective memory performance? The subjective experience of remembering gives one the impetus to act. This important role for remembering is particularly striking when it is absent, as in the case of amnesics. Although amnesics can be encouraged to guess about the past, and often do so correctly, they are unwilling to trust that information enough to act on it. In the absence of remembering, we can misattribute the effects of memory used as a tool to other causes and so unwittingly change our interpretation of the present. We illustrate such misattributions in the next section of the chapter. The contrasting case of confabulation also points to the importance of the subjective experience of remembering. An illusion of memory can be as compelling a basis for action as a "real memory", but may have disastrous consequences. We review illusions of memory in the final section of the chapter.

REPRESENTATION WITHOUT REMEMBERING:
MEMORY MISATTRIBUTIONS

One effect of the past is increased fluency of perception and thinking. Words read once are more easily re-read later; an idea considered once comes to mind more readily later. The fluency of perceptual and conceptual operations can be correctly attributed to the past and experienced as remembering. However, the effects of the past are often difficult to distinguish from other determinants of subjective experience.

The effects of the past can be misattributed to physical characteristics of the present. The possibility of misattributions of this sort arose in investigations of the effects of prior presentation of a word on the fluency of later visual perceptual identification (Jacoby & Dallas, 1981). Several subjects in those studies reported that some words stayed on the screen longer, and so were easier to report. The words thought to have been presented for a longer duration were words that had been read in an earlier phase in the experiment. Witherspoon and Allan (1985) actually varied the duration of presentations and required subjects to judge duration. Words that had been presented previously were judged as staying on the screen longer than new words. That is, the effects of prior experience were misattributed to a present difference in temporal duration. Similar misattributions occurred in an experiment in which subjects listened to sentences presented against a noisy background (Jacoby, Allan, Collins & Larwill, 1988). Their task was to judge the loudness of the background noise and it was found that they judged it less loud when the foreground sentences were old rather than new. The prior experience of hearing the sentences increased the fluency with which they were perceived and comprehended at test. The easy perception of the old sentences was misattributed to a lower background noise level.

The "mere exposure effect" in studies of aesthetic preferences may also be a case of the misattribution of the effects of prior experience (Jacoby, 1984; Mandler, Nakamura, & Van Zandt, 1987; Seamon, Brody & Kauff, 1983). Subjects in those studies have shown a preference for stimuli such as random polygons or short melodies that occurred in an earlier phase of the experiment, relative to new stimuli (Kunst-Wilson & Zajonc, 1980; Moreland & Zajonc, 1977). Prior exposure presumably produces more fluent processing of the old items relative to the new items. Because subjects are asked "Which do you prefer?", they may misattribute the fluent processing of items to a characteristic of the items—that they have a good form or are particularly pleasing. Such a misinterpretation of the effects of the past as a pleasing quality of the stimulus rather than as a feeling of familiarity points again to parallels between the feeling of familiarity and other affective experiences.

Prior experience may also influence subjective experience used as a basis for more cognitive judgments. To illustrate this possibility, consider the case of judging the quality of writing. We typically judge whether a paper is well-written by our subjective experience of the flow of the paper as we read it. However, that experience changes with re-reading. We become increasingly adept at anticipating examples and following previously difficult arguments. Unfortunately, we are unable to separate the contribution of prior readings to our current subjective experience of "good flow" from the contribution of the structure and style of the paper. The influence of the structure of the paper and our prior readings may be integrally combined determinants of subjective experience. In that sense, we may speak of subjective experience as a nonanalytic basis for judgment (see, for example, Jacoby & Brooks, 1984). The effects of the past are misattributed to the quality of writing.

Hindsight:
Subjective versus Objective Bases for Judgments

The example of the influence of prior experience on judging the quality of writing is similar to a hindsight effect. Once given the outcome of an uncertain event, people find it nearly impossible to ignore that outcome and make predictions that are equivalent to those of the naive subject (e.g., Fischhoff, 1975). By our view, giving people the outcome of an uncertain event robs them of a fundamental basis for assessing uncertainty—their subjective experience of that uncertainty. People's experience and interpretation of later events is influenced even when they are told to disregard the earlier event.

Jane Collins, a graduate student at McMaster, recently obtained a hindsight effect in the paradigm requiring subjects to judge the loudness of background noise. In one condition, subjects made noise judgments and judged the background noise less loud when old versus new sentences were in the foreground. Subjects in the second condition were told about this effect and warned to try to avoid the effect on their noise judgments. However, these informed subjects produced exactly the same pattern of results as did uninformed subjects. They were unable to "ignore" the effects of prior presentation of sentences when making noise judgments.

Similarly, once informed about the answer to a problem, the problem often appears easy. If we judge the difficulty of problems by trying to solve them, but solving is made easier by being told the answer earlier, we may underestimate the difficulty of the problem for others. The only way to escape such a hindsight bias is to shift to an alternative basis for making judgments. We examined this possibility in experiments aimed at a hindsight bias in judging the difficulty of anagrams for others (Jacoby & Kelley, 1987).

To illustrate the paradigm, judge how difficult it would be for most people to solve the anagram "fscar." If you are like most of our subjects, you use your own experience of solving the anagram as a basis for judging its difficulty for others. Suppose you had read the solution to the anagram, scarf, in a list of words in an earlier phase of the experiment. Reading the solution would make it easier to later solve the anagram. If you continued to use your own subjective experience as a basis for predicting for others, you would underestimate the difficulty of the anagram. The effect of prior experience would be misattributed to the difficulty of the anagram.

We asked subjects to rate the difficulty of anagrams for others. They did use their own subjective experience of solving an anagram to judge difficulty, as shown by the finding that speed of solving anagrams correlated highly with rated difficulty. Reading the solution words in the first phase of the experiment substantially reduced the time to solve the anagrams encountered in the next phase, and also resulted in those anagrams being rated as easier for others to solve relative to the ratings of subjects who had not previously read the anagram solution words. People apparently misattributed the effects of prior experience to the anagram's being easy.

Can people avoid a hindsight bias by using a more objective basis for judgments? To illustrate such an objective basis for judgments in the anagram experiment, we arranged a condition that forced subjects to give up subjective experience as a basis for judgments. In that condition, the solutions to anagrams were given immediately before each anagram, e.g., "scarf fscar." The influence of reading the solution was meant to be inescapable and to block the subjective experience of solving the anagram. We predicted that those subjects would rely on rules for judging the difficulty of anagrams, such as "common words are easier to solve."

Subjects shown the anagrams accompanied by solutions made their ratings more slowly than did the others, which is consonant with using rules rather than an immediate impression of difficulty. This use of a more objective basis for judgments did diminish the hindsight bias. Anagrams presented with their solution words were rated as being more similar in difficulty to new anagrams than were anagrams whose solution words had been presented earlier. To gain further evidence of a qualitative difference in the basis for judgments, we collapsed ratings across subjects, and compared the patterns of relative difficulty ratings for anagrams accompanied by solutions versus anagrams without solutions (c.f. Rubin, 1985). The relatively low correlation of difficulty ratings between those conditions (.30) is consistent with the claim of qualitatively different bases for judgment. The ratings in the two conditions in which subjects could actually try to solve the anagrams correlated .71.

Why did subjects who had earlier read the solution words not recognize that their subjective experience was flawed and, consequently, use a more analytic basis for judgments? First, the success of that strategy depends on the availability of a good theory of anagram difficulty. Perhaps, rightfully so, they had little faith in their theory. As a criterion measure of anagram difficulty, we used the average solution times for anagrams that were new. Ratings of the difficulty of anagrams that were old but rated alone correlated .79 with actual difficulty, but the correlation was only .31 when the solutions accompanied the anagrams. That is, the use of flawed subjective experience did produce better predictions than did the use of a theory. Second, judgments based on subjective experience present themselves with an immediacy that contrasts with slower, more analytic judgments. That immediacy may give judgments based on subjective experience a powerful veridical quality, regardless of their true validity.

The misattribution of prior experience to a difference in anagram difficulty is essentially a hindsight bias and could be seen as egocentrism of the sort found in some classic Piagetian demonstrations of children's predictions for others (c.f. Olson, 1986; Piaget & Inhelder, 1956). For example, children mistakenly rely on their own subjective experience when they predict what another person can see. We think such egocentric behavior is not a characteristic of a general developmental stage that is replaced by more sophisticated judgments later. As shown in the anagram experiment, even adults rely on subjective experience to make judgments for others, despite the invalidation of that subjective experience by the effects of the past. Instead of being stage-specific, egocentrism may be domain-specific (Dasen, 1977; Gelman, 1978; Piaget, 1972). We may escape egocentrism when we develop an alternative, more objective basis for judgment in a particular domain. However, in other domains, decisions based on subjective experience are decidedly more efficient and accurate than those based on theory.

Subjective experience is a nonanalytic basis for judgments (Jacoby, 1988; Jacoby & Brooks, 1984). Many factors jointly determine the experienced difficulty of a task or the readiness with which an idea comes to mind without the subject's awareness or understanding of the influence of the separate factors. Such nonanalytic judgments are global or comprehensive. They reflect the influence of factors that may be subtle and complex, and so not captured by more analytic judgments. However, nonanalytic judgments may be affected by irrelevant factors, as when each re-reading increases our sense that a paper flows well. In contrast, people have more control over the information that enters an analytic judgment. Particular factors can be given more or less weight or even be ignored when a theory is used. When people recognize the irrelevant influence of prior experience, they can shift to an alternative, more analytic basis for judgment, and so escape the influence of prior experience. This, of course, requires that one's theory is adequate to the task, and that one has the time and resources to use the theory.

Mistaking the Specific for the General:
Discriminating Between Sources of Familiarity

General knowledge can be mistaken for memory of a specific event. Such errors have been interpreted as evidence that people use general schemas or scripts to reconstruct what must have happened on a particular occasion, and so mistake the general for the specific (e.g., Alba & Hasher, 1983). In contrast, experiments that we describe hereafter demonstrate that the confusion between general knowledge and memory for specific events is symmetrical. People are unable to discriminate between the "episodic" familiarity produced by presenting an item in the experimental setting and the "semantic" familiarity produced by general knowledge. Consequently, memory for the specific can be mistaken for the general as readily as the general can be mistaken for the specific. Such symmetrical errors would be difficult to accommodate in a schema model of memory. However, this symmetry is consistent with an attributional analysis of memory. Familiarity does not specify its source but, rather, is attributed to a particular source depending on the details of the experimental situation.

Dosher (1984) demonstrated that people mistakenly "recognize" semantically related items on a test of episodic memory, and concluded that people are unable to discriminate between episodic and semantic familiarity. We have reached the same conclusion; subjects mistake memory of a particular episode for general knowledge on a test of famous names. Our experiments (Jacoby, Kelley, Brown & Jasechko, in press; Jacoby, Woloshyn, & Kelley, in press) show that the familiarity of a name produced by simply reading it in the experiment can be mistaken for the general familiarity that characterizes a famous name. Reading a name in the first phase of an experiment increased the probability that it would later be judged "famous."

This false fame is a misattribution similar to the hindsight effect. Familiarity is a nonanalytic basis for fame judgments that does not allow subjects to ignore the irrelevant effect of prior presentation of the name in the experiment. As in the anagram experiment, people could use an alternative, more analytic basis for judgments of fame. For example, they could call a name famous only if they could recall what the person did to become famous.

In our experiments, people did shift to a more analytic basis for judgments when faced with the possibility of confusion between sources of familiarity. In one experiment, subjects in a baseline condition made fame judgments without having previously read names in the experiment. Another group made fame judgments after having seen half of the names in a prior phase. Those subjects were told that the earlier presentation of the names was uninformative regarding actual fame because half of those names were famous and half were nonfamous.

The results from that experiment are presented in Table 19.1. By comparing the judgments of new famous and new nonfamous names, we see evidence of a

TABLE 19.1
Probability of Judging a Name Famous

Test Condition	Famous		Nonfamous	
	Old	New	Old	New
Condition 1 (Baseline)	—	.66	—	.39
Condition 2	.74	.63	.32	.23

qualitative shift in the basis for fame judgments produced by the possibility of confusion between sources of familiarity. The discrimination, d', between new famous and new nonfamous names was higher when old names were included in the test list (1.47) than it was in the baseline condition (1.11). The old non-famous names reduced the validity of familiarity as a basis for fame judgments, so subjects shifted to more analytic judgments. However, they did not com-pletely rely on the more analytic basis for judging fame. Old names were still more likely to be called "famous" (.53) than were new names (.43), and this was true regardless of whether the names were truly famous or nonfamous. The familiarity gained from prior presentation was still sometimes misattributed to fame.

If people had been asked to recognize names rather than judge their fame, they might have correctly attributed the familiarity of old names to its source in the experiment. That is, familiarity might serve as a basis for either fame or recognition memory judgments, depending on the question that is asked. Also, recognition may have a basis that is more analytic than is judging the familiarity of the name (e.g., Atkinson & Juola, 1974; Jacoby & Dallas, 1981; Mandler, 1980). For example, retrieval of study context could serve as an analytic basis for recognition memory judgments.

We (Jacoby & Kelley, 1987; Jacoby, Woloshyn & Kelley, in press) have argued that treating memory as an object for conscious recollection involves a different goal and a different focus of attention than does using memory as a tool to accomplish some present task. The notion is that conscious recollection re-quires an attention-demanding act that is separate from the unconscious influ-ences of memory. Conscious recollection of the context and other particulars of the prior presentation of an item can serve as a more analytic basis for recogni-tion memory decisions, but it requires more processing than that necessary to assess the familiarity of the item. It should be possible to limit attention so that a person could not use conscious recollection to recognize items, but prior presen-tation of a name would still increase familiarity as measured by the fame test.

To obtain this separation of conscious recollection and familiarity, recogni-tion memory performance was placed in opposition to the increased familiarity of a name gained from its prior presentation. To do so, we presented only non-

TABLE 19.2
Probability of Judging a Name Famous

	Type of Name		
	Famous	Nonfamous	
Test Condition	New	New	Old
Full Attention	.54	.18	.13
Divided Attention	.49	.14	.28

famous names to be read in the first phase of the experiment and informed subjects that the names were not famous. Prior presentation is now relevant to the fame judgment—recognizing a name as coming from the first phase allows one to be certain that the name is nonfamous. The fame judgment test was given either under conditions of full or divided attention. In the divided-attention condition, subjects engaged in a listening task while simultaneously judging the fame of names presented visually. Dividing attention was expected to make it impossible to consciously recollect the names, but not to impair the experience of familiarity of old names. Consequently, in the divided-attention condition, old nonfamous names should seem familiar but not be recognized, making them *more* likely to be judged famous than new nonfamous names. In contrast, when full attention is given to the test, subjects should be able to use conscious recollection to recognize old nonfamous names, allowing them to be certain that those names are nonfamous. Thus, with full attention at test, old nonfamous names should be *less* likely to be called famous than new nonfamous names. The results of that experiment are shown in Table 19.2.

The results of this experiment are consistent with our claim that conscious recollection is an act that is separate from assessing the familiarity of a presented item. The higher probability of calling old as compared to new nonfamous names "famous" in the divided-attention condition suggests that reading a name increased its familiarity, without the name being recognized as previously read. In tests of recognition memory, subjects can use familiarity or the more analytic retrieval of context as a basis for recognition memory. The fame judgment task directs subjects to misattribute familiarity to fame, leaving only the analytic basis for recognition. Divided attention at test eliminates that basis for recognition memory, while leaving familiarity intact.

The procedure of placing conscious recollection in opposition to unconscious influences of memory is likely to be generally useful for separating different uses of memory. In many experiments, the conscious use of memory dictates the same response as an unconscious use of memory. For example, increased probability of completing a word fragment due to prior presentation of the word could result from either an unconscious influence of memory or from active retrieval of the prior presentation. This creates difficulties for interpretation, because unconscious influences of memory could actually be due to conscious recollection (e.g., Richardson-Klavehn & Bjork, 1988). Placing conscious recognition in opposition to the unconscious use of memory eliminates this difficulty. For example, in our experiment, recognition of a name dictated a different response (calling the name "nonfamous") than did a gain in the familiarity of the name (calling the name "famous"). This allows us to be certain that the false fame effect as a measure of unconscious memory is not mediated by conscious recollection of the names from the prior presentation.

Divided attention at test prevents people from checking the bases for their first impressions, a form of monitoring. Even without divided attention, people differ widely in the degree to which they engage in such activity. The elderly may be particularly poor at monitoring. A common complaint about older people is that they tell the same story repeatedly. Perhaps this repetition of stories is similar to the phenomenon of old nonfamous names being called famous when attention is divided at the time of test. Having told a story may make the story more readily come to mind later in the presence of the same audience. The elderly may become repetitive in part because they fail to check why the story came to mind. In line with this possibility, we (Dywan & Jacoby, 1988) have found that the elderly are more susceptible to the false fame of old nonfamous names than are younger subjects. Consistent with claims made by Craik (Craik & Byrd, 1982), age produces effects that parallel those of dividing attention; in this case, producing confusion between sources of familiarity.

In summary, the effects of prior experience can be misattributed and so change the subjective experience of the physical stimulus, influence affective judgments, produce hindsight effects, and make nonfamous names seem famous. These effects on subjective experience are important, because we often act on our subjective experience. For example, if we experience a problem as easy to solve, we are likely to draw a very different conclusion about a person who fails to solve the problems than we would if we had experienced the problem as being difficult to solve.

Judgments of problem difficulty or fame were nonanalytic with respect to the factor of irrelevant prior experience. In both cases, subjects could use a more analytic basis for judgment that would allow them to escape the irrelevant effects of the past. Subjects in the fame study used a more analytic basis for judging fame when faced with confusion between sources of familiarity. Subjects in the anagram study did not change to theory-based judgments, perhaps because they were not sensitive to the effects of prior reading of solution words on later anagram difficulty, or perhaps because their theories were not particularly good predictors of anagram difficulty. An analytic basis for recognition memory requires extra attentional resources at retrieval to specify source. These studies point to two bases for recognition memory. Familiarity is a nonanalytic basis for recognition that we have tracked by measuring its misattribution to sources other than the past. A more analytic basis for recognition is conscious recollection, that is, the generation of additional details of an event that more narrowly specifies its source in the past.

Divided attention at test produced difficulty in specifying the source of familiarity. Memory for source or context may be particularly poor in the elderly and in some forms of amnesia (Hirst, 1982; Schacter, Harbluk & McLachlan, 1984; Winocur & Kinsbourne, 1978). One interpretation of poor memory for source is that it reflects a generally weakened or degraded memory trace (e.g., Mayes & Meudell, 1981). However, the difficulties in specifying source when attention is divided at test cannot be accounted for by a degraded memory trace, because, of course, the trace would be equivalent to that of unimpaired subjects in the full attention condition. Instead, divided attention at test may prohibit subjects from elaborating on the test cue, thus limiting opportunity for transfer from study to test.

REMEMBERING WITH AND WITHOUT MEMORY REPRESENTATIONS: BASES FOR THE SUBJECTIVE EXPERIENCE OF REMEMBERING

In the previous sections, we considered the use of memory without the corresponding experience of remembering. Using memory as a tool without awareness that one is doing so can result in misattribution similar to the cryptomnesia or unintentional plagiarism illustrated earlier in the case of Helen Keller. However, the use of memory for a prior event is often accompanied by the subjective experience of remembering. By our emphasis on misattributions, we run the risk of underestimating the validity of memory claims. The fluency that was misattributed to fame or to the difficulty of problems could as easily be correctly attributed to the past, and be quite diagnostic of the past. Also, people can use a more analytic strategy for remembering, such as attempting to generate details of the original experience. We first present evidence to show that fluency can be used as a valid basis for memory claims. Next, we return to a discussion of memory errors by considering confabulation—the subjective experience of remembering without a corresponding veridical representation. We argue that the more analytic basis for remembering nonetheless rests on subjective experience and is also open to deception and misattribution.

Perceptual Fluency as a Basis for Remembering

An important factor that guides the direction of the attribution is the goal that is set for the subject. When asked about the past, effects of the past on fluency are likely to be correctly attributed to their source. Such correct attributions are likely because effects on fluency are relatively specific to reinstating details of the prior occurrence, rather than being widely generalizable. To illustrate the specificity, consider the task of judging whether one previously read or heard a word. If some words are originally read and others are originally heard, the read words have a larger advantage in later visual identification (Jacoby & Dallas, 1981; Morton, 1979). Thus, relative differences in perceptual fluency could serve as one basis for remembering modality of presentation. An item that is read very easily at the time of test is likely one that was read during study. If subjects base their judgment of whether an item was read or heard on relative perceptual fluency, we should see a positive correlation between ability to perceptually identify an item and the probability of judging it ''read.''

To check this possibility, we (Kelley, Jacoby, & Hollingshead, 1988) presented a set of words to subjects in the first phase of an experiment. Half of the words were read by the subject and half were heard. In the second phase, the old words and a set of new words were presented briefly on the screen of a CRT and followed by a pattern mask. Subjects attempted to identify each word as it was presented. Immediately after they attempted to identify a word, it appeared in full view with the question ''OLD OR NEW?''. Next, subjects judged whether they had read or heard the item.

We expected that subjects would often use perceptual fluency as a basis for remembering modality. Therefore, we predicted dependence between perceptual identification and modality judgments. Of course, subjects could rely on other bases for remembering modality. Within our attributional analysis of remembering, subjects could assess transfer in their performance on other levels of analysis, perhaps conceptual rather than perceptual. However, because subjects were not instructed to study the modality of presentation, we anticipated that perceptual fluency would be the primary basis for judging modality.

Dependence between perceptual identification and modality judgments might simply reflect variations in trace strength or item differences (e.g., Watkins & Gibson, 1988). To guard against such interpretations, we attempted to change the size of the correlation by reducing subjects' reliance on perceptual fluency as a basis for remembering modality. Whereas subjects in the first condition only read or listened to a word, subjects in a second condition were given a mnemonic for remembering modality that was to be used during study. The mnemonic would provide an alternative basis for remembering modality and so reduce the size of the correlation between perceptual identification and modality judgments. Subjects were told to think of negative aspects of words they read and positive aspects of words they heard. So, for example, if the word ''rugby'' were read, they might think of rugby as a bruising, painful sport, but if the word ''rugby'' were heard, they might think of rugby as an exciting and fun sport. The mnemonic was reversed for half of the subjects.

Table 19.3 shows the probabilities of calling a word ''read'' conditionalized on perceptual identification performance for each of the two conditions. Those probabilities were computed using modality judgments only for those items that were called ''old.'' As illustrated by the conditional probabilities, the mnemonic

TABLE 19.3
Probability of Calling a Word "Read" Conditionalized
on Perceptual Identification (For Items Called "Old")

| | Study Conditions | |
	Incidental	Mnemonic
P("Read") | PI)	.59	.48
P("Read") | $\overline{PI}$)	.36	.39
Difference	.23	.09

condition led to a substantially lower correlation between perceptual identification and modality judgment on the later recognition test than did the incidental condition that simply read or heard words in the first phase of the experiment. This conclusion is supported by a comparison of gammas in the two conditions, a measure of the relationship between perceptual identification and modality judgments. The gamma in the incidental condition (.46) was considerably higher than that in the mnemonic condition (.23).

Perceptual fluency is one of several bases for remembering modality. The mnemonic reduced subjects' reliance on perceptual fluency by allowing them to use the strategy of regenerating other details at test regarding modality of presentation. When reading words at test, a negative or positive aspect of each word presumably came to mind that served as the basis for remembering modality. Such a basis for remembering is more analytic than perceptual fluency, but it nonetheless requires that subjects attribute those aspects coming to mind to a particular source. It is not a perfectly reliable indicator of past experience, as it could also be susceptible to influences other than the specific episode.

This study clearly illustrates the variable relationship between effects on perception and memory judgments. The degree of dependence between the two was a function of the basis used for an attribution of modality. Similarly, the variable relationship between effects in perception and recognition memory performance reflects the basis used for recognition decisions (e.g., Johnston, Dark & Jacoby, 1985).

Memory Illusions

We *know* we are remembering when we can follow up one idea with supporting details (c.f., Baddeley, 1982b). Each detail increases our confidence that we are remembering rather than inventing, particularly if the details are idiosyncratic and there is no other plausible source for those ideas coming to mind. In addition to generating supporting details as a basis for remembering, Marcia Johnson and her colleagues (e.g., Johnson & Raye, 1981) have discussed other bases for the experience of remembering. Memory representations of perceived events include more spatial and temporal information and greater sensory detail than do memory representations of imagined events. The ability to generate such details might also be evidence that one is remembering, rather than imagining, at test. In line with this possibility, Schooler, Gerhard, and Loftus (1986) found that people use the amount of sensory detail in a memory report to distinguish memory for actual events from memory for suggested events. Particularly vivid imagery may also indicate that one is remembering, rather than imagining (Johnson, Raye, Wang, & Taylor, 1979). Memory images may be more vivid than those that are invented at the time of test. However, it is interesting to note that Titchener (1928) made precisely the opposite claim. He argued that memory images are less vivid and more uncertain than are invented ones.

Generating supporting details, particularly sensory and temporal details, provides a basis for greater certainty that we are remembering than does familiarity based on perceptual fluency. Such an analytic basis for memory judgments sharpens the relationship between memory representation and the subjective experience of remembering. It is an analytic basis for remembering in that gaining additional evidence reduces the contribution of irrelevant sources of transfer to current experience. However, we see the more analytic basis for remembering as nonetheless relying on an attribution to the past and as susceptible to misattributions. It is as reasonable to talk about the ease with which an idea comes to mind or the ease of making an argument and the corresponding familiarity of ideas and arguments as it is to talk about the fluency of perceptual processing and the familiarity of an item's appearance. Analytic and nonanalytic bases of remembering are relative terms. A process is analytic to the extent that it excludes irrelevant factors. For example, we described the analytic process of judging fame by generating an accomplishment for which someone became famous. That process excluded the irrelevant influence of reading the name earlier in the experiment. But ease of generating an accomplishment could also be affected by an earlier phase in the experiment. Imagine an experiment in which subjects read names paired with accomplishments such as "Sebastian Weisdorf—composer" before attempting to judge the fame of names. Fluency can occur on any level of analysis, and irrelevant sources of fluency may contaminate it as a basis for judgment. For supporting details to be accepted as remembered rather than invented they must be experienced as familiar. The ease with which those details come to mind is likely our basis for their being experienced as familiar, allowing even the analytic basis for remembering to be misled.

Source Confusions.   Although the ability to produce elaborations can be used as a way of monitoring sources of familiarity, they can themselves form the basis of misattributions. One cause of memory illusions is people's own elaborations upon the past. In a study of hypermnesia for the recall of pictures (Dywan, 1984), subjects studied simple line drawings, including such items as a rabbit and a bicycle. They tried to recall the items every day for a week using a forced recall paradigm (see for example, Erdelyi & Kleinbard, 1978). They also rated their confidence in their recall of each item on a scale from zero to four, with zero indicating that the item was simply a guess.

It soon became clear that one does not need 30 years, as in the case of the two physicists, for asymmetries to emerge between information as perceived and information as remembered. As the week progressed, hypermnesia, an increase in correct responses, was accompanied by a steady increase in the proportion of responses that were false positives or false negatives. That is, many correct items were given confidence ratings of zero, and many new items were reported to be memories with various levels of confidence. Even items correctly reported were not necessarily remembered with appropriate details. For example, when reviewing the slides at the end of the study, one young man accused the experimenter of changing the slide of the bicycle. He agreed that he had seen a bicycle during the initial stimulus presentation and had, in fact, reported "bicycle" on each recall trial but insisted that it had been a racing bike rather than the touring bike on the slide. In fact, he insisted that the original slide had been of a bike very much like his own which is how he remembered it so well!

We propose that the items generated repeatedly gained fluency—items were generated more easily on each trial and would eventually seem familiar irrespective of accuracy. To the extent that this occurs, each attempt to retrieve information should decrease the likelihood of it being accurately remembered. We explored the extent to which this was true by varying the number of interpolated recall trials that subjects undertook over the course of a week followed by a test of recognition memory (Dywan, Segalowitz, & Otis, in preparation). We found that recognition was best when subjects were never given the opportunity to recall the slides at all. Even one recall attempt lowered recognition accuracy by one third. Again, recalling that a bicycle had been seen, for example, made people less able to identify the particular bicycle that had been presented.

This propensity toward intrusions and source confusion seems to be a natural and inevitable result of cognitive operations. No attempt was made to influence what subjects would remember in the repeated recall studies. The leading question paradigm developed by Elizabeth Loftus and her colleagues takes advantage of this natural propensity and gives it a nudge (e.g., Loftus, 1981; Loftus, Miller & Burns, 1978; Loftus & Palmer, 1974). She found, moreover, that confidence for suggested memories can be as great as for memories based on actual perceptions (e.g., Cole & Loftus, 1979), and that subjects could provide detailed descriptions of these suggested memories. On one occasion, a nonexistent tape recorder was described as being "small, black, in a case, with no visible antenna" (Loftus, 1979, p. 62). Thus, the experience of "really remembering" as a function of the ability to generate related information is an attribution that can be influenced by irrelevant sources.

Laurence and Perry (1983) made very effective use of a leading question by incorporating it into the hypnotic context—in effect, giving the propensity for incorporating intrusions a more powerful nudge. They instructed hypnotized subjects to relive the events of a night during the previous week. In the course of this recollection, subjects were asked whether they had been awakened by some loud noises and were allowed to elaborate on that suggestion. Upon awakening from hypnosis, many of the subjects stated that the suggested event had actually occurred. Even after they were told that the event had been suggested to them, many remained adamant that they had "heard" the noises and supported their assertion by referring to specific events that they believed had accompanied the noises.

Occasionally, subjects will try to impose a more objective criterion on their own experience of retrieval. Laurence and Perry (1983) reported that some of those who stated correctly that the noises had been suggested to them by the hypnotist reached this conclusion in a reasoned fashion. For example, one subject decided that the noises were suggested because they were more vivid than any noise he felt could occur in reality. When uncertain about the source of a "memory," the subject resorted to using an analytic, theory-based decision process. In this case, the theory helped.

A subject in the repeated recall paradigm tried to use a theory-based decision process with less success. When reviewing the slides at the end of the study, this subject was surprised when she saw that a rabbit had been one of the stimulus items. She explained that each time she attempted to recall the slides, the image of a rabbit had come to her. However, she never put "rabbit" down as a memory because her image was of a white furry rabbit on a green lawn and she knew that the slides had been black-and-white line drawings. Perhaps this subject had spontaneously elaborated on the concept she was trying to remember and, on the basis of that elaboration, rejected the persistent rabbit as a memory. She probably held an implicit theory that memory was made up of immutable representations and was unaware that one can elaborate on one's memories as well as on events that never, in fact, occurred.

Retrieval Experience. To confirm the notion that the experience of retrieval—familiarity—is not an intrinsic part of the memory representation but an attribution, the experience of retrieval must be modified without altering the content of the memory system. However, most experimental manipulations occur at the study or input phase. Leading questions raise plausible scenarios, suggestions are made about noises in the night, or repeated retrieval attempts leave a confusing residue of intrusion errors. All of these strategies modify the contents of memory to some extent, they produce source confusions but don't clearly separate the experience of remembering from that which is remembered.

However, it is possible to change the experience of remembering without modifying the contents of memory. One can manipulate the cues that subjects use to infer that they are remembering and in so doing create illusions of memory. Hypnosis allows us to do this because it provides an opportunity to observe the retrieval process under conditions in which some of Johnson's reality monitoring parameters (e.g., Johnson & Raye, 1981) are modified in predictable ways. We know, for example, that subjects report enhanced imagery during hypnosis (e.g., Crawford & Allen, 1983; Gur & Reyher, 1976; Rothmar, 1983). Hypnosis also induces a sense of effortless experiencing (Bowers, 1978). Thus, hypnosis ought to change the quality of items generated during retrieval making them more like remembered events—vivid, detailed, and effortlessly generated.

Using the repeated recall paradigm described earlier, we found that hypnosis can operate during retrieval to create memory illusions even when no attempt is made to mislead subjects (Dywan & Bowers, 1983). Subjects initially saw pictures and attempted to recall the pictures once each day for a week to establish a baseline with respect to recall and errors. On the eighth day, half of the subjects were hypnotized and half were given motivating instructions for recall. Both conditions led subjects to believe that they should be able to recall more items, but the memory reports of the high hypnotizables in the hypnosis condition were clearly most affected. They thought that more of the items that they generated during recall trials were memories and reported higher levels of confidence in these items relative to their nonhypnotized counterparts. The false illusion of remembering was apparent, however, because most of these "new memories" were not from the original stimulus set. Even if memory performance was not objectively improved, the subjective experience of remembering was enhanced.

Hypnosis is a dramatic example of the attribution process at work, but we believe that the effects are simply an exaggeration of what occurs in normal cognitive experience. We believe that hypnotic effects are related to the manipulation of attention as are a number of the other effects we have reported in this chapter. We have demonstrated, for example, that one can alter the attributions that subjects will make about familiarity by directing their attention away from the retrieval aspects of the task, that is, towards background noise, the difficulty of anagrams, or the judgment of fame.

Although internal context plays an important part in the experience of retrieval, it is clear that environmental context can also be influential. A very important part of the environmental context is social. The choice of question influences what is recalled, and an interviewer's response can have subtle but powerful effects on subjective experience. Simply leaning forward when a person reports an event may communicate that the statement is significant. If your audience treats your story as a memory, you will be more likely to give it the status of a memory yourself.

Thinking of the subjective experience of remembering as an attribution is of more than academic interest when one moves into applied settings. It is alarming to think that invalid memory reports can be produced and adamantly defended when the arena is not a psychology lab but a court of law. A case in point is that of Michael Kempinski (People vs. Michael Kempinski, 1980). The only witness to a murder reported that he had seen someone running away from the scene of the crime but that he did not see the person clearly. Videotapes of the questioning procedure are very revealing in that one can watch "memories" being created. The witness was hypnotized and told that everything he had seen was stored in his memory and that if he kept trying, the original events would return to him. As the witness began to produce some tentative details, the officer became noticeably more interested and encouraged him to keep going. The witness became more excited as new details "came to him," and he eventually recognized the assailant as being a student from the local high school. The vividness of imagined events combined with the validation by an authority figure led to the experience of remembering. The newly created "memory" led eventually to Kempinski's arrest and may have led to a conviction except that an ophthalmologist testified that it would have been impossible to make an identification beyond 25 feet in the prevailing light conditions. The witness who had supplied the description had been 250 feet away in conditions of semi-darkness.

From the perspective of signal detection theory, the influence of hypnosis on memory performance could be described as a beta effect (e.g., Klatzky & Erdelyi, 1985). Increases in correctly reported items are offset by corresponding increases in incorrectly reported items. However, our claim is not that hypnosis makes memory better, but, rather, that it makes memory *seem* better. Our emphasis is on the subjective experience of remembering. Defining memory as an objective recounting of the past, as has typically been done by memory theorists, is like defining a person's emotional state as an objective account of his or her present life situation. Depression, for example, can be experienced even when it is seemingly not justified by the objective circumstances of a person's life. We propose that the subjective experience of remembering, like sadness or joy, is a feeling that can exist somewhat independently of the objective reality.

CONCLUDING COMMENTS

Titchener (1928) noted the importance of studying the feeling of familiarity, or "memory consciousness." He remarked that the introduction of nonsense syllables to the study of memory was, in a way, unfortunate because the precision of results and potential for quantitative analysis forced the problem of understanding memory consciousness to the background. Concern with the subjective experience of remembering has only recently again been brought to the front (e.g., Jacoby, 1984; Klatzky, 1984; Lockhart, 1984; Tulving, 1983). Understanding subjective experience is important because we use it as a basis for action and decisions. This is most evident in the case of dense amnesics who retain the ability to express memory for a prior experience in their performance but lack the subjective experience of remembering. Nearly as disruptive is the unwarranted subjective experience of remembering that accompanies confabulation. We rely on the subjective experience of remembering to maintain contact with our own past, to act in the present, and to plan for the future.

We have argued that awareness of the past is not to be found in a memory trace. Rather, the feeling of familiarity is best treated as being similar to other affective reactions in its reliance on an attribution process. When the situation directs subjects to a task other than remembering, fluency resulting from prior experience is misattributed to contemporary causes. We described experiments in which memory used as a tool lowered the subjective experience of background noise, lowered estimates of the difficulty of anagrams, and increased the fame of nonfamous names. In each case, subjects' judgments were based on their subjective experience, and that subjective experience was altered by the use of memory as a tool. In some domains, subjects attempted to avoid or limit the effects of prior experience on judgment by shifting to more analytic, theory-based judgments. This research illustrates misattributions of the effects of prior experience that are analogous to the case of unintentional plagiarism. Having—and even using—a memory representation of a prior event is not sufficient to insure the subjective experience of remembering.

Next, we considered the opposite case, in which subjects falsely attribute current experience to the past, and so "remember" without a memory representation. In remembering, even more analytic judgments rest on familiarity and are open to misattributions. Vividness and distinctiveness may be two qualities of thought that produce an inference of remembering, rather than imagining or guessing. If we effortlessly generate a complex image of a birthday party that includes the number of guests, the presents they brought, and the kind of icing on the cake, we are likely to experience that as a memory rather than as a confabulation. In this regard, hypnosis produces a sense of effortlessness when producing vivid and detailed imagery. Hypnosis may not increase the accuracy of recall, but can increase the likelihood that one will have the subjective experience of remembering.

We end this chapter on a speculative note regarding the goal of remembering in determining subjective experience. For the subjective experience of remembering, ideas that come to mind must be attributed to one's own efforts, rather than to the situation. Consider an analogous situation in learning how to play golf. A parent might try to correct a child's golf swing by telling him or her exactly where to put his or her feet for the best stance, adjusting the child's hands until he or she has the proper grip, and then standing behind the child and guiding his or her arms through the arc of a perfect swing. The child might be able to hit a beautiful shot with such assistance, but it is unlikely that he or she will feel the satisfaction of making the shot. Rather, the child will credit his or her performance to the parent. Similarly, we can structure a situation such that it is guaranteed to evoke evidence of a prior experience, but the "rememberer" is unlikely to feel that he or she is remembering. In this regard, it is interesting to note that unaware uses of memory often occur when responses are heavily constrained by the task.

These concerns make amnesics seem well justified in their claims that they are not remembering even when they show effects of prior experience in their performance. Dissociations between effects in performance and remembering are often produced by tightly structuring the test. For example, detecting savings on a task depends on creating a close match between the training and test situations. The test so constrains responding that amnesics may very reasonably attribute their performance to the current test situation rather than to the past, and so not experience remembering. This point can be illustrated with an example provided by Talland (1968).

Talland asked a man who was amnesic some questions about his family, including details about the forthcoming wedding of a younger brother. In response to Talland's detailed questions, the amnesic was able to provide a full report of the wedding plans. Because the man was quite concerned about his memory disorder, Talland complimented him on his memory performance. However, the man would not accept the compliment because he was convinced that all the information he had given actually had been *told* to him by Talland. Talland termed this misattribution *probole*, which is the Greek equivalent for projection, but without a motivational component. He speculated that it was caused by the highly structured nature of the interview that "programmed the patient's responses step by step" (p. 154). Talland found this misattribution of one's own recall to the questioner to be a strikingly odd error. Perhaps not. The patient's experience of hearing about the details of his brother's wedding plans, rather than remembering them, may be analogous to the golfer who credits the situation rather than himself or herself for the good shot. Perhaps the patient's attribution is at least as defensible as Talland's.

How does all of this relate to Tulving's proposal of separate memory systems? Once again, Endel Tulving has helped to focus our attention on an issue that we agree is an important one: the basis for the subjective experience of remembering. However, to account for awareness of the past, we think the functions accorded an episodic memory system will have to be considerably broadened. The difference between aware and unaware uses of the past cannot be fully accounted for in terms of differences among underlying memory representations or the factors controlling their retrieval. Having—or even using—a memory representation of a particular prior experience is neither a necessary nor a sufficient condition for producing the subjective experience of remembering. Rather, subjective experience involves an attribution or unconscious inference that is as much a function of the present as it is a record of the past. It is doubtful that the processes that are responsible for the inferences underlying awareness are unique to the subjective experience of remembering. We have been struck by the similarities among the problems of explaining perceptual experience, awareness of the past, the experience of affect, and the attribution of responsibility in social settings. To understand people's awareness of remembering, we need to address issues beyond the scope of traditional memory theories. The focus of Tulving and others on data from amnesics is informative for speculations about the basis for awareness of the past; however, we doubt that any single anatomical structure that is responsible for adding awareness of the past to other functions of memory will ever be found. Even if such a structure were found, its functions could not be understood in the absence of a satisfactory analysis of the processes that underlie the subjective experience of remembering.

ACKNOWLEDGMENTS

This research was supported by a National Science and Engineering Research Council Grant to Larry Jacoby, and a Medical Research Council Fellowship to Jane Dywan. The authors express appreciation to Ann Hollingshead for her assistance collecting and analyzing data, and to Fergus Craik, Eric Eich, and Michael Ross for their comments on an earlier version of this chapter.

REFERENCES

Alba, J. N., & Hasher, L. (1983). Is memory schematic? *Psychological Bulletin, 2,* 203–231.

Atkinson, R. C., & Juola, J. F. (1974). Search and decision processes in recognition memory. In D. H. Krantz, R. C. Atkinson, R. D. Luce, & P. Suppes (Eds.), *Contemporary developments in mathematical psychology, Vol. 1: Learning, memory and thinking.* San Francisco, California: Freeman.

Baddeley, A. (1982a). Domains of recollection. *Psychological Review, 89,* 708–729.

Baddeley, A. (1982b). Amnesia: A minimal model and an interpretation. In L. Cermak (Ed.), *Human memory and amnesia* (pp. 305–336). Hillsdale, NJ: Lawrence Erlbaum Associates.

Bower, G. H. (1981). Mood and memory. *American Psychologist, 36,* 129–148.

Bowers, P. G. (1978). Hypnotizability, creativity and the role of effortless experiencing. *International Journal of Clinical and Experimental Hypnosis, 26,* 184–202.

Bowers, K. S., & Hilgard, E. (1986). Some complexities in understanding memory. In H. M. Pettinati (Ed.), *Hypnosis and memory* (pp. 3–18). New York: Guilford Press.

Broadbent, D. E., & Broadbent, M. H. P. (1975). Some further data concerning the word frequency effect. *Journal of Experimental Psychology: General, 104,* 297–308.

Brunswik, E. (1956). *Perception and representative design of psychological experiments.* Berkeley: University of California Press.

Cermak, L. S. (1984). The episodic/semantic distinction in amnesia. In L. R. Squire & N. Butters (Eds.), *The neuropsychology of memory* (pp. 55–62). New York: The Guilford Press.

Cohen, N. J., & Squire, L. R. (1980). Preserved learning and retention of pattern-analyzing skill in amnesia: Dissociation of knowing how and knowing that. *Science, 210,* 207–210.

Cole, W. G., & Loftus, E. F. (1979). Incorporating new information into memory. *American Journal of Psychology, 92*(3), 413–425.

Craik, F. I. M., & Byrd, M. (1982). Aging and cognitive deficits: The role of attentional resources. In F. I. M. Craik & S. E. Trehub (Eds.), *Aging and cognitive processes.* New York: Plenum.

Crawford, H. J., & Allen, S. N. (1983). Enhanced visual memory during hypnosis as mediated by hypnotic responsiveness and cognitive strategies. *Journal of Experimental Psychology: General, 112*, 662–685.

Dasen, P. R. (Ed.) (1977). *Piagetian psychology: Cross-cultural contributions.* New York: Gardner Press, Inc.

Dosher, B. A. (1984). Discriminating preexperimental (semantic) from learned (episodic) associations: A speed–accuracy study. *Cognitive Psychology, 16*, 519–555.

Dywan, J. (1984, June). *Hypermnesia and accuracy in recall.* Paper presented at the forty-fifth annual convention of the Canadian Psychological Association, Ottawa.

Dywan, J., & Bowers, K. (1983). The use of hypnosis to enhance recall. *Science, 222*, 184–185.

Dywan, J., & Jacoby, L. L. (1988). *Effects of aging on source monitoring: Differences in susceptibility to false fame.* Manuscript submitted for publication.

Dywan, J., Segalowitz, S., & Otis, L. (1988, June). *Recall interference and the prototype shift in recognition.* Paper presented at 41st annual convention of the Canadian Psychological Association, Montreal, Quebec.

Erdelyi, M. H., & Kleinbard, J. (1978). Has Ebbinghaus decayed with time? The growth of recall (hypermnesia) over days. *Journal of Experimental Psychology: Human Learning and Memory, 4*, 275–289.

Fischhoff, B. (1975). Hindsight is not equal to foresight: The effects of outcome knowledge on judgment under certainty. *Journal of Experimental Psychology: Human Perception and Performance, 1*, 288–299.

Gelman, R. (1978). Cognitive development. *Annual Review of Psychology, 29*, 297–332.

Gur, R., & Reyher, J. (1976). The enhancement of creativity via free imagery and hypnosis. *American Journal of Clinical Hypnosis, 18*, 237–249.

Hirst, W. (1982). The amnesic syndrome: Descriptions and explanations. *Psychological Bulletin, 91*, 435–460.

Jacoby, L. L. (1984). Incidental versus intentional retrieval: Remembering and awareness as separate issues. In L. R. Squire & N. Butters (Eds.), *Neuropsychology of memory* (pp. 145–156). New York: Guilford Press.

Jacoby, L. L. (1988). Memory observed and memory unobserved. In U. Neisser & E. Winograd (Eds.), *Remembering reconsidered: Ecological and traditional approaches to the study of memory* (pp. 145–177). Cambridge, MA: Cambridge University Press.

Jacoby, L. L., Allan, L. G., Collins, J. C., & Larwill, L. K. (1988). Memory influences subjective experience: Noise judgments. *Journal of Experimental Psychology, Learning, Memory and Cognition, 14*, 240–247.

Jacoby, L. L., & Brooks, L. R. (1984). Nonanalytic cognition: Memory, perception and concept learning. In G. Bower (Ed.), *The psychology of learning and motivation: Advances in research and theory* (vol. 18, pp. 1–47). New York: Academic Press.

Jacoby, L. L., & Dallas, M. (1981). On the relationship between autobiographical memory and perceptual learning. *Journal of Experimental Psychology: General, 110*, 306–340.

Jacoby, L. L., & Kelley, C. M. (1987). Unconscious influences of memory for a prior event. *Personality and Social Psychology Bulletin, 13*, 314–336.

Jacoby, L. L., Kelley, C. M., Brown, J. & Jasechko, J. (in press). Becoming famous overnight: Limits on the ability to avoid unconscious influences of the past. *Journal of Personality and Social Psychology.*

Jacoby, L. L., & Witherspoon, D. (1982). Remembering without awareness. *Canadian Journal of Psychology, 36*, 300–324.

Jacoby, L. L., Woloshyn, V., & Kelley, C. M. (in press). Becoming famous without being recognized: Unconscious influences of memory produced by dividing attention. *Journal of Experimental Psychology, General.*

James, W. (1892). *Principles of psychology.* London: MacMillan.

Johnson, M. K., & Raye, C. L. (1981). Reality monitoring. *Psychological Review, 88,* 67–85.

Johnson, M. K., Raye, C. L., Wang, A. Y., & Taylor, T. H. (1979). Fact and fantasy: The roles of accuracy and variability in confusing imaginations with perceptual experiences. *Journal of Experimental Psychology: Human Learning and Memory, 5,* 229–240.

Johnston, W. A., Dark, V., & Jacoby, L. L. (1985). Perceptual fluency and recognition judgments. *Journal of Experimental Psychology: Learning, Memory, and Cognition, 11,* 3–11.

Kelley, H. H. (1973). The process of causal attribution. *American Psychologist, 28,* 107–129.

Kelley, C. M., Jacoby, L. L., & Hollingshead, A. (1988). *Direct versus indirect tests of memory for source: Judgments of modality.* Manuscript submitted for publication.

Klatzky, R. L. (1984). *Memory and awareness.* New York: Freeman and Company.

Klatzky, R. L., & Erdelyi, M. H. (1985). The response criterion problem in tests of hypnosis and memory. *International Journal of Clinical and Experimental Hypnosis, 23,* 246–257.

Kunst-Wilson, W. R., & Zajonc, R. B. (1980). Affective discrimination of stimuli that cannot be recognized. *Science, 207,* 557–558.

Laurence, J. R., & Perry, C. (1983). Hypnotically created memory among highly hypnotizable subjects. *Science, 222,* 523–524.

Lockhart, R. S. (1984). What do infants remember? In M. Moscovitch (Ed.), *Infant memory* (pp. 131–143). Plenum Press: New York.

Loftus, E. F. (1979). *Eyewitness testimony.* Cambridge, MA: Harvard University Press.

Loftus, E. F. (1981). Mentalmorphosis: Alterations in memory produced by bonding of new information to old. In J. B. Long & A. D. Baddeley (Eds.), *Attention and performance IX* (pp. 417–434). Hillsdale, NJ: Lawrence Erlbaum Associates.

Loftus, E. F., Miller, D. G., & Burns, H. J. (1978). Semantic integration of verbal information into visual memory. *Journal of Experimental Psychology: Human Learning and Memory, 4,* 19–31.

Loftus, E. F., & Palmer, J. C. (1974). Reconstruction of automobile destruction: An example of the interaction between language and memory. *Journal of Verbal Learning and Verbal Behavior, 13,* 585–589.

Mandler, G. (1980). Recognizing: The judgment of previous occurrence. *Psychological Review, 87,* 252–271.

Mandler, G., Nakamura, Y., & Van Zandt, B. J. S. (1987). Nonspecific effects of exposure on stimuli that cannot be recognized. *Journal of Experimental Psychology: Learning, Memory, and Cognition, 13,* 646–648.

Mayes, A. R., & Meudell, P. R. (1981). How similar is immediate memory in amnesic patients to delayed memory in normal subjects?: A replication, extension and reassessment of the amnesic cueing effect. *Neuropsychologia, 19,* 647–654.

Mercer, B., Wapner, W., Gardner, H., & Benson, D. F. (1977). A study of confabulation. *Archives of Neurology, 34,* 429–433.

Moreland, R. L., & Zajonc, R. B. (1977). Is stimulus recognition a necessary condition for the occurrence of exposure effects? *Journal of Personality and Social Psychology, 4,* 191–199.

Morton, J. (1979). Facilitation in word recognition: Experiments causing change in the logogen model. In P. A. Kolers, M. E. Wrolstad, & H. Bouma (Eds.), *Processing of visible language, Volume 1.* New York: Plenum.

Neisser, U. (1982). *Memory observed.* San Francisco: Freeman.

Olson, D. R. (1986). The cognitive consequences of literacy. *Canadian Psychology, 27,* 109–121.

People vs. Michael Kempinski. (1980, October 21). No. W80CF 352 (Cir. Ct., 12th Dist., Will Co., IL, unrep.).

Piaget, J. (1972). Intellectual evolution from adolescence to adulthood. *Human Development, 15,* 1–12.

Piaget, J., & Inhelder, B. (1956). *The child's conception of space.* London: Routledge and Kegan Paul.

Polanyi, M. (1958). *Personal knowledge: Towards a post-critical philosophy.* Chicago: The University of Chicago Press.

Reed, G. (1974). *The psychology of anomalous experience: A cognitive approach.* Boston: Houghton Mifflin Co.

Reisenzein, R. (1983). The Schachter theory of emotion: Two decades later. *Psychological Bulletin, 2,* 239–264.

Richardson-Klavehn, A., & Bjork, R. A. (1988). Measures of memory. *Annual Review of Psychology, 39,* 475–543.

Rothmar, E. (1983). *The relationship between hypnotic ability and heart rate responsiveness to imagery.* Unpublished doctoral dissertation, University of Waterloo, Ontario.

Rovee-Collier, C. (in press). The joy of kicking: Memories, motives, and mobiles. In P. R. Solomon, G. R. Goethals, C. M. Kelley, & B. R. Stephans (Eds.), *Memory—An interdisciplinary approach.* New York: Springer Verlag.

Rubin, D. C. (1985). Memorability as a measure of processing: A unit analysis of prose and list learning. *Journal of Experimental Psychology: General, 114,* 213–238.

Schachter, S., & Singer, J. (1962). Cognitive, social, and physiological determinants of emotional states. *Psychological Review, 69,* 379–399.

Schacter, D. L., Harbluk, J. L., & McLachlan, D. R. (1984). Retrieval without recollection: An experimental analysis of source amnesia. *Journal of Verbal Learning and Verbal Behavior, 23,* 593–611.

Schooler, J. W., Gerhard, D., & Loftus, E. F. (1986). Qualities of the unreal. *Journal of Experimental Psychology: Learning, Memory, and Cognition, 12,* 171–181.

Seamon, J. G., Brody, N., & Kauff, D. M. (1983). Affective discrimination of stimuli that are not recognized: Effects of shadowing, masking, and cerebral laterality. *Journal of Experimental Psychology: Learning, Memory, and Cognition, 9,* 544–555.

Stuss, D. T., & Benson, D. F. (1986). *The frontal lobes.* New York: Raven Press.

Sutton, C. (1984). A breakdown in symmetry. *New Scientist, Jan. 26,* 34–35.

Talland, G. A. (1968). *Disorders of memory and learning.* Middlesex, England: Penguin Books Ltd.

Titchener, E. B. (1928). *A textbook of psychology.* New York: MacMillan.

Tulving, E. (1983). *Elements of episodic memory.* London and New York: Oxford University Press.

Tulving, E. (1985). How many memory systems are there? *American Psychologist, 40,* 385–398.

Warrington, E. K., & Weiskrantz, L. (1974). The effect of prior learning on subsequent retention in amnesic patients. *Neuropsychologia, 12,* 419–428.

Watkins, M. J., & Gibson, J. M. (1988). On the relationship between perceptual priming and recognition memory. *Journal of Experimental Psychology: Learning, Memory, and Cognition, 14,* 477–483.

Winocur, G., & Kinsbourne, M. (1978). Contextual cueing as an aid to Korsakoff amnesia. *Neuropsychologia, 16,* 671–682.

Witherspoon, D., & Allan, L. G. (1985). The effects of a prior presentation on temporal judgments in a perceptual identification task. *Memory and Cognition, 13,* 101–111.

Zillman, D. (1978). Attribution and misattribution of excitatory reactions. In J.H. Harvey, W. J. Ickes, & R. F. Kidd (Eds.), *New directions in attribution research* (vol. 2, pp. 335–368). Hillsdale, NJ: Lawrence Erlbaum Associates.

20 Consciousness and the Function of Remembered Episodes: Comments on the Fourth Section

Robert S. Lockhart
University of Toronto

The chapters in this section provide an abundance of material for discussion; they cover a vast range of topics and reveal the widely differing perspectives of their authors. Rather than attempting a systematic review of each, this commentary examines the relevance of each chapter to the general theme of consciousness and the function of episodic memory.

Our ability to remember particular past events undoubtedly serves many functions; but the major function of episodic memory probably lies in the flexibility it imparts to the processes by which we construct and revise rules, especially the kind of rules that enable us to comprehend past events and predict future outcomes. The point is best made with the help of a hypothetical example. Consider the plight of a person, say Smith, who suffers an allergic reaction while eating a meal. Smith needs to establish the cause of the reaction—a rule that will explain this present event and anticipate future reactions. Suppose the initially suspected food is a variety of shellfish, but that a subsequent meal containing this same food results in no allergic reaction, whereas an allergic reaction *is* obtained following a third meal in which the shellfish was not present. How should the hypothesis be revised? It is clear that an appropriate interrogation of the episodic memory for each of the three meals can serve as the basis for a revised hypothesis. Such an interrogation might, for example, establish what foods were common to the two meals associated with the allergic reaction, but was absent from other meals. That is, episodic memory creates the possibility of conducting effective *thought experiments*; hypotheses can be formulated and tested using conditions and outcomes that have already occurred. It is episodic memory that affords the retrospective assembling of these conditions and their associated outcomes.

An organism without episodic memory would be limited to rule learning of quite a different kind. For such an organism, hypotheses or associations formed as a consequence of a specific experience would exist in a semantic or procedural memory without reference to the contextual particularities of that event. Subsequent events might lead to the revision of this hypothesis, or to a modification of the strength of the association, but the irrelevant particularities of the first event would no longer be available. Smith may hold the initial belief that shellfish is the cause of the allergy, and even without episodic memory this belief may be weakened or discarded when a second meal containing the same food yields no reaction and a third meal without shellfish does. But it requires episodic remembering to establish subsequently what foods were common to the first and third meals and absent from the second meal, and to reformulate the hypothesis accordingly. This kind of inductive rule-refinement should not be possible for amnesics suffering from the forms of dissociation that Schacter talked about in chapter 18. That is to say, anticipations that are embodied in procedures or rules that are dissociated from the episodes under which they were acquired are not amenable to refinement though the recovery of additional contextual data that might be contained in an explicit memory for those episodes.

Insofar as everyday experience provides a series of informal experiments that serve to test our personal hypotheses about condition–outcome contingencies, episodic memory enables us to conduct these experiments, post hoc, with different arrangements of condition–outcome relationships. Thus, episodic memory provides a set of possible conditions, along with the corresponding results, that enables us to conduct everyday thought experiments. This argument is not a claim that episodic memory consists of an uninterpreted veridical snapshot that can be later consulted and interpreted; the claim is merely that episodic memory, despite its undoubtedly being a biased and selective representation of the actual event, is nevertheless a richer portrayal of the event than that contained in a single hypothesis of a condition–outcome relationship stripped of the particularities of its episodic context.

The effective functioning of episodic memory as a data base for thought experiments depends critically on the ability to discriminate past events from general knowledge, a discrimination that amounts to distinguishing data from theory, and, as in science, assigning authority to the former to modify or discard the latter. The effectiveness of the thought experiments conducted by our allergic Smith, depends on Smith being able to distinguish between the actual events (what foods were actually eaten) and non-episodic reconstructions of the events based on general knowledge. Only the former constitute valid data for the testing of revised hypotheses. This ability to distinguish episodic from non-episodic memory is the issue that Jacoby, Kelley, and Dywan addressed in chapter 19.

JACOBY ET AL.'S ECOLOGICAL MNEMICS

My main criticism of chapter 19 (Jacoby et al.) is the title, which, unlike the chapter itself, is unimaginative. It might have been more daringly called *Eco-*

logical Mnemics, because its ideas are very much in the tradition of Egon Brunswik and it could be argued that the basic thesis of the chapter stands in relation to memory theory as J. J. Gibson's *Ecological Optics* stands in relation to perception. The questions that Jacoby et al. ask of the experience of remembering are those questions that Brunswik asked of perceptual cues. Brunswik asked: What properties of proximal stimulation enable one to infer properties of distal objects or events; for example, that object A is further away than object B? Brunswik pointed out that the proximal stimulus contains cues, and these cues vary in their ecological validity: For relative distance judgments, occlusion is a cue of very high ecological validity. That is to say, it is difficult to imagine circumstances in which B occludes A yet is, in reality, further away. Size and clarity of image each have a degree of ecological validity, but are less valid than occlusion.

The question that Jacoby et al. asked is this: What is there about a *temporally* proximal (that is, present) experience that warrants the inference (or attribution) of a temporally distal (that is, past) event? Are memories identified *as memories* in virtue of phenomenological properties of the memory experience itself, properties that constitute cues possessing a certain degree of ecological validity? These are ancient philosophers' questions and their antiquity makes even more impressive the chapter's achievement, which is to phrase the questions in such a way as to gain some genuine empirical purchase on the problem and thereby to make some significant headway in solving it.

The headway is gained by identifying a number of different cues and assessing their validity. Familiarity based on perceptual fluency, for example, is a cue, but one of less than perfect validity because factors other than a past experience can influence the subjective sense of familiarity. Subjects seem to be aware of these factors and thus can be led to misattribute fluency to contemporary causes, or conversely, to misattribute contemporary causes to a past experience. These demonstrations of misattribution constitute a class of cognitive illusions analogous to those that have been catalogued in the domain of subjective probability. Such demonstrations are most valuable to the extent that they identify the procedures that under normal conditions serve to support valid inferences, that is, veridical remembering.

There is, however, a danger in becoming too enchanted by errors. The demonstration of a cognitive illusion such as a confabulated memory serves to make the point that episodic memory involves an error-prone attribution process, but it fails to address the more fundamental question of how cues acquire the degree of validity they do possess. How *is* the validity of cues acquired? For example, constructing contextual detail may, as Jacoby et al. claimed, increase confidence that we are remembering and not inventing, and this cue may be one of high validity, but how do we come to appreciate this validity? Jacoby et al. did not really address this question. This issue of memory validation, first raised in the context of child development by James Mark Baldwin (Baldwin, 1906; 1920; see also Lockhart, 1984; Ross & Kerst, 1978) remains one of the most interesting unexplored areas of human memory. It seems unnecessary to assume that these attributions are necessarily ''strategic inference processes,'' which is the way Schacter, at the end of chapter 18, interpreted Jacoby et al.'s argument. There are, of course, extensive discussions of this matter in the perception literature that date back at least to Helmholtz.

SCHACTER'S CAS

What does all this have to do with consciousness, the putative theme of this section? On this matter, Jacoby et al. were ominously silent. Clearly, consciousness and episodic memory are closely related; it is difficult to imagine episodic memories in an organism lacking consciousness in one form or another. But to say that episodic memory presupposes some form of consciousness is to say very little. Schacter's chapter, on the other hand, had a great deal to say about consciousness, or at least the neurophysiological conditions that are necessary to bring consciousness about. Consciousness became identified with entities such as pathways, structures, and brain locations, and we were told less about consciousness itself than we were about what structures it depends on. E. B. Titchener would have applauded. But a number of questions remain unanswered. How does Schacter's CAS distinguish between input from a perceptual module and input from declarative memory module? For example, how would DICE explain the errors of attribution that Jacoby et al. so thoroughly documented?

Schacter seems well aware of these difficulties and made a valiant attempt to relate structure and function: CAS is identified ''with one particular function: phenomenal awareness of ongoing mental activity.'' It is unclear to me in what sense the quoted phrase is a function; it seems more like a descriptive characterization of consciousness, so that the phrase might be translated as ''the function of CAS is to sustain consciousness.'' But this accusation of question begging is less than fair, because Schacter's arguments constitute a substantial refinement of our understanding of what consciousness might be. His claim that CAS is to be distinguished from memory or knowledge modules on the one hand and from the executive system on the other is a strong claim that will, as he suggested, raise questions that might not otherwise be investigated. In particular, it is not difficult to imagine how DICE and CAS might enable the allergic Smith to conduct his or her thought experiments, provided, of course, that it finds a way of reliably distinguishing episodic from non-episodic information.

EICH'S STATE DEPENDENCY

What lies at the basis of state dependency? Is it the case that the presence or absence of a drug merely induces differences in processing operations, so that state dependency is just an exotic means of demonstrating Tulving's ESP? Or is there something special, perhaps in terms of brain physiology, that is to be learned about memory processes by studying memory in the alcohol-bathed brain? Eich clearly wants to draw general conclusions—to develop a general theory of state dependency that would apply equally to drug states, mood states, and presumably the states induced by a semantic context. The danger is that too much generality makes the narrower, traditional concept of state dependency theoretically less interesting. All that would be left for the cognitive psychologist to do would be to catalogue the specific details for different states—drugs, moods, under the sea versus on land, semantic context effects, and so on, and so on. The specific details of these states may or may not have practical and clinical value, but all would demonstrate the same theoretical point.

It would be helpful to have a clearer account of what there is about Eich's results that is not apparent from simpler studies that manipulate semantic context. Is there an important difference between, on the one hand, presenting the word "light" to an intoxicated subject and noting that it is better remembered when tested in a similar intoxicated state, and, on the other hand, presenting the word "light" in the context of the prefix head and noting that it is better remembered when tested in the context of that same prefix?

One possible rebuttal to this apparent attempt to belittle the phenomenon of state dependency is that the state dependent effects are asymmetric, an asymmetry that results from (or can be understood in terms of) an asymmetric similarity function. Notice first that, as Tversky (1977) pointed out, there is no logical problem with Eich's claim that A might be more similar to B than B is to A. Indeed, there is no logical problem in saying that the similarity of A to B (from one perspective) is greater than the similarity of A to B (from a second perspective). Vodka and water are more similar visually than are vodka and water viewed psychopharmacologically. All similarity measures are conceptually relative, and it is frequently the case that the initial element of a pair induces a distinctive conceptual viewpoint. Thus, most people consider that Canada is more similar to the U.S. than the U.S. is to Canada for precisely the reasons that Eich mentioned. The question is whether the asymmetries in state dependent remembering can be understood in these terms. It is entirely possible that they can, but the evidence seems weak at present. First, there is little direct evidence that asymmetries of similarity of the type just mentioned are associated with the kind of memory differences that Eich described, although there is some indirect evidence in the redintegration literature (Horowitz & Prytulak, 1969; Lockhart, 1969). Second, one of the classic cases of state dependency (Godden & Baddeley, 1975) fails to show the expected asymmetry, assuming of course that land can be considered the reference (=sober) state and underwater as a non-canonical (=intoxicated) state. Nevertheless, the matter is one that should be pursued further; state dependency is a phenomenon that, when fully understood, is likely to reveal important properties of the memory system.

Granted that state dependency is a real feature of memory, we might ask about its functional significance. How, for example, might it assist our allergy sufferer, Smith? In the context of rule revision there is an obvious answer. State dependency can be viewed as a means of directing retrieval to precisely those episodes that are most likely to be relevant to rule revision. It makes good sense that events experienced in the state of suffering from an allergic reaction should be biased in favor of recalling previous events also experienced in this state. That is, state dependency is a way of mnemonically linking two events, the shared contexts of which are exceptional by virtue of being non-canonical and which are therefore likely to bring about the need for rule formulation.

BJORK'S INHIBITION

Bjork made a convincing case for the importance of inhibitory processes in memory retrieval. The data that he described add support to a point of view that is attractive on a priori functional grounds. To continue the analogy with perceptual processes that was begun in the comments on the chapter by Jacoby et al., the adaptive, functional significance of inhibition for memory retrieval would seem to be that of shaping and sharpening mnemonic contours. The particularly interesting aspect of this inhibition, or at least some forms of inhibition, is that it operates through retrieval mechanisms rather than on the to-be-retrieved material itself.

An interesting question that arises from Bjork's account of inhibition is its generality. How widely might it be applied? Can phenomena such as Tulving's ESP be subsumed under the general operating principles of inhibitory mechanisms, and their excitatory counterpart, priming?

The functional question is similar to the one raised by the phenomenon of state dependency. How does the memory system constrain retrieval in functionally useful ways? Bjork made an important point when he argued that it is frequently non-adaptive to recall too much. Inaccessibility, far from always being a negative thing, may under certain circumstances be highly adaptive. Updating would seem to be a good example. It is to be hoped that the functional significance of forgetting, or inaccessibility, is a topic that receives increased attention. A good case can be made that the issues constitute one of the most significant gaps in our present understanding of human memory.

MEMORY AND CONSCIOUSNESS

The four chapters reviewed in this section contain valuable insights into many aspects of human memory, but it is clear that much work remains to be done before we have a full and focused picture of the relationship between memory and consciousness. Some of the difficulty can be traced to the confusion of functionalist and structuralist modes of theorizing, especially with respect to memory systems. On what grounds are memory systems to be distinguished: functional, structural, or some convergence of evidence and creative synthesis of the two?

Schacter in particular drew our attention to this state of affairs when he raised the question of whether consciousness is a *property* of memory systems. I find it difficult, as does Schacter apparently, to give a clear meaning to the notion of a system having or not having awareness. It seems more profitable to pose the question in terms of the contribution to consciousness of various forms of remembering where the forms are distinguished in functional terms. It then becomes clear that episodic remembering is a major contributor to consciousness, if by episodic remembering we mean acts of remembering that have the concept of "self" along with "pastness" as criterial attributions. Indeed, an interesting way to approach the problem of defining episodic remembering functionally rather than structurally, is in terms of the rememberer's application to stored information of these two concepts as retrieval criteria. Thus, for example, the application of concepts such as food and allergy as retrieval criteria may yield considerable information from memory, but it is the additional application of the concepts of self and pastness which, if successful, would generate information that might be labelled episodic remembering. Consciousness is then the continuous Jamesian stream of acts of conception, and the quality of consciousness depends on the nature of the concepts themselves. Rather than talking about awareness being a property of memory systems, it is preferable to regard remembering as a cognitive activity that contributes to consciousness in ways that are to be understood in terms of the concepts being used to guide retrieval.

REFERENCES

Baldwin, J. M. (1906). *Thought and things: A study of the development of meaning and thought or genetic logic.* New York: MacMillan.

Baldwin, J. M. (1920). *Mental development in the child and the race* (3rd ed.). New York: MacMillan.

Godden, D. R., & Baddeley, A. D. (1975). Context-dependent memory in two natural environments: On land and underwater. *British Journal of Psychology, 66,* 325–332.

Horowitz, L. M., & Prytulak, L. S. (1969). Redintegrative memory. *Psychological Review, 76,* 519–531.

Lockhart, R. S. (1969). Retrieval asymmetry in the recall of adjectives and nouns. *Journal of Experimental Psychology, 79,* 12–17.

Lockhart, R. S. (1984). What do infants remember? In M. Moscovitch (Ed.), *Infant memory* (pp. 131–143). New York: Plenum.

Ross, B. M., & Kerst, S. M. (1978). Developmental memory theories: Baldwin and Piaget. In H. W. Reese & L. P. Lippsitt (Eds.), *Advances in child development and behavior* (vol. 12, pp. 183–229). New York: Academic Press.

Tversky, A. (1977). Features of similarity. *Psychological Review, 84,* 327–352.

Author Index

A

Abbott, D. W., 342
Abelson, R. P., 90
Abramowitz, R. L., 311, 312, 313, 327
Adams, J. K., 245
Alba, J. N., 405
Alexander, M. D., 137, 139, 142, 155
Alexander, M. P., 145
Allan, L. G., 401
Allen, S. N., 415
Allender, L. E., 64
Allport, D. A., 328, 365, 366
Amaral, D., 377
Amyes, E. W., 371
Anderson, C. M. B., 41
Anderson, J. R., 5, 36, 73, 74, 81, 195, 199, 206, 217, 218, 223, 229, 231, 237, 262, 263, 287, 288, 365
Anderson, P., 113
Andrewsky, E. L., 361
Appenzeller, T., 13, 36, 156
Armstrong, D. R., 167
Atkinson, R. C., 62, 313, 396, 406
Azam, M., 331

B

Baars, B. J., 363, 365, 369
Bachevalier, J., 115, 365, 366, 376
Baddeley, A., 395, 411
Baddeley, A. D., 8, 61, 110, 137, 142, 212, 213, 214, 218, 274, 278, 279, 280, 349, 357, 427
Bagheri, B., 317
Baillet, S. D., 83, 84
Bajo, M., 32
Baker, E., 123, 126
Baldwin, J. M., 425
Balota, D. A., 81, 205, 234, 237, 239, 245, 248, 262
Barclay, J. R., 62
Bargh, J. A., 359
Barris, R. W., 371
Barlow, M. C., 212
Barnhart, S. S., 342
Barry, H., 342, 343
Bartlett, J. C., 333, 334, 339
Bateson, P. P. G., 112
Batta, S. K., 346
Bauer, R. M., 111, 361, 375
Baveresco, J. L., 350
Becker, C. A., 237
Becker, J. T., 152, 156, 170
Begg, I., 26, 74
Belleville, R. E., 342
Bendtfeldt, F., 334, 339, 340, 341
Bennett, R. W., 277
Benson, D. F., 142, 145, 373, 374, 381, 393, 399

431

Subject Index

443